Transcultural English Studies

ross
ultures

Readings in the Post / Colonial

Literatures in English

102

ASNEL Papers 12

Series Editors

Gordon Collier
(Giessen)

†Hena Maes–Jelinek
(Liège)

Geoffrey Davis
(Aachen)

ASNEL Papers appear under the auspices of the
Gesellschaft für die Neuen Englischsprachigen Literaturen e.V. (GNEL)
Association for the Study of the New Literatures in English (ASNEL)

Frank Schulze—Engler, President
(English Department, J.W. Goethe University, Frankfurt am Main)

Formatting, layout and final editing: Gordon Collier

Transcultural English Studies

Theories, Fictions, Realities

ASNEL Papers 12

Edited by
Frank Schulze-Engler and Sissy Helff

With editorial assistance from
Claudia Perner and Christine Vogt-William

Amsterdam - New York, NY 2009

Cover design: Gordon Collier & Pier Post

The paper on which this book is printed meets the requirements of
"ISO 9706:1994, Information and documentation - Paper for
documents - Requirements for permanence".

ISBN: 978-90-420-2563-9
© Editions Rodopi B.V., Amsterdam – New York, NY 2009
Printed in The Netherlands

Table of Contents

TRANSCULTURAL REALITIES

TRANSCULTURAL FICTIONS

TEACHING TRANSCULTURALITY

Introduction

FRANK SCHULZE–ENGLER

T HE TITLE under which this volume of essays announces itself
may well seem preposterous. Isn't 'Transcultural English Studies'
simply too wide, an impossible label for an unlikely new meta-
discipline encompassing British Studies, American Studies, and the New
Literatures in English? Or isn't it simply too narrow, a retrogressive tag that
seeks to redirect the interdisciplinary practice of Postcolonial Studies to a
disciplinary past in English Studies that it has long since left behind? And
what, amidst the flurry of 'hybrid' concepts and 'trans'-terminology attempt-
ing to bring further innovation into the contemporary theoretical scene, is new
about the 'transcultural', anyway?

To start with the last question first: what is most strikingly new about the
transcultural is its sudden ubiquity. Following in the wake of previous concepts in cultural and literary studies such as creolization, hybridity and syncretism, and signalling a family relationship with terms such as transnationality, translocality, and transmigration, 'transcultural' terminology has
unobtrusively, but powerfully, edged its way into contemporary theoretical
and critical discourse. The four sections of this volume denote major arenas
where 'transcultural' questions and problematics have come to the fore:
theories of culture and literature that have sought to account for the complexity of culture in a world increasingly characterized by globalization,
transnationalization, and interdependence; realities of individual and collective lifeworlds shaped by the ubiquity of phenomena and experiences relating
to transnational connections and the blurring of cultural boundaries; fictions
in literature and other media that explore these realities, negotiate the fuzzy
edges of 'ethnic' or 'national' cultures, and participate in the creation of
transnational public spheres as well as transcultural imaginations and memo-

ries; and, finally, pedagogy and didactics, where earlier models of teaching 'other' cultures are faced with the challenge of coming to terms with cultural complexity both in what is being taught and in the people it is taught to, and where 'target cultures' refuse to sit still for pedagogical purposes.

The vantage point of many – though by no means all – of the essays in this volume are the New or Postcolonial Literatures in English. These literatures were originally often thought of in terms of a mosaic of more or less discrete (usually national) cultures characterized by an inherent difference from Britain and the USA. Today, the field of the 'New Literatures' has come to be seen as a world-wide network of anglophone literatures and cultures with increasingly fuzzy edges: Indian authors not only write in India, but also in the Caribbean, in South Africa, Canada, Australia, Britain, and the USA; anglophone African literature extends to a variety of new diasporic locations in Europe and North America that have come into existence in the wake of migration, transmigration, flight, and exile; and even where people stay put, ideas, texts, images, and sounds circulate through a globally interlinked network constituted by old and new media alike. The idea of 'locating' culture and literature exclusively in the context of ethnicities or nations is rapidly losing plausibility throughout an 'English-speaking world' that has long since been multi- rather than monolingual. Exploring the prospects and contours of 'Transcultural English Studies' thus does not entail giving free rein to meta-disciplinary ambitions but, rather, reflects a set of common challenges and predicaments that in recent years have increasingly moved centre-stage not only in the New Literatures in English but also in British and American Studies.

In exploring the theoretical consequences of ubiquitous transnational connections and trajectories joining the local and the global, many of the contributions to this volume critically engage with transcultural theories such as the concept of 'transculturation' developed by Fernando Ortiz in the 1940s and Wolfgang Welsch's more recent theory of 'transculturality'. Ortiz's 'transculturation' concept, set out in his seminal *Cuban Counterpoint,*[1] sought to explore processes of cultural transformation and exchange within a framework of fundamentally unequal and hierarchical relations between powerful nations (such as the USA) and less powerful ones (such as Cuba). As MARK

---

[1] Fernando Ortiz, *Cuban Counterpoint: Tobacco and Sugar*, tr. Harriet de Onís, (*Contrapunteo cubano del tabaco y el azúcar*, 1940; tr. Durham NC and London: Duke UP, 1995).

STEIN points out in his contribution to the present volume, Ortiz's main interest lay in exploring the manner in which seemingly 'weaker' cultures developed a capacity to move beyond a trajectory of straightforward 'assimilation'
and to accomplish a fusion of old and new cultural elements 'into a coherent
body.' While 'transculturation' undeniably opened up important new perspectives for analysing the dynamism and complexity of culture, it remained ultimately tied to the epistemological framework of 'national cultures' on the one
hand and to a structural configuration of dominating and dominated cultures
on the other. Yet it is precisely the practice of thinking of 'cultures' in terms
of 'national cultures' as well as the assumption that transcultural phenomena
occur in 'peripheral' rather than 'central' constellations that have been called
into question in recent transcultural debates. Several of the essays in this collection suggest that transculturality has long since become a constitutive feature of cultural transformations in Britain or the USA, and that the dynamics
of contemporary 'transculture' can no longer be understood in terms of classical dichotomies such as colonizer vs. colonized or centres vs. peripheries. As
the editors of a recent special issue on "Transcultural Britain" put it: "Transculturality [...] does not have to be minoritarian, diasporic, or dissident, but
rather is a constitutive feature of the culture at large."[2]

   The second major strand in current transcultural terminology has philosophical origins. In 1991, the German philosopher WOLFGANG WELSCH
published a first version of his seminal essay on transculturality which later
appeared in various revised forms and was subsequently translated into English, Italian, and Spanish.[3] For Welsch, transculturality cannot be understood
as a process related to a specific hierarchical relationship of societies and cultures (such as colonialism or imperialism), but instead needs to be perceived
as a specific quality of contemporary cultures that necessitates the development of new theoretical concepts. The main thrust of his original argument
(repeated in his own contribution to the present volume) is thus directed
against the 'separatist' idea of 'cultures' as self-enclosed entities which he
traces back to Johann Gottfried Herder's perception of culture as based on

---

[2] Bernd–Peter Lange & Dirk Wiemann, "Transcultural Britain: An Introduction," *Journal for the Study of British Cultures* 15.1 (2008): 6.

[3] For the English version, see Wolfgang Welsch, "Transculturality: The Puzzling Form
of Cultures Today," in: *Spaces of Culture: City, Nation, World*, ed. Mike Featherstone &
Scott Lash (London: Sage, 1999): 194–213; for other versions and translations, see fn. 1 of
Welsch's "On Acquisition and Possession of Commonalities" in the present volume.

"ethnic foundation, social homogenization, and intercultural delimitation."[4]
According to this argument, theories of 'intercultural' communication thus
create the very problem they set out to solve: they posit 'cultures' as separate
entities and people as 'belonging' to these separate entities, thereby failing to
acknowledge the fact that in an increasingly interconnected world, cultures
are increasingly intertwined and people often constitute their cultural identities by drawing on more than one culture. Welsch's concept of transculturality
challenges this spectral afterlife of Herderian cultural theory and moves towards a theoretical redefinition of cultural practices based on "identity configurations that have some elements in common while differing in other
elements, in their arrangement as a whole, and often in their complexity."[5]
This move is completed by the supplementary emphasis on human commonalities that Welsch introduces in his contribution to the present collection:
transculturality is now redefined in terms of both the 'permeation of cultures'
and 'determinants common to all cultures'. Welsch's concept of transculturality thus combines a long-term theory of culture (since cultures have always
been shaped by permeation and by universal human determinants, culture per
se can be argued to be transcultural) with an emphasis on the diagnostic need
to come to terms with the present dynamics of culture in an increasingly
globalized world.

As many of the contributions in the first section of this volume ("Theoretical Perspectives") point out, this present dynamic of culture is intricately
linked to the globalization of modernity. If it is true that culture can no longer
be thought of in terms of incommensurable separate units, it seems equally
true that our understanding of modernity needs to be decentred and divested
of proprietary notions that see modernity as essentially 'Western'. In a world
of 'multiple modernities', the transnational dimensions of culture can no longer
be thought of as extrinsic to essentially local cultures (GISELA WELZ),
'cultural authenticity' itself becomes the site of complex renegotiations of the
global and the local (VIRGINIA RICHTER), and anglophone literatures become a prime conduit for exploring the 'heterogeneity of the present' beyond
eurocentric (mis)representations of modernity (DIRK WIEMANN). The ethical
and political dimensions of these processes raise intricate questions of their
own, however. If it is true that the habitual identification of 'hybridity' with

---

[4] Welsch, "On Acquisition and Possession of Commonalities," page 5 below.
[5] See Welsch, "On Acquisition and Possession of Commonalities," page 10 below.

the subversion of Western master-discourses practised in postcolonial theory has lost much of its plausibility, it seems equally unconvincing to regard transculturality as a methodological panacea for cultural and literary studies. Several contributions to the "Theoretical Perspectives" section of this volume thus argue for the need to critically scrutinize the limitations and liabilities of transcultural approaches to culture and literature: transcultural and transnational continua such as the 'Black Atlantic' may entail not only commonalities and solidarity, but also rifts and dissonance (RUTH MEYER), the capacity of 'transcultural studies' to account for the experiences and lifeworlds of mobile groups such as refugees or illegal migrants needs to be critically addressed (SISSY HELFF), and transculturality may need to be supplemented by a 'cosmopolitanism from below' in order to avoid premature insouciance and political naivety in a world characterized by social and political inequality (PETER STUMMER).

Current debates on cosmopolitanism in philosophy and the social sciences may also be helpful in coming to terms with the "Transcultural Realities" explored in the second section of this volume. As Ulrich Beck has pointed out in his *Cosmopolitan Vision*, one of the salient features of "really existing cosmopolitanization" is a "banal" cosmopolitanism" that unfolds "beneath the surface or behind the façade of persisting national spaces": "My life, my body, my 'individual existence' become part of another world, of foreign cultures, religions, histories and global interdependencies, without my realizing or expressly wishing it."[6] In a similar vein, an important dimension of transculturality may be said to reside in a really existing 'transcultural transformation' of lifeworlds, experiences, and cultural practices in Europe and elsewhere that challenges a compartmentalized understanding of 'multicultural' societies in terms of a "benign cultural apartheid."[7] Coming to terms with these transcultural transformations and realities is, of course, also a major mainspring of literature, film, and art: in this respect the division of transcultural 'realities' and 'fictions' practised in this volume is at best a heuristic approximation. Realities, fictions, and theories are undoubtedly hard to separate in the real social world, but it may be useful to remember that transculturality is not only about (high) art and theory, but also about popular

---

[6] Ulrich Beck, *The Cosmopolitan Vision*, tr. Ciaran Cronin (*Der kosmopolitische Blick, oder: Krieg ist Frieden*, 2004, Cambridge: Polity, 2006): 19.

[7] Mike Phillips, "Broken Borders: Migration, Modernity and English Writing – Transcultural Transformation in the Heart of Europe," page 139 below.

culture and everyday life. The contributions to the "Realities" section of this volume all engage with culturally multiform lifeworlds and the transcultural suturing of the artistic and the mundane: with the complexity of language as a marker for transcultural experiences in anglophone literature in Israel (AXEL STÄHLER) and in Jewish-American writing (PASCAL FISCHER), with the conflicting semantic crossovers produced by attempts to impose a colonial semantic order upon recalcitrant oral systems of knowledge in the Ordnance Survey Memoir in Ireland (EDITH SHILLUE), but also with explorations of modern forms of indigeneity in Inuit filmmaking (KERSTIN KNOPF) and Maori literature (MICHAELA MOURA–KOÇOĞLU), and with the articulation of diasporic and local realities in Caribbean poetry (SABRINA BRANCATO).

If the representation of culturally complex experiences and lifeworlds is one side of the transcultural coin, the third section of this volume ("Transcultural Fictions") is centrally concerned with its flipside: specifically transcultural modes of literary, artistic, and filmic representation and the emergence of a 'transcultural imagination'. The 'location of transculture' is not only to be found in realities outside texts or in the texts themselves, but also in audiences that make sense of them according to 'new regimes of reference, norm, and value' drawing upon several cultural backgrounds; the transcultural potential of texts thus lies in their impact on the reader as well as in the modes of representation required to approximate the cultural complexity they engage with (MARK STEIN). The forms, functions, and limitations of such modes of representation are explored in several of the contributions to this section focusing on issues such as different portrayals of black British history in literature and on TV (ULRIKE PIRKER), the staging of cultural identities in terms of playfulness and performativity in black British Literature (BARBARA SCHAFF), or the depiction of cultural 'returns' to India in Bollywood cinema (CHRISTINE VOGT–WILLIAM). If, as Mike Phillips reminds us, "it is the artist's job to extend the reach of our imagination about the potential of real life,"[8] the question necessarily arises as to what extent transcultural realities give rise to transcultural forms of imagination – for example, in the puzzling social world of the Indian subcontinent, where cultural memory finds itself confronted with a shared history before and divergent national trajectories after Partition (NADIA BUTT), in the spatial arrangements and re-

---

[8] Mike Phillips, "Broken Borders: Migration, Modernity and English Writing – Transcultural Transformation in the Heart of Europe," page 149 below.

alignments of Native and non-Native lives in Canadian native fiction that do not resolve cultural conflicts and political tensions, but present them as "productively dynamic and as going beyond the mere contact zone,"[9] or in the century-old conflicts and negotiations over Scottish nationality and cultural identity that in the twentieth century have given rise to 'postcolonial' perspectives in Scottish Literature (SILKE STROH).

The last section of this volume ("Teaching Transculturality") takes one of the most important social functions of English Studies as its focus: the training of English teachers and the challenges of learning about culture in the English as a Foreign Language (EFL) classroom. In Germany and elsewhere, 'intercultural' paradigms are still deeply entrenched in school curricula bent on furthering dialogue between the pupils' 'own' and 'other' cultures. Cultural texts from non-Western locations are thus all too often introduced in terms of an ultimately static notion of 'cultural background' which these texts are supposed to relate to. Many of the cultural 'texts' to be found in the contemporary world (including those taught at schools and universities) no longer follow that logic, however; they are deeply imbued with transcultural experiences of negotiating between several cultures, of assembling individual or group identities from a large variety of sociocultural sources, of conflicts and compromises that destabilize and alter the very cultural frameworks that conventional notions of 'intercultural' understanding usually take for granted. These experiences are often enough reflected in the very classrooms where this teaching takes place: in many cases, the pupils themselves have to come to terms with transnational and transcultural experiences emerging from biographies that are no longer located in stable and largely unchanging cultural frameworks. 'Teaching transculturality' thus involves a heightened sensitivity towards and knowledge of transcultural processes of cultural conflict, negotiation, and fusion. The essays in this section of the volume explore possibilities of enhancing this sensitivity through confronting pupils at schools with culturally complex authors and their work (SABINE DOFF), promoting the notion of a 'cosmopolitan readership' in working with literary texts marked by cultural diversity in university classes (MICHAEL PRUSSE), exposing pupils to the challenging portrait of multicultural Britain in the works of Hanif Kureishi (LAURENZ VOLKMANN), utilizing cultural heterogeneity

---

[9] Katja Sarkowsky, "Beyond the Contact Zone? Mapping Transcultural Spaces in *Kiss of the Fur Queen* and *Monkey Beach*," page 337 below.

among Indian students to enrich the understanding of cultural complexity in contemporary African literature (BASHYAM SANKARAN), and initiating transcultural learning processes by opening up dialogue between African photographs, expository texts, and pupils' own responses in the EFL classroom (GISELA FEURLE and DETLEV GOHRBANDT).

As the thematic and spatial range of the contributions assembled in this volume testifies, the New Literatures in English themselves have long since become a transcultural field with blurred boundaries. Scottish 'postcolonial' literature or Israeli literature in English are ample proof that English-language literatures worldwide need to be seen as a discursive field rather than as an imaginary assembly of national literatures. 'Transcultural English Studies' thus stands for a genuinely transnational and transcultural perspective that is capable of encompassing both the literary practice of writers who can no longer be related to one particular 'national literary space' and the complex articulations that link individual works of literature not only to local or regional modernities with their specific social, linguistic, and cultural constellations, but also to the world-wide field of English-language literatures and specific forms of communicative interaction and political conflict engendered by it.

WORKS CITED

Beck, Ulrich. *The Cosmopolitan Vision*, tr. Ciaran Cronin (*Der kosmopolitische Blick, oder: Krieg ist Frieden*, 2004, Cambridge: Polity, 2006).

Lange, Bernd–Peter, & Dirk Wiemann. "Transcultural Britain: An Introduction," *Journal for the Study of British Cultures* 15.1 (2008): 3--10.

Ortiz, Fernando. *Cuban Counterpoint: Tobacco and Sugar*, tr. Harriet de Onís, (*Contrapunteo cubano del tabaco y el azúcar*, 1940; tr. Durham NC & London: Duke UP, 1995).

Welsch, Wolfgang. "Transculturality: The Puzzling Form of Cultures Today," in *Spaces of Culture: City, Nation, World*, ed. Mike Featherstone and Scott Lash (London: Sage, 1999): 194--213.

❮❖❯

THEORETICAL PERSPECTIVES

On the Acquisition and Possession of Commonalities

WOLFGANG WELSCH

Introduction

I N PHILOSOPHY, the term 'transculturality' was not at all common – in fact, it was not even in use – when I introduced it into the philosophical discourse on culture several years ago.[1] In the meantime, it has become more familiar in my discipline, though it still meets with reluctance. I am all the more glad that it has now come to be so widely used in the work of literary studies.

When I introduced the term 'transculturality', I thought it was a new one. Subsequently I learned that at least the adjective 'transcultural' had not been quite as exceptional, after all, in cultural studies since the 1960s. But at least I was giving it a new twist. In the older anthropological and ethnological dis-

---

[1] I presented a first version of the concept in 1991 under the title "Transkulturalität: Lebensformen nach der Auflösung der Kulturen," *Information Philosophie* 2 (1992): 5–20. Several extended versions have appeared in Italian, English, Spanish and German. The following are representative: "Transculturalità: Forme di vita dopo la dissoluzione delle culture," in *Paradigmi: Rivista di critica filosofica* 10/30 (1992): 665–89; "Transculturality: The Puzzling Form of Cultures Today," in *Spaces of Culture: City, Nation, World*, ed. Mike Featherstone & Scott Lash (London: Sage, 1999): 194–213; "Transculturalidad: La forma cambiante de las culturas en la actualidad," in *Democracia y ciudadanía en la sociedad global*, ed. Cristina Camachos Ramos, Miriam Calvillo Verlasco & Juan Mora Heredia (Aragón: Universidad Nacional Autónoma de México, 2001): 191–218; "Auf dem Weg zu transkulturellen Gesellschaften," in *Die Zukunft des Menschen: Philosophische Ausblicke*, ed. Günter Seubold (Bonn: Bouvier, 1999): 119–44.

cussion, 'transcultural' referred to transcultural invariances. My objective, on the contrary, was to use it to describe a strikingly new, contemporary feature of cultures originating from their increased blending. The main idea was that deep differences between cultures are today diminishing more and more, that contemporary cultures are characterized by cross-cutting elements – and in this sense are to be comprehended as transcultural rather than monocultural. It seemed to me (and still does) that the inherited concept of cultures as homogeneous and closed entities has become highly inappropriate in comprehending the constitution of today's cultures. So my basic intuition was that a conceptual update was necessary. In suggesting 'transculturality', I was trying to do what Hegel urged us philosophers to do: namely, to grasp our age in thought.[2]

I still think that I was on the right track at the time. Yet, in the meantime, I have come to suspect that my original conception is in need of a supplement. An essential point is missing. At present, most of us think of transcultural commonalities exclusively as a – highly welcome – effect of today's blending of cultures. Cultures, we think, were quite different formerly; now they are merging and thus commonalities are coming about. Cultural difference is the point of departure; commonalities are second-level acquisitions. Furthermore, when our view of cultural blending comes under attack, when opponents object that this development will end in uniformization, our response again shows our adherence to difference: we point out that these supposedly uniform cultures nevertheless exhibit new forms of inner diversity, that the transcultural networks which arise sometimes differ even from one individual to the next. We are thus, both conceptually and emotionally, bound to the concept of difference.

This view, I think, is in need of revision, for there *is* another type of commonalities, one *preceding* cultural difference. We tend to overlook the amount of commonalities humans already share before cultural differences get off the ground. What I have in mind here is, roughly, what was formerly referred to as universals: determinants common to all cultures. It is to this point that I wish to direct attention. In doing so, however, I will give the old issue of universals a new twist – so to speak, an update in the light of recent research in both the sciences and the humanities.

---

[2] See Georg Wilhelm Friedrich Hegel, *Elements of the Philosophy of Right*, tr. H.B. Nisbet (*Grundlinien der Philosophie des Rechts*, 1821; tr. Cambridge: Cambridge UP, 1991): 21.

My current picture is that transculturality – the existence of cross-cultural commonalities – is fostered by two quite different factors operating at very different levels (though there is, as I will show, also some connection). One is the current process of the permeation of cultures – a process creating commonalities by *overcoming* differences. The other is much older, and related to the human condition as such; it *underlies* all formation of difference. If we take *both* aspects into account, we might, I suspect, arrive at a more complete picture of transculturality altogether.

In the following, I will first summarize the main points of my previous account of transculturality and will then move on to discuss the importance and impact that universal-style commonalities have on our condition.

I: From the Concept of Single Cultures to Transculturality

1.   The Traditional Concept of Single Cultures

a. The Herderian framework

The conception of transculturality was initially meant to replace the older notion of single cultures – a concept that had been dominant since the end of the eighteenth century and was paradigmatically formulated by Herder in his *Another Philosophy of History for the Education of Mankind* (1774) and his *Outlines of a Philosophy of the History of Man* (1784–91).[3]

This older conception was characterized by three determinants: ethnic foundation; social homogenization; and intercultural delimitation. First, culture was to be the specific culture of a certain people – with, say, French culture being intrinsically different from German culture, or Slavic, or Japanese culture. Secondly, every culture was supposed to mould the whole life of the people concerned, making every act and every object an unmistakable instance of precisely *this* culture. Thirdly, *delimitation* towards the outside ensued: every culture was, as the culture of one people, to be distinguished and to remain separated from the cultures of other peoples.[4]

---

[3] Johann Gottfried Herder, *Outlines of a Philosophy of the History of Man*, tr. T. Churchill (*Ideen zur Philosophie der Geschichte der Menschheit*, 1784–91; tr. 1800; New York: Bergman, 1966). The work first appeared in four separate parts, each of five books, in the years 1784, 1785, 1787 and 1791, published by the Hartknoch press in Riga and Leipzig.

[4] To be sure, Herder's conception also contains elements which we may still value: the emphasis on 'everyday culture', or the equitable recognition of all cultures, so different from the Enlightenment's unificatory and eurocentric assessment. For views on Herder's

b. Problematic consequences arising from this conception

The three main traits of the conception – the emphasis on ethnicity, homo-geneity, and separation – have certainly become untenable today, both in de-scriptive and in normative terms.

Let me highlight just one point. Having noted that "each nation has its *centre* of happiness *in itself,* like every sphere its centre of gravity,"[5] Herder continues: "Everything that is still *similar* with my nature, that can be *assimi-lated* to it, I covet, strive for, make my own; *beyond that,* kind nature has armed me with *feelinglessness, coldness* and *blindness*; this can even become *contempt* and *disgust.*"[6] Thus Herder advocates the double feature of empha-sizing what is one's own and excluding what is foreign. "Prejudice," he says, "is good [...] for it renders *happy.*"[7] Conversely, any reference to another cul-ture that goes beyond use for its own ends is damaging, is "already *sickness.*"[8]

The basic flaw of this conception is to envisage cultures as closed spheres. Exclusion and conflict logically follow from this, for different spheres, each closed on itself, cannot communicate or mingle with each other but, as Herder states, can only "*collide*"[9] (this, incidentally, is the original version of the 'clash of civilizations').

2. The Concept of Transculturality

Today's cultures can obviously no longer be described as closed spheres or in terms of inner homogeneity and outer separation. Rather, they are charac-terized by a wide variety of mixing and permeations.[10] It is this new form of

---

possible contemporary relevance, see *Herder Today,* ed. Kurt Mueller–Vollmer (Berlin: de Gruyter, 1990).

[5] Johann Gottfried Herder, "This Too a Philosophy of History for the Formation of Humanity" ("Auch eine Philosophie der Geschichte zur Bildung der Menschheit" [1774]), in Johann Gottfried von Herder, *Philosophical Writings,* ed. & tr. Michael N. Forster (Cam-bridge: Cambridge U P, 2002): 297.

[6] Herder, "This Too a Philosophy of History," 297.

[7] "This Too a Philosophy of History," 297.

[8] "This Too a Philosophy of History," 297.

[9] "This Too a Philosophy of History," 297.

[10] We are mistaken when we continue to speak of German, French, Japanese, Indian, etc. cultures as if these were clearly defined and closed entities; what we really have in mind when speaking this way are political or linguistic communities, not truly cultural forma-tions.

cultures that I call transcultural, since it goes *beyond* the traditional concept of culture and *passes through* traditional boundaries as a matter of course. Let me briefly summarize the main points of my concept.

a. The macro-level: permeations

At the macro-level, contemporary cultures are multiply characterized by *hybridization* – on the levels of population, market products, and information. The entanglements are a consequence of migratory processes, as well as of communications systems and economic interdependencies – and, of course, dependencies as well. In most countries of the world, members of most other countries of this planet are to be found; in the case of market products (as exotic as these may once have been) the new condition is evident anyway; and, finally, the global networking of communications technology makes all sorts of information available everywhere.

Cultural mixing occurs not only (as is often too one-sidely stated) at the low level of Coke, McDonald's, MTV or CNN, but in highbrow culture as well. This has been the case for a long time – classical examples include Puccini and Chinese music; Gauguin and Tahiti; expressionism and African art; or Messiaen and India. The example of medicine is another case in point: whereas Western medicine is on the advance in Asian countries, in the West people are increasingly turning to acupuncture, Qigong, and Ayurveda.

The effects of permeation even affect basic cultural questions. Today the same basic problems and similar states of consciousness appear in cultures once considered to be fundamentally different. Pertinent examples are human-rights debates, feminist movements, and ecological awareness, all of which constitute powerful unifying factors across the cultural board.

In a nutshell: as a result of the increasing interpenetration of cultures there is no longer anything *absolutely foreign*. Accordingly, there is no longer anything *exclusively one's own*, either. Authenticity has become folklore, 'own-ness' simulated for others – to whom the indigene himself belongs.[11] In

---

[11] Conversely, the foreign is, as a matter of fact, considered part of one's own culture. In Kyoto, accompanied by Japanese friends, I entered a restaurant in which everything appeared genuinely Japanese and asked my companions whether everything there really was completely Japanese, including the chairs which we had just sat down on. They seemed astonished by the question, almost annoyed, and hastily assured me that everything there – even the chairs – was completely Japanese. But I knew the chairs: they were "Cab" chairs designed by Mario Bellini and produced by Cassina in Milan. Some minutes later I no longer even dared to ask about the crockery we were eating from (Suomi series plates

a culture's internal design there is today almost as much foreignness as in its external relations with other cultures.[12] The delimitation of one's own culture and foreign culture has become invalid.[13]

b. The micro-level: transcultural formation of individuals

Transculturality is gaining ground not only at the macrocultural level, but also at the micro-level of individuals. For most of us, multiple cultural connections are decisive in terms of our cultural formation. We are cultural hybrids. Today's writers, for example, are no longer shaped by a single homeland, but by different reference-countries. Their cultural formation is transcultural. As Amy Gutmann put it: "Most people's identities, not just Western intellectuals or elites, are shaped by more than a single culture. Not only societies, but people are multicultural."[14] And this is likely to become even more so in the future.[15]

---

produced by Rosenthal in Germany). What is astonishing is not that European furniture and crockery should be found in Japan, but that the Japanese held them to be products of their own culture. That the foreign and the home-grown have become indistinguishable for them serves witness to factual transculturality.

[12] From a sociological point of view, this is a familiar fact today: "people belong to many different cultures and the cultural differences are as likely to be within states (i.e. between regions, classes, ethnic groups, the urban and rural) as between states" – Anthony King, "Architecture, Capital and the Globalization of Culture," in *Global Culture: Nationalism, Globalization and Modernity: A Theory*, ed. Mike Featherstone (London: Sage, 1990): 409; "cultural diversity tends now to be as great within nations as it is between them" – Ulf Hannerz, *Cultural Complexity: Studies in the Social Organization of Meaning* (New York: Columbia UP, 1992): 231.

[13] Incidentally, this is reflected in a famous thesis in analytic philosophy. According to Quine and Davidson, the problem of translation between different societies and languages is structurally not at all unlike, and in no way greater or more dramatic than within one and the same society and language.

[14] Amy Gutmann, "The Challenge of Multiculturalism in Political Ethics," *Philosophy & Public Affairs* 22.3 (1993): 183.

[15] Sociologists have been telling us since the 1970s that modern lives are to be understood "as a migration through different social worlds and as the successive realization of a number of possible identities" (Peter L. Berger, Brigitte Berger & Hansfried Kellner, *The Homeless Mind: Modernization and Consciousness* [New York: Random House, 1973]: 77) and that we all possess "multiple attachments and identities" – "cross-cutting identities," as Daniel Bell put it (Bell, *The Winding Passage: Essays and Sociological Journeys 1960–1980* [Cambridge MA: Abt, 1980]: 243). What once may have applied only to exquisite subjects like Montaigne, Novalis, Whitman, Rimbaud or Nietzsche – major advocates and prophets of a pluralistic identity – seems to be becoming the structure of almost everybody

c. Cultural diversity of a new type

What is the result of this? Some intellectuals fear that the entanglements at the macro- and micro-levels will result in straightforward uniformization and the loss of cultural difference. That is wrong. For even if people draw on the same set of cultural elements, they will probably give those elements different weight and a different overall arrangement. And differences will, of course, be even greater when people draw on several and diverse cultural elements. Identity networks woven from partly the same and from partly different threads are not all of the same colour and pattern.

What changes is the *type* of cultural variety. Differences no longer emerge between different kinds of monolothic identities, but between identity configurations that have some elements in common while differing in other elements, in their arrangement as a whole, and often in their complexity.

d. Transculturality – already in history

A further point needs to be clarified: Transculturality is in no way completely new historically; in fact, it has been widespread in history.

---

today. Michel de Montaigne had stated: "I have nothing to say about myself absolutely, simply, and solidly, without confusion and without mixture, or in one word. [...] we are all patchwork, and so shapeless and diverse in composition that each bit, each moment, plays its own game" (Montaigne, *The Complete Essays*, tr. Donald M. Frame [Stanford CA: Stanford UP, 1992]: 242 and 244 resp. [II 1]). Novalis wrote that one person is "several people at once," since "pluralism" is "our innermost essence"; Novalis, *Schriften*, ed. Paul Kluckhohn & Richard Samuel, vol. 3: *Das philosophische Werk II* (Stuttgart: Kohlhammer, 1983): 250 and 571. Walt Whitman declared: "I am large [...] I contain multitudes" (Whitman, "Song of Myself," in *Leaves of Grass* [1855; New York: Penguin, 1985]: 84). Arthur Rimbaud stated: "Je est un autre" (Rimbaud, "Lettre à Paul Demeny" [15 May 1871], in *Œuvres complètes* [Paris: Gallimard, 1972]: 250). And Friedrich Nietzsche said of himself that he was "glad to harbour [...] not 'one immortal soul,' but many mortal souls within" (Nietzsche, *Menschliches, Allzumenschliches: Ein Buch für freie Geister, Zweiter Band, Sämtliche Werke: Kritische Studienausgabe in 15 Bänden*. vol. 2, ed. Giorgio Colli & Mazzino Montinari [Munich: Deutscher Taschenbuch Verlag, 1980]: 386 [II 17]); he also coined the formula of the "subject as a multitude" (Nietzsche, *Nachgelassene Fragmente: Juli 1882 bis Herbst 1885, Sämtliche Werke: Kritische Studienausgabe in 15 Bänden*, vol. 11, ed. Giorgio Colli & Mazzino Montinari [Munich: Deutscher Taschenbuch Verlag, 1980]: 650). On the issue of the plural subject, see both my "Subjektsein heute: Überlegungen zur Transformation des Subjekts," *Deutsche Zeitschrift für Philosophie* 39.4 (1991): 347–65, and my *Vernunft: Die zeitgenössische Vernunftkritik und das Konzept der transversalen Vernunft* (Frankfurt am Main: Suhrkamp, 1995), Part II, ch. XIV: "Transversalität und Subjektivität," 829–52.

Carl Zuckmayer once wonderfully described this in *The Devil's General*: "just imagine the procession of your ancestors – since the birth of Christ," General Harras says to Lieutenant Hartmann. And then he provides the full picture of Hartmann's ancestry:

> There was a Roman Captain, a dark fellow, brown as a ripe olive; he managed to teach Latin to his blonde girl on the banks of the Rhine; then a Jewish spice dealer came into the family, a serious man who converted to Christianity before the wedding and founded the Catholic tradition in the house. Then a Greek doctor, a Celtic Legionnaire, a Grisonian landsknecht, a Swedish Knight, one of Napoleon's soldiers, a deserting Cossack, a Black Forest raftsman, a wandering miller's apprentice from Alsace, a fat boatsman from Holland, a Magyar, a Pandour, an officer from Vienna, a French actor, a Bohemian musician; and all the whole mixed-up crowd that lived, brawled, drank, and sang and begot children along the River Rhine! That Goethe character, he came out of the same pot. Also a guy named Beethoven, and Gutenberg, and – ah, whatever, look it up in the encyclopedia! They were the best, my friend! The best in the world! And why? Because the nations mixed there like the waters from the springs and brooks and rivers that flow together in one great living stream.[16]

This, I think, is a realistic description of a 'people's' historical genesis and of the mixed constitution of its members. When today, in the age of globalization, we witness an interpenetration of cultures, this is not a completely new phenomenon; such permeation was already typical of cultures in the past, though perhaps to a lesser degree. Edward Said may well have been right in saying: "all cultures are involved in one another; none is single and pure, all are hybrid, heterogeneous, extraordinarily differentiated, and unmonolithic."[17]

---

[16] Carl Zuckmayer, "The Devil's General" (1946), tr. Ingrid G. Gilbert & William F. Gilbert, in *Masters of Modern Drama*, ed. Haskell M. Block & Robert G. Shedd (New York: Random House, 1963): 930 [translation modified].

[17] Edward W. Said, *Culture and Imperialism* (London: Chatto & Windus, 1993): xxix. Similarly, from a philosophical point of view, Jitendra N. Mohanty stated: "that talk of a culture which evokes the idea of a homogeneous form is completely misleading. Indian culture, or Hindu culture consists of completely different cultures. [...] A completely homogeneous subculture is not to be found"; Mohanty, "Den anderen verstehen," in *Philosophische Grundlagen der Interkulturalität*, ed. R.A. Mall (Amsterdam: Rodopi, 1993): 118 (my tr.). "The idea of cultural purity is a myth" (Mohanty, "Den anderen verstehen," 117, my tr.). Jacques Derrida says: *"what is proper to a culture is to not be identical with itself. [...] There is no culture or cultural identity without this difference with itself"*; Derrida, *The Other Heading: Reflections on Today's Europe*, tr. Pascale–Anne Brault &

e. Transcultural possession and further acquisition of commonalities

I have already made it clear why transculturality does not simply lead to uniformization but is intrinsically linked with the emergence of diversity of a new type.[18] Transcultural identity networks are not all the same in their repertoire and structure; the same elements are differently weighted and arranged.

So difference is not vanishing, but its *mode* is changing. Difference, as traditionally provided by single cultures, certainly is diminishing. Instead, differences between transcultural networks arise. These networks, however, also have some elements in common while differing in others. So there is always some overlap between them – "family resemblances," as Wittgenstein put it.

Michael B. Naas (*L'autre cap*, 1991; tr. Bloomington: Indiana U P, 1992): 9–10 (emphasis in the original). Rémi Brague has pointed out how European identity is characterized by the sense of its distance from a double origin of Greek culture and Judaic religion: "This specific relation [of Europe to culture] is a consequence of the phenomenon of cultural secondarity, and as such it takes on in Europe the intensity that we have seen. Culture cannot be, for the European, something that he possesses and that constitutes his identity. It will be on the contrary something fundamentally strange, that therefore makes an effort of appropriation necessary"; Brague, *Eccentric Culture: A Theory of Western Civilization*, tr. Samuel Lester (*Europe, la voie romaine*, 1992; tr. South Bend I N : St. Augustine's, 2002): 135–36. As soon as one observes the cultural fictions of purity more closely and realistically, they rapidly break up into a series of transcultural entanglements.

[18] Similar views to mine are put forward by Mike Featherstone, who argues "against those who would wish to present the tendency on the global level to be one of cultural integration and homogenization" (Mike Featherstone, *Consumer Culture & Postmodernism* [London: Sage, 1991]: 146) and by Ulf Hannerz, who says "that the flow of culture between countries and continents may result in another diversity of culture, based more on interconnections than on autonomy" (Hannerz, *Cultural Complexity*, 266). Incidentally, it is by no means evident that globalization processes are correctly defined when they are described only as a unilinear expansion of Western culture. One would, at the same time, have to be attentive to considerable alterations which the elements of the initial culture experience in the process of their acquisition. Stephen Greenblatt has pointed out such ambiguities in the "assimilation of the other." He describes this, for instance, in the way the inhabitants of Bali deal with video technology in a ritual context: "if the television and the V C R [...] suggested the astonishing pervasiveness of capitalist markets and technology, [...] the Balinese adaptation of the latest Western and Japanese modes of representation seemed so culturally idiosyncratic and resilient that it was unclear who was assimilating whom" (Stephen Greenblatt, *Marvelous Possessions: The Wonder of the New World* [Chicago: U of Chicago P, 1991]: 4). Ulf Hannerz discusses similar phenomena under the heading "creolization": the uniform trends of a 'world culture', he demonstrates, are quickly bound into national or regional cultural profiles and thereby experience considerable diversification and transformation (see Hannerz, *Cultural Complexity*, esp. 264ff.).

The result of this is a greater chance for communication, linking-up, and understanding than ever before. The common stock of overlapping elements – of commonalities that have arisen through the development of transcultural networks in the first place – provides a basis for further exchange and agreement. On an initial ground of commonalities, a second range of commonalities can be developed which may even be made up of elements that had previously not seemed capable of being agreed upon. Many of these second-level commonalities will be pragmatic in nature.

In short: transcultural orientations provide a first set of commonalities and, on their basis, allow for the development of subsequent commonalities. In other words: transcultural intersections lead to an *initial acquisition* of commonalities, and the *possession* of these consequently enables *further acquisitions*. This increased possibility for exchange and coming to terms with each other obviously represents a great advantage in transcultural constitution.

II :   Deeper-Level Commonalities

Having so far summarized my previous account of transculturality, I now turn to the complementary aspect announced in the introduction. As pointed out above, there are not only commonalities that *arise* through the permeation of cultures, but there are also commonalities that already *precede* and *underlie* the formation of cultures. I would now like to consider these deeper commonalities.

Does this mean addressing the notorious issue of cultural universals? Not directly, at least. First I would like to show that transcultural experience and exchange can, as a matter of principle, not be understood without assuming something 'universal' underlying cultural difference. If there were no common basis to cultures at all, then the fact that we can transfer semantic items (beliefs, thoughts, perceptions, yearnings, etc.) from one culture to another and integrate them into a context which originally was not theirs would be completely unintelligible. We usually consider it a matter of course that such transfers are possible – but we are far less willing to accept their condition of possibility.

Reference to cultural universals must reckon with resistance. In the realm of cultural studies, an extreme form of 'difference-thinking' is today dominant. Cultural studies flourish under its auspices; to refer to universals there seems almost a sacrilege. But all I want is, first, to urge us to use *both* eyes – to take a look *also* at elementary commonalities. And, second, our clarificatory work cannot simply take established preferences as its measure. It is important to see whether there are in fact deeper commonalities and what significance accrues to them for the understanding of cultural differences and for the acquisition of commonalities.

1. Fascination by Works of Art and Literature from Foreign Cultures

Let us consider the fascination that outstanding works of art or literature from foreign cultures can exert on us. Why do we fall under their spell?[19]

a. Mea res agitur

When confronted with such works, we sense a *mea res agitur*. As distant as the origin of these works may be in time and space, we nevertheless feel, strangely enough, that it is *we* who are at stake. Though not made for us, the works seem to address us; we feel attracted to them, fascinated by them. They appear to bear a promise or a challenge to which we respond. Some at least seem to develop an impulse and potential to improve and enlarge our sensitivity, our comprehension, and perhaps even our way of being.

So we take those works, however distant their origin in time or space may be, to be relevant to *our* orientation. We do not lock them into their original cultural context; rather, we experience them as transculturally effective. As a phenomenon, I think, this is wellnigh self-evident.

b. Objection to the modern dogma of cultural boundness

Yet this transcultural force tends to be overlooked in current theorizing, for in modernity we have become accustomed to thinking that everything is strictly bound to its cultural context. We take all production, experience, and cognition to be fully determined by their cultural framework, hence as restricted to it. This is the modern axiom *par excellence*.[20] It lurks behind the various forms of relativism, contextualism, and culturalism that today dominate the humanities and cultural studies. Culture-dependent aspects do exist, to be

---

[19] I first presented the following considerations in "Rethinking Identity in the Age of Globalization: A Transcultural Perspective" (in *Symposion of Beauty and Art: Festschrift für Tsunemichi Kambayashi*, ed. Hiroshi Okabayashi et al. [Tokyo: Keiso, 2002]: 333–46). An updated version appeared in the *International Yearbook of Aesthetics*, vol. 8: "Aesthetics and/as Globalization" (2004): 167–76.

[20] In recent years I have been developing an account and critique of this axiom, which I hope to be able to present in a forthcoming study under the working title "Beyond Modern Anthropocentrism."

sure. But *not only* these exist. With the axiom noted above – with this common prejudice of contemporary cultural studies (*'Kulturwissenschaften'*) – we are blinding ourselves to the obviously not culture-bound but transcultural potential of outstanding semantic items –works of art, for example.

Instead of spiriting this potential away through the beliefs decreed by modernity, we should be trying to give it an appropriate rendering. We need, I think, a theory that faces up to and is able to explain this transcending of context, this transcultural force of semantic items. Such a theory, it seems to me, does not yet exist.

c. This fascination is not culture-bound but transcends cultures

The fascination works independently of familiarity with the respective culture. If you go to Japan for the first time and visit the Ginkakuji temple in Kyoto, you will feel the strong magnetism of the place. You may have no idea of fifteenth-century Japanese culture, nor of the conditions in which the Shogun Yoshimasa created this environment. Yet you are irresistibly attracted and, after some time, may feel how the place alters your way of walking, behaving, thinking.

It is as if a previously unknown chord in our existence were being struck; a side we knew nothing about and which now suddenly resonates. In our culture, it was never brought to bear; now it blossoms. It is as if, until now, we had only realized part of our human potential; as if this were, in fact, richer than it had previously (whether monoculturally or transculturally) been developed.

2. How Are Such Phenomena to Be Explained?

a. Insufficiency of the hermeneutic approach

The standard explanation, that given by hermeneutics, fails. It claims that all understanding is ultimately determined by the cultural context one belongs to. But this is highly implausible.

If someone grew up in Paris and studied at Paris VIII St. Denis, this obviously would not in itself provide him with a deep understanding of St. Denis Cathedral, the foundational work of Gothic architecture. For this he must – like everybody else – acquire a lot of additional knowledge. But for this acquisition he is, again, not *per se* better prepared by a Parisian childhood than, say, by a childhood in Vancouver or Nagoya. None of these childhoods facilitates or rules out thorough understanding. (Today, it is American scholars who write the most informed and fascinating books on European art.)

In the same way, the primary fascination works in a way that is culture-independent in the clearest of senses. People from *every* cultural context experience the magnetism of the Ginkakuji temple. None of them, neither people from 'old Europe' (an expression coined by Napoleon, not by Donald Rumsfeld) nor any of the Japanese visitors lived in the period when this temple was erected. Neither contemporariness nor belonging to the 'effective history' really plays any role here.[21] It must instead be something in the human make-up as such that makes us receptive to the attraction of the place: something beyond the realm of specific cultural formation, something precultural, something related to human potential and constitution as such.

b. The deep subcultural dimension

Even if it were the case that we inevitably approach what is unknown to us through the set of views and possibilities provided by our cultural condition (as hermeneutics likes to think), it would still be true that we can experience the culture-transcending force of works like the Ginkakuji temple only because there is a framework-transcending dimension inherent in our cultural condition. In the course of our cultural formation, paths to any work, no matter how 'exotic', open up. Our cultural formation must in itself contain something that enables such paths to other cultures – and by no means just dead ends of remaining-with-oneself in a self-modelled Other, but paths that really lead to the Other.[22]

In other words, culture seems to contain two layers: one cultural, and another precultural. The culture we are acquainted with is itself one specific moulding of a more general structure. And owing to the latter's inherence and permanence we are capable of experiencing semantic items lacking any direct connection with our own cultural mould. This is just as in Chomsky's con-

---

[21] A second objection to the hermeneutic approach applies to the circle of self-shackling to which it hands over all understanding. Hermeneutics thinks one can only understand the Other in terms of the Self, albeit in terms of a successively extended Self. However, this has the consequence that one nowhere gets beyond the figure of remaining-with-oneself in the face of a self-modelled Other. No matter how much pirouetting, genuine understanding therefore counts as impossible. Conversely, with this consequence one can recognize that the hermeneutic view must be wrong – genuine understanding of the Other does exist.

[22] In this context, it is worth pointing out a statement of Ernst Tugendhat's: "I consider the idea that our possibilities of understanding are primarily bound to the Western tradition to be a prejudice" (Tugendhat, *Egozentrismus und Mystik. Eine anthropologische Studie* [Munich: C.H. Beck, 2003]: 135). (My tr.)

ception, wherein any language represents a specific moulding of universal grammar; this universal structure remains in place, so that learning other languages is possible through processes that draw on universal grammar.

I do not mind whether one takes this general structure to remain *below* the level of cultural moulding or to be *inherent* in the latter (which I would prefer) – I am urging only that we should be aware of this deeper layer and take it into account.

3. 'Universals'

Can we say more about this general structure – which so far I have only demonstrated that we must recognize? What precisely does it consist of? In what way is it inherent in us? And is it truly universal?

The current employment of the term 'universal' is anything but precise. 'Universal', I think, would have to refer to the universe or to something valid all over the universe, as it did – as a matter of course – in traditional usages of the term. But in its modern usage the term has become restricted to things on earth, and furthermore to just one species on earth, *homo sapiens*. In contemporary language, 'universal' just means 'valid for all humans'. Isn't that an impertinent reduction? Yet I will (so as not to complicate things unnecessarily) submit to using the expression in the modern standard sense.

I will now turn to the discussion of 'universals' in older anthropological and more recent scientific literature. Maybe this can help us understand better the deep culture-transcending layers of our constitution, capacities, and experience.

a. Universals in older anthropological and recent scientific discussion
aa. Unsatisfactory beginnings

'Universals' were a problematic feature from the start. When in 1873 Adolf Bastian (1826–1905), the 'father of German anthropology', stated that there are universal "elementary ideas" ('*Elementargedanken*') which culturally develop into "folk ideas" or ideas shared by a given people ('*Völkergedanken*'),[23] he had a hard time making this plausible, because – even according to his

---

[23] Adolf Bastian, *Controversen in der Ethnologie*, vol. I: *Die Geographischen Provinzen in ihren culturgeschichtlichen Berührungspuncten* (Berlin: Weidmannsche Buchhandlung, 1893), excerpts translated in Klaus–Peter Koepping, *Adolf Bastian and the Psychic Unity of Mankind: The Foundations of Anthropology in Nineteenth Century Germany* (St. Lucia: U of Queensland P, 1983): 171–73.

own conception – these "elementary ideas" are never directly observable, but only indirectly deducible from the manifest plethora of folk ideas. Are they more than fictions, then?

Bastian passed his idea on to his disciple Franz Boas, who became the leading figure in North American anthropology. But given the constitutively concealed character of the assumed universals it was no wonder that in the more pragmatic climate of thought in the USA the Boas school turned completely to the apparent diversity of cultures (think, for example, of Ruth Benedict, Margaret Mead, Edward Sapir, Alfred L. Kroeber) and developed the doctrine of cultural relativism and incommensurability so dominant in the first half of the twentieth century. In this view, there was simply no space for universals.

Against this doctrine, Bronislaw Malinowski claimed in 1941 that cultural universals obviously do exist. But the list he presented was quite disappointing. All he could bring forward were seven basic needs: metabolism, reproduction, bodily comforts, safety, movement, growth, and health.[24] Things were hardly any better with George P. Murdock's famous list of 72 human universals, published in 1945.[25] Murdoch proposed, for example, "tool making, gift giving, funeral rites, greetings, hair styles, hospitality, marriage, housing, taboos, inheritance rules, status differentiation."[26]

There were obvious objections. Did these universals have any explanatory force for the real design of cultures? Didn't they rather look like "empty

---

[24] Bronislaw Malinowski, "A Scientific Theory of Culture" in Malinowski, *A Scientific Theory of Culture and Other Essays* (Chapel Hill: U of North Carolina P, 1944): 91.

[25] George P. Murdock, "The Common Denominator of Cultures," in Murdock, *Culture and Society: Twenty-Four Essays* (Pittsburg: U of Pittsburgh P, 1965): 89.

[26] Here is the full list in alphabetic order: "Age-grading, athletic sports, bodily adornment, calendar, cleanliness training, community organization, cooking, cooperative labor, cosmology, courtship, dancing, decorative art, divination, division of labor, dream interpretation, education, eschatology, ethics, ethnobotany, etiquette, faith healing, family, feasting, fire making, folklore, food taboos, funeral rites, games, gestures, gift giving, government, greetings, hair styles, hospitality, housing, hygiene, incest taboos, inheritance rules, joking, kin-groups, kinship nomenclature, language, law, luck superstitions, magic, marriage, mealtimes, medicine, modesty concerning natural functions, mourning, music, mythology, numerals, obstetrics, penal sanctions, personal names, population policy, postnatal care, pregnancy usages, property rights, propitiation of supernatural beings, puberty customs, religious ritual, residence rules, sexual restrictions, soul concepts, status differentiation, surgery, tool making, trade, visiting, weaning, and weather control" (Murdock, "The Common Denominator of Cultures," 89).

frames" or "blanket categories"?[27] Kroeber even spoke of "fake universals."
Clifford Geertz resumed the criticism in 1966 by pointing out that in order to
bring cultural phenomena under such universal headings one must strip them
of all their specific content.[28] What good is it to classify Confucianism,
Calvinism, and Buddhism together as "religion" when one form teaches that
merit accrues from following rules whereas the other excludes precisely this,
and when in one case it is a religion with a godhead and in the other without
one? "And as with religion, so with 'marriage', 'trade' and all the rest,"[29]
Geertz points out and asks:

> Is the fact that 'marriage' is universal (if it is) as penetrating a comment on what
> we are as the facts concerning Himalayan polyandry, or those fantastic Australian
> marriage rules, or the elaborate bride-price systems of Bantu Africa?[30]

Geertz's conclusion reads: "rather than moving toward the essentials of the
human situation," looking for human universals "moves away from them."[31]
This certainly constituted a plausible critique.

bb. Refutation of radical cultural relativism
and the discovery of hard universals

The situation changed in the 1980s, however, when once-paradigmatic
'proofs' of radical cultural diversity were falsified: in 1983 Derek Freeman
demolished Margaret Mead's Samoa-myth[32] and Ekkehart Malotki did the
same with Benjamin Lee Whorf's once so influential declarations about Hopi
language.[33] The dogma of radical cultural relativism broke down in anthro-

---

[27] See Elmar Holenstein, *Menschliches Selbstverständnis* (Frankfurt am Main: Suhr-kamp, 1985): 125.

[28] Clifford Geertz, "The Impact of the Concept of Culture on the Concept of Man," in Geertz, *The Interpretation of Cultures: Selected Essays* (New York: Basic Books, 1973): 33–54.

[29] Geertz, "The Impact of the Concept of Culture," 40.

[30] "The Impact of the Concept of Culture," 43.

[31] "The Impact of the Concept of Culture," 39.

[32] Derek Freeman, *Margaret Mead and Samoa: The Making and Unmaking of an Anthropological Myth* (Cambridge MA: Harvard UP, 1983).

[33] Ekkehart Malotki, *Hopi Time* (Berlin: Mouton, 1983).

pology[34] (but has survived until the present day in cultural studies in America and Europe). As a consequence, scholars have become disposed to reconsider the issue of universals and also finally to pay attention to research which had already, some decades earlier, demonstrated the existence of universals of a much more solid type than those listed by Malinowski and Murdock.

Roman Jakobson had found out in 1953 that the sounds of natural human languages are not a random mix, but form a system constituted by a distinct number of underlying binary oppositions.[35] However, Brent Berlin's and Paul Kay's 1969 study *Basic Color Terms* represented the real breakthrough.[36] They showed, first, that whatever the number of basic colour terms in a specific culture is (ranging from two to eleven), the members of these cultures, despite dividing up the colour spectrum quite differently (depending on the available number of colour words), nonetheless agree almost completely when asked which specific colour chip (of which they were shown more than 300) represents the ideal or prototypical instance of a colour they have a word for. This consensus with respect to the focal points of colour terms proves that the basic experience of colour is not culturally determined but universal. Secondly, Berlin and Kay found that the order in which basic colour categories enter languages is not arbitrary. If a language has only two colour words they are always white and black; the third colour is always red; if a fourth is added, it will be either green or yellow; the fifth will be yellow or green; then come blue and brown; and finally purple, pink, orange, and gray. So there *are* strong universal regularities – sequences of constitution that apply in all cultures. Research on the classification of botanical and zoological life forms has since revealed similar developmental sequences.[37]

cc. Surface universals

In addition to these underlying universals, the existence of surface universals has also been established. Facial expression of emotions is one such case. Studies of children born deaf and blind show that the elementary expressions

---

[34] The doctrine of radical cultural relativism was revealed to be "a myth created by linguists and anthropologists"; see Donald E. Brown, *Human Universals* (New York: McGraw–Hill, 1991): 13.

[35] See Holenstein, *Menschliches Selbstverständnis*, 125.

[36] Brent Berlin & Paul Kay, *Basic Color Terms: Their Universality and Evolution* (Berkeley: U of California P, 1969).

[37] See Brown, *Human Universals*, 14.

of, say, happiness or sadness are not learned or imitated (children born deaf and blind are not capable of such learning), but form part of an innate behavioural repertoire which is the same across cultures.[38] Another well-known example – this time of universal gestures – is raising one's eyebrows as a way of initiating communication: "as an expression of friendly attentiveness, say when greeting at a distance, people in all cultures raise their eyebrows for a sixth of a second; at the same time they lift their head, following this they nod and a smile spreads."[39]

One might ask: are there not also cultural differences in these matters? Certainly. But they are only a *secondary* phenomenon. They do not concern the expressions as such but, rather, the willingness to display them publicly. This was brilliantly demonstrated by Paul Ekman and his associates (1969, 1972, 1973). They did a comparative study of Japanese (who allegedly have a tendency to mask facial expressions of emotions) and Americans (who are considered not to do so). The result was that the Japanese, when with others, do mask expressions or substitute one for another, while Americans do not. But when, so to speak, off-stage (alone) the Japanese and Americans respond in quite the same way. So the basic features of emotions and their facial expression are the same; differences only concern "display rules": i.e. culture-specific standards about the display of emotions.[40]

dd. Aesthetic universals

Another case in point are aesthetic preferences. Studies of infants (3–4 months) showed that they already prefer the same adult faces that we prefer as adults. They respond with greater interest to faces that also seem more

---

[38] See Irenäus Eibl–Eibesfeldt, "Universalien im menschlichen Sozialverhalten," in *Der ganze Mensch: Aspekte einer pragmatischen Anthropologie*, ed. Hans Rössner (Munich: Deutscher Taschenbuch-Verlag, 1986): 82 f.

[39] Eibl–Eibesfeldt, "Universalien im menschlichen Sozialverhalten," 89.

[40] See Paul Ekman, "Cross-Cultural Studies of Facial Expressions," in *Darwin and Facial Expression: A Century of Research in Review*, ed. Paul Ekman (New York: Academic Press, 1973): 215–18, as well as his "Afterword" to Charles Darwin, *The Expression of the Emotions in Man and Animals* (1872; Oxford: Oxford UP, 1998): 383–85. – The facial expressions for happiness, sadness, anger, and disgust are unambiguously universal; in addition (though apparently only in literate cultures) come those of fear and surprise (see Ekman, "Afterword," 390; see also Vicki Bruce, *In the Eye of the Beholder: The Science of Face Perception* [Oxford: Oxford UP, 1998]: 190).

interesting to us. This applies cross-culturally.[41] These early preference patterns are thus innate, not culturally acquired.

Furthermore, in the adult world patterns of preference concerning the opposite sex are very similar worldwide. This has been demonstrated for facial and bodily proportions. In a famous 1993 study, Devendra Singh found out that, from a male point of view, the ideal female waist–hip ratio (WHR) is 0.7. (For Europeans: this is very close to the famous 60:90 centimeter measure; and for Americans 24:36 inches might ring a bell).[42]

These body-related patterns of aesthetic preference are thus also universal. They do not, of course, determine our aesthetic preferences completely, since they are culturally transformed. Nonetheless, they represent a solid core that determines our *primary* choice.

❮❖❯

I have identified three groups of universals: deep (phonetic and linguistic) universals; surface (emotive and mimetic) universals; and, finally, aesthetic universals. All of these are factors which all people across all cultures share.

Recently I re-read Rousseau's complaint that "philosophy does not travel."[43] Were it to do so, then the "philosophical rabble" would not be able to propagate the "hackneyed" doctrine that "people are the same everywhere."[44] When one starts to travel, one is certainly fascinated by the variation. But when one travels a lot and travels far (and if one also gets around enough otherwise – say, in science), then one might increasingly notice how much we humans have in common.[45]

---

[41] See Judith H. Langlois et al., "Infant Preferences for Attractive Faces: Rudiments of a Stereotype?" *Developmental Psychology* 23 (1987): 363–69.

[42] Further universal marks of beauty are smooth skin, thick shiny hair, and symmetrical body; see Nancy Etcoff, *Survival of the Prettiest: The Science of Beauty* (Garden City NY: Doubleday, 1999).

[43] Jean–Jacques Rousseau, *Discours sur l'origine et les fondements de l'inégalité parmi les hommes* (1755; Paris: Gallimard, 1969): 142 (note X).

[44] Rousseau, *Discours sur l'origine*, 142–43 [note X].

[45] Darwin had already noticed the "similarity, or rather identity" of humans regarding elementary abilities and modes of behaviour. One can "hardly fail to be deeply impressed with the close similarity between the men of all races in tastes, dispositions and habits. This is shown by the pleasure which they all take in dancing, rude music, acting, painting, tattooing, and otherwise decorating themselves – in their mutual comprehension of gesture-language – and, as I shall be able to show in a future essay, by the same expression in their

b. Universals as the legacy of humanity's protocultural developments

In the following part of my essay, I will give the theme of universals a certain twist. Why, in fact, do we all have these things in common? Where do we have them from?

aa. The shaping of 'human nature' through
*   protocultural-biological feedback processes*

These processes are fairly well known today. They have taken shape in the course of human development and became frozen at a certain point in time as the reserves of 'human nature' – at a point in time *before* the spread of *homo sapiens* across the globe, hence *before the emergence of cultural diversity*. I want to go into this in greater detail.

One must bear in mind that the early humans (the Australopithecines, just like the early species of *homo*) enhanced – and in this way, as evolutionary theorists put it, 'selected' – certain biological features through protocultural activities in the process of becoming human. Human nature is not simply a product of nature, but in large part a human product – humans have themselves taken a role in producing their 'nature'.[46]

An obvious example of this is the fact that our bodies are largely hairless (along with simultaneous enhancement of our scalp hair) – which so clearly distinguishes us from our nearest biological relatives, the apes. This hairlessness is not to be explained, as was thought earlier, as an adaptation to climatic change (in that case, we should have lost the hair on our head first instead of enhancing it), but as a result of sexual selection.[47] Reducing hair growth – a

---

features, and by the same inarticulate cries, when they are excited by various emotions. This similarity, or rather identity, is striking, when contrasted with the different expressions which may be observed in distinct species of monkeys." Charles Darwin, *The Descent of Man, and Selection in Relation to Sex* (1871; Princeton NJ: Princeton UP, 1981): 232.

[46] This has been pointed out by Clifford Geertz: "there is no such thing as a human nature independent of culture" (Geertz, "The Impact of the Concept of Culture," 49); "culture [...] was ingredient, and centrally ingredient, in the production of that animal itself" ("The Impact of the Concept of Culture," 47).

[47] "Sexual selection" is the second major selection mechanism which Darwin, in addition to the natural selection set out in *Origin of Species* of 1859, presented in 1871 in *The Descent of Man* (the book's subtitle is "Selection in Relation to Sex" and the voluminous Part II is dedicated entirely to sexual selection). Only both procedures together provide the full picture of evolution. The theory of sexual selection at the same time builds a bridge to aesthetics: for sexual choice, the gradual development of aesthetic attractors, of so-called "ornaments" (which in the order of natural selection are costly and of no use, and indeed

means of distancing ourselves from our nearest ape relations – had become attractive,[48] and so in the choice of partner those candidates were preferred who already corresponded to this new human fashion to some extent. This preference then led to increased propagation of hairlessness in the genome of the species – until humans one day, having left behind their paradisiac proximity to animals, simultaneously (as the Bible recounts) discovered that they were human and "perceived themselves to be naked."[49] Through its effects on the gene pool, the ongoing aesthetic preference had produced a new, distinctive bodily feature of the human.[50]

---

often a hindrance) represent the decisive success factor, and the higher reproductive success then secures increased propagation of these aesthetic formations and of the correlatively growing aesthetic sense in the genome of the species. Sexual selection is a process that makes the bodies and attitude of future generations more aesthetic.

For Darwin, it was eminently important to pay attention to the dynamics particular to sexual, as distinct from natural selection. Only a few hours before his death, in a lecture to the Zoological Society, he expressed his conviction, against objections, that the theory of sexual selection is sound: "I may perhaps be here permitted to say that, after having carefully weighed, to the best of my ability, the various arguments which have been advanced against the principle of sexual selection, I remain firmly convinced of its truth." Charles Darwin, "A Preliminary Notice: On the Modification of a Race of Syrian Street Dogs by Means of Sexual Selection" (1882), *The Collected Papers of Charles Darwin* (Chicago: U of Chicago P, 1977): 278. Neo-Darwinism and sociobiology attempt to deny the independence of sexual selection, however, and (by means of a general perspective of 'fitness') to reduce all effects of sexual selection (including specifically aesthetic ones) to effects of natural selection ("the currency in which the success of every biological trait is measured" is "reproductive fitness"); see Eckart Voland, "Aesthetic Preferences in the World of Artifacts: Adaptations for the Evaluation of 'Honest Signals'?" in *Evolutionary Aesthetics*, ed. Eckart Voland & Karl Grammer (Heidelberg: Springer, 2003): 256. For a critique of this tendency, see my "Animal Aesthetics" (paper at the 16th International Congress of Aesthetics, "Changes in Aesthetics," Rio de Janeiro, 18–23 July 2004), available at: *Contemporary Aesthetics* 2 (2004), http://www.contempaesthetics.org/newvolume/pages/article.php?articleID=243 (accessed 1 March 2008).

[48] "As a matter of fact, the majority of parameters in human beauty are defined by enhancing differences with apes"; Winfried Menninghaus, *Das Versprechen der Schönheit* (Frankfurt am Main: Suhrkamp, 2003): 91.

[49] Genesis, 3:7.

[50] Incidentally, this is a specific aesthetic preference also in the sense that hairlessness is just an optical impression: in absolute numbers, the human body has as many hairs as – or even more than – many kinds of ape; it is simply that our hairs have become so minute and inapparent that the optical appearance of hair loss or nakedness originated (see Menninghaus, *Das Versprechen der Schönheit*, 88). In addition, sex-specific variations (generally stronger hair and especially beard growth in men) within the general tendency towards

Much of what one calls 'human nature' is a result of protocultural-biological feedback processes: biological provisions made protocultural activities possible and through feedback these in turn enhanced the corresponding biological factors. Not only have our bodies (starting with our upright gait) formed in such processes, but also our basic emotional and mimetic patterns, and even the specific shape of the human brain.[51]

What makes our brain so special is not, as one can often read, due simply to expansion of the cerebral cortex or increased differentiation in areas of the brain, but to a dramatic redistribution between external (sensorimotoric) and internal (reflexive) functions. In lower mammals (say, in rats, with which we nonetheless share 90 percent of our genome), the relationship between internal and external communication is 10:90 percent; conversely, in humans it is at least 90:10 percent.[52] We humans are experts in inner communication, world champions in reflection. It is *in this* that our peculiarity lies. We have generated this feature in a million-year-long feedback process in which protocultural activities such as tool use, the formation of social structures, and language have played a decisive role.[53]

---

hairlessness are to be explained as strategies of differentiation between the sexes (dimorphism).

[51] "His [man's] large and efficient brain is a consequence of culture as much as its cause. He does not have a culture because he has a large brain; he has a large brain because several million years ago his little-brained ancestors tried the cultural way to survival. Of course, the correct way to view this is a feedback process. [...] the cultural things themselves propelled him into getting a larger brain. It is not only the capacity for culture, then, that lies in the brain; it is the forms of culture, the universal grammar of language and behavior." Robin Fox, *Encounter with Anthropology* (1973; New Brunswick NJ: Transaction, 1991): 283.

[52] See Volker Storch, Ulrich Welsch & Michael Wink, *Evolutionsbiologie* (Berlin: Springer, 2001): 375. According to other sources, "the inputs from the sensory system and the outputs to the effectors" comprise only "a vanishingly small percentage of the connections"; see Wolf Singer, "Selbsterfahrung und neurobiologische Fremdbeschreibung – zwei konfliktträchtige Erkenntnisquellen," *Deutsche Zeitschrift für Philosophie* 52.2 (2004): 242 (my tr.); perhaps even only "one in 10 million threads is connected with the world, the others connect the brain with itself" (Manfred Spitzer, *Lernen: Gehirnforschung und die Schule des Lebens* [Heidelberg: Spektrum Akademischer Verlag, 2002]: 52 (my tr.).

[53] This picture results as the distillation of today's state of palaeoanthropological knowledge, which is itself nourished by many research disciplines. It is beyond the scope of this essay to set out the argument in detail. It will form part of my forthcoming study "Beyond Modern Anthropocentrism."

bb. 'Freezing' of the developmental state around 40,000 years ago

It is easy to see that a further increase in the dominance of reflexiveness would no longer have been advantageous. If humans had made the transition to a relation of 100% inwardly related functions as opposed to 0% outwardly related ones, they would actually have turned into the beings decribed by radical constructivists: they would have been able only to think up the world, but would no longer have been able to calibrate their constructions externally, and would eventually only have moved in fantasies. Steps in this direction were presumably in fact tried out, but for understandable reasons did not prove advantageous, and so the state already reached has remained – that in which the optimal relationship between heightened reflexive ability and indispensable sensorimotoric linkage to the world was attained.

In fact, it is today known that the development of the brain froze in this state an estimated 40,000 years ago and has since been conserved.[54] At that time – as surprising as this might initially sound – our whole bodily design and our emotional and mimetic repertoire (indeed, the whole human genome) became frozen in the state that had been reached in the wake of protocultural processes.[55] Since then, there has been no further development of humans in these respects.

cc. Universals: frozen standards

This has two consequences. First, it explains the existence of universals, which constitute the stocks of human nature then attained and which have been preserved thanks to the absence of further genetic change. Hence their universality – and their archaic character. To recapitulate: these universal factors concern our bodily form and the aesthetic preferences relating to them,

---

[54] The point in time may be located a maximum of 10,000 years earlier or later. The fact that the 'freezing' took place is uncontroversial.

[55] Wolf Singer has set out clearly what that means: if a Stone-Age baby were to grow up in our civilization it would be just as capable of learning-successes as our children. And owing to genetic commonalities concerning anatomy it would also look like one of our children. Conversely, if a twenty-first-century baby were to grow up in a Stone-Age culture it would simply turn out like a Stone-Age person; see Wolf Singer, *Der Beobachter im Gehirn: Essays zur Hirnforschung* (Frankfurt am Main: Suhrkamp, 2002): 44. All this also means that humanity has produced its later impressive cultural achievements with what are still Stone-Age brains. From this one can see that although our genetic provision does an awful lot, it is a long way from doing everything. Cultural progress must obviously rest on a mechanism of its own which can no longer be explained in terms of genetic logic.

elementary emotions and their facial expression, and finally basic neuronal structures (including phonetic and linguistic patterns). All these factors have remained unchanged and lie beneath the cultural evolution that followed.[56]

dd. Emergence of culture

The second consequence is likewise obvious. From now on, a further development of humans could take place *only* by way of culture. The genetic route had been exhausted, and cultural evolution, as everyone knows, no longer has any genetic repercussions. Now, it is a fact that precisely then – around 40,000 years ago, when our genetic development came to a standstill – that the cultural route was dramatically embarked upon. This simultaneity of the end of genetic evolution and the beginning of cultural evolution is no coincidence. Indeed, a strong congruence exists between both developments: the human biological make-up had become good enough through protocultural evolution to be able henceforth to carry cultural evolution (in particular, as described, the optimum brain configuration necessary for this had been achieved), and cultural evolution uses this make-up but does not change it.

Thus, 40,000 years ago, with the transition to the New Stone Age, cultural development accelerated: initially in the form of a dramatic explosion in the invention of tools, followed soon after by initial forms of art (first small statues, then cave paintings). The further course of cultural take-off is familiar to everyone: a good 10,000 years ago, the Neolithic revolution took place, with the first towns being built; around 6,000 years ago, the first advanced civilizations formed; and for about 200 years we have been witnessing attempts to develop a global culture.

As pointed out above, with the freezing of genetic development only the cultural route still remained open. This is why an acceleration and a take-off of a now genuinely cultural evolution came about, one decoupled from the genetic mechanisms of natural evolution and instead developing its own mechanisms of tradition – which in turn made further advances in cultural development possible.[57]

---

[56] They are genetically fixed and neurally anchored.

[57] In this perspective, it becomes for the first time explicable, without the traditional introduction of mythic kinds of external dimensions ('divine spark', nonnatural 'reason' that suddenly turns up in the midst of nature, etc.), how the emergence of genuinely cultural processes, together with their tendency to autonomization, could come about from the start-

ee. The global spread of homo sapiens
*   and the beginning of cultural diversification*

And now for the final two points of this survey of development. The rapid evolution of culture coincided precisely with the global spread of the species of *homo sapiens*. In the course of this development, all other kinds of humans died out. Precisely because it took the path towards a decisively cultural evolution, *homo sapiens* seems to have become conspicuously superior.

Only *after* this development, only in the further history of the successful model *homo sapiens*, did the formation of cultural difference occur, the further development of which has led to the different cultures that we know. Cultural diversity is a late product, on the basis of our common nature.

III: The Overall Picture:
Primary and Subsequent Commonalities

As I argued above, this scenario allows us to explain human universals. They correspond to the protocultural-biological make-up of humans that froze about 40,000 years ago. It is still at work in us. All later cultural development rests on this.

1. The Relevance of Universals – For Our
Self-Understanding and for Transcultural Tasks

One might, however, harbour doubts about whether the ongoing efficacy of this universal make-up is, in fact, of any real relevance. You may well have found the list of universals and their anthropogenetic explanation interesting – but ultimately not very important for your work, or for our self-understanding. The universals named seem to concern only very elementary, not higher, levels of human existence. How could they ever be relevant to a writer or literary theorist? I want to make three points in response to this impression and such reservations.

a. Self-understanding
aa. The significance of prelinguistic and precultural aspects
First: I don't think the ultimate grounds of the human are linguistic. To be sure, the human is a *zoōn logon echon*, a speaking and thinking being. But

---

ing-point of a protoculturally, biologically achieved state of development. After millions of years of preparation, the arrow of culture shot free of the bowstring of protoculture.

these activities, in their best moments, draw upon presentiments and certainties that are prelinguistic and precultural. As Thomas Nagel, an eminent philosopher, put it: "philosophy is not like a particular language. Its sources are preverbal and often precultural." And the big difficulty for philosophy, Nagel continues, is "to express [...] intuitively felt problems in language without losing them."[58]

Artists often express a similar belief. They feel driven by forces from the bedrock underlying the 'cultural'. Rcall, for instance, Paul Klee's endeavour to dwell "somewhat closer to the heart of creation."[59] Any number of writers have seen their vocation in putting wordless things into words.[60]

I take this prelinguistic and precultural dimension very seriously. It is the locus of our fundamental connectedness with the world. Through language *alone* we would never meet with the world. And the fact that the universals I named are precultural does not entail that they are noncultural. They are so neither in their (protocultural) genesis nor in their efficacy – they are still powerful within culture.

I once conducted a test concerning mimic expressions. Are we able to change them arbitrarily – for example, by substituting the expression of sadness for that of joy, and vice versa? And what happens if we do? Yes, with a lot of effort, we are able to switch them. But after a while one feels deeply uncomfortable and in serious danger – and is better advised to give up the experiment. We are better off going by the innate programme – rather than to an asylum. If we wanted to meddle with these old patterns, our cultural activity would also break down.

---

[58] Thomas Nagel, *The View from Nowhere* (Oxford & New York: Oxford UP, 1986): 11.

[59] "Diesseitig bin ich garnicht faßbar. / Denn ich wohne grad so gut bei den Toten, / wie bei den Ungeborenen. / Etwas näher dem Herzen der Schöpfung als üblich. / Und noch lange nicht nahe genug" [I cannot be grasped at all on this side. For I dwell as well with the dead as with the unborn. Somewhat closer to the heart of creation than usual. And yet not close enough by far]; Paul Klee, *Gedichte* (1920), ed. Felix Klee (1960; Zurich: Arche, 1980): 7. Cf. also (with a different accentuation) Jean Dubuffet, "Positions anticulturelles" (1951), *L'homme du commun à l'ouvrage* (Paris: Gallimard, 1973): 67–77.

[60] Cf. Hugo von Hofmannsthal: "the language in which it might perhaps have been given to me not only to write, but also to think, is neither Latin nor English nor Italian nor Spanish, but a language of which I do not know even one word, a language in which [mute] things speak to me"; Hofmannsthal, *The Lord Chandos Letter*, tr. Michael Hofmann (1902; London: Syrens, 1995): 20.

bb. The elementariness of the logical

My second response might come as a surprise. It is that, though our foundations are not linguistic, they are nonetheless *logical* in nature.

According to recent findings, the basic logical elements are anchored in
the brain's modes of neural processing. Logical particles such as 'and' and
'or', logical relations such as 'same', 'identical', and 'other', connectives
such as 'either/or', 'as well as', and 'if ... then', the quantitative categories
'one', 'many', 'all' as well as the qualitative categories of affirmation and
negation – all correspond to deep-seated operational modes of the neuronal
system. These lie at the level of the general algorithm underlying all of the
brain's specific functions (hence also the infamous 'modules'), which also
includes mathematical operations such as addition and subtraction or multi-
plication and division.[61]

Logic and mathematics are the elaborate *cultural articulations* of this *elementary neuronal logic*. No doubt they also lead the latter to unsuspected
heights, linked with many degrees of freedom, but their basic stock is
neurally anchored and their further development remains bound to this. Incidentally, this root is also capable of explaining the universal applicability of
logic and mathematics, and likewise of throwing light on both the old
theorem that the structure of the world is intrinsically logical and mathematical, and the modern view that precisely the mathematically based sciences
get closest to the core of things.

Thus, in our logical operations, too, we draw on a very old possession. It
works pervasively in all our activities. Feelings and their forms of expression,
aesthetic decisions, linguistic achievements: all are shaped by the elementary
arsenal of affirmation and negation, sameness and difference, exclusive or
inferential relationships.[62] One can hardly exaggerate the extent to which
logical elements shape the form of our simplest performances. Just try to
imagine how any sensation, perception, action or communication might be

---

[61] For a representative example from the mass of literature on the subject, see Christof
Koch & Idan Segev, "The Role of Single Neurons in Information Processing," *Nature:
Neuroscience Supplement* 3 (2000): 1171–77.

[62] The neural anchoring of these logical parameters is to be distinguished, however, from
the conscious use we make of logical forms. The neural provision in no way guarantees the
correctness of our reasoning. Not only can we make mistakes in our use of logical structures, but we can also consciously stage deceptions. It is just that correct and incorrect uses
alike are possible and can only be evaluated within the framework of the basic possession
of the logical forms.

possible or might appear without these patterns. You cannot – all determinacy would be dissolved.

The fact that we usually do not notice this logical impregnation of everything is simply the reverse side of its elementariness. "The real foundations of his enquiry," Wittgenstein once said, "do not strike a man at all."[63] We humans move in these elementary logical structures in the most matter-of-course manner – like fish in water.

Now, if it is the case that the logical structures are inherent in us as a neural possession, and if all our advanced cultural communication and rational methods rest on these, then the rejection of evolutionary biological and neurobiological research results – as currently often witnessed on the part of cultural studies and philosophy – is blind and foolish. The *formulation of logic* is a *cultural product*, to be sure; but the *structure and validity* of the logical is an *evolutionary product*. It is precisely when one recognizes the elementary importance of logical operations for all our sensations and understanding – and who could escape this insight? – that the extent to which an adequate understanding of the human must also include precultural dimensions becomes clear.[64]

---

[63] Ludwig Wittgenstein, *Philosophical Investigations*, tr. G.E.M. Anscombe (1953; New York: Macmillan, 1968): 50 [129].

[64] Such considerations have nothing to do with adopting an 'interpretative monopoly' from the biological sciences. It is simply a matter of considering empirical findings about the human as an empirical being – instead of making a show of ignoring them and continuing to tell obsolete stories based on a lack of information and false empirical assumptions. Conversely, however, it is also important to examine the findings provided by science with philosophical tools and to integrate them into a framework of philosophical conceptions. I am therefore decidedly not pleading in favour of any straightforward adoption of the, in fact often simplistic, interpretations ('philosophies') of the sciences. Nevertheless, I see the habit of simple rejection as having two disadvantages: for philosophy, because it keeps it at a regressive level; for cultural understanding, because it encourages amateur general interpretations based on precisely these philosophical reservations.

One should recall just once, in contrast to the prevalent present-day attitude, how energetically philosophers like Kant and Hegel endeavoured to take on the most recent scientific knowledge of their time. Kant became famous for his theory of the development of galaxies and solar systems based on Newtonian foundations (the Kant–Laplace theory), which he posited in his 1755 *Universal Natural History and Theory of the Heavens*; and with minimal scientific findings, but maximal application of reflection, the late Immanuel Kant (long before Darwin) developed the notion that humans might have originated when "an orangutan or a chimpanzee formed the organs that served to walk, to feel objects and to speak into the anatomy of a human, the most interior [trait] of which contained an organ for the use of the understanding and gradually developed through societal culture"; Kant,

b. Universals and transcultural communication

aa. Universals as elementary conditions of communication

Thirdly, the precultural potentials of our existence are still important, indeed indispensable, for present attempts to attain more commonalities between cultures.

First, however diverse the *content* of transcultural understanding may be, without the support of elementary *logical* forms we would not be able to grasp or communicate a single content, and would be equally incapable of entering into mutual comparison for the purpose of more closely determining what is common and what separates.[65]

Secondly, emotions and their expressions participate essentially in successful communication. A conversation is determined not only by views and arguments but is also guided by emotional proximity or distance. Often it is only growing emotional trust that makes participants able to really involve themselves with content and henceforth to actually move towards one another with *understanding*.

Anthropology from a Pragmatic Point of View, tr. Robert B. Louden (*Anthropologie in pragmatischer Hinsicht*, 1798; tr. Cambridge: Cambridge UP, 2006): 233. Furthermore, Kant entertained the idea of a common derivation of all creatures from a single "original mother"; *Critique of Judgment*, tr. Werner S. Pluhar (*Kritik der Urteilskraft*, 1790; Indianapolis IN: Hackett, 1987): 304; he called "a hypothesis like this" "a daring adventure of reason" – an assumption that is by no means "absurd" and "not inconsistent a priori, in the judgement of mere reason" (Kant, *Critique of Judgment*, 305). And Hegel's account of animals in the Encyclopaedia is an eloquent document of how eager he, too, was to adopt and to reflect on the state of scientific knowledge of his time.

It seems as though philosophers have, paradoxically, retreated to the ivory tower of pure speculation only after an immense wealth of scientific knowledge has become available. Already Adorno complained about this attitude of ignorance about science: "Among the tasks awaiting the attention of philosophy, by no means the last is the adaptation, without amateurish analogies and syntheses, of the results of experience gained in the natural sciences, to the province of the mind. [...] If the sole purpose of philosophy consisted in bringing the human intellect to the stage where it could identify itself with what it has learned about natural phenomena, instead of leaving mankind to live out its life like a troglodyte sheltering behind its own knowledge of the cosmos in which the imprudent species, 'homo', goes his graceless way, at least something would have been achieved." Theodor W. Adorno, "Why Philosophy" (1962), tr. Margaret D. Senft–Howie & Reginal Freeston, in *The Adorno Reader*, ed. Brian O'Connor (Oxford: Blackwell, 2000): 50–51.

[65] Pointing out the preference for ambiguity in some cultures over the clear either/or does not influence this. The 'as well as' is also part of the basic logical repertoire, as is ambiguity; although in each case a lot is excluded, this does not exclude everything.

To be sure, the elementary commonalites mentioned do not lead to success *on their own*. But *without them* the whole undertaking would be in vain – it wouldn't even get off the ground.

bb. Extending the range: need universals and culture universals

At this point it is time to extend the range of universals. Until now, I have only been pointing out universals in the strictest sense – those that are strictly common to *all* humans and human communities.

Based on these, however, there is also a second type of universals relating to elementary human needs, to life's demands, and to problem-solving strategies responding to them. Malinowski and Murdock were not wrong to list such universals. If all humans were not familiar with hunger or the need for protection and accommodation, human cultures would look quite different. However, the solution to these problems (posed by the *protocultural nature* of humans) already occurs on the *route of culture* – hence, for instance, strategies for storing provisions or accommodation differ greatly (also depending on the natural living environment). Geertz was right that with regard to such universal needs the analysis of culturally different problem-solving strategies cannot be dispensed with. Conversely, it would be just as wrong not to recognize the latter as being different solutions to the same kind of problems. As universal needs underlie these commonalities, I call them *need universals*.

It is important to see that it is precisely this dual structure (same need universals/different problem solutions) that enables an understanding of other cultural achievements. One attains understanding of an exotic type of housing because one is familiar with the problem of accommodation and because one can clarify for oneself, in view of the differing climatic and other circumstances, why the form chosen there is an appropriate solution to the problem as it exists under those conditions - a form not suitable to the problem at home, but just right for oneself if one were living in the other place. *Need universals* thus represent, in contrast to strict universals (which are of protocultural origin), the next-highest (protocultural-cultural) level that also contributes to transcultural understanding.

Further, there are universals that are completely *cultural* in kind. These arise from structural necessities that crop up in the cultural process, in particular with regard to the cultural mission of tradition, which is indispensable to any culture whatsoever. In this respect, analogous solutions often arise as a result of the same pressure created by problems. An example of this is the development of writing systems. Accordingly, I call these specifically *cultural* commonalities *culture universals*. These are, admittedly, features that are not common to *all* humans and human communities – there are also cultures without writing. These are thus commonalities between *many*, but not all, cultures – one might therefore also call them *semi-universals*. Although their forms vary culturally, these culture universals also represent transcultural points of contact: the writing of other cultures can be decoded and documents can be translated.

The table of universals is thus at least threefold: strict universals of a protocultural kind; need universals of a protocultural-cultural kind; and genuine culture universals. This table could presumably be extended further. What matters here is that on the basis of 'hard' universals the formation of higher-level (universal or semi-universal) commonalities is effected, commonalities that also contribute to the possibility of transcultural communication, and which are suitable to fill the gap between fundamental commonalities and current difference – or that between necessary and sufficient conditions for transcultural communication.

2.   Original Possession and Further Acquisition of Commonalities

The following overall picture thus emerges concerning the possession and acquisition of commonalities: Long before the culture-specific commonalities and differences that one usually focuses on, we humans already possess universal commonalities owing to the origins common to all of us. Through these commonalities, people were already connected before they began to differentiate culturally. If one wants to go back to an 'effective history', one should focus first of all on this one – it is common to *all* of us. And these old commonalities continue to operate. It is thanks to them, first, that what would not be possible or understandable in terms of cultural difference alone is possible: namely, that we are able to connect inwardly with the content of other cultures – from the initial fascination I attempted to describe, using the Ginkakuji temple as an example, through to highly elaborate forms of understanding.

The acquisition of transcultural commonalities currently sought for is still nourished by these old commonalities – indeed, would not be able to get going at all without them. To be sure, higher-level commonalities also have a role to play. But their formation and acquisition is possible only on the basis of these more elementary commonalities, and their use still depends on the latter. This is why I trust that this essay will have motivated readers to reconsider the importance of elementary commonalities. In this way, I believe, we can add a new perspective and give a new boost to the aim of promoting transcultural commonalities.

WORKS CITED

Adorno, Theodor W. "Why Philosophy" (1962), tr. Margaret D. Senft–Howie & Reginald Freeston, in *The Adorno Reader*, ed. Brian O'Connor (Oxford: Blackwell, 2000): 40–53.

Bastian, Adolf. *Controversen in der Ethnologie*, vol. I: *Die Geographischen Provinzen in ihren culturgeschichtlichen Berührungspuncten* (Berlin: Weidmannsche Buchhandlung, 1893).

Bell, Daniel. *The Winding Passage: Essays and Sociological Journeys, 1960–1980* (Cambridge MA: Abt, 1980).

Berger, Peter L., Brigitte Berger & Hansfried Kellner. *The Homeless Mind. Modernization and Consciousness* (New York: Random House, 1973).

Berlin, Brent, & Paul Kay. *Basic Color Terms: Their Universality and Evolution* (Berkeley: U of California P, 1969).

Brague, Rémi. *Eccentric Culture: A Theory of Western Civilization*, tr. Samuel Lester (*Europe, la voie romaine*, 1992; tr. South Bend IN: St. Augustine's, 2002).

Brown, Donald E. *Human Universals* (New York: McGraw–Hill, 1991).

Bruce, Vicki. *In the Eye of the Beholder: The Science of Face Perception* (Oxford: Oxford UP, 1998).

Darwin, Charles. *The Descent of Man, and Selection in Relation to Sex* (1871; Princeton NJ: Princeton UP, 1981).

——. "A Preliminary Notice: On the Modification of a Race of Syrian Street Dogs by Means of Sexual Selection" (1882), in *The Collected Papers of Charles Darwin* (Chicago: U of Chicago P, 1977): 278–80.

Derrida, Jacques. *The Other Heading: Reflections on Today's Europe*, tr. Pascale–Anne Brault & Michael B. Naas (*L'autre cap*, 1991; tr. Bloomington: Indiana UP, 1992).

Dubuffet, Jean. "Positions anticulturelles" (1951), in Dubuffet, *L'homme du commun à l'ouvrage* (Paris: Gallimard, 1973): 67–77.

Eibl–Eibesfeldt, Irenäus. "Universalien im menschlichen Sozialverhalten," in *Der ganze Mensch: Aspekte einer pragmatischen Anthropologie*, ed. Hans Rössner (Munich: Deutscher Taschenbuch-Verlag, 1986).

Ekman, Paul. "Afterword," in Charles Darwin, *The Expression of the Emotions in Man and Animals* (1872; Oxford: Oxford UP, 1998): 363–93.

——. "Cross-Cultural Studies of Facial Expressions," in *Darwin and Facial Expression: A Century of Research in Review*, ed. Paul Ekman (New York: Academic Press, 1973): 169–222.

Etcoff, Nancy. *Survival of the Prettiest: The Science of Beauty* (Garden City NY: Doubleday, 1999).

Featherstone, Mike. *Consumer Culture & Postmodernism* (London: Sage, 1991).

Fox, Robin. *Encounter with Anthropology* (1973; New Brunswick NJ: Transaction, 2nd ed. 1991).

Freeman, Derek. *Margaret Mead and Samoa: The Making and Unmaking of an Anthropological Myth* (Cambridge MA: Harvard UP, 1983).

Geertz, Clifford. "The Impact of the Concept of Culture on the Concept of Man," in Geertz, *The Interpretation of Cultures* (New York: Basic Books, 1973): 33–54.

Greenblatt, Stephen. *Marvelous Possessions: The Wonder of the New World* (Chicago: U of Chicago P, 1991)

Gutmann, Amy. "The Challenge of Multiculturalism in Political Ethics," *Philosophy & Public Affairs* 22.3 (1993): 171–206.

Hannerz, Ulf. *Cultural Complexity: Studies in the Social Organization of Meaning* (New York: Columbia UP, 1992).

Hegel, Georg Wilhelm Friedrich. *Elements of the Philosophy of Right*, tr. H.B. Nisbet (*Grundlinien der Philosophie des Rechts*, 1821; tr. Cambridge: Cambridge UP, 1991).

Herder, Johann Gottfried. "This Too a Philosophy of History for the Formation of Humanity" (*Auch eine Philosophie der Geschichte zur Bildung der Menschheit*, 1774), in Johann Gottfried von Herder, *Philosophical Writings*, ed. & tr. Michael N. Forster (Cambridge: Cambridge UP, 2002): 268–358.

——. *Outlines of a Philosophy of the History of Man*, tr. T. Churchill (*Ideen zur Philosophie der Geschichte der Menschheit*, 1784–1791; tr. 1800; New York: Bergman, 1966).

Hofmannsthal, Hugo von. *The Lord Chandos Letter*, tr. Michael Hofmann (1902; London: Syrens, 1995).

Holenstein, Elmar. *Menschliches Selbstverständnis* (Frankfurt am Main: Suhrkamp, 1985).

Kant, Immanuel. *Anthropology from a Pragmatic Point of View*, tr. Robert B. Louden (*Anthropologie in pragmatischer Hinsicht*, 1798; tr. Cambridge: Cambridge UP, 2006).

——. *Critique of Judgment*, tr. Werner S. Pluhar (*Kritik der Urteilskraft*, 1790; Indianapolis IN: Hackett, 1987).

King, Anthony. "Architecture, Capital and the Globalization of Culture," in *Global Culture: Nationalism, Globalization and Modernity. A Theory*, ed. Mike Featherstone (*Culture & Society* special issue; London: Sage, 1990): 397–411.

Klee, Paul. *Gedichte*, ed. Felix Klee (1920; 1960; Zurich: Arche, 1980).

Koch, Christof, & Idan Segev, "The Role of Single Neurons in Information Processing," *Nature, Neuroscience Supplement* 3 (2000): 1171–77.

Koepping, Klaus–Peter. *Adolf Bastian and the Psychic Unity of Mankind: The Foundations of Anthropology in Nineteenth Century Germany* (St. Lucia: U of Queensland P, 1983): 171–73.

Langlois, Judith H. et al. "Infant Preferences for Attractive Faces: Rudiments of a Stereotype?" *Developmental Psychology* 23 (1987): 363–69.

Malinowski, Bronislaw. "A Scientific Theory of Culture," in Malinowski, *A Scientific Theory of Culture and Other Essays* (Chapel Hill: U of North Carolina P, 1944): 1–144.

Malotki, Ekkehart. *Hopi Time* (Berlin: Mouton, 1983).

Menninghaus, Winfried. *Das Versprechen der Schönheit* (Frankfurt am Main: Suhrkamp, 2003).

Mohanty, Jitendra N. "Den anderen verstehen," in *Philosophische Grundlagen der Interkulturalität*, ed. R.A. Mall (Amsterdam: Rodopi, 1993): 115–22.

Montaigne, Michel de. *The Complete Essays*, tr. Donald M. Frame (Stanford CA: Stanford UP, 1992).

Mueller-Vollmer, Kurt, ed. *Herder Today* (Berlin: de Gruyter, 1990).

Murdock, George P. "The Common Denominator of Cultures," in Murdock, *Culture and Society: Twenty-Four Essays* (Pittsburgh PA: U of Pittsburgh P, 1965): 87–110.

Nagel, Thomas. *The View from Nowhere* (New York: Oxford UP, 1986).

Nietzsche, Friedrich. *Menschliches, Allzumenschliches: Ein Buch für freie Geister, Zweiter Band*, in Nietzsche, *Sämtliche Werke: Kritische Studienausgabe in 15 Bänden*, vol. 2, ed. Giorgio Colli & Mazzino Montinari (Munich: Deutscher Taschenbuch Verlag, 1980).

——. *Nachgelassene Fragmente: Juli 1882 bis Herbst 1885*, in Nietzsche, *Sämtliche Werke: Kritische Studienausgabe in 15 Bänden*, vol. 11, ed. Giorgio Colli & Mazzino Montinari (Munich: Deutscher Taschenbuch Verlag, 1980).

Novalis. *Schriften*, ed. Paul Kluckhohn & Richard Samuel, vol. 3: *Das philosophische Werk II* (Stuttgart: Kohlhammer, 1983).

Rimbaud, Arthur. "Lettre à Paul Demeny" (15 May 1871), in Rimbaud, *Œuvres complètes* (Paris: Gallimard, 1972): 249–54.

Rousseau, Jean–Jacques. *Discours sur l'origine et les fondements de l'inégalité parmi les hommes* (1755 ; Paris: Gallimard: 1969).

Said, Edward W. *Culture and Imperialism* (London: Chatto & Windus, 1993).

Singer, Wolf. *Der Beobachter im Gehirn: Essays zur Hirnforschung* (Frankfurt am Main: Suhrkamp, 2002).

——. "Selbsterfahrung und neurobiologische Fremdbeschreibung: Zwei konfliktträchtige Erkenntnisquellen," *Deutsche Zeitschrift für Philosophie* 52.2 (2004): 235–55.

Spitzer, Manfred. *Lernen: Gehirnforschung und die Schule des Lebens* (Heidelberg: Spektrum Akademischer Verlag, 2002).

Storch, Volker; Ulrich Welsch & Michael Wink, *Evolutionsbiologie* (Berlin: Springer, 2001).

Tugendhat, Ernst. *Egozentrismus und Mystik: Eine anthropologische Studie* (Munich: C.H. Beck, 2003).

Voland, Eckart. "Aesthetic Preferences in the World of Artifacts: Adaptations for the Evaluation of 'Honest Signals'?" in *Evolutionary Aesthetics*, ed. Eckart Voland & Karl Grammer (Heidelberg: Springer, 2003): 239–60.

Welsch, Wolfgang. "Animal Aesthetics," *Contemporary Aesthetics* 2 (2004): online http://www.contempaesthetics.org/newvolume/pages/article.php?articleID=243 (accessed 1 October 2007).

——. "Rethinking Identity in the Age of Globalization: A Transcultural Perspective," in *Symposion of Beauty and Art: Festschrift für Tsunemichi Kambayashi*, ed. Hiroshi Okabayashi et al. (Tokyo: Keiso, 2002): 333–46. Rev. & repr. in *International Yearbook of Aesthetics* 8 (2004): 167–76.

——. "Subjektsein heute: Überlegungen zur Transformation des Subjekts," *Deutsche Zeitschrift für Philosophie* 39.4 (1991): 347–65.

——. "Transculturalidad: la forma cambiante de las culturas en la actualidad," in *Democracia y ciudadanía en la sociedad global*, ed. Cristina Camachos Ramos, Miriam Calvillo Verlasco & Juan Mora Heredia (Aragón: Universidad Nacional Autónoma de México, 2001): 191–218.

——. "Transculturalità. Forme di vita dopo la dissoluzione delle culture," *Paradigmi: Rivista di critica filosofica* 10/30 (1992): 665–89.

——. "Transkulturalität – Lebensformen nach der Auflösung der Kulturen," *Information Philosophie* 2 (1992): 5–20.

——. "Transculturality: The Puzzling Form of Cultures Today," in *Spaces of Culture: City, Nation, World*, ed. Mike Featherstone & Scott Lash (London: Sage, 1999): 194–213.

——. "Auf dem Weg zu transkulturellen Gesellschaften," in *Die Zukunft des Menschen – Philosophische Ausblicke*, ed. Günter Seubold (Bonn: Bouvier, 1999): 119–44.

——. *Vernunft. Die zeitgenössische Vernunftkritik und das Konzept der transversalen Vernunft* (Frankfurt am Main: Suhrkamp, 1995).

Whitman, Walt. "Song of Myself," in *Leaves of Grass* (1855; New York: Penguin: 1985).

Wittgenstein, Ludwig. *Philosophical Investigations*, tr. G.E.M. Anscombe (1953; New York: Macmillan, 1968).

Zuckmayer, Carl. "The Devil's General" (1946), tr. Ingrid G. Gilbert & William F. Gilbert, in *Masters of Modern Drama*, ed. Haskell M. Block & Robert G. Shedd (New York: Random House, 1963): 911–58.

❮❖❯

Multiple Modernities
— The Transnationalization of Cultures

GISELA WELZ

D URING THE PAST DECADE, globalization has come within the purview of anthropology. Today, migration, mobility, and the social groups they produce – refugees, tourists, labour migrants – are on anthropology's research agenda. Increasingly, anthropologists study the cultural effects of the worldwide diffusion of commodities, technologies, and media products, as new communication and transportation technologies bridge huge distances in ever briefer intervals of time and release people from geographically restricted communities of interaction. Cultural artefacts – not just material things but also political ideas, scientific knowledge, images of the future, and interpretations of the past – travel further and more swiftly than ever before. They are available simultaneously almost everywhere. However, their accessibility is restricted to those social actors who have the economic means or the cultural capital to make use of them.

As a consequence of these transformations, anthropologists have abandoned established notions of how culture relates to territory. The Swedish social anthropologist Ulf Hannerz suggests that the well-established anthropological concept of cultures as "packages of meanings and meaningful forms, distinctive to collectivities and territories," was put to the test when anthropologists started to take a closer look at the "increasing interconnectedness in space": "As people move with their meanings, and as meanings find ways of travelling even when people stay put, territories cannot really contain

cultures."[1] Originally, the anthropological concept of culture referred to the
way of life of a bounded social group in a fixed and clearly defined geographical location or territory. Both the increased mobility and worldwide dispersal of populations, forming diasporas far from home, and the interpenetration of societies by things and ideas from elsewhere challenged the unspoken
anthropological assumption that "culture sits in places."[2] With globalization,
cultures ceased to be static objects. They would no longer hold still for ethno-
graphers to portray them, as James Clifford, the American historian and critical theorist of anthropology, so aptly puts it:

> Twentieth-century identities no longer presuppose continuous cultures or tradi-
> tions. Everywhere individuals and groups improvise local performances from
> (re)collected pasts, drawing on foreign media, symbols, and languages.[3]

As a consequence, cultural boundaries are much more difficult to fix, let
alone map onto territorial divides, as communication channels transgress and
migrant communities routinely cross them.

In anthropology, the term 'transnationalization' was adopted in order to
capture those cultural processes that stream across the borders of nation
states. 'Transnational' has increasingly become a blanket term in anthropology to describe any cultural phenomenon that extends beyond or cross-cuts
state boundaries and is an effect of the diffusion or dispersal of people, ideas,
and artifacts across huge distances, often in such a way that they cease to be
identified with a single place of origin. Anthropologists distinguish transnational processes from globalization. The latter they define as world-encompassing in scale, and embodied in economic and political processes whose
protagonists are multinational corporations, national governments, and supra-
national organizations. Conversely, the term 'transnational' "draw[s] attention to the growing involvement of other kinds of actors – individuals, kinship groups, ethnic groups, firms, social movements, etc.– in activities and

---

[1] Ulf Hannerz, "Introduction" to *Transnational Connections: Culture, People, Places*
(London & New York: Routledge, 1996): 8.

[2] See Arturo Escobar, "Culture Sits in Places: Reflections on Globalism and Subaltern
Strategies of Localization," *Political Geography* 20 (2001): 139–74.

[3] James Clifford, "The Pure Products Go Crazy," in Clifford, *The Predicament of
Culture: Twentieth-Century Ethnography, Literature, and Art* (Cambridge MA: Harvard
UP, 1988): 14.

relationships that transcend national boundaries."[4] Aihwa Ong, a USA-based anthropologist whose studies analyse the changing societies and cultures of contemporary Southeast Asia, asserts that transnationality as a term is best suited to symbolize the "condition of cultural interconnectedness and mobility across space" which has intensified under late capitalism. According to Ong, the prefix 'trans'

> denotes both moving through space or across lines, as well as changing the nature of something. Besides suggesting new relations between nation-states and capital, transnationality also alludes to the transversal, the transactional, the translational, and the transgressive aspects of contemporary behavior and imagination that are incited, enabled, and regulated by the changing logics of states of capitalism.[5]

The new concept of transnationalism in anthropology is not meant to reify a view of the world as "composed of sovereign, spatially discontinuous units"[6] but, rather, aims at destabilizing the very notion that cultures and societies are contained and indeed defined by the nation state.

The Shifting Grounds of Transnational Ethnography

The reorientation that anthropology has undergone, however, is not only a response to perceived empirical changes on the ground but, rather, a radical revision of the epistemological underpinnings of the discipline. Certainly, anthropologists in the past had been far from unaware of the translocal, even global, relations and exchanges that the societies and cultures they studied were entangled in. Yet, more often than not, they tended to view these processes as influences and forces impacting on their object of study from the outside. In an important way, then, those connections and trajectories that tie the local to the global were considered peripheral to the concerns of the dis-

---

[4] Ulf Hannerz, "The Global Ecumene as a Landscape of Modernity," in Hannerz, *Transnational Connections: Culture, People, Places* (London & New York: Routledge, 1996): 237. See also Hannerz, "Transnational Research," in *Handbook of Methods in Cultural Anthropology*, ed. H. Russell Bernard (Walnut Creek, London & New Delhi: Altamira, 1998): 235–56.

[5] Aihwa Ong, *Flexible Citizenship: The Cultural Logics of Transnationality* (Durham NC & London: Duke UP 1999): 4.

[6] Liisa Malkki, "National Geographic: The Rooting of Peoples and the Territorialization of National Identity Among Scholars and Refugees," *Cultural Anthropology* 7.1 (1992): 27.

cipline. They were conceptualized as "externalities,"[7] placed outside the realm of anthropological research practices, and excluded from what the discipline considered to be its knowledge domain.

By focusing on the interpenetration of societies and their increasing internal heterogeneity, anthropology thus reconfigured the concept of culture and started to address new phenomena under the heading of transnationalism. As a consequence, methodological issues also came to the fore with unexpected urgency. Can anthropologists still do ethnography where they used to, in rural communities, in urban neighbourhoods, in bounded social groups? The very constructedness of the notion of the field, and the epistemological groundings of ethnography as a "field science,"[8] became visible when anthropology started addressing cultures on the move. The challenge that new social phenomena of transnational mobility have begun to pose to anthropology made it evident that the field had never simply been 'out there', but had always been constructed by the anthropologist. It is not just a bounded place and social group that the anthropologist can discover and dwell among, but she or he sets the limits and defines the boundaries according to the conventions and rules of the discipline, most of them implicit and quite literally embodied in the practices of scholars doing fieldwork. In their volume *Anthropological Locations*, Akhil Gupta and James Ferguson have pointed out that the idea of the bounded field site, and the notion of what anthropologists do in the field, constitute the core identity of anthropology. They criticize, not unlike Clifford, the fact that the field seems so deceptively obvious a place that the complex processes that go into constructing it are obscured: "This mysterious space – not the 'what' of anthropology, but the 'where' – has been left to common sense, beyond and below the threshold of reflexivity."[9] According to these authors, the most pressing problem for anthropology lies in the fact that, while the discipline has obviously shifted its attention to translocal phenomena, its practice and its identity remain deeply implicated in an intensely local, immobile research method.

---

[7] See Marilyn Strathern, "Externalities in Comparative Guise," *Economy and Society* 31.2 (2002): 250–67.

[8] See Akhil Gupta & James Ferguson, "Discipline and Practice: 'The Field' as Site, Method, and Location in Anthropology," in *Anthropological Locations: Boundaries and Grounds of a Field Science*, ed. Akhil Gupta & James Ferguson (Berkeley: U of California P, 1997).

[9] Gupta & Ferguson, "Discipline and Practice," 5.

A number of other anthropologists have also raised the point that ethnography, conventionally understood as long-term participant observation in a narrowly circumscribed locale such as a village or a tribal community, is not particularly suited for research perspectives on transnational cultural processes. Fieldwork is a localizing, place-making knowledge practice in a double sense: the culture to be observed is fixed in place by anchoring the field in a specific and concrete geographical location, and the fieldworker locates herself or himself by establishing a bodily presence in this chosen place for a lengthy period of time, often a year or longer. In conventional ethnography, mobility is the privilege of the fieldworker who arrives from elsewhere and will again depart after her or his time is up. The privilege, however, is suspended during the actual period of fieldwork. Conversely, the people under study are thought to be immobile in a sustained manner. Obviously, then, anthropology was not particularly well-equipped in research methods when it came to the increase in transcultural mobility and communication that we are witnessing on an almost global scale. The classic approach of ethnography, the community study, turned out to be a slow and clumsy instrument under conditions of transnationalization. In recent years, the way in which ethnography has privileged perspectives on local communities and sedentary populations has been criticized vehemently.[10] James Clifford suggests that instead we should see local communities

> as much as a site of travel encounters as of residence. [...] To press the point: Why not focus on any culture's farthest range of travel while also looking at its centers, its villages, its intensive fieldsites? How do groups negotiate themselves in external relationships, and how is a culture also a site of travel for others?[11]

Sparked by this discontent, new methodological approaches were created, most notably the suggestion put forward by George Marcus to make ethnography multi-sited. The fields of multi-sited ethnography are constituted by migration routes, communication channels, commercial transactions, and

---

[10] See Gisela Welz, "Moving Targets: Feldforschung unter Mobilitätsdruck," *Zeitschrift für Volkskunde* 94.2 (1998): 177–94; Gisela Welz, "Siting Ethnography: Some Observations on a Cypriot Highland Village," *Anthropological Journal on European Cultures* 11 (2002): 137–58.

[11] James Clifford, "Traveling Cultures," in Clifford, *Routes: Travel and Translation in the Late Twentieth Century* (Cambridge MA & London: Harvard UP, 1997): 25.

lines of conflict and interfaces of contact alike. Mobile research projects are designed to connect various geographical sites and to bridge the distances separating them:

> Ethnography moves from its conventional single-site location, contextualized by macro-constructions of a larger social order, such as the capitalist world system, to multiple sites of observation and participation that cross-cut dichotomies such as the 'local' and the 'global,' the 'lifeworld' and the 'system.'[12]

As the site of ethnography can no longer be presupposed to be an unproblematic given, before a fieldworker can engage in multi-sited research he or she has to discover the trajectories of mobility and track the far-flung relations of communication that connect a social setting to others. The effects of this paradigm shift have made themselves felt not only in methodological discourse:

> Thinking in terms of multi-sited research provokes an entirely different set of problems that not only go to the heart of adapting ethnography as practices of fieldwork and writing to new conditions of work, but challenge orientations that underlie the entire research process that has been so emblematic for anthropology.[13]

Clearly, the advantages of mobile ethnography have been most evident in the anthropological exploration of transnational phenomena. The ready adoption of this innovative methodology, and of the new research agenda that goes with it, is predicated on a shift of attention in anthropology, away from isolated small-scale units towards social formations and cultural practices that transgress national boundaries, are dispersed geographically, and link local with translocal social actors and institutions.

Global Standards, Local Diversity

Many of the new research concerns of anthropology – not just migration and mobility, but media and computer mediated communication, statehood and supra-national governance, commodities and consumption, science and tech-

---

[12] George E. Marcus, "Ethnography in/of the World System: the Emergence of Multi-Sited Ethnography," *Annual Review of Anthropology* 24 (1995): 95.

[13] George E. Marcus, *Ethnography Through Thick and Thin* (Princeton NJ: Princeton UP, 1998): 3.

nology – today entail a turning-away from more established patterns of doing fieldwork and writing ethnography. Yet what remains unchanged about ethnographic fieldwork and what gives it its special advantage over other, less engaged and more distant methods of research is the fact that field-workers immerse themselves in the everyday lives of the people they study, becoming participant observers of social practices as they unfold. "In fieldwork you live where people live, you do what people do, and you go where people go." The anthropologist James Watson states that "increasingly, all over the world, people are going to McDonald's; they are also going to shopping malls, supermarkets, and video stores. If anthropologists do not start going with them, we will soon lose our raison d'être."[14] Watson, along with a team of East Asian colleagues in anthropology, decided to do just that, to accompany people going to McDonald's in five Asian metropolitan areas, Taipeh, Hong Kong, Seoul, Tokyo, and Beijing. The anthropologists Yunxiang Yan, James Watson, David Wu, Sangmee Bak, and Emiko Ohnuki-Tierney contributed to the book *Golden Arches East*, which contains five case studies, exploring "how McDonald's worldwide system has been adapted to suit local circumstances in five distinct societies."[15] The team found out that East Asian consumers have managed to transform McDonald's into local institutions and that this localization process has spawned McDonald's restaurants that not only differ from those in the USA or in Germany, but also show considerable variation between the East Asian cities studied. What consumers actually do when they frequent the hamburger place is very different from city to city, as are the cultural meanings that they are afforded: a popular after-school place for high-school students where they do their homework, a place for three-generation-family outings on a weekend, or else the equivalent of a high-priced restaurant where nouveau-riche couples go for dinner. The book is an enjoyable read and quite convincing in presenting evidence that the spread of fast food does not necessarily undermine the integrity of indigenous cuisines, nor can fast food chains unproblematically be called agents of global cultural homogenization. The study can be criticized, of course, for not paying sufficient attention to socio-economic inequities within the societies studied, to problematic labour relations within McDonald's, or to the detrimental ecological effects of food production for hamburger empires. However, the special

---

[14] Watson, James K., ed. *Golden Arches East: McDonald's in East Asia* (Stanford CA: Stanford UP, 1997): viii.
[15] Watson, *Golden Arches East*, ix.

achievement of the study is that it takes the term McDonaldization literally and examines the empirical value of the term. In popular social science discourses, this had become a synonym for the negative dimensions of globalization, for americanization and cultural imperialism. Yet, instead of finding cultural standardization, the researchers were confronted with a new cultural diversity as McDonald's is adapted and effectively indigenized in the various settings.

Anthropology had started to study globalization with the expectation and, indeed, fear that globalization would bring about a culturally homogenized world. Instead, the discipline was witnessing a surge of greatly increasing cultural diversity, an observation that contradicted everything that anthropologists were led to believe. Anthropology had come into being as a scholarly enterprise enquiring into pre-modern societies. Historically, the discipline of anthropology emerged as a systematic attempt to learn about traditional cultures which often did not possess written records of their history and cultural heritage. The specific methodology of ethnographic research – fieldwork and participant observation – was developed to meet this challenge. Throughout much of the nineteenth and twentieth centuries, anthropologists were intent on recording and salvaging traditional cultures before they crumbled under the onslaught of modernization. The global transformations underway today – the increase in transnational migration, the intensification of economic exchanges, and the global reach of media and consumer culture – in a sense are the epitome of the process of modernity, a global expansion and intensification of modernization. What modernization had fallen short of, the production of a single unified world culture, globalization for sure would achieve. This is what anthropologists assumed, as for decades they had observed the incursion of monetary economies and capitalist markets into tribal lifeworlds and indigenous social systems, turning them inside out and mangling them beyond recognition, leaving populations adrift in the rapidly growing urban slums of Third World mega-cities, bereft of their identities and cultural meanings. Globalization has intensified these modernization processes. In its wake, there has been no significant alleviation of poverty in many postcolonial societies, and the social inequalities within these societies, and between them and the prosperous and powerful societies of the West, have deepened. Meanwhile, new links of economic and political relations have been forged that often are called neocolonial.

Yet cultural difference has not disappeared – quite the contrary. Culturally, globalization is having some unexpected and, indeed, contradictory effects. It has not led to the emergence of a single, unified world culture. Of course, we can observe the worldwide diffusion of modern institutions – the bureaucratic state, formal education, mass media and telecommunications, health systems, and military infrastructures. The globalization of the capitalist economy has left no society on earth untouched. However, the consequences of these processes are – despite all prognoses and prophecies – not the same everywhere.[16] The globalization of modernity has produced both sameness and difference; uniformization and differentiation are evolving side by side. Even though globally standardized institutions and practices are being introduced and adopted all over the world, the increased interaction between societies does not automatically lead to any significant levelling of cultural contrasts. Rather, when local cultures interact with global imports, new amalgamations of tradition and modernity are produced that are unique to the time and place where they occur.

The Global Cultural Economy

Thus, new cultural forms grow out of historically situated articulations of the local and the global:

> The trappings of globalization – world markets, mass media, rapid travel, modern communication [...] have had the effect of greatly increasing cultural diversity because of the ways in which they are interpreted and the ways they acquire new meanings in local reception.[17]

In his attempt to theorize the global cultural economy for anthropology, Arjun Appadurai stresses the importance of mass mediated products – radio, television, music videos, movies – which in conjunction with migration processes come to the fore as "forces [...] that seem to impel (and sometimes compel) the work of the imagination."[18] This has been explored ethnographically by a number of anthropologists in their research on the audience reception of popular media formats. Sarah Dickey's study of the significance of

---

[16] See Samuel N. Eisenstadt, *Die Vielfalt der Moderne* (Weilerswist: Velbrück, 2000), Eisenstadt, ed. *Multiple Modernities* (New Brunswick NJ: Transaction, 2002).

[17] Ong, *Flexible Citizenship*, 10.

[18] Arjun Appadurai, "Here and Now," in Appadurai, *Modernity at Large: Cultural Dimensions of Globalization* (Minneapolis MN & London: U of Minnesota P, 1996): 4.

popular cinema for moviegoers in South India[19] and Lila Abu-Lughod's interpretation of how Egyptian audiences respond to television serials[20] show that
viewers use "crucial moments of the serial to confront their own positions in
their family, community, and class"[21] and, by doing so, diverge from intended
interpretations. The new readings they create vary within an audience of
viewers at one single location, as their responses are gendered and also specific to social classes and generations. Michael Herzfeld, in his highly informative overview of anthropological work on media reception, points to the new
and unexpected effects of cross-cultural media reception, such as the popularity of Indian films in Nigerian Hausa culture,[22] and to the ways in which
media consumption fuels a "creative retooling of social identities in interaction with media"[23] – an assessment that resonates with an assertion of Appadurai's:

> the consumption of mass media throughout the world often provokes resistance,
> irony, selectivity, and in general agency [...] It is the imagination, in its collective
> forms, that creates ideas of neighborhood and nationhood, of moral economies and
> unjust rule, of higher wages and foreign labor prospects. The imagination is today a
> staging ground for action, and not only for escape.[24]

For Appadurai, this is what links globalization with modernity. He claims that
globalization marks an era where modernity is, as he puts it, "at large."
According to him, anthropology challenges conventional assumptions about
modernization and has the potential to contribute to a new social theory of
modernity. Once anthropology starts to systematically address as 'sites of
modernity' precisely those cultural situations it once sought out because they

---

[19] Sara Dickey, *Cinema and the Urban Poor in South India* (Cambridge: Cambridge UP,
1993).

[20] Lila Abu-Lughod, "Modern Subjects: Egyptian Melodrama and Postcolonial Difference," in *Questions of Modernity*, ed. Timothy Mitchell (Minneapolis: U of Minnesota P,
2000): 87–114.

[21] Michael Herzfeld, "Media," in *Anthropology: Theoretical Practice in Culture and
Society* (Malden MA & Oxford: Blackwell 2001): 301. See also Purnima Mankekar,
*Screening Culture, Viewing Politics: An Ethnography of Television, Womanhood and
Nation in Postcolonial India* (Durham NC: Duke UP, 1999).

[22] Brian Larkin, "Indian Films and Nigerian Lovers: Media and the Creation of Parallel
Modernities," *Africa* 67.3 (1997): 406–39.

[23] Herzfeld, "Media," 308.

[24] Appadurai, "Here and Now," 7.

appeared to harbour relics of tradition, the discipline will reinvent itself as an *anthropology of modernity*. With this change, anthropology also abandons its earlier self-appointed task of documenting and salvaging traditional cultures before they succumb to modernization. It is not, however, giving up its role as a prime witness and quite often also a plaintiff, accusing colonial powers and neocolonial actors of "transforming colonized peoples into alienated human beings, as commodity relations dissolve pre-existing cultural relations among people, uprooting them from former ways life" and eroding their subsistence bases.[25] In an essay on the anthropology of modernity, Aihwa Ong asserts that "thus emerged a strong anthropological tradition to study the varied impact of the capitalist juggernaut on native social forms, subjectivity, and social change."[26]

Anthropologists, then, have always been close observers of what is actually happening when Western institutions make incursions into non-Western societies. One of the most prominent voices in anthropology, Clifford Geertz, who was well known for revolutionizing anthropological epistemology with his approach to cultural interpretation (namely, thick description), was also most knowledgeable about, and critical of, so-called development in Third-World countries. Four decades of fieldwork engagement with communities in Morocco and Indonesia gave him unique insights into how social change plays out on the ground, how 'progress' impacts on the everyday lives of communities, and what choices local people actually make when confronted with new options. In his book *After the Fact*, Geertz weaves a rich, ethnographically informed tale of this change, a change that is not so much a "parade that can be watched as it passes,"[27] following prescribed stations – traditional, modern, postmodern, or else feudal, colonial, independent – as a discontinuous and disjunctive process. It progresses by leaps and halts rather than smoothly, and, in its course, spawns surprising and largely unintended effects. Modern life in Morocco is totally unlike that in Indonesia, and both bear little resemblance to France or the USA. Geertz is at his best when he gives a thick description of an improvised and quite innovative ceremony in an Indonesian

---

[25] Aihwa Ong, "Modernity: Anthropological Aspects," in *International Encyclopedia of the Social and Behavioral Sciences* (Amsterdam: Elsevier, 2001), 9945.

[26] Ong, "Modernity," 9944.

[27] Clifford Geertz, *After the Fact: Two Countries, Four Decades, One Anthropologist* (Cambridge MA & London: Harvard UP, 1995): 4.

community.[28] The public event he selects is a graduation ceremony for adult students of an English language course. The course had been organized and marketed by the enterprising leader of a Muslim school of religious instruction. As if this concurrence were not incongruous enough, the ceremony described by Geertz turns out to be a hybrid event, hardly able to contain the contradictory cultural currents it tries to combine, some local, some national, some global, some Muslim, and some Western. Geertz reports how this event generates ironic self-reflection and puzzlement in the audience and, by extension, he evokes these responses in the readers of his book.

Poetic insights such as those afforded by a master like Geertz resonate with many other situations around the world, where cultural diversity, hybridity, and ironic effects are generated when local populations appropriate globally distributed commodities and media products – even if these are only hamburgers or music videos. Modernization and globalization are but two sides of the same coin. Observations of the contradictory and highly productive cultural effects of globalization can be linked fruitfully to a theory of modernity that incorporates the anthropological attention given to everyday life, social agency, and the ways in which people give meaning to the circumstances in which they find themselves. The globalization of modernity that we experience today, indeed, has from its inception been part and parcel of the trajectory of modernity, which has always been inherently global in scope and intent.[29]

Multiple Modernities

Anthropology engages with the place that cultural difference and cultural diversity occupy in the modern world. For Ulf Hannerz, with his lively interest in the to and fro of cultural flows between the centres and peripheries of the world, and the resulting hybrid and creolized cultural expressions, the imperative question is "How does modernity go with cultural difference?" He himself subscribes to a view of "modernity as a civilizational complex, spreading globally, affecting the cultures of ever more societies, and at the same time

---

[28] See Geertz, *After the Fact*, 143–51.

[29] Obviously, colonialism shares many important characteristics with modernization and globalization. It has been suggested that both colonial subjects and representatives of power had already been modern for centuries as they were part of the world-encompassing story-and-map of modernity. See Peter J. Taylor, *Modernities: A Geohistorical Interpretation* (Minneapolis: U of Minnesota P, 1999).

being itself reshaped in those locations,"[30] resulting in a heightened degree of diversity within interconnectedness, new cultural forms, expressions, and interpretations that are unique to the societies that employ them and can no longer be classified according to simple dichotomies of non-Western tradition and Western modernity.

Hannerz suggests two perspectives that may capture this state of affairs:

> As the civilization of modernity enters into contact with other cultures, changes and refractions result, so that one may see it alternatively as one increasingly internally diverse civilization or as multiple modernities."[31]

While Hannerz himself has been leaning towards the former notion – that modernity forms a framework in which cultural diversity manifests itself – an increasingly vocal group of his colleagues in anthropology have opted for the latter notion, proposing that each society or social group generates its very own version of modernity that is unlike any other. So, wherever we go, there are particular regional forms of modernity. These cannot simply be explained by the presence of relics of tradition that coexist with modern elements. Rather, this recent theoretical innovation in anthropology, talking of multiple or plural modernities, of the 'alternatively'[32] or 'otherwise'[33] modern, attempts to solve the "paradox that people in different world areas increasingly share aspirations, material standards, and social institutions at the same time that their local definition of and engagement with these initiatives fuels cultural distinctiveness."[34]

To talk of multiple modernities effectively collapses any contradiction or conflict between being modern and adhering to local cultural practices and beliefs. Rather, the notion of "alternative modernity" acknowledges the fact that in each society, there is a "social and discursive space in which the relationship between modernity and tradition is reconfigured," as Bruce Knauft

---

[30] Hannerz, "The Global Ecumene," 48.

[31] "The Global Ecumene," 44.

[32] Bruce M. Knauft, "Critically Modern: An Introduction," in *Critically Modern: Alternatives, Alterities, Anthropologies*, ed. Bruce M. Knauft (Bloomington: Indiana UP, 2002): 1–54.

[33] Michel–Rolph Trouillot, "The Otherwise Modern: Caribbean Lessons from the Savage Slot," in *Critically Modern. Alternatives, Alterities, Anthropologies*, ed. Bruce Knauft (Bloomington: Indiana UP, 2002): 220–37.

[34] Knauft, "Critically Modern," 2.

points out against the backdrop of his many years of ethnographic work in
Melanesia. He adds that this "reconfiguration is forged in a crucible of cultural beliefs and orientations on the one hand, and politicoeconomic constraints and opportunities on the other."[35] In a brilliant survey essay, Joel
Kahn summarizes recent moves in anthropology to pluralize the modern. As
an illustration, he employs his own ethnographies of Malaysian and Indonesian society and points out that these countries today can easily be interpreted as "wanting: modern perhaps, but incompletely modern at best,"
particularly according to standards set by conventional modernization theory
which inevitably raises points such as the "incomplete separation of public
and private," meaning incomplete secularization and the strong role of religion in public life, or the "failure of differentiation of economic and political
spheres," referring to social relations labelled as patronage and nepotism from
a Western perspective.[36] "Measured against the yardstick of modernist narratives," Kahn continues,

> Malaysia and Indonesia become 'other to the modern' in significant ways, forcing
> us back into the language of a liberal social evolutionism in which otherness was
> constituted as historically anterior to and, as a result, an incomplete or immature
> version of the modern, civilized self [...] Southeast Asia appears at best perversely
> modern, or to manifest various perverse forms of modernity. These may be ex-
> plained away as premodern survivals or invented traditions, but neither explanation
> does much to come to grips with what is apparently unique to such places.[37]

One possible answer to this predicament is to reconceptualize modernity in
the plural. Multiple modernities is about "alternative constructions [...] in the
sense of moral-political projects that seek to control their own present and
future,"[38] as Aihwa Ong succinctly puts it. These can no longer be denigrated
as deficient or labeled non-modern, pre-modern, or traditional. This conceptual pluralization of modernities has been welcomed as a liberatory move
within anthropological theoretical debates, breaking down the divide between
tradition and modernity. It allows anthropologists to acknowledge as modern
those cultural practices that coexist with capitalist modernity but do not con-

---

[35] Knauft, "Critically Modern," 25.
[36] Joel S. Kahn, "Anthropology and Modernity," *Current Anthropology* 42.5 (2001): 657.
[37] Kahn, "Anthropology and Modernity," 658.
[38] Ong, *Flexible Citizenship*, 23.

form in any narrow way to the Western European or US-American model of a modern way of life. The Indian historian Dipesh Chakrabarty points out that it is not sufficient to explain such forms as "inventions of tradition" or in terms of the idea of "the modernity of tradition";[39] as Timothy Mitchell has noted in the introduction to the anthology *Questions of Modernity*, such "invocations of the restored, contrived, or resistant powers of a tradition accept the notion that there is a universal narrative of modernity, against which local variations can be measured."[40] However, these are not residual elements or fragments of the past, nor simply an absence of modernity or indicators of its incomplete fulfilment. To talk of multiple modernities, then, means to explore the possibility of a heterogeneous account of the emergence of colonial modernity. According to Mitchell, Chakrabarty's work has been especially evocative of how

> colonialism has made European narratives a global heritage that inevitably structures any subsequent account of this modernity [...] A theme that emerges from studies of this kind is that in the production of modernity, the hegemony of the modern over what it displaces as 'traditional' is never complete. As a result, modernizing forces continuously re-appropriate elements that have been categorized as non-modern, such as religious elements, in order to produce their own effectiveness [...] failures do not indicate the inability of modern secular politics to delimit the traditional powers of religion. They show that producing a colonial modernity requires the production of groups and forces designated as non-modern yet able to contest the hegemony of the modernist politics that called for them.[41]

The different versions of modernity that are generated in different places, then, are no longer to be seen merely as aspects of the emergence of the 'real' modernity that are on the sidelines of the one plot that actually counts. Rather, anthropologists stress the fact that modernity is emerging beyond or on the margins of the geography of the West. These developments are not to be

---

[39] Dipesh Chakrabarty, "The Difference-Deferral of a Colonial Modernity: Public Debates on Domesticity in British Bengal," in *Subaltern Studies* 8, ed. David Arnold & David Hardiman (Delhi: Oxford UP, 1994): 81.

[40] Timothy Mitchell, "Preface" to *Questions of Modernity*, ed. Mitchell (Minneapolis: U of Minnesota P, 2000): xvi.

[41] Mitchell, "Preface," xviii–xix. See also Dipesh Chakrabarty, "Witness to Suffering: Domestic Cruelty and the Birth of the Modern Subject in Bengal," in *Questions of Modernity*, ed. Timothy Mitchell (Minneapolis: U of Minnesota P, 2000b): 49–86.

assessed in terms of "their contribution to the singular history of the modern."[42] Rather than focusing on the grand designs of colonial powers and modernizing states, anthropology starts looking at the local sites "where the modern is realized and continually translated, in its articulation with and production of the non-modern."[43] And this may happen at a neighbourhood grocery, a village school, a video store, a fast food parlour, but also in a government office, a conference room, or a research lab. Anthropology's fieldwork approach leads us to look closely at sites where we can observe modernity as it is socially produced, in the actual social practices of people who are engaged in the making of modernity.[44]

Recapturing the Critical Potential of Anthropology

In adopting this stance, social theory has come a long way from the 1960s and its conventional modernization theory, the epitome of which were standardized sociological measurements of the percentage degree of modernity acquired by individuals in so-called Third-World countries.[45] To conceptualize modernity in the plural also implies stressing that each society has the right to determine how and to what ends it wants to modernize. Yet some caveats are in order. If the conceptual switch from emphasizing a divide between tradition and modernity to acknowledging a multiplicity of modern cultures entails merely a celebratory attitude towards the hybridity that is generated by local–global encounters, then anthropology would fall back into older habits of essentializing non-Western cultures as 'Others'. Also, to indiscriminately declare contemporary cultural expressions as modern makes no sense, as it renders the designation meaningless. Joel Kahn warns that if we "reject any general understanding of modernity," this may well be an "escape route out of modernity altogether."[46] By the same token, to suggest that all social prac-

---

[42] Mitchell, "Preface," xii.

[43] Mitchell, "Preface," xxvi.

[44] For exemplary case studies, see, for instance, Michael Burawoy, "Introduction: Reaching for the Global," in *Global Ethnography: Forces, Connections, and Imaginations in a Postmodern World*, ed. Michael Burawoy et al (Berkeley: U of California P, 2000): 1–40.

[45] See Alex Inkeles & D.H. Smith, *Becoming Modern* (Cambridge MA: Harvard UP, 1974).

[46] Joel Kahn suggests viewing modernity as a product of contradictory cultural processes rather than – as liberal modernization narratives and also their critiques imply – as "a single cultural movement of liberty or discipline." Kahn asserts that these cultural processes entail a conflict between 'autonomy' and 'rationalization' rather than between tradition and

tices are legitimate as long as they can be explained as expressions of 'alternative modernity' implies an irresponsibly relativist stance that uses the multiple-modernities paradigm as an excuse to evade the responsibility of dissent, critique, and engagement. To talk of multiple modernities cannot simply mean to recognize everybody as modern. If we do not at the same time make visible and critique the inequalities and power asymmetries that are being produced by a globalizing economy and the new geopolitical world order, then the designation 'otherwise modern' or 'alternatively modern' is simply another way of saying 'backward', or of replacing the older labels 'premodern' or 'traditional'.

As much as anthropology welcomes the paradigm shift outlined above, at our peril we cannot, and must not, ignore the fact that, of course, Western centres of power continue to consider themselves more modern than anybody else. At the same time, a number of supranational institutions continue to claim the right to assess the accomplishment of modernity by political systems, economies, and cultures around the world, and whether they deserve benefits, support, and attention, or else are to be fined, sanctioned, and boycotted for their lack of 'good governance' and 'best practices'. The postcolonial scholar and social anthropologist Vassos Argyrou asserts that, through the process of modernization, non-Western societies do not acquire a Western identity; rather, "they constitute themselves as Western subjects" while at the same time "the West essentializes itself as the only true source of legitimate culture so that the practical manifestations of [non-Western] claims to modernity seem a poor version of the 'original'."[47] For Agyrou, it matters little whether we continue to use the term 'modernity' in the singular or plural mode so long as we do not pay attention to the mechanisms of domination and governmentality at work in the modern world order.[48] Timothy Mitchell has pointed out that modernity of the Western type always requires the non-universal, non-Western to define itself in contradistinction to it. The mode of

---

modernity. He gives examples from his fieldwork among Malay Muslims that show that "the theme of reconciling the apparently contradictory processes of rationalization ('globalization') and expressive meaning (understood as the expressive values of a particular people that we are wont to call their culture)" is central here as well. Kahn, "Anthropology and Modernity," 662.

[47] Vassos Argyrou, *Tradition and Modernity in the Mediterranean: The Wedding as Symbolic Struggle* (Cambridge: Cambridge U P, 1996): 178.

[48] See also Vassos Argyrou, *Anthropology and the Will to Meaning: A Postcolonial Critique* (London: Pluto Press, 2002).

production of modernity depends on "what remains heterogeneous to it" as its
constitutive outside:

> Yet in the very processes of the subordination and exclusion, it can be shown, such
> elements infiltrate and compromise that history. These elements cannot be referred
> back to any unifying historical logic or any underlying potential defining the nature
> of capitalist modernity, for it is only by their exclusion or subordination that such a
> logic or potential can be realized. Yet, such elements continually redirect, divert,
> and mutate the modernity they help constitute.[49]

Conclusion: Anthropology in and of Modern Societies

To adopt Mitchell's notion allows us to "acknowledge the singularity and
universalism of the project of modernity"[50] and, at the same time, to view
modernity as "something concrete, embedded in particular institutions and
cultural formations, but also a singular process that is global and multicultural
from its inception."[51] Ultimately, this calls on anthropology not just to reveal
the wide variety of modernities in non-Western societies but, rather, to apply
this research perspective to ourselves, to our own position as German, British,
Swiss or American scholars. Anthropologists need to historicize and cross-
culturally compare their very own versions of modernity. As Joel Kahn points
out, this new anthropology of modernity "compels us towards an ethnographic engagement with modernity in the West"[52] and, incidentally, picks up on
some longstanding research interests, especially among anthropologists of
Europe, who have been exploring the distinct formations of European modernities and their historical and cultural specificities.[53] This resonates strongly
with Dipesh Chakrabarty's intention to unmask the particular historical trajectory and power formation that has made it possible for Europe to claim
that it is everybody's heritage. Chakrabarty asserts that the "phenomenon of

---

[49] Mitchell, "Preface," xiii.

[50] Mitchell, "Preface," xiii.

[51] Kahn, "Anthropology and Modernity," 664.

[52] Kahn, "Anthropology and Modernity," 663.

[53] See James D. Faubion, *Modern Greek Lessons: A Primer in Historical Constructivism*
(Princeton NJ: Princeton UP, 1993); Jonas Frykman & Orvar Löfgren, *Culture Builders: A
Historical Anthropology of Middle-Class Life* (New Brunswick NJ: Rutgers UP, 1987);
Michael Herzfeld, *The Social Production of Indifference: Exploring the Symbolic Roots of
Western Bureaucracy* (Chicago & London: U of Chicago P, 1992); Paul Rabinow, *French
Modern: Norms and Forms of the Social Environment* (Cambridge MA: MIT Press, 1989).

'political modernity' – namely, the rule of modern institutions of the state, bureaucracy, and capitalist enterprise – is impossible to *think* of anywhere in the world without invoking certain categories and concepts, the genealogies of which go deep into the intellectual and even theological traditions of Europe." He suggests engaging in an operation he calls the provincializing of Europe, as

> European thought is at once both indispensable and inadequate in helping us to think through the experiences of political modernity in non-Western nations, and provincializing Europe becomes the task of exploring how this thought – which is now everybody's heritage and which affect us all – may be renewed from and for the margins.[54]

Anthropology may contribute to this operation once the discipline becomes aware of the fact that – as Aihwa Ong puts it[55] – it is both an extension of modernity and an instrument for its undoing.

WORKS CITED

Abu-Lughod, Lila. "Modern Subjects: Egyptian Melodrama and Postcolonial Difference," in *Questions of Modernity*, ed. Timothy Mitchell (Minneapolis: U of Minnesota P, 2000): 87–114.

Appadurai, Arjun. "Here and Now," in *Modernity at Large: Cultural Dimensions of Globalization* (Minneapolis & London: U of Minnesota P, 1996): 1–23.

Argyrou, Vassos. *Anthropology and the Will to Meaning: A Postcolonial Critique* (London: Pluto Press, 2002).

Argyrou, Vassos. *Tradition and Modernity in the Mediterranean: The Wedding as Symbolic Struggle* (Cambridge: Cambridge UP, 1996).

Burawoy, Michael. "Introduction: Reaching for the Global," in *Global Ethnography: Forces, Connections, and Imaginations in a Postmodern World*, ed. Michael Burawoy et al. (Berkeley: U of California P, 2000): 1–40.

Chakrabarty, Dipesh. "The Difference-Deferral of a Colonial Modernity: Public Debates on Domesticity in British Bengal," in *Subaltern Studies VIII*, ed. David Arnold & David Hardiman (Delhi: Oxford UP, 1994): 50–88.

——. *Provincializing Europe: Postcolonial Thought and Historical Difference* (Princeton NJ & Oxford: Princeton UP, 2000).

---

[54] Dipesh Chakrabarty, *Provincializing Europe: Postcolonial Thought and Historical Difference* (Princeton NJ & Oxford: Princeton UP, 2000): 16.

[55] Ong, "Modernity," 9944.

———. "Witness to Suffering: Domestic Cruelty and the Birth of the Modern Subject in Bengal," in *Questions of Modernity*, ed. Timothy Mitchell (Minneapolis MN: U of Minnesota P: 2000): 49–86.

Clifford, James. "Traveling Cultures," in *Routes: Travel and Translation in the Late Twentieth Century* (Cambridge MA & London: Harvard UP, 1997): 17–46.

———. "The Pure Products Go Crazy," in *The Predicament of Culture: Twentieth-Century Ethnography, Literature, and Art* (Cambridge MA: Harvard UP, 1988): 1–17.

Dickey, Sara. *Cinema and the Urban Poor in South India* (Cambridge: Cambridge UP, 1993).

Eisenstadt, Samuel N. *Die Vielfalt der Moderne* (Weilerswist: Velbrück, 2000).

———, ed. *Multiple Modernities* (New Brunswick NJ: Transaction, 2002).

Escobar, Arturo. "Culture Sits in Places: Reflections on Globalism and Subaltern Strategies of Localization," *Political Geography* 20 (2001): 139–74.

Faubion, James D. *Modern Greek Lessons: A Primer in Historical Constructivism* (Princeton NJ: Princeton UP, 1993).

Frykman, Jonas & Orvar Löfgren. *Culture Builders: A Historical Anthropology of Middle-Class Life* (New Brunswick NJ: Rutgers UP, 1987).

Geertz, Clifford. *After the Fact: Two Countries, Four Decades, One Anthropologist* (Cambridge MA & London: Harvard UP, 1995).

Gupta, Akhil, & James Ferguson. "Discipline and Practice: The Field as Site, Method, and Location in Anthropology," in *Anthropological Locations: Boundaries and Grounds of a Field Science*, ed. Akhil Gupta & James Ferguson (Berkeley: U of California P, 1997): 1–46.

Hannerz, Ulf. "Transnational Research," in *Handbook of Methods in Cultural Anthropology,* ed. H. Russell Bernard (Walnut Creek, London & New Delhi: Altamira, 1998): 235–56.

———. *Transnational Connections: Culture, People, Places* (London & New York: Routledge, 1996).

Herzfeld, Michael. "Media," in *Anthropology: Theoretical Practice in Culture and Society* (Malden MA & Oxford: Blackwell 2001): 294–315.

———. *The Social Production of Indifference: Exploring the Symbolic Roots of Western Bureaucracy* (Chicago & London: U of Chicago P, 1992).

Inkeles, Alex, & D.H. Smith. *Becoming Modern* (Cambridge MA: Harvard UP, 1974).

Kahn, Joel S. "Anthropology and Modernity," *Current Anthropology* 42.5 (2001): 651–64.

Knauft, Bruce M. "Critically Modern: An Introduction," in *Critically Modern: Alternatives, Alterities, Anthropologies*, ed. Bruce M. Knauft (Bloomington: Indiana UP, 2002): 1–54.

Larkin, Brian. "Indian Films and Nigerian Lovers: Media and the Creation of Parallel Modernities," *Africa* 67.3 (1997): 406–39.

Malkki, Liisa. "National Geographic: The Rooting of Peoples and the Territorialization of National Identity Among Scholars and Refugees," in *Space, Identity, and the Politics of Difference*, ed. James Ferguson & Akhil Gupta, *Cultural Anthropology* 7.1 (Special Issue 1992): 24–44.

Mankekar, Purnima. *Screening Culture, Viewing Politics: An Ethnography of Television, Womanhood and Nation in Postcolonial India* (Durham NC: Duke UP, 1999).

Marcus, George E. "Ethnography In/Of the World System: the Emergence of Multi-Sited Ethnography," *Annual Review of Anthropology* 24 (1995): 95–117.

———. *Ethnography Through Thick and Thin* (Princeton NJ: Princeton UP, 1998).

Mitchell, Timothy. "Introduction," in *Questions of Modernity*, ed. Timothy Mitchell (Minneapolis: U of Minnesota P, 2000): xi–xxvii.

Ong, Aihwa. "Modernity: Anthropological Aspects," in *International Encyclopedia of the Social and Behavioral Sciences* (Amsterdam: Elsevier, 2001): 9944–49.

———. *Flexible Citizenship: The Cultural Logics of Transnationality* (Durham NC & London: Duke UP, 1999).

Rabinow, Paul. *French Modern: Norms and Forms of the Social Environment* (Cambridge MA: MIT Press, 1989).

Strathern, Marilyn. "Externalities in Comparative Guise," *Economy and Society* 31.2 (2002): 250–67.

Taylor, Peter J. *Modernities: A Geohistorical Interpretation* (Minneapolis: U of Minnesota P, 1999).

Trouillot, Michel-Rolph. "The Otherwise Modern: Caribbean Lessons from the Savage Slot," in *Critically Modern: Alternatives, Alterities, Anthropologies*, ed. Bruce Knauft (Bloomington: Indiana UP, 2002): 220–37.

Watson, James K., ed. *Golden Arches East: McDonald's in East Asia* (Stanford CA: Stanford UP, 1997).

Welz, Gisela. "Moving Targets: Feldforschung unter Mobilitätsdruck," *Zeitschrift für Volkskunde* 94.2 (1998): 177–94.

———. "Siting Ethnography: Some Observations on a Cypriot Highland Village," in *Shifting Grounds: Experiments in Doing Ethnography*, ed. Ina–Maria Greverus, Sharon Macdonald, Regina Römhild, Gisela Welz & Helena Wulff, *Anthropological Journal on European Cultures* 11 (2002): 137–58.

◄❖►

Authenticity
— Why We Still Need It Although It Doesn't Exist

VIRGINIA RICHTER

I N CONTEMPORARY CRITICAL THEORY, constructivist views –
like the 'narrative turn' in history and ethnology, the notion of 'imagined communities', the critique of 'identity politics' in gender studies,
etc. – tend to predominate. The notion that we can have a 'direct' access to
reality, unmediated by linguistic, representational, and cultural conventions,
will find few adherents among university teachers, literary critics, and similar
groups familiar with recent theoretical debates. Nevertheless, we keep returning to the notion of 'authenticity' in the discussion of literary texts – or,
perhaps, this is the case only with specific kinds of texts. There still seems to
be a need for authenticity as both an aesthetic and an ethical category that is
drawn on in value judgements of literary works, films, and other forms of
symbolic representation. However, this need is addressed only obliquely in
critical writing, more like an embarrassing habit rather than an important
theoretical issue that needs to be explored in all its paradoxical twists and
turns.

The paradox of authenticity, as Jonathan Culler has remarked, lies in the
fact that "to be experienced as authentic [an object] must be marked as
authentic, but when it is marked as authentic it is mediated, a sign of itself,
and hence lacks the authenticity of what is truly unspoiled, untouched by
mediating cultural codes."[1] Consequently, the notion of authenticity is con-

---

[1] Jonathan Culler, *Framing the Sign: Criticism and Its Institutions* (Norman: U of Oklahoma P, 1988): 164.

ceivable only in a culture that realizes its own alienation from 'the natural', 'the pure', and 'the unspoiled'. In our postmodern culture, the authentic is inaccessible; it can be viewed only as a lost referent – in short, authenticity has been thoroughly deconstructed and discarded as the product of an impossible nostalgia for 'pure origins'. Indeed, it is precisely a sign of our mental arrival in the postmodern era that we accept this loss of the authentic experience not with melancholia, but with the ironic detachment of 'post-tourists' who are well aware of the secondary, mediated nature of their journey.

Nevertheless, in certain contexts authenticity still remains an important category of reference. This is particularly the case with books written by women, writers from ethnic minorities, or Holocaust survivors. Works written by authors whose identity is 'unmarked' – by and large, white heterosexual men – tend to be evaluated according to their aesthetic merit. One reason is the symbolic invisibility of a position that is 'just' human, described by Richard Dyer in his study on whiteness:

> As long as race is something only applied to non-white peoples, as long as white people are not racially seen and named, they/we function as a human norm. Other people are raced, we are just people.[2]

This invisibility of race – and, by analogy, of (male) gender and ('normal') sexuality – invests the position of enunciation with the greatest possible authority, with power, because it allows the claim "to speak for the commonality of humanity."[3] In the academic marketplace, this unmarked, 'normal' position of enunciation commonly entails – or used to entail – certain effects: the literary work in question, e.g., Joyce's *Ulysses*, is seen as a representation of the (universal) *conditio humana*, it is accepted as part of the 'Great Tradition', and it is valued for its complexity, its literariness, and its originality. But the example of *Ulysses*, written by an Irishman in exile about a Dublin Jew of Hungarian extraction, already indicates the complexity of the question. Even if Leopold Bloom's wanderings through Dublin can be seen as representing man's alienated condition in modernity or, even more generally, man's forlorn condition in life, or as a great formal achievement, the epitome of modernist literature, at the same time *Ulysses* is one of the most context-specific novels in literary history, accurate in its evocation of a concrete time

---

[2] Richard Dyer, *White* (London: Routledge, 1997): 1.
[3] Dyer, *White*, 2.

and space, up to the detail of lodging Bloom in a vacant house in Eccles Street, in order not to disturb any 'real' inhabitants. As the interests of literary criticism shifted in the course of the twentieth century, the Irishness of Joyce and of his novel came into focus. From this point of view, Joyce's depiction of a day in the life of a group of Dubliners is certainly 'authentic' – based on his own experience, information received from friends, documentary material, facts. Or is it? What is, for instance, the function of Bloom's Jewishness, if not to introduce an alienating element, a bar between the author and his character, in order to foreground precisely the fictionality, the literariness, the 'non-authenticity' of the text? Does not Joyce's deliberate removal from the scene, his self-imposed exile, gesture in the same direction? Does not the text stage its own authenticity, and thereby frame it, label it as 'truly Irish, made in Paris'? And what, then, is the best approach to the text: to consider it as the 'Great Modernist Novel', disregarding the context, or the opposite, its integration in the manifold contexts of British dominance, Irish politics, Catholicism, the web of Dublin life, Joyce's biography, and all the other conditions that allowed the emergence of this novel at that precise moment in time?

The problem of authenticity is even more evident in the contexts of postcolonial literature and of writings concerned with the Holocaust. In such cases, congruence either between a writer's life and his or her subject-matter is demanded, or between the subject-matter and the real experiences of the groups represented. In other words, equivalence between the signifiers of the fictional text and the real-life referents is presupposed. This claim of congruence is particularly strong in the case of autobiographies, biographies, and other non-fictional categories, but it has been equally made for works of fiction. In recent years, an apparent lack of such congruence has been perceived as extremely disturbing in two kinds of events: in cases of faked authorial identity, and in the ostensible misrepresentation of a particular ethnic group, religion, or community.

Several cases in which authors pretended to belong to a certain group, or innocently believed in their membership in a certain group, have created a stir, notably the examples of Benjamin Wilkomirski and of Mudrooroo: what makes these disclosures so explosive is not just the fact that these authors invented a new identity for themselves or unknowingly lived out a false identity – respectively, as Holocaust survivor (Wilkomirski) and as Aborigine (Mudrooroo) – but that they affiliated themselves with groups who had been victimized on a huge historical scale. Wilkomirski's act of reinventing an authorial identity and Mudrooroo's assumption of one were thus seen as illegitimate appropriations, as a second silencing, a second marginalization of these victims of genocide.[4] Wilkomirski misrepresented himself; to put it bluntly, he have lied about who he was; and Mudrooroo, after the exposure of his likely Afro-American/West Indian ancestry, stood as the unwitting compromiser of a whole people who had placed their faith in him as the prime articulator of their culture. Although questions of audience expectations and marketing are involved, the transgression concerns not so much literature itself as personal integrity, it is a moral, not an aesthetic question.[5] As a first step in my attempted approximation to authenticity, I would suggest distinguishing this kind of more or less deliberate authorial (self-)misrepresentation from other, trickier forms: i.e. I want to differentiate between sincerity and authenticity.[6]

The literary 'misrepresentation' of a community (a nation, an ethnic group, a religion) is differently circumstanced. It raises another set of questions: of literary representation as such, of the relation between text and reality, of truth and imagination. Without denying an author's social responsibility, which includes consideration for real-life models, individual or collective, of a literary work, the main problems raised in such debates about the 'correct',

---

[4] Since both cases have been extensively covered, I won't pursue these examples any further. On the 're-invention' of Colin Johnson as Mudrooroo Narogin and the attendant implications, see Adam Shoemaker, "Mudrooroo and the Curse of Authenticity," in *Mongrel Signatures: Reflections on the Work of Mudrooroo*, ed. Annalisa Oboe (Cross/Cultures 64; Amsterdam & New York: Rodopi, 2003): 1–23; on Wilkomirski, see Stefan Maechler, *The Wilkomirski Affair: A Study in Biographical Truth*, tr. John E. Woods (New York: Schocken, 1996).

[5] On the distinction between 'authenticity' as a literary and a moral question, see also Ulrike Erichsen, "A 'True-True' Voice: The problem of authenticity," in *Being/s in Transit: Travelling, Migration, Dislocation*, ed. Liselotte Glage (Cross/Cultures 41, ASNEL Papers 5; Amsterdam & Atlanta GA: Rodopi, 2000): 193–203. Erichsen offers one of the most lucid accounts of the question of authenticity in the context of deliberate falsifications and the critical problems they raise.

[6] I am aware that occasionally these terms are difficult if not impossible to separate. Geoffrey Hartman, for instance, links the authenticity of writing with the personal sincerity of the author: i.e. the uncompromising search for a 'true self' as the source of writing invested both with authenticity and authority. However, as his example – Henry Thoreau's withdrawal from a 'civilised' life perceived as inauthentic to a 'simple and sincere' life in rural nature – clearly shows, such a gesture may be simultaneously sincere on a personal level and yet marked by the paradox of authenticity: if authenticity were an untroubled term it would not be necessary to go looking for it in such an elaborate way. See Geoffrey Hartman, *Scars of the Spirit: The Struggle Against Inauthenticity* (New York: Palgrave Macmillan, 2002): 28.

the 'authentic' representation of particular groups are not of a social and moral nature, but concern the aesthetic integrity of the text. This integrity is threatened, on the one hand, by a too close adherence to the authentic: i.e. by the cliché,[7] and, on the other hand, by a too strong deviation, a breakdown of the 'representational pact' between author and reader that underpins realist fiction. In other words, a text that appears to be 'untrue' is also perceived as aesthetically flawed. But what is the measure of truth in a *fictional* text – a problem that has bothered authors and critics since the rise of the novel in the eighteenth century? Does not truth, like beauty, lie in the eye of the beholder – or, rather, in the expectations of the reader? I will return to this problem with regard to a concrete example, Monica Ali's recent debut novel *Brick Lane*, after pursuing the question of authenticity a little further on a theoretical level.

What is authenticity? Is it an aesthetic category, a marketing strategy, an ethical position? The OED offers the following definitions: authenticity is "the quality of being authentic, or entitled to acceptance, 1. as being authoritative or duly authorized"; "2. as being in accordance with fact, as being true in substance"; "3. as being what it professes in origin or authorship, as being genuine; genuineness"; "4. as being real, actual; reality". The adjective 'authentic' has nine different meanings, including the prevailing sense "3.a. entitled to acceptance or belief, as being in accordance with fact, or as stating fact; reliable, trustworthy, of established credit" and "6. Really proceeding from its reputed source or author; of undisputed origin, genuine. (Opposed to *counterfeit, forged, apocryphal.*)" Some obsolete meanings that are also of interest to the discussion of literary authenticity include: of authority, authoritative, entitled to obedience or respect; legally valid, having legal force; original, first-hand, prototypical; as opposed to *copied*; belonging to himself, own, proper. This array of meanings indicates what is involved in the question of

---

[7] According to Erichsen, the fact that 'authentic experience' can be imitated so easily and so convincingly – both Wilkomirski's and Mudrooroo's texts, as well as the supposed 'autobiography' of the female Aborigine Wanda Koolmatrie, in fact written by the white male Leon Carmen, have been hailed as particularly 'authentic voices', representative of their peoples' suffering – means that the concept of authenticity is emptied of its original meaning and reduced to cliché: "One could even argue that in a sense (from the reader's point of view) the 'false' voices are, paradoxically, more 'authentic' than the real thing – or, rather, the real voice; because the creators of such 'false' voices write with an eye to the expectations of the (dominant) reading public, they cater to the reader's need to stabilize his or her identity through a fiction of difference" (Erichsen, "A 'True-True Voice'," 201–202).

authenticity: the foundations of human relations such as truth, belief, trust, and respect; but also aspects constituting (literary) authority and (social) power: origin, value, property, and legal validity. When we talk about authenticity in literature, we negotiate basic social, moral, and even religious questions in relation to the symbolic production in our culture.

Such questions tended to be dismissed in literary criticism in the wake of poststructuralist 'textuality';[8] but if there is, as some critics maintain, an 'ethical turn' in the most recent theory, these issues will have to be addressed in a new way. However, at the moment the question of authenticity itself remains seriously under-theorized. For instance, in Derek Attridge's most recent book, *The Singularity of Literature*, an explicit reference to authenticity will be sought in vain, although the author aims at addressing precisely the interaction of the aesthetic and the ethical, an endeavour to which the term would seem to belong – indeed, to be indispensable.[9]

In the following, I would like to take a closer look at two theoretical models from which a concept of authenticity can be derived that, on the one hand, takes into account our postconstructivist scepticism about the authentic and that, on the other, does not fail to acknowledge its political effects. The first theoretical approach is Graham Huggan's analysis of ethnic autobiographies in the context of a global commodification of the exotic. These texts figure as examples of the paradox of authenticity mentioned earlier:

> authenticity is valued for its attachment to the material contexts of lived experience even as it is so palpably the *decontextualization* of the commodified artifact that enables it to become marketably authentic.[10]

While Huggan is highly critical of the commodification of ethnic writing in which not only certain features identified as 'authentic' semiotic markers, but "*authenticity itself* can be made to circulate as a commodity,"[11] he is equally

---

[8] Of course, this is a generalization that does not do justice to many poststructuralist critics; Foucault, to name but one example, addresses precisely the question of social authority and authorship. See Michel Foucault, "What is an Author?" in *Language, Counter-Memory, Practice: Selected Essays and Interviews*, ed. Donald Bouchard, tr. Donald Bouchard & Sherry Simon (Ithaca NY: Cornell UP, 1977): 113–38.

[9] See Derek Attridge, *The Singularity of Literature* (London: Routledge, 2004).

[10] Graham Huggan, *The Postcolonial Exotic: Marketing the Margins* (New York: Routledge, 2001): 158.

[11] Huggan, *The Postcolonial Exotic*, 158.

sceptical of a new essentialism on the side of critics who desire to maintain the purity of such writing. It is a truism in the postcolonial world that "the experience of multiply affiliated cultural subjects[12]" is no longer – if there ever was such a state – single and univocal. In the age of global cultural exchange and migrancy, identities are constructed as self-consciously hybrid. In consequence, Huggan posits something that could be called 'strategic inauthenticity', a double positioning of the ethnic writer in relation to a dual audience. An example would be the writing of black Australians for a white readership: this situation simultaneously creates an outlet for their work – without a white publishing industry and readers able and willing to purchase the books, there would be no opportunity to publish at all – and imposes certain constraints by dominant representational mechanisms. Such texts then take on the function of underpinning white Australian history instead of recuperating the historical tradition from which they emerged: "Authenticity functions here, we might say, less as a validating mechanism for collective Aboriginal consciousness than as a kind of cultural fetish reminding white Australians of the discrepancy between past material gains and present spiritual losses."[13]

Although this fetishization of authenticity is problematic, ethnic writers publishing in a Western context should not be accused of selling out. According to Huggan, writing for a dual audience, for 'one's own people' *and* for an international readership, opens up possibilities of an ironic and self-conscious engagement with issues of authenticity, identity, and origin. A deliberate 'misquoting' of authenticity, then, will give rise to empowerment and agency:

> The search for authenticity in such an obviously compromised context involves the reaching out to alternative readerships, including the people one regards as being one's own. As I have suggested, it also involves a reflexive approach to authenticity – one that plays on the expectations of the international 'market reader,' as well as on a readership more likely to be acquainted with the text's (inter)cultural nuances and representational codes. Perhaps, in this sense, the most fitting paradox of Native authenticity is that it can be used for self-empowering purposes, even as its potential is recognised as a mechanism for the representation of otherness and as an objectifying market tool. And if Aboriginal writers remain constrained to some extent by a commodified discourse of authenticity that serves majority interests,

---

[12] Huggan, *The Postcolonial Exotic*, 156.
[13] *The Postcolonial Exotic*, 160–61.

several of them have proved singularly adept in 'playing the market' to their own ideological ends.[14]

What Huggan proposes here is in fact a performative concept of authenticity that is quite close to Judith Butler's theory of identity formation. Butler is the second theorist I would like to draw on in my reflections on authenticity, although this is a term that does not explicitly make an appearance in her writings. But her engagement with questions of identity, agency, and reality from a pronounced anti-essentialist perspective can be made very productive for a reconsideration of authenticity.

As is well known, Butler has developed her theory of the performative construction of identity with a particular focus on gender. The thesis she put forward in *Gender Trouble* is, very briefly, that there is no pre-existing sexual identity that constitutes the gendered subject through representation, but that gender is produced by performative gestures determined by a genealogy of heterosexual norms. This means, on the one hand, that each individual is constrained by the historicity of such norms. Gendered identities cannot be transformed by a simple act of will. On the other hand, there is a limited space in which agency and change are possible. Subjects can respond to the appellation of the norm in a skewed way – in a 'queer' way – which will result in the "denaturalization and mobilization of gender categories": "The replication of heterosexual constructs in non-heterosexual frames brings into relief the utterly constructed status of the so-called heterosexual original."[15] This denaturalization of gender norms is what Butler calls 'doing gender'.

The initial reception of *Gender Trouble* was very controversial. Butler was criticized mostly because her notion of performativity, based on speech-act theory,[16] was confused with theatrical performance, with role-playing. In *Bodies That Matter* she made it clear that she did not simply advocate the assumption of alternative roles, but that in fact she aimed at a radical deconstruction of the sex–gender difference itself: there is no biological essence prior to its performative realization. Butler is one of the keenest critics of identity politics, including the gay and lesbian variety. Nevertheless, she does not fully repudiate the strategic use of terms such as 'women' that have been

---

[14] Huggan, *The Postcolonial Exotic*, 176.

[15] Judith Butler, *Gender Trouble: Feminism and the Subversion of Identity* (New York: Routledge, 1990): 31.

[16] Cf. J.L. Austin, *How to Do Things with Words* (Oxford: Clarendon, 1975).

criticized by other feminists as essentialist, universalist, and eurocentric. In her argument for what she calls a 'radical democratic project', she draws on Slavoj Žižek's concept of the 'political signifier':

> Political signifiers, especially those that designate subject positions, are not descriptive; that is, they do not represent pregiven constituencies, but are empty signs which come to bear phantasmatic investments of various kinds. No signifier can be radically representative, for every signifier is the site of a perpetual *méconnaissance*; it produces the expectation of a unity, a full and final recognition that can never be achieved. Paradoxically, the failure of such signifiers – 'women' is the one that comes to mind – fully to describe the constituency they name is precisely what constitutes these signifiers as sites of phantasmatic investment and discursive rearticulation. It is what opens the signifier to new meanings and new possibilities for political resignification.[17]

This means that encompassing designations like 'women' – but also, in our context, terms like 'Aboriginal', 'Native American', 'black British' – are not based on representation: there is no iconic or indexical relation between sign and referent, but, at the utmost, a symbolic relation: i.e. one that is arbitrary and contingent. Such designations therefore can never include the full range of experience of the subjects summoned by them. Identity labels such as 'women', 'gays', or 'black British' always are, and always have to be, 'inauthentic' (my term): they *must* miss the density and complexity of lived experience. But it is precisely in this perpetual *méconnaisance* between appellation and individual experience that Butler locates the possibility of freedom and agency:

> The incompletion of every ideological formulation is central to the radical democratic project's notion of political futurity. The subjection of every ideological formation to a rearticulation of these linkages constitutes the temporal order of democracy as an incalculable future, leaving open the production of new subject-positions, new political signifiers, and new linkages to become the rallying points for politicization.[18]

---

[17] Judith Butler, *Bodies That Matter: On the Discursive Limits of 'Sex'* (New York: Routledge, 1993): 191.

[18] Butler, *Bodies That Matter*, 193.

This position has two implications for the question I started with: why do we need authenticity although it doesn't exist? First, the incompletion of every ideological formulation opens up the way to a productive critique of identity labels, as Butler has shown in respect of the term 'women'. In the postcolonial context this would mean that labels like 'Commonwealth Literature' or 'black British Writing' are necessary because they constitute a political signifier which, however, by necessity fails to represent the subjects invoked. A label designating a group identity is therefore always constituted as "a permanent site of contest,"[19] as a field that structurally resists closure. In other words, we need authenticity *because* it doesn't exist. Secondly, identity positions cannot be simply dismissed, since they are bearers of phantasmatic investments: the task for an 'anti-descriptivist' policy in Butler's sense is precisely to work on a 'rearticulation' of these positions, not to abandon them completely. According to Butler, it is precisely the failure of representation – the structural impossibility of authenticity – that opens up the way to a discursive rearticulation of the political signifier. It is *because* we live in an era of globalization, migration, and displacement, not in spite of it, that stories about identity, which are always also stories about its loss, continue to be told and read. But in the process, these identities are constantly reformulated.

In order to add a further turn of the screw to the question of authenticity, I would now like to take a critical look at the constructivist positions I have advocated so far. Butler in a way tries to have her cake and eat it: her concept allows her to operate with signifiers like 'women' as empowering political master narratives on the understanding that these signifiers are always already deconstructed, performative, non-referential. Like denial in psychoanalysis, always affirming what it sets out to negate, objections to identity labels are automatically recuperated as necessary parts of the process of political resignification. But what happens if one takes referential claims seriously? Are collectives or individuals entitled to reject representations of themselves on the grounds of inaccuracy, distortion, falsification – in a nutshell, because of their lack of authenticity? And can such protests be linked to the identity of the real author?

---

[19] Butler, *Bodies That Matter*, 221.

To clarify these questions further, let me briefly consider the debates in the British press following the publication of Monica Ali's *Brick Lane*.[20] The author, the daughter of an English mother and a Bangladeshi father, was born in Dhaka and grew up in England; an Oxford graduate, she worked in marketing before she started to write after the birth of her two children. Her heroine Nazneen is a Bangladeshi village girl who has to cope with her transplantation to London following her contracted marriage. The story certainly is not 'authentic' in the sense of describing the author's own experiences or even her social background. Nor does Ali claim authenticity in this referential sense; in her Acknowledgements, she points to research she did on Bangladeshi women garment workers and thus explicitly grants the '(re)constructed' and biographically remote nature of her work. The 'experiences' of Nazneen, her husband Chanu, her sister Hasina, and the other characters are clearly fictional, but linked to an extra-textual reality in two ways: on the side of production, they are based not just on research into the social background of the characters, but also on oral family traditions;[21] on the level of paratexts, the title *Brick Lane* associates the novel with an existing referent, a street in East London. Through this choice of title, Ali performs the contrary move to Joyce's insertion of his novel in the 'Great Tradition' of European letters: while Joyce, through a title referring to the *Odyssey*, staged the fictionality and literariness of his text, Ali connects her novel to a concrete geographical place and its inhabitants. This gesture is far from being a claim to 'authentic' representation, but it allows – possibly even invites – a mimetic reception of the text by its various reading publics. The ambivalent effects of both the title and the text, closely connected to the publishers' marketing strategies, are epitomized in the blurb of the paperback edition: "Profoundly humane and beautifully rendered, *Brick Lane* captures a world at once unimaginable and achingly familiar." This sentence moves between the aspirations of belonging to ethnically unmarked, 'just human' 'great literature' – the representation of universal values ("humane") and the novel's aesthetic quality ("beautifully rendered") – and the claim of representational relations to an exotic, hidden

---

[20] Monica Ali, *Brick Lane* (New York: Scribner, 2003). I am grateful to Florian Stadtler (University of Kent at Canterbury) for perspicacious comments and for material on *Brick Lane*.

[21] In the Acknowledgements, Ali thanks her father "for handing down stories" (Ali, *Brick Lane*, 543), but stresses simultaneously the aspect of fiction, of 'making' and 'forming' that is constitutive of the literary text.

world in our midst. The real author's privileged relations to this separate world are, for example in the view of the Man Booker judges, clearly based on her ethnic identity, as 'a Bangladeshi writing for Bangladeshis'.[22]

For which audience is the world of Brick Lane "at once unimaginable and achingly familiar"? Three groups can be posited for whom the play with authenticity in the title – the evocation of a real-life referent – has different implications: (1) readers with no connection to the Bangladeshi expatriate community in London; (2) middle-class British Bengalis who have only a vicarious knowledge of the East End community; (3) members of that community itself: i.e. inhabitants of Brick Lane, most of whom are not, like Ali, middle-class Bengalis but lower-class Sylhetis. The phrase from the blurb seems to suggest that the book was primarily written for the first two groups of readers, for whom it functions as a kind of fictional guidebook. The immediate success of the novel indicates that Ali met the expectations of these readers, whereas the public reactions of parts of the Bangladeshi East Enders are more troubled.

The journalist Fareena Alam celebrates the 'documentary' value of Ali's novel, its mimetic and instructive function as "a rare account of the British Bengali diaspora experience": "This is why I found Monica Ali's new book *Brick Lane* so important and so revealing. [...] It celebrates the humanity and complexity of a community which even Bengalis like me know little about."[23] In her article, Alam acknowledges the problematic aspects of reading a novel as a mine of information on an ethnic group:

> But we would rarely ask other writers the same questions that are asked of Monica
> Ali. Is Nick Hornby criticised for failing to represent the true London in his comic

---

[22] The novelist DJ Taylor, one of the judges for the Man Booker prize for which Ali's novel was shortlisted in 2003, is quoted as saying "If Monica Ali wants to write about Brick Lane, which as a Bangladeshi she presumably knows a good deal about, then she should be free to do so"; see Matthew Taylor, "Brickbats Fly as Community Brands Novel 'Despicable'," *The Guardian* (3 December 2003): 5. This argument seems to imply that the Bangladeshis know about Brick Lane just as the Chinese know about dry cleaning: the point of the criticism levelled against Ali was precisely that she knows as much, or as little, as any Londoner who did not grow up in Tower Hamlets and who is not part of the community.

[23] Fareena Alam, "The Burden of Representation," *The Observer* (13 July 2003): online http://books.guardian.co.uk/departments/generalfiction/story/0,,997000,00.html#article_co ntinue (acc. March 1, 2008).

treatments of North London angst? [...] It seems that only 'ethnic' writers carry a
burden of 'representation' whether they want to or not.

But while she deplores the 'burden of representation', Alam simultaneously
places Ali's work firmly in the real-life context of Brick Lane by interviewing
drug-rehabilitation workers, local politicians, community activists, and "the
waiter at my local Indian restaurant." Her defence of the novel against criticism voiced by some members of the community – in particular a long ac-
cusatory letter by the Greater Sylhet Welfare and Development Council
(GSWDC) – largely rests on the claim, substantiated by many interviews,
that Ali's representation of the community's problems is by and large correct
and, moreover, that her portrayal of the women in particular is much more
positive than Ali's detractors (many of whom have not read the novel) assume. In other words, Brick Lane is both authentic and politically correct.

The accusations made in the open letter to the author by members of the
GSWDC are also considered in an article by Ian Jack, an editor of the literary
journal *Granta*. Jack, on the one hand, turns the tables on Ali's critics by asking how representative they are of their community – "it is probably safe to
assume that [the GSWDC's] leaders are mainly men"[24] and therefore unsym-
pathetic to the novel's female protagonists' struggles for emancipation. On
the other hand, Jack places the debate in the context of Ali's deliberate evocation of representationality and of the marketing of the novel. If not Ali herself, then at least her publishers draw attention to the referentiality of the
book's setting – for example, by having the book-launch in the rooms of an
old brewery in Brick Lane:

> Forgivable then, surely, that the people in *Brick Lane* might think that the book was
> about them, their beliefs and behaviour, in one way or another. So far as I could
> tell, very few (or possibly none) of them had been invited to the party.[25]

This observation highlights one of the problems of ethnically marked literature: a commodification of the exotic and the authentic that is based on the
simultaneous exclusion of the represented objects: i.e. the real people (who,
despite everything, exist).

---

[24] Ian Jack, "It's only a Novel...," *The Guardian* (20 December 2003): 7.
[25] Jack, "It's only a Novel...," 7.

The debate about Brick Lane shows the many contradictions surrounding the issue of authenticity. (1) The reference to an author's ethnic (gendered, class, sexual etc.) identity harbours the danger of assuming a monolithic Other for whom the author is supposed to speak. (2) This return to a representational paradigm entails the devaluation of 'minority discourse': according to Ulrike Erichsen, the reference to authenticity, applied only to ethnically or otherwise 'marked' writing,

> strengthens and reifies the differences between mainstream and marginal writers. The desire for an authentic voice retains essentialist notions of culture and identity, privileging 'concrete experience' over reflecting the formation of discursive subject-positions.[26]

(3) Even an ironic or strategic approach to authenticity as advocated by Huggan and Butler is highly problematic, although it is supposed to result in the empowerment of the subaltern group in question. The irony might go undetected, so that an essentialist image is further fixed. In addition, the interests of the represented group might in fact be silenced by a representation directed at least in part at a Western audience; this is further complicated by the possibility that these interests might be entirely irreconcilable with a postcolonial or radical democratic agenda. In the case of Brick Lane, the GSWDC members can be said to give voice to a patriarchal, fundamentalist position that is wholly at odds with a radical democratic notion of empowerment, but also with liberal beliefs. (4) Reading a text for its referential value is tantamount to not reading it as a literary text; this includes both the positive (Fareena Alam's celebration of Brick Lane as a true account of the Bangladeshi community) and the negative reception (the GSWDC's rejection of this account as false and shameful). (5) The debate also reveals what is at stake concerning the function of literature in contemporary society. From a Western, post-Enlightenment perspective, the freedom of imagination and the critical licence of literature are paramount. From a fundamentalist position,[27] this view is unacceptable. One person's freedom of speech can be another's

---

[26] Erichsen, "A 'True-True Voice'," 202.

[27] Quite explicitly, I do not want to limit this term to religious, in particular to Islamic fundamentalism, although this seems to be suggested by the context of the debate. Views of gender or 'family values' can be equally deep-seated and equally pernicious, in the East as in the West.

blasphemy. The problems resulting from this clash, not only on a political level but also for literary theory, reached a critical point, of course, in the Rushdie affair.[28]

As this summary shows, the problems inherent in the issue of authenticity are heavily loaded with different, often contradictory assumptions and beliefs. To reformulate the 'paradox of authenticity': it is a deeply flawed and dangerous term; but our collective investment in it is so high that even after decades of deconstructivism and anti-essentialism it is impossible to get rid of it. It was my purpose in this essay, not to offer a recipe for a better use of authenticity, but to suggest that its contrary impulses should be acknowledged. Too often, authenticity functions as a silent subtext in critical approaches to ethnically marked texts. At a point where central theoretical concepts like difference, identity, and nationalism are being reconsidered in postcolonial studies, the vexed problem of authenticity should also be put on the agenda.

WORKS CITED

Alam, Fareena. "The burden of representation," *The Observer* (13 July 2003): online http://books.guardian.co.uk/departments/generalfiction/story/o,,997000,00.html#article_contin ue (accessed 1 March 2008).

Ali, Monica. *Brick Lane* (New York: Scribner, 2003).

Attridge, Derek. *The Singularity of Literature* (London: Routledge, 2004).

Austin, J.L. *How to Do Things with Words* (Oxford: Clarendon, 1975).

Butler, Judith. *Bodies That Matter: On the Discursive Limits of 'Sex'* (New York: Routledge, 1993).

——. *Gender Trouble: Feminism and the Subversion of Identity* (New York: Routledge, 1990).

Culler, Jonathan. *Framing the Sign: Criticism and Its Institutions* (Norman: U of Oklahoma P, 1988).

Dyer, Richard. *White* (London: Routledge, 1997).

Erichsen, Ulrike. "A 'True-True' Voice: The Problem of Authenticity," in *Being/s in Transit: Travelling, Migration, Dislocation*, ed. Liselotte Glage (Cross/Cultures 41, ASNEL Papers 5; Amsterdam & Atlanta GA: Rodopi, 2000): 193–203.

Foucault, Michel. "What is an Author?" in *Language, Counter-Memory, Practice: Selected Essays and Interviews*, ed. Donald Bouchard, tr. Donald Bouchard & Sherry Simon (Ithaca NY: Cornell UP, 1977): 113–38.

---

[28] See Frank Schulze–Engler, "Riding the Crisis: *The Satanic Verses* and the Silences of Literary Theory," in *Fusion of Cultures?* ed. Peter O. Stummer & Christopher Balme (Cross/Cultures 26, ASNEL Papers 2; Amsterdam & Atlanta GA: Rodopi,1996): 193–203.

Hartman, Geoffrey. *Scars of the Spirit: The Struggle Against Inauthenticity* (New York: Palgrave Macmillan, 2002).

Huggan, Graham. *The Postcolonial Exotic: Marketing the Margins* (New York: Routledge, 2001).

Jack, Ian. "It's only a Novel...," *The Guardian* (20 December 2003): 7.

Joyce, James. *Ulysses* (1922; New York: Random House, 2002).

Maechler, Stefan. *The Wilkomirski Affair: A Study in Biographical Truth*, tr. John E. Woods (New York: Schocken, 1996).

Schulze–Engler, Frank. "Riding the Crisis: *The Satanic Verses* and the Silences of Literary Theory," in *Fusion of Cultures?* ed. Peter O. Stummer & Christopher Balme (Cross/Cultures 26, ASNEL Papers 2; Amsterdam & Atlanta GA: Rodopi,1996): 193–203.

Shoemaker, Adam. "Mudrooroo and the Curse of Authenticity," in *Mongrel Signatures: Reflections on the Work of Mudrooroo*, ed. Annalisa Oboe (Cross/Cultures 64; Amsterdam & New York: Rodopi, 2003), 1–23.

Taylor, Matthew. "Brickbats Fly as Community Brands Novel 'Despicable'," *The Guardian* (3 December 2003): 5.

❖

Shifting Perspectives
— The Transcultural Novel

SISSY HELFF

Introduction

FOR SOME TIME NOW, literary critics have been tackling globalization and its effects on culture and literature over the last few centuries with a keen interest in the acceleration and limitedness of movements, on the one hand, and increased cultural exchange, on the other. While 'traditional' English literary studies mainly focused on Britain and its national imagination, the study of postcolonial literature and the New Literatures in English[1] introduced a distinctly anti-imperial perspective by focusing

---

[1] The term "New Literatures in English" started to emerge in the 1970s and became associated with critics such as Dieter Riemenschneider and Bruce King. The term denotes the attempt to pay special critical attention to the changed socio-political situation in the former Commonwealth countries by redefining the literary and cultural tradition of those countries. However, more recently the term has become more heavily contested. The South African postcolonial scholar Graham Huggan, for example, has claimed in *The Postcolonial Exotic: Marketing the Margins* (London: Routledge, 2001) that the term suggests an implicit blandness which is far too evasive and apolitical, while "matching the revived interest in nationalist ideologies within Europe itself" (234). These terminological conditions, according to Huggan, mark the term "New Literatures" as "another inconvenient term of convenience" (235). However, Frank Schulze–Engler reminds us that "the New Literatures are related not only to contexts of 'other' cultures, but also to contexts of an increasingly globalised modernity that challenge us to ask questions beyond the parameters of the paradigms sketched out [by postcolonial projects]"; "Reading After the Postcolonial Deluge: Texts and Contexts in the New Literatures in English," in *Transgressions: Cultural Interventions in the Global Manifold*, ed. Renate Brosch & Rüdiger Kunow (Trier: Wissen-

on authors and their creative writing from Commonwealth countries. Striving
for a more distinct disciplinary profile, scholars soon designated the Commonwealth regions as their sole research topics. However, in the last decade
or so this situation has become somewhat more complex, with the formation
of Black and Asian British Literary Studies, which forcefully claims Great
Britain as a region of minority literature. Seen from this angle, we certainly
witness a different quality of interest in and engagement with globalized
modes of textuality. Publications such as Arjun Appadurai's *Modernity at
Large* (2000), James Clifford's *The Predicament of Culture* (1988), Iain
Chambers's *Migrancy, Culture, Identity* (1995), and Wolfgang Welsch's
Grenzgänge der Ästhetik (1996) bring home to us the fact that we have
entered a new era with different predicaments.[2] In the course of these developments a new field within English literary studies has begun to emerge:
Transcultural English Studies. While this field is, 'methodically speaking',
still in its infancy, it is hardly possible to ignore the flourishing production of
critical studies and texts dealing with this particular subject-matter.[3]

In the light of these developments, my essay follows a threefold project. It
opens with a brief and rather eclectic survey of the study of transcultural English literature by describing this currently still rather unsystematically developed avenue within English literary studies. In the second part, I seek to
develop the concepts of the intercultural and transcultural novel by presenting
my thoughts about a recent study on the intercultural novel. In doing so, I
address several problems confronting literary critics working with postcolonial and transcultural narratives. Finally, I introduce my definition of the

---

schaftlicher Verlag Trier, 2005): 111. In this respect, Schulze–Engler proposes that "the New
Literatures will remain an essential part of modern English Studies as well as a fascinating
body of literary texts [...] even if the enthusiasm for postcolonial theory should abate in
coming years" (111).

[2] Arjun Appadurai, *Modernity at Large* (Minneapolis & London: U of Minnesota P,
2000); James Clifford, *The Predicament of Culture* (Cambridge MA: Harvard UP, 1988);
Iain Chambers, *Migrancy, Culture, Identity* (London: Routledge, 1995); Wolfgang Welsch,
Grenzgänge der Ästhetik (Stuttgart: Reclam, 1996).

[3] See, for example, Alastair Pennycook's *Global Englishes and Transcultural Flows*
(London: Routledge, 2007), *Studying Transcultural Literary History*, ed. Gunilla Lindberg–
Wada (Berlin & New York: Walter de Gruyter, 2006), *Across the Lines: Intertextuality and
Transcultural Communication in the New Literatures in English*, ed. Wolfgang Klooss
(Cross/Cultures 32, ASNEL Papers 3; Amsterdam & Atlanta GA: Rodopi, 1998) and
Inter- und Transkulturelle Studien: Theoretische Grundlagen und Interdisziplinäre Praxis,
ed. Heinz Antor (Heidelberg: Winter, 2006).

'transcultural novel'. What follows in the last part is a contextual reading of
Oonya Kempadoo's *Tide Running* (2001), an Indo-Caribbean narrative which
perfectly exemplifies features and narrative modes of the transcultural novel.
A major focus will be on the mode of unreliable narration.[4] It is argued that,
in *Tide Running*, the cultural practice of narrative unreliabity represents transculturality on a mimetic level.

Any critical account of English transcultural literary studies should reckon
with the fact that in the neighbouring disciplines of literary studies – cultural
anthropology, philosophy, and cultural studies – transcultural and transnational approaches have become commonplace and established concepts in the
last fifteen years or so.[5] This newly emerging research horizon doubtless also
confronted, and still confronts, these disciplines with serious methodological
predicaments and challenges. Cultural anthropology, for example, found itself
increasingly at risk of losing its concrete 'place of action', the field.

In English literary studies, critics wonder whether transcultural approaches
offer perspectives that add anything that could not be addressed by postcolonialism. One result of this theoretical debate within English literary
studies is certainly rooted in an imprecise employment of postcolonial and
transcultural key concepts, terminologies, and methodologies. More recently,
and especially against the backdrop of the dawning demise of postcolonial
theory within English literary and cultural studies,[6] critics have begun to enquire into the possibility of a distinct postcolonial and/or transcultural aesthetics that could not only help them to get a firmer grasp on their own field
of interest, postcolonial and/or transcultural literatures, but might also con-

---

[4] For an overview of approaches to unreliable narration, see, for example, Wayne
Booth's classic *The Rhetoric of Fiction* (Chicago: U of Chicago P, 1995) as well as the
more recent collection *Unreliable Narration: Studien zur Theorie und Praxis unglaubwürdigen Erzählens in der englischsprachigen Erzählliteratur*, ed. Ansgar Nünning (Trier:
Wissenschaftlicher Verlag Trier, 1998).

[5] See, for example, Gisela Welz and Wolfgang Welsch's essays in this volume, as well
as Arjun Appadurai's "Global Ethnoscapes: Notes and Queries for a Transnational Anthropology," in *Recapturing Anthropology: Working in the Present*, ed. Richard G. Fox (Santa
Fe NM: School of American Research 1991): 48–65, Welsch's *Grenzgänge der Ästhetik*,
and *The Cultural Studies Reader*, ed. Simon During (London & New York: Routledge, 2nd
ed. 1999).

[6] In "What was Postcolonialism?" Vijay Mishra and Bob Hodge discuss the possible
demise of postcolonialism, but set out to reinforce its current validity and pointedly state
"We have not come to announce the 'end of postcolonialism,' as the ends of so many other
movements have been announced, usually in vain"; *New Literary History* 36 (2005): 375.

tribute to safeguarding the future validity of their discipline. Accordingly, the British postcolonial scholar John McLeod enquires "whether the protocols of postcolonial theory are always suitably sensitive in bearing witness to the aesthetics and politics of the literatures which are termed 'postcolonial', especially writing which has emerged in the 1990s."[7]

McLeod alludes to the fact that numerous postcolonial approaches to literature and culture almost obsessively remain tied to notions of difference, diversity, and the subversive in their reading of cultural encounters, and thus at times become bogged down in unbridgeable cultural difference. Clearly, it would be a folly to deny that culture as an analytic concept always resembles a matrix of various cultural codes, modes, and histories. This argument points to the conceptual strength of transcultural criticism, especially when it highlights processes of cultural amalgamation as the very foundation of 'culture'. These processes are 'limitless' in a geographical, historical, and also sociopolitical sense and show no particular preference for either difference or homogeneity. In this respect, they do not necessarily entail subversive manoeuvres – they simply exist and need to be reckoned with. Conceptualizing transcultural life in a globalized modern world, therefore, challenges postcolonial concepts such as hybridity (which always implies and thus relies on notions of subversion).

Guided by similar concerns, Frank Schulze-Engler supports a change in perspective, since "transnational and transcultural connections have long since become the lived reality [...] shaping modern literature in 'Western' and 'non-Western' settings alike."[8] For him, postcolonial methodology is problematic, since it irrefutably echoes an 'alterity industry' which simply cannot do justice to the transcultural dimensions of culture.[9] While I mostly agree with this argument, I also have some reservations concerning the scope of transcultural criticism. In understanding transculturality as an amalgama-

---

[7] John McLeod, "'Wheel and Come Again': Transnational Aesthetics Beyond the Postcolonial," *Hungarian Journal of English and American Studies* 7.2 (2001): 85.

[8] Frank Schulze–Engler, "Literature in the Global Ecumene of Modernity: Amitav Ghosh's *The Circle of Reason* and *In an Antique Land*," in *English Literatures in International Contexts*, ed. Heinz Antor & Klaus Stierstorfer (Heidelberg: Winter, 2000): 375–76.

[9] For a critique of the shortcomings of the transcultural paradigm, see Huggan, "Derailing the 'Trans'? Postcolonial Studies and the Negative Effects of Speed," in *Inter- und Transkulturelle Studien: Theoretische Grundlagen und Interdisziplinäre Praxis*, ed. Heinz Antor (Heidelberg: Winter 2006): 55–61, and McLeod, "'Wheel and Come Again'."

tion of cultures, there would ultimately seem to be little space for describing experiences which express the liminality of groups that represent the margins of society such as refugees and illegal migrants. Interestingly enough, these groups often live in no-man's land (such as the highly 'protected' detention-camps at international airports) or seek to survive as illegal migrants in urban liminal zones. Consequently, they do not appear on any immigration record. Their existence in non-places becomes a challenging space for any criticism.

While transcultural theory, as introduced by German-based English lite-rary studies, seems particularly appropriate for an analysis of radicalized dia-sporic situations, liminal groups including gypsy clans and asylum seekers who actually never officially arrive and settle anywhere do not feature in transcultural criticism. Although I do believe in the overall conceptual valid-ity of transculturality as a means to reflect and describe modern transcultural life, there is no denying that a major shortcoming is the development of a 'regionalism' which includes neither the refugee experience of living in non-places nor migrant experiences which are not somehow rooted in Britain's colonial legacy. Seen from such an angle, the recent application of transcul-turality (which constitutes a central theoretical concept for describing cultural globalization in high modernity) runs the danger of reducing the multi-regional and multicultural reality of modern societies.

Charting the Way for Transcultural Narration

In *Fictions of Migration*, Roy Sommer offers a definition of intercultural fiction in order to illuminate new perspectives within literary studies.[10] Som-mer provides an incisive reading of intercultural narration by applying his theory of the intercultural novel to contemporary novels in Britain. In his ap-proach to genre, he distinguishes between the paradigms of interculturality, transculturality, and multiculturalism. He comes to the conclusion that classi-fications of genre, such as minority literature in Great Britain, or even the homogeneous concept of black British literature, are far too reductive because these terminologies do not capture the dynamics of social and cultural change

---

[10] See Roy Sommer, *Fictions of Migration: Ein Beitrag zur Theorie und Gattungstypo-logie des Zeitgenössischen Interkulturellen Romans in Großbritannien* (Trier: Wissen-schaftlicher Verlag Trier, 2001).

in the last few decades in Britain.[11] In his interdisciplinary analysis of cultural
theory, which serves as a theoretical foundation for his literary analysis, Sommer defines transculturality as a subcategory of interculturality:

> The paradigm of interculturality embraces transculturalism as a second central con-
> cept beside multiculturalism. To distinguish between the multicultural discourse of
> identity, as a reaction to the demographic developments, and the concept of trans-
> culturalism, this study views transculturalism as an approach that ascribes a posi-
> tive connotation to cultural hybridity, cosmopolitan globalisation and ethnic
> fragmentation while establishing them as counter models to exclusively national or
> ethnic identities. Therefore transcultural concepts are marked by a utopian mo-
> ment: They develop optimistic counter approaches to the 'classic' models of multi-
> cultural assimilation and alteration to the extent of approaching visions of dissolu-
> tion of fixed cultural identities. However, transculturality can neither be understood
> as an alternative to nor as a rivalling model of multiculturalism, but as its further
> development. Both discourses can be viewed as an intercultural continuum of the
> discursive evaluations and negotiations of ethnic variety and cultural hybrid-
> isation.[12]

Sommer's differentiation between interculturality, transculturality, and multiculturalism is problematic for several reasons. His model places transculturality next to multiculturalism in a conceptual space circumscribed by interculturality and differentiates between multiculturalism and transculturality

---

[11] For further discussion of theories based on the ostensibly 'natural' link between
literature, culture, and region, see Mark Stein's *Black British Literature: Novels of Transformation* (Columbus: Ohio State UP, 2004): 16.

[12] "Das Paradigma der Interkulturalität umfaßt neben der Multikulturalität als zweites
zentrales Konzept die Transkulturalität. In Abgrenzung zum multikulturellen Identitäts-
diskurs als einer Reaktion auf demographische Entwicklungen werden hier als trans-
kulturell diejenigen Ansätze bezeichnet, die der kulturellen Hybridisierung, kosmopoliti-
schen Globalisierung und ethnischen Fragmentierung als Gegenmodellen zu exklusiven
nationalen oder ethnischen Identitäten grundsätzlich positiv gegenüberstehen. Charakteris-
tisch für transkulturelle Konzepte ist daher ein utopisches Moment: Sie entwickeln opti-
mistische Gegenentwürfe zu den 'klassischen' multikulturellen Assimilations- und Dif-
ferenzmodellen bis hin zu Visionen von der Auflösung fester kultureller Identitäten.
Transkulturalität ist jedoch nicht als Alternative oder 'Konkurrenzmodell' zur Multikulturalität zu verstehen, sondern als deren Weiterführung. Beide Diskussionszusammenhänge
lassen sich als ein interkulturelles Kontinuum der diskursiven Bewertung und Verarbeitung
von ethnischer Vielfalt und kultureller Hybridisierung auffassen" (tr. S. Helff); Sommer,
Fictions of Migration, 48.

mainly by aligning the latter with utopian ideas. This hypothesis thus characterizes the intercultural and the multicultural as referring to the social world,
whereas the transcultural embraces utopian world scenarios. This, of course,
is questionable, since there are many experiences relating to transculturality
which cannot possibly be connected with a utopian realm. It is thus of considerable importance to read transculturality as a paradigm which is not solely
informed by utopian moments but, rather, by strong ambivalences.[13]

As I have argued elsewhere,[14] in order to find one's bearings in these
ambivalences it is crucial to pursue the connection between culture and modernity. Scholars such as Nina Glick Schiller and Iain Chambers treat transnational oscillations as common modern practices that produce new transnational social spaces and transcultural identities. In contrast to Sommer's
definition, their notion of transculturality focuses on the need to view culture
against the background of modernity and increasingly connected lifeworlds.
Culture, they remind us, must be seen as a dynamic process involving multiple modes of behaviour and life-style.[15] Following this train of thought,
transculturality cannot be evaluated as a subcategory of interculturality, because it describes a different set of social preconditions related to the situation
of modern globalized worlds. Hence, transculturality not only highlights a
shift in the perspective and in the description of life, but also indicates a
changed reality of life altogether.[16] In this context, it can be argued that more
recent questions concerning the description and theorizing of difference and
alterity occur in a far more self-reflexive context than in the 1970s and early
1980s, something that becomes evident not only in the cultural turn in social
and anthropological studies but also in critical approaches to literature.[17]

---

[13] Thus, there is neither a utopian moment in the transcultural lifeworld of a Nepalese
sexworker in Mumbai nor in the transcultural experiences of an illegal Russian bricklayer in
Germany.

[14] See my *Unreliable Truths: Indian Homeworlds in Transcultural Women's Writing*
(forthcoming)

[15] See Nina Glick Schiller, Linda Basch & Cristina Blanc–Szanton, "From Immigrant to
Transmigrant: Theorizing Transnational Migration," in *Transnationale Migration*, ed. Lud-
ger Pries (*Soziale Welt*, Sonderband 12, 1997): 121–40, and Chamber's *Migrancy, Culture,
Identity*.

[16] For further discussion see Helff, "Signs Taken For Truth: Orchestrating Transcultural
Aesthetics through Narrative Unreliability, in *Anglistentag 2006 Halle: Proceedings*, ed.
Sabine Volk–Birke & Julia Lippert (Trier: Wissenschaftlicher Verlag Trier, 2007): 200–10.

[17] For further discussion of the cultural turn in social and anthropological studies, see
Reckwitz, *Die Transformation der Kulturtheorien* (Weilerwist: Velbrück Wissenschaft,

Sommer, by contrast, discards all these considerations and repudiates the critical potential of transculturality by separating it from the social world. In this respect, he transfers this concept from a socio-political discursive level onto a philosophical level, where transculturality remains an elegant category exclusively aligned with cultural utopianism. On this discursive plane, transculturality remains untouched by and effectively isolated from the social world. As a consequence, Sommer's reading of transcultural, intercultural, and multicultural literature suggests a literary criticism that is demarcated by a semiotic meta-theory. Within this theoretical realm, culture is assumed to be non-dynamic, static, and distinctive. For this reason, Sommer's criticism remains on a discursive level and hardly allows any recontextualization with regard to modern social life. In this respect, his theory is scarcely suitable for describing and analysing the cultural dynamics of transforming societies as represented in the literature of an increasingly globalized world.

Undoubtedly, a neat categorization of transcultural literature is hardly feasible, not only because transculturality is a very recent concept within literary studies, but also because categories will always be prone to lose their apparent rigidity and leak into each other. The question thus remains: what characterizes the narrative mode of a transcultural novel?

The Transcultural Novel: A Case Study

Whereas formal and structural criteria hardly serve to set off the transcultural novel from multicultural or intercultural narratives, the latter accommodate themselves well to characterization by means of thematic concerns. One more general feature of the transcultural novel is its self-doubting characters, whose actions are dominated by uncertainty, a mind-set which thereby frequently influences the whole narrative. In this respect, the transcultural novel, particularly in contrast to intercultural narratives, introduces more radically individualized realities. A common imagined community is thus lost to the main protagonists, since transcultural characteristics challenge essentialist modes of identity construction. This is also why the transcultural novel is increasingly marked by ostensibly bizarre narrative situations in which self-doubting perspectives interact with obviously questionable views of the world. This

2000). A critical reflection on the New Literatures and their reception can be found in Graham Huggan's *The Postcolonial Exotic*. In this study, Huggan investigates the important question of the extent to which the cultural capital of the New Literatures is "bound up in a system of cultural translation operating under the sign of the exotic" (viii).

struggle with transculturality within and beyond the novel is demonstrated not only on the level of plot but also in the patterns of narrating a story. The narrated worlds often run up against diverse idealized notions of cultural nationalism – for instance, imagined homogeneous national cultures and conventional concepts of home and gender roles. Thus, they often oscillate between intercultural and transcultural imaginaries. Transcultural narration is a process in which the narrative and the reader are constantly crossing and shifting boundaries between intercultural and transcultural spaces. For this reason, I will speak of a 'transcultural novel' if one of the following aspects applies: first, if the narrator and/or the narrative challenge(s) the collective identity of a particular community; second, if experiences of border crossing and transnational identities characterize the narrators' lifeworld (*Lebenswelt*); and third, if traditional notions of 'home' are disputed. All these indicators have a particularly high impact on modes of storytelling, especially if the narrative introduces an unreliable narrator, because the latter challenges both the structure of a text and the reader's perception.

An interdisciplinary approach to narratology that connects a contextualized approach to narrative unreliability with individualized modern worlds therefore provides a viable methodology for gaining insights into the deeper structure of the novels.[18] In this respect, it is important to realize that the dramatizing and storytelling strategies in transcultural novels have the power to redefine and modify processes and experiences in the social world. At the same time, these strategies sometimes reflexively generate a focus on the act of storytelling by utilizing metafictional devices within the narrative itself.[19] Onya Kempadoo's *Tide Running* perfectly exemplifies how narratives function as engines of cultural representation and reproduction while negotiating alternative realities which are intrinsically based on specific modernities. The text follows agendas of the social world by retrieving untold histories and by rewriting already recorded history. Hence, it re-imagines geographical loca-

---

[18] See my "Signs Taken For Truth."

[19] Metafiction, with its stylistic devices, investigates the nature of novel-writing or storytelling and therefore directly addresses the act of fiction-making. This narrative technique often dismantles the illusions of realism and omnipresent narrative perspectives within a text. These metafictive devices are common in contemporary fiction in general, particularly in the New Literatures in English. For a more detailed discussion of metafiction, see Patricia Waugh's *Metafiction: The Theory and Practice of Self-Conscious Fiction* (London: Routledge, 1991), and *Metafiction*, ed. Mark Currie (London: Longman, 1995).

tions, rewrites histories, and challenges imagined communities while describing the protagonists' lives.

Kempadoo's novel is set on the Caribbean island of Tobago, where the two main protagonists, Bella and Cliff, meet and fall in love. The love story is a tale of expectations, great hopes, and even greater disillusionment. Cliff's Tobagonian home is marked by his absent father, strong religious beliefs, and the artificial realities of the shows he watches on TV. He feels neither at home in his ancestral house nor loved by his family. Accordingly, Cliff is depicted as an acerbic man who does not show much emotion, although there are moments when the reader catches a glimpse of his inner vulnerability. He is an introverted, laconic man whom the reader mainly gets to know through narrative fragments of his world of thought. Cliff's life is turned upside down when he by chance encounters the Trinidadian woman Bella. Through these two narrator-protagonists, *Tide Running* contrasts the homeworlds of two characters with conflicting personalities and differing needs.

Bella, unlike Cliff, is searching for an emotional bond; she feels a strong desire to get to know her 'roots' and thus begins her exciting search for the 'heart' of Tobago. This desire is partly fulfilled when she and her husband Peter purchase a mansion on Tobago. Yet, when Bella first meets Cliff her longing to connect to her imaginary homeland merges with the dream of a sexual fusion with the young Tobagonian. In fact, Bella's yearning for this emotional bond, which on the surface addresses Cliff but in fact relates to her cultural heritage, is the driving force behind the encounter between the two narrator-protagonists. And it is this energy that she initially mistakes for love. Bella's hunger is satisfied when she eventually embarks on a triangular love relationship with Cliff and her husband Peter. However, the differing needs of the characters become a point of contention, and Bella finally has to pay a high price for her obsession: Cliff later steals Bella's money and takes Peter's car without permission. After this, Bella is forced to realize that her picture of Cliff was nothing more than a figment of her imagination. Thus she finds herself in a predicament in which she has to understand that stories always have more than one perspective on reality and truth and are therefore always meant to be questioned. Her final self-reflexive awakening is depicted in the closing pages of the novel:

I should've seen clear through his skin to the green in him. And through his cool and talk and moves. I should've looked through the eye-slits of his mask, touched the rough inside, smelt breath still damp on it. How many times his shell sat here with us while he showed off outside?[20]

The novel depicts Bella's personal development, which is mirrored in the shift from an unreliable narrator to an awakened, self-reflexive narrator. Her final realization suggests that her imagined self-construction based on the idea of a shared ethnic origin cannot easily be transferred to her lover Cliff. It is the dilemma of their different worlds – their differing social backgrounds and their respective values – that deeply influences and finally separates the two protagonists.

While the love-relationship symbolizes on the plot level the difficult and ambiguous quest for home and belonging in a modern Caribbean nation, on the level of storytelling the text introduces the narrative phenomenon of polyphony. This latter term denotes the narrative strategy of multivoiced storytelling, and it is the tension created by the clash of voices that is crucial to the multiperspectival narrative structure in *Tide Running*. The polyphonic voices speaking in the text mainly represent the two narrator-protagonists Bella and Cliff. Their voices come across in distinct dialects that not only reflect their diverse cultural backgrounds but also highlight their dissimilar social worlds. By confronting Cliff's voice, which is mainly employed to describe his inner world of thought, with Bella's perspective, which narrates the plot and thus propels the storyline, the novel sets up a frictional interface between the narrator-protagonists' dissimilar perceptions, which materializes in a mode of narrative unreliability. To foreground Bella's and Cliff's ambivalent experiences and their doubts about their experienced realities, their struggles are translated into unreliable narratives. This becomes obvious when Cliff visits Bella and her English husband Peter at Bella's place. In a situation of mounting intensity, all of the characters involved experience different realities. When Bella invites Cliff and his brother into her home and displays her naked body in front of the young men, Cliff is deeply confused. He finds the situation rather bizarre, as the whole scene corresponds neither to his experiences of gender roles nor to his own behavioural patterns. Bella, however, believes that she is now experiencing his inner self:

---

[20] Oonya Kempadoo, *Tide Running* (London: Macmillan, 2001): 198. Further page references are in the main text.

> In one glance down the long white corridor they saw the swing of my walk, how
> my arms hung, the white of my teeth. It let them see right through my clothes and
> see my whole self, where the sweat forms under my breast, the dent on my chest
> bone. Showed me their insides too, and I could see their different selves in the way
> they stared. (57)

Bella does not register Cliff's confusion and thus remains an outsider to him. Her outsider status is not only illustrated in her behaviour but also in her luxurious home, since Cliff's feeling of alienation is intensified by the movie-like scenery. Cliff is genuinely impressed by the architecture and furnishings, which he compares to the artificial reality he knows from advertising and TV. But these images so overwhelm and alienate him that he begins to feel profoundly dissociated, imagining somebody else sitting on the film-set wearing his sneakers:

> Inside that house make you feel like you on TV. All the colours showing up. My
> shirt feel whiter, me pants feel bluer. I look me Nikes setting there on the clean
> floor. Look like it wasn't my foot, is a shiny photo, a ad. Michael Jordan or one
> a'them fellas. (51)

The two passages quoted above illustrate their shared misunderstanding. While Bella eventually harshly awakes and starts accepting her own wrong judgements, Cliff, who is finally sent to prison, is even more strongly bound to his own dreamlike unreliable perspective. *Tide Running* depicts Bella's life as oscillating between intercultural and transcultural imaginations. Her compulsive quest for home is mirrored in her ambivalent relationships to her Tobagonian lover and to her English husband. With her essentialist dream of a bonding with Cliff shattered, she comes to the realization that Peter, her husband, is the one who really understands her.

The novel represents a transculturality which is based on a conglomeration of various fictive and narrative characteristics, ranging from the intercultural to the transcultural. In this regard, Bella's unreliable perspective finally challenges essentialist modes of identity construction and thus describes the limits of an intercultural approach to identity formation in a globalized world. In the light of this observation, it is doubtful whether the function of imagination and narration as represented through art and fiction in particular constitutes the most crucial difference between fictional and non-fictional texts. This is not to say that everything is a narrative but, as Mieke Bal puts it, that "practically everything in culture has a narrative aspect to it, or at the very least, can be perceived, interpreted as narrative."[21] Her cultural analysis highlights the importance of a necessary interpretative turn in narratology:

> What I propose we are best off with in the age of cultural studies is a conception of narratology that implicates text and reading, subject and object, production and analysis, in the act of understanding. In other words, I advocate a narrative theory that enables the differentiation on the place of narrative in any cultural expression without privileging any medium, mode, or use; that differentiates its relative importance and the effect of the narrative (segments) on the remainder of the object as well as on the reader, listener, viewer. A theory, that is, which defines and describes narrativity, not narrative; not a genre but a cultural mode of expression.[22]

In *Tide Running*, the narrative device of transcultural narrative unreliability negotiates new subject positions which are often torn between intercultural and transcultural behavioural patterns. In this respect, narrated unreliability formulates the tension and the ambivalences between intercultural and transcultural narrative patterns. Unreliability, in *Tide Running* and more generally, is therefore an important source of information for determining what makes a novel a piece of transcultural narration. Transcultural narration not only emerges from and combines different cultural traditions; it also highlights and struggles with its own transcultural content. Together with a situation of unreliable narration, the transcultural novel, with its deep currents of doubt, represents the transcultural qualities of modern life far better than narrative patterns claiming absolute authority about truth and identity.

WORKS CITED

Appadurai, Arjun. *Modernity at Large* (Minneapolis & London: U of Minnesota P, 2000).
——. "Global Ethnoscapes: Notes and Queries for a Transnational Anthropology," in *Recapturing Anthropology: Working in the Present*, ed. Richard G. Fox (Santa Fe NM: School of American Research, 1991), 48–65.
Ashcroft, Bill, Gareth Griffiths & Helen Tiffin. *The Empire Writes Back: Theory and Practice in Post-Colonial Literatures* (London & New York: Routledge, 1989).

---

[21] Mieke Bal, "Close Reading Today: From Narratology to Cultural Analysis," in *Grenzüberschreitungen: Narratologie im Kontext/ Transcending Boundaries: Narratology in Context*, ed. Walter Grünzweig & Andreas Solbach (Tübingen: Gunter Narr, 1999): 19.

[22] Bal, "Close Reading Today," 21.

Bal, Mieke. "Close Reading Today: From Narratology to Cultural Analysis," in *Grenz-überschreitungen: Narratologie im Kontext/ Transcending Boundaries: Narratology in Context*, ed. Walter Grünzweig & Andreas Solbach (Tübingen: Gunter Narr, 1999): 19–40.

Beck, Ulrich. *Risikogesellschaft: Auf dem Weg in eine andere Moderne* (Frankfurt am Main: Suhrkamp, 1986).

Booth, Wayne. *The Rhetoric of Fiction* (Chicago: U of Chicago P, 1995).

Chambers, Iain. *Migrancy, Culture, Identity* (London: Routledge, 1995).

Clifford, James. *The Predicament of Culture* (Cambridge MA: Harvard UP, 1988).

Currie, Mark, ed. *Metafiction* (London: Longman, 1995).

During, Simon, ed. *The Cultural Studies Reader* (London & New York: Routledge, 2nd ed. 1999).

Glick Schiller, Nina; Linda Basch & Cristina Blanc–Szanton. "From Immigrant to Trans-migrant: Theorizing Transnational Migration," in *Transnationale Migration*, ed. Ludger Pries, *Soziale Welt*, Sonderband 12 (1997), 121–40.

Helff, Sissy. *Unreliable Truths: Indian Homeworlds in Transcultural Women's Writing* (Cross/Cultures; Amsterdam & New York: Rodopi, forthcoming, 2009).

——. "Signs Taken For Truth: Orchestrating Transcultural Aesthetics through Narrative Unreliability," in *Anglistentag 2006 Halle: Proceedings*, ed. Sabine Volk–Birke & Julia Lippert (Trier: Wissenschaftlicher Verlag Trier, 2007): 200–10.

Huggan, Graham. *The Postcolonial Exotic: Marketing the Margins* (London: Routledge, 2001).

——. "Derailing the 'Trans'? Postcolonial Studies and the Negative Effects of Speed," in *Inter- und Transkulturelle Studien: Theoretische Grundlagen und Interdisziplinäre Praxis*, ed. Heinz Antor (Heidelberg: Winter 2006): 55–61.

Kempadoo, Oonya. *Tide Running* (London: Macmillan, 2001).

Klooss, Wolfgang, ed. *Across the Lines: Intertextuality and Transcultural Communication in the New Literatures in English* (Cross/Cultures 32, ASNEL Papers 3; Amsterdam & Atlanta GA: Rodopi: 1998).

Linberg–Wada, Gunilla, ed. *Studying Transcultural Literary History* (Berlin & New York: Walter de Gruyter, 2006).

McLeod, John. "'Wheel and Come Again': Transnational Aesthetics Beyond the Post-colonial," *Hungarian Journal of English and American Studies* 7.2 (2001): 85–99.

Mishra, Vijay, & Bob Hodge. "What was Postcolonialism?" *New Literary History* 36 (2005): 375–402.

Nünning, Ansgar. "Unreliable Narration zur Einführung: Grundzüge einer kognitiv-narrato-logischen Theorie und Analyse unglaubwürdigem Erzählens," in *Unreliable Narration: Studien zur Theorie und Praxis unglaubwürdigen Erzählens in der englischsprachigen Erzählliteratur*, ed. Ansgar Nünning (Trier: Wissenschaftlicher Verlag Trier, 1998).

Pennycook, Alastair. *Global Englishes and Transcultural Flows* (London: Routledge, 2007).

Schulze–Engler, Frank. "Reading After the Postcolonial Deluge: Texts and Contexts in the New Literatures in English," in *Transgressions: Cultural Interventions in the Global Manifold*, ed. Renate Brosch & Rüdiger Kunow (Trier: Wissenschaftlicher Verlag Trier, 2005): 101–13.

——. "Literature in the Global Ecumene of Modernity: Amitav Ghosh's *The Circle of Reason* and *In an Antique Land*," in *English Literatures in International Contexts*, ed. Heinz Antor & Klaus Stierstorfer (Heidelberg: Winter, 2000): 375–76.

Sommer, Roy. *Fictions of Migration: Ein Beitrag zur Theorie und Gattungstypologie des Zeitgenössischen Interkulturellen Romans in Großbritannien* (Trier: Wissenschaftlicher Verlag Trier, 2001).

Stein, Mark. *Black British Literature: Novels of Transformation* (Columbus: Ohio State UP, 2004).

Waugh, Patricia. *Metafiction: The Theory and Practice of Self-Conscious Fiction* (London: Routledge, 1991).

Welsch, Wolfgang. *Grenzgänge der Ästhetik* (Stuttgart: Reclam, 1996).

◄❖►

The Dangers of Diaspora
— Some Thoughts About the Black Atlantic

RUTH MAYER

D IASPORA STUDIES – studies of transnational interrelations, cultural contact zones, and cosmopolitan conditions – have come to
replace regional studies, as well as traditional literary and cultural
scholarship concerned with national traditions and constellations. The concept of the 'Black Atlantic', in particular, has received much attention in the
context of this rearrangement of focus. My own work testifies to the pro-
ductivity of Paul Gilroy's metaphor, which envisages a black history of modernity "that defiantly reconstructs its own critical, intellectual and moral
genealogy in a partially hidden public sphere of its own."[1] In what follows,
however, I would like to point out an inflationary use of the term, whereby I
would first like to place the debates on diasporas and transnationalism in an
historical context – they are, after all, to be seen as a reaction to Cold-War
discourses of literature as a self-contained and ahistorical phenomenon. In the
USA, in particular, the Cold-War practice of literary and cultural analysis
was very much demarcated by the logic of exceptionalism, favouring an
isolationist approach to the study of the USA. I will develop my critique of
current practices and concepts on the grounds of an engagement with this
earlier approach, and I will argue that there are more analogies between the
outdated doctrines of exceptionalism and today's fashionable theories than
might at first meet the eye.

---

[1] Paul Gilroy, *The Black Atlantic: Modernity and Double Consciousness* (London:
Verso, 1993): 37–38.

I would like to begin with a brief history of what could be regarded as a
master text from my discipline – a text with which American studies came
into its own in the 1950s. Perry Miller's study *Errand into the Wilderness*
(1956) traces what has later been called "the Puritan origins of the American
self,"[2] a history of thought which Miller made out to be unique and exceptional – American in contrast to European or English traditions. By leaving
Europe and settling in America, the new 'promised land' and the 'city on the
hill' for all the world to watch, Miller argues, the Puritans initiated a new
history of thought and culture and thus inaugurated "the uniqueness of the
American experience."[3]

This line of reasoning might sound a little surprising coming from a scholar who made his name in the American academy of the Cold-War period. Yet
in his preface to the study, Miller chose an odd way of enacting his own initiation into the field of American studies. The preface states that the quest for
the origin of the American self started, surprisingly enough, in Africa. In the
1920s, Miller recounts, as a young college drop-out disillusioned with a life
of books and theory in which everything seemed already said and done, he
hired out on an oil tanker crossing the Atlantic, looking for "adventure"
where a British traveller of the nineteenth century might have looked for it,
too: in Africa. He did not find what he was looking for. Like so many of his
European contemporaries, Miller was disappointed by Africa, which did not
seem to live up to the high expectations of exoticism and jungle thrill he had
entertained. Yet "The adventures that Africa afforded were tawdry enough,"
he writes in his introduction to *Errand into the Wilderness*, "but it became the
setting for a sudden epiphany (if the word be not too strong) of the pressing
necessity for expounding my America to the twentieth century."[4] At Matadi,
on the "banks of the Congo," while engaged in the trivial occupation of
supervising, "in that barbaric tropic, the unloading of drums of case oil,"
Miller first encounters the "mission" which was to shape his entire academic
career – the mission of recording America from 'the beginning': "it seemed
obvious that I had to commence with the Puritan migration."[5]

---

[2] Sacvan Bercovitch, *The Puritan Origins of the American Self* (New Haven CT: Yale
UP, 1975).
[3] Perry Miller, *Errand into the Wilderness* (Cambridge MA: Harvard UP, 1956): ix.
[4] Miller, *Errand*, vii.
[5] Miller, *Errand*, viii.

With this curious anecdote, Miller exemplarily and certainly unconsciously brings to the fore a pattern of representation in American cultural history in which Africa or, rather, africanity, is always there yet never present. His insistence on perceiving Africa as an uncultured and ahistorical wilderness, as the space of uninscribed and alien 'otherness' from which the study of the 'self' takes off, must seem doubly problematic. First, he refuses to see the Congo – or America, as it were – as part of a whole or, rather, as part of a web. By thus blinding himself, he also refuses to perceive American (literary and cultural) history as something that is intricately and inextricably interlinked with world history.[6]

In keeping with his line of reasoning, Miller explicitly excludes that other and 'earlier' beginning of North American colonization (the Jamestown colony in Virginia) from his study. Indeed, to start an American cultural history with Virginia would have meant telling a different story. After all, the first African slaves in North America arrived in Virginia with its plantation culture; a circumstance made all the more ironic by the fact that these Africans entered the New World a year before the Puritans made it to Plymouth Rock.

One could, of course, go even further back in time. Columbus's pilot Pedro Niño, Paul Gilroy reminds us, was an African. To look for a 'pure' beginning for 'Project America' or the project of americanization is to engage in simplification – America was always already inscribed with difference, and not only because the continent was by no means an uninhabited wilderness, as Miller had it, but also because, from the very outset of the colonial venture(s), Africans were involved in the process of settlement and takeover. Thus, to focus on America in isolation is to present a picture with many blind spots.

Yet to criticize isolationism and exceptionalism in cultural studies these days is not considered very radical. In fact, to call for a transnational perspective in literary and cultural studies has almost become a ritual in recent years; the very existence of the Association of the Study of the New Literatures in English (ASNEL) is a case in point. At this juncture, I would like to contrast

---

[6] Numerous critics have taken issue with Miller's preface; the most extensive and insightful critique is by Amy Kaplan, "'Left Alone with America': The Absence of Empire in the Study of American Culture," in *Cultures of United States Imperialism*, ed. Amy Kaplan & Donald Pease (Durham NC: Duke UP; 1993): 3–21. See also Gesa Mackenthun's introduction to her study *Metaphors of Dispossession: American Beginnings and the Translation of Empire, 1492–1637* (Norman: U of Oklahoma P, 1997).

the first anecdote with a second. While the story around Perry Miller illustrates the need for a transatlantic perspective, what follows elucidates some of the dangers inherent in contemporary theories of transnationality and diasporic identity.

When Miller was looking for a job on a ship which would bring him to Africa in the early 1920s, he might have crossed paths with another young man, who was just as eager to leave the USA behind and who also had dropped out of school (Columbia University, New York City). Langston Hughes felt that real life was somewhere else, and he, too, sailed to Africa in the early 1920s, as a member of the crew on a merchant steamer. Yet the incentive and outcome of his travels were quite different: the African-American poet claimed to have gone on the voyage in order to get in touch with his own roots. This time the journey seems to have been more satisfactory – in fact, Hughes seems to have experienced an epiphany of his own, a kind of pan-Africanist vision to counter Miller's culture-shocked fantasy of retreat. This is how Hughes recorded his first sightings of Africa in his autobiography:

> And finally, when I saw the dust-green hills in the sunlight, something took hold of me inside. My Africa, Motherland of the Negro peoples! And me a Negro! Africa! The real thing to be touched and seen, not merely read about in a book.[7]

His experience while travelling down the west coast of Africa seems to be in keeping with this first impression; in his autobiography he revels in memories of a "wild and lovely" country, with "dark and beautiful" people, "the palm trees tall, the sun bright, and the rivers deep."[8] All these were clichés of africanity which hardly allow for more of a sense of the actual place than Miller's vague allusion to the "edge of a jungle in central Africa."[9] Yet, while Miller registered indifference and alienation, Hughes seems to have relished the difference of the African experience. The only drawback he jots down is: "The Africans looked at me, and would not believe I was a Negro."[10]

---

[7] Langston Hughes, *The Big Sea* (1940; New York: Hill & Wang, 1963): 10.

[8] Hughes, *The Big Sea*, 11.

[9] Miller, *Errand*, viii. For a more detailed discussion of the workings of 'africanity', see my *Artificial Africas: Images of Colonialism in the Times of Globalization* (Lebanon OH: UP of New England, 2002).

[10] Hughes, *The Big Sea*, 11.

Writings such as these made critics such as David Chioni Moore argue that Hughes' career "enmeshed itself within the broader Black Atlantic" and thus requires something other than nationalist paradigms of analysis.[11] Yet while Hughes was indubitably an internationally relevant writer whose many travels and whose political activism makes him an important figure not only in the USA, but also in African and European literary and cultural debates, I am not quite sure that I agree to the statement that his writing on Africa testifies to a Black Atlantic sensitivity. Things are more complicated than that. Hughes's autobiographical text was written in 1940, at a time when he felt it more important than ever before to express his critique of colonialist and neocolonialist business ventures, as well as to present a perfect continent in the exploitative grip of European and American imperialism. This imperative did not quite chime with the ambivalences of the actual 'first encounter' of the young American with West Africa and made him purge the autobiographical text of almost all indications of culture-shock or alienation. Thus, a piece which he published in the New York magazine *Crisis* shortly after he returned allows for a considerably greater sense of difference and distance. Here, Hughes describes his impressions of Matadi, hence of the very same place that triggered Perry Miller's revelation, where Hughes, too, was engaged in the activity of supervising African workers unloading the ship. Where Miller remembers only the jungle, Hughes focused on the workers. He admits to be horrified by the "dirtiest, saddest lot of Negro workers seen in Africa,"[12] where no communication and no bonding took place.

While the horror of this sight is mediated by colonial critique in the *Crisis* piece, Hughes is even more explicit in his private notes about a feeling of alienation, mixed uneasily with a sense of cultural superiority. "Hughes's first impression [of Africa] was of crudeness and absurdity," claims his biographer Arnold Rampersad on the basis of the letters that the young poet wrote home. "I have laughed until I can't," Hughes wrote to his mother about the local dress code, and concludes: "It's a scream."[13]

---

[11] David Chioni Moore, "Local Color, Global 'Color': Langston Hughes, The Black Atlantic and Soviet Central Asia, 1932," *Research in African Literatures* 27.4 (1996): 50.

[12] Langston Hughes, "Ships, Sea and Africa: Random Impressions of a Sailor on His First Trip Down the West Coast of the Motherland," *Crisis* 27 (December 1923), 70, quoted in Arnold Rampersad, *The Life of Langston Hughes*, vol. 1 (New York: Oxford UP, 1986): 76–77.

[13] Langston Hughes, Letter to Carrie M. Clark, July 3, 1923, quoted in Rampersad, *The Life of Langston Hughes*, 73–74.

In these letters, the impression of a noble country with regal inhabitants and classical scenery communicated in the autobiography collapses, and gives way to a much more realistic sense of distance. This is, after all, Hughes' very first transatlantic trip, and journeys do have a tendency to run counter to pre-formulated programmes and projections. Yet, in Hughes' poetry of the period, the ambivalent experience did not register at all; he continued to celebrate Africa precisely along the lines he had laid out for its celebration quite some time before he travelled there. In fact, his celebratory stance became even more pronounced after 1923. The backdrop to a re-invigorated project of promoting africanity in America, however, is definitely not constituted by Hughes' trip to Africa, but by another transatlantic trip he undertook, less than a year after returning from Africa – this time to Europe. In Rotterdam, he jumped ship and made his way to Paris, where he lived for several months in 1924. He mentions, in particular, the chance to "see the famous collection of African sculpture belonging to [the collector] Paul Guillaume,"[14] and thus seems to confirm Henry Louis Gates, Jr.'s insight that the "route to Africa [...], for black as well as white Americans and Europeans, is by way of the Trocadéro [i.e. the Ethnographic Museum with its huge African collection in Paris]."[15]

It was on these grounds, those of expressionist Primitivism, that Hughes celebrated Africa in the years to follow. With this, his response to Africa doubtless differs glaringly from Perry Miller's response. In his manifesto of black art, "The Negro Artist and the Racial Mountain" of 1926, he conjures up the "eternal tom-tom beating in the Negro soul" to defy and disclaim everything that Miller cherished – an established culture of "white teachers [...], white books, pictures, and papers, and white manners, morals and Puritan standards."[16] Yet if Hughes, in contrast to Miller, acknowledges the 'africanism' at the heart of American culture, his africanism still has little to do with Africa – or even a diasporic consciousness at that.

For Hughes and for many other black travellers in the twentieth century, the Atlantic was indeed an important site of identification, and it was

---

[14] Hughes, *The Big Sea*, 186.

[15] Henry Louis Gates, Jr., "Europe, African Art and the Uncanny," in *Africa: Art of a Continent*, ed. Tom Philipps (Munich: Prestel, 1995): 30.

[16] Langston Hughes, "The Negro Artist and the Racial Mountain" (1926), in *The Norton Anthology of African American Literature*, ed. Henry Louis Gates, Jr. & Nellie Y. McKay (New York: Norton, 1997): 1270.

certainly no accident that Hughes chose to entitle his autobiography *The Big Sea*, indicating a transatlantic dimension and thrust in his life. Yet the blackness of this Atlantic is often a marked construct rather than a reliable framework or alternative 'public sphere', as Gilroy has it. A case in point is the following anecdote from *The Big Sea* about an encounter of Caribbean and American blacks in Lagos Africa. A fight broke out between a British freighter and Hughes' ship, the *S.S. Malone*:

> The main thing I remember was that crew-solidarity outweighed race that day, because there were on the British ship quite a few Negroes – West Indian Negroes, and on our ship, George and I and the two Puerto Ricans were definitely colored. But when the white boys on our boat yelled: "Get them limeys [slang for British sailors]! Get them niggers!" and we met the British crew on the dock head on, George and the Puerto Ricans and I yelled, too: "Get them niggers! Get them limeys!" And after them we went. In the heat of the fight, we forgot we didn't like the word nigger applied to ourselves.[17]

The fight that ensues is more a matter of entertainment, depicted in largely comical terms, than of serious conflict. But the alliances opening up (or, rather, not opening up) here, indicate that categories such as 'diasporic identities' or 'transcultural communities' do not really apply. To take the notion of a 'black Atlantic' too seriously is to miss much of the dynamic and flexibility involved in identification.

Hence, although it is to be conceded that for an analysis of literary and cultural processes of exchange, the concept of the 'black Atlantic' has proven immensely productive in the last decade, its impact on more basic, less immaterial forms of exchange is worrying. I am thus of the view that this concept threatens to deflect from the central problems of the black diaspora in the twentieth and twenty-first centuries, given the fact that heterogeneity, discrepancy, and glaring differences are so much more pervasive between the different groups of 'Africans' worldwide than a common basis, be it as evanescent and floating as the imagery of the sea. Whenever we concentrate on concrete instances of encounter and exchange, problems arise which studies such as Gilroy's and many other contemporary accounts of diasporic culture hardly allow for. I do not share Joan Dayan's very basic and very categorical critique of Gilroy's book, but she has a point when she writes:

---

[17] Hughes, *The Big Sea*, 116.

In Gilroy's potent images of the 'diasporic cultural innovation', in what he calls 'the black Atlantic network', he never once considers how political realities – a chaos of instrumentalisation and greed – merge with a destructive syncretism.[18]

Indeed, one tends to forget these days, now that hybridity and syncretism have become concepts with generally positive connotations and seem to have completely replaced the older values of purity and homogeneity, that the appropriations and adaptations, the mergings and mixings that arise from uneven cultural encounters are not always positive for everybody involved. Especially when the encounter at stake is among black people, rather than one between black and white people, we are prone to lose sight of very basic economic and political realities, and to see new communities, alliances, and solidarity, where often enough projection, suspicion, and misunderstandings evolve on both sides. Thus it is all the more important to look closely at who is appropriating what for which purpose.

Let me give another example of this discrepant and variegated history. Almost thirty years after Langston Hughes was there, Paris was still a much-favoured metropolis for white and black Americans. In the 1950s, it became the chosen city of two other famous black American writers – Richard Wright and James Baldwin. And Baldwin tells us of another instance of black Atlantic reality which took place in this city. In a magazine piece written in 1950 for the American journal *The Reporter*, he relates his encounter with North African students in Paris, an encounter which could have taken the guise of a diasporic union of the marginalized. Yet Baldwin reaches quite bleak conclusions with regard to the prospect of a diasporic political mobilization:

> They face each other, the Negro and the African, over a gulf of three hundred years – an alienation too vast to be conquered in an evening's good-will, too heavy and too double-edged ever to be trapped in speech. This alienation causes the Negro to recognize that he is a hybrid.[19]

---

[18] Joan Dayan, "Paul Gilroy's Slaves, Ships, and Routes: The Middle Passage as a Metaphor," *Research in African Literatures* 27.4 (1996): 11. For an interesting critical take on Gilroy's approach, see also Laura Chrisman, "Journeying to Death: Paul Gilroy's *The Black Atlantic*," in Chrisman, *Postcolonial Contraventions: Cultural Readings of Race, Imperialism and Transnationalism* (Manchester: Manchester UP, 2003): 73–88.

[19] James Baldwin, "Encounter on the Seine: Black Meets Brown," in Baldwin, *Notes of a Native Son* (1955; Boston MA: Beacon, 1984): 122.

For Baldwin, the identity of the 'Negro', the African American, configures itself in stark contrast to a 'European' and an 'African' sense of selfhood, and just like Perry Miller – if with very different implications – he ends up evoking an America very much at variance with the rest of the world, an exceptional America with very specific problems and people, especially when it comes to its minorities.

Ironically, at exactly the same time that Baldwin formulated these thoughts, Frantz Fanon approached the issue from another angle in *Black Skin, White Masks* (1952), demarcating the situation of postcolonial Africans as no less 'hybrid' and artificial than that of African Americans, if definitely laid out along different lines. Yet the fact that similar projects of reconceptualization went on in North Africa, in Paris, and in the USA does not mean that easy alliances open up between the aggrieved communities involved. Frantz Fanon writes in *The Wretched of the Earth* (1961):

> The Negroes of Chicago only resemble the Nigerians or Tanganyikans in so far as they were all defined in relation to the whites. But once the first comparisons had been made and subjective feelings were assuaged, the American Negroes realized that the objective problems were fundamentally heterogeneous. The test cases of civil liberty whereby both whites and blacks in America try to drive back racial discrimination have very little in common in their principles and objectives with the heroic fight of the Angolan people against the detestable Portuguese colonialism.[20]

Obviously, this is not to say that transnational alliances cannot be forged and put to use for minority purposes worldwide. But it is a reminder that often enough such alliances are illusory, based on projections and false ascriptions, and that to take them for granted is to ignore the very complexity of the problems at stake. One last example may illustrate this danger.

I have focused on the experience of African Americans abroad – in Africa and in Europe – up to now. Let us now invert this perspective and cast a glance at the situation of Africans in the USA. As Rosemary J. Coombe and Paul Stoller have shown in their analysis of the contact zone constituted by Harlem, New York, things are just as complicated for the Songhay men from the Niger, who sell all kinds of consumer goods in Harlem, as they were for the young Langston Hughes in Matadi. Increasingly, Coombe and Stoller

---

[20] Frantz Fanon, *The Wretched of the Earth*, tr. Constance Farrington, preface by Jean–Paul Sartre (*Les damnés de la terre*, 1961; New York: Grove, 1963): 216.

found, these African vendors offer paraphernalia of africanity in the streets of
Harlem:

> Knowing something about the history and plight of African Americans, a few
> Songhay speaking migrants accept the fact that the 'Africa' African Americans
> 'need' is not the Africa they know. In the Harlem market context they are prepared
> to renounce recognition of the complexities of the Africa from which they come,
> and make a gift of the more unencumbered significance it has acquired in the local
> community. Most of them easily engage in marketing the fetishes of an imaginary
> Africa and the signs of an utopian America – learning to read their market, media
> culture, and the marks of fame that appeal to African Americans.[21]

If Coombe and Stoller end on a conciliatory note, focusing on the "few"
Songhay traders who might have an insight into the intricacies of the needs
and desires evident in their business, the predominant feeling of these sellers
most likely is not understanding but rather puzzlement, amusement, or indifference. The Songhay vendors and their African-American clients live in
different worlds, even though they live in one city; their paths cross daily, but
to think of them as part of the same social group – an imaginary 'diasporic'
culture – would mean to resort to racial categorization.

Thus this phenomenon, like the phenomena discussed before, warrants a
warning: not to take the metaphors of the Black Atlantic and of diasporic
identity at face value and not to focus too strongly on them. While there may
be links between blacks in the UK, in the USA, in the Caribbean, and in
Africa, there are also numerous ruptures, and in many respects these ruptures
are more important than the commonalities. To insist otherwise is to fall prey
to an illusion which Benedict Anderson has commented on with respect to
contemporary identity politics and the myth of "'diasporic' collective subjectivities." The advocates of such models of thought, Anderson argues, confuse
a "certain contemporary vision of cosmopolitanism" with historical reality –
thus seeing 'members' of groups where historically and culturally all sorts of
identificatory categories may have been relevant.[22] To come back to the

---

[21] Rosemary J. Coombe & Paul Stoller, "X Marks the Spot: The Ambiguities of African
Trading in the Commerce of the Black Public Sphere," in *The Black Public Sphere*, ed.
Black Public Sphere Collective (Chicago: U of Chicago P, 1995): 269–70.

[22] Benedict Anderson, "Nationalism, Identity, and the World-in-Motion: On the Logics
of Seriality," in *Cosmopolitics*, ed. Pheng Cheah & Bruce Robbins (Minneapolis: U of
Minnesota P, 1991): 131.

examples at hand: the Africans did not acknowledge Hughes' blackness, and James Baldwin did not conceive of himself as part of a global black community, either. We should be aware of the danger of essentializing and reifying the very categories brought into discursive circulation to provide a way out of essentialist structures of identification. If care is not taken, the very terminology of diasporic identities and cultures will come dangerously close to the essentialist notion of a national tradition laid out in Perry Miller's *Errand into the Wilderness* – if translated onto a global scale. The very complexities of modernity and its global networks of people and resources call for a vocabulary which reflects rather than distracts from material conflicts, cultural hierarchies, and the subtle and not so subtle shadings that organize and differentiate ethnic groups worldwide.

WORKS CITED

Anderson, Benedict. "Nationalism, Identity, and the World-in-Motion: On the Logics of Seriality," in *Cosmopolitics*, ed. Pheng Cheah & Bruce Robbins (Minneapolis: U of Minnesota P, 1991): 117–33.

Baldwin, James. "Encounter on the Seine: Black Meets Brown," in Baldwin, *Notes of a Native Son* (1955; Boston MA: Beacon, 1984): 117–23.

Bercovitch, Sacvan. *The Puritan Origins of the American Self* (New Haven CT: Yale UP, 1975).

Chrisman, Laura. *Postcolonial Contraventions: Cultural Readings of Race, Imperialism and Transnationalism* (Manchester: Manchester UP, 2003).

Coombe, Rosemary J., & Paul Stoller. "X Marks the Spot: The Ambiguities of African Trading in the Commerce of the Black Public Sphere," in *The Black Public Sphere*, ed. Black Public Sphere Collective (Chicago: U of Chicago P, 1995): 253–78.

Dayan, Joan. "Paul Gilroy's Slaves, Ships, and Routes: The Middle Passage as a Metaphor," *Research in African Literatures* 27.4 (Winter 1996): 7–14.

Fanon, Frantz. *The Wretched of the Earth*, tr. Constance Farrington, preface by Jean–Paul Sartre (*Les damnés de la terre*, 1961; New York: Grove, 1963).

Gilroy, Paul. *The Black Atlantic: Modernity and Double Consciousness* (London: Verso, 1993).

Gates, Henry Louis, Jr. "Europe, African Art and the Uncanny," in *Africa: Art of a Continent*, ed. Tom Philipps (Munich: Prestel, 1995): 27–30.

Hughes, Langston. "The Negro Artist and the Racial Mountain" (1926), in *The Norton Anthology of African American Literature*, ed. Henry Louis Gates, Jr. & Nellie Y. McKay (New York: W.W. Norton, 1997): 1267–71.

——. *The Big Sea* (New York: Hill & Wang, 1963).

Kaplan, Amy. "'Left Alone with America': The Absence of Empire in the Study of American Culture," in *Cultures of United States Imperialism*, ed. Amy Kaplan & Donald Pease (Durham NC: Duke UP; 1993): 3–21.

Mackenthun, Gesa. *Metaphors of Dispossession: American Beginnings and the Translation of Empire, 1492–1637* (Norman: U of Oklahoma P, 1997).

Mayer, Ruth. *Artificial Africas: Images of Colonialism in the Times of Globalization*
    (Lebanon NH: UP of New England, 2002).
Miller, Perry. *Errand into the Wilderness* (Cambridge MA: Harvard UP, 1956).
Moore, David Chioni. "Local Color, Global 'Color': Langston Hughes, the Black Atlantic,
    and Soviet Central Asia, 1932," *Research in African Literatures* 27.4 (1996): 49–70.
Rampersad, Arnold. *The Life of Langston Hughes*, vol. 1 (New York: Oxford UP, 1986).

❖

The Times of India
— Transcultural Temporalities in Theory and Fiction

DIRK WIEMANN

T HE PROTAGONIST in Kiran Nagarkar's novel *Cuckold* (1997) is an early sixteenth-century Rajput prince who, at first sight, appears to be profiled as the paragon of a well-behaved character in an historical novel: namely, a fictionally fleshed-out native informant who takes the reader, willing to suspend disbelief, on a guided tour through a past made legible, and 'credible', for the occasion. As both focalizer and part-time narrator, Nagarkar's prince proves a rich source of information concerning the hard and soft facts of historically remote Rajputana, from economics to military strategies, gender relations to religion, dietary habits to courtly codes of conduct and intricacies of kinship and inheritance. In all of this, the prince seems very much a child of his times, safely located in a sufficiently exoticized temporal elsewhere when, for example, "smallpox was nothing but the visitation of a devi [goddess],"[1] or a member of the royal family could trace his family tree back to "[his] ancestor, the Sun-God" (48). Yet *Cuckold* is not a simple period piece; it neither reconstructs Rajputana as a chronotope, however imaginatively, nor does it reinvent the inaccessible structure of feeling of a bygone era. The novel, instead, re-presents the feudal Rajput system as a past that refuses to stay in place.

The seemingly premodern prince, for instance, obviously sports a wristwatch – how else could he check that it is exactly "nine seventeen in the

---

[1] Kiran Nagarkar, *Cuckold* (Delhi: Harper Collins, 1997): 149. Further page references are in the main text.

morning" (50), arrange meetings for "six o'clock sharp" (20), or inform us
about the resumption of a particular military move at precisely "seven thirty-
five in the morning" (235)? Not only does the Maharaj Kumar subject himself
to well-nigh Taylorist time-discipline but he also revels in other modernisms.
If, on his neatly planned working days, the prince confers first with the head
of the "Institute of Advanced Military Tactics and Strategy" (16), then with a
civil engineer from "the Department of City Planning" (3); if he rejoices in
the state's additional source of income after "the tourist traffic had gone up by
a hundred and fifty percent" (394); if he introduces the king's steward as the
"PM to the Rana, my father" (27); if a spendthrift member of the royal family
does not get any further loans after "his IOUs came due" (29); – then those
conspicuous and apparently anachronistic interpolations seem to mark very
unlikely intrusions of wildly proleptic moments into a traditional system. Yet
they simultaneously signify nothing but integral components of that system:
the historical Rajput states, in fact, *had* a bureaucracy that organized city
planning and military instruction; the king *was*, after all, represented by a
political dignitary whose office would correspond roughly to that of a prime
minister. If, thus, the Rajput system holds ample referentiality for the antici-
patory terms employed by Nagarkar, 'anachronism' – if there is any – arises
primarily from a peculiar mode of signification that is strategically employed
in order to play out *Cuckold*'s more fundamental ambition: to uncover the
present in the past, and, by extension, the past in the present. Thus, historical
difference is straddled by acts of translation:

> We have two prime ministers among us *Suryavanshis, the descendants of the Sun-
> god*. Father is a *Diwan or prime minister* to *Eklingji, the five-headed Shiva* who is
> our family deity and whose kin and representative he is on earth. Pooranmalji who
> had just entered is PM to the Rana, my father. (27; emphases mine)

While the narrator at first sight simply seems to translating opaque 'vernacular'
terms – *Suryavanshis, Diwan, Eklingji* – for the non-vernacular reader's benefit,
his role clearly exceeds that of a mere native informant, inasmuch as the
sequence quoted performs one act of literal translation in order to elucidate
another, more complex one: the parameters of sovereignty in feudal Rajputana in the discharge of power first from Shiva to the King as the god's
deputy, then to the PM as the King's stand-in. Nagarkar's trick consists partly
in the structural similarity that pertains between these two different levels of
exchange (one of linguistic meaning, the other of political authority), both of
which operate on the principle of replacing one term, in a conventionalized
mode, by another. Two parallel lines of representation thus emerge, neither of

which, however, will escape the dynamics of the ineluctable slippage of the
signifier: The translation of "Diwan" as "prime minister" gets undermined by
the application of that same signifier to Pooranmalji, who is *not* the Diwan
but, in his capacity as the king's representative, the "Pradhan" (as we learn
later; 542); this latter office, at the political level, serves as a stand-in, not for
the absent ultimate sovereign (Shiva) but for another absent referent (the
king), which, in turn, is yet another representative – the place-holder of the
absent Shiva. Although these two distinct instances of representation – Diwan
and Pradhan – occupy different positions in the sign chain of political author-
ization, they can be subsumed under the name "prime minister" because they
operate on one and the same principle: the representation of an absent,
superior, and ultimately transcendent authority. To substitute the modernist
term 'prime minister' for both 'Diwan' and 'Pradhhan' ensures that the transfer of authority from the god as ultimate sovereign to the latter's first- and
second-degree representations in the realm of the political proper becomes
uncannily commensurate with dominant contemporary political theories and
entrenched structures; for, very obviously, it would only take a rewriting of
that ultimate sovereign's name not as Shiva but as 'the People' – an equally
metaphysical point of reference – to arrive at the genuinely modernist conceptualization of the State's legitimacy as "the *representation* of the whole
population."[2] If the Rajput *raison d'état* with its hierarchies of political representative authority is ultimately derived from transcendent categories, its
structural likeness to modern political systems – underscored by the trans-
latory efforts of Nagarkar's text – emphasizes how "the adoption of the field
of immanence as the exclusive terrain of the theory and practice of politics"[3]
has as yet by no means been achieved with modernity. If, thus, a distinctly
obsolete formation amazingly comes to serve as a mirror image of the present, the neat demarcation-lines between those temporal units that historical
discourse posits as distinct epochs begin to blur. Only on this condition can
both 'Diwan' and 'Pradhan' pass for versions of prime ministership. By extension, it becomes plausible that Nagarkar's prince should inhabit the world
of the Rajputs whose state is run by a "Diwan," as well as that of his reader,
where heads-of-state are called "PM." In short, *Cuckold*'s play with historical
difference suggests the juxtaposition of seemingly incompatible temporalities

---

[2] Michael Hardt & Antonio Negri, *Empire* (Cambridge M A & London: Harvard U P,
2000): 105.

[3] Hardt & Negri, *Empire*, 377.

not as the coexistence of different 'stages' of social time-constructions (mythic and secular, premodern and modern, residual and emergent, cyclic and linear, 'Indian' and 'Western'), but defies such binarisms of clearly distinct and culturally specific temporalities in favour of a fusion that articulates a complex and transcultural heterogeneous time.

This latter term already indicates the polemic built into the project I am trying to delineate: heterogeneous time, obviously, implies dissent from its Other: i.e. homogeneous time constructed as chronological and continuous, linear, irreversible, and organizing the commensurability of all points in time. Walter Benjamin, who first introduced the term, equates homogeneous empty time with clock-time,[4] which is, in Benjamin's critique, the temporality of progressivism and 'historicism'. Now, if there is any temporality that could arguably be labelled as specific to modern Western culture, it is clock-time, which today appears as schematized "global time."[5] With irritating triumphalism, David Landes – one of the authoritative historians of time-keeping and its effects – sums up his investigations as a victory march of naturalized clock-time:

> I would not want simply to say that time measurement and the mechanical clock made the modern world and gave the West primacy over the Rest. That they did. But the clock in turn was part of a larger, open, competitive Western attitude towards knowledge, science, and exploration. Nothing like this attitude was to be found elsewhere. Attitude and theme came together, and we have all been the beneficiaries, including those civilizations and societies that are now learning and catching up.[6]

Needless to say, there is no such thing as a homogeneous and uniform modern 'West' vis-à-vis a retarded 'Rest'. All the same, eurocentrist chronopolitics served to implement such a dichotomy, which became a constitutive part of the colonialist imagination in which "the 'out there' was almost always a

---

[4] Walter Benjamin, "Theses on the Philosophy of History," in *Illuminations*, tr. Harry Zohn (New York: Schocken, 1968): 260–62; German original version "Über den Begriff der Geschichte" (1940), in Benjamin, *Gesammelte Schriften* I.2, ed. Rolf Tiedemann & Hermann Schweppenhäuser (Frankfurt am Main: Suhrkamp, 1980): 701–703.

[5] See Soraj Hongladarom, "The Web of Time and the Dilemma of Globalization," *The Information Society* 18 (2002): 241–49.

[6] David S. Landes, "Clocks and the Wealth of Nations," *Daedalus* 132.2 (Spring 2003): 26.

'back then'."[7] One historical example, picked at random, may help to illustrate this: around 1870, the English colonial officer Henry Maine suggested that administrators in British India "had to keep their watches set simultaneously to two longitudes";[8] of course, Maine is not only talking about technical time-reckoning here but more crucially insinuates that Indian development was 'lagging behind'. His is a chronopolitical statement that, as Johannes Fabian would have pointed out, posits the modern Western subject by way of "denying coevality to its Other."[9] Maine's recommendation of a two-dialled watch construes an historicist gulf between the modern and the pre-modern; in order to posit British time as modern time, however, Maine has to efface the fact that two-dialled watches were a prerequisite in England itself deep into the 1850s. In fact, as Nigel Thrift elaborates, the transformation of Britain into one uniform time zone was not effectively achieved until 1855, by which year approximately 98 percent of the public clocks in Great Britain had finally been set to Greenwich Mean Time, and only in 1880 was the synchronization of Britain formally sanctioned. Read in this context, Maine's counsel harks back to a not-so-distant past where in Britain itself "watches could be bought showing local and Greenwich time."[10]

Certainly, the longevity of such temporal pluralism is not merely a technicality but, rather, an indicator of a plurality of socially constructed times, and also of intense and widespread resistance to the imposition of modern clock-time in the West, especially its disciplinary aspects in the organization of industrial labour processes. The time-discipline that industrial capitalism demands gets consistently re-fractured on the ground, and – as E.P. Thompson suggests – "we may doubt how far it was ever fully achieved."[11] Instead

---

[7] D. Graham Burnett, "Mapping Time: Chronometry on Top of the World," *Daedalus* 132.2 (Spring 2003): 16.

[8] As quoted in Thomas R. Metcalf, *Ideologies of the Raj: The New Cambridge History of India* III.4 (Delhi: Cambridge UP, 1997), 66.

[9] Johannes Fabian, *Time and the Other: How Anthropology Makes Its Object* (New York: Columbia UP, 1983): 152.

[10] Nigel Thrift, "Owners' Time and Own Time: the Making of a Capitalist Time Consciousness, 1300–1800," in *The Sociology of Time*, ed. John Hassard (London: Macmillan, 1990): 126.

[11] E.P. Thompson, "Time, Work-Discipline and Industrial Capitalism," *Past & Present: A Journal of Historical Studies* 38 (December 1967): 90. Thompson's narrative may be read as a complement to the manifold aesthetic and philosophical explorations – from Romanticism to High Modernism and beyond – of (mostly) personal time as deviant from, and

of one homogeneous time zone entirely subsumed under capital, then, even
the heartlands of the first Industrial Revolution are better grasped as heterochronic – shot through with "slices in time [...] when men arrive at a sort of
absolute break with their traditional [read: normalized] time."[12] Arguably,
High Modernism's dissident preference for the unsystematic, excessive, and
contingent may, as Fredric Jameson or Mary Ann Doane suggest,[13] itself be
read as a structurally necessary concomitant of intensified rationalization, a
compensatory gesture whose function it was to uphold the horizon of some
'outside' of structure, and "to make tolerable an incessant rationalization."[14]
Postcolonial critics such as Homi K. Bhabha, Partha Chatterjee or Dipesh
Chakrabarty would be the last to deny this internal heterogeneity of the West,
but they are not primarily committed to its archaeology. Instead, they are
interested in elucidating how the West, however heterogeneous, was nevertheless historically "orchestrated as a unified effect with telling consequences
for the non-West."[15] The interrogation of what Javeed Alam calls "entrenched
modernity,"[16] therefore, does not necessarily entail wholesale dismissal of
modernity, but much rather enables a critical approach that claims modernity
for itself without subscribing to its dominant embodied form. Hence, instead
of nostalgic recourse to nativist or other purist myths of origin, the spectral
"unembodied surplus" of modernity comes to serve as a crucial point of reference: "What remained unutilized from entrenched modernity is a surplus
which we can draw upon and which the West was incapable of or is, perhaps,
disinclined now to draw upon."[17]

---

beyond the measure of, the clock. Benjamin's own intervention obviously forms an attempt
to politicize precisely the High Modernist aesthetic of the epiphany.

[12] Michel Foucault, "Of Other Spaces" ("Des Espaces Autres"), tr. Jay Miskowiec, *Diacritics* 16.1 (Spring 1986): 26.

[13] See Fredric Jameson, *Postmodernism: Or, The Cultural Logic of Late Capitalism*
(London & New York: Verso, 1991): 302–13; Mary Anne Doane, *The Emergence of Cine-
matic Time: Modernity, Contingency, the Archive* (Cambridge MA & London: Harvard
UP, 2002): 1–33.

[14] Doane, *The Emergence of Cinematic Time*, 11.

[15] R. Radhakrishnan, "Postmodernism and the Rest of the World," in *The Pre-Occupation of Postcolonial Studies*, ed. Fawzia Afzal–Khan & Kalpana Seshadri–Crooks (Durham NC & London: Duke UP, 2000): 55.

[16] Javeed Alam, "Modernity and Its Philosophical Visions," in *The Making of History:
Essays Presented to Irfan Habib*, ed. K.N. Panikkar, Terence J. Byers & Utsa Patnaik (New
Delhi: Tulika, 2000): 405.

[17] Javeed Alam, "Modernity and Its Philosophical Visions," 423.

With reference to the genealogy of time, the social historian Sumit Sarkar has demonstrated how the clock and the schematized time it produces made a surprisingly late entry into South Asia, in spite of intensive European commerce from the sixteenth century (the setting of Nagarkar's novel) onwards. Only with the construction of railway and telegraph networks starting in the 1850s, the inauguration, in India, of English schools with their rigid time-tables, and the establishment of a modern bureaucracy did rigorous clock-time discipline become an issue along with the varied responses to its implementation. Sarkar explores how this newly imposed temporal order was appropriated and represented by Bengali office clerks who translated the rigours of clock-time discipline as symptoms of the dark age of Brahminical lore, *Kaliyuga* – a motif which "enjoyed a kind of revival precisely alongside the spread of clock-time."[18] What in the dominant, Western perspective passes for modern time, then, gets articulated by Sarkar's clerks with a reactivated concept of time that oscillates between the mythic and the historical, the cyclic and the linear, in an excessively indeterminate fashion. While the four ages, or *yugas*, of Brahminical orthodoxy are each endowed with precise duration (*Kaliyuga*, for example, spans 420,000 years), they make up a combined unit that repeats itself time and again. Thus, as Romila Thapar puts it, "elements of [...] linear time do occur even within the broadly cyclic,"[19] since the *yugas* form "fragmentary arcs within the cycle that take on the role of linear time. The dichotomy between cyclic and linear becomes increasingly vague."[20] Clock-time inserted into such a temporal structure gets reformulated as specific to the dark age of Kali, hence integrated into a superior cosmic framework.

In this vein, Nagarkar rewrites the birth of the clock and the advent of homogeneous empty time in India as a Hindu legend. The embedded micro-narrative of the minor goddess Charani Devi, recalled by the narrator as a story from his childhood, recounts a cosmic crisis among the gods that motivates a temporal paradigm shift:

---

[18] Sumit Sarkar, *Beyond Nationalist Frames: Relocating Postmodernism, Hindutva, History* (Delhi: Permanent Black, 2002): 26.

[19] Romila Thapar, *Time as a Metaphor of History: Early India* (Delhi: Oxford UP, 1996): 44.

[20] Romila Thapar, *Time as a Metaphor of History*, 31.

> Time was suffering from advanced symptoms of megalomania. He was the frame-
> work or the boundaries within which everything that happened, happened. The
> demons, the gods, space and the cosmos were time-bound. [...] Little wonder that
> Time began to perceive himself as cause and consequence, the begetter and begot-
> ten, as the beginning and the end. It wasn't just that he had delusions of grandeur, it
> appeared that he was what he claimed to be: omnipotent, omniscient, and omni-
> present. (60)

After the gods' attempts to negotiate with Time had failed, and Time straight-
away refused to behave, catastrophe seemed inevitable: "Time was about to
ingest the three worlds" (60). It is in that moment of cosmic danger that
Charani Devi appears on the scene and saves the worlds in an act that does to
Time what Time had threatened to do to the world:

> She was gathering together the million and one strands of Time; [...] her fingers
> picked up the loose ends and the unbroken threads, endless stretches of pre-history,
> history-to-be, and the simultaneous present which is the same second multiplied by
> all the points in space, [...] she bundled it up helter skelter, no beginning, no mid-
> dle, no end, no order, just one monstrously big ball the size of the cosmos. Then the
> Devi opened her mouth and swallowed all of it in one gulp. (60–61)

Time the devourer, obviously heterogeneous, is thus himself devoured –
which, of course, effects a new and different crisis: "Time had stopped dead.
And so had everything else. Because life, as we all know, can only occur on
the axis of time with its three sharp and fluid divisions: the past, the present
and the future" (61). There is only one way out of this deadlock: Since the
gods cannot run the risk of releasing Time from the dungeon of Charani
Devi's belly, they have to convince the Devi that she has to fulfil one more
task in order to save the world from both Time and timelessness. This, in fact,
will be a "long, lonely and loveless vigil" (62): i.e. the domestication of
unruly Time by way of its transformation into homogeneous empty time.
Shiva succeeds in persuading the Devi to unravel the tapeworm of Time and
to release it in regular rhythm and measured bits:

> And so Charani Devi sits in the temple and delicately, oh so delicately, coaxes a
> fraction of a milimetre of the worm from her mouth. She can never close her mouth
> for if she does, all mankind and devilkind and all godkind will be forever frozen in
> suspended animation. (62)

Thus the Devi is herself transformed into a clock, churning out measured and
disciplined time. Time-discipline, Nagarkar's embedded legend seems to

suggest, first of all requires that Time itself be disciplined; if the issue of the Devi's ever-open mouth is homogeneous empty time, however, this latter is firmly inserted into a cosmological framework in which the clock – modernity's "key-machine" according to Lewis Mumford[21] – is itself a goddess, encased in a temple for worship. In Partha Chatterjee's and Dipesh Chakrabarty's accounts, machine worship comes to figure as one of the many indicators of the subcontinent's complex modernity, "an everyday fact of life in India, from taxis to scooter-rickshaws, minibuses and lathe machines."[22]

Partha Chatterjee is best known for his extensive critique of Indian nationalism as a political ideology, which, in his reading, turns out to be a derivative discourse: In India, as elsewhere in the decolonizing world, nineteenth-century European nationalism was adopted and reproduced so that, as a result, nation-states emerged that "were invariably shaped according to contours outlined by given historical models."[23] Chatterjee's analysis of colonial and postcolonial nationalism includes a rigorous interrogation of nation-time as powerfully posited by Benedict Anderson in *Imagined Communities*. As is well known, Anderson describes the imagined community of the nation as a "sociological organism moving calendrically through homogeneous empty time."[24] Since it facilitates the very synchronicity that is indispensable for the act of imagining the political community of the nation, homogeneous empty time forms a crucial structural precondition for the modern nation to emerge as a coherent entity. Yet, as Chatterjee interjects, "homogeneous empty time is not located anywhere in real space – it is utopian,"[25] hence not descriptive of any social reality whatsoever. Like the concept of the nation itself, homogeneous empty time is imposed on a fundamentally heterochronic present; and it is precisely the silenced yet persistent presence of alternative forms of community that, though "relegated

---

[21] Quoted in David S. Landes, *Revolution in Time: Clocks and the Making of the Modern World* (Cambridge MA: Harvard UP, 1983): xix.

[22] Dipesh Chakrabarty, *Provincializing Europe: Postcolonial Thought and Historical Difference* (Delhi: Oxford UP, 2001): 78.

[23] Partha Chatterjee, *Nationalist Thought and the Colonial World: A Derivative Discourse?* (Delhi: Oxford UP, 1986): 21.

[24] Benedict Anderson, *Imagined Communities: Reflections on the Origins and Spread of Nationalism* (London & New York: Verso, 1991): 26.

[25] Parha Chatterjee, "Anderson's Utopia," in *Grounds of Comparison: Around the Work of Benedict Anderson*, ed. Jonathan Culler & Pheng Cheah (New York & London: Routledge, 2003): 166.

to the primordial zone of the natural,"[26] explodes the apparent homogeneity
of the present by ensuring the pervasive coexistence of different temporalities, all of which decidedly partake of "the here-and-now of modernity."[27] In
such a configuration, homogeneous empty time – far from being neutral –
continuously produces those 'historicist' fictions that effectively hierarchize
the world in ever new formulations of allochronic discourses. For homogeneous empty time "linearly connects past, present and future, creating the possibility for all of those historicist imaginings of identity, nationhood, progress."[28] It is, in short, the utopian "time of capital,"[29] which engenders the
latest and most successful version of historicism and enables advocates, but
also ruthless critics, of capitalist subsumption to conceive of the present as
composed of coexisting historical stages. Modernity, in Chatterjee, does not
work that way at all, since it is predicated on the "presence of a dense and
heterogeneous time" which he illustrates with a couple of examples that
might immediately stem from Rushdie, Vikram Seth, or Kiran Nagarkar:

> industrial capitalists waiting to close a business deal because they hadn't yet had
> word from their respective astrologers, or industrial workers who wouldn't touch a
> new machine until it had been consecrated with appropriate religious rites [...]. To
> call this the copresence of several times – the time of the modern and the times of
> the premodern – is only to endorse the utopianism of Western modernity.[30]

Chatterjee's example of factory workers engaged in machine worship certainly finds an echo in Nagarkar's clock-goddess; it also tacitly refers to a sequence in Dipesh Chakrabarty's account of workers' struggles in early-
twentieth-century Bengal jute mills.[31] In his later work, Chakrabarty theorizes
that notion of unevenly dense, heterogeneous time more rigorously – not as
anomalous but as the standard temporality of the real.[32] "Heterotemporality,"

---

[26] Partha Chatterjee, *The Nation and Its Fragments: Colonial and Postcolonial Histories*
(Delhi: Oxford UP, 1993): 239.

[27] Partha Chatterjee, *The Nation and Its Fragments*, 237.

[28] Partha Chatterjee, "Anderson's Utopia," 166.

[29] Partha Chatterjee, "The Nation in Heterogeneous Time," unpublished manuscript,: 3.

[30] Partha Chatterjee, "Anderson's Utopia," 166.

[31] Dipesh Chakrabarty, *Rethinking Working-Class History: Bengal 1890–1940* (Delhi:
Oxford UP, 1996): 89–92.

[32] I emphasize this in order to make sure that neither of the two embraces Benjamin's (or,
more generally speaking, European High Modernity's) high rhetoric of emergency and

"timeknots," and "entangled time" are Chakrabarty's coinages for an argument that addresses and assesses the conceptualization of both the past and the present: In his assault on the universalizing 'stageist' narrative of economic transition, Chakrabarty turns to Marx's scattered observations on surplus value that were supposed to form the fourth volume of *Capital*. From these neglected writings – a clear instance of Alam's 'unembodied surplus of modernity' – he excavates a Marx who proposes a multiplicity of pasts beyond the teleology of capital and modernity, a world that exceeds the universal history of transitions to the capitalist mode (and thereafter to socialism and the classless society). There is, then, in Marx himself the concession that not all history is one long teleological move towards capitalism and beyond; that not all pasts can be reduced to antecedents of the present (capitalist-modern) mode; "that the total universe of pasts that capital encounters is larger than the sum of those elements in which are worked out the logical presuppositions of capital."[33] All the same, in Marx (and, more surprisingly so, in Chakrabarty) the universal history of capital (i.e. the conceptualization of history in terms of subsequent modes of production) remains intact, with the proviso that it be supplemented by those elements that capital encounters "not as antecedents established by itself, not as forms of its own life-process."[34] While the familiar terrain of the grand transition narrative constitutes what Chakrabarty in *Provincializing Europe* labels "History 1," those pasts "that do not lend themselves to the reproduction of the logic of capital" (64) constitute "History 2," "a category charged with the function of constantly interrupting the totalizing thrusts of History 1" (66).

The monolateral script of the transition narrative is thus replaced by a principal pluralism. Chakrabarty's reading of Marx forecloses any notion of a 'universal' capital; more generally speaking, his objective is the heterogenization, from within, of a concept ('capital') that in some dominant discourse is deemed to be categorically homogeneous. In the heterogenizing perspective

---

messianistic epiphany in which homogeneous empty time gets suspended (only) in a moment of being/moment of danger.

[33] Dipesh Chakrabarty, *Provincializing Europe*, 66.

[34] Marx, quoted in Chakrabarty, *Provincializing Europe*, from *Theories of Surplus Value*; for the German original, see Karl Marx, *Theorien über den Mehrwert* (MEW 26.3; Berlin: Dietz, 1968): 460: "Diese ältren Formen findet es [das industrielle Kapital] vor in der Epoche seiner Bildung und seines Entstehens. Es findet sie als Voraussetzungen vor, aber nicht als von ihm selbst gesetzte Voraussetzungen, nicht als Formen seines eigenen Lebensprozesses."

of *Provincializing Europe*, the "globalization of capital is not the same as capital's universalization" (71); nor does Chakrabarty stop short at the internal pluralization of capital, but explicitly extends his diagnosis to the category of the present as such, suggesting, with Heidegger, that "not-being-a-totality [were] a constitutional characteristic of the 'now'" (250).

Far from implementing a unilateral and monocultural formation on a global scale, the present is shot through with historical difference, since "no global (or even local, for that matter) capital can ever represent the universal logic of capital, for any historically available form of capital is a provisional compromise made up of History 1 modified by somebody's History 2s."[35] If, therefore, the present is conceptualized as so radically plural that it is not possible for any particular element to claim to represent the whole in any way, then the present becomes thinkable as the site of a pervasive permeability of concepts, languages, cultures, temporalities. What in an historicist version of time can be branded as 'archaic' thus turns out to be necessary and integral to the present:

> Pasts are there in taste, in practices of embodiment, in the cultural training the senses have received over generations. They are there in practices I sometimes do not even know I engage in. This is how the archaic comes into the modern, not as a remnant of another time but as something constitutive of the present.[36]

In this reading, Nagarkar's Rajput prince, with his genuinely modern time-discipline coupled with his interaction with demons and gods, would not embody anachronism – in fact, anachronism itself is now unthinkable – but the heterogeneity of the present, and any time.

WORKS CITED

Alam, Javeed. "Modernity and Its Philosophical Visions," in *The Making of History: Essays Presented to Irfan Habib*, ed. K.N. Panikkar, Terence J. Byers & Utsa Patnaik (New Delhi: Tulika, 2000): 405–39.

Anderson, Benedict. *Imagined Communities: Reflections on the Origins and Spread of Nationalism* (London & New York: Verso, rev. ed. 1991).

Benjamin, Walter. "Theses on the Philosophy of History," in *Illuminations*, tr. Harry Zohn, intro. Hannah Arendt (New York: Schocken, 1968): 253–64.

---

[35] Dipesh Chakrabarty, *Provincializing Europe*, 70.

[36] *Provincializing Europe*, 251.

——. "Über den Begriff der Geschichte" (1940), in *Gesammelte Schriften* I.2, ed. Rolf Tiedemann & Hermann Schweppenhäuser (Frankfurt am Main: Suhrkamp, 1980): 691–704.

Burnett, D. Graham. "Mapping Time: Chronometry on Top of the World," *Daedalus* 132.2 (Spring 2003): 5–19.

Chakrabarty, Dipesh. *Rethinking Working-Class History: Bengal, 1890–1940* (Delhi: Oxford UP, 1996).

——. *Provincializing Europe: Postcolonial Thought and Historical Difference* (Delhi: Oxford UP, 2000).

Chatterjee, Partha. *Nationalist Thought and the Colonial World: A Derivative Discourse?* (Delhi: Oxford UP, 1986).

——. *The Nation and Its Fragments: Colonial and Postcolonial Histories* (Delhi: Oxford UP, 1993).

——. "Anderson's Utopia," in: *Grounds of Comparison: Around the Work of Benedict Anderson*, ed. Jonathan Culler & Pheng Cheah (New York & London: Routledge, 2003): 161–70.

——. "The Nation in Heterogeneous Time" (MS).

Doane, Mary Anne. *The Emergence of Cinematic Time: Modernity, Contingency, the Archive* (Cambridge MA & London: Harvard UP, 2002).

Fabian, Johannes. *Time and the Other: How Anthropology Makes Its Object* (New York: Columbia UP, 1983).

Foucault, Michel. "Of Other Spaces" ("Des Espaces Autres"), tr. Jay Miskowiec, *Diacritics* 16.1 (Spring 1986): 22–27.

Hardt, Michael, & Antonio Negri. *Empire* (Cambridge MA & London: Harvard UP, 2000).

Hongladarom, Soraj. "The Web of Time and the Dilemma of Globalization," *The Information Society* 18 (2002): 241–49.

Jameson, Fredric. *Postmodernismm, Or, The Cultural Logic of Late Capitalism* (London & New York: Verso, 1991).

Landes, David S. *Revolution in Time: Clocks and the Making of the Modern World* (Cambridge MA: Harvard UP, 1983).

——. "Clocks and the Wealth of Nations," *Daedalus* 132.2 (Spring 2003): 20–26.

Marx, Karl. *Theorien über den Mehrwert* (MEW 26.3; Berlin: Dietz, 1968).

Metcalf, Thomas R. *Ideologies of the Raj: The New Cambridge History of India*, III.4 (Delhi: Cambridge UP, 1997).

Nagarkar, Kiran. *Cuckold* (Delhi: HarperCollins, 1997).

Radhakrishnan, R. "Postmodernism and the Rest of the World," in *The Pre-Occupation of Postcolonial Studies*, ed. Fawzia Afzal–Khan & Kalpana Seshadri–Crooks (Durham NC & London: Duke UP, 2000): 37–70.

Sarkar, Sumit. *Beyond Nationalist Frames: Relocating Postmodernism, Hindutva, History* (Delhi: Permanent Black, 2002).

Thapar, Romila. *Time as a Metaphor of History: Early India* (Delhi: Oxford UP, 1996).

Thrift, Nigel. "Owners' Time and Own Time: The Making of a Capitalist Time Consciousness, 1300–1800," in *The Sociology of Time*, ed. John Hassard (London: Macmillan, 1990): 105–29.

Thompson, E.P. "Time, Work-Discipline and Industrial Capitalism," *Past & Present: A Journal of Historical Studies* 38 (December 1967): 56–97.

◄❖►

Lakshman's Journal
— An Essay in Narratology
and the Barbs of Transculturality

PETER STUMMER

S IGNIFICANTLY ENOUGH, there were, from the very beginning, two completely different editions of Shashi Tharoor's *Riot* (2001): the American one with a well-poised, highly respectable aesthetic decor, and the Indian [Other] one that sported a small-format, catastrophe-mongering appearance in loud garish colours.

The following article will first discuss the novel from the perspective of a multilayered tradition of cross-culturality; it will then try and penetrate its allegedly postmodern narratological façade; and, finally, it will seek to critique it from a transnational point of view. My thesis, in a nutshell, is that the novel, rather than belonging to the Indian narrative spectrum proper, tends to be part and parcel of the Indian expatriate political discourse within the USA before 9/11, when many expatriate Indians were worried about the public image of Hinduism in India because of the reports on Hindu fundamentalism and the activities of the Vishwa Hindu Parishad (which implied – as the *Times of India* put it – that "Hindutva [was] out of the closet"[1]).

Let us briefly look at various traditions of cross-culturality which have exerted some influence on the novel. First there is the Cross-Cultural Reciprocity Tradition, which can be looked at in four different forms: colonial

---

[1] Anon., "Running Riot," *The Times of India* (1 September 2001): online http: //timesofindia .indiatimes.com/cms.dll/articleshow?catkey=2114117552&art_id=1288446596&sType=1 (accessed 15 March 2008).

echoes; expatriate precursors; cross-cultural comparisons; and postcolonial
inside inspections. The first need not concern us for too long. This is the type
of 'transnational anglomania', from transatlantic partnership to war-monger-
ing cronyism in politics, where writers straddle the fence between Great Britain and the USA – for example, Bill Bryson or Alistair Cooke, who, if Jan
Morris is to be trusted, "most Britons assume is American while most Americans are damned sure he's a Brit."[2] D.B.C. Pierre's *Vernon God Little* (2003)
is the most recent if somewhat more dubious example of this transnational
anglomania. There are a good many contemporary British narratives with distinct traces of colonial nostalgia that qualify for our consideration. There is
Amit Chaudhuri's *Freedom Song* (1998), for instance, which surely seeks to
improve the image of Calcutta's Hindus, and the combined efforts of Meera
Syal, Nisha Minhas, and Monica Ali. *Sari & Sins* (2003) and *Brick Lane*
(2003), in particular, with their female emancipatory agenda and their enlightened treatment of arranged marriages, clearly use the Indian subcontinent
as a contrasting backcloth to enhance the effect of wry comments on the immigrant community in England, whether it is Bengali-speaking or not. Thus
the observation of Nazneen, the eighteen-year-old heroine of *Brick Lane*, that
poor women in a Tower Hamlets council flat can truly be fat,[3] in all probability is not so funny from a Bangladeshi rural perspective as it is supposed to
be from an English middle-class point of view.

Ruth Prawer Jhabvala and Gita Mehta, too, certainly had an interest in
applied cross-culturality, although they both had, first and foremost, a keen
and observant eye for spiritual deficiencies in the West and thus primarily
tended towards satirical overtones with regard to the First World. In Mehta's
Karma Cola (1979), we read:

> A guru who has an ashram in Western India with a large number of foreign fol-
> lowers, confided to a correspondent from Time magazine, "My followers have no
> time. So I give them instant salvation. I turn them into neo-sanyasis."[4]

Inter alia, there is a clear line from Jhabvala's *How I Became a Holy Mother*
(1976) and *Karma Cola* to Anita Desai's *Journey to Ithaca* (1995) and the
film *The Guru* (2002) by Daisy von Scherler–Mayer. Like Tharoor, Mehta, in

---

[2] Jan Morris, "The President Steps Down," *New Statesman* (15 March 2004): 43.
[3] Monica Ali, *Brick Lane* (New York: Scribner, 2003): 48.
[4] Gita Mehta, *Karma Cola: Marketing the Mystic East* (London: Collins, 1979): 107.

Snakes and Ladders (1997), has written a portrait of India; other expatriates, such as Farrukh Dhondy, or Bharati Mukherjee, Anita Desai or Rohinton Mistry, repeatedly wrote critical narratives about Bharat Mata, Mother India, with or without echoes of Mehboob Khan's famous film of 1957.

Of greater interest for our purpose, however, is a somewhat different and slightly more postcolonial tradition. It is indeed cross-cultural, but seeks to turn the tables on the hegemonic West with regard to the USA. Paule Marshall's *Brown Girl, Brownstones* (1959), which describes gender-specific acculturation problems experienced by a group of Afro-Barbadians in New York, can duly be considered a kind of prototype. Sushama Bedi's *Havana/ The Fire Sacrifice* (1989 in Hindi and 1993 in English) clearly follows this pattern, including female empowerment. The title refers to a sacrificial ritual that goes back to a type of reformed Hinduism introduced in 1875 by Swami Dayananda Sarasvati, and provides a structural framework for the novel. The central, self-sacrificing and hard-working mother figure enables her daughters to study medicine in the USA. Their husbands arrive later in full expectation of cushy jobs. The medical profession is seen as the model of easy money-making. The men still rely on the support system of the extended family, whereas the young women, with varying degrees of success, try to make the most of the opportunities available on the basis of individual effort. Much is seen critically, most of all the societal undercurrent of violence. Guddo, the mother, a model of strength, is robbed on the subway, and one granddaughter, Radhika, goes astray and is gang-raped and stabbed to death at night in front of a discotheque. On the other hand, it is remarkable how the range of readily available stipends and scholarships, also for newcomers, is taken for granted and eagerly made full use of. Perhaps there is a connection with the fact that the author has settled in the USA and teaches Hindi literature. The outside view, then, has actually become an inside one.

Basically, Jhumpa Lahiri follows the same pattern in *The Namesake* (2003), though with greater literary ambition. However, being of the next generation, she has not been called a "Boston Brahmin" for nothing.[5] Just like Bharati Mukherjee, or presumably Chitra Divakaruni, she is well into the process of dropping her hyphenated existence and settling into the status of an American writer, *tout court*. The comparison that is most instructive, how-

---

[5] Sumit Mitra & Arthur J. Pais, "Jhumpa Lahiri: Boston Brahmin," *India Today* (24 April 2000): 89.

ever, is with Anurag Mathur's *The Inscrutable Americans* (published in India in 1991 and in the USA in 1997). The novel was a bestseller in India and the film version of it was quite a hit in the USA. It is sometimes described as a hilarious *Bildungsroman*, which is perhaps carrying the praise somewhat too far, but it certainly is very funny in many places. The protagonist, Gopal Kumar, is a twenty-year-old student of chemical engineering, heir apparent, appropriately enough, to a National Hair Oil factory in Madhya Pradesh, who spends a year on a small university campus, Eversville, in the USA, somewhere in the sticks. Further sources of cross-cultural hilarity are his ignorance of spoken American English (often exemplified by the token American student, Randy Wolff, delegated by the Dean to look after him) and, of course, his ignorance of American mores, particularly where sexual behaviour is concerned, since he derives most of his assumptions about American sexual conduct from his knowledge of pornographic magazines and videos. Furthermore, he exchanges extremely stilted letters with his younger brother back home in India, which – scattered throughout the text – not only give the novel some extra structure, but also unobtrusively differentiate between the limited point of view of the protagonist and a covert authorial narrator. Often it is obviously a case of *ridendo dicere verum*. This is most clearly the case when Gopal gets to know the star of the football team, a black guy nicknamed the Peacock, six feet six inches tall, mostly wearing colourful shirts and reflecting sunglasses, who explains the colour bar and the race problem of the country to him by using the example of this small-town set-up: the black folks disappear behind a borderline of junk, guarded over by white hoodlums, in order to become more or less invisible to the wider community.[6]

That this 'outside' perspective has almost become a pattern is demonstrated by the debut novel of a young Nigerian, Ike Oguine, entitled *A Squatter's Tale* (2000). The background there is the oil boom in Nigeria, which introduces Obi, the central character, to dubious financial transactions in the banking business as long as it lasts. When the crash comes and the bubble bursts, he sees going to the States as the only way out and buys himself a passage as well as illegal entry. Obi learns the hard way about the American Dream. What is most significant in *The Fire Sacrifice* as well as in *A Squatter's Tale* is the tendency to differentiate between brown and black or, for that

---

[6] This is certainly a more direct observation on racism in the USA than Anita Desai's sly insinuation of racially motivated ostracism in the short story "The Artist's Life" from her collection *Diamond Dust* (New York: Vintage, 2001).

matter, between black and black. In Bedi's text, the Indians try to stay aloof from African Americans and relationships are fended off as much as possible. In Oguine's tale, much is made of the difference between Nigerian immigrants, sometimes successful professionals, and African Americans, who more often than not are seen as gangsters, trying to rip off the young Nigerian. The irony lies in the fact that the expected Nigerian network of former friends and acquaintances and even relatives eventually comes in for serious criticism as well.

So the model was all there for Tharoor: the perspective of a relatively naive protagonist, the indirect comparison between two countries, and the unobtrusive employment of letters, diaries, and such material. It might have been accidental, but it just so happened that *The Inscrutable Americans* was re-issued when *Riot* was first published. 2001 also happened to be the year of publication of *Recovering Rude* (2000), a novel, written by the Calcutta-born Montreal-based writer-playwright Rana Bose, which also uses the device of a man's diary being recovered by some dubious character for political purposes. Again it seems that all the ingredients of Tharoor's novel were in the air.

Riot begins with the death of twenty-four-year-old Priscilla, an American girl who is found stabbed to death in the aftermath of a violent Hindu–Muslim confrontation in Zalilgarh, a small place in the region east of New Delhi. The American press gets on to the murder case and sends an investigative reporter, Randy Diggs. The divorced parents of the girl get their act together, too, and travel to India to make enquiries of their own. It turns out that their daughter had an affair with the District Magistrate of the area, V. Lakshman, nicknamed Lucky. The regional Superintendent of Police, Gurinder Singh, is a Sikh and Lakshman's best friend. Between them, they try to handle the 'riot' of the title (we are in the year 1989 and witness a foreshadowing of the Babri Masjid–Ram Mandir controversy in Ayodhya in 1992) and eventually manage to hush up the private affair.

Priscilla had been working for an organization called Help-US, the latter part of the name ambiguously designating both the USA, which finances it, and the self-help angle of the Indian women, for whom the organization is intended in order to raise awareness about population control. Freely offering birth-control pills to married women of both religions, Priscilla treads on many toes and underestimates the intricacies of arranged marriages and the circumstances of institutionalized violence against women in matrimony. She clearly gets into difficulties when she seeks to help Fatima, a mother of seven, with an abortion while her husband is away. Kadambari, an indigenous aide

with the women's project, unsuccesfully tries to introduce her to a more differentiated view of the matter with regard to female empowerment, when she
tells her about the fate of her nineteen-year-old sister Sundari, which name,
ironically enough, means 'the beautiful'[7] – over seventy-five percent of her
body is burnt, wounds which were inflicted when her mother-in-law, infuri-
ated by her reluctance to shoulder the manifold household chores she sought
to saddle her with, started first to beat her and, on finding out that she was
pregnant with only a daughter, doused her sari with kerosene and set fire to it.
V. Lakshman, aged thirty-three, is a relatively dark Indian from the South
with a wife, Geetha, and a small daughter, Rekha; he hardly knows any Urdu
and has an English education which he is very proud of. He finds it natural to
defend the fact that his marriage had also been an arranged one. On an ideological level, we encounter a confrontation between the views of Professor
Mohammed Sarwar, a liberal Muslim scholar, and Ram Charan Gupta, a
leading Hindu zealot, mediated through the interviews the journalist Randy
Diggs conducts with both of them.

Priscilla's corpse had been found near the Kotli, an old ruin, somewhat out
of town, where the lovers used to have their romantic meetings. Partly, the
exotic attractiveness of India goes back to Priscilla's childhood years, when
her father had been engaged in introducing the charms of Coca Cola to the
Indians, discovering in the long run, to his dismay, that India thought it could
do very well without the benefits of the American beverage. It turns out that
the daughter caught him *in flagrante delicto* with his Indian secretary having
sex *a tergo*, a memory which, until one of the late encounters at the Kotli, had
been at the base of her own inhibitions.

It just so happens that playwright Tony Kushner put a reworking of his
play *Homebody/Kabul* on stage in 2004.[8] The original was completed in
2001 and was set in 1998: a solitary British housewife, living in a dysfunctional family, is infatuated with Afghanistan on the basis of an outdated travel
guide, goes there, and disappears. Again the similarities with Tharoor are

---

[7] Shashi Tharoor, *Riot: A Novel* (New York: Arcade, 2001; New Delhi & London:
Viking, 2001): 246.

[8] I am grateful to Tiffany Knight of the University of Southern California for pointing
this out to me; see Tony Kushner, *Homebody/Kabul* (London: Nick Hern, 2002, rev. definitive ed. 2004), Peter Marks, "Tony Kushner, Replaywright," *Washington Post* (8 March
2004): C01, and Peter Marks, "'Homebody/Kabul': Land of Lost Chances," *Washington
Post* (10 March 2004): C01.

quite striking; the daughter, who goes to Kabul with her father to search for her mother, is actually called Priscilla.

Formally, Tharoor's novel is a "file folder,"[9] as the American critic Lorraine Adams aptly puts it; it is not enough to call it, as Shyamala Narayan does, "a truly post-modern novel."[10] The book is a collage of newspaper clippings, transcriptions of interviews, letters (especially by Priscilla to female friends of hers in the USA), extracts from diaries and scrapbooks and, of course, Lakshman's poems. These texts also vary accordingly in their layout and their typographical make-up. Stylistically, the various texts range from highly academic language (when arguments about Hinduism and Islam in India are exchanged) to the Superintendent's tough-guy lingo and the faulty English of Priscilla's superior in the Help-US organization, which provides a kind of comic relief.

Despite the postmodern narratological façade of his novel, Tharoor painstakingly acknowledges his sources (such as the IAS officer Harsh Mander's report about sectarian violence in Madhya Pradesh, or the killing of Amy Biehl from Palo Alto by a black mob in South Africa). Tharoor has emphasized his intention that each of his novels should be different and, also formally, cover some new ground; in *Riot*, his starting-point was clearly a satirical one. In an interview about his novel, he firmly rejected any connection with colonial precursors, such as *Passage to India* or *Heat and Dust*, and emphatically placed the novel in the context of a global world-view:

> My novel is not about a torrid East–West encounter in a colonial setting; it's about todays's people in our increasingly globalizing world, where collision and confluence seamlessly cross national and ethnic boundaries.[11]

Asked about his having lived outside India for over twenty-five years, and about his demanding work for the United Nations in New York, "as Kofi Annan's eyes and ears," he maintained that geography was merely circum-

---

[9] Lorraine Adams, "Carried Away – *Riot: A Love Story* by Shashi Tharoor," *Washington Post* (28 October 2001): BW03.

[10] Shyamala A. Narayan, "India," *Journal of Commonwealth Literature* 37.3 (2002): 65.

[11] Sandip Roy–Chowdhury, "Love in the Time of Riots: Shashi Tharoor takes on a communal tinderbox in *Riot*" (interview), *India Currents* (1 October 2001): online http://www.indiacurrents.com/news/view_article.html?article_id=d8ae8ac5dc9d34c6e0b41 cd7cbaf8062 (accessed March 15, 2008).

stantial, that he was an expatriate but not an émigré, and that he still carried his Indian identity and his Indian passport with him.

If this is so, one must wonder with Claudia Wenner of the *Franfurter All-gemeine Zeitung*[12] why Tharoor made Gurrinder, the Sikh head of police, not only a hard drinker but also someone who dismisses the anti-Sikh pogrom of 1984 in the wake of Indira Gandhi's assassination, playing down the 3,000 killed in the process. Even worse, Tharoor makes him negligent of his duty, possibly for reasons of friendship, since he repeatedly suppresses evidence. It might only be a weak joke on the part of the narrator, it is true, when Gur-rinder identifies the vibrator in Priscilla's handbag as an electric hair-brush. It starts to become more serious, however, when he also suppresses Priscilla's scrapbook. And his behaviour is really difficult to stomach when he finally suppresses the postmortem finding that Priscilla had been with child.

This leads us to the weaknesses of the central character, Lakshman. On the plot level, it certainly demands quite some willing suspension of disbelief when one learns that Lakshman, in the process of riot control, completely for-gets about Priscilla, who is waiting for him in the usual ruins of the Kotli. Slightly more plausible, though not at all more positive, are his reservations concerning Priscilla's former sexual activities. Although rather dark himself, he resents the fact that a former partner of Priscilla's had been an African American. In a letter to a friend, Priscilla ruminates about Lakshman's mul-tiple personalities, which do not match: district administrator, passionate lover, traditional husband and father, and the closet writer who fantasizes about a masterpiece he will write one day on an American campus.[13] His poetry writing is indeed a problem, as is his tendency to trot out bons mots by Oscar Wilde, some genuine, some made up. It is rather odd that so many con-temporary writers, from Arundhati Roy to Monica Ali and Shashi Tharoor, should still tend to employ some type of babu outlook. With the women authors, such a character is a means of deflating male pomposity, even though this may be somewhat dated. However, if Tharoor uses elements of such a cliché figure for his central character, this will surely impair his 'higher pur-pose'. Lakshman's journal is unconvincing and often stilted – for instance, when he tells himself he cannot really "abdicate his husbandhood" (201) by

---

[12] Claudia Wenner, "Aufruhr in Ayodhya: Shashi Tharoors heikler Roman gegen den Fundamentalismus" (Riot in Ayodhya: Shahshi Tharoor's controversial novel against fun-damentalism), *Frankfurter Allgemeine Zeitung* (13 June 2003): 34.

[13] Shashi Tharoor, *Riot*, 242. Further page references are in the main text.

leaving with Priscilla for America. He is insincere and eager to combine the reassuring groove of traditional marriage with the excitement of an extra love affair, which would be all very well if it were not for the fact that Lakshman is also the vehicle and the mouthpiece for the serious message of the author. He denies any knowledge about what Priscilla's business could have been at the Kotli, and he denies to the mother's face having been intimate with Priscilla at all.

Unfortunately, he is at the same time concerned with intricate notions of truth in tolerant Hinduism (137), which seemingly relativizes the moral absolutism of the other established world religions, yet seeks to corroborate the teachings of that "great Hindu monk Swami Vivekananda and his electrifying statement at the World Parliament of Religions in Chicago in 1893" (146), thereby underwriting some notion of truth after all. This argument is born out by the fact that it is exactly this *Weltanschauung* that Tharoor has been repeatedly expounding in his regular column in *The Hindu*, because, as he says, the Swami "articulated best the liberal humanism that lies at the heart of his (and my) creed."[14] Against this background, sensibly enough, the 'common enemy' are "the forces of sectarian division that would, if unchecked, tear the country apart."[15] Not all of his readers were convinced, however, when he recommended "Hinduism as culture rather than as religion" which can "easily be embraced by non-Hindus if it is separated from religious faith and treated as a heritage to which all may lay claim."[16]

This certainty of the professed creed jars somewhat with the fashionable vagueness of the novel's ending. The helper Kadambari obviously turned informer; thus Lakshman's wife Geetha knew about her husband's affair and sought spiritual sustenance from a sadhu at the temple who, in turn, informed the fanatic Ram Charan Gupta, who would have loved to catch Lakshman with his pants down in more than one sense. Then one of Gupta's frustrated menials could have committed the murder, or it might have been the revenge

---

[14] "The Enemy Lies Within," *The Hindu, Online Edition* (5 January 2003), http://www.hinduonnet.com/thehindu/mag/2003/01/05/stories/2003010500430300.htm (acc. March 15, 2008).

[15] "The Enemy Lies Within."

[16] "Strengthening Indianness," *The Hindu, Online Edition* (19 January 2003), http://www.hinduonnet.com/thehindu/mag/2003/01/19/stories/2003011900240300.htm (acc. March 15, 2008).

of Ali, wife-bashing husband to Fatima, whom Priscilla had supported against the will of her husband in the attempt of an abortion.

Ultimately it does not really matter who committed the murder, since the uppermost goal of the narrative enterprise is the face-saving of the Hindu majority's image in the USA. To substantiate this claim, let me point out the diversity of the debate among the Indian diaspora in the USA and maintain that Tharoor seeks, at least to some degree, to plug in to this discussion as well.[17] Several newspapers have been involved in this debate; there is *India Abroad*, there is the Manhattan-based *News India–Times*, there is *India Star* with its many reviews, and there is *Khabar*, which has been catering to the South Asian community of Georgia for about ten years now. The Indian journal *Manushi*, started by Madhu Kishwar in 1978 and subtitled "about women and society," is also frequently accessed on the internet. In *India Star*, a contributor attacked the "Brood of Opinion Writers" who, in his view, had been irresponsibly demonizing the Hindus in India for American consumption in the competing *India Abroad* and had created an image of Hinduism in India that had to be corrected.[18] Tharoor agrees with the analyses of Kishwar and Varshney, who both publish in the USA and argue that neither city, Ayodhya nor Ahmedabad, represents India.[19] According to this view, rural India is practically a stranger to sectarian violence. Most sectarian riots are planned by evil-minded politicians who employ criminal gangs and provide religious pretexts for their own clearly political ends. Citizens must understand these motives and learn how to counteract the methods used by the purveyors of ethnic and religious hatred.

It is noteworthy that Tharoor enthuses about *The Future of Freedom* by Fareed Zakaria, a former editor of *Foreign Affairs* and now editor of *Newsweek International*.[20] The book is about democracy and maintains that 'electoral democracies' are not the answer to everything; as Tharoor approvingly

---

[17] See, for example, Shashi Tharoor, *India: From Midnight to the Millennium* (New York: Arcade, 1997).

[18] Ramesh N. Rao, "India Abroad's Brood of Opinion Writers – Analysts or Ideologues?" *India Star: A Literary–Art Magazine*, http://www.indiastar.com/closepet1.htm (accessed 15 March 2008).

[19] See Madhu Kishwar, *Religion at the Service of Nationalism and Other Essays* (New Delhi: Oxford UP India, 1998), and Ashutosh Varshney, *Ethnic Conflict and Civic Life: Hindus and Muslims in India* (New Haven CT: Yale UP, 2002).

[20] "A Call for Self Control," *The Hindu, Online Edition* (27 April 2003), http://www.shashitharoor.com/articles/hindu/selfcontrol.php (acc. March 15, 2008).

states, "*The Future of Freedom* asserts simultaneously that in many parts of the world democracy needs more democratisation, and that in America the process has gone too far."[21]

Much as I have criticized *Riot* as a novel, I should like to appreciate it up to a point as political prose and use it as inspiration for a new argumentational model. As I have tried to show, the demonstratively transcultural also functions locally. Ideally, there would be next to no differentials in the reciprocity of the here and there. Starting with Walter Mignolo's post-occidental reason and his Darcy Ribeiro-derived border gnosis,[22] we should proceed to a truly transcultural perspective on the basis of Seyla Benhabib's "flexible citizenship" which transcends the nation-state.[23] In thus creating a newly conceived, near-utopian cosmopolitanism from below, we might be able to call into being a critical counterweight to globalization as it actually exists today: as trendy as it is uncontrolled. In this manner, it may be possible to tame and civilize a process which, in the words of the Australian committed journalist John Pilger, has so far been dominated solely by corporatism, and which has failed to respond to the "globalisation of poverty, a world where most human beings never make a phone call and live on less than two dollars a day, where – according to UN sources – 6,000 children die every day from diarrhoea because most have no access to water."[24] With regard to strengthening Indian political activism in the USA, Indian initiatives in Georgia, documented in an eleven-page-long appeal in *Khabar*,[25] might constitute a beginning, since there the passionate argument is in favour of political participation by Indian Americans, both on grassroots and on institutional levels. In view of the astounding prosperity of the community, it should be possible to overcome the widespread political apathy documented in the lack of citizenship and voter registration and embrace the long-term vision of possible political clout in Congress to influence US policies towards India.

---

[21] "A Call for Self Control."

[22] Walter D. Mignolo, *Local Histories/Global Designs: Coloniality, Subaltern Knowledges, and Border Thinking* (Princeton NJ: Princeton UP, 2000).

[23] See Seyla Benhabib, *Claims of Culture: Equality and Diversity in the Global Era* (Princeton NJ & Oxford: Princeton UP, 2002).

[24] John Pilger, *The New Rulers of the World* (London: Verso, 2002): 2.

[25] Harin Contractor & Parthiv Parekh, "From Political Apathy to Activism," *Khabar* 7.10 (October 2002): 20–32.

WORKS CITED

Adams, Lorraine. "Carried Away – *Riot: A Love Story* by Shashi Tharoor," *Washington Post* (28 October 2001): BW03.

Ali, Monica. *Brick Lane* (New York: Scribner, 2003).

Anon. "Running Riot." *The Times of India* (1 September 2001): online http://timesofindia .indiatimes.com/cms.dll/articleshow?catkey=2114117552&art_id=1288446596&sType=1 (accessed 15 March 2008).

Bedi, Sushama. *The Fire Sacrifice*, tr. David Rubin (*Havana*, 1989; tr. Oxford & Portsmouth NH: Heinemann, 1993).

Benhabib, Seyla. *Claims of Culture: Equality and Diversity in the Global Era* (Princeton NJ & Oxford: Princeton UP, 2002).

Bose, Rana. *Recovering Rude: A Novel* (Montreal: Véhicule, 2000).

Chaudhuri, Amit. *Freedom Song* (London: Picador, 1998).

Contractor, Harin, & Parthiv Parekh. "From Political Apathy to Activism," *Khabar* 7.10 (October 2002): 20–32.

Desai, Anita. *Journey to Ithaca* (London : Heinemann, 1995).

——. *Diamond Dust* (New York: Vintage, 2001).

Jhabvala, Ruth Prawer. *How I Became a Holy Mother and Other Stories* (London: John Murray, 1976).

Kishwar, Madhu. *Religion at the Service of Nationalism and Other Essays* (New Delhi: Oxford UP India, 1998).

Kushner, Tony. *Homebody/Kabul* (London: Nick Hern, 2002, rev. definitive ed. 2004).

Lahiri, Jhumpa. *The Namesake* (Boston MA: Houghton Mifflin, 2003).

Marks, Peter. "Tony Kushner, Replaywright," *Washington Post* (8 March 2004): C01.

——. "'Homebody / Kabul': Land of Lost Chances," *Washington Post* (10 March 2004): C01.

Marshall, Paule. *Brown Girl, Brownstones* (New York, Random House, 1959).

Mathur, Anurag. *The Inscrutable Americans* (Calcutta: Rupa, 1991; Novato CA: New World Library, 1997).

Mehta, Gita. *Karma Cola: Marketing the Mystic East* (London: Collins, 1979).

——. *Snakes and Ladders: A View of Modern India* (London: Secker & Warburg, 1997).

Mignolo, Walter D. *Local Histories/Global Designs: Coloniality, Subaltern Knowledges, and Border Thinking* (Princeton NJ: Princeton UP, 2000).

Minhas, Nisha. *Sari & Sins* (London: Pocket, 2003).

Mitra, Sumit, & Arthur J. Pais. "Jhumpa Lahiri: Boston Brahmin," *India Today* (24 April 2000): 89.

Morris, Jan. "The President Steps Down," *New Statesman* (15 March 2004): 43.

Narayan, Shyamala A. "India," *Journal of Commonwealth Literature* 37.3 (2002): 65–66.

Oguine, Ike. *A Squatter's Tale* (Oxford & Chicago: Heinemann, 2000).

Pierre, D.B.C. *Vernon God Little: A 21st Century Comedy in the Presence of Death* (London: Faber & Faber, 2003).

Pilger, John. *The New Rulers of the World* (London: Verso, 2002).

Rao, Ramesh N. "*India Abroad*'s Brood of Opinion Writers – Analysts or Ideologues?" *India Star: A Literary–Art Magazine*, http://www.indiastar.com/closepet1.htm (accessed 15 March 2008).

Roy–Chowdhury, Sandip. "Love in the Time of Riots: Shashi Tharoor takes on a communal tinderbox in *Riot*" (interview), *India Currents* (1 October 2001): online: http://www .indiacurrents.com/news/view_article.html?article_id=d8ae8ac5dc9d34c6e0b41cd7cbaf80 62 (accessed 15 March 2008).

Tharoor, Shashi. *India: From Midnight to the Millennium* (New York: Arcade Publishing, 1997).

———. *Riot: A Novel* (New York: Arcade, 2001; New Delhi & London: Viking, 2001).

———. "The Enemy Lies Within," *The Hindu*, Online Edition (5 January 2003), http://www.hinduonnet.com/thehindu/mag/2003/01/05/stories/2003010500430300.htm (accessed 15 March 2008).

———. "Strengthening Indianness," *The Hindu*, Online Edition (19 January 2003), http://www.hinduonnet.com/thehindu/mag/2003/01/19/stories/2003011900240300.htm (accessed 15 March 2008).

———. "A Call for Self Control," *The Hindu*, Online Edition (27 April 2003), http://www.shashitharoor.com/articles/hindu/selfcontrol.php (accessed 15 March 2008).

Varshney, Ashutosh. *Ethnic Conflict and Civic Life: Hindus and Muslims in India* (New Haven CT: Yale UP, 2002).

Wenner, Claudia. "Aufruhr in Ayodhya: Shashi Tharoors heikler Roman gegen den Fundamentalismus" (Riot in Ayodhya: Shahshi Tharoor's controversial novel against fundamentalism), *Frankfurter Allgemeine Zeitung* (13 June 2003): 34.

Zakaria, Fareed. *The Future of Freedom: Illiberal Democracy at Home and Abroad* (New York: W.W. Norton, 2003).

◄❖►

TRANSCULTURAL REALITIES

Broken Borders

— Migration, Modernity and English Writing — Transcultural Transformation in the Heart of Europe

MIKE PHILLIPS

WALTER BENJAMIN made a speech in Paris during the 1930s in which he talks about rescuing artists' work from fashion and argues that some photographers of the time had turned what he calls the struggle against misery into an object of consumption; he goes on to say that for a writer's work to be a means of production rather than an article of consumption it should have an organizing function. For this to happen it is also necessary for the writer to have a teacher's attitude – a writer who does not teach other writers teaches nobody.

Now, the question is how to do this, and it's interesting to be thinking about it in a moment when we're discussing such issues as migration, nationality, citizenship, and culture, not in an abstract mode, not as an academic topic or a theoretical issue, but in terms of a living reality, which will decide how we can live together in a new Europe – both inside our traditional borders, and as a result of a growing movement of people between countries.

Paradoxically, at a moment like this, theoretical issues, ideas, become increasingly influential, and suddenly they emerge as newspaper headlines over which the juggernauts of right and left clash like blind armies in the night. But, of course, as Gramsci might have said, every man is a philosopher and, of course every man and every woman is involved in the processes by which culture connects all the operations of our political, social and economic life.

Therefore, for me, literature and criticism are not merely the site of my work. Instead, the whole network and my work inside and outside of it has to be part of this present attempt to reconcile new populations, new cultures, and new struggles over cultural and social territory in Europe as a whole. But I need now to identify myself, as I do in my routine business every day, and try to locate what I am doing in this continuing debate about culture and identity.

Here I am, an interesting contradiction. Classically, an intellectual who has emerged from the working class, a black writer with various kinds of origins and interests in the regions inhabited by Fanon's *The Wretched of the Earth*,[1] but I am also a member of the post-industrial club of wealthy populations. To be here at all, in Frankfurt, is to have both feet firmly planted in the condition of the West. The poorest and most oppressed among us enjoys a life which millions would envy, for obvious reasons.

But the temptation for someone in my position is to engage in what Gayatri Spivak calls "retrospective hallucination."[2] She says that the ruling elites in the Third World, along with professionals and intellectuals who have their origins in the Third World, reconstruct their own history or, to put it another way, re-invent their roots, which they claim spring from an historical world of uninterrupted ethnicity and nationhood that existed before the take-over of imperialist and colonial culture.

This re-invention becomes a rhetorical trope that locates such people in a traditional stereotype within which cultures are fixed and separated in history, partly because this particular view of culture has been, in our time, the official gateway to the transnational academic and business world in Europe and the USA. I think of the Trinidadian novelist V.S. Naipaul, who resurrected his role in an Indian caste system that his family had abandoned when they went to the Caribbean, and who, consistent to the end, has recently been supporting the attempts of Hindu nationalists to link themselves with a pure pre-Muslim Hindu culture. But the history of postcolonial and migrant intellectual effort is layered with this kind of affirmation, and the rhetoric, during the last couple of decades, has also begun to conflate a reconstructed nationhood with the historical roots of migrant identity. That is to say, the spokesmen and spokeswomen of migration now tend to trace migrant identity to a precolonial and autonomous ethnicity, an autonomous nationhood, an ancient paradise, from which the migrants have been somehow exiled. Of course, migrant academics, writers, and artists have not been slow to identify themselves with this over-arching popular narrative.

---

[1] Frantz Fanon, *The Wretched of the Earth*, tr. Constance Farrington, preface by Jean–Paul Sartre (*Les damnés de la terre*, 1961; New York: Grove, 1963).

[2] Gayatri Spivak, "Who Claims Alterity?" in *Remaking History*, ed. Barbara Kruger & Phil Mariana (Seattle W A : Bay, 1989): 275.

We are also forced, I would say, into this position by a framework of popular racism which calls on us to trace the history of cultures through a kind of arena of separate development, as if cultures existed in a series of boxes, distinct from each other, and distinct from the world in which they exist. The result of the tradition of retrospection is that, for the migrants, their assertion of dignity, self respect or even humanity is supposed to be a constant recall of an imagined cultural tradition, an instant recollection of exclusive cultural roots, as if there was no other way of convincing society about their worth.

But as a black writer with a migrant background, now a citizen of a European country, Britain, I have to be conscious that my actual experience offers a continual challenge to this rhetoric of retrospection. For instance, English is my native language. Like most Caribbeans and many Africans, I grew up speaking both standard English and a dialect of standard English. In the retrospective tradition, it has become fashionable to interrogate our Atlantic dialects for African survivals, but it is equally possible and rather more obvious to trace the dominant influence of Elizabethan English, the language of Shakespeare and the King James Bible, along with a number of archaic regional dialects, notably from the seafaring southwestern coast of England. The point, however, is that, as a reader and writer, my experience of language located me in a tradition where such figures as Chaucer, Shakespeare, and Dickens figured largely, and drawing upon the richness and complexity of my own language involved my entering and exploring a culture which had evolved at some distance from the circumstances in which I had grown up. According to the arguments of postcolonial retrospection, this was transgressive behaviour – a rejection of the task of reconstructing one or the other nativist tradition. But as every genuine artist knows, creativity is a matter of grappling with the landscape in which you find yourself. It seemed to me, when I began to write fiction, that resurrecting an imagined utopia in order to describe my identity would be a sterile approach, an intellectual cul-de-sac, whose likely consequence might have been to shut me off from my environment rather than to liberate me for constructive engagement with my fellows.

So I want to distinguish my approach to migration from what I would like to call traditional forms of migration studies: that is, the sort of study which springs from certain major lines of sociological enquiry, and which places the phenomenon of migration – the act of people moving across borders to settle in different places – in the context of social conflict and political anxiety. I want to make this distinction because it seems to me that this sociological thematization has had the effect of persistently distorting our understanding both of cultures and of the cultural consequences of migration.

Of course, sociological enquiry forms an integral part of the background to the study of any aspect of migration. After all, it is essential to count numbers in order to understand where people are, what they are doing, and how to help. We have become very good at this in Britain. We know, for instance, that migrants and the children of migrants have been excluded from certain occupations, that our system of public education has allowed a shameful proportion of migrant children to emerge without useful qualifications. We know that recruitment of migrants and their children into the police force, the Civil Service, and so on has been blocked by discrimination. We know also many of the mechanisms which control this situation. The real problem, however, is to find solutions – and after two decades of revelation, discussion, and retraining, there is now a growing realization that, if there is any answer to the problems we face, it lies in an understanding and a remodelling of the political and social culture we inhabit.

Britain began to tackle the issue earlier than its Continental neighbours, partly because our colonialist history created conditions in which migration became a central political issue during the mid-twentieth century, partly because our cities and a number of our institutions had already begun to be reshaped by the fact of migration. On the other hand, this also led to an early realization that a purely sociological approach to these issues was not entirely useful. It became apparent, therefore, that culture was the only medium that could provide a framework for the solutions which had to be sought.

In Britain, the product of this understanding was the concept of multiculturalism. Some scholars, notably Wolfgang Welsch,[3] have already outlined cogent and convincing critiques of multiculturalism in the theoretical field, but I want to discuss the term here within specific historical circumstances and to outline specific consequences which flow from its use, because multiculturalism was, of course, a term already in use in various settings, but in Britain it achieved popular status as a response to specific conditions. Every country approaches its identity with a certain flexibility which allows it to attach new labels to whatever its citizens perceive to be the contemporary condition of life. For instance, in the 1960s when London was thought to be on

---

[3] See Wolfgang Welsch's essay "On Acquisition and Possession of Commonalities" in the present volume.

the cutting edge of fashion, popular music, and style, the city was referred to as 'swinging London'; a trivial example, but one gets the point.

In the case of 'multiculturalism', it is crucial to note that it entered our popular vocabulary during a specific period (in the second half of the 1990s) and within a specific context. When my brother Trevor and myself began working on the TV programme and the book about the Windrush at the end of 1996,[4] it seemed to us that 'multicultural' was a term that was making claims about British society which were more or less false. So we used the title "The irresistible rise of multiracial Britain." But between the conception and the actual anniversary of the Windrush landing, a number of things happened. First, the murder of Stephen Lawrence and the subsequent McPherson enquiry which characterized a number of British institutions and authorities as 'institutionally racist'. This was a drama which played itself out in front of the TV cameras and in the daily headlines of tabloid newspapers. Secondly, Labour won the General Election and ushered in the first age of New Labour. Thirdly, there was a campaign for the mayor's office in London which was won by Ken Livingston, the man who had originally created a species of rainbow coalition to support the Greater London Council.

In hindsight, the political and social anxiety of the Stephen Lawrence affair, the rebranding instincts of New Labour, and the political opportunism of the mayoral campaign were all gathered up and reflected in the long aftermath of Windrush. It was also obvious that we needed a new brand name to describe what was happening to the British population, especially in our major cities. Up to that point, 'multiracial' had been a more or less acceptable code word for the changing population in our cities, and the eclipse of the term is instructive. Clearly, multiracialism would not serve, partly because of the difficulties of definition; multiracialism was rather too closely associated with Afro-Caribbeans and a number of ethnic groups were uncomfortable with the term. In any case, multiracialism served as a persistent reminder of conflict and oppression, the sort of thing the politicians in particular wanted us to forget. For example, our Minister of Culture, Chris Smith, was deeply committed to a cultural diversity that would feature the inclusion of homosexuals, language groups, and so on. So multiculturalism emerged from this background as an emblem of a diversity which had an official imprimatur

---

[4] Mike Phillips & Trevor Phillips, *Windrush: The Irresistible Rise of Multi-Racial Britain* (London: HarperCollins, 1998).

or, to put it another way, had become part of an official strategy for
containing the implications of a social and political crisis.

But multiculturalism offered different meanings to different people. It was
more or less devoid of challenging content, since the phrase merely referred
to the existence of different cultures in the same place, while for a number of
people it was, at the same time, symbolic of elements they hoped to embrace:
equality, tolerance, and so on. Ironically, even the right-wing and racist parties, deadly opponents of multiracialism or what they might have described as
race-mixing, recognized the advantages of a multicultural arrangement in
which each 'culture' could maintain its exclusivity behind various social barriers.

The problem has been that, on the one hand, multiculturalism plied a
rhetoric about the coexistence of cultures from all over the world; we demonstrated that by supporting Hindu religious festivals and the Notting Hill Car-
nival, among other things. We had a high visibility of black and Asian people,
especially in popular entertainment and music. Obligatory respect was paid
by politicians and public figures to the idea that there were several different
cultures in Britain which enjoyed equal status.

The reality of life in the multicultural state was, however, very different.
Multiculturalism had its shareholders, of course; the rubric had made life
easier for a number of institutions and authorities, who were able to retreat or
delay such issues as equal-opportunity recruitment by putting a multicultural
policy in place which devoted relatively insignificant funding to supporting
religious festivals and oral reminiscing. Multinational corporations and local
enterprises also benefitted hugely from the commodification of identity that
was implicit in our operation of the multicultural. On the other side of the
equation were a relatively small number of artists, entertainers, entrepreneurs,
and administrators from the ethnic minorities, whose task it was to execute
the strategy.

At the same time, we had a developing tradition of discrimination and
marginalization towards those people who came from the cultures we were
celebrating. The idea of cultural diversity also started to become a useful tool
for maintaining the barriers originally put in place by racial discrimination.
To put it crudely, the argument said 'you have a culture which we will support and praise, but that implies that we don't have to make room in our culture for you'. Thus multiculturalism, instead of being a process which made
connections between social, political, and economic conditions, became a sort
of bridge which allowed various people to step lightly from one phase of

history to another imaginary phase without having to dabble in the dangerous waters of cultural conflict.

Now, one can see the potential in this for a kind of benign cultural apartheid, which is precisely why the organizing principle of my own writing is concerned with trying to understand how migration fits into a framework of theoretical argument about the development of art and letters in the English language, rather than trying to recover notions of ethnic or cultural purity. The exploitative potential of the multicultural concept has precisely to do with its reading of cultures as autonomous and isolated from each other in history, but it is true that migration and its cultural effects can be read in entirely different ways. It is also true that the trends associated with migration have begun to set in motion decisive changes in the way that cultures, their relationships, and their interactions are understood.

The first thing is to identify the object of discussion. Migration is not, of course, a twentieth-century phenomenon. People were moving across borders long before there were borders. The populations of every continent owe their origins to various kinds of migration, and they have not stopped moving ever since. I am not going to argue the virtues of migration, if only because the thing was self-evident even before we ever heard of famous migrants like Arnold Schwarzenegger (arguably Austria's most successful migrant). Migration has nearly always been associated with a species of dramatic intervention in the social, cultural, and political forms of particular locations. We habitually speak of these movements of peoples in terms of conquest, invasion, and imperialist ideology, fostering the idea that when two cultures meet the superior culture inevitably destroys or drives out its inferior. We also talk about civilization as a matter of ownership, in which the conquerors imposed their culture or took over the cultures they found. Imperialist Europe and its emigrants even believed that they introduced the idea of culture to territories in which such notions did not exist. I am thinking here about Joseph Conrad and his novella *Heart of Darkness*[5] – a title which became part of the English language to describe Africa – and in a sense we see these notions persisting in the attitudes that the Palestinian academic Edward Said described as Orientalism.[6] There are obvious connections between these ideas about civilization and our attitudes to nationality and citizenship which were born and nurtured

---

[5] Joseph Conrad, *Heart of Darkness* (London: Dent & Sons, 1902).
[6] Edward W. Said, *Orientalism* (London: Routledge & Kegan Paul, 1978).

here in Europe, because the themes that run through the development of the nation-state were concerned not only with who belonged to the nation and why, but also with where the boundaries lay between inclusion and exclusion.

But while there is no doubt that the ideology of race and nation which policed these boundaries pervades the practice of European artists and writers in the modern period, there were also other interesting ways of talking about nationhood, rooted in other kinds of reality. It can also be argued that artists and writers have persistently chosen other paths through which they have opened up an avenue of escape from the straitjacket of nation and nationality, as well as from the limitations of race and ethnicity.

As has become obvious from the above, I am concerned with trying to understand how migration fits into the development of arts and letters in Britain over the last century. This is partly because I want to challenge the notion that, in the world of ideas, migration represents a sudden and alien incursion into the ecology of the arts in Europe. The meaning of the phenomenon is not forged in an isolated crucible where only migrants live, but instead, the effects of migration are part of how modernity and modernization have shaped our world, in particular the world of culture and the arts.

In this process, I cannot talk about migration as if it were merely an aspect of race and racism – not because those things do not deserve a focus, but because the issues of migration go well beyond anxieties about the colour of people's skins. I also cannot talk about migration without discussing modernity, because modernity offers us new insights into migration.

For instance, there is a moment in Europe, the start of the Enlightenment and the extraordinary movements of the eighteenth century, where the nation state emerges to dominate the rhetoric of identity as well as to define the boundaries between inclusion and exclusion. One product of Enlightenment thought that went along with the development of the nation-state was a secularization which encouraged Europeans to question the religious rubric in which the soul and its relationship with the City of God was the index of the individual. The result of this questioning was a state of mind in which the self could be identified with the idea of the nation. You can collect a bundle of characteristics, assemble them into a single personality, and offer this individual as a synonym for the nation. The nation itself could be thought of, or described, as an individual – for example, the French Marianne, the American

Uncle Sam, the English John Bull and so on – all products of this junction between individuals and the symbolism of the nation.

But as we pass through the nineteenth century, our ideas about what constituted the individual self change radically. In Freud,[7] we see the argument
that we are not born as ourselves – we acquire a self which is already stressed
and divided by internal conflict, fractured into ego, superego, and unconscious – and these things are held together by entering into a symbolic order
of language and culture. So we arrive at the end-point of the European Enlightenment, already in a condition of serious doubt about the status of the
individual self. This is a climax which brings on industrialism, control of
information and centralization of its distribution, capitalism, military power.

Modernism goes hand in hand with this development: it entails aesthetic
self consciousness, interest in language, rejection of realism in favour of 'the
real', abandonment of linearity in favour of montage and simultaneity,
Romanticism or emphasis on the value of aesthetic experience, depth and universal mytho-poetic meaning, privileging fragmentation, valorizing of avant-
garde culture.

Modernist poets like T.S. Eliot provide us with illuminating descriptions of
these states of mind – the beginning of "The Lovesong of J. Alfred Prufrock,"
for instance, in which you can read this divided consciousness, this new
awareness of a fragmented identity:

> Let us go then, you and I,
> When evening is spread out against the sky
> Like a patient etherised upon a table;
> Let us go, through certain half deserted streets,
> The muttering retreats
> Of restless nights in one-night cheap hotels
> And sawdust restaurants with oyster–shells[8]

In true modernist style, poets like Eliot reflected on the unreliability of words
themselves, how they crack and break down into imprecision. This is a metaphor for the way in which identity in modern times could never hold a single

---

[7] Henk de Berg, *Freud's Theory and Its Uses in Literary and Cultural Studies: An
Introduction* (Rochester N Y : Camden House, 2003).

[8] T.S. Eliot, "The Lovesong of J. Alfred Prufrock" (1915), in *The Waste Land and Other
Poems* (1940; London: Faber & Faber, 1975): 9.

irreducible form – "Things fall apart / the centre cannot hold," which is the
famous quotation from Yeats, his contemporary.[9]

James Joyce goes further in highlighting the nature of language as a reflection of fragmented identity: parodies of advertising, journalism, literature,
science, colloquial speech, and classical analogies all get tossed in to focus on
the tools we use to construct meaning. What emerges in *Finnegans Wake* is
what Joyce calls "the waters of babalog"[10] in which meaning breaks down
and flows into the shape of the narrative; the waters re-creating and creating
new meanings and contradictory statements.

This brings us back to our particular tranche of modernism, migration,
which has been going on while all this history has been in process. In the century before the last one, the Enlightenment brought the concepts associated
with non-Christian, non-representational, pre-industrial art into the Western
canon. The Cubists and their cohorts, after all, imported ideas about 'the
Primitive' to justify their disdain for neoclassical and realist modes. After all,
the transcultural has been walking among us for a very long time.

What is important, however, is the notion that the migrations which alter
cultural perspectives in the twentieth century do not emerge from isolated
moments of inspiration or compulsion. Instead, they are the resolution of
processes which were set in motion during preceding centuries by the operations of the most powerful nation-states. After all, what did the empires of the
nineteenth century give their subjects? They gave them modernity in the
shape of speed, industrialization, the irresistible export of capital, instanta-
neous communication, centralized authority, universal surveillance, a culture
of quasi-liberal despotism.

One difficulty for the imperial mission was reconciling the political libe-
ralism of the Enlightenment with its most important achievement, the nation-
state, within the framework of a rapidly expanding transnational capitalism.
The logic of the nation was to impose cultural barriers between itself and the
others who existed in the outer darkness. At the same time, the corporate
needs of trade and military dominance drove its members outwards to engage
with those others, but rationality itself created social and cultural stresses
which could only be resolved by a political rhetoric that justified despotism of
one kind or the other.

---

[9] W.B. Yeats, "The Second Coming" (1920), in Yeats, *Selected Poetry* (London: Macmillan, 1974): 99.

[10] James Joyce, *Finnegans Wake* (London: Faber & Faber, 1939): 103.

Modernity provided an arena in which all these different elements operated. As a result of the movements of the last three centuries or so, we had in
the late-twentieth century a globalized space in which the movements of
migrants into regions like Europe resembled an instruction manual about the
effects of global culture on our ideas about identity and the nature of the self.

In effect, migration in the twentieth century was one of those extraordinary
trends that created an impact which forced the realization that we lived in the
middle of a peculiar break with the past. In addition, we were moving towards a new aesthetic where the boundaries between art and culture were to
become blurred, where culture and commerce could not easily be distinguished one from the other, where art and everyday life could be the same,
where the constant flow of signs and images turned in a perpetual conversation about meaning. Ironically, the practice of a modernist aesthetic coexisted
comfortably with a traditional view about the ownership of cultures. Joyce
himself, in *The Portrait of The Artist as a Young Man*, has Stephen Daedalus
say, after a conversation with an Englishman: "the language in which we are
speaking is his before it is mine [...] His language, so familiar and so foreign,
will always be for me an acquired speech. I have not made or accepted its
words."[11] What stands out here is the sheer oddity of the sentiment from one
of the premier exponents of the English language, someone who shaped the
way we speak and understand its idioms, and this apparent contradiction is a
demonstration of the way in which the traditional view of culture could survive hand in hand with modernist practice.

Artists are called upon to occupy a particular role in the business of ar-
ranging and fixing identity, because the pursuit of any kind of artistic endeavour is a public statement. Art and artists emerge from history, and at the
same time re-create a history of their own activities. So, in talking about the
relationship between black British artists, black British identity, and some of
the dilemmas discussed here, I need to address what it means to be black British, because, although we use the label all the time nowadays, it is largely the
practice of artists that has called this label into being, and what they have
done goes beyond a cosmetic multiculturalism and begins a reconfiguration
of identity. In fact, we needed this term to describe a particular shift in aware-

---

[11] James Joyce, *A Portrait of the Artist as a Young Man* (1916; St Albans: Triad, 1977):
172.

ness which had to do not only with ourselves but also with what was happening inside the UK.

We know a great deal about the constitutional and legal framework within which British citizenship has evolved over the last fifty years. This was a political struggle, which went on over the space of fifty years and opened up new categories of British identity, and made a new statement about citizenship in Britain. It is also clear that the process is not at an end. It has made possible a constitutional statement about our citizenship, which does not depend on ethnicity or racial origins. But, at the same time, this political formula does not account for the way individuals perceive themselves. My passport tells me where I can go, for instance, and even what I am able to do in certain cases. But it does not tell me who I am. This 'who I am', however, goes to the heart of a fundamental issue: the problem of how our notions of self are constructed.

Many postcolonial writers tended to suggest that an individual's identity was an autonomous entity – an *a priori* characteristic of skin colour or geographical location, something to do with the individual's relationship to a particular ethnic group or a particular place, a particular piece of territory, and they were accordingly concerned with mapping the outlines of an authentic self which sprang out of a specific historical continuity, and whose health could be determined by the extent to which it resisted the invasion of alien elements and cultural dominance. It is this background that makes the phrase 'black British' necessary and challenging, because, in the circumstances, it constituted a new argument about identity, which altered certain boundaries and created new possibilities.

For instance, the conventional way of talking about migration in Britain almost always focuses on the 'moment of arrival', because there is always a demand that the ethnic minorities should be framed within this 'moment of arrival' – a moment which appears to value and privilege the arrival but which also is a much more powerful argument that defines cultures as separate and alien to each other and extends that definition into the past. But this moment of arrival is an imaginary moment, because there were lots of black people in Britain before then, and we have begun to discover that the history of the black British community truly begins, not with the moment of arrival, but with a routine daily negotiation about crossing boundaries and barriers, about expanding limits. At the heart of this routine negotiation is a reshaping of the self, and in the process what emerges is a divided, fragmentary, contradictory consciousness, which we were obliged to take for granted.

Now, I would argue that any individual consciousness is determined or over-determined by compulsory relationships and external processes. No one is a simple and autonomous unity. This is the point at which we all emerged from the long transformation of the post-Enlightenment world. In the case of the black British, we were obliged to be conscious of the sense in which our selves were characterized by compulsory relationships with the people and the environment we found in the UK. This environment was composed of any number of different things, it was made up of a bundle of economic and social features, forming a horizontal marketplace of cultures, coercive pressures, as well as a set of narratives about identity, about what people were.

So our reshaping of identity was determined by a continuing negotiation about the nature of language, about the meanings of behaviour, about things that were said, about how to learn, what we learned and what we taught. It was determined also by the internal play between a specific and singular history: i.e. the history of our own families, the history of the group to which that family belonged, and the historical circumstances which dominate the lived experience of a person or persons in this arena. For instance, the coming into being of the whole concept of black Britishness is associated with a number of historical crises which are very important in the life of our community – the Notting Hill riots, the struggle against the 'Sus Law', the New Cross fire, the death of Stephen Lawrence, and so on. These historical circumstances frame the way we see ourselves and the way that vision of ourselves develops. All these elements and more go to make up the identity of any individual. What makes the narrative British is that these things took place within specific geographical and cultural limits and were determined by the conditions and processes operating within the limits of these particular boundaries.

So the development of the concept 'black British' is complex; it takes place over time and exists in a creative tension with a modernist conception of self-hood and a particular concept of individuality. It takes this reconstituted individual out of the private realm into the public arena – a shift which immediately creates an argument about the recasting of national identity.

But black artists in Britain work within the framework of race thinking. Audiences and people in general look at our work with the question in mind, "What is he saying about us? Does he like us? Is he attacking us? Is he condemning us?" rather than asking: "What is he saying?" If I say that we live in a framework where racial divisions determine our view of almost everything, I am not making an accusation, merely stating a class of fact which accounts for many things. It accounts, for instance, for the fact that the inventiveness and creativity of black British artists has traditionally been submerged in a narrative about race, so that the productions of Caribbean, African-American, Asian or African artists are somehow perceived as offering the same view of the world as that of a 'black British' artist. This is a consequence of a framework of ideas dominated by race, as well as by generations of the "retrospective hallucination" pinpointed by Spivak.[12]

Most black British artists, however, come from a peasant or semi-rural, working-class background which never completely shared in the nationalist, postcolonial reconstruction of Third-World history. The reality in which their work is grounded happens to be this routine renegotiation of identity in their new homes, where the historical formation of diasporic blackness, as well as universalist notions about an 'uncorrupted' identity, or about unbroken connections with black roots, have no actual connection with their day-to-day experiences. This leads to a fundamental academic error, where contemporary critics periodize very different tendencies and individuals within a simplistic framework determined by their race and the place where they happen to be, without a sense of the vital differences about the intellectual landscape which shapes and contains them.

In fact, the authentic identity of many migrant communities begins with the tension of operating several different selves at the same time. One sees this most clearly if one lives through the process of operating a new language, new religious ideas, and new manners with some of the new East European migrants. The consequence of this tension is that, as migrant artists, the choices we make are often transgressive or at least unrecognizable within a context which demands from us an unambiguous black outline – 'black', that is, in terms of a rigidly stereotyped conception of culture.

Until very recently, typically the general context in which black British writers' work was received tended to regard us as another group of blacks who simply happened to be where we were, only notable for the colour of our skins, while the demand from us was to reproduce the 'drama of race'. In the present day, it is possible to see an equivalent being created where the drama that is demanded from East Europeans is the drama of difference – a drama rooted in the distinction between rich and poor.

The suggestion here is that, typically, as artists, our major struggle is not so much with dramatic manifestations of racism, although we struggle with

---

[12] See note 2 above.

those too. You walk around London, and in some parts of it you can easily get the sense that you are in a vibrant, multiracial, multicultural community. You will see lots of black people on television, reading the news, for example. This will happen everywhere in Europe as minorities settle in – but it will become increasingly apparent that the struggle we are engaged in is fundamentally concerned with the routine daily endeavour of representing who we think we are, within our specific circumstances, with unlocking and exploring the specific history from which we emerge and with finding outlets for that enterprise.

By contrast, in the past, black artists in the UK were, traditionally, more rigidly confined behind the barriers of ethnicity, where we were required to sketch out a picture of an alien identity. On the other hand, the necessity of breaking free of these limits, in order to talk about the changes which were occurring in our own lives, and about our relationship with our new environment, is precisely what gives the work of black British artists its radical tenor, and the potential for radicalizing our nation's view of culture and what it means.

Again, I want to distinguish this enterprise from the postcolonial process in which artists are concerned with a very different view of identity. Our work, therefore, has generally described the process of becoming a different kind of individual self, a process which takes place in a sustained dialogue or conversation with all the elements that go to make up this new self; and we clearly see the emergence here of a new consciousness, which springs from the time and place that contains it and is linked to various other narratives about migration, about urban experience, about tensions between nationality and citizenship.

So what you are reading when you read my books, for instance, is a part of the mechanism by which the concept of the black British came into being, a way of seeing, a reconfiguration of selfhood, which is a necessary precondition of the transcultural process, and, on the other side of the equation, all this has had a specific and interesting effect on the culture and identity of the UK.

We, the British, recognized this fact in what I describe as the cosmetic rhetoric of British multiculturalism, but this is precisely why the term and the concept have had to be challenged, because the rhetoric of inclusion conceals the fierceness and intensity of the struggle we are presently waging over cultural territory and over the identity of the state. At this moment in Britain, we face a long constitutional argument associated with Celtic nationalism. The establishment of parliaments in Scotland and Wales is only the beginning of a debate about the retention or dissolution of the British Union. In the last few years another argument has emerged: what does it mean to be English for someone who, whether or not they were born there, lives in and identifies with the country England, as opposed to any other constituent country of the British Union?

If we use that definition, a substantial part of the English population now has fairly recent origins in Ireland, Scotland, Wales, Central and Eastern Europe, Africa, Asia, and the Caribbean. This fact is rapidly rendering archaic the long-held view of Englishness as an ethnic club, and we now begin to recognize that we are in the middle of a cultural struggle to re-interpret exactly what Englishness and Britishness mean, to re-interpret who has the right to say who we are, and towards what we should be sympathetic. This struggle is partly the result of a sort of sympathetic vibration provoked by the significance of the changes going on in the body of migrants.

Black British and Asian writing is within the epicentre of this vibration, and central to the recognition that a new debate has begun to organize categories of identity, opening up a new landscape. Within this landscape we begin to go beyond the pre-existing, the *a priori* definition of our nationhood which I heard my fellow citizens outline as I grew up. They used to say: 'We know what we are, because that is what we are. And if you have to talk about it, you are not one of us'. British writing of every kind now has begun (albeit with a certain tentativeness) to take advantage of the opportunities opened up by this new debate where people are not saying, 'We know what we are'. Instead, they are saying, 'We don't know what we are and we have to decide'.

I speak now about the writers of migration, rather than about migrant writers, because in this new atmosphere it becomes the task of writers from any and every part of the population to understand and explore new meanings.

At the same time, this new landscape of debate, argument, and discussion within England and Britain points to the potential throughout Europe for assembling an alternative to our traditional ideas of identity and its congruence with traditional ideas about the nation. This is because it is actually taking place in the context of discussions which are cranking up all over this continent: Germany, France, Italy, and the countries of Central and Eastern Europe.

The major features which the black British experience and its literature make explicit in this discussion are the phenomenon of migration, movement, and mobility, the renegotiation of selfhood, the historicizing of new identities and the reconstitution of a dominant culture to reflect again new identities which are often in conflict. All these things together can flow, separate, join up in the same space, coexist. They not only coexist, but actually offer the possibility of re-creating a single culture with very different facets.

So the meanings associated with this experience seem to open up a transcultural vista where it may become possible to accommodate all these elements in the same space without massacres, daily murders, orders. In this vision we see the future transformed, and it is a vision on which artists who emerge from the transcultural experience of migration have been nurtured, because there was no other way. And if it is a dream, it is the artist's job to extend the reach of our imagination about the potential of real life and to dream dreams about how things could be if we had the will.

Works Cited

Conrad, Joseph. *Heart of Darkness* (London: Dent & Sons, 1902).

de Berg, Henk. *Freud's Theory and Its Uses in Literary and Cultural Studies: An Introduction* (Rochester N Y: Camden House, 2003).

Eliot, T.S. "The Lovesong of J. Alfred Prufrock" (1915), in Eliot, *The Waste Land and Other Poems* (1940; London: Faber, 1975): 9–14.

Fanon, Frantz. *The Wretched of the Earth*, tr. Constance Farrington, preface by Jean–Paul Sartre (*Les damnés de la terre*, 1961; New York: Grove, 1963).

Joyce, James. *A Portrait of the Artist as a Young Man* (1916; St Albans: Triad, 1977).

——. *Finnegans Wake* (London: Faber & Faber, 1939).

Phillips, Mike, & Trevor Phillips. *Windrush: The Irresistible Rise of Multiracial Britain* (London: HarperCollins, 1998).

Said, Edward W. *Orientalism* (London: Routledge & Kegan Paul, 1978).

Spivak, Gayatri Chakravorty. "Who Claims Alterity?" in *Remaking History*, ed. Barbara Kruger & Phil Mariana (Seattle W A: Bay, 1989): 269–92.

Yeats, W.B. "The Second Coming" (1920), in Yeats, *Selected Poetry* (London: Macmillan, 1974): 99.

◄❖►

From the Belly of the Fish
— Jewish Writers in English in Israel: Transcultural Perspectives

AXEL STÄHLER

D
IASPORIC WRITING, transcending borders and cultures, is, by its very nature, a test case for transcultural and transnational studies. But what about diasporic writing that has come home? There is a sizable community of Jewish writers in English in Israel.[1] Yet their position is a difficult one, for they suffer severe problems of integration into the culture of their, usually freely, chosen homeland, whose language, at least for artistic purposes, they cannot or do not want to adopt: "For many of these writers," Karen Alkalay–Gut observes, "there is a degree of 'Diaspora' in their work, a sense of a cultural, literary and personal center elsewhere, that is concurrent with a varying but steady commitment to Israel as the homeland." This phenomenon, "of being physically Home in the Holy Land, but native and/or loyal to another language," has been labelled by Alkalay–Gut a "double diaspora" and qualified as "almost unique to the Zionist experi-

---

[1] Karen Alkalay–Gut, herself a poet writing in English, a professor of English at Tel Aviv University, and Chair of the Israel Association of Writers in English (IAWE), estimates that there are about "500 professional and semi-professional writers of literature in English in Israel, in addition to at least a thousand people who make writing their hobby"; Alkalay–Gut, "Double Diaspora: English Writers in Israel," *Judaism* 51 (2002): 459.

ence."[2] "Most Anglos," she concludes, "remained loyal to English, and either deserted writing or Israel, or fell silent."[3]

My purpose, in this article, is to have a closer look at those who did not fall silent and who did not only continue to write in English in their chosen homeland but also gave their concerns a voice by organizing themselves into a professional body. For it seems to me that an exposition of the cultural 'loquation',[4] of the transcultural spot Jewish writers in English in Israel find themselves in may well contribute to an understanding of what constitutes Jewish literature in English. For one thing, the diasporic origins of most anglophone Jewish writers in Israel to some degree appear like a cross-section *en miniature* of Jewish existence in the anglophone diaspora. With all due caution, their 'loquation' may therefore perhaps be considered in some ways to be paradigmatic of the larger context. In addition, the very tenacity with which they adhere to the diasporic language even in Israel suggests a particular force of cohesion which relates them both to the cultural contexts of the anglophone world and to each other. And this, too, may perhaps be seen as paradigmatic, and as a version *en miniature* of the transcultural and transnational intertwinings of Jewish literature in English in the global context.[5]

In 1997, the Israel Association of Writers in English (I A W E),[6] itself established in 1980, issued an anthology of poems that were, as it says on the

---

[2] Alkalay–Gut, "Double Diaspora," 458–59. Usually, the term "double diaspora" is understood 'quantitatively' rather than 'qualitatively' and alludes to consecutive displacements within the diaspora; see, for example, Sophia Lehmann, "In Search of a Mother Tongue: Locating Home in Diaspora," *MELUS* 23 (1998): 101, 111, and the discussion of "double or even triple diasporization" in Monika Fludernik, "The Diasporic Imaginary: Postcolonial Reconfigurations in the Context of Multiculturalism," in *Diaspora and Multiculturalism*, ed. Monika Fludernik (Cross/Cultures 66; Amsterdam & New York: Rodopi, 2003): xxvi.

[3] Alkalay–Gut, "Double Diaspora," 459.

[4] A contraction of 'location' and the Latin *loquor* ('to talk, to speak'; cf. 'locution'), this self-fashioned 'neologism' alludes to Homi Bhabha's *The Location of Culture* (London: Routledge, 1993). It will subsequently be used to signify the inseparable connection between language and culture and to refer to the Jewish writers' situation and self-positioning between languages and cultures.

[5] For Jewish writing in English, see also *Anglophone Jewish Literature*, ed. Axel Stähler (London & New York: Routledge, 2007).

[6] In April 2004, membership was forty-seven, according to an e-mail communication from Mark L. Levinson, I A W E mailclerk, from 15 April 2004.

IAWE website, "culled from the first several issues of *Arc*."[7] *Arc*, first published in 1982 and appearing annually, is, again as advertised on the IAWE website, "a continuing literary showcase for the members of the IAWE (Israel Association of Writers in English) and for other Israeli citizens and residents. It includes both original works in English and translations into English from the many other languages of Israeli writers."[8] A 'distillate' of *Arc*, *English Poetry from Israel*, according to the blurb, is an anthology that

> presents a sampling of poets writing in English in Israel. Of various backgrounds and native cultures, they left their homelands of their own choice, not because of a tragic past, hostile government or social persecution. And yet, at some level, they remain foreigners within this community: often a unique opportunity for independence and perspective.[9]

The anthology was edited by the poets Karen Alkalay–Gut, Lois Unger, and Zygmunt Frankel, and Frankel also designed the collection's cover illustration. This shows, next to the prominent lettering of the title, a stark, woodcut-like image of a hunched human figure inside the belly of a fish. The allusion to Jonah is obvious but not necessarily self-explanatory. Why, then, was this

---

[7] Quoted from http://www.geocities.com/iawe_mailbox/pubs.html (accessed 10 April 2008).

[8] Quoted from http://www.geocities.com/iawe_mailbox/pubs.html (accessed 10 April 2008).

[9] A point worth noting is that the IAWE publications are programmatically open to all (not only Jewish) writers in English who are citizens of, or resident in, Israel, see http://www.geocities.com/iawe_mailbox/pubs.html (accessed 10 April 2008). Yet statements like this seem to apply exclusively to the Jewish particular, and in fact none of the writers represented in *English Poetry from Israel* is of non-Jewish origin. The anthology includes poems by the following thirty-eight poets: Ada Aharoni, Karen Alkalay–Gut, Rachel Tzvia Back, Ruth Beker, Gavriel Ben–Ephraim, Edward Codish, Eugene Dubnov, Elazar (= Larry Freifeld), Zygmunt Frankel, Shalom [Seymour] Freedman, William Freedman, Robert Friend, Gershom Gorenberg, Aloma Halter, Jean Kadmon, Shirley Kaufman, Sharon Kessler, Olga Kirsch, Charles Kormos, Orit Kruglanski, Lami (= Lami Halperin), Mark L. Levinson, Simon Lichman, Fay Lipshitz, Rochelle Mass, Joanna Morris, Shimon Palmer, Reena Ribalow, Riva Rubin, Raquel Sanchez, Reva Sharon, Richard E. Sherwin, Norman Simms, Elaine M. Solowey, Lois Ungar, Roger White, Chayym Zeldis, and Linda Zisquit. In the "Introduction" to *Arc* 13, explicit mention is made of the fact that only Jewish writers contributed to this volume, although its thematic focus might have been of particular interest also to Arab-Israeli authors; see Jeff Green (= Jeffrey M. Green) & David Margolis, "Introduction" to *Arc: Journal of the Israel Association of Writers in English* 13 (1999): 1.

particular 'emblematic' image chosen for the evidently programmatic self-presentation of the IAWE? I will return to this later in my essay.

The programmatic quality of *English Poetry from Israel* is elaborated on in more detail in the editors' preface on "The English Poet in Israel."[10] Here, the Israeli anglophone writers' alleged independence is emphasized once more, as is their continuing alienation within the society they elect to live in. Their predicament is largely attributed to their choice of language:

> Some have the common problem of learning a language. Some have never tried to learn Hebrew and exist comfortably among their countrymen in this multicultural society. Others speak perfect Hebrew but remain loyal to their mother tongue.[11]

That it should be possible to escape exposure to other cultures in a multicultural society seems to belie the very concept of transculturality, and I would suggest that, on closer scrutiny, none of the poems in *English Poetry from Israel* stands in splendid isolation. Indeed, any such notion seems to be revoked by the next paragraph, which is, in effect, a proclamation of the transculturality of the anglophone Israeli writer – the result of border crossings, temporal and geographical as well as cultural and national or political:

> There are writers who perceive their foreignness a handicap, and others who see it as an opportunity for independence and perspective. Even within this small community of writers, there are marked differences. Geography and atmosphere play a part: Jerusalem writers often have different subject matter or moods than Tel Aviv writers, and those in the desert and kibbutzim may have alternative narratives to relate. Background and native culture are additional factors. A poet steeped in the American tradition will begin from a different position than another brought up on British literature. But there is one factor which unites them all – an obstinate, sometimes even perverse, affection for the English language.[12]

As is suggested here, *English Poetry from Israel* appears to be mainly a document of the diversity of writers in English in Israel, the contributors to the

---

[10] Karen Alkalay–Gut, Lois Unger & Zygmunt Frankel, "The English Poet in Israel," in *English Poetry from Israel*, ed. Karen Alkalay–Gut, Lois Unger & Zygmunt Frankel (Tel Aviv: IAWE, 1997): 7.

[11] Alkalay–Gut, Unger & Frankel, "The English Poet in Israel," 7.

[12] Alkalay–Gut, Unger & Frankel, "The English Poet in Israel," 7.

anthology hailing from all over the anglophone diaspora,[13] conjoined only through their choice of language and the common experience of foreignness. (Their 'Jewishness', quite intriguingly, is not explicitly evoked as common ground; perhaps because it is taken for granted, although the publications of IAWE are open to contributions by non-Jewish Israelis as well.[14])

Yet I would argue that *English Poetry from Israel* should be considered in conjunction with the two issues of *Arc* immediately following its publication. They both concern themselves with set topics and progressively aim at a thematic coherence lacking in the earlier volume. In fact, if seen together, all three publications seem to follow a continuous course of narrowing their focus. Since editorship of *Arc* rotates,[15] this may not have been a deliberate editorial policy, yet in effect it seems to amount to a homing-in on what appears to be the central problematic of being a writer in English in Israel: the multiple and polydirectional processes of transculturation in a sustained encounter with cultural differences while still retaining the diasporic language.

Published just a few months after the anthology in autumn 1997 as a prose special and edited by Haim Chertok and Shalom Freedman, *Arc* 12 gathers contributions which are meant to "reflect some aspect of contemporary Israeli life or culture."[16] The vagueness of the thematic criterion, insufficiently defined and retrospectively acknowledged as "nettlesome"[17] by the editors, was further narrowed down in *Arc* 13. This was published after a lengthy interval

---

[13] According to the biographical notes appended to Alkalay–Gut, Unger & Frankel, ed., *English Poetry from Israel*, 68–72, of the thirty-eight contributors to the anthology more than half (twenty) were born and raised in the USA (another three, born elsewhere, spent a substantial time there before emigrating to Israel); only four were born in Britain (three lived there for a while), another three in South Africa and two in Canada; three come from Eastern Europe and are not native English speakers at all; one emigrated from Germany (via the USA), one from Egypt, one was born in France and then lived in many other countries, and only one is a native of Israel; two do not reveal where they originate from. It is tempting to see this configuration as reflecting not only the spectrum of anglophone countries of origin but also numerical proportions. However, I am not aware of any demographic survey on this subject, and for the time being this suggestion must therefore remain purely conjectural.

[14] See note 10.

[15] "Because editorship is rotated from one issue to the next, *Arc* demonstrates how aesthetic tastes and concerns vary even within the English-speaking community of Israel." Quoted from http://www.geocities.com/iawe_mailbox/pubs.html (accesed 10 April, 2008).

[16] Haim Chertok & Shalom [Seymour] Freedman, "Introduction," *Arc: Journal of the Israel Association of Writers in English* 12 (1997): 4.

[17] Chertok & Freedman, "Introduction," 4.

in summer 1999 and was given the punning title "Expatriates and Ex-Patriots" by its editors, Jeff Green and David Margolis. Intriguingly, after the programmatic effort of *Arc* 13, the journal's next issue, published in spring 2000, was "self-edited"[18] and seems to be pervaded by a certain flavour of indecision.[19] Far from giving any concerted statement of purpose or definition of collective identity, *Arc* 14, in what appears to be almost a gesture of retraction, seems to be the product of a retreat behind the notion of diversity and eschews articulation of the common, and sometimes perhaps unsettling, experience of transculturation programmatically.

This had been strongly emphasized by Green and Margolis in their "Introduction" to *Arc* 13. There, they state that "we hoped to encourage Israeli writers in English to explore the stimulating but perhaps uncomfortable space in which we function as writers in a language that is foreign to the place where we live."[20] The 'place' they refer to, obviously the state of Israel, is the contact zone of a varied multi- and, invariably, transcultural encounter, in certain respects perhaps even more varied than in the diaspora. For in Israel, the encounter with the other 'Self' – born Israelis and Jewish returnees from the global diaspora and their different cultural backgrounds, religious and secular – compounds past and present encounters with the individual's diasporic origins in a narrowly confined, and possibly 'claustrophobic',[21] space with encounters with various 'Others'. All of this takes place in a highly charged and potentially violent atmosphere under constant international scrutiny.

All of those encounters are thematically present in the IAWE publications. Yet the most basic one remains the continuous encounter with the English language and whatever this entails:

> We have [...] not given up the language we brought from the diaspora, which also means that we are still engaged in dialogue with the place we came from. Our memories of that place color our experiences in Israel, and our experiences in Israel

---

[18] "A Word of Explanation," *Arc: Journal of the Israel Association of Writers in English* 14 (2000): 4.

[19] While, in "A Word of Explanation," 4, it is claimed once again that "it is important to foster creativity in English and the other languages that writers brought to Israel, along with other precious cultural luggage," the main intention of this issue was "to introduce [members] to one another as to the public at large."

[20] Green & Margolis, "Introduction," 1.

[21] See Sidra DeKoven Ezrahi, *Booking Passage. Exile and Homecoming in the Modern Jewish Imagination* (Berkeley: U of California P, 2000): 20.

color our responses to that place when we return to it, either physically or in memory.[22]

Central to Green's and Margolis' description are the categories of experience (past and present) and of memory, which is relevant to all three temporal dimensions. Through memory past experiences reverberate into the present and, compounded with those of the present, inform expectations of the future. Any disruption of the interconnectedness of the three temporal dimensions threatens individual and collective identification schemata. This disruptive experience has been rendered evocatively by Linda Grant in her award-winning novel *When I Lived in Modern Times* (2000). In an attempt to re-create the historical consciousness of an Anglo-Jewish immigrant to postwar Mandate Palestine, the British-based author shows her narrator suffering from what amounts, in effect, a split personality. For all her memories, she says, "were in the English language and what I saw when I opened my eyes was in Hebrew, so how could I know what I was anymore."[23] Later, she remembers: "I felt as if we were all half here and half somewhere else, deprived of our native languages, stumbling over an ugly ancient tongue. We knew that we were to be re-made and re-born and we half did and half didn't want to be."[24] She has the feeling as if she were living in two spaces at the same time, as if there were two Palestines at odds with each other:

> As much as I felt that I belonged heart and soul to Zion, it was the British whose taste and idioms, language and dress, cooking and habits I knew and understood. The British were the only people who did not seem like foreigners to me, although they were the colonial, the oppressive power. They were the enemy and the paradox of my life was that the ways of the enemy were partly mine too.[25]

The experience of disruption and paradox, similar to that rendered by Grant, yet finally transcended, is also the subject of Mordechai Beck's "My Aliyah Story," published in *Arc* 13. The prose sketch of the Jerusalem-based writer ends with the British-born narrator lifting the commemorative mug of the

---

[22] Green & Margolis, "Introduction," 1.

[23] Linda Grant, *When I Lived in Modern Times* (London: Granta, 2000): 55.

[24] Grant, *When I Lived in Modern Times*, 106.

[25] *When I Lived in Modern Times*, 106.

coronation of Elizabeth II, which he brought along to Israel, and aiming it at the kitchen wall. "At that precise moment," he says,

> the years of psychological and emotional colonialism unwind inside me. The memories and nostalgia that have shackled my heart and soul pour out and turn into wings. I open the window and test the air with my new lungs. Weightless, I step out of the room and slowly, effortlessly, rise.[26]

What the narrator has finally achieved is *aliyah*. (The Hebrew word referring to Jewish immigration in the Land of Israel literally means 'to ascend, to rise'.) Beck's prose sketch chronicles three stages of *aliyah*, during the first of which the narrator perceives himself unredeemably as the 'Other', indelibly, as it seems, conditioned by his British upbringing: "Israel, says one of my inner voices, will always remain in parentheses, will never be the thing itself."[27] The second stage he experiences as one of transition: "How long does it take to make this aliyah – the internal ascent – the transcendent sort that allows you to look back and down at what you were before and continue on your way? I haven't, it seems, reached that point. I'm in permanent transition."[28] Doubts are the corollary of this stage: "But do I really want to be transformed so radically; isn't all this talk of 'ascending' just a metaphysical trap, a necessary myth justifying mundane realities?"[29] In the end, it is trivial divorce news from the British royals which makes him recognize: "So they're human after all!"[30] The myth sustaining his own continuing Britishness shattered, he gropes for the fated mug.

The question remains, however, what the narrator in Beck's prose sketch actually rises to. Obviously, he still adheres to English as his preferred language of artistic expression, although it is central to the foreignness he experiences, as he had suggested earlier: "Between the unresolved yearnings, I wonder exactly what is it that I can't get rid of. Is it the English language,

---

[26] Mordechai Beck, "My Aliyah Story (In Three Parts)," *Arc: Journal of the Israel Association of Writers in English* 13 (1999): 24.

[27] Beck, "My Aliyah Story," 22.

[28] "My Aliyah Story," 22–23.

[29] "My Aliyah Story," 23.

[30] "My Aliyah Story," 24.

with its delicate cadences and subtle turns of phrase, the rich allusions of its poetry, the hard clarity of its no-nonsense, sceptical philosophy?"[31]

In his poetry collection *Giving Myself Away* (2001), Jeffrey M. Green, writer, poet, and translator (and the co-editor of *Arc* 13), originally from Greenwich Village but now living in Jerusalem, addresses the language issue most explicitly in "Trains, the English Language, and the Jewish Imagination."[32] The first part of the poem reiterates a 'Jewish' joke: of the Nazi ordering a Jew in a fully occupied train compartment to remove his suitcase from the seat it is perched on. When the Jew, reading a Yiddish paper, doesn't show himself to be impressed, the Nazi gloatingly heaves the suitcase out of the window – the punch-line being, of course, that the suitcase was not the Jew's at all. The (in view of its historical setting) rather ambivalent story then provides the material for an extended metaphor which the poet engages to reflect on his own 'loquation':

> Do you have to love a language to use it well
> Why should I care more about your English
> Than the Jew in that joke
> Cared about the stranger's suitcase?

The English language, it is implied here, is foreign to the Jewish poet; it is the language of the Other ("your English") and, it seems, expendable like the stranger's suitcase. How it came to be the language of the Jewish poet talking here is explained in the following lines:

> Two stops ago, my lucky grandparents
> Boarded the American train.
> Where it came from meant little enough to them,
> And what has its destination to do with my history?
> I never felt at home with English.[33]

The metaphor of the train not only connotes an essential foreignness in the diaspora. It also constitutes an attempt to divorce the anglophone diaspora

---

[31] Beck, "My Aliyah Story," 23.

[32] First published in *Arc: Journal of the Israel Association of Writers in English* 14 (2000): 62–64.

[33] Jeffrey M. Green, "Trains, the English Language, and the Jewish Imagination," in Green, *Giving Myself Away* (Tel Aviv: Sivan, 2001): 6.

(particularly America) and its language from both collective and individual
Jewish history or, at the very least, to highlight its episodic character in that
history. This, of course, goes right against William D. Rubinstein's argument
that the English-speaking world provides an "appropriate matrix for Jewish
history."[34] To the speaker, the English language ostensibly is merely a useful
tool, because:

> Were I not to the language born,
> I'd have had to learn it,
> Envying native speakers, maybe
> Having more fun with the language.

It is precisely the global currency, the common, and almost 'indecent', avail-
ability, of English hinted at here which adds to the speaker's unease with the
diasporic language:

> But where's the intimacy
> When so many speakers tongue it?
> Talking English is like making love
> With the bedroom door wide open and the shades up.[35]

Yet, still, the speaker remains saddled with his English. In the fourth, concluding, section of the poem he acknowledges his bond to the language and, it
seems to me, the at least partial validity of ascriptions of this bond from the
'outside'. Furthermore, the reference to the common Jewish vernacular of the
generation of his grandparents may even hint at its replacement with English
as, in the terms of Cynthia Ozick, a "New Yiddish"[36]:

> I'm a Hebe, and the Goyim didn't have it all wrong.
> My grandparents read Yiddish papers on the train.
> But that's my valise in the luggage rack above my head.[37]

---

[34] W.D. Rubinstein, *A History of the Jews in the English-Speaking World: Great Britain*
(London: Routledge, 1996): 1.

[35] Green, "Trains, the English Language, and the Jewish Imagination," 7.

[36] Cynthia Ozick, "Toward a New Yiddish," (1970) in Ozick, *Art & Ardor: Essays* (New
York: Alfred A. Knopf, 1983).

[37] Green, "Trains, the English Language, and the Jewish Imagination," 7.

However, like many of his fellow Israeli writers in English, Green seems to find it difficult to find a market for his work in English, and this raises the question at whom the voice of anglophone writers in Israel is directed. In an academic book of his, *Thinking through Translation* (2001), Green refers resignedly to his own literary production in English: "Since I live in Israel," he says, "far away from the literary markets of the English-speaking world, I cannot hope to interest publishers in projects of my own."[38] Later, in the same book, he adds:

> I identify much more strongly with Israeli culture than with American or British culture. So much so that I have begun to write and publish in Hebrew, although this remains difficult for me. I will never master Hebrew the way I know English, yet I want to address the people where I live, whom I know, in their own language, rather than speak to people abroad, who are strangers to me.[39]

Although, to the uncharitable critic, this may seem like making a virtue of necessity, Karen Alkalay–Gut confirms in her essay on English writers in Israel that there is hardly a readership for anglophone Israeli literature in that country: "English readers in Israel do not seem to need speakers for their cause, and prefer their country of origin when it comes to literature, assuaging their cultural hunger with imported books."[40] On the other hand, it seems difficult for Israeli writers in English to reach a significantly large audience in the anglophone world.

However, recently, as Karen Alkalay–Gut notes, "the Web has not only validated the use of English in Israel and provided English writers with a stage, a market, and an audience, but has also give[n] the means to fulfil a sense of political purpose, whether for dissension and/or support."[41] Of course, some Israeli writers in English are published in anglophone countries, not least among them Karen Alkalay–Gut herself or, to name two authors not affiliated with the IAWE, Simon Louvish and Naomi Ragen. Louvish has been published in the UK by Heinemann and other well-established publishers in hardcover and in paperback editions. Yet, it may be symptomatic that his novel *The Days of Miracles and Wonders* (1997), first published in

---

[38] Jeffrey M. Green, *Thinking through Translation* (Athens: U of Georgia P, 2001): 86–87.
[39] Green, *Thinking through Translation*, 89.
[40] Alkalay–Gut, "Double Diaspora," 462.
[41] "Double Diaspora," 457.

Edinburgh by Canongate, appeared in the USA in the "Emerging Voices" series of Interlink Books and that Louvish finds it increasingly difficult to have his more recent work published. In contrast, Naomi Ragen's bestselling novels are hugely popular in the USA. Their atypical success may be due, to some extent, to their subject-matter: in many of her books, Ragen explores the world of ultra-orthodox Jewry – arguably, to many American Jews a Jewish 'Other' that holds an ambivalent fascination. Yet in Israel, Ragen became known only after her books were translated into Hebrew.[42]

Certainly, many questions remain: is anglophone Jewish literature in Israel a literature of (im-)migration, of return, or of exile? Or is it truly transnational? And are those who produce it Jewish writers, Israeli authors, Americans or British in exile, or all of these? Which is to say: is the transculturality of anglophone Jewish writers in Israel argued for in this essay an indicator of the validity of the concept of a Jewish literature in English, and is their 'loquation' paradigmatic of the global context? What, if any, are the distinctive features of Jewish literature in English with respect to other literatures in English and to other Jewish literatures? Is there really anything "centrally Jewish," as suggested by Ozick in 1970[43] and implied by the Yiddish critic Ba'al Makhshoves much earlier,[44] connoting an essentialist notion of Jewishness controlling inclusion and exclusion? Shouldn't we, rather, think in terms of the formation of cultural allegiances (in the sense of Benedict Anderson's concept of 'imagined communities'[45]), of which an important factor is language? And where will this lead us?

From the outset, I was aware that I would not be able to provide answers to all the questions raised in this article. Rather, it has been my objective to stimulate an awareness of, and an academic interest in, the transnational and transcultural dimension of Jewish literature in English. And if, as Sophia Lehmann argues, to create "a mother tongue which incorporates both history and contemporary culture and experience is tantamount to creating a home within

---

[42] See Alkalay–Gut, "Double Diaspora," 463.

[43] Ozick, "Toward a New Yiddish," 169.

[44] See Ba'al Makhshoves (= Israel Isidor Elyashev), "One Literature in Two Languages" (1918), tr. Hana Wirth–Nesher in *What is Jewish Literature?* ed. Hana Wirth–Nesher (Philadelphia PA: Jewish Publication Society, 1994): 74.

[45] As Lehmann, "In Search of a Mother Tongue," 104, argues in reference to Carole Boyce Davies' work on Caribbean identity. See Benedict Anderson, *Imagined Communities: Reflections on the Origin and Spread of Nationalism* (London: Verso, rev. ed. 1991).

the diaspora,"[46] then the very tenacity with which Jewish writers from the anglophone diaspora adhere to their English 'mother tongue' even in Israel may not only prove Lehmann's point. By the same token, it seems to me that the phenomenon of the 'double diaspora' of anglophone Jewish writers in Israel may, in turn, sustain the claim that it is, indeed, reasonable to make the distinction of a Jewish literature in English, precisely because it links those authors with their cultural rather than with their chosen national homeland and because the cultural affinities of the countries of the anglophone diaspora are sustained in the Israeli setting by their work and by their interrelation.

An aspect not mentioned by Lehmann, yet arguably a decisive factor also in the creation of a 'linguistic' home within both the diaspora and the double diaspora, is the future perspective. Future expectations project continuity and are essential for the construction of identities, both individual and collective,[47] and, I would add, for constructions of 'home'. With regard to the 'loquation' of Jewish literature in English in Israel, this perspective is ambivalent: Rooted in the anglophone diaspora, as is the individual past of (most of) those who produce it,[48] its present in Israel is determined by transcultural encounters, merging, as Green and Margolis suggest, memory and present experiences. The question is, however, whether anglophone Jewish writing in Israel has a future. A second generation of writers in English has as yet not developed in Israel, and this is one of the major differences to Jewish writing in English from the diaspora, whose diversity and vibrancy seem to expand continuously across the generations. Of the thirty-eight contributors to *English Poetry from Israel*, only Orit Kruglanski was born in the country (in Tel Aviv), and she writes both in English and in Hebrew.[49] Ultimately, time may

---

[46] Lehmann, "In Search of a Mother Tongue," 115.

[47] See, for example, Karmela Liebkind, "Ethnic Identity: Challenging the Boundaries of Social Psychology," in *Social Psychology of Identity and the Self Concept*, ed. Glynis M. Breakwell (Surrey Seminars in Social Psychology; London: Surrey UP / Academic Press, 1995): 171.

[48] With a few exceptions: Zygmunt Frankel, who emigrated to Israel in 1952, was born in Poland, deported to Siberia, and lived for a while in Belgium and England; Charles Kormos was born in Romania but later also lived in England before he emigrated to Israel; Gavriel Ben-Ephraim made *aliyah* from the USA in 1970 but is originally from Germany; Eugene Dubnov emigrated to Israel from Estonia in 1971. For biographical details, see Alkalay–Gut, Unger & Frankel, ed., *English Poetry from Israel*, 68–70.

[49] See the brief biography of Kruglanski in *English Poetry from Israel*, ed. Alkalay–Gut, Unger & Frankel, 70.

put anglophone Jewish literature in Israel to the test: will it prove to be not only productive but also re-productive? Or will it turn out, in the long run, to be sterile, like some cross-breeds, and dependent on the steady, if trickling, influx of 'expatriates'[50] from the anglophone Jewish diaspora?

In this article I concentrated largely on what appears to be an 'institutional' voice of Israeli writers in English, because, to some degree and against the odds, it is an amplified voice, and intended to be heard. Nevertheless, I am very much aware of the possibility that this voice may be distorted and that it is not necessarily representative of the variety of individual voices of writers in English in Israel. Still, in conclusion I would like to return to the cover illustration of *English Poetry from Israel*.

In the Book of Jonah, the runaway prophet is saved by the fish from drowning, but its belly certainly is not a place in which he feels comfortable. Is this why the IAWE writers chose for their self-presentation the image of Jonah in the belly of the fish? Because, like Jonah who was separated by the blubber and the deep seas from his fellow men, they inhabit an uncomfortable place of in-between-ness,[51] a place that is neither here nor there, and a place, perhaps, that makes you wonder who you are and where you really belong? Is that what the experience of transculturality means to them? Is it a trap? Does it spell isolation, imprisonment? Or is it a place of transition, one located in time rather than in space? A place from which *aliyah* will finally be achieved through the gullet of the fish?

The image of the writer in the belly of the fish may call to mind George Orwell's 1940 essay "Inside the Whale" and Salman Rushdie's 'postcolonial' critique of Orwell's endorsement of political quietism. To Orwell, inspired by "the essential Jonah act of allowing himself to be swallowed, remaining passive, *accepting*"[52] (an act he perceives as being performed by Henry Miller):

---

[50] See Alkalay–Gut, "English Writing in Israel," 13: "That I have concentrated upon dead writers [in this essay] might seem to indicate that the phenomenon of foreign-language writers in Israel is a disappearing one. While this is true of writers using languages such as Polish and Hungarian (whose average age in the Writers' Associations is well over 50), among the English writers there is a constant influx of new talent."

[51] Cf. Homi K. Bhabha, *The Location of Culture*, 1.

[52] Quoted from Rushdie, "Outside the Whale" (1984), in Rushdie, *Imaginary Home-lands: Essays and Criticism, 1981–91* (London: Granta / Penguin, 1992): 95; cf. George Orwell, "Inside the Whale," in *The Complete Works of George Orwell*, vol. 12: *A Patriot After All 1940–1941*, ed. Peter Davison (London: Martin Secker & Warburg, 1998): 107.

seemingly there is nothing left but quietism – robbing reality of its terrors by simply submitting to it. Get inside the whale – or rather, admit you are inside the whale (for you are, of course). Give yourself over to the world-process [...] simply accept it, endure it, record it. That seems to be the formula that any sensitive novelist is now likely to adopt.[53]

Not surprisingly, Rushdie, in his "Outside the Whale" (1984), emphatically argues against this. "The truth is," he maintains, "that there is no whale. We live in a world without hiding places,"[54] and "outside the whale the writer is obliged to accept that he (or she) is part of the crowd, part of the ocean, part of the storm."[55] Yet for Orwell – and to my mind, Rushdie, intent on emphasizing the writer's political responsibility, does not do full justice to this aspect – being in the whale is also transitional: "until the world has shaken itself into its new shape."[56] These are the concluding words of Orwell's essay and, written in the early years of the war, when literature must have seemed but an inefficient defence against modern arsenals, they may, perhaps, be taken as an expression of hope and of the vision of a time when the enforced quietism would be no more.

Whether a reference to Orwell's or Rushdie's essays be intended by the editors of *English Poetry from Israel* must remain conjectural. More readily appreciated is, certainly, the allusion to the Book of Jonah and it may also serve to answer the question of the value of being 'inside' or 'outside': Questioned by the sailors of the storm-tossed boat, Jonah not only reaffirms his Jewish identity, incidentally giving a concise definition of what it means to him to be Jewish – "I *am* an Hebrew; and I fear the LORD, the God of heaven, which hath made the sea and the dry *land*" (Jon 1:9); from the belly of the fish Jonah cries out in utter despair to God: "And the LORD spake unto the fish, and it vomited out Jonah upon the dry *land*" (Jon 2:10).

---

[53] Quoted from Rushdie, "Outside the Whale," 95; cf. Orwell, "Inside the Whale," 111.

[54] Rushdie, "Outside the Whale," 99.

[55] "Outside the Whale," 100.

[56] Orwell, "Inside the Whale," 112.

WORKS CITED

Alkalay–Gut, Karen. "Double Diaspora: English Writers in Israel," *Judaism: A Quarterly Journal of Jewish Life and Thought* 51 (2002): 457–68.

——. "English Writing in Israel," *Arc: Journal of the Israel Association of Writers in English* 13 (1999): 3–13.

Alkalay–Gut, Karen, Lois Unger & Zygmunt Frankel. "The English Poet in Israel," in *English Poetry from Israel* (1997), ed. Alkalay–Gut, Unger & Frankel, 7.

——, ed. *English Poetry from Israel* (Tel Aviv: IAWE, 1997).

Anderson, Benedict. *Imagined Communities: Reflections on the Origin and Spread of Nationalism* (1983; London: Verso, 1991).

Anon. "A Word of Explanation," *Arc: Journal of the Israel Association of Writers in English* 14 (2000): 4.

Ba'al Makhshoves (= Israel Isidor Elyashev). "One Literature in Two Languages" (Tsvey shprakhen: Eyn eyntsiker literatur, 1918), tr. Hana Wirth–Nesher, in *What Is Jewish Literature?* ed. Wirth–Nesher, 69–77.

Beck, Mordechai. "My Aliyah Story (In Three Parts)," *Arc: Journal of the Israel Association of Writers in English* 13 (1999): 21–24.

Bhabha, Homi K. *The Location of Culture* (London: Routledge, 1993).

Chertok, Haim, & Shalom Freedman. "Introduction" to *Arc: Journal of the Israel Association of Writers in English* 12 (1997): 4.

Ezrahi, Sidra DeKoven. *Booking Passage: Exile and Homecoming in the Modern Jewish Imagination* (Berkeley: U of California P, 2000).

Fludernik, Monika, ed. "The Diasporic Imaginary: Postcolonial Reconfigurations in the Context of Multiculturalism," in *Diaspora and Multiculturalism: Common Traditions and New Developments*, ed. Fludernik (Cross/Cultures 66; Amsterdam & New York: Rodopi, 2003): xi–xxxviii.

Grant, Linda. *When I Lived in Modern Times* (London: Granta, 2000).

Green, Jeff (= Jeffrey M. Green), & David Margolis. "Introduction" to *Arc: Journal of the Israel Association of Writers in English* 13 (1999): 1.

Green, Jeffrey M. *Giving Myself Away* (Tel Aviv: Sivan, 2001).

——. *Thinking through Translation* (Athens: U of Georgia P, 2001).

Israel Association of Writers in English (IAWE). http://www.geocities.com/iawe_mailbox/pubs.html (accessed 10 April 2008).

Lehmann, Sophia. "In Search of a Mother Tongue: Locating Home in Diaspora," *MELUS* 23 (1998): 101–19.

Liebkind, Karmela. "Ethnic Identity: Challenging the Boundaries of Social Psychology," in *Social Psychology of Identity and the Self Concept*, ed. Glynis M. Breakwell (Surrey Seminars in Social Psychology; London: Surrey UP / Academic P): 147–85.

Louvish, Simon. *The Days of Miracles and Wonders: An Epic of the New World Disorder* (Edinburgh: Canongate, 1997).

——. *The Days of Miracles and Wonders. An Epic of the New World Disorder* (Emerging Voices; 1997; New York: Interlink, 1999).

Orwell, George. "Inside the Whale" (1940), in *The Complete Works of George Orwell*. vol. 12: *A Patriot After All, 1940–1941*, ed. Peter Davison (London: Martin Secker & Warburg, 1998): 86–115.

Ozick, Cynthia. "Toward a New Yiddish" (1970), in Ozick, *Art & Ardor: Essays* (New York: Alfred A. Knopf, 1983): 151–77.

Rubinstein, W.D. *A History of the Jews in the English-Speaking World: Great Britain* (Studies in Modern History; London: Routledge, 1996).

Rushdie, Salman. "Outside the Whale" (1984), in Rushdie, *Imaginary Homelands: Essays and Criticism, 1981–91* (London: Granta / Penguin, 1992): 87–101.

Stähler, Axel, ed. *Anglophone Jewish Literature* (London & New York: Routledge, 2007).

——. "Introduction: Jewish Literature(s) in English? Anglophone Jewish Writing and the 'Loquation' of Culture," in *Anglophone Jewish Literature* (London & New York: Routledge, 2007): 3–32.

Wirth–Nesher, Hana, ed. *What is Jewish Literature?* (Philadelphia P A : Jewish Publication Society, 1994).

◀❖▶

Linguistic Dimensions
of Jewish-American Literature

PASCAL FISCHER

I N HIS SEMINAL ARTICLE "Transculturality: The Puzzling Form of Cultures Today," Wolfgang Welsch presents his idea of transculturality primarily with reference to current developments in a globalized world.[1] According to him, envisaging cultures as internally uniform and externally clearly delineated is not only inappropriate in view of "the inner complexity of modern cultures"[2] but also politically dangerous. Instead, cultural conditions should be seen as "characterized by mixes and permeations."[3] In spite of his examples, including electronic communication technology and the worldwide distribution of consumer goods, Welsch is well aware that many of the elements that define transculturality have been of importance for a long time; in his supplementary remarks, he makes it quite clear that the concept is germane to other historical periods as well.

A look at my field of interest, anglophone Jewish-American immigrant literature of the late-nineteenth and the early-twentieth centuries, really corroborates the validity of this assessment as well as the validity of the concept of transculturality. My investigation concentrates on language, since it is the linguistic dimension of Jewish-American narrative literature that most vividly

---

[1] Wolfgang Welsch, "Transculturality: The Puzzling Form of Cultures Today," in *Spaces of Culture: City, Nation, World*, ed. Mike Featherstone & Scott Lash (London: Sage, 1999): 194–213.

[2] Welsch, "Transculturality," 195.

[3] "Transculturality," 197.

illustrates the hybrid nature of cultures on a macro-level and of individual identities on a micro-level. It is, however, not the aim of this article simply to use literature as a pool of examples to explain cultural phenomena or as a mere reflection of social and cultural reality. On the contrary: by focusing on language and the different ways authors deal with languages, I centre on the literariness of their works. My approach, which applies linguistic methodology, therefore serves a twofold purpose: it draws attention to the importance of languages within fictional worlds and serves to promote a better understanding of the fabric literary works are made of.[4] Thus it sets out to counter a lamentable tendency in some studies of immigrant writing, for even though language usually occupies a very prominent position in transcultural spaces, literary critics have not devoted sufficient attention to it. Too often, the main concern still focuses on fostering the collective consciousness of a particular group, instead of scrutinizing the literary make-up of individual works. In the case of Jewish immigrant literature, a linguistic approach is particularly rewarding.

The history of Jewish immigration to America can be divided into three major phases. After the small wave of Sephardic immigration from Western Europe in the seventeenth and eighteenth centuries came a larger one from Germany in the nineteenth, which was followed by the mass influx of Jews from eastern Europe around the turn of the last century.[5] More often than not, these great waves of immigration are imagined to have been confrontations between one monolithic culture and another monolithic culture. Depending on the period and the ambitions of the immigrants involved, the outcome has been presented as either a gradual process away from the source culture towards the target culture (known as assimilation) or the establishment of a hyphenated Jewish-American identity. The reality is, of course, far more complex. Particularly eastern European Jewry, the most relevant group for

---

[4] For a general introduction to the diverse ways in which literary criticism can profit from linguistics, see *Literature and Linguistics: Approaches, Models, and Applications*, ed. Marion Gymnich, Ansgar Nünning & Vera Nünning (Trier: Wissenschaftlicher Verlag Trier, 2002).

[5] See Eli Faber, *A Time for Planting: The First Migration, 1654–1820* (*The Jewish People in America* 1, ed. Henry L. Feingold; Baltimore MD: Johns Hopkins UP, 1992), Hasia R. Diner, *A Time for Gathering: The Second Migration, 1820–1880* (*The Jewish People in America* 2, ed. Henry L. Feingold; Baltimore MD: Johns Hopkins UP, 1992), and Gerald Sorin, *A Time for Building: The Third Migration* (*The Jewish People in America* 3, ed. Henry L. Feingold; Baltimore MD: Johns Hopkins UP, 1992).

our discussion here, was extremely heterogeneous and had various points of contact with the outside world. Furthermore, the individual strategies taken up to adapt to the new realities in America also differed widely.

I want to argue that a close analysis of the ways Jewish authors deal with languages in their fictional works on the immigrant experience can provide deep insights into the multiformity of Jewish culture and identity both in Europe and in America. For Jews, more than for other immigrant groups, language played a major role in constructing and signalling identity. Lacking a homeland of their own, the group was to a large extent bound together by language. Hana Wirth–Nesher's image of language as homeland for the Jews and Jonathan Boyarin's metaphor of the book as a portable homeland are just two more recent formulations of an older notion.[6]

Jews from Poland, Russia or the eastern parts of the Austro-Hungarian Empire did not share a country of origin but they did share a language: Yiddish. The Yiddish word ייִדיש (*yidish*) not only means 'Yiddish' but also 'Jewish', and the ability to speak the language was considered one of the most important hallmarks of Jewishness. Since it was only Jews who spoke Yiddish, the language served to secure the distinctiveness of the group of immigrants. Several Jewish-American novels of the early-twentieth century illustrate the fact that those Jews who came from a cultural background other than that of the mass of East European immigrants, and were therefore not able to speak Yiddish, were often regarded with suspicion. Samuel Ornitz's *Allrightniks Row* relates how Jewish immigrants from the Balkans, whose mother tongue is the Jewish-Spanish Ladino, move into a house in the Jewish ghetto: "At first the neighbors thought they were not Jews because they did not speak Yiddish."[7] While Ornitz, who grew up in the Yiddish immigrant environment of New York's Lower East Side, nevertheless stresses the unifying aspect of Yiddish, the German-Jewish writer Sidney Nyburg emphasizes the dangers of too heavy a reliance on Yiddish for Jewish self-definition. When, in Nyburg's *The Chosen People*, the posh Rabbi Graetz, the head of an established German reformed congregation, comes to the bed of a dying

---

[6] Hana Wirth–Nesher, "Language as Homeland in Jewish-American Literature," in *Insider/Outsider: American Jews and Multiculturalism*, ed. David Biale, Michael Galinsky & Susan Heschel (Berkeley & Los Angeles: U of California P, 1998): 212–30.

[7] Samuel Ornitz, *Allrightniks Row "Haunch Paunch and Jowl": The Making of a Professional Jew*, intro. Gabriel Miller (1923; Masterworks of Modern Jewish Writing; New York: Markus Wiener, 1986): 44.

Jewish immigrant from Russia, whose Yiddish he doesn't understand, he is contemptuously called a "goy," a non-Jew, by the Russian immigrant.[8] The language barrier epitomizes a cultural barrier within the Jewish community that can only be overcome with considerable difficulty.

But while Yiddish was an indication of otherness and uniqueness, the mixed nature of the language is also proof of a continuous process of exchange and interaction and opens up links to other cultures outside the Jewish communities. The Germanic basis, the Hebrew component, and the Slavic influences together form the triangular structure of Yiddish. More than the speakers of other European languages, which are also hybrid historically, the speakers of Yiddish were highly aware of the different constituents of their language.[9] This "component-consciousness," which was described in detail by the Yiddish scholar Max Weinreich,[10] stresses historical relations and therefore emphasizes the transcultural status of eastern European Jewry. Right at the beginning of Elias Tobenkin's novel *Witte Arrives,* the narrator describes how the Russian-Jewish immigrants Masha Witkowski and her children get on the train after their arrival in the harbour of New York:

> Then came the train with a welcome surprise – a conductor who greeted them in German. There was a difference of centuries between the German which the American conductor spoke and the ghetto Yiddish of Masha Witkowski and her children. Nevertheless she and her children were cheered to the marrow. With a man who spoke German they felt kinship. Masha even took it as a good omen. She put her questions in the most cosmopolitan Yiddish she could summon to her command.[11]

Jewish immigrant authors writing in English in the first decades of the twentieth century were confronted with the problem of how to represent Yiddish as the language of the immigrant masses and as a sign of their ethnic identity.

---

[8] Sidney L. Nyburg, *The Chosen People*, intro. Stanley F. Chyet (1917; Masterworks of Modern Jewish Writing; New York: Markus Wiener, 1986): 64–65.

[9] Benjamin Harshav, *The Meaning of Yiddish* (Berkeley: U of California P, 1990); David Roskies, "Coney Island, USA: America in the Yiddish literary imagination," in *The Cambridge Companion to Jewish American Literature*, ed. Michael P. Kramer & Hana Wirth–Nesher (Cambridge: Cambridge UP, 2003): 71–72.

[10] Max Weinreich, *History of the Yiddish Language*, tr. Shlomo Noble & Joshua A. Fishman (*Geshikhte fun der yidisher shprakh*, 1973; tr. Chicago & London: U of Chicago P, 1980): 656–57.

[11] Elias Tobenkin, *Witte Arrives* (1916; New York: Gregg, 1968): 2–3.

Abraham Cahan, Ezra Brudno, Elias Tobenkin, Mary Antin, Samuel Ornitz, Anzia Yezierska, and Henry Roth all portray Jewish characters who – at least partly – converse in Yiddish. But how is this done in novels that are written in the English language? One cannot find any lines of Yiddish written with Hebrew characters in a single novel or story of the immigrant period. There is, however, some transliterated Yiddish. After her positive experience with the German-speaking conductor, Masha Witkowski in Tobenkin's novel tries her luck in addressing a policeman: *"Sprechen Sie Deitsch?"*[12] But this is the only Yiddish or German-Yiddish sentence in the whole book. In Henry Roth's *Call it Sleep*, we overhear a brief exchange of words between the newly arrived Genya and her husband Albert, who has already spent some time in America and now picks up his wife at the immigration office:

"Gehen vir voinen du? In Nev York?"
"Nein. Bronzeville. Ich hud dir schoin geschriben."[13]

The individual transliteration systems used in Jewish-American literature can throw light on the way the authors experienced the relation of their mother tongue to German. In the examples given, Tobenkin and Roth both follow the German orthographic convention in using the letter combination <sch> to express the phoneme /ʃ/. The same system of romanization, which was still dominant in Yiddish studies at that time, is also characteristic of Samuel Ornitz and Anzia Yezierska – for instance, when they write the word "schnorrer". Abraham Cahan, on the other hand, who generally stressed Jewish cultural autonomy and wanted to mark off Yiddish from German, transliterates the Yiddish letter *shin* ש with <sh>. By relying on the same grapheme for the palatal fricative in Yiddish words as in the surrounding English text, he can consistently follow the principle of phonographic rendering of spoken language within one system. Analogous to this is the authors' handling of the Yiddish letter *tsadhe* צ, which represents the sound [ts]: while Ornitz writes a simple <z> in words like "ziegelle" ('goaty'), Cahan sticks to the English spelling and inserts <tz> – for instance, in "tzimess" ('a sweet dish with carrots and turnips').

---

[12] Tobenkin, *Witte Arrives*, 7.
[13] Henry Roth, *Call it Sleep* (1934; New York: Cooper Square, 1970): 12.

As the direct presentation of transliterated Yiddish hinders communication with the anglophone reader, one usually finds hardly more than a few lines of Yiddish. But some authors still use the technique to make the reader experience the sound and temperament of the language.

For others, a simple metalingual remark that the characters speak Yiddish is enough. Sidney Nyburg avoids the pitfalls of representing a language he was not too familiar with by having recourse to indirect speech, usually in the form of content paraphrase or diegetic summary, whenever his characters converse in the foreign idiom.[14] But it is not only in the case of indirect discourse that the narrator performs the function of interpreter for the reader. Also novelists who prefer scenes with direct speech often 'translate' their characters' Yiddish; for example, in his *The Rise of David Levinsky*, Abraham Cahan presents Yiddish predominantly as standard English.[15]

A further and very popular way of rendering Yiddish can be labelled "devised translational interference."[16] Again Yiddish dialogues are 'translated' into English, but not into immaculate idiomatic English, but English that contains a few Yiddish elements to remind the reader of the source language. The most common device is the use of stereotypical interjections like *Nu*, *Ach*, or *Oi weh*! These interjections, which are profusely employed by Anzia Yezierska and Michael Gold, are problematic, since they contribute to the cliché of the Jew as effeminate, whining, and weak. In German literature, mainly by Gentile writers, these linguistic topoi signallizing the Jew had been used throughout the nineteenth century.[17] Authors like Yezierska, Ornitz, and Brudno also incorporate Yiddish lexical words in the translated passages of Yiddish dialogue. Many of them are considered typical of Jewish culture and do not have a one-to-one English translation, like *gefilte fish*, *treif* ('not kosher'), or *shadkhan* ('Jewish marriage broker'). But these authors sometimes also use Yiddish words that have a direct equivalent in English. It is

---

[14] See, for example, Nyburg, *The Chosen People*, 201; cf. the direct speech in the English dialogue on the pages that follow, 202–203.

[15] Abraham Cahan, *The Rise of David Levinsky* (1917; New York: Penguin, 1993).

[16] Meir Sternberg, "Polylingualism as Reality and Translation as Mimesis," *Poetics Today* 2.4 (1981): 227.

[17] Florian Krobb, "'Durch heutige Sprache und Kunstform wieder beleben...': Expressions of Jewish Identity in German Literature around 1848: Salomon Kohn, Hermann Schiff, Leopold Kompert," *German Life and Letters* 49.2 (1996): 160; Hans Peter Althaus, "Soziolekt und Fremdsprache: Das Jiddische als Stilmittel in der deutschen Literatur," *Zeitschrift für deutsche Philologie* 100 (1981): 218.

striking that in his novel *Yekl: A Tale of The New York Ghetto*, Abraham Cahan inserts words like *poritz* ('nobleman') and *taté* ('father') most frequently in the speech of his most traditional character, the young immigrant woman Gitl.[18] Her cultural identity seems to be so strongly defined by her Jewishness that her language should appear not to be completely translatable into English.

Although Yiddish is very often employed to characterize backwardly orientated immigrants, Jewish-American authors indicate that this language doesn't remain unchanged, either. It is, on the contrary, much influenced by English – just as much as every individual is affected by the surrounding culture of the New World. Yiddish had always been very open to adopting new vocabulary from other languages, but the influx of words was amazingly high in America. Far from presenting a simple dichotomy between Yiddish and English, the authors under discussion here show different ways in which Yiddish is permeated by the new idiom. Abraham Cahan makes a point of differentiating between the Yiddish spoken in Boston and the Yiddish of the Lower East Side of New York. Of the main character Yekl in Cahan's early novel we learn: "He spoke in Boston Yiddish, that is to say, in Yiddish more copiously spiced with mutilated English than is the language of the metropolitan Ghetto in which our story lies."[19] While Cahan discriminates between two Jewish immigrant localities that, owing to their size, differ as far as contact with the English speaking population is concerned, Henry Roth makes a distinction between two age groups: while the lexicon of the fairly isolated Genya remains practically unchanged in America, her son David has taken up many new words while roaming the streets of New York's immigrant quarter – much to the distress of his mother, who complains: "Your Yiddish is more than one-half English now. I'm being left behind."[20]

Although in the Russian census of 1897, 98 percent of the Jewish population stated that they had Yiddish as their mother tongue,[21] it would be grossly wrong to imagine eastern European Jewry as monolingual. Many Jews had at least some knowledge of the languages surrounding their villages, *shtetlekh*

---

[18] Abraham Cahan, *Yekl and The Imported Bridegroom, and Other Stories of Yiddish New York* (1896; Mineola N Y : Dover, 1970).

[19] Cahan, *Yekl*, 2.

[20] Roth, *Call it Sleep*, 154.

[21] Joshua A. Fishman, *Yiddish: Turning to Life* (Amsterdam & Philadelphia P A : John Benjamins, 1991): 86.

or urban Jewish quarters. As artisans, merchants or shopkeepers, they needed Polish, Ukrainian or Russian to interact with the local communities.

This external bilingualism, as it was termed by Max Weinreich,[22] is reflected very often in Jewish American literature of the immigrant period. In *Yekl*, even the rustic title figure is able to speak a few words of Russian and the orthodox David Levinsky in Cahan's principal novel is taught "a smattering of Russian" one hour a day at the Talmudic school, the *yeshiva*, of his Russian home town.[23] The first-person narrator David nevertheless stresses that it was mainly those who had to some extent assimilated into the larger populations who had a fairly sound knowledge of a non-Jewish language. He comments on the Jews who live "like Gentiles": "These fellows spoke Russian instead of Yiddish and altogether they belonged to a world far removed from mine. [...] To me they were apostates, sinners in Israel."[24] The fact that in Henry Roth's novel *Call it Sleep* Genya and her sister Bertha, who originate from Galicia, speak Polish fluently gives us an important indication that they belonged to the 'enlightened' part of the Jewish community back home. The *Haskala*, the Jewish enlightenment, encouraged the learning of Polish and German, the languages of trade in the region, whereas the religious movement of Chassidism strictly opposed any non-Jewish languages.[25] Genya also reads German romances in the original, thus documenting her level of education as well as her affinity with the dominant culture in the Austro-Hungarian Empire. In Roth's novel of the year 1934, German still has positive connotations as the language of romantic poesy, while in novels of the 1940s and 1950s, for example in Bernard Malamud's writing, German is now the fear-inspiring language of the perpetrators.

Eastern European Jewry was not only characterized by this external bilingualism, but also by an internal bilingualism, also referred to as diglossia.[26] Jews used Yiddish for everyday communication and Hebrew for religious purposes, particularly for liturgy and the study of the Torah. When Jewish-

---

[22] Weinreich, *History of the Yiddish Language*, 247.

[23] Cahan, *The Rise of David Levinsky*, 27.

[24] *The Rise of David Levinsky*, 42.

[25] Raphael Mahler, "The Social and Political Aspects of the Haskalah in Galicia," in *Studies in Modern Jewish Social History*, ed. Joshua A. Fishman (New York: KTAV, 1972): 62, 77.

[26] Weinreich, *History of the Yiddish Language*, 247–314; Joshua A Fishman, *Language in Sociocultural Change* (Stanford CA: Stanford UP, 1972): 137–40.

American authors make religion an important aspect in their works, very often Hebrew comes in as a central component of Judaism.

But just as in the case of Yiddish, immigrant authors had to find means of rendering spoken Hebrew in English novels. A very common technique was to use archaic English as a substitute. The German-American Jew Ludwig Lewisohn translates the Kiddush, the Hebrew prayer that is recited over a cup of wine, in the following way: "Praised beest thou, O Eternal, our God, King of the world, for Thou hast created the fruit of the vine!"[27] Lewisohn obviously wanted to emphasize the sacral character of the *losh-kodesh*, the Holy Tongue, by adapting this antiquated style. The convention of using archaisms to suggest the Holy Language can be seen as an influence of Christian Bible translations. Reformed Jewish congregations who substituted English for Hebrew for the first time often drew on these translations. That the application of this technique by Jewish writers is in fact a powerful example of transcultural permeations becomes more evident if we take a look at Abraham Cahan's novel *The Rise of David Levinsky*, where the title hero, a young Talmud scholar, feels impelled to recite Psalm 104 from his Hebrew prayer book while crossing the Atlantic towards America:

> "Thou who coverest thyself with light as with a garment, who stretchest out the heavens like a curtain: who layeth the beams of his chambers in the waters: who maketh the clouds his chariot: who walketh upon the wings of the wind."[28]

This is precisely the wording of the King James Version of the Bible. The fact that the Russian-Jewish immigrant writer Cahan used this Christian translation of the ancient Hebrew text to represent Ashkenazic Hebrew is also proof that an author's decision to write in the English language almost inevitably weds him to the Christian tradition.

To convey something of the fascination that Hebrew exerts on many Jews, several Jewish-American authors directly present transliterated Hebrew on the page. In Henry Roth's *Call it Sleep*, the child David is completely enthralled by the *losh koydesh*, the Holy Tongue he learns in *kheyder*, the religious school, even though he is not yet able to understand its meaning. Roth makes the English reader experience Hebrew as David does: where the semantic content is inaccessible, the attention is concentrated on the sound:

---

[27] Ludwig Lewisohn, *The Island Within* (1928; Syracuse NY: Syracuse UP, 1997): 9.
[28] Cahan, *The Rise of David Levinsky*, 86.

"Beshnas mos hamelech Uziyahu vawere es adonoi yoshav al kesai rum venesaw, vshulav malaiim es hahahol. Serafim omdim memal lo shash kanowfayim, shash kanowfayim lawehhad, beshtayim yahase fanav uvishtayim yahase raglov uvishtayim yaofaif."

　　All his senses dissolved into the sound. The lines, unknown, dimly surmised, thundered in his heart with limitless meaning, rolled out and flooded the last shores of his being.[29]

It is the centrality of the *losh koydesh* for Jewish identity that secured its place in Jewish-American writing well into the second half of the twentieth century. There is even an example of a Hebrew word printed in Hebrew letters: Cynthia Ozick wrote the word *hashem* ('the holy name') in Hebrew characters.[30]

　　Even though the internal bilingualism of Yiddish and Hebrew was still intact in most Jewish communities in eastern Europe in the nineteenth century, things gradually began to change. While the Chassidic movement raised the status of Yiddish by using it more frequently for religious discourse in order to grant a greater section of the Jewish population access to spiritual experience, the *maskilim*, the adherents of the Jewish enlightenment, began writing treatises as well as fictional literature and poetry in Hebrew to lend authority to their ideas. Ludwig Lewisohn's *The Island Within*, the first part of which is set in eastern Europe, echoes this functional change when the enlightened Shimen tries to convince his more traditional friend Mendel of the dependability of the *maskilim* and their leader by referring to their use of Hebrew:

> Here today in our midst, in our congregation, God has raised up a man who is inditing new songs in the lashon kodesh, the holy language. No, he is no meshumet, no renegade. He sings even as sang the prophets of Israel.[31]

It is, however, Yiddish that the true Jewish model of the novel, the Chassid Hacohen, uses to mark off his ethnic identity. That Lewisohn gives prominence to Yiddish and not to Hebrew as the quintessence of Jewishness is a blow to those who want to read *The Island Within* as a Zionist novel.[32] Most

---

[29] Roth, *Call it Sleep*, 343.

[30] See Wirth–Nesher, "Language as Homeland," 220.

[31] Lewisohn, *The Island Within*, 13.

[32] See Allen Guttmann, *The Jewish Writer in America. Assimilation and the Crisis of Identity* (New York: Oxford UP, 1971): 103; Andrew Furman, "A New 'Other' Emerges in

Zionists tied their hopes for a Jewish state closely to the resuscitation of Hebrew as a language for everyday communication while rejecting Yiddish as a supposedly effeminate language around the turn of the century. The revaluation of Yiddish by the assimilated German-American Jew Lewisohn is a prerequisite for what he called the rediscovery of his Jewish identity. It was, moreover, a prerequisite for finding his voice as a writer, since he appears to be strongly influenced by the traditions of Yiddish storytelling. These are particularly apparent in the way Lewisohn tries to teach the reader by example.[33] In his general appreciation of eastern European Jewry and its language, Lewisohn shows many parallels to Jewish authors in Germany and Austria like Arnold Zweig, Alfred Döblin, and Joseph Roth: their quest for an authentic Jewish existence had also led them to identification with and sympathetic portrayal of eastern European Jews and their language.[34] Lewisohn, however, shares a widespread prejudice of his time, according to which there is a unique and pathological Jewish discourse – a prejudice that was also particularly prevalent in Germany.[35] In Lewisohn's view as expressed in the novel, the attempt to escape one's Jewishness in a relentless struggle for assimilation leads to hysteria, which finds its expression in language. His character Victor, who is in many ways depicted as a Jewish caricature type, impersonates the self-hating Jew: "The voice heard only itself. It roared at the top of a world fallen silent. Victor stood and talked. And his talk was immensely intelligent. Only it was tireless, tense with a half-mad intensity."[36]

Of course, for those Jewish-American writers who had emigrated from the Russian pale of settlement, the question of rediscovering their Jewish identity, so essential for their well-established German-American brethren, was not yet on the agenda. Their novels and stories concentrate on the effort of fellow immigrants to come to terms with life in a new country and to become amer-

---

American Jewish Literature: Philip Roth's Israel Fiction," *Contemporary Literature* 36.4 (1995): 639.

[33] Pascal Fischer, *Yidishkeyt und Jewishness. Identität in jüdisch-amerikanischer Literatur unter besonderer Berücksichtigung der Spache: Cahans "Yekl", Lewisohns "The Island Within", Roths "Call it Sleep", Malamuds "The Assistant"* (Heidelberg: Winter, 2003): 293–94.

[34] Noah Isenberg, *Between Redemption and Doom: The Strains of German-Jewish Modernism* (Lincoln: U of Nebraska P, 1999): 70–72.

[35] See Sander L. Gilman, *Jewish Self-Hatred: Anti-Semitism and the Hidden Language of the Jews* (Baltimore MD: Johns Hopkins UP, 1986).

[36] Lewisohn, *The Island Within*, 105.

icanized. Most eastern European Jews tried to get rid of Yiddish and learn English as quickly as possibly as a presumably infallible sign of their cultural assimilation. This difficult process is depicted extensively in Jewish-American immigrant literature, often humorously, sometimes critically, but mostly benevolently. Sara Smolinsky in Anzia Yezierska's novel *Bread Givers* manages not only to emancipate herself from the rigid orthodoxy of her father but also to learn English well enough to teach immigrant children. However, when she does pronunciation exercises with her pupils she inadvertently slips back into the immigrant language, only to be corrected by her colleague Mr Seelig, a Jewish immigrant himself.[37] The English language classroom is also the setting of a collection of stories called *The Education of Hyman Kaplan* by Leonard Q. Ross (= Leo Rosten), where most of the humour arises from Mr Kaplan's stumbling attempts to master the rudiments of the new idiom.[38]

Many Jewish-American writers strove hard to produce a realistic rendering of Jewish immigrant speech, sometimes referred to as 'Yiddish English' or 'Yinglish'.[39] In doing this, they were following the fashion of American dialect literature at the end of the nineteenth century. Although Henry James used the term "invasion" to describe the plethora of dialect writing in America, it is evident that it was mainly an American trend which was adopted be the newcomers.[40] But the notion of an exchange from single culture to single culture is again rather misleading when it comes to explaining the multidimensional influences that constituted a vogue within America's transcultural spaces.

Like the authors of American 'local color writing', Jewish immigrant authors had to find ways to present non-standard spoken English in their literary works. Generally, novelists have at their disposal a wide variety of possibilities to represent deviations in the fields of phonetics, morphology, syntax, and on the textual level. The different techniques applied by Jewish-American writers not only illustrate their ingenuity and inventiveness but also

---

[37] Anzia Yezierska, *Bread Givers*, foreword & intro. Alice Kessler (1925; New York: Persea, 1999): 271–72.

[38] Leonard Q. Ross (= Leo Rosten), *The Education of Hyman Kaplan* (New York: Harcourt, Brace, 1937).

[39] For a discussion of the advantages and disadvantages of these terms as well as alternative designations, see my *Yidishkeyt und Jewishness*, 231–32.

[40] Gavin Jones, *Strange Talk: The Politics of Dialect Literature in Gilded Age America* (Berkeley & Los Angeles: U of California P, 1999): 1.

give us clues to the diverse functions their literary dialect should fulfil. While some authors restrict themselves to a slightly different word order in the speech of their characters, others try to convey the immigrant speech as realistically as possible on all linguistic levels. This is, of course, particularly problematic in the area of phonetics and graphemics, since the phonographic character of the English spelling system has been undermined in the course of the centuries. Therefore, it cannot always be determined which pronunciation a specific spelling should hint at.

In contrast to regional varieties of English, the deviations in immigrant speech are to a large part due to what linguists later called interference or language transfer from the native language. When it comes to representing these interferences, Abraham Cahan was the most meticulous of all Jewish-American writers, especially in his novel *Yekl*. The narrator informs us that the English spoken in the dancing school of the Jewish immigrants was "broken and mispronounced in as many different ways as there were Yiddish dialects represented in that institution."[41] However, it is not this metalingual remark that is most striking but the minuteness with which Cahan depicts the language transfer from the individual Yiddish dialects.

The protagonist Yekl, who comes from Lithuania, lengthens certain vowels in English words: *pitch*, *kick* and *mister* are pronounced as *peetch*, *keeck* and *meester*. This can easily be explained by his native north-eastern Yiddish, the only Yiddish dialect that does not distinguish between long and short vowels.[42] Yekl's articulation is a consequence of the phenomenon of 'divergent negative transfer': the target language distinguishes between two phonemes, here between /ɪ/ und /iː/, where the native language possesses only one. In cases like this, there is a high probability that the learner perceives both phonemes of the target language simply as allophones of one phoneme and pronounces only one variant.[43] The character Mamie, who is from Poland and therefore probably speaks central-eastern Yiddish, never makes this mistake.

---

[41] Cahan, *Yekl*, 17.

[42] Dovid Katz, "Zur Dialektologie des Jiddischen," in *Dialektologie: Ein Handbuch zur deutschen und allgemeinen Dialektforschung* 1.2., ed. Werner Besch et al. (Berlin & New York: Walter de Gruyter, 1983): 1030; Solomon A. Birnbaum, *Yiddish: A Survey and a Grammar* (Toronto: U of Toronto P, 1979): 218.

[43] Elaine E. Tarone, "The Phonology of Interlanguage," in *Interlanguage Phonology: The Acquisition of a Second Language Sound System*, ed. Georgette Ioup & Steven H. Weinberger (Cambridge MA: Newbury House, 1987): 71–72.

The English word *round* is pronounced *roynd* by Yekl but *rawnd* by his Jewish-Polish shopmate, just as the pronunciation for the corresponding vowel in Yiddish is [ɔɪ] in the north-eastern dialect and [ɔ:] in the central-eastern one.[44] The most striking feature of the novel's literary dialect is, however, the protagonist's articulation of the English alveolar fricative [s] as the palatal fricative [ʃ]: *business* comes out as *beeshnesh*, *cent* as *shent* and so on. Yekl's buddy Joe, on the other hand, seems to be unable to enunciate the [ʃ]-sound: *she* is substituted by *se*. Yekl and Joe are both speakers of the north-eastern, or Lithuanian dialect of Yiddish, parts of which don't distinguish between [s] and [ʃ]. In this variant, called *sabesdiker losn*, the sibilant is pronounced "intermediate between š and s, with varying degrees of palatality,"[45] according to Uriel Weinreich. It can be inferred that Yekl and Joe are compatriots but do not come from the same region in Lithuania. Cahan really had the knack of conveying sophisticated differentiations.

The crucial thing is that this pronunciation feature clearly marks the speaker as a Lithuanian Jew, a *litvak*. Many comedians made fun of this provincial type by imitating just this element of the accent. With Yekl, Abraham Cahan introduces a character who parades his assimilation by speaking English, but the way Yekl pronounces English reveals the true Yekl, an incorrigible *litvak*, who still partly belongs to the Old World. What is more, Cahan's painstaking differentiation between dialects, which are still visible – respectively audible – in the characters' English, documents his refusal to present his group of immigrants as a uniform block. Apart from dialectal variation, Cahan draws our attention to further factors that influence the English of the characters. We are, for instance, told that female immigrants usually speak English more fluently than men, and that the contact with people outside the immigrant quarters is crucial for learning the language. Thus there is not *the* immigrant experience but as many immigrant experiences as there are individuals. By their form alone, the Yinglish dialogue in *Yekl* illustrates not only the hybridity of Jewish immigrant culture but also its inner differentiation and complexity or, in short, its transcultural character.

---

[44] That is the Yiddish proto-vowel U4 (54) that occurs in words like מויז "moys" ('mouse'); Ulrike Kiefer, *Gesprochenes Jiddisch: Textzeugen einer europäisch-jüdischen Kultur* (Tübingen: Niemeyer, 1995): 20–24; 298.

[45] Uriel Weinreich, "Sábesdiker Losn in Yiddish: A Problem of Linguistic Affinity," *Word: Journal of the Linguistic Circle of New York* 8 (1952): 362.

Henry Roth's approach to Yinglish is a similar one. While he does not distinguish between dialectal influences, he clearly differentiates between age groups. The suffix "-ingk" instead of "ing," obviously a consequence of the lack of a phoneme [ŋ] in Yiddish, is almost exclusively used by the adults in *Call it Sleep* and hardly ever by their children. The same pertains to Yiddish conjunctions in the English of the immigrants: the word *oder* instead of *or* can only be found in those passages that render the speech of grown-ups. However, Roth not only makes a distinction between the English of the children and that of their parents, but also between individual children. The most striking example is the character Benny, who has a speech impediment. Roth presents his defect together with the immigrant dialect, which makes his speech almost unintelligible: In Benny's sentence "I'm fylyoist t' stlmook,"[46] we can, however, detect those elements that are due to his lateral emission, the letters y and l, and the Yinglish element <oi> for [ɔɪ] instead of English <i> for [ɜ:] and are thus led to the correct sentence "I'm first to smoke."

But apart from the individualizing tendency of Roth's literary dialect, it also establishes connections to other immigrant groups who do not speak standard English, either. The language of Italian and Irish immigrants as well as of David's Polish playmate Leo is made accessible by very similar means. Leo's sentence "Jews is the Chris'-killers," for instance, semantically expresses the animosity against the Jews, but, by disregarding the subject–verb concord, it ironically shows the same grammatical mistake that can be seen in the language of Jewish characters, thus linking the immigrant groups on the level of linguistic form.

Far from depicting Jewish culture as homogeneous and separate, Jewish-American literature of the end of the nineteenth century and the beginning of the twentieth presents many shades and layers of Jewish culture: regional, social, and religious variations, the gradual changes it underwent, and the sudden upheavals it was confronted with. Thus these works shed light on the exchanges with the non-Jewish populations in Europe as well as in America while stressing the interconnectedness of the Old and the New World. All of these aspects of transculturality are accentuated by the use of different languages. To analyse the linguistic dimension of Jewish-American immigrant literature therefore means highlighting its transcultural character.

---

[46] Roth, *Call it Sleep*, 489.

WORKS CITED

Althaus, Hans Peter. "Soziolekt und Fremdsprache: Das Jiddische als Stilmittel in der deutschen Literatur," *Zeitschrift für deutsche Philologie* 100 (1981): 212–32.

Brudno, Ezra. *The Fugitive: Being Memoirs of a Wanderer in Search of a Home* (Garden City NY: Doubleday, Page, 1904).

Cahan, Abraham. *The Rise of David Levinsky* (1917; New York: Penguin, 1993).

——. *Yekl and The Imported Bridegroom, and Other Stories of Yiddish New York* (1896; Mineola NY: Dover, 1970).

Diner, Hasia R. *A Time for Gathering: The Second Migration, 1820–1880* (*The Jewish People in America* 2, ed. Henry L. Feingold; Baltimore MD: Johns Hopkins UP, 1992).

Faber, Eli. *A Time for Planting: The First Migration, 1654–1820* (*The Jewish People in America* 1, ed. Henry L. Feingold; Baltimore MD: Johns Hopkins UP, 1992).

Fischer, Pascal. *Yidishkeyt und Jewishness: Identität in jüdisch-amerikanischer Literatur unter besonderer Berücksichtigung der Spache: Cahans "Yekl", Lewisohns "The Island Within", Roths "Call it Sleep", Malamuds "The Assistant"* (Heidelberg: Winter, 2003).

Fishman, Joshua A. *Language in Sociocultural Change* (Stanford CA: Stanford UP, 1972).

——. *Yiddish: Turning to Life* (Amsterdam & Philadelphia PA: John Benjamins, 1991).

Furman, Andrew. "A New 'Other' Emerges in American Jewish Literature: Philip Roth's Israel Fiction." *Contemporary Literature* 36:4 (1995): 633–53.

Gilman, Sander L. *Jewish Self-Hatred: Anti-Semitism and the Hidden Language of the Jews* (Baltimore MD: Johns Hopkins UP, 1986).

Gold, Michael. *Jews Without Money* (1930; New York: Carroll & Graf, 1985).

Guttmann, Allen. *The Jewish Writer in America: Assimilation and the Crisis of Identity* (New York: Oxford UP, 1971).

Gymnich, Marion, Ansgar Nünning & Vera Nünning, ed. *Literature and Linguistics: Approaches, Models, and Applications* (Trier: Wissenschaftlicher Verlag Trier, 2002).

Harshav, Benjamin. *The Meaning of Yiddish* (Berkeley: U of California P, 1990).

Isenberg, Noah. *Between Redemption and Doom: The Strains of German-Jewish Modernism* (Lincoln: U of Nebraska P, 1999).

Jones, Gavin. *Strange Talk: The Politics of Dialect Literature in Gilded Age America* (Berkeley & Los Angeles: U of California P, 1999).

Katz, Dovid. "Zur Dialektologie des Jiddischen," in *Dialektologie: Ein Handbuch zur deutschen und allgemeinen Dialektforschung* 1.2., ed. Werner Besch et al. (Berlin & New York: Walter de Gruyter, 1983): 1018–41.

Kiefer, Ulrike. *Gesprochenes Jiddisch: Textzeugen einer europäisch-jüdischen Kultur* (Tübingen: Niemeyer, 1995).

Krobb, Florian. "' Durch heutige Sprache und Kunstform wieder beleben...': Expressions of Jewish Identity in German Literature around 1848: Salomon Kohn, Hermann Schiff, Leopold Kompert," *German Life and Letters* 49:2 (1996): 159–70.

Lewisohn, Ludwig. *The Island Within* (1928; Syracuse NY: Syracuse UP, 1997).

Mahler, Raphael. "The Social and Political Aspects of the Haskalah in Galicia," in *Studies in Modern Jewish Social History*, ed. Joshua A. Fishman (New York: KTAV, 1972): 58–79.

Nyburg, Sidney L. *The Chosen People*, intro. Stanley F. Chyet (1917; Masterworks of Modern Jewish Writing; New York: Markus Wiener, 1986).

Ornitz, Samuel. *Allrightniks Row "Haunch Paunch and Jowl": The Making of a Professional Jew*, intro. Gabriel Miller (1923; Masterworks of Modern Jewish Writing; New York: Markus Wiener, 1986).

Roskies, David. "Coney Island, USA: America in the Yiddish Literary Imagination," in *The Cambridge Companion to Jewish American Literature*, ed. Michael P. Kramer & Hana Wirth–Nesher (Cambridge: Cambridge UP, 2003): 70–91.

Ross, Leonard Q. (= Leo Rosten). *The Education of Hyman Kaplan* (New York: Harcourt, Brace, 1937).

Roth, Henry. *Call it Sleep* (1934; New York: Cooper Square, 1970).

Sorin, Gerald. *A Time for Building: The Third Migration* (*The Jewish People in America* 3, ed. Henry L. Feingold; Baltimore MD: Johns Hopkins UP, 1992) [=].

Sternberg, Meir. "Polylingualism as Reality and Translation as Mimesis," *Poetics Today* 2.4 (1981): 221–39.

Tarone, Elaine E. "The Phonology of Interlanguage," in *Interlanguage Phonology: The Acquisition of a Second Language Sound System*, ed. Georgette Ioup & Steven H. Weinberger (Cambridge MA: Newbury House, 1987): 70–85.

Tobenkin, Elias. *Witte Arrives* (1916; New York: Gregg, 1968).

Weinreich, Max. *History of the Yiddish Language*, tr. Shlomo Noble & Joshua A. Fishman (*Geshikhte fun der Yidisher shprakh*, 1973; tr. Chicago & London: U of Chicago P, 1980).

Weinreich, Uriel. "Sábesdiker Losn in Yiddish: A Problem of Linguistic Affinity," *Word: Journal of the Linguistic Circle of New York* 8 (1952): 360–77.

Welsch, Wolfgang. "Transculturality: the Puzzling Form of Cultures Today," in *Spaces of Culture: City, Nation, World*, ed. Mike Featherstone & Scott Lash (London: Sage, 1999): 194–213.

Wirth–Nesher, Hana. "Language as Homeland in Jewish-American Literature," in *Insider/ Outsider: American Jews and Multiculturalism*, ed. David Biale, Michael Galinsky & Susan Heschel (Berkeley & Los Angeles: U of California P, 1998): 212–30.

Yezierska, Anzia. *Bread Givers* (1925; New York: Persea, 1999).

◄❖►

Eluding Containment
— Orality and the Ordnance Survey Memoir in Ireland

EDITH SHILLUE

T HE CONTEMPORARY POSTCOLONIAL DISCUSSION of the nineteenth-century Ordnance Survey of Ireland asserts an imperialist intent in the classification and categorization of Irish culture through the memoir project of the cartographic survey.[1] Ethnographic discourse, which informed the inquiry, remains the culprit in an elision, if not eradication, of Irish indigenous culture. Utilizing only Michael Hechter's sociological discussion of Britain's 'Celtic Fringe', Ireland resembles the colonial interventions generated out of a dualistic centre–periphery superstructure.[2] Yet the Ordnance Survey was a part of the larger transition taking place in Europe in the wake of the Enlightenment. As such, it is an interesting arena within which to explore complex cultural tensions sourced from multiple hierarchies. This essay refuses a binarist approach to the contact zone of the memoir apparatus within the Ordnance Survey. Instead, we can explore the

---

[1] See Mary Hamer, "Putting Ireland on the Map," *Textual Practice* 3.2 (1989): 192–195; Gerry Smyth, *Space and the Irish Cultural Imagination* (London: Palgrave, 2000); Angáele Smith, "Landscape Representation: Place and Identity in Nineteenth-Century Ordnance Survey Maps of Ireland," in *Landscape, Memory and History: Anthropological Perspectives*, ed. Pamela Stewart & Andrew Strathern (London: Pluto Press, 2003): 71. See also Maureen G. Hawkins, "'We Must learn Where We Live': Language, Identity and the Colonial Condition in Brian Friel's *Translations*," in *Eire–Ireland* 38 (2003), 23–37.

[2] Michael Hechter, *Internal Colonialism: The Celtic Fringe in British National Development, 1536–1966* (London: Routledge & Kegan Paul, 1975): 18–19.

project as evidence of transitions in both Irish and British intellectual and linguistic arenas. Its outcome, then, cannot be considered simply in terms of
victory or defeat, but should, rather, be recognized as a series of perpetual
adjustments born of continual linguistic negotiation.

As subject-matter, the memoir apparatus provides us with a look at the research practices and outcomes of metropolitan intellectual communities in
contact with rural culture. The picture is one of ambivalence and confusion,
with representation of linguistic and oral culture a particularly revealing
aspect. Evidence within the archive and the 1837 published memoir reveals a
complex engagement with indigenous Irish cultural hierarchies. The Ordnance Survey memoir apparatus explored this diverse cultural arena and came
up with a voluminous amount of material on Gaelic culture. Yet examination
of these materials also exposes the failings and inadequacies of the project's
rationalist framework.

The paradox and ambivalence of the metropolitan–rural relationship lies in
the fact that the project clearly attempted to record the Gaelic environment.
What the project workers collected would then be contained within a 'rational'
intellectual framework dependent on many of the practices of mathesis. The
Ordnance Survey of Ireland failed in its objective more because of the inadequacy of the framework than because of any single underlying contempt
for indigenous culture on the part of project workers. Place-names, the starting-point of the memoir project, are also the starting-point of postcolonial
discussion. Yet this exploration reveals, above all, the complexity of the linguistic landscape early in the nineteenth century. Unprepared for language
shift and a domestic institutional and literary hierarchy, the survey utilized
Procedures of Intervention to contain and control Ireland's largely oral,
mythico-historical toponymy.

When appointed Director of the Ordnance Survey in Ireland, Thomas
Colby attempted to develop a statistical memoir that would differ from the
work of his predecessors. He and Thomas Larcom (who took over leadership
of the memoir project in 1828) combined the scholarly practices of British
and Irish antiquarianism with the needs and practices of a utilitarian scheme
for an expanding capitalist marketplace. This generated a natural tension that
would be further exacerbated by parliamentary inquiry with regard to its

cost.[3] In the 1837 volume, the *Ordnance Survey Memoir of Londonderry*, Colby instructed readers on ways to navigate "a work so entirely new in its design, and so varied and elaborate in its details."[4] This new design can be traced to the expansive nature of the inquiry, which included exploring everything from antiquities to zoology. But maybe postcolonial research would be more fruitful if we examined the diversity of *inquiry materials*, the most famous of which are the name books, but which also include questionnaires, geological tables, and the collection and reporting of public and church records. How (and if) these materials were utilized reveals a complex arena of cultural negotiation rather than an English steam-rolling of Gaelic purity. With regard to place-names, Colby developed a self-correcting system of inquiry that would simultaneously capture Gaelic origins and generate recognizable anglicized forms. Field-engineer instructions include specific responsibilities for capturing Gaelic place-names through a taxonomy of phonetic and orthographic representations, including a record of the authority from which the information was taken. Situational and descriptive materials were to be included in another column, including a record of what Colby termed "any remarkable events"; overall, it was five columns, within which the information was to be contained. After collection, the project's internal Gaelic authority, John O'Donovan among others, would follow through parishes and townlands, verifying the work of the engineers. This appears to be a search for suitable indigenous names properly represented as Gaelic in origin. The task, however, was not well received. Much of the work was ignored and at some point made entirely voluntary[5] – this is a central factor in the resulting instability of the apparatus. In fact, archival materials show a consistent failure to accommodate the prescribed format of questionnaires and tables, with many left blank and accompanied by narratives.[6] This evidence reflects the transitional or mixed nature of the linguistic environment into which the sur-

---

[3] See Report of the Commissioners appointed to inquire into the facts relating to the Ordnance Memoir of Ireland [OSM Report] (1844) HC [527] XXX: i–xvi.

[4] Thomas Colby, *Ordnance Survey Memoir of Londonderry* (Dublin: Hodges & Smith, 1837): 6.

[5] John H. Andrews, *A Paper Landscape: The Ordnance Survey in Nineteenth-Century Ireland* (2000; Dublin & Portland OR: Four Courts, 2001): 149.

[6] See Royal Irish Academy Ordnance Survey materials: Box 21/II/2 Henry Maturin from Clondavaddog in response to a questionnaire; 21/XII/2 John Ewing from "Glen-Columb-Kill"; SS/Donegal II/XII 'Miscellaneous materials" including multiple differing responses to a Statistical Enquiry on Coast Fisheries.

vey was wandering. The resulting contradictions reveal the inadequacy of the project's rationalist approach, coupled with a heteroglossia within Irish rural culture. Mikhail Bahktin has defined 'heteroglossia' as placing context in a primary position. He notes:

> At any given time, in any given place, there will be a set of conditions – social, historical, meteorological, physiological – that will insure that a word uttered in that place and at that time will have a meaning different than it would have under any other conditions; all utterances are heteroglot in that they are functions of a matrix of forces practically impossible to recoup, and therefore impossible to resolve.[7]

The nineteenth century in Great Britain, with residues of the discourse of the preceding era and the revolutionary rationalism that came with the Enlightenment, presents us with a shifting linguistic landscape in the metropolitan centre. Using Bahktinian thought within a politicized framework rather than a purely literary one, the Irish periphery becomes a complex social and linguistic environment, and the notion of the implementation of monolithic anglocentric orthodoxy is too simple. At the very least, there is a persistent confrontation between the oral and the written. The rural environment of Ireland, at an advanced stage of language change (from Gaelic to English), presents us with a similar complexity, informed by multiple old and new stratifications.

Mixing forms of spoken and written language was a distinctive element in rural Irish culture. However, it was one with its own hierarchy. Irish-language literati were markedly disparaging of 'unlettered' people, pushing oral transmission and storytelling into second-class status after the manuscript or written text.[8] Ironically, from the sixteenth century onward Gaelic literature was a consistent linguistic cross-fertilization between the oral and written that lent vibrancy to both forms.

Ireland was (and remains) a place where residual orality had significant influence. Walter J. Ong's definition of the elements of orality helps us understand how Irish responses to the survey's historical inquiry yielded mixed results. The survey was particularly at odds with copiousness, empathy, and

---

[7] M.M. Bahktin, *The Dialogic Imagination: Four Essays*, ed. Michael Holquist, tr. Caryl Emerson & Michael Holquist (Austin: U of Texas P, 1986): 428.

[8] Daithi Ó Hógain, "Folklore and Literature, 1700–1850," in *The Origins of Popular Literacy in Ireland: Language Change and Educational Development, 1700–1920*, ed. Mary Daly & David Dickson (Dublin: Trinity College, 1990): 1.

situational rather than abstract forms of information.[9] When and if field-workers sought to elicit linguistic or historical information, they frequently received it in forms rapidly losing value in the intellectual and political institutions of the British centre. Thus, questions utilizing inductive reasoning elicited responses containing elements of orality; subsequently, the answers had to undergo successive refinements. Apart from conforming to the actual size and shape of the name books, collected information was subject to approximation, delimitation, transcription, translation, and systematization.[10] While reflecting the colonial relationship to a certain extent, the place-name archive in Ireland is more complex than a mere imposition of English. The disruptive influence of internal cultural and linguistic factors was to be a distinguishing characteristic of the memoir.

Central to our understanding of the Ordnance Survey as a transitioning intellectual endeavour is the persistence of the cohesive power of relationships in a rural setting. Dependent on a Linnaean taxonomy, the task of capturing culture and place-names within the mathesis persistently missed the cohesive and holistic nature of the subject-matter. Working within this limited framework, the survey apparatus overlooked the fluidity that informed an environment regularly marked by political and cultural negotiation. Fluidity was interpreted within the mathesis as instability. Thus, both Colby and his marketplace competitor Samuel Lewis, who wrote a *Topographical Dictionary of Ireland,* refer to the 'unsettled' nature of names in the landscape.[11] Systematization of Gaelic toponymy presumed a consistent homogeneity that would accommodate the simplicity and rigour of their apparatus. Yet, paradoxically, Irish names were unsettled, as Colby noted. They did not reflect original purity but, rather, multiple historical relationships. Through orality – through oral inquiry as required by Colby and Larcom – the interconnectedness of Irish landscape and human experience disrupted the categorizations of the survey apparatus.

---

[9] See Walter J. Ong, *Orality and Literacy* (London: Routledge, 1988): 36–68. Discussion of the nature of mixed literate–oral environments can be found in Jack Goody, *Literacy in Traditional Societies* (Cambridge: Cambridge UP, 1968); see also Ruth Finnegan, *Literacy and Orality* (Oxford: Basil Blackwell, 1988): 140–60.

[10] Michel Foucault, *Archaeology of Knowledge*, tr. A.M. Sheridan Smith (*L'Archéologie du savoir*, 1969; London: Routledge, 1990): 58–59.

[11] See Samuel Lewis's introduction to his *Topographical Dictionary of Ireland* (London: S. Lewis, 1837).

Oral versions of local history were founded on relationships or collective memory – elements not of purity but, rather, of internal struggle and cultural negotiation. Colby's instructions to capture orthography and local pronunciation were not executed with any system of phonetic standardization or, for that matter, by workers with a minimum level of linguistic understanding. Thus, the orderly ideal of the memoir apparatus was disrupted in multiple ways – first, by a refusal on the part of many to record the requested information; next, by the disagreements and rationalizations pursued by O'Donovan; and, finally, by the awkward nature of the English equivalents. Multiple diverging meanings were regularly recorded by field engineers as well as rather non-sensical names, such as "Margery's horse" for the town of Mevagh or 'Bonyfoble' as a phonetic transcription of the Gaelic for 'Moville'.[12] These English place-names codified idiosyncratic representations based on gaelicized orthography, or, when expedient, the entire process fell back on ecclesiastical and land ownership records. Thus, their sources reveal meaning divorced from community relationships.

Corporeality, Credibility, Authority

Another theoretical approach to the subject may help us to understand the complexity of the dynamic between survey workers and the environment. Michel de Certeau's discussion of Foucault's analysis of the infrastructure of power ultimately urges us to examine what he calls a "'polytheism' of scattered practices" that persist in spite of the tendency toward centralized panoptic practices of the state. The victory of "one among their number" is a result, not of originary coherence but, rather, of a mistaken association of technology and the control of heterogeneity.[13] This critique of Foucault's regressive history suggests instability in metropolitan responses to heterogeneous communities and, applied to the Ordnance Survey, helps us to see how it received the discourse of rural Irish communities, whose communication and cultural practices were grounded in contextualized orality.

---

[12] *Ordnance Survey Memoirs of Ireland/Donegal, 38*, ed. Angelique Day & Patrick McWilliams (Belfast: Institute for Irish Studies, Queen's University Belfast, 1999): 54, 64.

[13] Michel de Certeau, *The Practice of Everyday Life*, tr. Steven Rendall (*Arts de faire*, 1980; Berkeley: U of California P, 1988): 48.

Central to our understanding of de Certeau's rescue of orality is the corporeal experience of communication.[14] Such an approach is apposite to the Ordnance Survey and O'Donovan's unique mandate. Applied to the inquiry of local naming practices and folk culture, the memoir aspect of the cartographic project takes on a completely different hue, bringing the dynamics of language (in both Gaelic and English) into sharp relief. If objectification through sight, or surveying the landscape, rendered the Irish passive, then dialogic engagement of indigenous names and events overturned the colonial relationship, forcing the agent of colonialism out of a type of deafness and into an environment where he had no authority. In fact, archival evidence shows not an objectification of Gaelic language and culture but, rather, a complex arena of reception. It is one that reveals English biases, but more often and more interestingly reveals the Irish rural cultural arena as a complex scene of negotiation and transition. O'Donovan literally followed in the footsteps of the engineers and officers, listened to native speakers, and held the name books up to their scrutiny, wrenching authority from an English centre to a Gaelic one – if only momentarily. As his letters reveal, the historical sources for place-names and local history were notoriously fluid.

Only through intervention could the memoir worker be the agent of 'naming' and even of bringing 'the Other' into being through a linguistic articulation specific to scientific discourse. Even in this case, as the archives reveal, the workers themselves were without 'naming' agency but, rather, brought forward materials to decision-makers that were later re-interpreted and re-presented.[15] The paradox of the Irish context is the mixed preservationist and transformative aims of the nomenclature project. It neither denied the existence of the landscape prior to the cartographic gaze (or the survey's inquiry) nor did it fully transform (i.e. anglicize) toponymy. Translation and orthography aiming to duplicate the Gaelic origins created idiosyncratic names instead, which were multiply removed from the locale and relationships they represented. Examples of more overt imperial interventions in the

---

[14] Michel de Certeau, *The Practice of Everyday Life*, 115–53.

[15] See J.H. Andrews on the compilation of place-names and the process of decision making – a rather simple one, since an administrator would choose from a range of choices available (*A Paper Landscape*, 125).

landscape are found in ceremonial events such as the re-naming of Dún Laoghaire as Kingstown by George IV in 1821.[16]

An analysis of letters and archive materials reveals that both the preservationist and the colonizer were in a hopeless position with regard to nomenclature in Ireland. The landscape – for the Irish – was the first, most active agent of representation. Its literary-mythic foundation points not to a delusional national character but to a host of fluid relationships and a physical environment seen as a naturally produced representation of that hierarchy. O'Donovan's letters from Meath are particularly revealing in discussing the pre-Christian origins of place-names and landscape topography, suggesting that the history department was overturning not just the symbols of the Anglo-oriented centre, but those of a Catholic hierarchy that was invested in translating pagan landscape icons into Christian/monastic symbols. In his August 1836 discussion of "Broad Boyne," or *Brugh na Boinne*, O'Donovan challenged the antiquarian interpretations of both the place-name and the topography, by pointing to extensive evidence for pagan, not monastic Christian, origins of landscape icons. In Meath he writes:

> That many ancient Irish churches were erected within the rings of Pagan Raths and Cashels cannot be doubted, as Fenagh within the Cashel of King Fergna, and perhaps Inishmurray &c,[sic] but it is also certain that the early Christian converts raised mounds and Cashels around their Monasteries in imitation of the mode of fortification practiced by their fathers.[17]

After the Gaelic lexicon and its localized adaptation, the pre-Christian and literary foundation of Irish toponymy constituted a third arena of 'foreignness' that the survey's epistemology had to navigate. The Irish informants

---

[16] Joep Leerssen, *Remembrance and Imagination: Patterns in the Historical and Literary Representation of Ireland in the Nineteenth Century* (Field Day Essays and Monographs; Cork: Cork UP, 1996): 78. See also James Murphy, *Abject Loyalty: Nationalism and Monarchy in Ireland During the Reign of Queen Victoria* (Cork: Cork UP, 2001): 8, and W.E. Vaughan, *A New History of Ireland* (Oxford: Clarendon, 1989), vol. 5: 67–68.

[17] John O'Donovan, *Ordnance Survey Letters/Meath*, ed. Michael Herity (Dublin: Four Courts, 2001): 22, 77–80, 84–92. See also *Ordnance Survey Letters/Donegal*, ed. Michael Herity (Dublin: Four Courts, 2000): 122, for assertions about Lough Derg and the oral tradition that it was visited by Saint Patrick. See also *Ordnance Survey Letters/Clare*, ed. Maureen Comber (Ennis: CLASP Press, 1997): 10–11 for an explanation of the corruption of a name that generates an Irish Saint, Banala, who never appears in any Gaelic manuscripts.

had no such restrictions. The answers to the inquiry are copious and frequently referred to as fabulous or superstitious.

The flexibility and abundance of names and places in Donegal were particularly vexing for O'Donovan, as he was unable to find any particular 'standard' for areas away from the metropolitan centre. He wrote in September 1835 that he was exhausted by the multiple names he received from local sources and wished to demand an oath from informants before they spoke to him.[18] Frequently this diversity of response was received by the project as dishonesty. In fact, O'Donovan himself would discard much of the information he received in the field, relying instead on the authority of a manuscript source.

The survey was in a similar situation negotiating representational authority in Scotland. The work of the linguist John Munro Mackenzie added a layer of intellectual authority to the project that undermined the assertion of the British centre. As indigenous authority increased, the centre administration reasserted itself and discarded the indigenous contribution.[19] Combined with information about the heterogeneity of Irish culture, we can begin to see the Irish landscape as one informed by a wider range of relationships than that commonly expressed in the dualistic Irish-English connection. The outcome of such a challenging inquiry is exemplified in the Londonderry memoir, where the Dinnseanchas tradition jostles for room alongside archaeological essays, biographies of corporation overseers and ecclesiastical histories.[20]

Reading the Internal Milieu

In the Ordnance Survey memoirs, the communities and landscape records studied were part of the social urge toward proud 'self-knowledge', which also informed public response. In studying the project, we cannot merge cartographic image and place-name archive, since such an intellectual move would distract us from an exploration of naming within Ireland's Gaelic milieu. We can read Gaelic Ireland with as much rigour as we read the English expansion. If we are to assume that 'naming' was a crude imperial inter-

---

[18] John O'Donovan, *Ordnance Survey Letters/Donegal*, 3.

[19] For a discussion of the Scottish mapping project, see Charles W.J. Withers, "Authorizing Landscape: 'Authority', Naming and the Ordnance Survey's Mapping of the Scottish Highlands in the Nineteenth Century," *Journal of Historical Geography* 26.4 (2000): 544.

[20] Thomas Colby, *Ordnance Survey Memoir of Londonderry*, 221–30.

vention, what are we to make of the fluid history of names that preceded anglicization?

What the memoir workers and project administrators did in response to the oral information they received is a fine reflection of the strangeness and complexity of the tasks assigned. Archival and published materials show just how effective the intervention could be in producing a text to accommodate contemporary intellectual discourse. An antiquities memorandum filed on 26 February 1833 by J. Stokes, J.B. Williams and C.W. Ligar illustrates the administrative transformation of materials: the entire memorandum is in narrative form – with no tables or charts, only illustrations of antiquities or famous sites (St. Columb's Stone, for example), accompanied by descriptions of physical size, origins, and speculation on causes of decay. The description of a "Tower at Cassino" is composed of a physical description of the tower and speculation about origins and modern interventions: i.e. masonry and roofing, new doors, etc. It runs to six pages. The category "traditions relative to the tower" is most revealing:

> A Catholic named Decain (?) who lives near Fox's corner at St. Columb's springs in Derry stated this day that that saint had "something to do with the tower." Also that he had a monastery at Graves in the Bishops demesne.
>
> The age of the tower is thought to be very great. It is said by one person to be older than St. Columb.
>
> No connexion [sic] heard between the tower and any particular tribe or place.
>
> A person named Hacket was heard this day telling Mrs. McGarrigle at her lodging house in 157 Bishop Street that at Doagh in the border of the County Donegal and Derry a Catholic peasant prophesy (?) and Irish manuscript containing "Brief history of the Chieftains of Derry and Tyrone." Further information is most probably in that manuscript. Mr. Hacket's relations live near Muff."[21]

This information was eventually presented in the Londonderry memoir through exclusion and revision and finally appeared within the "History" section of the city of Londonderry, where the rather informal trail of tellers was revised into a formalized reference. The frog of narrative and local tale was transformed into the prince of scientific discourse through rewriting, delimitation, and transfer (from one "field" to another, as described by Foucault), and published thus:

---

[21] National Archives of Ireland, Ordnance Survey Papers, OS/95/1/11.

In the charter of Derry it is called "Columb-kille's Tower." In Raven's plan of the city, in 1621, it appears as a very high and slender belfry; but it is incorrectly represented as square – a common error in the plans made by English artists in Ireland in that and earlier times, as appears from any old maps among the manuscripts in the library of Trinity College. *In the popular traditions of Derry and its vicinity this tower is still invariably spoken of as a lofty round tower, built by St. Columb himself, and many legends are current of its miracle-working silver bell.* It has been erroneously supposed by the rev. Mr. Sampson that 'the old windmill,' so memorable during the siege, and still existing as a pigeon house at the Cassino, was the remains of this tower."[22]

Delimitation and transfer can be seen in the notes and informant's influence on the History section with relation to the round tower, but the section from a broad perspective is a fine example of the privileging of the manuscript source, the *Annals of the Four Masters*, with translation and systematization of the Gaelic record into the context of the memoir. The section is preceded by the following statement: "It may be proper to state that in all instances, where the authority is not cited throughout the following notices, they are to be considered as taken from the Irish originals of the *Annals of the Four Masters*."[23] The search for originary purity in Ireland is a vexed endeavour. In fact, as the memoir project advanced, the plurality of hierarchies within native culture began to emerge, rendering it more difficult for the survey apparatus to maintain classificatory coherence.

A number of elements influence the indigenous relationship to landscape. Prior to the modern era, English administrative culture had actually adapted itself to the geographical and toponymic practices of Ireland. Other elements that were a part of Gaelic culture exert significant influence on how local populations perceived the meaning and use of landscape, revealing a pre-existing heterogeneity in Irish culture rather than a pure Gaelic unity. Gender, religious practice, bardic and manuscript traditions, and administrative procedure were all elements that generated internal tensions in the Gaelic milieu.

The exclusion of women from secular and religious learning, as well as bardic traditions in sixteenth-century Ireland, generated a record of history that shows women at the mercy of local or personal bardic and religious male figures. Literate or poetic women were given less status than those who

---

[22] Thomas Colby, *Ordnance Survey Memoir of Londonderry*, 25 (my emphasis).
[23] Colby, *Ordnance Survey Memoir of Londonderry*, 25.

performed duties that reflected well on male spouses.[24] The status of male spouses was also a significant influence in women's right to own and inherit property.[25] The suppression of the presence of women was a mark of Gaelic legal culture;[26] women were also forbidden to engage in public satire – a central element in political relationships. Mary Condren's assertion that place-names and Christian celebrations were born of the violation of women is found in the Ordnance Survey archives, which include records of place-names born of rape; under 'culture', the marginalization/shunning of women as 'witches' was categorized as mere 'superstition'.[27] In fact, a number of archive materials reveal a female alterity that was entrenched by the eighteenth and nineteenth centuries. Reports show that pagan practices and related female behaviour were strictly marginalized and policed elements of spiritual practice, with the Catholic church a particularly effective pacifying agent.

Most historical sources point to an inherent fluidity of meaning in Irish local history, but one that can also be seen as having its own internal structure and regulations.[28] Further, much of the work produced by Deirdre Flanagan reminds us that the anglicization of place-names was a 'blanket' over a voluminous set of names within Irish provinces, counties, baronies, and townlands. She asserts, also, that the instability of English names is a matter of historical record.[29] Clearly, we can see that the civic institutions – in choosing to standardize place-names – were engaging not just with a parallel civic or legal infrastructure, but with a way of conveying/communicating historical events.

We can perhaps see memoir workers as members of a community who were pursuing new, scientific epistemologies to organize/standardize the records of centre institutions. Outside of the cartographic representations, the

---

[24] Katharine Simms, "Women in Gaelic Society during the Age of Transition," in *Women in Early Modern Ireland*, ed. Margaret MacCurtain & Mary O'Dowd (Dublin: Wolfhound, 1991): 32–40.

[25] Keith Nicholls, "Women and Property in the Sixteenth Century," in *Women in Early Modern Ireland*, ed. MacCurtain & O'Dowd, 18–28.

[26] Fergus Kelly, *A Guide to Early Irish Law* (Dublin: Dublin Institute for Advanced Studies, 1995), 137.

[27] *Ordnance Survey Memoirs of Ireland County Donegal, 39*, ed. Angelique Day & Patrick McWilliams (Belfast: Institute for Irish Studies, Queen's University Belfast, 1999), 172.

[28] Georges Denis Zimmerman, *The Irish Storyteller* (Dublin: Four Courts, 2001), 33.

[29] Deirdre Flanagan, "Place-Names as Historical Source Material," *Ulster Local Studies* 1.1 (1975): 6–10.

project was part of a form of administration that reflected the centralizing tendency that would come to full flower from 1850 onward. In O'Donovan and other cultural workers on the Ordnance Survey as a whole, the preservationist tendency is apparent, but O'Donovan was able to straddle the oral and chirographic communities. The work was not simply a matter of clarifying, but required a capacity to enter into the oral world, negotiate its meanings, and in some ways translate the world-view not simply from Irish into English but from the realm of the oral into the chirographic, manuscript, and print context. The inherent richness and the complex struggle that came of the meeting of communities and institutions were confined and undermined by the forms of categorization with which the workers were forced to record their observations. Indeed, the regular experience of encountering local history through collective memory was an encounter with the orality of indigenous Irish culture and the maintenance of historiography. Its truth value is of less interest for study than how orality itself undermined the survey's execution.

WORKS CITED

Primary Materials

National Archives of Ireland, Ordnance Survey Papers. OS/95/1/11

Royal Irish Academy Ordnance Survey materials: Box 21/II/2 Henry Maturin from Clondavaddog in response to a questionnaire. 21/XII/2 John Ewing from "Glen-Columb-Kill". SS/Donegal II/XII "Miscellaneous materials".

Ordnance Survey Memoirs of Ireland/Donegal, 38. ed. Angelique Day and Patrick McWilliams (Belfast:Institute for Irish Studies, Queen's University Belfast, 1999).

Report of the Commissioners appoint to inquire into the facts relating to the Ordnance Memoir of Ireland, (1844) HC [527] XXX.

Secondary Materials

Andrews, John H. *A Paper Landscape: The Ordnance Survey in Nineteenth-Century Ireland* (2000; Dublin & Portland OR: Four Courts, 2001).

Bahktin, M.M. *The Dialogic Imagination: Four Essays*, ed. Michael Holquist, tr. Caryl Emerson & Michael Holquist (Austin: U of Texas P, 1986).

Colby, Thomas. *Ordnance Survey Memoir of Londonderry* (Dublin: Hodges & Smith, 1837).

Comber, Maureen, ed. *Ordnance Survey Letters/Clare* (Ennis: CLASP Press, 1997).

Certeau, Michel de. *The Practice of Everyday Life*, tr. Steven Rendall (*Arts de faire*, 1980; Berkeley: U of California P, 1988).

Finnegan, Ruth. *Literacy and Orality* (Oxford: Basil Blackwell, 1988).

Flanagan, Deirdre. "Place-Names as Historical Source Material," *Ulster Local Studies* 1.1 (1975): 6–10.

Foucault, Michel. *Archaeology of Knowledge*, tr. A.M. Sheridan Smith (*L'Archéologie du savoir*, 1969; London: Routledge, 1990).

Goody, Jack. *Literacy in Traditional Societies* (Cambridge: Cambridge UP, 1968).

Hamer, Mary. "Putting Ireland on the Map," *Textual Practice* 3.2 (1989): 192–95.

Hawkins, Maureen. "'We Must learn Where We Live': Language, Identity and the Colonial Condition in Brian Friel's *Translations*," *Eire–Ireland* 38 (2003): 23–36.

Hechter, Michael. *Internal Colonialism: The Celtic Fringe in British National Development, 1536–1966* (London: Routledge & Kegan Paul, 1975).

Kelly, Fergus. *A Guide to Early Irish Law* (Dublin: Dublin Institute for Advanced Studies, 1995).

Leerssen, Joep. *Remembrance and Imagination: Patterns in the Historical and Literary Representation of Ireland in the Nineteenth Century* (Field Day Essays and Monographs; Cork: Cork UP, 1996).

Lewis, Samuel. *Topographical Dictionary of Ireland* (London: S. Lewis, 1837).

Murphy, James. *Abject Loyalty: Nationalism and Monarchy in Ireland During the Reign of Queen Victoria* (Cork: Cork UP, 2001).

Nicholls, Keith. "Women and Property in the Sixteenth Century," in *Women in Early Modern Ireland*, ed. Margaret MacCurtain & Mary O'Dowd (Dublin: Wolfhound, 1991): 18–28.

O'Donovan, John. *Ordnance Survey Letters/Meath*, ed. Michael Herity (Dublin: Four Courts, 2001).

——. *Ordnance Survey Letters/Donegal*, ed. Michael Herity (Dublin: Four Courts, 2000).

Ó Hógain, Daithi. "Folklore and Literature, 1700–1850," in *The Origins of Popular Literacy in Ireland: Language Change and Educational Development, 1700–1920*, ed. Mary Daly & David Dickson (Dublin: Trinity College, 1990): 1–13.

Ong, Walter J. *Orality and Literacy* (London: Routledge, 1988).

Simms, Katharine. "Women in Gaelic Society During the Age of Transition," in *Women in Early Modern Ireland*, ed. Margaret MacCurtain & Mary O'Dowd (Dublin: Wolfhound, 1991): 32–40.

Smith, Angáele. "Landscape Representation: Place and Identity in Nineteenth-Century Ordnance Survey Maps of Ireland," *Landscape, Memory and History: Anthropological Perspectives*, ed. Pamela Stewart & Andrew Strathern (London: Pluto Press, 2003): 71–88.

Smyth, Gerry. *Space and the Irish Cultural Imagination* (London: Palgrave, 2000).

Vaughan, W.E. *A New History of Ireland*, vol. 5 (Oxford, Clarendon, 1989).

Withers, Charles W.J. "Authorizing Landscape: 'Authority', Naming and the Ordnance Survey's Mapping of the Scottish Highlands in the Nineteenth Century," *Journal of Historical Geography* 26.4 (2000): 532–54.

Zimmerman, Georges Denis. *The Irish Storyteller* (Dublin: Four Courts, 2001).

❖

Atanarjuat – Fast Running and Electronic Storytelling in the Arctic

KERSTIN KNOPF

T HE THREE-HOUR FEATURE FILM *Atanarjuat: The Fast Runner* is one of the most celebrated Canadian films of the past few years. It is the first Inuit dramatic film made in Inuktitut to receive nation-wide and international attention. The film was screened at various film festivals and program theaters in the world and won six Genie Awards including Best Picture, and the *Caméra d'Or* for Best First Feature at the Cannes Film Festival in 2001.[1] After a brief synopsis of the film's plot, this essay will outline the community approach underlying this film project and discuss its ethnographic potential in opposition to Western ethnographic filmmaking. It will broach the issue of translating oral tradition into film and video and attempt to single out characteristics of an Inuit filmmaking style. In doing so, the film will be positioned in the context of transculturality.

The presently discussed concept of transculturality goes back to Fernando Ortiz's idea of transculturation, which he employs in order to describe phenomena of meeting, colliding, and mixing cultures in Cuba. He argues that transculturation is a process of constant disadjustment and readjustment as well as of deculturation and acculturation, thereby creating new cultural phenomena.[2] The concept of transculturality goes beyond the notion of vari-

---

[1] Paul Apak Angilirq, *Atanarjuat: The Fast Runner* (Toronto: Coach House, 2002): 7.

[2] Fernando Ortiz, *Cuban Counterpoint: Tobacco and Sugar*, tr. Harriet de Onís (*Contrapunteo cubano del tabaco y el azúcar*, 1940; tr. Durham NC & London: Duke UP, 1995): 97–103.

ous single cultures meeting and mixing, and presupposes that modern cultures are marked by an inner differentiation and complexity on vertical and horizontal levels, which offer moments of commonalties and connections to other cultures. Transcultural identities are constantly negotiated at these interfaces of various different cultural influences; in Wolfgang Welsch's words, "work on one's identity is becoming more and more work on the integration of components of differing cultural origin."[3] Modern cultural patterns are no longer defined by a polarization and/or amalgamation of monolithic and clearly defined cultures, but by a transcultural network formed by the coexistence and intermingling of single cultures that have transformed into transcultures. This transcultural network relies on cultural commonalties and overlaps, and on cultural distinctions and specificity at the same time.[4] Transcultural phenomena thus necessitate cultural dialogue, interaction, and enrichment.[5]

The development of transculturality in Canada's Arctic was clearly triggered by Western contact, colonization, christianization, and the implementation of Canadian assimilation politics. As a direct result of Euro-American and Euro-Canadian expansionist politics, beginning in the 1920s the Inuit economy changed from a subsistence mode of production based on self-sufficient hunting into a capitalist mode of production based on the fur trade, subsequently modifying the pattern of hunting activities and making the Inuit economy dependent on traders. After the collapse of the fur trade, the Inuit economy changed into a wage-labor economy that rested on Inuit employment in southern companies which were established in the Arctic and which predominantly exploited natural resources. These developments resulted in widespread unemployment and poverty, because only a minor share of the increasing Inuit labor force could be employed, labor was relatively poorly paid, most were seasonal jobs, and permanent jobs were often given to southern non-Inuit laborers, and the socio-economic effects of such industrialization projects on local communities were often catastrophic. The creation of National Parks and so-called 'outpost camps', and the development of an

---

[3] Wolfgang Welsch, "Transculturality: The Puzzling Form of Cultures Today," in *Spaces of Culture: City, Nation, World*, ed. Mike Featherstone & Scott Lash (London: Sage, 1999): 197–99.

[4] Wolfgang Welsch, "Transculturality: The Puzzling Form of Cultures Today," 203, 208.

[5] Virginia H. Milhouse, Molefi Kete Asante & Peter O. Nwosu, ed., *Transcultural Realities: Interdisciplinary Perspectives on Cross-Cultural Relations*, ed. Milhouse et al. (Thousand Oaks CA, London & New Delhi: Sage, 2001): ix–x.

Inuit art industry could not alleviate this disastrous economic situation. The present Inuit economy is a coexistence and combination of several income sources: full-time and seasonal wage labor, traditional sustenance through hunting, fishing, and trapping, art and crafts production, and welfare.[6]

The transformation of the economic system and the christianization of the Arctic was a simultaneous process, and in 1918 the first Bibles were translated into Inuktitut. For example, in 1921–22 the evangelist Inuk moved to Igloolik in order to convert this community to Christianity, and in 1931 the first Catholic mission was established three kilometers north of Igloolik. Canada's official assimilation policy involved the introduction of a formal education system, transmitting eurocentric knowledge, values, and beliefs in day and residential schools, and a massive population relocation program, urging Inuit to move to government-built and -controlled permanent settlements.[7] These Western influences resulted in transformations in the social, economic, educational, and residential structures; traditional Inuit ways of life were effectively destroyed, the traditional self-sufficient hunting economy disrupted, and the tradition of orally communicating cultural knowledge severely undermined.[8] Modern Inuit cultural identities are, in the sense of transculturality, constant negotiations of Inuit and Western cultural, socio-economic, and political components, which are the result of the forcible imposition of Western values, beliefs, economic structures, and modes of living. This transcultural process, however, is not only a unilateral Inuit acculturation that involves retaining Inuit cultural and economic distinctions and specificity, but has also been marked by transcultural tendencies that have worked the other way around, as non-Inuit settlers and fur traders in the Arctic adopted Inuit hunting techniques and an Inuit subsistence mode, and Inuit terminology enriched Western Arctic semantics.[9]

After the introduction of Western media (mainstream Canadian television) to the Arctic, which had similar devastating effects on Inuit cultural tradi-

---

[6] See Ronald Quinn Duffy, *The Road to Nunavut: The Progress of the Eastern Arctic Inuit since the Second World War* (Kingston & Montreal: McGill–Queen's U P, 1988): 131–95.

[7] See Jean–Philippe Chartrand, "Survival and Adaptation of the Inuit Ethnic Identity: The Importance of Inuktitut," in *Native People, Native Lands: Canadian Indians, Inuit and Metis*, ed. Bruce Alden Cox (Ottawa: Carleton U P, 1992): 241–42, 249–50; Angilirq, *Atanarjuat: The Fast Runner*, 7.

[8] See Zacharias Kunuk, "I First Heard the Story of Atanarjuat From my Mother," in Angilirq, *Atanarjuat: The Fast Runner*, 13.

[9] Chartrand, "Survival and Adaptation of the Inuit Ethnic Identity," 247.

tions, language use, and identity formation, the Inuit developed a self-control-led media system beginning in 1980 with the implementation of the Inukshuk project that ran seventeen hours of Inuit-produced programming each week.[10] Following the success of this project, the Inuit Broadcasting Corporation (IBC) was licensed in 1981 and started to broadcast in allocated slots on CBC North. On account of continual lobbying of various Indigenous organizations, TeleVision Northern Canada (TVNC) emerged in 1992 from the fusion of the IBC with other local Indigenous broadcasters and provided pan-Arctic cross-cultural broadcasting tailored to the information and entertainment needs of Northern communities. TVNC broadcast in various northern Indigenous languages belonging to fifteen different language groups besides English and French.[11] In 1999, TVNC became the Aboriginal Peoples Television Network (APTN) with a country-wide broadcast license. As the first national Indigenous television network in the world, its programs consist of Indigenous documentaries, news magazines, drama, entertainment specials, children's series, cooking shows, and educational programs, which are broadcast in English, French, Inuktitut, Cree, Micmac and other Indigenous languages.[12]

The film *Atanarjuat: The Fast Runner* is part of a self-controlled, de-colonized, and transcultural Inuit media discourse. Set in the area between Baffin Island and the Melville Peninsula, the film is an electronic retelling of an ancient Inuit legend that is a central story in the Inuit oral tradition and one that the filmmakers heard as children. The story has didactic functions, as it admonishes listeners not to let envy, rivalry, and personal interests overtake the sense of responsibility and community that is of utmost importance for

---

[10] John Greyson & Lisa Steele, "The Inukshuk Project – Inuit TV: The Satellite Solution," in *Video re/View: The (Best) Source for Critical Writings on Canadian Artists' Video*, ed. Peggy Gale & Lisa Steele (Toronto: Art Metropole & V Tape, 1996): 57–60.

[11] Lorna Roth, "Television Broadcasting North of 60," in *Images of Canadianness: Visions on Canada's Politics, Culture, Economics*, ed. Leen d'Haenens (Ottawa: U of Ottawa P, 1998): 154–61; Lorna Roth, "First Peoples' Television Broadcasting in Canada," http://www.museum.tv/archives/etv/F/htmlF/firstpeople/firstpeople.htm (accessed 1 March 2008); "Explore North: Milestones in Television Broadcasting in Northern Canada," http://www.explorenorth.com/library/weekly/more/bl-milestones.htm (accessed 1 March 2008).

[12] Beverly Singer, *Wiping the War Paint off the Lens: Native American Film and Video* (Minneapolis: U of Minnesota P, 2001): 93; "Aboriginal Peoples Television Network," http://www.aptn.ca/corporate/corporate_home_html (accessed 1 March 2008).

survival in the Arctic.[13] It is the legend of an unknown shaman putting a curse on a small nomadic Inuit community, infesting it with evil, and upsetting the spiritual balance and solidarity.

After the community leader Kumaglak is killed with the help of his son Sauri, Sauri himself becomes the manipulative leader who weakens his old rival Tulimaq through ridicule and mistreatment because Tulimaq and his family suffer from the curse that brings bad luck and bad hunting. Tulimaq's two sons Amaqjuaq and Atanarjuat and Sauri's daughter Puja and son Oki grow up in this climate of rivalry and hatred. Amaqjuaq, the Strong One, and Atanarjuat, The Fast Runner, soon change the power relations in the community by becoming the best hunters and ridiculing the Sauri/Oki family. Community relations come to boiling point when the beautiful Atuat, Oki's promised wife-to-be, reveals her feelings for Atanarjuat, who then wins her in a head-punching contest. Oki is the embittered loser on a physical and emotional level. Puja, Oki's scheming sister, is also in love with Atanarjuat, and, with Oki's encouragement, manages to accompany Atanarjuat on his summer caribou hunt because his pregnant wife needs to stay at the summer camp. She seduces Atanarjuat, who, apparently out of a sense of responsibility, takes her home as his second wife. When Puja seduces her brother-in-law Amaqjuaq, the brothers' relationship is seriously strained. Puja walks to Oki's camp, complaining that Atanarjuat had tried to kill her, whereupon Oki resolves to avenge 'the shame' and kill Atanarjuat, his hated rival. Returning to Atanarjuat's camp, Puja manages to reconcile with Atuat and Amaqjuaq's wife Uluriaq. Knowing that Oki will take blood revenge, she arranges events so that the brothers are asleep in their tent after an exhausting hunt and the three women have gone to collect bird's eggs. The two brothers are attacked by Oki's gang while they are asleep. Amaqjuaq is speared to death but Atanarjuat escapes through the help of a good spirit. Naked and barefoot, he runs across the ice, trying to escape from his three pursuers. He succeeds with the help of the same good spirit and finds his way to Qulitalik and his family, where he is hidden and nursed back to health. Years back, they had fled the evil and embittered community. Shaman Qulitalik sustains Atanarjuat's spiritual power and supports his endeavor to end the evil haunting curse. In the meantime, Oki has killed his father Sauri, thus becoming community

---

[13] Kunuk, "I First Heard the Story of Atanarjuat From my Mother," 13; Nancy Wachowich, "Interview with Paul Apak Angilirq," in Paul Apak Angilirq, *Atanarjuat: The Fast Runner*, 17.

leader, and has raped Atuat to claim her as his wife. Returning with Qulitalik, Atanarjuat finally defeats Oki and restores peace and harmony in his community.

The film *Atanarjuat* was made by the first independent Inuit-owned production company, Igloolik Isuma Productions, founded in 1990 by the director and hunter Zacharias Kunuk, the now deceased producer Paul Apak Angilirq, the elder and actor Paulossie Qulitalik, and the New York-born video artist Norman Cohn, the only non-Inuit member.[14] The film was co-produced and partly financed through the Aboriginal Filmmaking Program of the National Film Board of Canada[15] and further financed through the Canadian Television Fund and Telefilm Canada. Directed by Kunuk, written by Apak Angilirq, and photographed by Cohn, the film was realized in an 'Inuit-style of community-based media production'.[16] Like the three-hour Canadian TV drama *Big Bear*,[17] this film was shot on Indigenous land, here Nunavut, the first Indigenous-controlled territory in Canada. The all-Inuit cast consisted entirely of Igloolik residents and comprised both experienced actors and first-time performers. The production also employed an almost exclusively Inuit crew, mixing expert filmmakers and film novices who trained hands-on on the set. A few southern professionals were involved in pre- and postproduction processes, including music composition, editing, and the training of Inuit film novices in make-up, sound recording, continuity, stunts, and special effects.[18] The production, coming in at 1.9 million Canadian dollars, employed sixty Igloolik Inuit as cast, crew, and support staff, and together with other production expenditures supported the local economy of the Igloolik community with 1.5 million Canadian dollars.[19] Just as the production money of the film *Big Bear* benefited the weak economy of a Cree reserve community, *Atanarjuat*'s production money supported the community of Igloolik

---

[14] "About Isuma," http://www.isuma.ca/about (accessed 1 March 2008).

[15] "Production Diary," http://www.atanarjuat.com/production/ (accessed 1 March 2008).

[16] The filmmakers of Igloolik Isuma Productions define this community-based media production as an approach to filmmaking that would "preserve and enhance Inuit culture and language; [...] create jobs and economic development in Igloolik and Nunavut; and [...] tell authentic Inuit stories to Inuit and non-Inuit audiences worldwide"; http://www.isuma.ca/about (accessed 1 March 2008).

[17] Gil Cardinal, dir., *Big Bear*, prod. Doug Cuthand, writ. Rudy Wiebe & Gil Cardinal (Télé-Action Bear Inc., Big Bear Films, Canada, 1998; 180 min.)

[18] "Production Diary," http://www.atanarjuat.com/production/ (accessed 1 March 2008).

[19] "Production Diary," http://www.atanarjuat.com/production/ (accessed 1 March 2008).

that, like other Arctic communities, has an unemployment rate of sixty per-cent and suicide rates ten times higher than the national average.[20] Money acquired to film a myth of the oral tradition, an intellectual property of Inuit culture, is returned to at least one community. Thus, the appropriation of this cultural knowledge for a market outside of the Inuit community is 'compen-sated' through financing that comes from that outside community.

Adjusting the process of filmmaking to extreme Arctic conditions does not only mean shooting on widescreen digital betacam and transferring the material later to 35 mm film,[21] but in this case involved having crew and cast live in conditions and dwellings similar to those of their ancestors in order to reduce the notoriously high production costs of Arctic films.[22] It is repeatedly stated that crew and cast had to go seal and caribou hunting in order to sustain themselves.[23] The community approach also involves the remaking of tradi-tional clothes, tools (*ulu* – curved women's knife, seal-oil lamps), hunting weapons (forked *kakivak* – fish spear, *unaaq* – spear, *sakku* – harpoon head), sleds (*qamutik* – sled made of caribou antlers, bone, and sinew), a kayak (*qajaq* – one-man canoe), caribou goggles (*iggak*), igloos (*qaggiq* – large ceremonial igloo), and seal-skin tents.[24] All of these items were re-created mostly by local artists and elders after traditional models which either belong to cultural knowledge handed down orally from generation to generation or

---

[20] "Production Diary," http://www.atanarjuat.com/production/ (accessed 1 March 2008). *Statistics Canada* in 2001 gives an employment rate for Igloolik of 40.0 percent and for Nunavut of 56.2 percent. Official unemployment rates in the same year are 28.4 percent for Igloolik and 27.8 percent for Nunavut. See "Statistics Canada: Community Profile – Igloolik,"

http://www12.statcan.ca/english/profilo1/CPo1/Details/Page.cfm?Lang=E&Geo1=CSD&Code1=6204012&Geo2=PR&Code2=62&Data=Count&SearchText=Igloolik&SearchType=Begins&SearchPR=01&B1=All&Custom= (accessed 1 March 2008).

[21] Raúl Gavez, "In Conversation with Norman Cohn," *Montage* (Spring 2002): 12. Kunuk clarifies that using film technology would have been impossible because it would have taken too much time to send the rushes south to get developed and back before the filmmakers would have been able to see what they have filmed. Raúl Gavez, "Epic Inuit: In Conversation with Zacharias Kunuk," *Montage* (Spring 2002): 11.

[22] "Sets," http://www.atanarjuat.com/art/sets.php (accessed 1 March 2008).

[23] Eric Beltman, "Atanarjuat: The Fast Runner," http://www.flipsidemovies.com/atanarjuat.html (accessed 1 March 2008).

[24] "Probs, Caribou Goggles," http://www.atanarjuat.com/art/goggles.php (acc. March 1, 2008); "Probs, Hunting Tools," http://www.atanarjuat.com/art/tools.php (accessed 1 March 2008); "Probs, Qamutik," http://www.atanarjuat.com/art/qamutik.php (accessed 1 March 2008).

are based on the journals of William Edward Parry, leader of the British expedition to Igloolik in 1821–23.[25] The kayak was rebuilt according to drawings made of an almost two-hundred-year-old kayak from the British museum, taken there by this expedition. This is an interesting circumstance, showing that the filmmakers relied on cultural knowledge that has been made part of the Western anthropological museum discourse. Because anthropologists can read cultures that are different from their own only within the framework of thought of their own cultures, the cultural knowledge that they convey in their notebooks, film/video, and later books and museums is subject to misinformation and information gaps where the dimensions and materiality of objects cease to be an immanent factor. For reconstruction, the framework of thought and cultural knowledge of the cultures studied is necessary in order to correct misinformation and fill information gaps. In the case of the kayak and other props, Inuit cultural knowledge was indispensable for determing how these objects are made and how to acquire the materials. Thus, the re-appropriated anthropological knowledge about Inuit is only valid in combination with Inuit oral cultural knowledge. By reconstructing a pre-contact Inuit way of life and reviving the traditional making of costumes, tools, weapons, and means of transportation, the film-production takes an active part in preserving these traditions and sustaining Inuit cultural knowledge.[26] In the same vein, translating this myth into film/video continues the tradition of storytelling in a modified way and preserves this oral knowledge for future generations.[27]

---

[25] This expedition was part of Parry's second attempt of four to find the Northwest Passage, here via the Hudson Bay and Repulse Bay. Edward Struzik, *Northwest Passage: The Quest for an Arctic Route to the East* (Toronto: Key Porter, 1991): 69, 86; "Probs, Qajaq," http://www.atanarjuat.com/art/qajaq.php (accessed 1 March 2008); "Cast and Characters," http://www.atanarjuat.com/cast/ (accessed 1 March 2008).

[26] Paul Apak Angilirq explains that the research for the movie revealed many traditional activities that were no longer performed. He points out that the remaking of traditional tools and clothes and redoing of ancient cultural activities will help to promote traditional Inuit culture in contemporary Arctic communities; Wachowich, "Interview with Paul Apak Angilirq," 21. Nancy Wachowich also recounts that actors were transforming into their characters, growing their hair, learning rituals and rules of behaviour, and practising Old Inuktitut, which is not just a passive learning of cultural tradition and language through viewing a film, but an active reviving and re-learning of these. Nancy Wachowich, "Comments by Nancy Wachowich," in Angilirq, *Atanarjuat: The Fast Runner*, 23.

[27] In an interview, Paul Apak Angilirq expresses his view that making such films is a way of preserving oral knowledge and the cultural tradition; Wachowich, "Interview with

As Indigenous filmmaking is in constant dialogue with colonial filmic discourse which has objectified and stereotypified colonized cultures and established them as the 'inferior Other', an Arctic film must necessarily be in dialogue with Robert Flaherty's ethnographic film *Nanook of the North* of 1922. As a prospector, Flaherty had undertaken four expeditions (1910, 1911, 1913, 1915) into the Arctic and sub-Arctic, all financed by Sir William Mackenzie, the Canadian railway magnate. During the latter two, Flaherty collected impressions and ideas and shot footage for a film about the North that was accidentally burned during editing in Toronto.[28] His fifth expedition in 1920 was subsidized by the French fur trading company Revillon Frères, a competitor of the Hudson's Bay Company that foresaw the advertising potential of an Arctic film, and led him to Port Harrison (a Frères trading post) on the Eastern shore of the Hudson Bay.[29] Here Flaherty set up camp, undertook filming expeditions, and processed the filmed material that was to become the film *Nanook*. The film invokes the documentary format,[30] pretending to record Inuit life by following Nanook and his family during their hunting trips and everyday activities. In reality, Flaherty compelled his objects to re-enact a traditional, pre-contact, primitive way of life without Western influence. His approach entailed occluding location and time of what was presented, homogenizing different Inuit cultural groups, and erasing the identities of his characters. The people he filmed were Itivimiut from Hopewell Sound, the real

---

Paul Apak Angilirq," 19–21. Similarly, Zacharias Kunuk claims that filming traditional oral knowledge is a way to collect these old stories and retain them for the future and that the film is "one way of bringing back lost traditions"; Raúl Gavez, "Epic Inuit: In Conversation with Zacharias Kunuk," 12.

[28] Paul Rotha, "Nanook and the North," *Studies in Visual Communication* 6.2 (1980): 35–45.

[29] Sherrill Grace, "Exploration as Construction: Robert Flaherty and *Nanook of the North*," *Essays on Canadian Writing* 59 (Fall 1996): 126.

[30] John Grierson and Richard Griffiths termed *Nanook* a documentary film, and Griffith referred to Flaherty as "the father of documentary film," a 'fact' that entered film history seemingly unquestioned. Accordingly, Flaherty's realism in *Nanook* was hailed; see Grace, "Exploration as Construction," 127, 134, 137. Brian Winston, on the other hand, distinguishes between critics who see Flaherty as the father of documentary and prime 'poet' of the cinema and others who criticize his practice of reconstruction and his paternalistic attitude towards his filmed objects. He defines this attitude of superiority and practice of dramatic reenactment as "major factors in documentary's flawed methodological and theoretical foundations"; see Brian Winston, "The White Man's Burden: The Example of Robert Flaherty," *Sight and Sound* 54.1 (1984): 58–59.

name of Nanook was Allakariallak, his 'wife' Nyla (played by Alice Nuva-
linga) and 'son' Allegoo (played by Phillipoosie) were not Allakariallak's
real family.[31] The actors were only allowed to wear traditional clothes and to
use traditional tools and hunting weapons, as if to lend the film anthropological authenticity. Flaherty managed to film a walrus hunt as it was done in
pre-contact times, during which his 'actors' at one point were in considerable
danger and asked him to intervene with a rifle, which Flaherty, for the sake of
his picture, refused to do.[32] Any sign of Western contact that had influenced
Inuit cultural activities was banned from his film. This essentializing attempt
to preserve 'authentic' pre-contact Indigenous cultures on celluloid only reflects the maker's constructed, clichéd, and ethnocentric image of 'the Inuit'.

Flaherty was infatuated with the universal theme of humanity fighting
against natural forces, of people living and surviving in harsh environments,
which was also to become the central theme in two other films by him,
Moana: A Romance of the Golden Age (1926) and *Man of Aran* (1934). *Man
of Aran* is a dramatic story set on the Aran islands of Ireland, portraying a
nuclear family that tries to make a living in the barren environment by fishing
and growing potatoes. The custom of shark hunting, abandoned ninety years
earlier, was re-enacted for the film, delivering some exciting and thrilling
pictures.[33] *Moana* is shot in the Samoan islands, where Flaherty looked for
communities who did not yet have Western contact, but he could not find
any, as the missionaries were always one step ahead. Because this environment was not so hostile as in *Nanook* and *Man of Aran*, the story of man
fighting against a harsh environment would not have worked that well. Thus,
Flaherty's film focuses on a love story and the tattooing initiation ceremony
of Ta'avale alias Moana, a custom that was almost extinct by the time of
Flaherty's filming.[34] Nevertheless, Flaherty here retained the element of
threatening natural forces in the shape of a group of wild boars.

The subtitle *A Romance of the Golden Age* is itself a romantic revitaliza-
tion of the concept of the golden age inscribed by Flaherty in colonial film

---

[31] Grace, "Exploration as Construction," 129, 135.

[32] Eric Barnouw, *Documentary: A History of Non-Fiction Film* (Oxford: OUP, 1993):
36–37.

[33] "Flaherty's Man of Aran," http://www.iol.ie/~galfilm/filmwest/19aran.htm (accessed 1
March 2008).

[34] Barnouw, *Documentary*, 47–48; Frances Flaherty, "Flaherty: Samoa," *Filmkritik* 5/245
(1977): 255–60.

discourse.[35] Flaherty's three films are clearly manifestations of colonialist politics: exploration of foreign, exotic worlds, mapping these 'other' worlds in film discourse, and objectifying them in films that combine an anthropological desire for knowledge with an interpretation that harks back to preconceived eurocentric notions of these worlds. The cultural and natural backgrounds of these films differ, but the patterns of storytelling are the same: a fictitious family with invented names is followed during everyday activities that are mostly staged. Abandoned customs are reintroduced and signs of Western influence banished. Subsequently, all three films are nostalgic re-enactments of an exoticized, 'pure' past of the three different cultures. The paradox is that Flaherty was aware of the devastating influences of Western contact and that he as explorer and filmmaker was part of the colonizing process. Like anthropologists, he resolved "to capture on film the nature of rapidly vanishing cultures," a practice that became known as 'salvage ethnography'.[36] On the one hand, Flaherty expressed sensitivity towards the cultures he studied, which is testified to by his (however paternalistic) practice of filming that necessitated the collaboration of the people being filmed and by the fact that he spent considerable time living with these cultures (sixteen months at Port Harrison and more than a year in Safune, Samoa).[37] On the other hand, he nourished the idea that the people being studied should revere him, even consider him as the 'Big White Chief', which conditioned his attitude of being a member of a superior culture who had the right to film 'vanishing' inferior cultures. Winston terms this attitude the "divine right of

---

[35] Seafarers and explorers of the sixteenth century were immersed in the discourse of the golden age established in Hesiod's, Ovid's, and Virgil's writings and were subsequently searching for terrestrial paradise and medieval and Renaissance wonders such as Eldorado or the Fountain of Eternal Youth on foreign continents. The notion of a mythic world, a space where laws of physics and logic were suspended, was born in the very moment of the European discovery of new continents, and the belief in golden-age wonders foreclosed an objective assessment of climatic and agricultural conditions the seafarers and explorers encountered in the new world. Their accounts of the new world presented it as golden land and terrestrial paradise, thus approximating the golden age discourse and palliating encountered realities. See Gesa Mackenthun, *Metaphors of Dispossession: American Beginnings and the Translation of Empire, 1492–1637* (Norman & London: U of Oklahoma P, 1997): 36–37; Carmen Judith Galarce, *La novela chilena de exilio (1973–1987): El caso de Isabel Allende* (New York: Maiten, 1994): 131.

[36] Barnouw, *Documentary*, 45.

[37] Paul Rotha, "Nanook and the North," 45; Flaherty, "Flaherty: Samoa," 260.

film-makers,"[38] which aligns anthropological filmmaking with the colonial
concept of Manifest Destiny.

As in Flaherty's *Nanook*, Kunuk's *Atanarjuat* also has ethnographic traits,
since he presents pre-contact Inuit culture and remade traditional props,
taking his time to show everyday activities in the camp such as eating raw
seal meat, skinning animals, preparing the runners of a sled, and building a
ceremonial igloo. Furthermore, he contextualizes traditional competitions and
entertainment games such as a women's *ajaja* singing,[39] a men's head-punching contest, and a contest where the corner of the opponent's mouth is pulled.
Kunuk does not, however, present a traditional wedding, initiation rituals,
burial ceremonies or the like, which most often form essential elements of
Western ethnographic films, and which would have been legitimized by the
film's plot as one generation grows up, Atanarjuat and Amaqjuaq marry, and
Kumaglak, Amaqjuaq, and Sauri die. Thus we can conclude that Kunuk is not
interested in giving a complete ethnographic picture of his Inuit culture. In
contrast to Western ethnographic films, Kunuk presents these ethnographic
facts embedded in a dramatic story that is set in pre-contact times, which
justifies the staging of a pre-contact life style. Kunuk shows aspects of Inuit
life from an inside perspective, uncommented and just 'in passing'. These
aspects support a narrative, instead of being the sole purpose of a film that
looks at an 'other', 'exotic' culture from the outside.

In a documentary that revisits Inukjuak, the location of Flaherty's film, the
manager of the local T V station, Moses Naquaq, presents some clips of
Nanook of the North and comments on serious flaws and misrepresentations
in Flaherty's film. He explains that the characters in *Nanook* wear polar bear
pants, although these were not typical of the region where he filmed, that
Nanook seals an igloo entrance from outside instead of from inside as it is
done, that for lighting reasons the tops of the igloo props were cut off, and
that the characters were filmed practically outside.[40] The character of Nanook
is ridiculed, as he has to pretend at a trading post that he has never seen a
gramophone before, and Flaherty shows him wondering about it and actually
biting into the record. In the same vein, one of the children swallows castor
oil that it was given before. This trading post scene is a staged example of the

---

[38] Winston, "The White Man's Burden," 59.

[39] "Sets," http://www.atanarjuat.com/art/sets.php (accessed 1 March 2008).

[40] Claude Massot, dir., *Nanook Revisited*, writ. Claude Massot & Sebastien Regnier
(IMA Productions, La Sept, Films for the Humanities, USA, 1994; 60 min.).

first-contact-game 'I give you an object and you will certainly misuse it, making a fool out of yourself but making me laugh' – and this is the whole intention. Flaherty was here playing on the animal instinct of checking out whether or not encountered objects are food by sniffing or tasting, thereby attributing a non-human trait to the Inuit. Furthermore, Flaherty staged a seal hunt by having two ice holes connected by a rope under the ice; Nanook, after having harpooned 'the seal', pulls at one end of the rope while others off-screen pull at the other end to imitate a seal being hauled out of the water. The seal hunt scene works to parody Inuit hunting activities by rendering it as slapstick comedy. In both scenes, a Western filmmaker ridicules individuals of the 'other' culture and presents them as deficient, animalistic, and unable to engage in cultural activities, clearly constructing his own culture as superior and the one studied as inferior.

In his references to Flaherty's film *Nanook*, Kunuk uses the strategy of subversive quotation. He quotes directly in one scene when Atanarjuat returns from a fishing trip and paddles ashore, similar to Nanook's arrival at a shoreline. Whereas, in Flaherty's film, this scene triggers laughter and again borders on mockery of the Inuit as Nanook's whole family and a puppy one after the other emerge from the one-man canoe, Kunuk neutralizes this scene by creating a rather idyllic and romantic picture of the fisherman returning home to his family. Kunuk too, uses polar bear pants, but instead of having everybody wear them and creating a pan-Inuit mishmash, he has only the shaman wear such pants in order to distinguish him as a shaman and to stress that he is a stranger from another part.[41] Similarly, Kunuk only suggests a seal hunt by showing his characters patiently waiting at different breathing holes, again neutralizing Flaherty's parody with solemn pictures. In stark contrast to Flaherty's *Nanook*, which centers on hunting activities, in *Atanarjuat* we often see men bringing home the bag on sleds, but we do not see an animal being killed. It is hard to believe that this is a case of political correctness in the sense of 'No animals were harmed during or in connection with the production of this film', because the filmmakers themselves are hunters and hunting is a necessary activity for survival in the Arctic. Rather, it seems that the hunting actions as such were not crucial elements in the plot, sustaining the claim that the objective of the film was not the presentation of ethnographic details. With *Atanarjuat*, Kunuk averts an objectifying colonial gaze by

---

[41] "Costumes," http://www.atanarjuat.com/art/costumes.php (accessed 1 March 2008).

creating an autonomous gaze at his own culture, where the people behind and in front of the camera as well as the people working on the set form a horizontally organized team as opposed to the vertically organized film teams characteristic of most Western filmmaking.[42] The people being filmed cease to be studied objects and become creative subjects. In this way, Kunuk subverts the ethnographic subject/object relation and undermines a latent self/other dichotomy that is inherent in Western films about Indigenous cultures.

When Indigenous filmmakers translate oral knowledge into the medium of film and video, they have to be aware of certain changes that they subject the material to. The oral tradition is an oral medium, functioning through continuous retelling of the same legends. Each telling brings about minor adjustments and changes that depend on the conditions, atmosphere, and audience as well as on the storyteller. The oral tradition is not correspondent with Western modes of transmitting knowledge such as print or film, but constitutes a medium of the moment. As soon as words are spoken, they are gone, and with them, the information they contain that cannot be retrieved later (except in the same mode with a new telling). Only when oral information is transformed into the Western media of video/film and print, can it be retrieved again and again without the authority of the sender/storyteller. The filming of such a legend removes this oral knowledge from its original narrative context. The immediate and primary quality of the mythtelling is lost and replaced by a secondary mythtelling through the filmmakers. Words and performance of one storyteller now become an omniscient story constructed, acted out, and realized by a group of people. The means of transmitting information, the audiovisual impulses, are alienated by electronic recording. Furthermore, the filming freezes one version of the legend and breaks with the continuum of change and adaptation of the story. Screening the film for a non-Inuit audience also removes this oral knowledge from the cultural context that is necessary to maintain its function. For filmmakers, there is also the issue of the language in which the oral knowledge should be rendered, as employing English subjects oral knowledge to colonial influence and loss of the cultural context of the words spoken. Employing the traditional language secures the cultural context of the spoken words, but limits the film audience. The filmmaking team of *Atanarjuat* has solved the problem by having all the

---

[42] "Filmmaking Inuit-Style," http://www.atanarjuat.com/production/filmaking.php (accessed 1 March 2008).

actors speak Inuktitut and providing English subtitles. Of course, the subtitles distract the viewers' attention from the visuals, but they seem to be the best pragmatic choice for getting round the language problem. Fewer of the younger Inuit generation speak their traditional language, and by choosing to film in Inuktitut, the filmmakers are helping to revive this language.[43]

Kunuk and his team have taken great pains in order to render this myth as close as possible to its model from the Inuit oral tradition. The team recorded eight Igloolik elders telling their versions of this myth and combined these into one final version. Elders were also consulted for cultural and linguistic accuracy during the various stages of the scriptwriting process.[44] At no point does the film allow viewers to draw any conclusion about the time period in which the story takes place, thereby supporting the fact that this is a timeless myth. Non-Inuit viewers are taken into a cultural and contextual limbo, where they find themselves positioned in a culture which they can hardly relate to and faced with a legend they are not acquainted with. For Western viewers, this mythic space is constructed in a threefold way. First, viewers are aware that they are watching an Inuit legend translated into film, where a DVD player, VCR, or computer is their storyteller. They view the film within their own cultural contexts, which are different from the non-Western, almost non-rational space presented in the film, where myth is more believable. Secondly, the film contextualizes shamanic activities and displays items that have shamanic power (e.g., the walrus-tooth necklace of the camp leader). Here, Western viewers are confronted with activities and items that in their cultures are usually exoticized and most often defined as belonging to the sphere of myth. Thirdly, much of the story's action is motivated by shamanic power which is again understood as unreal and supernatural: there is the evil curse, to begin with; later, help is called through a seal oil lamp; then there is

---

[43] In spite of the development of a formal Canadian education system in the 1950s, which at the beginning employed English exclusively and discouraged the use of Inuktitut (this policy was gradually abandoned in the present-day Nunavut area in the 1970s), the use of Inuktitut remained quite strong with adults. In 1984 over ninety percent of Inuit in the eastern Arctic were reporting Inuktitut as their home language; see Chartrand, "Survival and Adaptation of the Inuit Ethnic Identity," 242–49. However, today very few Inuit children in Nunavut speak, or even understand Inuktitut, and language revival programs are set up to counter this situation. See, for example, http://www.nunavut.com/nunavut99 /english/our.html#3 (accessed 1 March 2008).

[44] Wachowich, "Interview with Paul Apak Angilirq," 19; Norman Cohn, "The Art of Community-Based Filmmaking," in Angilirq, *Atanarjuat: The Fast Runner*, 25.

Atanarjuat's escape from the camp where his brother is killed because a shamanic spirit distracts the murderers' attention; and, finally, a shamanic spirit helps Atanarjuat to make a superhuman jump across a wide crack in the ice and to find his way across the ice to the old couple, running naked and barefoot for an incredibly long distance.[45] On the other hand, this film presents a universal story of love and hate, sex and rape, envy and rivalry, pride and resentment that is not unique to Inuit cultures. It could have happened anywhere and anytime in the world, and could be part of other world mythologies. There is much humor in the film, many bodily jokes, references to sex life in songs and conversations, and also a love and a rape scene. This universality, coupled with the autonomous presentation of Inuit culture from an inside perspective, works toward demystifying and de-exoticizing the material filmed.

The most striking contrast with classical Western narrative films is *Atanarjuat*'s slow pace, which is reminiscent of long, slow processes of storytelling. It takes a long time for the narrative to unfold, the camera lingers on cultural details, and the film contains long stretches with nobody speaking, allowing viewers to take in the powerful landscape images. The film runs for three hours and one could speculate that the screen time is close to the time it would take to tell this legend in reality. Thus, the length and slow pace position the film in the sphere of the oral tradition. The filmmakers avoid fast cuts, and most shots are realized as longer takes. In accordance with this, the cinematography supports the mythic character. Extremely long shots reveal the vastness and beauty of the arctic landscape. The camera highlights the sometimes bluish, yellowish, and greyish nature of snow and ice in the unique Arctic light. Whiteness outweighs subdued brownish and greyish colors of washed-out rocks in summer camps, sea grass, and the inside space of igloos. Greyish, brownish, and whitish clothes made out of the skins of Arctic animals complement this space of whiteness.

Besides the many long shots, there is an unusually high number of close-ups of objects and characters' faces, feet, and other body fragments. Sometimes characters move so close to the camera that viewers get the impulse to pull back. This effect is only partly owing to the fact that the team filmed in closed igloos and summer tents where there is not much space. Many 'point

---

[45] The filmmakers provide a map of the localities of the myth, and the length of Atanarjuat's run can be estimated as approximately thirty kilometers. See "The Legend on the Land," http://atanarjuat.com/legend/legend_land.php (accessed 1 March 2008).

of view' shots, a shaky hand-held camera when filming competitions, fights, dramatic unrest, and a camera tied to sleds or a cameraperson with a hand-held camera on a sled when filming movements of people, lend the film an immediacy and sense of closeness that helps to bridge the cultural and spatial difference of filming and viewing contexts.

The camera work and extensive mobile framing almost make the viewers feel that they are part of the picture. Close-ups of feet walking and running, and long walking and running sequences, group the film together with early Navajo films[46] and one film by the Hopi filmmaker Victor Masayesva.[47] Exemplary here are the sequences of Tulimaq returning from his hunt (2.30 min.) and of Atanarjuat escaping across the ice (5.30 min.), both photo-graphed from various angles. There are many unusual low angle shots, as in Tulimaq's return sequence, showing a dog's face, the hunter's feet, and the hunter's face from below. At another point, the camera is just pointed up-ward, featuring the heads of three men from below with the background of the sun shining through the igloo roof and rendering the snow transparent. Or the camera is positioned on the ground, showing Atanarjuat and his pursuers as tiny little figures moving within the vast Arctic landscape. By positioning the camera on the ground, the filmmakers can even take in the part of the ground that is immediately before the camera and which would have been cut off if shot from a straight angle. The frame compositions are similar in most outside sequences because of the character of the flat land: there is a horizon-tal line dividing the screen, showing varying proportions of land/ice/snow and sky. Since the bright Arctic light is of sufficient quality for filming, no artificial light seems to be used and the outside sequences are rendered in high-key lighting. Quite a few *contre-jour* shots, which are considered flaws in classical narrative films, enhance this sense of natural lighting. In se-quences taking place inside igloos, there seem to be only seal oil lamps as diegetic light sources and these sequences are usually rendered in low-key lighting. It is difficult to assess whether or not artificial light is employed

---

[46] Mike Anderson, *Old Antelope Lake* (15 min.); Susan Benally, *A Navajo Weaver* (20 min.); Johnny Nelson, *The Navajo Silversmith* (20 min.); Maxine Tsosie & Mary Jane Tsosie, *The Spirit of the Navajo* (20 min.) (all part of the "Navajos Film Themselves" project by Sol Worth and John Adair, 1966); see Sol Worth & John Adair, *Through Navajo Eyes: An Exploration in Film Communication and Anthropology* (Albuquerque: U of New Mexico P, 1997).

[47] Victor Masayesva, dir./prod./writ., *Itam, Hakim Hopiit* (IS Productions, USA, 1984; 58 min.).

here, but it is obvious that the filmmakers did not employ the classical three-point lighting system. Blurred shots, superimpositions, long dissolves, and slow motion effects complement the catalogue of salient techniques. These stylistic techniques are not unique to Indigenous filmmaking and might also be used by Western filmmakers, but their distinct combination creates a unique film style that is conditioned by the Arctic.

In conclusion, this film is a transcultural film product in the sense of integrating components of Inuit and Western cultural origin. Western film technologies are adapted to Arctic conditions and to an Inuit story. The traditional props were reconstructed and remade on the basis of Inuit cultural knowledge combined with Western anthropological research contained in museums and print. Traditional storytelling is adapted to Western ways of storytelling (filmmaking) and Inuit filmmakers become electronic storytellers, whereas in their traditional cultures they would not necessarily have been storytellers. The film itself is a bilingual product, both Inuktitut and English being spoken during the making of the film and both languages being present in the film product.[48] Thus, parallel to the assimilation of Inuit ways of life to Western modes of living, Inuit cultural expression approximates Western modes of expression, while still retaining Inuit culture to a considerable degree. The Inuit filmmakers avail themselves of Western film technology and apply it according to their own modes and concepts of film. In basic aspects, the film stays close to Western film conventions: it has a consistent, linear narrative, a classical cause-and-effect chain, events and interpersonal relations dynamizing the plot. It also has temporal and spatial continuity, continuity editing, and a conventional placement of sound with a composed musical score, which nevertheless integrates traditional music into the composition. These basic aspects of classical filmmaking are complemented and realized with individualistic techniques such as the slow pace, many long shots and close-ups of faces and feet, long walking and running sequences, many low angles, hand-held cameras and extensive mobile framing, no classical lighting, blurred shots, superimpositions, long dissolves, and slow-motion effects. The mythic story embedded in an Inuit cultural context and realized with these individual stylistic techniques and an Inuit community-based approach to filmmaking

---

[48] The script was written parallel in Inuktitut and English, the Inuktitut script being the basis for the filming, the instructions and dialogue for the actors, and the English script for the proposals for the Canadian funding institutions. See Cohn, "The Art of Community-Based Filmmaking," 25.

produce a transcultural film code. This transcultural film code exists at the interface between Inuit cultural activities and oral knowledge, Arctic conditions, Western filmmaking conventions, and Western colonial influences. The film belongs to a transcultural and decolonized film discourse that consciously merges Indigenous cultures and colonial influences.

WORKS CITED

Apak Angilirq, Paul. *Atanarjuat: The Fast Runner* (Toronto: Coach House, 2002).

Barnouw, Eric. *Documentary: A History of Non-Fiction Film* (Oxford: Oxford UP, 1993).

Chartrand, Jean–Philippe. "Survival and Adaptation of the Inuit Ethnic Identity: The Importance of Inuktitut," in *Native People, Native Lands: Canadian Indians, Inuit and Metis*, ed. Bruce Alden Cox (Ottawa: Carleton UP, 1992): 241–55.

Cohn, Norman. "The Art of Community-Based Filmmaking," in Angilirq, *Atanarjuat: The Fast Runner* (2002), 25–27.

Flaherty, Frances. "Flaherty: Samoa," *Filmkritik* 5/245 (1977): 255–67.

Galarce, Carmen Judith. *La novela chilena de exilio (1973–1987): El caso de Isabel Allende* (New York: Maiten, 1994).

Gavez, Raúl. "Epic Inuit: In Conversation with Zacharias Kunuk," *Montage* (Spring 2002): 10–14.

——. "In Conversation with Norman Cohn," *Montage* (Spring 2002): 12–13.

Grace, Sherrill. "Exploration as Construction: Robert Flaherty and *Nanook of the North*," *Essays on Canadian Writing* 59 (Fall 1996): 123–46.

Greyson, John, & Lisa Steele. "The Inukshuk Project – Inuit TV: The Satellite Solution," in *Video re/View: The (Best) Source for Critical Writings on Canadian Artists' Video*, ed. Peggy Gale & Lisa Steele (Toronto: Art Metropole & V Tape, 1996): 57–63.

Kunuk, Zacharias. "I First Heard the Story of Atanarjuat From my Mother," in Apak Angilirq, *Atanarjuat: The Fast Runner* (2002), 13–15.

Mackenthun, Gesa. *Metaphors of Dispossession: American Beginnings and the Translation of Empire, 1492–1637* (Norman & London: U of Oklahoma P, 1997).

Milhouse, Virginia H., Molefi Kete Asante & Peter O. Nwosu, ed. *Transcultural Realities: Interdisciplinary Perspectives on Cross-Cultural Relations* (Thousand Oaks CA, London & New Delhi: Sage, 2001).

Ortiz, Fernando. *Cuban Counterpoint: Tobacco and Sugar*, tr. Harriet de Onís (*Contrapunteo cubano del tabaco y el azúcar*, 1940; tr. Durham NC & London: Duke UP, 1995).

Quinn Duffy, Ronald. *The Road to Nunavut: The Progress of the Eastern Arctic Inuit since the Second World War* (Kingston & Montreal: McGill–Queen's UP, 1988).

Roth, Lorna. "Television Broadcasting North of 60," in *Images of Canadianness: Visions on Canada's Politics, Culture, Economics*, ed. Leen d'Haenens (Ottawa: U of Ottawa P, 1998): 147–66.

Rotha, Paul. "Nanook and the North," *Studies in Visual Communication* 6.2 (1980): 34–60.

Singer, Beverly. *Wiping the War Paint off the Lens: Native American Film and Video* (Minneapolis: U of Minnesota P, 2001).

Struzik, Edward. *Northwest Passage: The Quest for an Arctic Route to the East* (Toronto: Key Porter, 1991).

Wachowich, Nancy. "Interview with Paul Apak Angilirq," in Apak Angilirq, *Atanarjuat: The Fast Runner* (2002), 17–21.

——. "Comments by Nancy Wachowich," in Apak Angilirq, *Atanarjuat: The Fast Runner* (2002), 23.

Welsch, Wolfgang. "Transculturality: The Puzzling Form of Cultures Today," in *Spaces of Culture: City, Nation, World*, ed. Mike Featherstone & Scott Lash (London: Sage, 1999): 194–213.

Winston, Brian. "The White Man's Burden: The Example of Robert Flaherty," *Sight and Sound* 54.1 (1984): 58–60.

Worth, Sol, & John Adair. *Through Navajo Eyes: An Exploration in Film Communication and Anthropology* (Albuquerque: U of New Mexico P, 1997).

Internet Sources

"Isuma – Independent Inuit Film." http://www.isuma.ca/about (accessed 1 March 2008).

"Atanarjuat (The Fast Runner)," http://www.atanarjuat.com (accessed 1 March 2008).

"Aboriginal Peoples Television Network," http://www.aptn.ca/corporate/corporate_home _html (accessed 1 March 2008).

Beltman, Eric. "Atanarjuat: The Fast Runner," http://www.flipsidemovies.com/atanarjuat .html (accessed 1 March 2008).

"Explore North: Milestones in Television Broadcasting in Northern Canada," http://www .explorenorth.com/library/weekly/more/bl-milestones.htm (accessed 1 March 2008).

"Flaherty's Man of Aran," http://www.iol.ie/~galfilm/filmwest/19aran.htm (accessed 1 March 2008).

"Nunavut: Our Language, Our Selves," http://www.nunavut.com/nunavut99/english/our .html#3 (accessed 1 March 2008).

Roth, Lorna. "First Peoples' Television Broadcasting in Canada," http://www.museum.tv /archives/etv/F/htmlF/firstpeople/firstpeople.htm (accessed 1 March 2008).

"Statistics Canada: Community Profile – Igloolik," http://www12.statcan.ca/english/profil01 /CP01/Details/Page.cfm?Lang=E&Geo1=CSD&Code1=6204012&Geo2=PR&Code2=62 &Data=Count&SearchText=Igloolik&SearchType=Begins&SearchPR=01&B1=All&Cust om= (accessed 1 March 2008).

Filmography

Anderson, Mike. *Old Antelope Lake* ("Navajos Film Themselves" project, Sol Worth & John Adair, 1966; 15 min.)

Benally, Susan. *A Navajo Weaver* ("Navajos Film Themselves" project, Sol Worth & John Adair, 1966; 20 min.)

Cardinal, Gil, dir. *Big Bear*, prod. Doug Cuthand, writ. Rudy Wiebe & Gil Cardinal (Télé-Action Bear Inc., Big Bear Films, Canada, 1998; 180 min.)

Kunuk, Zach, dir. *Atanarjuat: The Fast Runner*, prod. Zacharias Kunuk, Paul Apaq Angilirq & Norman Cohn, writ. Paul Apak Angilirq & Norman Cohn (Lot 47 Films, Canada, 2001; 172 min.)

Masayesva, Victor, dir./prod./writ. *Itam, Hakim Hopiit* (IS Productions, USA, 1984; 58 min.)

Massot, Claude, dir. *Nanook Revisited*, writ. Claude Massot & Sebastien Regnier (IMA Productions, La Sept, Films for the Humanities, USA, 1994; 60 min.)

Nelson, Johnny. *The Navajo Silversmith* ("Navajos Film Themselves" project, Sol Worth & John Adair, 1966; 20 min.)

Tsosie, Maxine, & Mary Jane Tsosie. *The Spirit of the Navajo* ("Navajos Film Themselves" project, Sol Worth & John Adair, 1966; 20 min.)

⊰❖⊱

Manifestation of Self and/or Tribal Identity?
— Māori Writing in the Global Maelstrom

MICHAELA MOURA–KOÇOĞLU

> We have been dispossessed. We have been marginalized.
> In many places our cultures, yours and mine, have been
> destroyed. We occupy the borderlands of White society.
> We live only by the White man's leave within White
> structures that are White driven and White kept [...]
> There is no future for indigenous people unless you
> obtain your sovereignty.
> — Witi Ihimaera, *The Uncle's Story* (326)

T HIS PASSAGE from Witi Ihimaera's recent novel set at an international conference for First Nation Peoples in Canada vigorously
confronts the reader with a heated discourse currently escalating
among indigenous peoples worldwide. Minorities such as the San across
Southern Africa and the Métis in Canada or indigenous majority people such
as the Aymara and Quechua in South America all constitute aboriginal people
who inhabited specific territories before other dominant cultures arrived and
were then subjected to a period of colonialism with concomitant suppression
and disenfranchisement. The issue of cultural autonomy or even sovereignty
is on the top of their political agenda due to dilemmas inherent in postcolonial
societies.

With regard to their socio-economic situation, indigenous peoples nowadays often continue to live at the margins of their respective societies, many
of them being denied equal rights to the dominant culture. In addition, economic and military domination was followed by cultural supremacy, trigger-
ing ongoing conflicts of identification among these ethnic groups. These

conditions have generated and reinforced vigorous cultural and socio-political movements within the societies concerned. Identity discourses have moved centre-stage: on the one hand, indigenous ethnic groups succeeded in retaining a distinct culture and tradition; on the other, syncretism and hybridization intrinsic to culture contact are characteristic of their daily lives. Thus, the assertion of indigenous identity has become of paramount importance, but is faced with new challenges today: while efforts to create awareness of indigenous concerns were previously directed at the descendants of the former colonists with a local focus, globalization has allowed indigenous discourse to shift onto a global trajectory.

Globalizing processes, in the past, were mostly seen as a force contradicting locality, with negative implications particularly for indigenous populations. However, the winds have changed recently in academic discourse. The renowned social theorist Anthony Giddens, among many others, holds that globalization is "the reason for the revival of local cultural identities in different parts of the world."[1] In the past decade, theorists from diverse disciplines have come to dominate current discourse with the common proclamation of a vital link between globalization and localization.[2] The general consensus is that representations of identity: i.e. particularistic manifestations, are inexorably intertwined with ubiquitous global and thus universalistic processes: "The *idea* of nationalism (or particularism) develops *only* in tandem with internationalism."[3] Thus, formulations and interpretations of particularism, the most important being self-identities, are now routinely linked to globalization and concomitant processes. Roland Robertson puts forward the thesis that identity construction is bound to global processes: "Globalization has involved and continues to involve the institutionalized construction of the individual."[4]

This essay enquires into the implications of this contention for indigenous peoples engaged in the construction of cultural identities, peoples who feel

---

[1] Anthony Giddens, *Runaway World: How Globalisation Is Reshaping our Lives* (New York: Routledge, 2003): 13.

[2] Among important contributions are Roland Robertson, *Globalization: Social Theory and Global Culture* (London: Sage, 1992), *Global Culture: Nationalism, Globalization and Modernity*, ed. Mike Featherstone (London: Sage, 1990), Jonathan Friedman, *Cultural Identity and Global Process* (London: Sage, 1994), and *Global Modernities*, ed. Mike Featherstone, Scott Lash & Roland Robertson (London: Sage, 1995).

[3] Robertson, *Globalization*, 103.

[4] Robertson, *Globalization*, 104–105.

the urge to renegotiate the contemporary understanding of their culture, because they have experienced major setbacks based on colonial encounters and their associated effects. Undoubtedly, the "discovery or assertion of native values to overcome the alienation from the self or native culture"[5] ensues from the colonial experience, as Arif Dirlik states. He rightly regards identity discourses as a necessary consequence of colonialism, intensified by the syncretism and hybridization inherent to postcolonial societies. The increased politicization of identity discourses within these societies, this essay argues, is reinforced vehemently by globalization and associated developments.

The focus of this essay lies on the current identity discourse of the Māori people in Aotearoa/New Zealand which is evolving along different trajectories. Political discourse is dominated by the ideal of a bicultural society, with ramifications ranging from cultural autonomy to sovereignty and even separatism. Within cultural discourse, the definition of indigenous identity itself is being disputed. One direction calls into question the generic notion of 'Māori' itself, thus highlighting a tribal, hence particularistic, identity allegedly preserved over more than 200 years after colonial contact. In view of the inherent dilemmas for indigenous peoples within postcolonial societies, such a radical stance appears comprehensible in defence of ethnic identities. Nevertheless, the notion of a fixed cultural identity is highly problematical, since the concept is subject to cultural construction and change.[6] The fact that over ninety percent of Māori have lived in urban areas since the beginning of the 1980s, and that many of them have lost their ties to their *iwi* (tribe) and even *whanau* (extended family), renders the propagation of tribal identities for all Māori people in contemporary Aotearoa/New Zealand a questionable proposition.[7] But, however residual or symbolic tribal identity for some mem-

---

[5] Arif Dirlik, "Rethinking Colonialism: Globalization, Postcolonialism, and the Nation," *Interventions* 4.3 (2002): 442.

[6] See Eric Hobsbawm & Terrence O. Ranger, *The Invention of Tradition* (Cambridge: Cambridge UP, 1983), and Joane Nagel, "Constructing Ethnicity: Creating and Recreating Ethnic Identity and Culture," *Social Problems* 41.1 (February 1994): 152-76.

[7] See James E. Ritchie, *Tribal Development in a Fourth World Context: The Maori Case* (Honolulu, Hawai'i: East–West Center Association, 1990). The author can be considered one of the fiercest contemporary supporters of tribal identity. Ritchie renders a somewhat nostalgic account of tribal life, dismissing any other form than tribal development as a solution to the diverse social, political, and cultural dilemmas the Māori have to face. However convincing the argument might be for Māori who have strong tribal ties even today,

bers of the Polynesian minority has become today, for others the validity of the tribal concept has to be acknowledged and must not be ignored.

Another direction is the construction of the cultural group of 'Māori' itself which evolved in the nineteenth century, finding expression in various movements to unify the diverse tribes in an effort to counter colonial intrusion. While the main rationale obviously had been opposition to European domination, activities such as the King Movement, starting in 1850, had fundamental repercussions on Polynesian islander society in cultural domains: this period laid the foundations for the emergence of a Māori identity, with implications up to the present.

Whether in favor of tribal or of Māori identity, both sides refute the 'one nation of one people' maxim that is regarded as a residue of an assimilation policy that began in the nineteenth century and is favoured even today by some Pakeha, the white Europeans. Repressing characteristics of a culture by ignoring and shutting out its obvious diversity with the aim of imposing a unilaterally defined identity is arguably not expedient to developing a viable and modern New Zealand identity, neither for Pakeha nor for Māori. Increasingly, scholars from both sides have realized the multi- and transcultural ramifications of the question of cultural and national identity:

> We must recognize, in New Zealand of all places, that our culture comprises many different beliefs and behaviours that stem from many different roots. Whatever identity we have must include that great variety of cultural patterns.[8]

In their long struggle for equality, it can be regarded as no small success that the specificity of Māori as a component of a national identity is no longer being denied. In order to tackle the fundamental question of identity for Māori people, however, it is essential to explore the extent to which the syncretisms and hybridities inherent in postcolonial societies reinforce local particularisms, on the one hand, and contribute to the emergence of multi- and transcultural societies, on the other. The following discussion of two recent novels by Māori aims at showing how the complexity of this prevailing identity discourse reverberates in contemporary indigenous writing and what

---

Ritchie completely fails to address the inherent predicaments of urbanized and 'westernized' members of the minority group.

[8] Bill Willmott, "Introduction: Culture and National Identity," in *Culture and Identity in New Zealand*, ed. David Novitz & Bill Willmott (Wellington: GP Books, 1989): 6.

tactics Polynesian minority writers have developed to negotiate subjective and personal as well as cultural and ethnic identities.

The Search for Identity in Paula Morris's *Queen of Beauty*

As a new Māori literary voice, Paula Morris, in her acclaimed first novel, engages in a search for identity embedded in an immanent global/local predicament: unable to build herself a life overseas, the protagonist returns home to Aotearoa/New Zealand for a family gathering. Confrontations with her own and her family's memories finally enable her to stop trying to escape from her past and thus allow her to actively embrace her hybrid identity.

Introduced as Virginia Seton, a researcher for an historical novelist working in New Orleans, the protagonist comes to realize that she lives in an in-between world where she has found neither her own identity nor her vocation: she assists a novelist but does not write herself; she lives with two roommates, Bridget and Jake, and thus has not started to build a real home for herself; she spends most of her time with her friend Arthur, whom she feels attracted to, but with whom she has not started a serious relationship. When her roommates move to another city, Virginia loses her chosen world just before returning to Aotearoa/New Zealand for Christmas and her sister's wedding.

With a storyline switching between the present and the past of different family members, Morris ingeniously incorporates Māori words and concepts into her text without providing translations or interpretations. Like other Māori authors such as Patricia Grace and Witi Ihimaera, the author thus unobtrusively compels the reader to deal actively with Māori culture and language, adding a distinctive quality to the text. Regarding Māori culture, the reader encounters diverse interpretations of contemporary Māoriness:

> When my auntie heard I was going to St Luke's, you know what she said? "Watch out for the Asians." [...] Basically, they're not to be trusted," said Tania [...] "Asians are the new Polynesians, but worse. That's what people think. You know, at least the Polynesians are sort of like Māoris. Brown and affable and overweight. They like playing cricket and rugby, picnics at the beach, that kind of thing. But Asians – they're completely alien. Who knows what they're up to." (179)

The author evidently does not refrain from exposing biased views, instead explicitly representing cultural prejudices existing among the Polynesian minority itself. Morris thus calls into question the justification for negotiating identity merely on a bicultural basis. While Māori as descendants of the

precolonial population clearly hold a special role in the cultural realm of Ao-
tearoa that goes back to the controversial 1840 Treaty of Waitangi negotiated
between Māori and Pakeha, the often extremely restricted focus of Māori
activists on the binary relationship Māori versus Pakeha does not take into
account the contemporary multicultural reality of Aotearoa/New Zealand and
fails to address predicaments of other minorities, whether from Polynesia,
Melanesia, Micronesia, or other pacific and Asian areas. Although *Queen of
Beauty* does not explicitly negotiate the predicaments of other minorities, the
author deserves recognition for being one of the few Māori authors to allude
to this problematic.

   With regard to the issue of cultural identification among the Polynesian
minority itself, Morris portrays more distinctive stances and underlines inter-
generational divisions. Some of Virginia's family members disregard Māori
culture and values in their own lives, thus discarding any trace of that heritage. For others, recognition and reinforcement of cultural roots are evidently
crucial to forming a viable self-identity. For instance, the reader learns that
Virginia's cousin Errol Tucker works for the Waitangi Tribunal and is thus
actively engaged in the pursuit of Māori customary rights. Virginia's brother
Robert Seton epitomizes what might be called the modern Māori who has
successfully constructed his own subjective hybrid identity. On the one hand,
he engages in activism through his legal profession; on the other, he develops
his own individual life-style out of his cultural roots. This is evident in his
habit of buying Māori art and design for his apartment, which is even recognized by his culturally less sophisticated sister: "'Rob only gives ethnic
presents,' said Julia. 'He's a Pacifica purist. He's even got paua shell lino on
his bathroom floor'" (273). By deliberately modifying and merging traditions
with modern values and ideals, Robert evidently succeeds in overcoming the
challenges of a complex identificatory process, and strategically creates a
hybrid identity that is viable for him. For Errol and Robert – however disparate their notions of Māori identity might be – unequivocal identification
seems to come naturally.

   Virginia, by contrast, embodies a more ambiguous and volatile character,
unable or unwilling to decide when asked about her perception of home and
identity: "'You mean about coming back, or about being Māori or Pākehā?
I'm not sure about the first, and as for the second, I don't think it's a choice,
really. I'm both'" (228). The protagonist's predicament evidently relates to
Roland Robertson's understanding of the global/local dynamic: globalization
allows Virginia to search for her self overseas, but she cannot create a home
for herself in a different cultural context without reflecting on her identity and

heritage. With everyone around her, including her American friends, ignorant of her origins, she starts calling into question her own ignorance and disavowal of her roots. When drawn back home, the protagonist is confronted with her own and her family's past, thus underpinning local concerns including Māori land rights and cultural activism.

Instead of digging up stories and legends of a different culture for a stranger, Virginia ends up researching her own family history, not only Māori but Pākehā as well, strongly reinforcing the image of a syncretistic and hybrid identity. Her search for pieces of family history primarily based on oral accounts sets up a strong link with traditional Māori orality and – to my mind, most strikingly – the concept of *whakapapa*, the recital of Māori genealogy. When Virginia literally brings one piece of family history to light by finding the graveyard of a family member whose story was intended to be buried and forgotten, she eventually recognizes that her own story will not begin or be complete without her past. In the end, she comes to realize that she truly is Virginia Ngātea Seton of Māori descent and that her family history is an important part of her identity which she had neglected and almost given up. This awareness enables her to take her life into her own hands and start shaping it.

The author chose to portray neither a traditional setting nor one that is biculturally focused but, rather, to provide a global and cosmopolitan background for her characters to evolve their subjective identities – identities in which the tribal perspective is of no significance at all, but where an ethnic identity, conspicuously a transcultural identity with Māori and Pākehā components shaped by an American life-style, is outlined as one viable way of encountering the complex process of identity formation in today's Aotearoa/ New Zealand.

To be Māori Is Not Enough:
Forming a New Tribe in *The Uncle's Story*

Witi Ihimaera, one of the most prominent Māori writers to have paved the way for Māori literature in English, has recently created a new focus in his literary work. His novel *The Uncle's Story* centres on a pursuit of identification in two directions: the protagonist Michael Mahana, a Māori arts counselor, brings himself to disclose his homosexuality to his family. His 'coming out' triggers off his discovery of a family secret. Both schemes are designed to support Michael's process of gaining a viable self-identity. The underlying story of Māori activism represents the framework of the novel: the negotiation of indigenous concerns via an international platform of First Nations, in which the protagonist represents a driving force. Thus, the character of Michael Mahana not only incorporates traditional Māori values and traditions but, more importantly, adds a new quality to the perception of Māori identity. By not only voicing indigenous issues but also proposing ways to live as First Nation Peoples in a globalized twenty-first century, Ihimaera has succeeded in giving Māori literature a fresh direction.

The novel's protagonist, whose life has been shaped as much by his Māori ancestry as by his homosexuality, sets out to fight against his double marginalization and for his right to an idiosyncratic and hybrid identity. On disclosing his sexual orientation to his family, Michael learns about a family secret that was to be forever buried: the love story of his Uncle Sam and an American soldier. While fighting in Vietnam, Sam discovers his sexual orientation and meets his first love, Cliff Harper. When his secret is detected by his family, neither his bravery in Vietnam, where he upheld the warrior family's *mana*, nor his position as the first-born saves him from humiliation by his father, rendered in explicit detail in an appalling scene. Only on being dishonoured and outcast can Sam bring himself to give up his family and commit himself to his true identity. Tragically, however, he dies in an accident before being able to declare to Cliff his recognition of their love, and his life is erased from the family books. Michael unearths his uncle's story and fulfils the task of finally telling Cliff Harper the truth.

Against the tragic life of Uncle Sam, Michael Mahana is led to question and redefine his own identity, fashioned explicitly around the universalization of particularism, as Roland Robertson would call it. Michael shifts his personal fate onto a global stage by speaking in front of an assembly of First Nations, where he calls into question the all too common practice of denial and ignorance of homosexuality:

> The issue here is that for too long all of you who come from traditional cultures have profited by the efforts of those gay men and women who, for love of their nations, developed the songs, the poems, the dances, the arts of all of us. [...] But they are people who, to do their work, had to pretend they did not exist. (344)

Michael and his companions win the fight for the recognition of "peoples of two spirits" among the First Nation Peoples. The author does not merely stage personal and tribal identity on a global platform, but goes further in proposing a new way of life for gay women and men of Māori heritage: Michael and his lesbian comrade-in-arms, Roimata, become involved in the creation of an innovative form of tribe consisting of homosexual Māori. The scheme advocated culminates in a scene with utopian overtones in which the protagonist and his friends accompany the body of a gay Māori boy back to his ancestral ground for burial. When some of the family refuse to welcome the funeral procession on the *marae* (the central place of assembly) by not calling them onto the grounds, as tradition prescribes, Michael nonetheless decides to bring the body onto the *marae*:

> We are a people. We are a tribe. We bring our dead. If tradition has to be broken, then I will break it. Nobody will stop us from burying our own among the people where they belong. The time for hiding ourselves and our dead is past. (365)

By blurring the boundaries of tradition, the author underlines the stance that Māori identity is subject to renegotiation and construction. In the setting of the story, the confessing homosexuals' act of bringing the dead Māori boy who died of HIV back to his family group at first appears as a genuine confrontation with conservative traditionalists. It is highly significant, however, that the protagonist is highly concerned about violating the traditional *tangi* (burial) protocol by moving onto the *marae* without being invited to do so. Thus, it becomes clear that the new 'gay tribe' is a functional unit that adheres to traditional Māori values, but bends the rules to achieve acknowledgement and respect by their people.

The novel's underlying framework theme of projecting local claims for cultural recognition and socio-economic concerns onto a global platform corresponds to a process of glocalization, signifying the indispensable interaction between the global and the local.[9] As Ihimaera's novel shows, glocalization has found its way into the cultural practice of ethnic minorities. A striking

---

[9] See the discussion of the term 'glocalization' in Roland Robertson, "Glocalization: Time–Space and Homogeneity–Heterogeneity," in *Global Modernities*, ed. Mike Featherstone, Scott Lash & Roland Robertson (London: Sage, 1995): 28–32. Robertson opts for replacing the term globalization with glocalization: originally a Japanese business term used in economics to denote the process of micromarketing (global markets adapting to local conditions), the term, for Robertson, suggests that globalization, with its tendency towards homogenization, and locality, with its dynamic of heterogenization, represent complementary rather than antagonistic tendencies. For an application of 'glocalization' to contemporary Māori writing, see Dieter Riemenschneider, "Contemporary Maori Cultural Practice: From Biculturalism towards a Glocal Culture," *Journal of New Zealand Literature* 18–19 (2000–2001): 139–60.

example is the conference of First Nation Peoples, where indigenous peoples "find support for local demands from transnational networks."[10]

Ihimaera seamlessly interweaves the quest for personal and cultural identity in *The Uncle's Story*. On the one hand, the author pays his tribute to tribal identification:

> She [Roimata] had dressed entirely in black and had placed three white feathers in her hair. I was reminded that her mother was from Taranaki and that, by wearing the feathers, Roimata was acknowledging her ancestral links with Parihaka, the village which had been the great site of resistance during the Land Wars. (324)

On the other hand, it becomes obvious that Ihimaera blends the concept of tribe by asserting an idiosyncratic identity, one that explicitly combines cultural with gender identification by incorporating members from diverse *iwi* who have diverse sexual orientations. By foregrounding the double challenge for indigenous homosexuals on a quest for personal and cultural identity, the author suggests new forms of living together while at the same time upholding Māori traditions. However utopian the author's view of a gay tribe may seem, Ihimaera has transcended traditional and modern values to generate a syncretistic and hybrid identity, not least because of cultural dynamics that are generated and reinforced by a globalized world.

In a society such as Aotearoa/New Zealand, in which individual identities are shaped by multicultural and transcultural processes, there thus seems to be hope for the acknowledgement and respect of cultural difference. Through their literary works, the authors discussed above have not only created respect for a different culture and emphasized the importance of one's cultural heritage: Morris and Ihimaera have succeeded in transcending divergent cultural values and concepts and in constructing very subjective hybrid identities, thus creating selves that are viable against the background of the globalized twenty-first century.

---

[10] Jan Nederveen Pieterse, "Globalization as Hybridization," in *Global Modernities*, ed. Mike Featherstone, Scott Lash & Roland Robertson: 49.

WORKS CITED

Dirlik, Arif. "Rethinking Colonialism: Globalization, Postcolonialism, and the Nation," *Interventions* 4.3 (2002): 428–48.

Featherstone, Mike, ed. *Global Culture: Nationalism, Globalization and Modernity* (London: Sage, 1990).

——, Scott Lash & Roland Robertson, ed. *Global Modernities* (London: Sage, 1995).

Friedman, Jonathan. *Cultural Identity and Global Process* (London: Sage, 1994).

Giddens, Anthony. *Runaway World: How Globalisation is Reshaping Our Lives* (New York: Routledge, 2003).

Hobsbawm, Eric, & Terrence O. Ranger. *The Invention of Tradition* (Cambridge: Cambridge UP, 1983).

Ihimaera, Witi. *The Uncle's Story* (Honolulu: U of Hawai'i P, 2000).

Morris, Paula. *Queen of Beauty* (Auckland: Penguin, 2002).

Nagel, Joane. "Constructing Ethnicity: Creating and Recreating Ethnic Identity and Culture," *Social Problems* 41.1 (February 1994): 152–76.

Pieterse, Jan Nederveen. "Globalization as Hybridization," in *Global Modernities* (1995), ed. Featherstone, Lash & Robertson, 45–68.

Riemenschneider, Dieter. "Contemporary Maori Cultural Practice: From Biculturalism towards a Glocal Culture," *Journal of New Zealand Literature* 18–19 (2000–2001): 139–60.

Ritchie, James Ernest. *Tribal Development in a Fourth World Context: The Maori Case* (Honolulu, Hawai'i: East–West Center Association, 1990).

Robertson, Roland. *Globalization. Social Theory and Global Culture* (London: Sage, 1992).

Willmott, Bill. "Introduction: Culture and National Identity," in *Culture and Identity in New Zealand*, ed. David Novitz & Bill Willmott (Wellington, NZ: GP Books, 1989): 1–20.

◄❖►

Transcultural Perspectives in Caribbean Poetry

S ABRINA B RANCATO

I N THE CURRENT REVISION of canonical notions of culture, Caribbean literature finds itself in a pioneering position. It is increasingly
being recognized that all cultures are transnational, in that they are no
longer seen as strictly bounded to a particular location: they participate in a
continuous exchange and therefore constantly renegotiate their own identity
and challenge simplistic definitions. Culture – if we can avoid throwing the
word into the dustbin – has to be understood as 'transculture': i.e. an on-going
hybridization, a process of embracing and releasing; no longer an island but,
rather, an ocean of waves.

Within Caribbean studies, plurality and syncretism have long been considered the foundation of a Caribbean aesthetic, and research on Caribbean
cultural identity has often drawn on theories highlighting the openness and
flexibility characterizing the region, one major example being the use of
chaos theory by Antonio Benítez–Rojo.[1] The notion of 'transculturalism' has
informed more than one description of the development of Caribbean literature. Alison Donnell and Sarah Lawson Welsh highlight the transcultural
dimension at the very root of Caribbean experience and literature: "The literature of this region, like its history, has *by necessity* developed from acts of

---

[1] Antonio Benítez–Rojo, *The Repeating Island: The Caribbean and the Postmodern Perspective*, tr. James Marannis (*La isla que se repite: El Caribe y la perspectiva postmoderna*,
1989; Durham NC: Duke UP, 1992).

negotiation and crossing between different cultures."[2] For this reason Caribbean literature is consonant with the theoretical tropes of current cultural
developments:

> We are now familiar with literatures of movement, with mobile cultural identities,
> and with flexible notions of aesthetic and cultural value. As readers of Caribbean
> literature we need to be aware that these seemingly postmodern tropes do not arrive
> as abstract theory but rather emerge from the lived reality of mobility, plurality and
> relativity over the centuries. The cultural specificity of Caribbean literature is not at
> risk in this almost postmodern configuration as these features are distinctly Carib-
> bean ones.[3]

In the Caribbean cultural landscape, literary praxis thus anticipates theory.
Caribbean poetry is transcultural both at the stylistic level and at the level of
subject-matter. It could be defined as a transcultural literary genre, since it
springs from the combination of different cultural traditions, both local (slave
songs, calypso, folk music, reggae, popular culture) and foreign (Western
classics, West African griots, the Harlem Renaissance, the American modernist tradition). The transcultural nature of the genre has in fact been thoroughly
and systematically explored by Laurence Breiner, who traces the different
relations which link the poetics of the region to Europe, Africa, and America.[4]
     The creole continuum, so widely employed by Caribbean poets, is itself a
transcultural product. As Edward Kamau Brathwaite highlights in his definition of nation language,

> it may be in English: But often it is in an English which is like a howl, or a shout or
> a machine-gun or the wind or a wave. It is also like the blues. And sometimes it is
> English and African at the same time.[5]

---

[2] Alison Donnell & Sarah Lawson Welsh, "General Introduction" to *The Routledge
Reader in Caribbean Literature*, ed. Donnell & Welsh (London: Routledge, 1996): 25 (my
emphasis).
[3] Donnell & Lawson Welsh, "General Introduction," 25.
[4] Laurence A. Breiner, *Introduction to West Indian Poetry* (Cambridge: Cambridge UP,
1998).
[5] Edward Kamau Brathwaite, *History of the Voice: The Development of Nation Language in Anglophone Caribbean Poetry* (London & Port of Spain: New Beacon, 1984): 13.

While stressing the African connection, Brathwaite also observes that the use of nation language in poetry owes a lot to a Western poet, T.S. Eliot, who introduced "the notion of the speaking voice, the conversational tone," which Caribbean poets incorporated into their "environmental expression."[6] A similar process of transculturation in the assimilation of different traditions is recognizable in Christian Habekost's definition of dub poetry:

> In the wider context of cultural dynamics, dub poetry functions as a connecting link between the 'black' oral tradition and the 'white' literary tradition. For Caribbean culture it represents both the 'African presence' and European influences.[7]

Bruce King also stresses the creative richness of the region, which challenges all restrictive notions of West Indian culture and highlights its transnational character instead: "The iambic pentameter, dub and rap are part of the mix, not mutually exclusive. Much of what is thought of as authentic is an adaptation of recent African or African-American fashions."[8]

As for the subject-matter, Caribbean poetry is deeply concerned with the cultural dynamics of the region and its people, and therefore articulates transcultural constructions of individual and collective identity. To discuss certain aspects of the transcultural dimension of Caribbean poetry, we might distinguish four different categories of analysis: transculturation; transculturality; transnational connections; and transculturalism/transnationalism.[9] These categories can also be considered as progressive stages of the transcultural process tending towards transnationalism as a worldview or an ideology.

I: Transculturation

Transculturation, a term coined in the Caribbean, is not a new concept. The Cuban sociologist Fernando Ortiz first employed the word in the 1940s in the

---

[6] Brathwaite, *History of the Voice*, 30–31.

[7] Christian Habekost, *Verbal Riddim: The Politics and Aesthetics of African-Caribbean Dub Poetry* (Cross/Cultures 10; Amsterdam & Atlanta GA: Rodopi, 1993): 1.

[8] Bruce King, "Introduction" to *West Indian Literature*, ed. King (1979; London: Macmillan, 1995): 4.

[9] I use the terms 'transculturalism' and 'transnationalism' as synonyms, although, while the first is employed more generally, the second is preferred when the emphasis is placed on the overcoming of boundaries of national identities.

context of a study on Afro-Cuban culture,[10] and, since then, it has been used to describe the process of assimilation, through selection and invention, of a dominant culture by a marginal group. The concept of transculturation thus implies, on the one hand, a wide difference in terms of the power held by the two cultural groups which come into contact and, on the other, a resourceful creativity which allows the marginal group to mould the material received to their own advantage. The concept proves particularly useful in the literary context of the Caribbean.

Reference has already been made to the adaptation of the English language in the region as a process of transculturation. But, of course, the literary tradition attached to English as a metropolitan language has also been adapted to local realities and experiences both in the colonial and in the postcolonial context: the counter-discursive practice of 'writing back', the intertextuality through which Caribbean writers establish a dialogue with the metropolitan tradition, and the creativity which allows them to subvert metropolitan tropes can all be seen as part of a phenomenon of transculturation.

Derek Walcott's epic poem *Omeros* is probably the most widely known poetic work to bridge Caribbean and Western traditions. As has been observed, this work "has ensured that readers of Caribbean literature remain aware of the creative and positive possibilities of intertextual relations with classical and canonical work."[11] Other interesting examples of transcultural intertextuality are provided by Amryl Johnson's *Gorgons*[12] and Marlene Nourbese Philip's *She Tries Her Tongue: Her Silence Softly Breaks*.[13] Both works make use of cornerstones of Greek mythology: the story of Medusa, whose look turns everything into stone, in the first case; and the rape of Proserpina by Ade in the second. Johnson and Nourbese Philip transplant these myths into the reality of the Caribbean to rewrite a local history marked by injustice and dispossession. But apart from these major works, let us consider other minor but no less interesting examples of counter-discursive and creative intertextuality.

---

[10] Fernando Ortiz, *Cuban Counterpoint: Tobacco and Sugar*, tr. Harriet de Onís (*Contrapunteo cubano del tabaco y el azúcar*, 1940; tr. Durham NC: Duke UP, 1995).

[11] Donnell & Lawson Welsh, "1930–49: Introduction," in *The Routledge Reader in Caribbean Literature*, 116.

[12] Amryl Johnson, *Gorgons* (Coventry: Cofa, 1992).

[13] Marlene Nourbese Philip, *She Tries Her Tongue: Her Silence Softly Breaks* (London: Women's Press, 1993).

Una Marson's poetic work inscribes itself in the English tradition (and Marson acknowledges her indebtedness to the canon), but nevertheless constitutes a challenge to the tradition by adapting it to her personal condition as a black woman. Her poem "Politeness," for example, is a response to William Blake's "The Little Black Boy," where the black child pities himself for being trapped in a black body: "And I am black, but O! my soul is white."[14] Rewriting this poem, Marson does not revert to the trope associating blackness with filthiness and whiteness with purity but simply extends Blake's assumption to white people and, acting as a spokesperson for the black race, she counters: "They tell us / That our skin is black / But our hearts are white. / We tell them / That their skin is white / But their hearts are black."[15] In another poem, "To Wed or Not to Wed," she dramatizes women's musings on the convenience and the risks of marriage by using Hamlet's best-known soliloquy to wonder: "To wed, or not to wed: that is the question: / Whether 'tis nobler in the mind to suffer / The fret and loneliness of spinsterhood / Or to take arms against the single state / And by marrying, end it?"[16] The parody, of course, serves as a reminder of the fact that women have much more concrete decisions to take before even thinking of indulging in transcendental reflections on existence. Years later, Grace Nichols would draw on the same Shakespearean soliloquy for her cheeky poem "With Apologies to Hamlet," where she parodies the old conflict between art and life by challenging the sacral character of poetic inspiration with an insistence on the urges of physiology: "To pee or not to pee / That is the question / Whether it's sensibler in the mind / To suffer for sake of verse / The discomforting slings / Of a full and pressing bladder / Or to break poetic thought for loo / As a course of matter / And by apee-sing end it."[17] In her comparative reading of Marson's and Nichol's poems, Denise deCaires Narain observes:

> In refusing to parallel exactly the phrasing and weight of Shakespeare's lines, and in replacing Hamlet's existential angst with the figure of the woman poet 'dying for

---

[14] William Blake, "The Little Black Boy" (1798), in *The Norton Anthology of English Literature*, ed. Stephen Greenblatt (1962; New York: W.W. Norton, 1993), vol. 2: 30.

[15] Una Marson, "Politeness" (1937), in *The Penguin Book of Caribbean Verse in English*, ed. Paula Burnett (Harmondsworth: Penguin, 1986): 170.

[16] Una Marson, "To Wed or Not To Wed" (1929), in *The Penguin Book of Caribbean Verse in English*, ed. Burnett, 161.

[17] Grace Nichols, *Lazy Thoughts of a Lazy Woman and Other Poems* (London: Virago, 1989): 6.

a pee', Nichols challenges the idea of the thinker-poet as a transcendental 'I'.
Instead, the writing of poetry is placed firmly within the realms of the ordinary and
the embodied.[18]

Although Marson's rewriting appears to the contemporary reader to be much
less subversive than Nichols's, deCaires Narain points out that, given that
Marson was writing at a time when anti-patriarchal discourses were not a
widespread practice, her poem anticipates Nichols's challenge.

Two other beautiful but less irreverent examples of a creative revision of
received Western tropes are found in Lorna Goodison's "The Mulatta as
Penelope" and "The Mulatta and the Minotaur," both rewritings of Greek
myths. In the "The Mulatta as Penelope," the myth is not reversed but subjected to scrutiny and modified in a womanist mode so as to celebrate
womanhood and motherhood. Penelope does not go out to sea, as might be
expected in a feminist poem, but does not wait for her man either: "this time /
I will not sit and spin and spin / the door open to let the madness in / till the
sailor finally weary / of the sea / returns with the souvenirs and a claim / to
me."[19] Goodison's Penelope is a mulatto woman and a mother: perhaps coun-
tering the historical dispossession of black women in the New World, where,
as slaves, they were denied control over their body and their children, Goodison makes her Penelope dry her hair in the sun and look after her child, rejoicing in herself. "The Mulatta and The Minotaur" is a peculiar love story
across the centuries. Both the mulatta and the minotaur are creatures of mixed
blood, and the minotaur, in Greek mythology confined in a labyrinth for
being the result of the shameful relations of a woman with a bull, here becomes a disarming lover with a god-like figure.[20] In both poems, a myth is
revisited to redeem the victims of injustice.

A subversion of the concept of transculturation as it has been defined in
ethnography is enacted in Louise Bennett's widely known poem "Colonisation in Reverse," where the poet describes how the increasing massive pres-

---

[18] Denise deCaires Narain, *Contemporary Caribbean Women's Poetry: Making Style*
(London: Routledge, 2002): 16.

[19] Lorna Goodison, "The Mulatta as Penelope" (1983), in Goodison, *I Am Becoming My
Mother* (London: New Beacon, 1986): 25.

[20] Goodison, "The Mulatta and The Minotaur" (1983), in *I Am Becoming My Mother*, 31.

ence of Jamaican migrants in England turns "history upside dung."[21] The idea of Caribbean people 'colonizing' England could be read as a reversal of an historical event, of the kind enacted in Brathwaite's *Masks*, where the poet reverses the Middle Passage voyage into a return to Africa.[22] In Bennett's poem, the decision to represent the Windrush through a parody of colonization could be seen as having a touch of revenge in it. But there is more than that: the irony and humour of the text, together with the cheerful tone of the performance, celebrate the hybridizing power of diasporic groups in the metropolis and suggest that the British are no longer going to be British. Here it is Jamaican culture that imposes itself on the motherland, and it is thus the British who are in a certain sense 'forced' to go through a process of transculturation. The poem closes with the speaker wondering mockingly how the brave British, who have faced wars and worse events, are going to stand that process. Not only history is turned upside down, but the actual structure of power implied in the concept of transculturation. Here, it is the marginal group that imposes its culture on the dominant one. As Carolyne Cooper observes in her reading of the poem, "the 'margins' move to the 'centre' and irreparably dislocate that centre."[23]

II: Transculturality

One of the main concerns of Caribbean literature is a preoccupation with identity and self-definition, both at the individual and at the collective level, and an exploration of multiple cultural traditions. To account for these multiple ethnic and cultural roots, Caribbean identity has often been articulated in terms of creolization and hybridity. While acknowledging the validity of both terms and continuing to use them, I nevertheless prefer the term 'transculturality' as a more general term covering both phenomena, creolization and hybridity. Whereas 'creolization', being geographically bounded, excludes the diasporic dimension of Caribbean people living or born abroad, 'transculturality' accounts for both the diasporic and the local reality. As for 'hybrid-

---

[21] Louise Bennett, "Colonisation in Reverse" (1966), in *Hinterland: Afro-Caribbean and Black British Poetry*, ed. E.A. Markham (London: Bloodaxe, 1989): 62–63.

[22] Edward Kamau Brathwaite, *Masks* (London: Oxford UP, 1968).

[23] Carolyn Cooper, *Noises in the Blood: Orality, Gender and the 'Vulgar' Body of Jamaican Popular Culture* (Warwick University Caribbean Studies; London: Macmillan, 1993): 175.

ity', the term is often unsatisfactory, in that it lacks both a dynamic connotation and an explicit reference to the cultural dimension contained in the word 'transculturality'.

This concern with identity, which bears the burden of history, is evident in Derek Walcott's probably most-quoted verses, where one of his multiple poetic selves attempts a self-definition leading to nothing more than a new unresolved dilemma: "I'm just a red nigger who love the sea, / I had a sound colonial education, / I have Dutch, nigger, and English in me, / and either I'm nobody, or I'm a nation."[24] Walcott articulates in his poetry the difficulty of Caribbean people in coming to terms with their plural ancestry, and at times a deep sense of despair emerges in his verses: "I who am poisoned with the blood of both, / Where shall I turn, divided to the vein? / I who have cursed / The drunken officer of British rule, how choose / Between this Africa and the English tongue I love?"[25] Transcultural identity is problematic, especially when the focus is placed on the colonial experience and on the oppression of a group by a dominant one. This produces a sense of fragmentation and the impression that something has been lost forever. In "Cockpit Country Dreams," Olive Senior beautifully dramatizes the consequences of cultural oppression on individual and collective identity through the voice of a child who feels divided and erased: "Now my disorder of ancestry / proves as stable as the many rivers / flowing round me. Undocumented / I drown in the other's history."[26]

Nonetheless, the transcultural dimension of Caribbean identity is not always experienced with a sense of loss, but is often seen as a source of enrichment. It is interesting to observe that transculturality is generally celebrated in ethnic terms. Race is often used as a visible mark of hybridization which is nevertheless also perceived as cultural. George Campbell, for example, gives us a sense of the Caribbean as a melting pot and of the poetic persona as representative of it when he writes: "Dark peoples / Singing in my veins / Fair peoples / Singing in soft strains // Oh, when lift my hand and

---

[24] Derek Walcott, "The Schooner *Flight*," in Walcott, *The Star-Apple Kingdom* (London: Jonathan Cape, 1980): 3–5.

[25] Derek Walcott, "A Far Cry from Africa," in Walcott, *In a Green Night* (London: Jonathan Cape, 1962): 18.

[26] Olive Senior, "Cockpit Country Dreams" (1985), in *Hinterland: Afro-Caribbean and Black British Poetry*, ed. E.A. Markham (London: Bloodaxe, 1989): 219.

pray, / I bow with blue eyes / Dark hands / Red hair // My prayer is life."[27] But Campbell is a colonial poet and his verses reveal a sense of detachment which makes his transcultural claim sound unconvincing. Grace Nichols, a poet of the diaspora, similarly traces her mixed ancestry in her beautiful poem "Tapestry," but in her case the transcultural pattern of identity is made personal and unique: "An African countenance here / A European countenance there / An Amerindian cast of cheek / An Asianic turn of eye / And the tongue's salty accommodation / The tapestry is mine."[28] Lorna Goodison embraces her multiple ethnic roots in a similar way:

> It all belongs to me. I had a poem which I have never published that said something like 'All of it belongs to me', because my great grandfather was a man called Aberdeen, who obviously came from Scotland. And my great grandmother came from Guinea, and because they had a mating and produced my grandmother, who looked like an American Indian – I have relatives who look like Egyptians and my son is an African prince – all of it belongs to me. If somebody tells you, take some and leave some, that is his or her problem. I am not going to do that. All of it belongs to me![29]

Identity, as these poets stress, cannot be split into compartments, and privileging one aspect of one's heritage over the other is part of a self-deceptive and fruitless ideology of cultural identity.

III: Transnational Connections

Transculturality does not necessarily mean having mixed ancestry and carrying in oneself different cultural traditions. A transcultural subject is also a person strongly connected with a culture other than the one dominant in his/ her place of birth or residence, a person, in other words, with multiple belongings. The feeling of belonging here and there can be more or less problematic

---

[27] George Campbell, "When I Pray," in Campbell, First Poems (Kingston, Jamaica: City Printery, 1945): 33, quoted (with different lineation) in Victor Stafford Reid, "The Cultural Revolution in Jamaica after 1938," address delivered at the Institute of Jamaica (1978); repr. (excerpt) in *The Routledge Reader in Caribbean Literature*, ed. Alison Donnell & Sarah Lawson Welsh (London: Routledge, 1996): 180.

[28] Nichols, *Lazy Thoughts of a Lazy Woman*, 57.

[29] Wolfgang Binder, "An Interview with Lorna Goodison," *Commonwealth: Essays & Studies* 13.2 (1991): 57.

depending on the degree of attachment to one's own roots and of adjustment to the host culture. 'Where do I belong?' is the key question underlying much of the literature produced by writers in the diaspora. When the subject's location physically shifts: i.e. when someone's life is marked by geographical movement, it may be more useful to speak of transnational connections. This term proves especially helpful to describe the ways in which writers in the diaspora articulate identity, since expatriate writers are obviously more concerned with the problem of belonging than their counterparts in the Caribbean, and experience a need to be 'connected' (hence the widespread use of the epistolary form in poems on migration and exile).

It is not surprising that in early poems exile should be articulated as a painful experience and that the notion of home should remain unquestioned: one belongs to the place one comes from and remains a stranger in the host country (this sense of 'unbelonging' is obviously also exacerbated by the experience of racism). Una Marson's "Quashie Comes to London" exemplifies the immigrant's belonging to a single place: "It's den I miss me home sweet home / Me good ole rice an' peas / An' I say I is a fool fe come / To dis lan' of starve an' sneeze / [...] It not gwine be anoder year / Before you see me face, / Dere's planty dat is really nice / But I sick fe see white face."[30] What is surprising is that more recent poems should reproduce exactly the same model. James Berry's "Lucy's Letter" presents a similar pattern: the immigrant is still an outcast in the host country and longs to go back home: "Leela, I really a sponge / you know, for traffic noise, / for work noise, for halfway / intentions, for halfway smiles, / for clockwatchin' an' col' weather. / I hope you don' think I gone / too fat when we meet. / I booked up to come an' soak / the children in daylight."[31] Of course, Berry is expressing here the frustrations of working-class people compelled to become expatriates out of necessity. Nonetheless, the fact that patterns of home and belonging should remain unchanged in a span of little less than half a century (Marson's poem was written in 1937) is still striking.

But other poets offer a different version of exile. In Merle Collins's "Seduction," expatriation is still painful but is experienced in a different and more ambivalent way: the immigrant still misses home, but the host country

---

[30] Una Marson, "Quashie Comes to London" (1937), in *The Routledge Reader in Caribbean Literature*, ed. Donnell & Lawson Welsh, 136–37.

[31] James Berry, "Lucy's Letter" (1975), in *The Routledge Reader in Caribbean Literature*, ed. Donnell & Lawson Welsh, 380–81.

is home to her children and she lazily accommodates to it. Her sense of belonging is shaken: "Going home becomes harder, she says / cold winter is
homely / the fire replaces the sun / and yet there's a longing / for the places
that gave me a longing / for leaving. / So what keeps me wandering still / she
wonders / New roots, she says, new shoots / and home moving further
away."[32] Longing is experienced in both places; belonging is somewhere in
between. Here it is a transnational subject speaking and establishing multiple
connections.

Joan Anim–Addo's "Our world" reshapes the concepts of home and belonging at a collective level. The poet traces the history of black people, a
history of forced displacement and exploitation: "Liverpool! Bristol! Spanish
Town! Lisbon! / Yes. We have graced many ports with nakedness / and
marked how our shame began." A mother's voice then exhorts her child to
claim the whole world as home: "Since, my child, we have journeyed so /
then this world bearing our footprints is plainly ours."[33] The dimension of
suffering is still there, recalled and emphasized by the phonetic proximity of
the adverb 'plainly' to 'painly', but this claim is evidently an attempt to in-
validate the sense of loss attached to the experience of dislocation. A similar
process, a focus on the burden of history with a final assertiveness and a renewed consciousness of identity and belonging, one's place in the world, is
the main theme of Grace Nichol's collection *i is a long memoried woman*,
charting the journey of a black woman through the centuries and finally
exorcizing the brutality of historical dispossession through rebirth. In the
epilogue, where the woman claims her coming to voice, she chants: "I have
crossed an ocean / I have lost my tongue / from the root of the old / one / a
new one has sprung."[34]

The insistence on cultural and geographical roots in these and other poems
proves that the need to belong somewhere is still very important. Nevertheless, there is an acceptance of the experience of dislocation and a re-evaluation
of this experience as an element of enrichment which envisages the possibility of development of a new concept of cultural identity based on movement and flexibility. The more one experiences, the more one becomes, as

---

[32] Merle Collins, *Rotten Pomerack* (London: Virago, 1992): 15–16.

[33] Joan Anim–Addo, *Haunted by History* (London: Mango, 1998): 21.

[34] Grace Nichols, *i is a long memoried woman* (1983; London: Karnak House, 1990): 87.

Ahdri Zhina Mandiela's short poem "I am" beautifully expresses, "i / used to be/ a lot of things / now / I am/ more."[35]

IV: Transculturalism/Transnationalism

While transculturality is a condition deriving from factors as diverse as having mixed ancestry or belonging to different cultural groups, transculturalism can be understood as a way of conceiving of identity which tends to overcome the boundaries of national identity. It is, in other words, an ideology which acknowledges the futility of fixed constructed categories such as 'nation' or 'culture' and engages in a more flexible concept based on movement and continuous ex/change.

Caribbean poets, who have been deeply concerned with questions of identity and belonging, show an increasing tendency to deal with this subject at a personal level by overcoming notions of group identity and focusing instead on the multifaceted nature of the individual subject. The focus is often placed on the concept of home, no longer to be identified as a country but, rather, as a private space, no matter where it is, where one feels comfortable. This idea has been developed by women poets in particular. Lorna Goodison, Joan Anim–Addo, Merle Collins, and Grace Nichols, among many others, have devoted a number of poems to the home, by representing a woman, often the poet herself, finding her voice and fulfilling her needs in a space of her own. Identity thus becomes a private, domestic matter. One may be more or less bound to a country or a cultural group, but ultimately one belongs to one's own everyday life, a private space which may change every day.

Grace Nichols's poem "Wherever I Hang" is symbolic of this tendency to overcome the need to belong to a single place/country and to focus instead on the personal and day-to-day life. The narrating voice is that of a Caribbean woman who has left her country to live in England, and the poem, which takes the traditional form of the letter home, dramatizes the process of adjustment of the immigrant subject to the host country. In the beginning, the attachment of the woman to her country of origin is evident in her referring to it as "me land, me home," whereas a sense of hostility towards the host country can be detected in the distance implicit in the expression "this place

---

[35] Ahdri Zhina Mandiela, "I Am," in *Creation Fire: A CAFRA Anthology of Caribbean Women's Poetry*, ed. Ramabai Espinet (Toronto: Sister Vision, 1990): 265.

call England." A sense of estrangement is the dominant feeling in the first part of the poem, where the woman notices "De misty greyness / I touching the walls to see if they are real." At first, there is an effort to maintain the bond with the original country ("I sending home fotos of myself"), but slowly she begins to change her "calypso ways" and adapts to local habits – for example, by "Never visiting nobody / Before giving them clear warning."

Nichols shows the immigrant subject as fragmented, divided between two countries, belonging here and there: "Now, after all this time / I get accustom to the English life / But I still miss back-home side." But the poem's closing line reveals a determination to make a home of any place the self inhabits: "Wherever I hang me knickers – that's my home."[36] Referring to this line, Denise deCaires Narain observes, on the one hand, that Nichol's use of the peculiarly English word 'knickers' suggests that "the process of acculturation is well established" and, on the other, that Nichols inscribes "a female speaker into a role more usually associated with men, that of the roving male lover who refuses to be anchored to one woman (as captured in the refrain of the popular song 'Wherever I Lay My Hat that's My Home')."[37] Nevertheless, the narrative voice of the poem does not really refuse to be anchored anywhere; she simply acknowledges her transcultural condition, which no longer allows her to identify completely with a single country, and therefore resolves to define herself by hanging on to her own self. In this way, the concept of home becomes flexible and hinges on the body and day-to-day life. "Wherever I Hang" shifts the focus of belonging from the geographical and cultural dimension to the personal and offers a vision of the transcultural subject as one who overcomes divisions and is able to feel at home anywhere, no longer an alienated immigrant but, rather, a down-to-earth, everyday cosmopolitan.

To argue that Caribbean poetry promotes a transcultural/transnational ideology would be pushing things too far, since it is undeniable that much of the poetry being published in recent years still deals with dispossession and exile, articulating a sense of fragmentation and loss or, especially in the case of dub poetry with its strong political agenda, a confrontational stance which is for obvious reasons still far from celebrating transculturality. Nevertheless, it has to be acknowledged that, in the way in which several Caribbean poets approach questions of identity and belonging, a world-view based on trans-

---

[36] Nichols, *Lazy Thoughts of a Lazy Woman*, 10.
[37] deCaires Narain, *Contemporary Caribbean Women's Poetry*, 190.

culturalism is emerging and giving a different shape to the perception of one's place in the world. The fact that women poets have been at the forefront of developing this perspective may indicate a significant gender difference in the way transcultural identity is perceived and articulated. But that is an area yet to be explored.

WORKS CITED

Anim–Addo, Joan. *Haunted by History* (London: Mango, 1998).

Benítez–Rojo, Antonio. *The Repeating Island: The Caribbean and the Postmodern Perspective*, tr. James Marannis (*La isla que se repite: El Caribe y la perspectiva postmoderna*, 1989; Durham, NC: Duke UP, 1992).

Bennett, Louise. "Colonisation in Reverse" (1966), in *Hinterland* (1989), ed. Markham, 62–63.

Berry, James. "Lucy's Letter" (1975), in *The Routledge Reader in Caribbean Literature* (1996), ed. Donnell & Lawson Welsh, 380–81.

Binder, Wolfgang. "An Interview with Lorna Goodison," *Commonwealth: Essays & Studies* 13.2 (1991): 49–59.

Blake, William. "The Little Black Boy" (1798), in *The Norton Anthology of English Literature* (1993), ed. Greenblatt, 30.

Brathwaite, Edward Kamau. *History of the Voice: The Development of Nation Language in Anglophone Caribbean Poetry* (London & Port of Spain: New Beacon, 1984).

——. *Masks* (London: Oxford UP, 1968).

Breiner, Laurence A. *An Introduction to West Indian Poetry* (Cambridge: Cambridge UP, 1998).

Burnett, Paula, ed. *The Penguin Book of Caribbean Verse in English* (Harmondsworth: Penguin, 1986).

Campbell, George. "When I Pray," in Campbell, *First Poems* (Kingston, Jamaica: City Printery, 1945): 33, quoted (with different lineation) in Victor Stafford Reid, "The Cultural Revolution in Jamaica after 1938," address delivered at the Institute of Jamaica (1978); repr. (excerpt) in *The Routledge Reader in Caribbean Literature*, ed. Alison Donnell & Sarah Lawson Welsh (London: Routledge, 1996): 180.

Collins, Merle. *Rotten Pomerack* (London: Virago, 1992).

Cooper, Carolyn. *Noises in the Blood: Orality, Gender and the 'Vulgar' Body of Jamaican Popular Culture* (Warwick University Caribbean Studies; London: Macmillan, 1993).

deCaires Narain, Denise. *Contemporary Caribbean Women's Poetry: Making Style* (London: Routledge, 2002).

Donnell, Alison, & Sarah Lawson Welsh, ed. *The Routledge Reader in Caribbean Literature* (London: Routledge, 1996).

Espinet, Ramabai, ed. *Creation Fire: A CAFRA Anthology of Caribbean Women's Poetry* (Toronto: Sister Vision, 1990).

Goodison, Lorna. *I Am Becoming My Mother* (London: New Beacon, 1986).

Greenblatt, Stephen, ed. *The Norton Anthology of English Literature*, vol. 2 (1962; New York: W.W. Norton, 1993).

Habekost, Christian. *Verbal Riddim: The Politics and Aesthetics of African-Caribbean Dub Poetry* (Cross/Cultures 10; Amsterdam & Atlanta GA: Rodopi, 1993).

Johnson, Amryl. *Gorgons* (Coventry: Cofa, 1992).

King, Bruce, ed. *West Indian Literature* (1979; London: Macmillan, 1995).

Mandiela, Ahdri Zhina. "I Am," in *Creation Fire* (1990), ed. Espinet, 265.

Markham, E.A., ed. *Hinterland: Afro-Caribbean and Black British Poetry* (London: Bloodaxe, 1989).

Marson, Una. "Politeness" (1937), in *The Penguin Book of Caribbean Verse in English* (1986), ed. Burnett, 170.

——. "To Wed or Not To Wed" (1929), in *The Penguin Book of Caribbean Verse in English* (1986), ed. Burnett, 161.

——. "Quashie Comes to London" (1937), in *The Routledge Reader in Caribbean Literature* (1996), ed. Donnell & Lawson Welsh, 136–37.

Nichols, Grace. *i is a long memoried woman* (1983; London: Karnak House, 1990).

——. *Lazy Thoughts of a Lazy Woman and Other Poems* (London: Virago, 1989).

Nourbese Philip, Marlene. *She Tries Her Tongue: Her Silence Softly Breaks* (London: Women's Press, 1993).

Ortiz, Fernando. *Cuban Counterpoint: Tobacco and Sugar*, tr. Harriet de Onís (*Contrapunteo cubano del tabaco y el azúcar*, 1947; tr. Durham NC: Duke UP, 1995).

Reid, Victor Stafford. "The Cultural Revolution in Jamaica after 1938," address delivered at the Institute of Jamaica (1978); repr. (excerpt) in *The Routledge Reader in Caribbean Literature* (1996), ed. Donnell & Lawson Welsh, 177–81.

Senior, Olive. "Cockpit Country Dreams" (1985), in *Hinterland* (1989), ed. Markham, 217–19.

Walcott, Derek. *Omeros* (New York: Farrar, Straus & Giroux / Noonday, 1990).

——. *The Star-Apple Kingdom* (London: Jonathan Cape, 1980).

——. *In a Green Night* (London: Jonathan Cape, 1962).

◄❖►

TRANSCULTURAL FICTIONS

The Location of Transculture

MARK STEIN

> Every transculturation [...] is a process in which both parts of the equation
> are modified, a process from which a new reality emerges, transformed
> and complex, a reality that is not a mechanical agglomeration of traits, nor
> even a mosaic, but a new phenomenon, original and independent. To
> describe this process the word *trans-culturation* [...] provides us with a
> term that does not contain the implication of one certain culture toward
> which the other must tend, but an exchange between two cultures, both of
> them active, both contributing their share, and both co-operating to bring
> about a new reality of civilization.[1]

J ACKIE KAY, it could be argued, is not a 'transcultural' author by any
description; she grew up in a white family in Scotland, has lived in
Britain all her life, and continues to do so. However, as a black woman
in a white country; as a member of a visual minority; as a Scottish woman in
England; and as a homosexual in a heterosexist culture, Kay may well qualify
for inclusion in an emergent transcultural canon. And yet, are such biological,
social, and biographical parameters at all appropriate or even helpful in the
context of transcultural writing? Kay's texts reflect transcultural experiences
and predicaments and they do, indeed, undermine "habitual classification of
literary texts in terms of national or regional literatures." Dealing with questions such as cultural 'belonging' and linguistic variety, phenotype and

---

[1] Bronislaw Malinowski, "Introduction" to Fernando Ortiz, *Cuban Counterpoint: Tobacco and Sugar*, tr. Harriet de Onís (*Contrapunteo cubano del tabaco y el azúcar*, 1940; tr.
Durham N C & London: Duke U P, 1995): lviii–lix.

racism, transgender issues and transracial adoption, her texts themselves –
formally as well as thematically – can be profitably considered within a transcultural framework. This, however, raises the question of how the transcultural can be formalized and where it can be located. With transcultural products often approximating a modernist aesthetic (consider Kay's use of jazz,
of multivocality/dialogism, intermediality, and intertextuality), locating them
primarily in formal terms is not unproblematic. However, locating transculture in the sphere of the author rather than her texts is not a workable option,
either. My essay, therefore, seeks to problematize the concept of transcultural
writing (and reading) by probing various ways of localizing transculture –
without denying some of its uses.

I : The Counterpoint of Transculture

This essay will focus on the location of transculture. The concept is not
treated as a given but, instead, a series of questions is raised about what transculture is and how it can be identified. In the process, I shall query a number
of conceptualizations of transculture and transculturation, before moving to
the work of Jackie Kay in the second part of my essay.

In *Notes Towards the Definition of Culture* (1948), T.S. Eliot writes that
religion and culture encompass "the *whole way of life* of a people, from birth
to the grave, from morning to night and even in sleep."[2] And although he
warns not to conceive of culture as "completely unified,"[3] for Eliot culture is
tied to a people, to an ethnic or national group, and therefore governs large
territories with defined borders. This goes back to Herder's understanding of
culture as a whole, an entity which makes "every act and every object an unmistakable instance of precisely *this* culture."[4] Here culture is seen as homogenous, all-encompassing, and exclusive: membership is restricted to "precisely *this* culture," a culture that in turn *authorizes* both acts and objects,
thereby effectively engendering them.

---

[2] T.S. Eliot, *Notes Towards the Definition of Culture* (New York: Harcourt, Brace 1948):
29 (emphasis in the original).

[3] Eliot, *Notes Towards the Definition of Culture*, 30.

[4] Wolfgang Welsch, "Transculturality: The Puzzling Form of Cultures Today," in *Spaces
of Culture: City, Nation, World*, ed. Mike Featherstone & Scott Lash (London: Sage, 1999):
194 (emphasis in the original).

Identities which cut across distinct frames of reference; multiple identities which have recourse to several cultures; attachments which link up discrete cultural territory: such transgressions bring to crisis a traditional understanding of culture and have, for some time now, promoted conceptualizations of transculture. In his well-known essay "Transculturality: The Puzzling Form of Cultures Today," and also in his keynote "On the Acquisition and Possession of Commonalities" at the conference "Transcultural Anglophone Studies" (see the present volume, above), the philosopher Wolfgang Welsch has observed that, today, "the multitude of varying ways of life and lifestyles" makes it impossible for conceptualizations such as Herder's and Eliot's to "cope with the inner complexity of modern cultures."[5] But not only does the increased internal complexity, the heterogeneity, of culture today mean that Eliot and Herder's concepts have been superseded. Following Adorno, Welsch makes a plea for a conception "beyond the contraposition of ownness and foreignness."[6] The proverbial binary of Self and Other, the opposition between sameness and difference, as this might be expressed in postcolonial studies or between "ownness and foreignness," as Welsch puts it, is no longer viable. Conceiving of cultures as separate and clearly delineated entities that are socially homogeneous and ethnically consolidated is no longer satisfactory. Instead, Welsch argues that contemporary cultures are characterized not only by internal difference and distinction but also by "overlaps."[7] They can thus no longer be conceived of as discrete entities. It is the concept of transculture that he draws on in this situation:

> Transculturality is gaining ground moreover, not only on the macrocultural level, but also on the individual's micro-level. For most of us, multiple cultural connexions are decisive in terms of our cultural formation. We are cultural hybrids. Today's writers, for example, emphasize that they're shaped not by a single homeland, but by differing reference countries [and] literature[s]. [...]
>
> Sociologists have been telling us since the 1970s that modern lives are to be understood 'as a migration through different social worlds and as the successive realization of a number of possible identities' (Berger, Berger and Kellner, 1973: 77), and that we all possess 'multiple attachments and identities' – 'cross-cutting identities,' as Bell put it (Bell, 1980: 243). What once may have applied only to

---

[5] Welsch, "Transculturality," 195.

[6] Welsch, "Transculturality," 196.

[7] Welsch, "Transculturality," 203.

outstanding persons like Montaigne, Novalis, Whitman, Rimbaud or Nietzsche,
seems to be becoming the structure of almost everybody today.[8]

It is of significance that in this passage a slippage occurs from the notion of
transculture to the concept of cultural identity; a slippage from the macro- to
the micro-level; from collectivity to the individual and his or her identity.
This is because the relationship between transculture and the individual agent
or an individual cultural product is not interrogated. "We are all hybrid," it is
being suggested. Is that a *result* of transculture? Or does the (presumed) fact
that we are "all hybrids" in effect *produce* transculture? This would take us
right back to Herder's perception of single acts as specific instances of a
given culture (albeit pluralized culture) – when this is precisely what Welsch
had set out to leave behind.[9]

Clearly, it would be folly to deny the existence of a relationship between
individuals, on the one hand, and culture, on the other. This is not my point.
But how does the individual's alleged hybridity relate to culture's transculturality? What is the relationship between individual agent or cultural product
and transculture? How might their interconnectedness work? How does the
implied mediation transpire? Are individuals simply the bearers of a cultural
imprint – a culture chip, if you like – which is, moreover, genetically
inflected, if we follow Welsch's recent 'update' of his transculturality essay
in the present volume? Or is culture, conversely, a mere symbolic reflection
of the ways of life that are adopted by individuals? Neither of these extreme
positions would be satisfactory. However, it is issues such as these that we
need to address. They are among the central questions in the conundrum that
is transculturality.

Citing V.S. Naipaul and Salman Rushdie as examples, Welsch also suggests that novelists themselves insist on being "shaped not by a single homeland"; therefore their "cultural formation is transcultural," he concludes.[10]
Postcolonial writers, by definition, practice at the intersection of several his-

---

[8] Welsch, "Transculturality," 198.

[9] Frank Schulze–Engler, in an essay on the challenge posed by transnational culture to
the study of literature, has noted, however, that Welsch's pointed critique of Herder does in
fact elide the complexity of Herder's work. Nevertheless, critiquing Herder's concept of
culture is a strategically crucial starting-point in the discussion of transculturality. See
Schulze–Engler, "Transnationale Kultur als Herausforderung für die Literaturwissenschaft,"
Zeitschrift für Anglistik und Amerikanistik 50.1 (2002): 65–79.

[10] Welsch, "Transculturality," 198.

torical, political, and cultural terrains, but I am less interested in their own formation than in the impact their writing has: i.e. the impact of their writing (which is notation) when it is enunciated and rehearsed by others. Arguably, it is cultural practitioners such as writers whose work is of particular import in the production and the location of transculture. I shall address this idea when turning to Jackie Kay's work.

Writing eight years before T.S. Eliot, the Cuban anthropologist Fernando Ortiz (1881–1969) launched the term 'transculturation' in his study *Contrapunteo cubano del tabaco y el azúcar*.[11] With regard to the dynamic context of colonial and postcolonial Cuba, he suggested a concept designed to undermine the homogenizing impact of the acculturation model. Instead of the unilateral process of acculturation, Ortiz emphasized "toma y daca," give and take, thereby pointing to the bilateral and even multilateral dimension of his concept. Deculturation, acculturation, and neoculturation – partial cultural loss for each immigrant group, concomitant assimilation of elements of other cultures (European, African, Asian, indigenous), and, finally, the creation of a new Cuban culture – are the three stages in which transculturation proceeds according to Ortiz.[12] The outcome is the fusion of old and new cultural elements into a coherent body. However, this is not conceived of as a process that is then over and done with, but one that continues with each new generation.

Therefore, "the real history of Cuba is the history of its intermeshed transculturations,"[13] Ortiz advises, and he indeed includes a precolonial sweep (to Palaeolithic Indians) in his account. Stressing that transculturation is not a

---

[11] Fernando Ortiz, *Cuban Counterpoint: Tobacco and Sugar*, tr. Harriet de Onís (*Contrapunteo cubano del tabaco y el azúcar*, 1940; tr. Durham NC and London: Duke UP, 1995).

[12] There is some disagreement as to whether Ortiz's concept of transculturation consists of two or three phases. Ortiz initially mentions the two phases of "disadjustment and readjustment [...] of deculturation and acculturation – in a world, of transculturation" (*Cuban Counterpoint*, 98). But then, a few pages on, he suggests that transculturation consists not only of acculturation ("the acquisition of another culture") but also of a deculturation (102) and in "addition [...] neoculturation" (102–103). Fernando Coronil, however, in the new introduction to Ortiz's study, claims that "transculturation suggests two phases [...] 'deculturation' [... and] 'neoculturation.'" By contrast, Nicholas Mirzoeff speaks of transculturation as a "three-way process." See Fernando Coronil, "Introduction" to Fernando Ortiz, *Cuban Counterpoint: Tobacco and Sugar*, tr. Onís (1995), xxvi, and Nicholas Mirzoeff, "Transculture: From Kongo to the Congo," in *An Introduction to Visual Culture* (London: Routledge, 1999): 131.

[13] Ortiz, *Cuban Counterpoint*, 98.

one-way process, he contends that immigrant groups and their cultures are "always exerting an influence and being influenced in turn."[14]

Ortiz, as has been noted above, was referring to a colonial as well as a postcolonial and, notably, New World context. Likewise, Mary Louise Pratt deploys transculturation as a "phenomenon of the contact zone,"[15] a process where subjugated or marginalized peoples determine what they absorb from the materials and codes transmitted by the dominant or metropolitan culture. However, Pratt also importantly asks, "how does one speak of transculturation from the colonies to the metropolis," of the ways "the periphery determines the metropolis"?[16] While Pratt's question of the impact of transculturation on so-called metropolitan centres is crucial, she fails to pursue the transculturation from colony to metropolis in her own study. Benita Parry has criticized Pratt for merely citing "the latter's obsessive need to present and represent its peripheries and its others to itself."[17] Parry writes that "whereas the peripheries can readily be shown to have appropriated and redeployed materials from the centre, what emerges [from Pratt] is that the centre was *unable* to recognize the materials from the periphery as constituting Knowledge."[18]

Going beyond Pratt, Nicholas Mirzoeff suggests that, by the late-twentieth century, transculturation has also reached the West: i.e. those cultures that previously saw themselves as the cultural centres. He not only suggests that "transculture offers a way to analyze the hybrid, hyphenated, syncretic global diaspora in which we live,"[19] but adds that "in the era of global diaspora and interconnection, all culture is transculture."[20] This rather vague notion of all culture constituting transculture is anything but satisfactory, however. Raised to this level of generality, the concept, clear enough in Ortiz's context, loses its capacity to provide apposite definitions and make necessary distinctions.

---

[14] Ortiz, *Cuban Counterpoint*, 98.

[15] Mary Louise Pratt, *Imperial Eyes: Travel Writing and Transculturation* (London: Routledge, 1992): 6.

[16] Pratt, *Imperial Eyes*, 6.

[17] *Imperial Eyes*, 6.

[18] Benita Parry, *Postcolonial Studies: A Materialist Critique* (London: Routledge, 2004): 8–9.

[19] Mirzoeff, "Transculture," 131.

[20] Mirzoeff, "Transculture," 159.

II: Nobody and No Body

Jackie Kay is one of the most versatile writers working in Britain today. She has published drama, short stories, poetry, and novels for adults and children. She writes for page and stage, for screen and radio. Her BBC poetry documentary *Twice Through the Heart* became an English National Opera song cycle. Born in Edinburgh, Scotland, in 1961, Kay did not grow up with her Scottish birth mother and Nigerian father. She and her brother were adopted transracially and brought up in Glasgow by a white working-class family.

This essay will focus on only one of her texts, the novel *Trumpet*, and on the strategies of notation and enunciation performed in – and by – the text. *Trumpet* is a love story and a lament, looking back to the life of the jazz trumpeter Joss Moody. Told from a multiplicity of perspectives, the novel reveals that Joss, who lived with his adopted son Colman and his wife Millie, was in fact anatomically female. His wife was his only confidante, so that Colman is very surprised and upset upon seeing his father in the funeral parlour, realizing his biological sex for the first time.

Joss frees himself from the materiality of his body – not by gender-reassignment, but by living as a 'transgenderist' (before this term had been coined). As a transgenderist, Joss possesses a commitment to living as a man, a commitment that is more substantial than the terms 'transvestite' or 'cross-dresser' could indicate.[21] Joss, we read, learned to walk like a man, talk like a man, dress like a man, blow his horn like a man. While he continues to send money to his mother, signing the cards he sends along as 'Josephine', he otherwise, by all accounts, lives as a man.

There are the stories our bodies tell, and there are those we tell ourselves. When Joss was courting Millie in 1950s Scotland, he kept his biological sex from her. When he finally does take her into his confidence, unwrapping the long bands he ties around his chest, uncovering his breasts, Millie sees a resemblance between the "outline of a corpse in a movie" and his "clothes spreadeagled on my floor."[22] Not only a second skin, his clothing and binding, which aid Joss to appear a man, also constitute his second body – a body that is dead when lying on the floor, but alive when worn. A second

---

[21] Jay Prosser, *Second Skins: The Body Narratives of Transsexuality* (New York: Columbia UP, 1998): 176.

[22] Jackie Kay, *Trumpet* (London: Picador, 1998): 21. Further page references are in the main text.

body that is *also* real. On seeing a corpse in Joss's garments, Millie paradoxically endows them with potential life.

It emerges, then, that Joss's male identity is produced performatively; it is
not based on the materiality of his physical body but on his ability to project a
male-gendered person to his family, friends, colleagues, and to himself. Joss
thereby *propagates* a view of identity that transcends the material body and
relies upon performance and enunciation. Performance and enunciation work
in conjunction with an audience, with recipients who in turn share in the
performance and further contribute to its enunciation. For example, Millie's
marriage to Joss, their life as husband and wife, lends strong support to Joss's
male identity, and also reveals her own interest and investment in his (their)
performance. By unwittingly accepting Joss's maleness, the members of his
band, too, lend it support; Joss's drummer, Big Red McCall, writes in a letter
that he would "fight anyone" who commented on Joss's high voice (159).

Like Big Red's letter, most sections of *Trumpet* have focalizers other than
Joss and therefore present a version of Joss. But in the novel's central chapter,
Joss himself is the focalizer. Here we read about Joss's aspiration to leave behind materiality. It is not blood that is coursing through his veins: "music is
his blood. His cells." In the final analysis, therefore, "blood doesn't matter,"
and none "of the particulars count for much" (135). This passage, which describes Joss playing his music and in effect losing himself in this performance
– and yet celebrates self-creation – continues:

> All his self collapses – his idiosyncrasies, his personality, his ego, his sexuality,
> even his memory. All of it falls away like layers of skin unwrapping. He unwraps
> himself with his trumpet. Down at the bottom, face to face with the fact that he is
> nobody. Playing the horn is [...] about being nobody coming from nothing. The
> horn ruthlessly strips him bare till he ends up with no body, no past, nothing. (135)

Joss makes it clear that he is nobody and no body. Aided by his trumpet, he
frees himself from the materiality of his being. Further, he feels he can free
himself from the grip of history, from his background, even from himself.
What remains is the act of enunciating his sound, playing his music. This
belief in enunciation takes the place of a fixed and recognizable identity. As
we shall see below, this position on the performativity of identity is provocative for Joss's son Colman, who asks his father about their African origins
and his grandfather.

III: "My life is a fiction now"

Joss's performance retains some of its capacity to project masculinity even beyond death. Understandably, the funeral director Albert Holding is dismayed when he undresses Joss Moody. But, more startlingly, he experiences Joss's power as "a woman who persuaded him, even dead, that he was a man, once he had his clothes on" (115). Yet this power no longer works for Colman; he is more deeply affected than the funeral director is by their discovery. Joss's maleness no longer resonates with his son, and this has repercussions for Colman himself. He becomes disorientated and can no longer trust himself, or others. He protests that his father "has made us all unreal" (60) because he no longer feels sure of who he is. Not only has Colman been adopted, therefore feeling a more tenuous link to Millie and Joss. On account of his sex (and because of his death), his adoptive father has all of a sudden become more distant.

Millie likewise feels "strange." Being herself is no longer "a certain thing" for her, because without her husband life has become a "fiction" (154). Although their bereavement demoralizes both Millie and Colman, their responses are ultimately different. While Millie wishes to continue to defend Joss's image, her life with him, and to preserve his memory, Colman embarks on a destructive search for his father's origins. His anger about having been excluded from his father's secret causes a vulnerability which is exploited by a callous reporter. Sophie Stones is working on a sensationalist biography of Joss/Josephine Moody. She plans to ghost-write this book and then publish it in Colman's name, hoping that the book's success will seal her fame. Millie, who is already hunted by journalists from the novel's onset, is also persecuted by Sophie and Colman: her son betrays his mother's confidence, and Sophie and Colman travel towards the remote Scottish cottage in Torr to which Millie has fled, interviewing "witnesses" to Joss's life on the way.

The novel is not only told through a range of focalizers; it also blends a range of text types. Chapter titles include "House and Home," "Editorial," and "Cover Story"; there are also recurrent generic headings such as "People: *The Doctor*" or "People: *The Registrar*." These are clear references to journalistic convention, specifically to the sections that make up our newspapers. This feature complements the novel's engagement with representation and mediatization. It also raises questions about different means of communicating, of claiming stories, and of authenticating them. In the tabloid journalist Sophie Stones we encounter a representative of a culture that feeds on stories and risks wrecking lives in the process. However, the novel does not allow us simply to point the finger at Stones. Not only is she portrayed as caught up in a media world where her desperate measures are wellnigh dictated by her career; given the novel's structural reliance on newspaper headlines, the reader, too, is implicated in the scenario. After all, we are consuming the stories as they are dished up. The early parts read like a thriller, with the reader wanting to find out what Millie is running from (a crime?) and what mystery enveloped Joss; the novel's suspense thus also raises the question of how different the readers of *Trumpet* are from those Stone writes for. While empathizing with Millie for being persecuted by journalists to the point of fleeing the country, Kay's readers are, paradoxically, at once implicated in this mediatized universe – a universe where a good story is hard currency and where Joss's story hits the headlines because readers pay for the broadsheets and tabloids printing them.

IV: "My own country is lost to me now"

Ortiz considered his concept of transculturation to be both "fundamental and indispensable" not only in the context of Cuba but also, "for analogous reasons, of that of America in general."[23] In this sense, jazz is an *American* art form, a transcultural art form, drawing as it does on West African, European, and North American musical traditions. It came into being at the end of the nineteenth century and it may serve as an emblem of the processes of transculturation described in *Cuban Counterpoint*. The turn of the century was also the time when the HMS *Spiteful* landed at Greenock, carrying Joss's father from an unnamed African port to Glasgow. John Moore, as he renamed himself, arrived sensing that the white people standing by the docks "*were* the last century" while he – "like a wild thing"[24] – represented the new one. Ortiz specifically considers migration (including forced migration) as a root factor in transculturation, and inasmuch as Joss represents a transcultural force, it is significant that his father had a migrant biography. Despite his symbolic freight of representing cultural change, John Moore dies when Joss is eleven years old, and leaves his son missing "holding his black hand" (276). Joss not only loses his connection to Africa, and a guiding hand, but also someone who could "clap in rhythm" (276) to his singing and dancing. Joss felt he was on his own from then on – despite his Scottish mother. Not only the lines of

---

[23] Ortiz, *Cuban Counterpoint*, 103.
[24] Kay, *Trumpet*, 272–73 (emphasis in the original).

this father's hand were gone, but also with them his perceived connection to his father's African family.

Kay takes up an historical instance of a transgenderist jazz musician, the story of the American pianist Billy Lee Tipton, an account of whose career was published in the same year as *Trumpet*.[25] The novel thereby transposes its source across the Atlantic, from the USA to Scotland, underscoring not only the diasporic link shared by Joss and Colman, but also the transcultural traffic for which jazz (and Joss) may stand. Practising a New World art form, Joss is musically an agent of transculturation. Via its origins, jazz, moreover, affiliates him with Africa, the continent to which he was also connected patrilineally. Further, Joss himself uses his music to connect with Africa; but this is a "Fantasy Africa," the title of his very first hit. Millie relates that he "had built up such a strong imaginary landscape within himself that he said it would affect his music to go to the real Africa" (34). According to Joss, every member of the black diaspora "has a fantasy Africa" because it is "all in the head" (34). Joss's meditation on diasporic relationships with Africa and its reliance upon the imagination is significant; he has grown up at many removes from the African part of his cultural heritage, yet has learnt not only to lay claim to it but also to invent it first. (Likewise, he suggests to his son that he is Scottish, although he grew up in London.) This indicates that the African diaspora is viewed by Joss not as a collectivity of blood relations but, instead, as an imagined community, one that relies upon affiliation, not filiation. He is therefore not in need of a *concrete*, material connection but prefers to himself originate such connections; he does not rely upon a notation, records, positive facts, but is happy to enunciate an affiliation to Africa by way of jazz.

When quizzed about his family history and the relationship between father and son, Joss tells Colman that they are related "in the way it mattered":

---

[25] Billy Lee Tipton evolved from a cross-dressing musician early in his career to a transgenderist; he married, had adoptive children, wore chest bindings, left his audience and collaborators unaware of his anatomical sex, and when, upon his death, his story made headlines around the world, family members, including some of his former wives, were shocked by the news. There are, then, some parallels between Joss and Tipton, but Kay's novel merely draws on aspects of the Tipton story, rather than fictionalizing his life. See Diane Wood Middlebrook, *Suits Me: The Double Life of Billy Tipton* (Boston MA: Houghton Mifflin, 1998).

He felt that way too about the guys in his bands. He said you make up your own
bloodline, Colman. Make it up and trace it back. Design your own family tree –
what's the matter with you? [...] Any of theses stories might be true [...] You pick.
You pick the one you like best and that one is true. (58–59)

His father's constructivist approach to genealogy and to cultural identity is
highly frustrating for the adoptive son. Although Colman didn't consider Joss
his biological father, he is nevertheless intent on finding out about Joss's
background. And even after Joss's death and the revelation it brings, he investigates his father's life, spurred by Sophie Stones. Gathering hard facts
about his father – and thereby contravening his father's principles – is a project motivated by revenge on Colman's part. But at the end of his life, Joss
had felt a need to communicate to his son what he knew of his own father's
background. He drafted a letter to Colman and with it bequeathed him all his
documents, certificates, and correspondence. Colman's curiosity to know
hard facts could thereby be satisfied. Yet Joss does *not* leave behind a clear
lineage, an unambiguous record, a straightforward legacy. Partly on account
of his transgendered life, its fabrication, and his creativity, Joss's papers will
not provide Colman with all the certainty he seeks. The papers do constitute a
notation, a documentation of Joss's life. But do these papers pertaining to
Josephine Moore, to Joss Moody, in their incongruous nature reflect Joss's
'true' life? Was not the life that Joss chose and projected, which he enunciated, finally his truer life?

But the gesture that Joss performs by writing this letter and handing down
his papers is highly significant: it acknowledges Colman's need and, curi-
ously, it does forge a material connection between the two, placing Joss's
future in his son's hands. Intriguingly, Joss feels he is becoming Colman's
son by way of this gesture (277).

Questions concerning biography and historiography; suspicions about the
inadequacy of records; misgivings about transposing lived life to a different
medium: certainly all of these apply not only to Joss's documents but also to
the narrative as a whole. Like Colman, the reader is confronted with a multiplicity of testimonies and statements pertaining to Joss's lives. Although they
do not add up to a complete picture and are in some cases contradictory, the
novel assembles many voices into a montage that constitutes *Trumpet*. By
contrast, neither the four-CD set "The Best of Moody: The Man and the
Woman" planned by Columbia Records, nor Sophie Stones's "Josephine/
Joss Moody," each promising a *definitive* perspective on Joss's life, actually
get published. There is resistance, then, to fixing Joss, to rendering his life
story transparent, and to pinning him down in a linear narrative. Instead,

Trumpet offers us pieces to rehearse, fragments that can be enunciated and in this fashion be brought to life. In this sense, Joss becomes the readers' son also.

The trumpet, the musical instrument, is a means of enunciating, of voicing a story without putting it into words, thereby allowing Joss to address a multitude of audiences. The air passing through the instrument is the same air that is emitted from it. But once set in motion it touches the audience; it becomes a connective medium that communicates with others and, indeed, affects them. The novel, too, has such an affective potential.[26] I am suggesting, then, that there is an analogy between Joss's impact on his fellow musicians, his family, his audience, on the one hand, and the novel's potential impact on its readership, given the way in which it involves and implicates the reader.

In the first part of this essay, I made an objection to Welsch's passing over the individual and the individual cultural product in the process of transculturation and therefore set out to enquire into the relationships between individual agent, cultural product, and the process of transculturation. It has emerged that Joss is not simply the bearer of an imprint, whether cultural or genetic/biological imprint, and that Joss can be considered an agent of transculturation, a transcultural force; further, the novel as a cultural product has the potential to elicit transculturation effects by confronting and implicating its readers.

It is possible to ground Joss's practice of transculture, to relate it to various influences he claims, and to tally up many of the elements he combines; it is, in other words, possible to locate his practice. However, crucially, I do not wish this to be confused with the notion of a Bhabhian Third Space, in which the translations, adaptations, and appropriations performed by Joss and by Kay's book entail a spatialized concept. *Trumpet* makes it clear that Joss is perceived differently by different people with whom he lived and worked. There is no single negotiated space that he has carved out for himself; with his wife, son, mother, and drummer, for example, a range of distinct relationships existed – for which the novel provides a notation in multiple stories. In practising transculture, Joss loses cultural elements (such as the more conventional, one-to-one relationship between anatomical sex and gender identity), acquires cultural elements (jazz music and also Scottish and African

---

[26] A more sustained argument for such affective and transformative potentials of literary fiction is made in my *Black British Literature: Novels of Transformation* (Columbus: Ohio State U P, 2004).

cultural elements), and creates new, recognizable cultural forms (his fantasy Africa, his gender identity, and his musical style).

Such a process of transculturation is related to (but not identical with) bi-directional cultural translations, about which Homi Bhabha has said that they also exceed "appropriation or adaptation":

> It is a process through which cultures are required to revise their own systems of reference, norms and values, by departing from their habitual or 'inbred' rules of transformation. [...] negotiating with the 'difference of the other' reveals the radical insufficiency of sedimented, settled systems of meaning and signification; it demonstrates, as well, the inadequacy of those 'structures of feeling' (as Raymond Williams would have put it), through which we experience our cultural authenticity and authority as being somehow 'natural' to us and part of a national landscape.[27]

Bhabha's notion of cultural translation has a narrower scope than the concept of transculturation employed here; it merely entails the *revision* of reference, norm, and value systems, whereas transculturation denotes the creation of these systems anew. But transculturation also institutes and follows new rules of transformation in producing new regimes of reference, norm, and value, regimes that draw upon several cultural backgrounds. In such an *evolved* context, cultural authenticity and authority are denaturalized and require reconstruction.

In this sense, *Trumpet* and its protagonist do more than perform cultural translations: Joss introduces *difference* into the contexts he reshapes; the novel confronts its readers with a transcultural force. While it would be false to conflate the transgender and transcultural energies of this novel, the text is very clearly tied to debates that have shaped Britain in the 1990s and continue to shape it today. The text's affective potential, its impact on the reader, and the complexity not only of Joss's life but also of the modes of representation employed to approximate it might constitute a transcultural potential of Kay's text. I am therefore proposing to read Kay's novel *Trumpet* as a work that represents the exceeding of traditions; Joss, the jazz musician, faced with the incongruence of his gender identity and his anatomical sex, forges a transgendered identity, living the life of a married man. What makes me suggest that Joss leads a life in transculture – that he, as Rüdiger Kunow might put it,

---

[27] Homi Bhabha, "The Vernacular Cosmopolitan," in *Voices of the Crossing*, ed. Ferdinand Dennis & Naseem Khan (London: Serpent's Tail, 2000): 141.

practices "trans"[28] – is the fact that Joss travels *symbolically* between distinct cultural traditions and in the process reveals interconnected forms of life and art without "prior existence within the discrete world of any single culture or language."[29] In other words, there is no precedent for Joss's life, no template, and no single cultural heritage in any given cultural context that would accommodate him. In the process of his *symbolic* travels – for Joss is not a migrant, does not in fact travel – and of these symbolic crossings, he not only reveals overlapping forms of life and art: Joss, whose very name resonates with the type of music he performs, stitches together distinct patterns and thereby enunciates new melodies, new stories.

WORKS CITED

Bhabha, Homi. "The Vernacular Cosmopolitan," in *Voices of the Crossing*, ed. Ferdinand Dennis & Naseem Khan (London: Serpent's Tail, 2000): 133–42.

Coronil, Fernando. "Introduction" to Fernando Ortiz, *Cuban Counterpoint* (1995): ix–lvi.

Eliot, T.S. *Notes Towards the Definition of Culture* (New York: Harcourt, Brace, 1948).

Kay, Jackie. *Trumpet* (London: Picador, 1999).

——, & Conor Murphy. *Twice Through the Heart* (London: English National Opera, 1997).

Kunow, Rüdiger. "People of the Crossing: The Subcontinental Diaspora in the United States," in *Transgressions: Cultural Interventions in the Global Manifold*, ed. Renate Brosch & Rüdiger Kunow (Trier: Wissenschaftlicher Verlag Trier, 2005): 1–18.

Malinowski, Bronislaw. "Introduction" to Fernando Ortiz, *Cuban Counterpoint* (1995): lvii–lxiv.

Middlebrook, Diane Wood. *Suits Me: The Double Life of Billy Tipton* (Boston MA : Houghton Mifflin, 1998).

Mirzoeff, Nicholas. "Transculture: From Kongo to the Congo," in Mirzoeff, *An Introduction to Visual Culture* (London: Routledge, 1999): 129–61.

Ortiz, Fernando. *Cuban Counterpoint: Tobacco and Sugar*, tr. Harriet de Onís (*Contrapunteo cubano del tabaco y el azúcar*, 1940; tr. Durham NC & London: Duke UP, 1995).

Parry, Benita. *Postcolonial Studies: A Materialist Critique* (London: Routledge, 2004).

Prosser, Jay. *Second Skins: The Body Narratives of Transsexuality* (New York: Columbia UP, 1998).

Pratt, Mary Louise. *Imperial Eyes: Travel Writing and Transculturation* (London: Routledge, 1992).

Schulze–Engler, Frank. "Transnationale Kultur als Herausforderung für die Literaturwissenschaft," *Zeitschrift für Anglistik und Amerikanistik* 50.1 (2002): 65–79.

---

[28] Rüdiger Kunow, "People of the Crossing: The Subcontinental Diaspora in the United States," in *Transgressions: Cultural Interventions in the Global Manifold*, ed. Renate Brosch & Rüdiger Kunow (Trier: Wissenschaftlicher Verlag Trier, 2005): 2.

[29] Bhabha, "The Vernacular Cosmopolitan," 141.

Stein, Mark. *Black British Literature: Novels of Transformation* (Columbus: Ohio State UP, 2004).

Welsch, Wolfgang. "Transculturality: The Puzzling Form of Cultures Today," in *Spaces of Culture: City, Nation, World*, ed. Mike Featherstone & Scott Lash (London: Sage, 1999): 194–213.

Witmer, Robert, & Rick Finlay. "Notation," in *The New Grove Dictionary of Jazz*, ed. Barry Kernfeld (London: Macmillan, 2nd ed. 2002): 167–75.

❮❖❯

"Final Passages"?

— Representations of Black British History in Caryl Phillips's Novel and Its Television Adaptation

EVA ULRIKE PIRKER

LACK BRITISH HISTORY has become a topic of interest in different discursive fields – for instance, cultural studies, postcolonial studies, and debates on national and collective identities. A relatively new development is its omnipresence in the media – no longer exclusively those addressing an arthouse or scholarly clientele, but the mass media. In the past few years, public broadcasting houses have included television drama, television documentary, and other formats about the black British experience and its historical roots. This interest is certainly connected with the generational threshold that is currently being crossed – the 'Windrush' generation (the largest of the West Indian waves of migrancy to Britain) is dying out. While the historicity of the black experience has only lately entered public awareness, it has long been a concern for black writers and filmmakers in Britain. Their works, however, were largely perceived by an exclusive audience. Nevertheless, Kobena Mercer had already anticipated a shift in the perception of representations of 'black themes' in the late 1980s:

> black film-making is a marginal cultural practice, but as it expands and becomes
> progressively de-marginalized, its oppositional perspectives reveal that the tradi-

tional structures of cultural value and national identity are themselves becoming increasingly fractured, fragmented and de-centered.[1]

Mercer touched on a point that was to become another important factor in the process of making the highly politicized issue of black history[2] compatible with mainstream concerns in the 1990s: the debate on Britain's national history. The fervour of the debate becomes evident when one takes a look at the numerous programmatic declarations produced by the visual-studies departments of institutions, media corporations, and governmental think-tanks. The question of how to rewrite or represent a national history is inseparably linked with the question of national identity. That the latter is not a matter of fate but can and must be invented and actively constructed seems to be a matter of consensus. Mark Leonard, for instance, points out in *Britain^{TM}: Renewing Our Identity* (a study published by the think-tank Demos in 1997):

> Nations have been recreating their identities throughout recorded history. Monarchs, emperors, popes and parliaments all used icons, myths and ceremonies to tell the world what they stood for and what made them special. Today, nations use new tools – logos and branding techniques, advertising campaigns and festivals, speeches and trade fairs – to project their identity to the outside world. [...]
>
> But the main reason why this needs to be done is that a gulf has opened up between the reality of Britain as a highly diverse society and the perception around the world that Britain remains a backward-looking island immersed in its heritage.[3]

---

[1] Kobena Mercer, "Recording Narratives of Race and Nation," in *Black Film, British Cinema: Papers from the ICA Conference February 1988* (London: Institute of Contemporary Arts, 1988): 5.

[2] Mercer notes that a "consistent motivation for black film-makers has been to challenge the predominant stereotypical forms in which blacks become visible [...] as some intractable and unassimilable Other on the margins of British society and its collective consciousness. It is in relation to such dominant imagery that black film-making has brought a political dimension to this arena of cultural practice." Kobena Mercer, "Recording Narratives of Race and Nation," 8. The theme of black history, traditionally seen as a collective memory of trauma or 'victims' memory' in Aleida Assmann's sense, has been a highly sensitive theme in this context. In the course of the 1990s, however, the obligation of black filmmakers and writers towards such a 'collective consciousness', the obligation to be political, seems to have lost some of its impetus. For the concept of a 'victims' memory' and other forms of collective memory, see Aleida Assmann & Ute Frevert, *Geschichtsvergessenheit – Geschichtsvergessenheit: Vom Umgang mit deutschen Vergangenheiten nach 1945* (Stuttgart: Deutsche Verlags-Anstalt, 1999): 41–49.

[3] Mark Leonard, *Britain^{TM}: Renewing Our Identity* (London: Demos, 1997): 15.

Leonard sees diversity (both ethnic and cultural generally) as one of the several facets that determine the basis on which Britain's national identity should be constructed. The historicity of visible communities' experience, however, is not taken into account when he looks at national identity-shaping aspects of British history. This "missing history" was addressed by Chris Smith in his keynote lecture at the Arts Council's national conference *Whose Heritage* in 1999:

> It's said that truth is the first casualty of war. But how does truth fare in the face of ignorance? Without a recorded history, nothing else can follow: no celebration of achievement; no development of a common cultural heritage. This results in immigrant populations looking outside these shores for their history and cultural points of reference. By recording their contribution and place in British history, we give people their roots, and give their cultures proper recognition and an appropriate stature within and beside the traditional Anglo-Saxon and Celtic cultures.[4]

Smith expresses the need to remodel history accordingly; he sees this as "the need to provide a more complete version of the truth."[5]

The Arts Council and other major cultural, media, and broadcasting institutions have begun to implement strategies to help improve the representation of issues of interest in and from the visible communities of Britain; black British history has become one of the popular themes in this context. It appears, however, that the essence of this strongly supported theme remains unclear. A number of questions remain open: what does black British history look like? Whose history is it? Who can give an account of it? When did it start? Where is it possibly leading? Although the term 'black British history' has become popular, as can be seen in the recent annual celebration of a "Black History Month,"[6] it evades definition. It is thus not surprising that existing contributions to the discourse on black British history have been heterogeneous in their modes of representation, their use of a wide range of media, their target-audience, and their approach to the subject-matter of black British history. The examples discussed in this essay are contributions by

---

[4] Chris Smith, "Opening Address," in Whose Heritage? The Impact of Cultural Diversity on Britain's Living Heritage, National Conference, Manchester, 1999, ed. The Arts Council of England (London: The Arts Council of England, 1999): 8.

[5] Chris Smith, "Opening Address," 8.

[6] See, for instance, the website www.Black-History-Month.co.uk (accessed 5 April 2008).

Caryl Phillips: his first novel, *The Final Passage* (1985) and his later epony-
mous television adaptation of that novel for Channel 4.[7]

Both the film adaptation and the novel tell the story of the Caribbean
newlyweds Michael and Leila, who make their journey across the ocean in
the wave of other migrants in the late 1950s. Interestingly, the novel and its
adaptation, written a decade later and for a mass medium, give remarkably
disparate accounts of black British history. While the film, broadcast at peak-
time in summer 1996, foregrounds the narration of a 'general' history of West
Indian mass migration from a 1990s perspective and uses the characters to
illustrate that history, the novel focuses on the development of the individual
characters, with the historical context as backdrop. The two products can thus
be said to represent two discourses, two ways of telling one story.

Leila and Michael, the protagonists, grow up on a small Caribbean island,
the name of which is not specified.[8] While Leila, a mulatto girl, is raised by a
single mother, Michael's parents leave their young son to his poor grandparents and emigrate to the USA. When the educated working girl Leila and
the jobless but free-spirited Michael meet, the latter already has a child by
another woman, Beverly, with whom he has been carrying on a relationship
while on the island. Michael and Leila go out together, she gets pregnant, and
they marry against the will of Leila's mother, who deeply disapproves of the
relationship. Michael senses this, and walks out of the wedding reception.
Leila's mother, seriously ill with cancer, goes to England for surgery. After

---

[7] Caryl Phillips, *The Final Passage* (London: Faber & Faber, 1999); Peter Hall & Caryl
Phillips, *The Final Passage* (London: Channel Four Productions, UK 1996). Research on
(television) adaptations of novels largely concentrates on the 'classics' of English literature.
For general insights, see *The Classic Novel: From Page to Screen*, ed. Robert Giddings &
Erica Sheen (Manchester: Manchester UP, 2000), *Adaptations: From Text to Screen,
Screen to Text*, ed. Deborah Cartmell & Imelda Whelehan (London: Routledge, 1999), and
John Caughie, "A Culture of Adaptation: Adaptation and the Past in British Film and Tele-
vision," *Journal for the Study of British Cultures* 5.1 (1998): 55–66. For a detailed overview
and case-study discussions of black British film (including adaptations of literary texts), see
Barbara Korte & Claudia Sternberg, *Bidding for the Mainstream: Black and Asian British
Film since the 1990s* (Amsterdam: Rodopi, 2004), of which chapter 6, "1990s Television
Drama: Mainscreening Black and Asian History," 179–203, offers an analysis of Hall's and
Phillips's *The Final Passage* with regard to the production's mainstream intentions.

[8] The Caribbean part of the TV drama was shot on location in St Lucia. This is, however,
not mentioned in the film. Neither are the names of the towns ("Baytown," "St Patrick,"
etc.) indicative of a specific island. These names can be found all over the formerly British
West Indies.

the birth of her son Calvin, Leila decides to follow her mother. Michael turns up again and wants to come along, to start afresh "as a family"[9] in the mother country. In London, their expectations are disappointed in every imaginable way. Instead of a fine place, the mother's lodgings prove to be a bedroom in a house crammed with West Indian immigrant men who take shifts using the few beds. The elderly Earl, apparently a friend of the mother, informs the in a state much worse than when she left the island. The family has to find a place to live, which is not easy: rooms or houses for rent are generally not available to 'coloured' people. Leila ultimately rents a run-down terraced house from an estate agency. Michael disapproves but moves in along with her. The problems in their marriage, apparently rooted in a lack of communication, mount; Michael begins a relationship with a white woman and leaves his wife. Apart from an Irish neighbour and a social worker, Leila has nobody to turn to.

The adaptation gives the story a closed ending that shows an elderly Leila who is visited by her adult son Calvin. Both have 'made it' in England. The novel's conclusion is open and leaves the reader feeling uncomfortable. Here, young Leila, pregnant again, turns away from the world in distrust. Visions of her home crop up which could be read as anticipations of a return but are, rather, her refuge in a world of illusions. Leila in London seems to have lost every connection to the world and retreats into madness.

The adaptation presents the traditional *Bildungsroman* plot – the linear progress of the protagonist's struggle to find his/her place in the world. The plot of the novel also follows a developmental trajectory, but in the form of a downward spiral culminating in the protagonist's total estrangement from and distrust of the world surrounding her. Phillips's novel can thus hardly be read as a *Bildungsroman*, neither in the traditional nor in the modern version of the genre, in which the aim of finding one's place in the world is replaced by the aim of finding or coming to terms with the self. Leila, the protagonist, lacks any concept of self: her sole orientation is the mirror which those around her hold up to her. In the course of events, this mirror becomes cracked, dysfunctional, and thus only reflects a distorted picture, which accounts for the protagonist's increasing and ultimately overwhelming desperation. This is illustrated in a passage from the closing chapter of the novel, "Winter":

---

[9] This expression is used by the commenting narrator in the novel (Phillips, *The Final Passage*, 95); in the adaptation, they are Michael's words (Hall & Phillips, *The Final Passage*, Part One, closing scenes).

Leila stopped at a window and listened to her son speaking, though he could not as
yet speak. She watched his image reflected in the glass as he spoke with unsurety.

"Mommy, is that Santa Claus there, that man with the white beard and
moustache, that man with a red suit and a red face?" […]

"Yes, Calvin, that's Santa Claus," said Leila.

Calvin looked at her as she confirmed the man's identity, then he looked back at
the man.

"Why is Santa Claus white?"

Leila could not answer her own question. (202)

Not only is there confusion about the speaker (Leila's inner voice or a voice
Leila projects onto Calvin), but also unclarity about the object spoken about.
The existence of the object, Santa Claus, is only revealed in direct speech and
not commented on by the narrator. One could see it as the reflection of a real
man dressed up as Santa Claus or as a Santa Claus dummy behind the window. The dressing-up and the idea of reflection contribute to the impression
of confusion in Leila's head and culminate in the confusion brought about by
the questioning of a prominent image that stands for the seeming distinctiveness of the mainstream culture's heritage, a 'white Christmas'. The question
of Santa Claus's skin colour ultimately links up with the question of Leila's
own neither-black-nor-white skin colour, which in turn reflects her dilemma
of belonging neither here nor there. The issue is explicitly addressed in an
earlier passage in "Winter," a passage that again involves the image of the
mirror:

In England Leila had suddenly found herself, her light skin starved of the sun,
growing paler by the day. But she was more coloured than she had ever been
before, and not shame exactly, but feelings of inadequacy prevented her from looking back into the mirror. (194–95)

The mirror can be read as a metaphor for emptiness and futility; it only gains
meaning through the objects that it reflects. Phillips repeatedly makes use of
imagery that suggests emptiness in connection with Leila. In a passage on the
sexual acts between Michael and Leila, the latter is described feeling "as if
she were a tunnel" (189); a few pages further on, the reader learns that "the
thought of being pregnant again filled Leila with something, though it was
neither fear nor happiness" (192). The use of the terms "tunnel" and the
phrase "filled […] with something" suggest an empty vessel. This and the
recurrent image of Leila clutching her baby add to the impression that she
tragically lacks a concept of self that could strengthen her and give her an

identity in a world that does not readily provide constructs of identity for migrant, in-between figures.

The novel is organized in five parts, with one central part entitled "England." It recounts the mother's dying and uses analepses that lead to the mother's past and thus provide the reader with explanations about Leila's background and character that would otherwise remain enigmatic, such as her silence. Leila seeks communication and answers unasked questions, to gain knowledge about the past and herself when she goes to see her mother, but does not reach her goal: the exchange between mother and daughter in the English hospital remains superficial, as can be seen in the following passage:

> Her mother paused. "And how is your husband?"
>
> "Things are fine," said Leila.
>
> Her mother laughed quietly.
>
> "You don't change at all, do you? Still the diplomat." [...]
>
> Leila fought back the tears in her eyes. She had always felt a child could never understand the illogicality of a parent's love until the child was a parent itself. But sadly, though Leila now felt she understood her mother a little better, her mother did not seem to have changed in her feelings towards her. That she loved her she did not doubt, but, as always, Leila wished there was something more, something that would make her mother more like a friend. As it was they just sat and stared at each other. The pain of illness, the pain of marriage, the pain of a journey across the world and the happiness of a small baby for them both to share, nothing seemed to be able to bring them together and this first exchange had been more interview than conversation. (123–24)

While the older woman remains a stranger to her own child, the reader of the novel learns more about the mother through the commenting, heterodiegetic narrative voice – about her having been regularly raped by a great-uncle who then also died before her eyes, and about later lovers who, after they had left, made her feel "used, like a canvas upon which an artist has toyed in light pencil" (125). After giving birth to a light-skinned baby girl, she demands money from three white men, "accusing them all of being the father and threatening to expose them as molesters if they even so much as looked at Leila" (126). The men, who look at their supposed daughter from a distance, "happily paid the money safe in the knowledge that they had a real relationship with the island that would live on after they left" (126). The woman's wit leaves a bitter-sweet taste – sweet in the sense that the idea of just revenge is evoked here; bitter, because the sexual relationships of white colonials with black slave women is one of the uncomfortable colonial memories that live on in the descendants of those generally involuntary liaisons.

The adaptation does not equip Leila's mother with a comparable past. Here, viewers learn only that she disapproves of Michael – they are left to make guesses about her own experiences with men. She appears as one of the sources for Leila's concerns and sorrows, but is not given the substantial and enigmatic quality of the mother in the novel, who remains nameless throughout the narrative. In the television drama, she gives the impression of being the loving mother who is put off by her daughter's foolishness but is too weak to do anything about it. One important point, however, is reflected in novel and film alike: without complaining about her current state, she makes it clear that she could never see England as her home. England, however, is the place in which she dies and is buried, a place that 'swallows' her. This power and dominance of the unloved place is illustrated by the image of the English soil that covers her in both novel and film; in the novel, she is, furthermore, figuratively 'buried' by the text: the part of the novel that allows insight into her past is entitled "England."

While the circumstances of her mother's death contribute to Leila's increasing desperation in the novel, they appear in a different light in the adaptation. The mother's death is one of the many hardships that Leila encounters but ultimately overcomes. Leila's most striking characteristic, her silence, something that has puzzled critics of the novel,[10] is also attached to her character in the television drama. Whereas, in the novel, the silence increases and ultimately gains the power to destroy Leila, in the adaptation the silence is broken at the end. The positive ending is in accordance with the design and aim of the production, which was to give an account of a successful black British (hi)story. However, the prime concern of the adaptation is even more basic: the representation of black British history as an important part of British history in the nation's "most potent medium."[11] As Caryl Phillips says,

> [the West Indian presence in Britain] struck me as being the most important change of the social fabric of Britain in the second half of the twentieth century, and though it had been done in fiction [...] it hadn't been seen on the most potent

---

[10] See, for instance, C.L. Innes, "Wintering: Making a Home in Britain," in *Other Britain, Other British: Contemporary Multicultural Fiction*, ed. Arthur Robert Lee (London: Pluto Press, 1995): 25.

[11] Maya Jaggi, "The Final Passage: An Interview with Writer Caryl Phillips," in *Black British Culture and Society: A Text Reader*, ed. Kwesi Owusu (London: Routledge 2000): 157.

medium in Britain – television. Caribbean migration has made a phenomenal impact – whether it's the music on Top of the Pops, or football.[12]

A little irony can be seen in the fact that although the adaptation succeeds in showing the transformation of Britain through migration, the transforming agents, the migrants, come from a place that is still permeated by British culture and colonial myths.[13] The protagonists in the film are drawn as types, as a representative immigrant couple in the 1960s with 'representative problems'. Especially Michael's character is depicted one-dimensionally: he stands in an almost stereotypical way for the black man who badly wants to fulfil his role as bread-winner but has trouble finding a job. He has not been raised to take responsibility and is not only a womanizer, but ultimately always dependent on women. In the adaptation, Leila is thus quickly associated with the figure of the victim who in the end becomes a kind of victorious heroine. She is the more pragmatic of the two, the one who ultimately 'makes it' in England and is able to stand on her own feet, despite the hardships she encounters. The marriage fails in the film as in the novel – in the adaptation, however, the reasons for this failure are clearly shown as Michael's responsibility. The second part of the television drama draws heavily on the novel's fourth part, "The Passage," which gives a detailed account of the events in London; here, however, they are approached from a different angle. In the film version, the difficulties Leila and Michael encounter in England are much more foregrounded than in the novel, which centres on the couple's (especially Leila's) problems communicating. The novel increasingly focuses on Leila. "The Passage," for instance, is almost exclusively about her, although the distance established by the novel's continuously heterodiegetic, externally focalized narrative voice is maintained here. In the adaptation, the scenes shift between Leila's and Michael's experiences: at the very end, the viewers encounter an old Michael who is sought out by his son Calvin, while the Michael in the novel ultimately disappears.

---

[12] Maya Jaggi, "The Final Passage: An Interview with Writer Caryl Phillips," 157.

[13] A powerful image is, for instance, Leila's and her friend Millie's workplace, a typists' pool in a government office. A white, portly supervisor is placed as if on a throne before a herd of black female typists. Despite the comfort of a fan and the official atmosphere that is conveyed by the British flag and a picture of the Queen, the man is sweating. The rhythmical clacking of the typewriters could be seen as alluding to the rhythms of the drums used in black slaves' field work a century earlier. The girls' giggling, however, renders the situation comical. Peter Hall & Caryl Phillips, *The Final Passage*, Part One, establishing scenes.

The diverging developments in film and novel reflect disparate conceptualizations of black British history: while the film shows characters that can
be read as representatives of *the* black British community of the first and even
the second generation, the novel foregrounds the individual, unique features
of its characters. The characters in the novel are hardly 'prototypical' migrants. While the film presents black British history as the history of a group
with a collective memory, the novel intimates that although there may have
been a phase of collective migration, the individual stories are as divergent
and disparate as those who play the leading roles in them; it thus questions
the possibility of one representative account of a black British history or any
collective history.

The realization of Phillips's project of rendering black British history in
the popular, if expensive format[14] of the two-part television drama certainly
required conceptual concessions.[15] Apart from the depiction of characters, the
most striking deviations from the novel are the simplification of plot and
structure. In each part of the television drama, framing ring compositions are
used. The first part is embedded in a ring that describes Leila's queuing up for
the ship while Michael takes his time to turn up. In an analepsis that takes up
most of the time in this part, an account is given of the events that have led to
the family's sea-passage. The closing half of the frame does not end on the
ship, but with the protagonists' train-journey to London, where they are faced
with their first disappointing findings. In contrast to the respective part in the
novel, entitled "The End," the frame in part one of the television drama does
not end in a mixture of uncertainty and hopeful expectations, but literally as a
dead end, an end to illusions about the new place.

The tone alters in the second part. Here the frame structure employs scenes
of the adult Calvin, who is driving through London to go and see his mother,
determined to find out more about his/their past. Calvin's driving parallels
Leila's journey across the ocean in the first part: she goes to see her mother.
In the novel, the hopes that Leila projects onto her mother in her quest for
communication, understanding, and identity are explored in detail. In contrast

---

[14] Cf. Barbara Korte & Claudia Sternberg, *Bidding for the Mainstream*, 203.

[15] In a personal communication in February 2004, Phillips indicated that although collaboration in a co-production like *The Final Passage* is "never 'easy', [...] making the story
slightly more 'upbeat'" was his decision: "I felt that things had improved in Britain, and
that the country was full of 'survivors'. I wanted to pay tribute to those that stayed on and
survived."

to Leila in the novel, however, Calvin in the adaptation succeeds in his pursuit of answers. In the frame of the second part, set in the late 1980s/early 1990s, communication replaces silence; solutions for a dilemma are found. The second part thus ends on a positive note and shows the success of Leila and Calvin: Leila has made her way to a comfortable middle-class existence, she is living in a terraced house and the only thing that disturbs her is that she is a bit "bored."[16] This may express loneliness, but also a certain degree of luxury: she has worked all her life and is now retired and only has the passing of time to worry about, which is further illustrated by the fact that she does not know what day it is. Her problems are those of well-to-do Western elderly people. Calvin is fully immersed in the urban working sphere, employed in the service/sales sector, and cruising the metropolis – the streets of which show a 'multicultural' population – in his little Volkswagen. This cruising of the place can be seen as knowing one's environment, claiming the place to a certain degree as one's own or home. The same sort of cruising has been seen in part one of the drama, in which Michael cruises the island on his scooter, in turn *his* home, *his* environment, *his* territory.[17] The motion described by driving around the city, however, shows another parallel to part one. Both frames, the one in the first part and the one in part two, are connected with moving or aiming at something. The ship crosses the ocean; the car navigates the streets of London. The ship holds a mass of people who share the same dream; the car holds the young individual of the early 1990s who goes to find out about his past and identity.

As shown above, the two works diverge greatly in their presentation of the story. Although the general theme and characters remain the same in the film, two stories are told in the novel and the film, and two images of black British history are presented. The adult Calvin, introduced in the adaptation, is a child of the 1990s, a decade in which multiculturalism becomes an ideal or at least a political issue in Western societies. That the plot of the novel does not serve as the basis for this development may be due to the fact that a broader awareness of the existence of black British success only emerged in the 1990s and this development could not be anticipated at the time the novel was written. On the other hand, the author may deliberately have chosen not to tell a

---

[16] Peter Hall & Caryl Phillips, *The Final Passage*, Part Two, establishing scenes.

[17] The idea that the male driving around functions as a "spatial signifier" in the adaptation is also expressed by Barbara Korte and Claudia Sternberg. See Korte & Sternberg, *Bidding for the Mainstream*, 202.

success story or to provide the problems raised with simple solutions. The film's focal point is England, not merely in its representation of the movement of mass migration, but especially in its creation of the image of black people planting roots and prospering on English soil, whatever the obstacles.

Leila's voicelessness stands metonymically for the voicelessness of a whole generation of black Britons. Just like Leila's silence in the film *The Final Passage*, this collective silence was broken in the 1990s and has been replaced by widespread negotiations that obviously find an impressive audience. One can certainly argue that the representation of black British history as a history that follows a linear development towards prosperity and final success is to a great extent one-sided and by no means representative of the experiences of the individual members of the black British community. One can criticize these representations as not doing justice to the uniqueness of the individual experience and question the existence of *one* black British history; one can expose it as a typical construct of a collective memory, which draws more from the need of a group to give a meaning to their existence than from past realities that evade representation.[18] Ultimately, one can express great discomfort with the use of the mass medium of television and the choice of the popular format of the two-part drama for a complex issue such as black British history. Although these points are to some degree justified and need to be addressed in theoretical discourses about black British history and the question of its representation, one must take into account the fact that precisely these sometimes simplifying and therefore deficient productions have the advantage of being extremely effective in their capacity to address a large audience. To leave the issue of black British history to discourses of theory and works of arts, literary texts or films that exclusively address an intellectual audience would certainly be equally insufficient. The popularity and media presence of black British history offer new perspectives of looking at the phenomenon and demand thorough investigation. This media presence has helped raise general awareness of the topic; in representing one side of the picture, it challenges viewers and critics to question it and thus continue

---

[18] Aleida Assmann stresses the functionality of memory and maintains that collective memory often serves as a group-strengthening force. The danger in this process lies in the sometimes inadequate rendering of history for the sake of giving it a meaning. See Aleida Assmann & Ute Frevert, *Geschichtsversessenheit – Geschichtsvergessenheit, 35 and Aleida Assmann, Erinnerungsräume: Formen und Wandlungen des kulturellen Gedächtnisses* (Munich: C.H. Beck, 1999): 130–45.

the discussion. The conversation is no longer an exclusive one, a discourse among researchers in postcolonial studies or practitioners of black British cultural studies – new participants from various backgrounds and learning have been invited to take part.

WORKS CITED

Assmann, Aleida. *Erinnerungsräume: Formen und Wandlungen des kulturellen Gedächtnisses* (Munich: C.H. Beck, 1999).

Assmann, Aleida, & Ute Frevert. *Geschichtsversessenheit – Geschichtsvergessenheit: Vom Umgang mit deutschen Vergangenheiten nach 1945* (Stuttgart: Deutsche Verlags-Anstalt, 1999).

"Black History Month," http://www.Black-History-Month.co.uk (accessed 5 April 2008).

Cartmell, Deborah, & Imelda Whelehan, ed. *Adaptations: From Text to Screen, Screen to Text* (London: Routledge, 1999).

Caughie, John. "A Culture of Adaptation: Adaptation and the Past in British Film and Television," *Journal for the Study of British Cultures* 5.1 (1998): 55–66.

Giddings, Robert, & Erica Sheen, ed. *The Classic Novel: From Page to Screen* (Manchester: Manchester UP, 2000).

Hall, Peter, & Caryl Phillips. *The Final Passage* (London: Channel Four Productions, 1996).

Innes, C.L. "Wintering: Making a Home in Britain," in *Other Britain, Other British: Contemporary Multicultural Fiction*, ed. Arthur Robert Lee (London: Pluto Press, 1995): 21–34.

Jaggi, Maya. "*The Final Passage*: An Interview with Writer Caryl Phillips," in *Black British Culture and Society: A Text Reader*, ed. Kwesi Owusu (London: Routledge, 2000): 157–68.

Korte, Barbara, & Claudia Sternberg. *Bidding for the Mainstream: Black and Asian British Film since the 1990s* (Amsterdam: Rodopi, 2004).

Leonard, Mark. *Britain™: Renewing Our Identity* (London: Demos, 1997).

Mercer, Kobena. "Recording Narratives of Race and Nation," in *Black Film, British Cinema: Papers from the ICA Conference February 1988*, ed. Kobena Mercer (London: Institute of Contemporary Arts, 1988): 4–14.

Phillips, Caryl. *The Final Passage* (London: Faber & Faber, 1999).

Smith, Chris. "Opening Address," in *Whose Heritage? The Impact of Cultural Diversity on Britain's Living Heritage*, National Conference, Manchester, 1999, ed. Arts Council of England (London: Arts Council of England: 1999): 7–11.

◄❖►

Trying to Escape, Longing to Belong
— Roots, Genes and Performativity in Zadie Smith's *White Teeth* and Hari Kunzru's *The Impressionist*

BARBARA SCHAFF

AN INCREASINGLY IMPORTANT PHENOMENON in British literature is the representation of mixed race, hybrid or hyphenated identities, reflecting the situation in a post- or transnational world. In postcolonial theory, all terms which denote flexibility, movement, mix, or anything with the prefix 'trans-' have long been regarded as positive values. In the global world, transcultural movements and cultural crossovers have been hailed as signifiers of a powerful destabilization of essentialism and binary oppositions. Homi Bhabha has defined the margin as the exciting place from where creative subversion can be started, and has attached the power of transgression and transformation to hybrid identities.[1]

The former negatively loaded term 'hybridity', which originally stems from nineteenth-century racist discourse, has thus undergone a re-evaluation. Nowadays, it signifies a positive concept, a ferment which changes culture, an energy field of different forces, or a 'Third Space' where different elements encounter and transform each other. In the wake of centuries of migration, of colonization, globalization, and productive cultural exchanges, the positive notion of hybrid cultural identities seems more than appropriate. Homi Bhabha has argued enthusiastically that nations and cultures must be

---

[1] See Homi K. Bhabha, *The Location of Culture* (1994; London & New York: Routledge, 2003): 251.

understood as performative narrative constructs that arise from the hybrid interactions and negotiations of interstitial cultural spaces.[2] According to Bhabha, national memory is always the site of the hybridity of history, and he claims that "the very possibility of cultural contestation, the ability to shift the ground of knowledges, or to engage in the 'war of position', marks the establishment of new forms of meaning, and strategies of identification."[3] Similarly, Stuart Hall has re-evaluated the older model of black identity as a unifying concept, and has replaced it with a new politics of representation where "'black' is essentially a politically and culturally *constructed* category, which cannot be grounded in a set of fixed trans-cultural or transcendental racial categories and which therefore has no guarantees in nature."[4]

Likewise, postcolonial writers have discarded holistic or homogeneous concepts of nations and identities, and have replaced them by stories of flexible and transgressive global urban identities, living in the creative contact zone of the in-between. Protagonists move across boundaries and cultural spheres, endeavouring to discard their 'hereditary burden' and create new cultural and racial unions and fusions. Salman Rushdie and Hanif Kureishi were among the first to explore the role of the migrant who knows that all views of the world are incomplete, which is why he can choose whatever or whoever he or she wants to be out of myriad combinations. Rather than deploring the fate of the displaced migrant, Rushdie and Kureishi consequently both define the space of the in-between as one of immense creativity and possibility.

This optimistic view of the situation of the migrant has been reconsidered in two recent debut novels by two young British novelists who also bring matters of transculturalism and hybrid identities into focus and explore the relationship between genetic determination, history, and cultural choice. Zadie Smith and Hari Kunzru have similar biographical experiences: an immigrant family background, hyphenated identities, Oxbridge education, and the enormous hype accompanying the launch of their first books. This hype catapulted them directly into the heart of the British literary establishment, thus paradoxically reversing the situation of their novels' protagonists, who are all far from being well-integrated.

---

[2] Bhabha, "DissemiNation: Time, Narrative and the Margins of the Modern Nation" (1990), in Bhabha, *The Location of Culture*, 139–70.

[3] Bhabha, "DissemiNation: Time, Narrative and the Margins of the Modern Nation," 162.

[4] Stuart Hall, "New Ethnicities" (1988), in *The Post-Colonial Studies Reader*, ed. Bill Ashcroft, Gareth Griffiths & Helen Tiffin (London: Routledge, 2002): 225.

Both writers are concerned foremost with the notion of identity, and they push these issues into new directions, re-evaluate racial ambiguity, and address the complex problems of multiracial or hyphenated identities. They are aware of the complex tensions in postmodern conditions, where selfhood has become fragmented and unstable, and identities are continuously constituted performatively as, in the words of Judith Butler, "a stylized repetition of acts."[5] They do not, however, encompass an identity model which is merely performative, but instead place a new emphasis on matters of roots and origins and explore what it means 'to belong' in a contemporary global culture. If Bhabha somewhat dismissively describes one side of modernity as the "narcissism of organic culture, the onanistic search for the origins of race,"[6] then Smith and Kunzru regard the issue of identity and subject-formation under two aspects, a performative self-enactment, on the one side, and a clear consciousness of origins and history, on the other.

Even though both novels have the same concern – a rather less enthusiastic attitude towards the positive evaluation of hybridity – these issues are addressed differently. Zadie Smith's urban transcultural protagonists remain in constant struggle against their histories, but despite migration, education, globalization and self-fashioning, they still cannot root out the influences of their origins. Smith uses a temporal axis in order to relate the dominant concerns of her protagonists to their roots: i.e. their collective cultural memories, and their geographical origins. Hari Kunzru, conversely, arranges his narrative along a spatial axis of different interstitial spaces and of different cultural and geographical zones in which his protagonist navigates issues of identity. The story is constructed as a nomadic movement, where binary oppositions of space, but also of class, race, and gender, can be transgressed.

One clue to Zadie Smith's concept of identity is the title and central metaphor of her novel. As an extended metaphor, teeth appear in various images in the novel's table of contents: "Teething Trouble," "Root Canals," "Molars," and "Ripping Teeth." 'White Teeth' is an ambiguous image. It signifies the elimination of racial difference as well as its confirmation: On the one hand, all human beings have white teeth, despite the colour of their skin. On the other, there is an episode in the novel about the war experience of a British soldier that foregrounds the significance of racial difference. The

---

[5] Judith Butler, *Gender Trouble: Feminism and the Subversion of Identity* (London: Routledge, 1990): 140.

[6] Bhabha, *The Location of Culture*, 245.

soldier remembers how, when fighting in the Congo, he could identify his ad-
versaries by the whiteness of their teeth:

> When I was in the Congo, the only way I could identify the nigger was by the
> whiteness of his teeth, if you see what I mean. Horrid business. Dark as buggery, it
> was. And they died because of it, you see?[7]

This episode shows that to look different may be deadly under certain circumstances. And if it is not deadly, it may at least define your role and position in
society. Apart from that, white teeth are also closely linked to class. Irie
Jones, the young female protagonist of *White Teeth*, daughter of a – toothless
– Jamaican mother and an English father, will overcome the limitations of her
underprivileged social background and become a dentist in the end. Her job
will be to remove bad, damaged teeth and to seal root canals – metonymically, for Irie, being a dentist means being able to cope with her heritage and
cultural memory.

A dominant theme of the novel is the relation of one's position in society
to one's looks or, to put it less neutrally, the determining influence of one's
physical appearance. The fate of all figures is in a way linked to their genetic
heritage: no performance can help them escape the way they look. Irie suffers
from her physical inheritance; she has her grandmother's "substantial Jamaican frame, loaded with pineapples, mangoes and guavas; the girl had weight;
big tits, big butt, big hips, big thighs, big teeth."[8] As long as the dominant discourse of female beauty is still determined by images of anorexic blondes,
Irie appears as an alien and a misfit in this land of English roses: access
denied. Even Shakespeare's dark lady, whom she hopes to adopt as a possible
role model which would help her to integrate, turns out to be dark in a different way: "Is she black?" Irie asks her English teacher, and is disappointed
by her answer:

> "No, dear, she's dark. She's not black in the modern sense. [...] Besides, he says
> very clearly, *In nothing art thou black, save in thy deeds* [...]. No, dear, she just has
> a dark complexion, you see, as dark as mine, probably." Irie looked at Mrs Roody.
> She was the colour of strawberry mousse.[9]

---

[7] Zadie Smith, *White Teeth* (2000; Harmondsworth: Penguin, 2001): 172.

[8] Smith, *White Teeth*, 265.

[9] *White Teeth*, 271–72.

Far from rejoicing in the cultural position of the 'in-between' and exploring possibilities of undermining culturally encoded notions of feminine beauty, Irie is intent upon fighting the genes of her black mother.[10] She undertakes several unsuccessful attempts to redefine her appearance: she wants to slim down and wants her hair straightened, but in doing so she betrays her origins and turns into a freak. Due to the manipulations of the hairdresser, she loses her curly hair and gets straight hair from an Indian woman glued to her head.

If the body is a material reminder of one's origins that cannot be transgressed so easily, so is the burden of a collective past and history. There are two generations in *White Teeth*, who both deal differently with the notion of cultural roots. Samad Iqbal is a first-generation immigrant who feels dislocated and alienated in London. He has not fully arrived in London, and still has the status of a migrant in an intermediate position. He represents a diasporic identity and only survives with the help of the intact memory of his roots, home, history, and community. For him, Pakistan serves as a means of orientation, a mental construct, existing in a fractured, discontinuous relationship with the present. It is a concept which gives him security, an imaginary, mythic, and illusory space which retains an emotional influence, shapes his identity, and compensates for his humiliation. In short, it is, in Rushdie's terms, an "imaginary homeland."[11] Samad takes refuge in his family's history and constructs a glorious past in order to overcome the shortcomings of his existence as a waiter in an Indian restaurant. He is obsessed with his roots, which he regards as his authentic self. He continuously tells and retells the family history to friends and family in order to keep it and to shape broken fragments into a coherent narrative which guarantees a coherent identity.

The second generation in *White Teeth*, however, show a different attitude towards their origins and histories. They are neither able to compensate for their shortcomings by a shared collective memory of a better past, nor are they able to experience the status of hyphenated identities as culturally

---

[10] Oliver Gross has a different view of Irie's development. While he is aware of the protagonists' difficulties in defining their identity against both 'homeland' and 'mother country', he nevertheless foregrounds a kind of transcultural harmony as the novel's most distinctive feature. Gross, "Finding Brown Strangers Really Stimulating: Xenophobia and the Second Generation in Zadie Smith's *White Teeth*," in *Xenophobic Memories: Otherness in Postcolonial Constructions of the Past*, ed. Monika Gomille & Klaus Stierstorfer (Heidelberg: Winter, 2003): 39–49.

[11] Salman Rushie, *Imaginary Homelands: Essays and Criticism, 1981–1991* (London: Granta/Penguin, 1991).

enriching. Rather, they all try to escape from the obsession of their parents' generation with the past, searching for, as Irie exclaims, "'neutral spaces. And not this endless maze of present rooms and past rooms and the things said in them years ago and everybody's old historical shit all over the place'."[12]

This neutral space is the blank page which can be inscribed anew every day. Identity, then, is performed and constructed, but it is definitely not one's fate. Samad Iqbal's sons, the twins Millat and Magid, develop into totally different characters: the constantly rebellious Millat joins a radical fundamentalist Islamic street crew, while his brother Magid is sent to university in Bangladesh and turns into a well-educated, conformist lawyer. Depicting the twins' development, Smith tackles the old question of whether one's identity is formed by genetic disposition or by one's social surroundings. She has no easy answer. The archive of a collective cultural identity is radically refused by the younger generation, yet seems impossible to discard altogether. The roots one has in one's genes, in family history or national history, may be hidden, unseen like the roots of our teeth, but they still exist. As Smith extends her teeth metaphor, she ironically shows that the 'root canals' of her protagonists, even if they try to discard their inheritance and to rely on a performative, self-assertive concept of identity, inexorably link their fate to their origins. Against conscious memory, which is remodelled and shaped to corroborate certain concepts of identity, Smith positions unconscious memory, body memory, or genetic disposition which contradicts ideas of performative selfhood. This is ironically highlighted at the end of the novel, when Irie learns that she is pregnant but does not know who the father of her child is. It might be either Millat or Magid, and as they are twins, no genetic test would ever provide her with conclusive evidence. In order not to build up an unproductive binary opposition here between two different and irreconcilable kinds of identity, I would like to point to Bakhtin's concept of hybridity as a means of communication where one language adds a new dimension of meaning to another.[13] Seen from this perspective, *White Teeth* appears as a truly hybrid novel, where different concepts of identity in a global world are seen as a

---

[12] Smith, *White Teeth*, 514.

[13] Bakhtin's concept of hybridity has been lucidly linked to postcolonial theory by Nikos Papastergiadis in "Tracing Hybridity in Theory," in *Debating Cultural Hybridity: Multi-Cultural Identities and the Politics of Anti-Racism*, ed. Pnina Werbner & Tariq Modood (London: Zed, 1997): 257–81.

productive site of conflict and negotiation. They inform and enrich each other while simultaneously battling each other, thus signifying the complex and paradoxical qualities of identity in a global world.

If Smith, in her story about three generations, negotiates concepts of trans-cultural and hybrid identities more in temporal terms and relates them to memory and origins, Hari Kunzru develops his ideas about hybridity along spatial lines. His novel *The Impressionist* is a picaresque black *Bildungs-roman*,[14] set in colonial India in the 1920s. It starts with the strange con-ception of the protagonist Pran Nath, who is the result of a rather sudden en-counter between an Indian woman and an English forestry expert during a monsoon flood. His fate is determined by his racial ambiguity. As a neither Indian- nor English-looking person, he is able to pass as both. He changes his identity according to circumstances, learns to perform and mimic roles, and continually re-invents himself, as and when the occasion or the people he encounters require. His bizarre adventures are due to the fact that he can ap-pear to be either Indian or white. In the course of this episodically structured novel, Pran Nath is evicted from his Indian home, sold as a prostitute in female clothes to a Maharaja, from whom he escapes to live in Bombay for a while with a Scottish minister and his wife. There he takes on the name and persona of a young Englishman whom he had met by acciden and who had died in his presence. As Jonathan Bridgeman, he travels to England, is edu-cated at a British boarding school, and proceeds to Oxford, where he falls in love with Astarte Chapel, the beautiful daughter of a professor of ethnology. Ironically, Pran Nath has learnt too well how to mimic Englishness: In Paris, Astarte abandons him for a black musician, because she is in search of a true and authentic 'native', and Pran appears too English for her. At the end of the novel, Pran Nath joins Professor Chapel on a trip to an imaginary African country to do some field research. All the members of the expedition except Jonathan are killed by an African tribe; all trace of him is lost. After all the various efforts of self-education and of finding a secure place for himself within a community, he vanishes into nothingness, because he has no concept

---

[14] Mark Stein has convincingly shown how the genre of the black *Bildungsroman* reinforces heterogeneity, transgresses national boundaries and establishes new subject-posi-tions – these features apply equally to Hari Kunzru's *The Impressionist* (London: Hamish Hamilton, 2002). Stein, "The Black British *Bildungsroman* and the Transformation of Brit-ain," in *British Literature and Culture in the 1990s*, ed. Barbara Korte & Klaus Peter Müller (Tübingen: Gunter Narr, 1998): 89–105.

of identity apart from performance, no history, no roots. He remains the migrant with a lost past and an unintegrated present – a zero identity. The novel ends on a very postmodern note on travelling: "For now the journey is every thing. He has no thoughts of arriving anywhere. [...] Tomorrow he will travel on."[15] In Kunzru's novel, travelling does not mean the liberating cultural position of choice, but the compulsive meandering movement of a rootless protagonist who is forever searching for a place of his own.

As a literary construct, Pran Nath appears to be the ideal hybrid subject. His story evokes issues of origin and encounter; he is born of the transgression of racial, cultural, class, and gender boundaries. Pran is rootless in the sense that he does not share any cultural memory or history, and this is why he is always 'en route'. This pun was coined by Paul Gilroy,[16] and his ideas about the relationship between identity and family history or collective memories also apply to Kunzru's depiction of Pran Nath. He cannot rely on prefabricated holistic concepts of culture and history, and therefore has to forge a new narrative across cultural boundaries. In his analysis of Hanif Kureishi's autobiographical essay "The Rainbow Sign," John MacLeod uses Gilroy's pun in order to highlight the creative quality of the 'in-between'. He could have referred equally well to Kunzru's protagonist:

> He does not have secure roots which fix him in place, in a nation or an ethnic group; rather, he must continually plot for himself itinerant cultural routes which take him, imaginatively as well as physically, to many places and into contact with many different people. [...] The grounded certainties of roots are replaced with the transnational contingencies of routes.[17]

The consequence of these contingencies of routes is a relationship between the present and the past that must always be accommodated to circumstances. It is flexible and never fixed. This does, however, also imply a fundamental lack in the narrative concerning the coherence of the hero's identity. Pran Nath is displaced from the beginning, he never had a place where he belonged – he has no roots. His identity is not a given, his being is definitely not defined by where he comes from. Instead, like a chameleon, he adapts to his

---

[15] Hari Kunzru, *The Impressionist*, 481.

[16] Paul Gilroy, *The Black Atlantic: Modernity and Double Consciousness* (London: Verso, 1993).

[17] John MacLeod, *Beginning Postcolonialism* (Manchester: Manchester UP, 2000): 215.

circumstances so easily, that, without a past, his being is determined only by where he is now.

Kunzru places his novel in a period when the binary opposition between the colonizer and the colonized was still the working condition of the Empire. Essentialism means the notion of a genetically determined selfhood, a racial concept of identity. In contrast to the various ideas of identity outlined on the level of the narrative, Kunzru's main protagonist Pran is set in stark contrast to these notions. Several other protagonists in Kunzru's novel believe in essentialist identity models: the Presbyterian minister in Bombay, who is an ardent phrenologist, or Jonathan Bridgeman's girlfriend, who falls in love with an African because of his black authenticity. Pran Nath, however, is the initially blank page in the typically English empiricist tradition of identity concepts, based on John Locke's influential thesis that the mind is born as a blank upon which all knowledge is inscribed in the form of human experiences.[18] Pran Nath's role, however, is that of an impostor, who is able to mimic others perfectly because he has no identity of his own, no roots, no origin, no memory. In his various adaptations of role models in the colonial context, Pran Nath's manipulations of identity also mirror and subvert conventional colonial strategies of going native. Here, for instance, Richard Burton's impersonations as a "Persian wanderer, a Darwaysh,"[19] during his pilgrimage to Al-Madinah and Meccah, or T.E. Lawrence's sheik garments come to mind as the prototypical manifestations of this kind of colonial appropriation. In the colonial context, mimicry has been read as a symbol for the unstable economies of identity production. Homi Bhabha locates in mimicry the site of an ambivalence and uncertainty that destabilizes the fixed notions of an imperial self and its Other in colonial discourse.[20] Kunzru reverses this model, and shows instead that the mimicry of the colonized subject violates even more any notion of stable selfhood. The mimicry of his protagonist not only destabilizes any concept of integrity and wholeness, but, in its multiple performances, produces a non-entity, a complete void. The performative exploration of Pran Nath's identity culminates in a scene where

---

[18] John Locke, *An Essay Concerning Human Understanding* (1690; Harmondsworth: Penguin, 1998).

[19] Sir Richard Burton, *Personal Narrative of a Pilgrimage to Al-Madinah & Meccah* (1893; New York: Dover, 1964): 2.

[20] Bhabha, "Of Mimicry and Man: The Ambivalence of Colonial Discourse," in *The Location of Culture*, 85–92.

Pran Nath as the Englishman Jonathan Bridgeman visits a cabaret in Paris and is fascinated by the appearance of an impressionist:

> One after the other, characters appear. One with a deep baritone voice. Another with a little cap and a hectoring way of talking. Each lasts a few seconds, a minute. Each erases the last. The man becomes these other people so completely that nothing of his own is visible. A coldness starts to rise in Jonathan's gut, cutting through the vodka. He watches intently, praying that he is wrong, that he has missed something. There is no escaping it. In between each impression, just at the moment when one person falls away and the next has yet to take possession, the impressionist is completely blank. There is nothing there at all.[21]

Instantaneously, Pran Nath understands that this is just what he is himself: Jonathan Bridgeman, the ultimate hybrid identity, travelling across border-lines of gender, culture, class, and race, is nothing more than a momentary impression.

This state of identity, however, is experienced as painful and unfulfilling. Far from enjoying his missing roots and lacking integration as a liberating experience, Pran Nath longs to belong to a community, a nation, a cultural or geographical space. This desire makes him perform different roles according to the respective situation, but on the whole he is unable to build up an identity by forging the single events into a coherent story. Kunzru pushes the concept of a performative subjectivity and hybrid identity to the farthest possible extreme: his protagonist adopts information, attitudes, behaviour from any cultural zone he comes into contact with, but he is never really contaminated by these contacts. They never become an integral part of his personality. In almost all the reviews of Kunzru's book, this insubstantiality of the main protagonist was declared the book's major flaw. It has the strange effect that readers feel quite at a loss with a hero if incoherent dimensions whose fate does not affect them and who appears inauthentic, not homogeneous – in short: a hollow impersonator. The construction of the protagonist as an 'emotionally unavailable' character results in a lack of empathy in the reader.[22] If this effect of the novel was regarded by some readers as a literary deficiency, one could also, with regard to performative concepts of identity, highlight this

---

[21] Kunzru, *The Impressionist*, 419.

[22] Susannah Meadows, "Son of a Sort of a Goddess," *New York Times Book Review* (12 May 2002), Desk: 27.

as the book's most interesting and rewarding literary strategy. Pran Nath is inaccessible, not because Kunzru lacked the means of detailed and vivid description and was unable to connect individual episodes into a coherent narrative but, rather, because he wanted to take the concept of an identity that has no cultural roots whatsoever to its logical consequence. Seen from this perspective, hybridity may begin to lose some of its charms.

Smith and Kunzru both belong to a new generation of writers that looks back from the twenty-first century on the history of migration with perceptive irony. These writers share a concern with the complex issues of hyphenated, hybrid identities and explore their multifarious fissures, gaps, and contradictions. Smith and Kunzru draft various concepts of transcultural identity in temporal and spatial terms, and they both develop the notion of identities constructed via narrative, told and retold according to changing circumstances. They are not, however, bent on denying the importance of origin and roots. On the contrary, they both place their stories in the strange and complex area of tension between their protagonist's desire to escape from fixed, essentialist notions of identity that are based on the idea of origins and roots, and the desire to belong to a community, to share cultural values and a history with somebody, to belong. The concept of an origin, of history and roots, is, however, not meant in a deterministic way. History in both novels – as family history or the history of an ethnic group – plays an important part in the complex process of identity-formation, because it transmits a sense of belonging, without determining the subject in a totalizing way. Smith very much underlines the importance of individual choice in her protagonists. This language of belonging is what Homi Bhabha finds disquieting, because – in the grander scope of the nation – it is precisely here that social cohesion becomes repellent as a totalitarian, holistic concept of community and collective experiences.[23] Smith and Kunzru, by contrast, seem to opt for a less antagonistic model of identity. They display conflicting and unresolved constructivist and performative notions of identity and conceptualize a sense of origin and history that is in no way teleological or deterministic, but serves as a basis for the free interplay of all possible options.

---

[23] Bhabha, *The Location of Culture*, 142.

WORKS CITED

Ashcroft, Bill, Gareth Griffiths & Helen Tiffin, ed. *The Post-Colonial Studies Reader* (London & New York: Routledge, 2002).

Bhabha, Homi K. *The Location of Culture* (1994; London & New York: Routledge, 2003).

Butler, Judith. *Gender Trouble: Feminism and the Subversion of Identity* (London: Routledge, 1990).

Burton, Richard. *Personal Narrative of a Pilgrimage to Al-Madinah & Meccah* (1893; Mineola NY: Dover, 1964).

Gilroy, Paul. *The Black Atlantic: Modernity and Double Consciousness* (London: Verso, 1993).

Gross, Oliver. "Finding Brown Strangers Really Stimulating: Xenophobia and the Second Generation in Zadie Smith's *White Teeth*," in *Xenophobic Memories: Otherness in Postcolonial Constructions of the Past*, ed. Monika Gomille & Klaus Stierstorfer (Heidelberg: Winter, 2003): 39–49.

Hall, Stuart. "New Ethnicities" (1988), in *The Post-Colonial Studies Reader* (2002), ed. Ashcroft, Griffiths & Tiffin, 223-27.

Kunzru, Hari. *The Impressionist* (London: Hamish Hamilton, 2002).

Locke, John. *An Essay Concerning Human Understanding* (1690; Harmondsworth: Penguin, 1998).

MacLeod, John. *Beginning Postcolonialism* (Manchester: Manchester UP, 2000).

Meadows, Susannah. "Son of a Sort of a Goddess," *New York Times Book Review* (12 May 2002), Desk: 27.

Papastergiadis, Nikos. "Tracing Hybridity in Theory," in *Debating Cultural Hybridity: Multi-Cultural Identities and the Politics of Anti-Racism*, ed. Pnina Werbner & Tariq Modood (London: Zed, 1997): 257–81.

Rushdie, Salman. *Imaginary Homelands: Essays and Criticism, 1981–1991* (London: Granta/Penguin, 1991).

Smith, Zadie. *White Teeth* (London: Hamish Hamilton, 2000).

Stein, Mark. "The Black British *Bildungsroman* and the Transformation of Britain," in *British Literature and Culture in the 1990s*, ed. Barbara Korte & Klaus Peter Müller (Tübingen: Gunter Narr, 1998): 89–105.

❖

Fictions of Transcultural Memory

— Zulfikar Ghose's *The Triple Mirror of the Self* as an Imaginative Reconstruction of the Self in Multiple Worlds

NADIA BUTT

> Already a fictitious past occupies in our memories the place of another, a
> past of which we know nothing with certainty – not even that it is false.[1]
>
> The past is what you remember, convince yourself you remember, or pre-
> tend to remember.[2]

T HIS ESSAY SETS OUT to negotiate the idea of fictions of transcultural memory with reference to the semi-autobiographical novel
The Triple Mirror of the Self (1992) by Zulfikar Ghose, an Amer-
ican-based writer of Pakistani origin. By focusing on the fictional(izing)
nature of memory in the face of our "moving world,"[3] my aim is to examine
the central character's re-invention of the self in diverse cultures and continents – a self that is as much imaginary and fictional as it is real in the flash-

---

[1] Jorge Luis Borges, "Tlön, Uqbar, Orbis Tertius" (1961), in *Labyrinths* (Harmondsworth: Penguin, 1970): 42–43.

[2] Thomas P. Adler, "Pinter's *Night*: A Stroll Down Memory Lane," *Modern Drama* 17
(1974): 461–65.

[3] For a broader view of contemporary cultural transformations in relation to transcultural
phenomena, see "Performing Arts and South Asian Literature," ed. Shirley Chew, special
issue of *Moving Worlds: A Journal of Transcultural Writing* 5.2 (2006).

back narration of the novel.[4] Ghose's transcultural fictions of memory[5] point to mnemonic processes that are resonant with the narrator–protagonist's fantastic experiences in heterogeneous cultural landscapes. These experiences begin to take the form of contradictory stories once he recollects them in a new country and continent, leaving him in a state of constant doubt about the reality of his past. Hence, memory and fiction are not only indispensable to his tales of multiple cultural encounters, but also pervade his perception of self and identity throughout the novel.

The Triple Mirror is a complex novel because it is a novel-within-a-novel. By employing memory patterns in structuring the novel, Ghose invites the reader to witness not only his character's journey through three continents and cultures, but three lives that he is destined to live as a migrant. The three parts of the novel, entitled "The Burial of the Self," "Voyager and Pilgrim," and "Origins of the Self," display the narrator–protagonist's constant struggle with various versions of the past in rediscovering his personal identity in an era of globalization and modernity.[6] Part One is set in Brazil and introduces the narrator–protagonist, Urimba Pons; Part Two shows a new transformation

---

[4] For deeper insights into the relationship between the imaginary and the fictive, see Wolfgang Iser, *The Fictive and the Imaginary: Charting Literary Anthropology* (*Das Fiktive und das Imaginäre: Perspektiven literarischer Anthropologie*, 1993; tr. Baltimore MD & London: Johns Hopkins UP, 1993): 222–38. See also Paul John Eakin, *Fictions in Autobiography: Studies in the Art of Self-Invention* (Princeton NJ: Princeton UP, 1985). Eakin argues that "autobiographical truth is not fixed but an evolving content in an intricate process of self-discovery and self-creation, and, further, that the self that is the centre of all autobiographical narrative is necessarily a fictive structure" (3).

[5] For concepts and definitions of the transcultural and transculturality, see Wolfgang Welsch, "Tranculturality: The Puzzling Form of Cultures Today," in *Spaces of Culture: City, Nation, World*, ed. Mike Featherstone & Scott Lash (London: Sage, 1999): 194–231. For further perspectives on the theory of the transcultural in literary studies, see Frank Schulze–Engler, "Von 'Inter' zu 'Trans': Gesellschaftliche, kulturelle und literarische Übergänge," in *Inter- und Transkulturelle Studien: Theoretische Grundlagen und interdisziplinäre Praxis*, ed. Heinz Antor (Heidelberg: Winter, 2006): 41–53.

[6] For a detailed perspective on self-identity in an era of globalization and modernity, see Anthony Giddens, *Modernity and Self-Identity: Self and Society in the Late Modern Age* (Oxford: Polity, 1991), particularly ch. 1 ("The Contours of High Modernity"): 10–34. For different approaches to theories of globalization and modernity, see Enrique Dussel, "Beyond Eurocentrism: The World-System and the Limits of Modernity" in *The Cultures of Globalization*, ed. Fredric Jameson & Masao Miyoshi (Durham NC & London: Duke UP, 1998): 3–31, and Roland Robertson, "Glocalization: Time-Space and Homogeneity-Heterogeneity," in *Global Modernities*, ed. Mike Featherstone, Scott Lash & Roland Robertson (London & New Delhi: Sage, 1995): 25–44.

of Urimba as Jonathan Archibald Pons in America; Part Three takes us to pre-
Partition India, where Urimba/Pons is Roshan. In the following analysis of
the novel, however, these parts are treated as three distinct phases of transcultural memory.

Theorizing Fictions of Transcultural Memory: Reflections
on the Self in the Age of Globalization and Modernity

The notion of cultural memory – which became particularly influential in the
humanities through the works of Maurice Halbwachs – is concerned with the
construction of collective identities through memory practices.[7] Since the
notion of cultural memory has been widely discussed in a eurocentric context,
as in the works of Pierre Nora from France and Aleida Assmann from Germany, I have chosen to prefix it with 'trans' not only to broaden the spectrum
of cultures of remembrance and negotiations of cultural identities, but also to
locate memory in "the global ecumene of modernity"[8] in order to grasp new
configurations across geographical and cultural boundaries.

The concept of transcultural memory is premissed on the dynamic of
"overlapping territories and intertwined histories" highlighted by Edward
Said:[9] people are likely to have multiple cultural belongings in an era of enormous cultural crisscrossing. As a result, their diverse cultural associations
may generate multiple memories in the process of recollection. This leads us
to consider the imperative of "intertwined memories" that are emblematic of
today's increasingly interconnected world. By exploring the mode of transcultural memory, I endeavour to show that, in the wake of movement and migration as well as of political and social change, memories of today's individuals are no longer an outcome of a singular world but are rooted in "multiple

---

[7] See Maurice Halbwachs, *On Collective Memory*, tr. Lewis A. Coser (*La mémoire collective*, 1939; Chicago & London: U of Chicago P, 1992); Astrid Erll & Ansgar Nünning,
"Where Literature and Memory Meet: Towards a Systematic Approach to the Concepts of
Memory Used in Literary Studies," in *REAL: Yearbook of Research in English and American Literature* 21, ed. Herbert Grabes (Tübingen: Gunter Narr, 2005): 261.

[8] See Ulf Hannerz, "The Global Ecumene of Modernity," in Hannerz, *Transnational
Connections: Culture, People, Places* (London: Routledge, 1996): 44–55.

[9] See Edward W. Said, *Culture and Imperialism* (1993; New York: Vintage, 1994), ch. 1
("Overlapping Territories, Intertwined Histories"): 3–61.

times"[10] and "contact zones."[11] We may realize amidst global flows that our memory of any given situation is now more and more multiform, because plurality tends to characterize the practice and act of memory in contemporary times. Therefore, memory should be conceived of as being "dynamic, changing, and plural"[12] in our "runaway world"[13] rather than a product of a singular (Western or non-Western) cultural sphere.

The idea of a fictional self takes inspiration from recent approaches to individual and cultural memory that have tended to emphasize not only the socially constructed nature of the self but also its fictional(izing) aspects. In his influential account of the creation of an autobiographical self, Paul John Eakin, for instance, illustrates the constructive nature of autobiographical remembering and "the fact that our sense of continuous identity is a fiction, the primary fiction of all self narration."[14] On closer analysis, the notion of continuous identity thus turns out to be nothing but "a fiction of memory":[15] i.e. an imaginative (re)construction resulting from a subtle interplay between fiction and reality, past and present.

Transcultural memory as a running thread in Ghose's novel unites the three lives of the same man, lives lived in South America, Europe, and Asia.

---

[10] The psychologists Joseph E. McGrath and Janice R. Kelly postulate that "time as experienced has many facets, many nuances, many ramifications." In negotiating the relationship between time and human psychology, they introduce the term "multiple times." The term "multiple times" is defined as "the myriad time frames within which individuals can 'locate' themselves at any given instant." See McGrath & Kelly, *Time and Human Interaction: Towards a Social Psychology of Time* (New York & London: Guilford, 1986): 49 (emphasis in the original).

[11] See Mary Louise Pratt, "Introduction: Criticism in the Contact Zone," in Pratt, *Imperial Eyes: Travel Writing and Transculturation* (London & New York: Routledge, 1992): 6. While Pratt employs the term 'contact zone' in terms of colonial encounters, the use of 'contact zone' in this essay aims at addressing the space of cultural plurality in today's transcultural world.

[12] Paul John Eakin, *How Our Lives Become Stories: Making Selves* (Ithaca N Y & London: Cornell U P, 1999): 98. Like Eakin, Daniel L. Schacter claims that memories are always complex constructions and not literal recordings of reality; therefore, like individual memories, cultural memories may be seen as an "imaginative reconstruction of past events." See Schacter, *Searching for Memory: The Brain, the Mind, and the Past* (New York: Basic Books, 1996): 101.

[13] See Anthony Giddens, "Introduction" to *Runaway World: How Globalisation is Reshaping our Lives* (London: Profile, 2002): 1–19.

[14] Eakin, *How Our Lives Become Stories*, 94.

[15] *How Our Lives Become Stories*, 95.

When he travels, his culture travels with him,[16] hence each time when he enters a new territory, his "native culture" merges into "the foreign," making him see a new image of his cultural identity in the mirror of the self. Soon the three aspects of the self, in line with the three phases of his existence, become his destiny as he lives with multiple identities and cultural loyalties. *The Triple Mirror* is thus not merely a mirror of the self but a mirror of today's evolving cultures in an age of worldwide cultural encounters. Furthermore, it constitutes a mirror of "intertwined cultural memories" in the global setting as filtered through the imagination of the narrator–protagonist.

Transcultural memory, however, also serves as a schema of narration. The narrator–protagonist's constant movement back and forth in the past and present in three separate parts of the novel reflects the ambivalence of remembering opposing worlds in narration and the mind's uncanny capacity to recall memories of far-flung regions – which may or may not be true, as the narrator himself claims.

Phase One: Recollecting Entangled Histories of the Self

Part One, "The Burial of the Self," written in the first person, is based on the first incarnation of the narrator–protagonist, which takes place in Suxavat. The natives of this mysterious region name him after "the immigrant tree: Urimba, the scattered one."[17] The type-name reinforces the migrant texture of the protagonist's existence and the fact that he is fated to reincarnate "the scattered one"; in this way Urimba or Urim symbolizes the individual in today's deterritorialized world,[18] "where places are no longer the clear supports of our identity."[19]

---

[16] For further insights into the role of travel and cultural translation, see James Clifford, "Traveling Cultures," in Clifford, *Routes: Travel and Translation in the Late Twentieth Century* (Cambridge MA: Harvard UP, 1997): 17–46.

[17] Zulfikar Ghose, *The Triple Mirror of the Self* (1992; London: Bloomsbury, 1994): 3. Further page references are in the main text.

[18] See Arjun Appadurai, *Modernity at Large: Cultural Dimensions of Globalization* (Minneapolis: U of Minnesota P, 1996), Chapter Two: "Disjuncture and Difference in the Global Cultural Economy," 27–47.

[19] David Morley & Kevin Robins, "No Place Like *Heimat*: Images of Home(land)," in *European Culture in Space and Place: Theories of Identity and Location*, ed. Erica Carter, James Donald & Judith Squires (London: Lawrence & Wishart, 1993): 5.

Urim's first love is Horuxtla, "the daughter of illusions," who always changes roles like his changing self, inviting him to review his lost past through the forces of memory, as he states: "Should all the coincidences of my life, the vagaries of circumstance that exiled me from one continent to another until I arrived at this still centre [...] lead to my possession of Horuxtla" (4). In Ghose's fictional realms, time and memory are always relevant, as the narrator–protagonist emphasizes that his mind has a tremendous power to imagine past, present, and future not as separate segments of time but as inextricably intertwined. This extraordinary capacity of the mind to "invent" and "construct" assists him in cogitating the mystery of his multiple selves:

> My mind has an uncanny capacity to transform an imagined future into an accomplished past; and I know, too, that I am quite capable of pretending that what has already happened has not yet happened and is something I wish to occur in the future. In the grammar of self-deception, I change tenses by the hour. What has become of you! I have lived so long in so many worlds that it is not merely a trick of the imagination to have the sense of not having been born yet. (4–5)

Before we finally reach the last part, which is set in a yet undivided India, we are reminded in parts one and two of the novel that the journey of the narrator–protagonist's self begins and culminates in India at the time of Partition. Nevertheless, he alludes to the haziness of his origins, because his memories, situated in divergent worlds, play tricks on him.

> I will say nothing of the memories that invaded my mind then. Life in America, in European cities, in India – I will say nothing of the history of passions which may well be the sum of a confusion of dreams with their conversion of dull events into marvellous fictions and their disguising of pain into the grotesquely masked creatures at a Kathakali dance that I may or may not have seen on a wooden platform one autumn evening in a park in Madras. (6)

While still in Suxavat before moving on to narrate the story of the self in California, London, and Bombay, he recollects a Canadian poet whom he had told that he was going to India. At this recall, he is suddenly confused to hear echoes of his native land India within the domain of foreign Brazil: "So far west, it is uncertain the territory is still Brazil. But the suburban train, is it not Bombay, going from Sion to Victoria Terminus?" (7). This practice of remembering distant worlds creates a dreamlike state for him, especially as past and present run parallel in his memory and imagination. As his individual and cultural past overshadows the present, it eventually leads him to imagine the past both as a centripetal and as a centrifugal force in the present.

In the fictionalizing process of transcultural memory, the name of a woman of Brazilian origin, Horuxtla, evokes a memory of Indian mountains, and thus Horuxtla echoes a forgotten landmark of time. This realization also hints at his astounding journeys to different continents of the world:

> I could not call the region *Horuxtla*, I suddenly realized. This great range of mountains already had a name, which I remembered. It was of Indian origin though somewhat altered by the European conquerors of the region […] Staring at the high peaks, in a land of origins, the sound I heard was The Hindu Kush. (97)

The place Suxavat reminds Urim of some hidden truths of the self that he needs to reconstruct in order to come to terms with his continuously changing present life:

> I seemed physically to enter other states of being which were not my own immediate being and yet which belonged to no one other than myself. I realized that this was the force of memory... My memory was also the repository of fabulous fictions of the self. (75)

Although he is aware that his remnants of memory are anything but reliable, he is nevertheless convinced that memory is indeed a key to solving the riddle of the self.

Ghose's narrator–protagonist emphasizes the doubling of his self and identity by using the mirror as a device. In chapter six of part one, "The Mirrored Man," we are introduced to the mirrored man Jonathan Archibald Pons from America, who is the hated Other of the narrator–protagonist. By elaborating the mirror metaphor in relation to the self, place, and culture, Ghose is simultaneously concerned with the theme of illusion and reality, on the one hand, and, on the other, with the manner in which the artist imagines reality and by doing so constructs new images of cultural reality. In chapter thirteen, "The Theory and Practice of Illusions," Ghose's narrator–protagonist gives his reader the example of a hologram, saying "There you have perfect proof that the artist is the inventor of reality and that reality is only an illusion" (79). In this way, the affinity between memory and fiction is stressed through the tension between illusion and reality, since the self is invariably caught between

these warring poles in its efforts to define itself. Consequently, the narrator–
protagonist is at times the author himself and on other occasions the subject
of his own story in "rewriting the self."[20] *The Triple Mirror* thus often hinges
on metafiction, as Ghose aims to address the novelist's struggle with reality
parallel to the protagonist's struggle with complex truths of self and identity.

On leaving Suxavat, Urim is once again overwhelmed by echoes from the
past. He recollects the time of Partition without directly mentioning India or
its British rulers, but recounts the tragic incident at Jellianwallah Bagh where
thousands of innocent freedom fighters, along with a huge rally of innocent
people, were killed or wounded by British troops under the command of
General Dyer, who was known for his brutality. In fact, the narrator wants to
show the reader that he is unable to seek connections in his memory himself,
and instead draws on disjointed episodes from a remote past to narrate entangled histories of the self:

> On one such occasion, there was a continuous firing of a succession of guns, pro-
> ducing in my mind the image of a crowd of people forced into a small clearing and
> massacred. I could still see nothing, but a picture seemed to be lit up before my
> eyes of a crazed English general commanding his soldiers to shoot at a crowd trap-
> ped in a square, and I was about to pity myself for having begun to hallucinate
> when I remembered a name, General Dyer [...] as if a terrible past had begun to
> heave out of that jungle's darkness, giving me the impression that I stood upon
> layers of centuries which were projecting fragmented mirror images of one another
> through cracks in the humus. (87)

It is important to keep in view that the narrator–protagonist contains within
himself the time and history of centuries. Time and again, he fears being cut
off from his lost Indian past amidst rapid cultural transformations in the present. However, as he is a living epitome of historical and cultural metamorphoses, he is always confronted with a present that is entangled with a multi-
valent past, composed of his "many-cultured"[21] histories.

---

[20] Mark Freeman, *Rewriting the Self: History, Memory, Narrative* (London & New York:
Routledge, 1993): 3.

[21] Dirk Hoerder, Yvonne Hébert & Irina Schmitt, *Introduction to Negotiating Transcultural Lives: Belonging and Social Capital Among Youth in Comparative Perspective*, ed.
Hoerder, Hèbert & Schmitt (Göttingen: V&R unipress, 2005): 17.

Phase Two: Translating Self amid Cultural Diversity and Interconnectedness

Part Two of the novel, "Voyager and Pilgrim," depicts yet another journey of Ghose's narrator–protagonist to a new continent and a new culture. This time, Urim metamorphoses into a man of letters from California, renamed Jonathan Archibald Pons. The resuscitation of the past in the present, as manifested by an imaginative reconstruction of the self in the process of remembering, draws our attention to the idea of translation of self and culture, for both translation and memory[22] are marked by a "boundary-crossing and by a re-alignment of what has become separate."[23]

Translation of culture and identity is fundamental to the dialectic of "intertwined memories" in Ghose's fictional realms. As the narrator–protagonist is constantly moving between past and present, east and west, translation in terms of names, culture, history, and language occurs as a new understanding of temporal and spatial truths of the self and identity. For example, in Part Two, Chapter Ten ("You"), he recollects how in his reincarnation in England, his name Shimmers was translated into English as "brightness, a light as something that shimmers" (179). This translation reminds him of a lost fragment of his translated past in India when the same Shimmers was called Roshan, which also means 'shimmer' in his native language.

In Chapter Four, entitled "The Incomplete Text," the narrator–protagonist comes across a bundle with the name Urim; Urim is one half of his self that keeps haunting him in his second incarnation as a professor of literature in the second section of the novel. The novel once again involve elements of metafiction. The narrator–protagonist becomes the author of his stories, making the reader forget the authorial presence momentarily. However, he has a mysterious feeling in the process of an imaginative reconstruction of the self that some kind of power outside himself is narrating his story. He remains sceptical about whether it might be the power of the past, the power of memory, or the power of translation. Eventually, he holds a text in his hand which he calls "The Burial of the Self," and discloses, in sheer surprise:

---

[22] For further insights into memory and translation, see Gabriel Motzkin, "Memory and Cultural Translation," in *The Translatability of Cultures: Figurations of the Space Between*, ed. Sanford Budick & Wolfgang Iser (Stanford CA: Stanford UP, 1996): 265–81.

[23] Wolfgang Iser, "Coda to the Discussion," in *The Translatability of Cultures: The Figurations of the Space Between*, ed. Sanford Budick & Wolfgang Iser (Stanford CA: Stanford UP, 1996), 297.

What's more, I was present in the text, making an appearance in a city called Natal
and a somewhat convenient exit from a frontier town called Xurupà. I can testify
that I have never been to either of those two places [...] I place my own name
between quotation marks because I do not accept that I am the person represented.
And yet, the use of my name is not a coincidence; and though the ludicrous person
seen to bear my name performs actions that I never did yet I know that Urim was
thinking of *me* when he invented that person. (120, emphasis in the original)

Conscious of the ambivalence of his "intertwined memories," the narrator–
protagonist feels a compulsion to reconstruct (in the capacity of an artist who
is a creator of stories, and a migrant who is a weaver of plural cultural belongings) the past according to the needs and demands of the present. It is not
only the past-ness of memory but its present-mindedness that causes awe and
wonder in him as the mind invokes memory episodes according to present
exigencies. In other words, current necessities are projected onto the past in
order to make it translatable into the present. This mutuality ultimately decides the nature of the past invoked. It is the present and the past, located in
many worlds simultaneously, that make him challenge individual and cultural
reality in the wake of proliferating cross-cultural relations all over the globe.
For him, there is no one ultimate present and no one final past. In fact, by exploring different facets of his self in the light of both past and present, the
narrator–protagonist tries to makes sense of the multidimensional character of
a modern world in constant flux.

His past experienced in far-off regions, along with multiple cultural memories, ultimately acquires an illusory dimension in the acts of recall. Just as
past and present run parallel, so, too, does the conflict between truth and
fiction in the stories of his self. He proclaims at last:

Though the pursuit of truth may be no more than a succession of conjectures in
which the mind weighs speculative fictions, I have most excitingly this to relate,
that in pursuing my researches on three continents [...] to sculpt the figure of the
man whom I sometimes believe to be my adversary, sometimes my nemesis, and
occasionally my friend, [...] I have finally found myself confronting the man who
might have been real. (193–94)

The narrator–protagonist's constant struggle with a variety of civilizations on
three distant continents – Asia, Europe, and America – not only calls for a
new approach to history and memory, but also unravels to him multiple puz-
zles of the self. He finally comprehends that the image of the man he has been

constructing in his journeys to such distant lands as America and England culminates in his native land India:

> It came to me in an old Moghul palace [...] in the heart of India, where I found myself in a hall of mirrors and suddenly perceived the true identity of my man, knew at last what the story was that I had to tell, the fiction that there was to invent yet of the century that was all but dead and become a memory [...] that reality, poor thing, has no existence at all. (194)

Phase Three: Discovering India as a Landmark of Time and Memory in Plural Worlds

Part Three, "Origins of the Self," is set in India at the time of Partition, and this time the protagonist is called Roshan, meaning 'light' in Urdu and Hindi (the national languages of now-independent India and Pakistan). The protagonist is thus transfigured into an Indian version of the anglicized Shimmers who is introduced to us as Urim in part one and Jonathan Archibald Pons in part two of the novel. From the far-flung lands of Brazil and California, the reader is suddenly thrown into the East. The subcontinent, surrounded by the greatest mountain ranges, becomes the ultimate symbol of time and memory.

This phase introduces us to Roshan's first encounter with a loss of home and a sense of exile that actually ensues from his transnational and transcultural adventures documented in part one and two of the novel. In contrast to the previous two parts, memory acquires a strong political dimension in part three, since the novelist sets Roshan's story in the most crucial phase of India's struggle for independence from British rule.

The political past of the pre-Partition subcontinent comes alive as fourteen-year-old Roshan recollects political debates about the division of his homeland into Hindu-dominated India and Muslim-dominated Pakistan as a consequence of the imperial policy of 'divide and rule'. Being Muslim himself, he tries to understand the conflict between Hindu nationalism and the Muslim obsession with partition, but cannot make head nor tail of it all, as his best friends in the neighbourhood and at school are Hindus and Sikhs. However, rivalry between Hindus and Muslims on the political scale is also reflected in private life when Roshan feels disgusted with the idea of touching the penis of his Hindu friend Chandru or is dismayed when a Hindu boy fancies his younger sister Zakia. Both these domestic episodes represent the influence of political separatism on the national scale that the political leaders have injected into the independence movement.

In the heat of many discussions at his parental home on the independence movement in relation to Gandhi's and Jinnah's ideology of freedom,[24] Roshan makes an effort to see an India beyond political boundaries and beyond an insular adult vision. In other words, he occupies himself with the soul of India, which he considers to be the "soil of his self's origins" (225). But this soil of origins falls victim to insurmountable ethnic tension and conflict which ends up in dividing not only land and territory, but also history and cultural memory. These divided memories, cast by the partition of subcontinent in 1947, pervade the realm of memory in his future incarnations as Urim and Pons in the garb of "intertwined memories."

Roshan's love affair as a teenager with a twenty-seven-year old Hindu primary-school teacher constitutes the most exciting as well as the most painful episode of Part Three. When, just at the time of Partition, he recovers from a severe beating inflicted on him, as a Muslim boy, by Miss Bhosle's brothers as punishment for his having a liaison with their sister, Roshan is awakened to a different world. His ideal of a united multicultural India is shattered. In Chapter Thirteen, "Time's Outcast," the power of memory seizes Roshan completely when physical recovery from the beating matures his sensibility towards temporal and spatial as well as political and social realities. He feels as if he were not only born again but is ready to be reincarnated:

> His memory was so vivid, he sometimes felt himself present again in some past event and was astonished, when he realized he had only been remembering, at the reappearance of forgotten tastes and smells. Sometimes it seemed the remembered event was not one from the past but from the future, but that, he was convinced, was merely a confusion in his brain [...] He had no system of reckoning time [...] and could only float among random appearances of images of events that claimed to be his reality. (303)

During his travels and migration, the memory of Partition and his memories of childhood begin to flow into his present life in distant places of the world as he tries to understand the story of his life. Memory and imagination begin to preoccupy him, and he cannot separate fact from fiction in the remembered

---

[24] For Mohandas Karamchand Gandhi (1869–1948), the foremost political and spiritual leader of the Indian Independence Movement, see Louis Fischer, *The Life of Mahatma Gandhi* (1951; New York: HarperCollins, 1997); for Muhammad Ali Jinnah (1876–1984), the president of the All India Muslim League who struggled for the creation of Pakistan, see Stanley Wolpert, *Jinnah of Pakistan* (Oxford: Oxford UP, 2002).

events or situate memory in any time-frame: "When he attempted to focus on the present it dissolved instantly into the past and he fell into the habit of re-enacting events in his memory [...] Sometimes the discovery of his condition seemed merely an imagined event" (304).

Despite memory's magical spell on him, conventional divisions of time become wholly redundant, as he does not live between past and present any longer but among past, present, and future simultaneously: "Whether it was a past or a future moment, or merely the eternally self-deleting present, seemed vastly irrelevant" (305). The reader notices that this is the stage where memory starts to draw upon fictions, since at this very stage he loses his hold on conventional temporal and spatial demarcations. The partition of the subcontinent stops the clock for him by thrusting him into a state of timelessness that is the state of eternal exile. In this state of timelessness, he is driven to reassemble his self and identity with the help of his imagination each time from scratch by repossessing lost vestiges of a remote past.

His train journey from India to newly created Pakistan, another symbol of the protagonist's many journeys in different continents, makes him consider the need to recollect and to invent the past once it is gone. After he is expelled from his own land because of an unavoidable political-cultural revolution, he feels a need to preserve the cultural past – real, imagined or fictive – in his memory so that he can view it in later years as a starting-point for his evolving self and identity no matter how (un)reliable the mnemonic process may be.

The protagonist's final confrontation with his moment of truth leads him to reflect on the dynamic of "intertwined memories." He manages to recognize not only his migrant condition but also various landmarks of time from Europe and Asia that permeate the domains of his vast imagination.

> Your father is calling to you to look. But you are already seeing and in your mind you are looking at more than you can see because what you are seeing you will re-vision many years later when you come to stand on the banks of the Thames, the mystery of primeval water with its source in the Himalayas, and there is a throbbing within you because your father has said he is taking you to the mountains, it is as if the blood that pulsed within the heaving surface of primeval water and you are certain that the Indus is within you. (341)

Soon land, border, country turn out to be myriad shades of memory – memory which is as much fictional as real, since place and space, located in time past or time present, seem to be a figment of the imagination, especially when the mind is engaged in evoking long-forgotten episodes from a dull and distant past. The narrator–protagonist looks at the Hindu Kush, "The head of India" (343) previously associated with Horuxtla in his prior incarnation, that no invader from the outside could ever conquer. Eventually, India, "this land of origins – this crunched up vertically thrusting land of suggestive distortions in exile" (343), draws Roshan to an unbreakable bond with his past and his native land: it is only through this bond that he comprehends the significance of transcultural memory within his being and that he recognizes a sense in his many journeys and travels to strange countries and continents around the globe.

Conclusion

The division of the subcontinent as a fundamental political revolution in the history of India, now divided into three independent nation-states, proves to be the prologue in the fantastical life of Urim / Pons / Shimmers / Roshan to the act of remembering multiple worlds, their eternal antagonism and interconnectedness. After the eventual loss of home / land, Roshan develops a deeper consciousness of self and culture, history and memory; in other words, "*how newness enters the world*"[25] from the channels of political, social, and economic change. The movement of newness as modernity is thus integral to his renewed understanding of his individual and collective cultural past. He arrives at the conclusion that, once the self is cut off from its origin, it begins to undergo a life-long process of translation despite the fact that translation is always coupled with its double, the untranslatable. It is reincarnated again and again as it travels to a new country and culture, and is thus always a fiction and a myth – but a fiction and a myth that is always in the making and in perpetual quest of its origins and its ultimate reality. Thus, while recollecting the transcultural phenomena in each of his new incarnations, the narrator–protagonist strives not only to reconcile himself with his plural lives in an age of cultural transgressions but also with the triple mirror of the self in a narrative world-within-a-world.

---

[25] Salman Rushdie, "In Good Faith" (1990), in Rushdie, *Imaginary Homelands: Essays and Criticism, 1981–1991* (London: Granta / Penguin, 1991): 394 (emphasis in the original).

WORKS CITED

Adler, Thomas P. "Pinter's *Night*: A Stroll Down Memory Lane," *Modern Drama* 17 (1974): 461–65.

Appadurai, Arjun. *Modernity at Large: Cultural Dimensions of Globalization* (Minneapolis: U of Minnesota P, 1996).

Borges, Jorge Luis. *Labyrinths* (Harmondsworth: Penguin, 1970).

Chew, Shirley, ed. "Performing Arts and South Asian Literature," Special Issue of *Moving Worlds: A Journal of Transcultural Writing* 5.2 (2006).

Clifford, James. *Routes: Travel and Translation in the Late Twentieth Century* (Cambridge MA: Harvard UP, 1997).

Dussel, Enrique. "Beyond Eurocentrism: The World-System and the Limits of Modernity" in *The Cultures of Globalization*, ed. Fredric Jameson & Masao Miyoshi (Durham NC & London: Duke UP, 1998), 3–31.

Eakin, Paul John. *Fictions in Autobiography: Studies in the Art of Self-Invention* (Princeton NJ: Princeton UP, 1985).

——. *How Our Lives Become Stories: Making Selves* (Ithaca NY & London: Cornell UP, 1999).

Erll, Astrid, & Ansgar Nünning. "Where Literature and Memory Meet: Towards a Systematic Approach to the Concepts of Memory Used in Literary Studies," in *REAL: Yearbook of Research in English and American Literature* 21, ed. Herbert Grabes (Tübingen: Gunter Narr, 2005): 261–94.

Fischer, Louis. *The Life of Mahatma Gandhi* (1951; New York: HarperCollins, 1997).

Freeman, Mark. *Rewriting the Self: History, Memory, Narrative* (London & New York: Routledge, 1993).

Giddens, Anthony. *Modernity and Self-Identity: Self and Society in the Late Modern Age* (Oxford: Polity, 1991).

——. *Runaway World: How Globalisation is Reshaping our Lives* (London: Profile, 2002).

Ghose, Zulfikar. *The Triple Mirror of the Self* (1992; London: Bloomsbury, 1994).

Halbwachs, Maurice. *On Collective Memory*, tr. Lewis A. Coser (*La mémoire collective*, 1939; Chicago & London: U of Chicago P, 1992).

Hannerz, Ulf. *Transnational Connections: Culture, People, Places* (London: Routledge, 1996).

Hoerder, Dirk, Yvonne Hébert & Irina Schmitt, ed. *Negotiating Transcultural Lives: Belonging and Social Capital among Youth in Comparative Perspective* (Göttingen: V&R unipress, 2005).

Iser, Wolfgang. *The Fictive and the Imaginary: Charting Literary Anthropology* (*Das Fiktive und das Imaginäre: Perspektiven literarischer Anthropologie*, 1993; tr. Baltimore MD & London: Johns Hopkins UP, 1993).

——. "Coda to the Discussion," in *The Translatability of Cultures: The Figurations of the Space Between*, ed. Sanford Budick & Wolfgang Iser (Stanford CA: Stanford UP, 1996), 294–304.

McGrath, Joseph E., & Janice R. Kelly. *Time and Human Interaction: Towards a Social Psychology of Time* (New York & London: Guilford, 1986).

Morley, David, & Kevin Robins. "No Place Like *Heimat*: Images of Home(land)," in *European Culture in Space and Place: Theories of Identity and Location*, ed. Erica Carter, James Donald & Judith Squires (London: Lawrence & Wishart, 1993): 3–32.

Motzkin, Gabriel. "Memory and Cultural Translation," in *The Translatability of Cultures: Figurations of the Space Between*, ed. Sanford Budick & Wolfgang Iser (Stanford CA: Stanford UP, 1996): 265–81.

Pratt, Mary Louise. *Imperial Eyes: Travel Writing and Transculturation* (London & New York: Routledge, 1992).

Robertson, Roland. "Glocalization: Time–Space and Homogeneity–Heterogeneity," in *Global Modernities*, ed. Mike Featherstone, Scott Lash & Roland Robertson (London & New Delhi: Sage, 1995): 25–44.

Rushdie, Salman. *Imaginary Homelands: Essays and Criticism, 1981–1991* (London: Granta/Penguin, 1991).

Said, Edward W. *Culture and Imperialism* (1993; New York: Vintage, 1994).

Schacter, Daniel L. *Searching for Memory: The Brain, the Mind, and the Past* (New York: Basic Books, 1996).

Schulze-Engler, Frank. "Von 'Inter' zu 'Trans': Gesellschaftliche, kulturelle und literarische Übergänge," in *Inter- und Transkulturelle Studien: Theoretische Grundlagen und interdisziplinäre Praxis*, ed. Heinz Antor (Heidelberg: Winter, 2006): 41–53.

Welsch, Wolfgang. "Tranculturality: The Puzzling Form of Cultures Today," in *Spaces of Culture: City, Nation, World*, ed. Mike Featherstone & Scott Lash (London: Sage, 1999): 194–231.

Wolpert, Stanley. *Jinnah of Pakistan* (Oxford: Oxford UP, 2002).

◄❖►

Routes to the Roots
— Transcultural Ramifications in *Bombay Talkie*

CHRISTINE VOGT–WILLIAM

> Sunrise, burning heat
> Nothing is as travelled as a Bombay street
> Contradictions, city of extremes
> Anything is possible in Bombay Dreams
> Some live and die in debt
> Others making millions on the Internet
> Contradictions, city of extremes
> Anything is possible in Bombay Dreams[1]
>
> The journey home
> Is never too long
> Some yesterdays always remain
> I'm going back to where my heart was light
> [...]
> I want to feel the way that I did then
> I'll think my wishes through before I wish again
> Not every road you come across
> Is one you have to take
> No, sometimes standing still can be
> The best move you ever make[2]

---

[1] Don Black, Raza Jaffrey, Preeya Kalidas & A.R. Rahman, "Bombay Dreams," from the musical *Bombay Dreams*; lyrics on http://www.allthelyrics.com/lyrics/bombay_dreams _soundtrack/bombay_dreams-lyrics-75250.html (accessed 15 March 2008).

[2] Black, Jaffrey, Kalidas & Rahman, "The Journey Home," from the musical *Bombay Dreams*; lyrics on http://www.allthelyrics.com/lyrics/bombay_dreams_soundtrack/the_journey_home-lyrics- 75246.html (accessed 15 March 2008).

T HE IDEA OF 'BOMBAY TALKIE' explored in this essay relates
         to fertile 'boundary breaking' ground particularly suited to investi-
         gating transgressive artistic and literary practice. My essay is based
on a film and a novel that both coincidentally bear the title 'Bombay Talkie':
although the term 'Bombay Talkie' was initially confined to the Bollywood
film industry, it has broken through genre and cultural barriers and has now
gained currency in various manifestations in film and literature.

   Bombay Talkie, the film, was produced by the Indian film director Ismail
Merchant and the Hollywood producer James Ivory, while the novel *Bombay
Talkie* was written by the South Asian-American author Ameena Meer.[3] Although both texts were created independently of each other, they do have
something in common besides their title: both the film and the novel address
the idea of a return to India as a transcultural strategy in effecting identity
negotiations. The film is about a white woman trying to 'return' to herself in
an India which she perceives to be spiritual, while the novel is about a South
Asian-American woman who actually returns to India, where her parents
came from, in order to get acquainted with that side of her cultural heritage.

   In this essay, I work with the premise that roots and transculturality are not
mutually exclusive and that roots can in themselves be transcultural, thus
questioning and even upsetting the notion that roots are the basis of an
authentic cultural identity. The search for roots leads many Indian diasporics
back to their ideas of their relationship to India, as shaped by their consumption of 'Indianness' in film, literature, and music. Given the diversity of cultural facets in India, these influences are intrinsically of a transcultural nature.
In this respect, it is interesting to note that Bombay, the Indian metropolis that
has lent its name to the term 'Bombay Talkie', is itself a transcultural construct, as Rushdie observes through his protagonist Saleem Sinai in *Midnight's Children*. Bombay was initally named 'Mumbai', after the goddess
Mumbaidevi, by the Koli fishermen, the first known inhabitants of the region.
The first colonial power to settle in India, the Portuguese, named the city
'Bom Bahia' because of its harbour, which sheltered the Portuguese merchant
ships and men-of-war. When the British came, they called it 'Bombay', a
British citadel, "fortified, defending India's West against all comers."[4] This

---

   [3] *Bombay Talkie*, dir. James Ivory, writ. Ruth Prawer Jhabvala & James Ivory (Merchant
Ivory, UK 1970); Ameena Meer, *Bombay Talkie* (London: Serpent's Tail, 1994).
   [4] Salman Rushdie, *Midnight's Children* (1981; London: Vintage, 1995): 92.

itself is a telling example of the diverse cultural resources which are so much part of India's socio-historical landscape.

The History of *Bombay Talkie*

The term 'Bombay Talkie' was coined back in the mid-1930s as the name of a Bombay film production studio launched by a husband-and-wife team, Himansu Rai and Devika Rani. It marked the age when movies with sound first came into being in the Bombay movie industry. The beginning of this age, the so-called 'talkies' era, also marked the genesis of the Hindi movie song.[5] Today 'Bombay Talkie' is synonymous with Bollywood and the Hindi film.[6]

The 'Bombay Talkie' formula – Meera Syal refers to them as 'masala movies'[7] – consists of the elements of melodrama, action, suspense, music, and, of course, the ever-present love story. The Talkie films were thus already entities of cultural fusion: the "immense complexity of the genre, indeed its novel-like flexibility, means that enbedded in the form are texts of extraordinary variety."[8] Bollywood is in itself a cross-genre cultural production, an amalgamation of foreign and Indian aesthetics (as is evident from the name Bollywood – a contraction of 'Bombay', the location of India's movie industry, and 'Hollywood', the cinema capital of the Western world), and is a vital aspect of Indian indigenous cultural modernity. As Vijay Mishra observes, "although the narrative form locates itself in tradition, textual ideology is firmly grounded in modernity."[9] The term 'Bombay Talkie' itself has thus left the original Bollywood film context to crop up in South Asian dia-

---

[5] Vish Krishnan, "The History of Hindi Filmi Music," http://www.cs.colostate.edu/~malaiya/music_hist.html (accessed 15 March 2008).

[6] See Rushdie's reference in *Midnight's Children*: "Melodrama piling upon melodrama; life acquiring the colouring of a Bombay talkie" (148); see also Jennifer Takhar, "Bollywood Cinema in Rushdie's Fiction," http://www.postcolonialweb.org/pakistan/literature/rushdie/takhar16.html (accessed 15 March 2008); Chapter 4: "Abhilash Talkies" in Arundhati Roy, *The God of Small Things* (London: Flamingo, 1997); and Vijay Mishra's references to 'Bombay Talkies' or the 'talkies' in *Bollywood Cinema: Temples of Desire* (London: Routledge, 2002).

[7] Meera Syal, "Prepare for Planet Bollywood" (15 May 2002): online http://www.thisislondon.co.uk/theatre/article-575209-details/Prepare+for+planet+Bollywood/article.do (accessed 15 March 2008).

[8] Mishra, *Bollywood Cinema*, xviii.

[9] Mishra, *Bollywood Cinema*, 4.

spora cultures in Western countries, and has become transcultural in a geographical as well as generic sense, crossing oceans and manifesting itself in diverse other contexts such as literature and music.

The Merchant–Ivory film does not follow the given Bollywood formula as such but, rather, is a product of transcultural collaboration between Hollywood elements and those of Bollywood. It is interesting to note that the American producer James Ivory and the Indian director Ismail Merchant make up one of the longest-lasting transnational film partnerships in the history of cinema. Along with the screenwriter Ruth Prawer Jhabvala, Merchant and Ivory, whose collaboration began in 1961, are best known for their literary adaptations such as *A Room With a View, Howard's End*, and *The Remains of the Day*.[10] Jhabvala herself is a Booker Prize-winning novelist, who also belonged to the ranks of Indian women writers who published prolifically in the 1970s and 1980s.[11] *Bombay Talkie*, produced in 1970, stars the Merchant–Ivory regulars, the Indian actor Shashi Kapoor and the late Jennifer Kendall, sister of the British actress Felicity Kendall.[12]

The novel, written by the South Asian-American writer Ameena Meer, addresses issues of cultural negotiation faced by second-generation South Asian-American immigrants and is thus concerned with interpenetrative cultural influences, personal agency, and the complexities of modern diasporic life. As in the film adaptation, the idea of return is also embodied in the female protagonist in the novel, who returns to India because she considers the country an appropriate site to resolve the conflicts she faces in her life.

---

[10] Merchant Ivory Productions was originally formed with an eye towards making films in India for the export market, and Bombay Talkie is an example of these earlier, lesser-known films, which was produced in 1970 for US$ 200,000. After Merchant Ivory's breakthrough with *Shakespeare Wallah, Bombay Talkie* marked another step in a series of early Indian-based films made by the remarkable trio of Ivory, Merchant and screenwriter Jhabvala.

[11] Of Polish-German descent, Jhabvala is married to an Indian architect and lived a considerable part of her life in India. She now divides her time between India, London and New York.

[12] The couple went on to star in the Merchant-Ivory production of *Heat and Dust*, based on the 1975 novel of the same name by Ruth Prawer Jhabvala.

Negotiating Transcultural Lifestyles

Modern lives are to be understood in a transcultural context in terms of a migration that implies not only physical movement but also movement through diverse psycho-social landscapes, and should consequently be seen as the successive realization of a number of possible identities.[13] Transculturality is thus a consequence of the inner differentiation and complexity of modern cultures which also interpenetrate or emerge from one another.

The general idea today is that cultures cannot be conceived of as being anything other than hybrid: "Cultures today are in general characterized by hybridization. [...] For most of us, multiple cultural connexions are decisive in terms of our cultural formation. We are cultural hybrids."[14] The idea of transculturality, as I address it here, is related to cultural hybridity. Although I do not read the terms 'tranculturality' and 'cultural hybridity' as being necessarily synonymous, I propose that the sense of one's cultural hybridity is a prerequisite of one's attempts to act, read, and live transculturally.

Thus the 'reality' of culture is always a consequence of one's notions of culture: i.e. what one deems valuable as cultural resources and how one perceives and implements them. The transcultural components chosen are then accepted and integrated into the cultural perceptions that one applies to one's life constellation. In the *Bombay Talkie* film and the *Bombay Talkie* novel, the two protagonists' 'return' to India can thus be read as attempts at transcultural living, whereby they gain access to the diverse pools of cultural resources both from the USA and from their stay in India, in order to pursue their personal goals in identity negotiation. 'Transcultural' readings should thus also take into account the element of transgression of cultural boundaries. This is all the more significant in both the film and the novel, since the female protagonists engage in transgressive behavioural strategies in their negotiations of foreign Indian cultural terrain.

---

[13] Wolfgang Welsch, "Transculturality: The Puzzling Form of Cultures Today," in *Spaces of Culture: City, Nation, World*, ed. Mike Featherstone & Scott Lash (London: Sage 1999): 194-213.

[14] Wolfgang Welsch, "Transculturality: The Puzzling Form of Cultures Today," 198.

Returning: Routes and Roots

Two different kinds of 'return' are addressed here: the geographical relocation through travel, however temporary, is very much linked to a psychological return to one's self. To effect a 'return' to something that one is not
familiar with is, of course, very much a paradox. For these protagonists, India
represents a primeval and psychological rootedness, perhaps even stability,
authenticity, and, of course, the much-touted spirituality. Thus a 'return' to
the roots could symbolize a return to a new form of self-perception through a
merging of selected cultural aspects, whereby lost or non-existent abilities
and convictions and thus a sense of balance can be regained. Again, the
'return' implicit in the settings of the *Bombay Talkie* film and the *Bombay
Talkie* novel can be seen as a transcultural strategy for both protagonists.

The Return of the White Memsahib

The film *Bombay Talkie* concerns the lives and loves of an egocentric young
filmstar, Vikram (played by Shashi Kapoor), a disillusioned writer of sensa-
tional novels, Lucia (played by Jennifer Kendall), and a scornful young poet,
Hari (played by Zia Mohyeddin), and is set in the frenetic movie world of
India's cinema capital. The interactional dynamic of this love triangle forms
the pivot of the film: "Stardom and a marriage are shattered as the battle of
the egos, of who will walk out on whom, rages and all three are hurtled to de-
struction in spite of themselves."[15]

Interestingly enough, Lucia Lane herself is not an American woman native
to American soil. She is an Englishwoman who married an American man
and migrated to the USA. She settled there and made a career for herself as a
writer of sensationalist fiction. Lucia's relocation to India in the 1970s was
symptomatic of a time when the Beatles travelled to India to find inspiration
for their music, and the 'return to spirituality' phenomenon was common
among Western individuals: "Generations of Westerners have travelled to
India in the hope that some of its spirituality will rub off, and thus help them
to get closer to Enlightenment than they would if they just stayed at home."[16]
In the film, Lucia travels to India, ostensibly to find inspiration for her next
best-selling novel, but she is actually out to find some meaning in her life.

---

[15] Judith Crist, "*Bombay Talkie*" (Review), *New York* (23 November 1970): 77.
[16] "Indian Spirituality: The Swamis," *The Economist* (18 December 2003): 5.

Lucia does not 'return' to India in the real sense of the word; rather, she relocates to India. India seems to be a space on which to project Lucia's own preconceptions, which she manipulates in order to effect a return to a sense of rootedness in herself.

Disillusioned with her life – with four failed marriages, writer's block, and an estranged teenage daughter in Switzerland – Lucia wants to create a new home base for herself in India. She attempts to live transculturally in Bombay on her own terms, by appropriating certain cultural aspects of India that fascinate her. She tries to fashion a new hybrid life-style against the backdrop of an intrinsically hybrid Bollywood, which appears more conducive and accommodating to the personal eccentricities of a disillusioned Western artist. She decides to take up with the young Indian actor Vikram in order to gain a foothold; she does this without any scruples, disregarding the fact that, despite Bollywood's ostensible modern permissiveness, this transgression is frowned upon in Indian society, as it is in Western countries. The interesting point here is that in 1970, the basic assumption was that the 'spiritual' Indian man could temporarily save the alienated Western woman, but the option of their leading a married life together would raise questions of miscegenation.[17]

An instance of Lucia's attempted transcultural transgression is when she uses the tradition of *rakshabandhan* to present Vikram with a personal gift. *Rakshabandhan* is an important festival in India where brothers and sisters re-establish their sibling bonds. Women, both young and old, bind specially made bracelets (*rakhi*) of multicoloured silk and gold and silver threads (often lavishly decorated with sequins and semi-precious stones) on their brothers' wrists. This ritual reinforces the relationship between brother and sister and serves to remind them of the brother's duty to love and protect his sister, while the sister ensures the brother's spiritual and corporeal welfare through the symbolic tying of the bracelet on his arm.[18] Lucia walks in un-invited on a private family ceremony at Vikram's home and presents an expensive wristwatch which she wants to bind on Vikram's wrist. Lucia's inappropriate intrusion is a way of marking Vikram as her property, binding him

[17] Interestingly enough, Shashi Kapoor and Jennifer Kendall were husband and wife in real life.
[18] See "Festivals of India: The Rakshabandhan Festival," http://www.kamat.com/kalranga/festive/rakhi.htm (accessed 15 March 2008), and "Hinduism: Rakhi – The Thread of Love," http://hinduism.about.com/library/wekly/aa080800a.htm (accessed 15 March 2008).

to her before his family. When Vikram's wife Mala politely tries to stave off Lucia's more than obvious advances towards her husband by explaining the significance of the ritual within the family, Lucia feigns obtuseness and plays the part of the confused but well-meaning and finally offended white memsahib. This is one example among several of an attempted transculturality that can be read as a colonizing gesture in the context of orientalism. This gendered colonizing reverses the original set-up of a white colonial master laying claim to a feminized India.

Lucia's attempts to establish a new mode of living for herself in the hybrid setting of Bollywood social circles are thwarted at nearly every turn. The first obstacle presents itself in the person of a former Bollywood starlet turned psychic palm-reader, a close friend and mentor of Vikram's. Lucia insists that the lady tell her future by reading her palm. Obviously, the psychic does not condone Vikram's relationship with the American woman and only reluctantly complies with Lucia's wish, pointing out that Lucia's interference in the social observances and structures is quite out of order and against the grain: "There are people, even though they are not bad people, yet they harm others."

Lucia suddenly becomes aware of her limitations in the face of what she perceives to be India's conservative and mystic traditionalism and is thrown off balance; hers is a failed transculturality. As this route to a modicum of rootedness proves thorny, Lucia turns to a more renowned and fashionable source of spirituality – the swami, or guru, who would lead her to a much-needed personal enlightenment. However, Lucia hits a dead-end here as well: the swami proves to be an egomaniac surrounded by fawning females, of both Indian and Western origin. Feeling uncomfortably inadequate, she resumes her romantic affair with Vikram. Her second attempt to get what she wants on her own terms fails miserably, in that the object of her affections does not seem at all serious about having a proper relationship with her; his reputation as an actor and his marriage are both destroyed as he bandies about with Lucia, despite his better judgement. Both Lucia and Víkram engage in power games, trying to get the upper hand over each other. In the end, both are punished for their arrogance, and Vikram is disposed of in true Bollywood melodramatic style: he is murdered by his rival for Lucia's affections after the couple splits up.

The Return of the Second-Generation
Non-Resident Indian Woman

The 'return' addressed in the novel *Bombay Talkie* is based on how second-generation South Asian-Americans, especially in the 1990s, engage in the transcultural process of negotiating their diasporic identities. The return of diasporic South Asians or NRIs (non-resident Indians) to the subcontinent is a phenomenon currently being addressed in Bollywood, as observed by Vijay Mishra and Deepa Shah.[19] Mishra points out the inherent transculturality in diasporic perceptions of one's own roots, using his own background as a Fijian-Indian diasporic to illustrate this:

> In Fiji this fragment society constructed a largely mythical – some would say illusory
> – India which had little basis in fact. My own India had grown through the myths [...]
> and like all mythical relationships, mine too had an implicit capacity to distort and
> magnify. Yet, these myths or, more accurately, ideologies, since they were imaginary
> systems of belief, framed our ambivalent relationship to Mother India.[20]

Elizabeth Russell sees the negotiation of diasporic identity in the light of a "reterritorialization of the diaspora." Russell considers Chandra Mohanty's "temporality of struggle" in Ameena Meer's novel:

> The real crossing of boundaries in *Bombay Talkie* does not correspond to a geo-
> graphical East/West dichotomy, but to a violent challenging of stereotyped identities
> and traditions. In the case of a culture steeped in religious tradition like the Hindu,
> everything has a place and duties assigned to it and as long as a woman respects this
> setup she will be valued. The tensions begin when the Indian woman comes into
> contact with other powerful discourses that offer her a reallocation in society. When
> this "double vision" occurs, when she finds herself in an in-between space, at the
> crossroads of different [...] cultures, she must be aware that her privileged position
> of "double vision" is critical.[21]

---

[19] See "Chapter 8: Bombay Cinema and Diasporic Desire" in Mishra, *Bollywood Cinema*, 235–69. See also Deepa Shah, "Hooray for Bollywood," *The Observer* (24 March 2002): online http://observer.guardian.co.uk/print/0,,4380329-102281,00.html (accessed 15 March 2008). The return of the NRI is significant as a trope both on the 'internal' filmic level and on the 'external' financial and production levels of Bollywood cinema.

[20] Mishra, *Bollywood Cinema*, x.

[21] Elizabeth Russell, "Cross-Cultural Subjectivities: Indian Women Theorizing in the Diaspora," in *Caught between Cultures: Women, Writing and Subjectivities*, ed. Elizabeth Russell (Cross/Cultures 52; Amsterdam & New York: Rodopi, 2002): 93.

In *Bombay Talkie*, a young South Asian-American woman, Sabah al Hussein, 'returns' to India, hoping to negotiate her cultural loyalties and perhaps find a way to satisfy her parents' expectations and her own desires in life. She hopes to find some form of happy medium between the cultural value systems she encounters in India and her need to be able to define herself as an American.

Issues of cultural viability are often at the root of this negotiation, which, however, also evinces a conservative edge exacerbated by immigrant nostalgia for a 'home' the second generation NRIs have only ever experienced at second hand through their parents. In the framework of the diaspora, the articulation of second-generation identities takes shape in a transcultural frame of reference. This form of transculturality works with the more or less unconscious premise that cultural boundaries are permeable in order to access chosen cultural resources to effect identity negotiations. As Sunaina Maira has observed, the exploration of ethnic identities is a significant rite of passage for those who do not have frequent access to Indian cultural systems, and one of the resources that they avail themselves of is the return to India, where their parents hail from.[22] Maira points out that many of the younger generation, either in late adolescence or in young adulthood, feel the need for this geographical and psychological return to their ancestral country, a kind of symbolic going back to find out what their parents had been enthusing about: "This shift stems from many layers of experience, many of them with emotional significance, that give rise to wishes to learn more about family history or to feel a sense of belonging."[23]

Sabah in the novel *Bombay Talkie* has to come to terms with herself as an Indian diasporic woman, especially with regard to her sexuality. Living in America, she is still set apart by her fellow university students as being different and exotic: "'You're so lucky you're Indian, I mean you're already so spiritual and everything'" (9) Yet Sabah does not necessarily feel just Indian; she reflects "What the hell is wrong with her? [...] Why should she feel different from any other American girl?" (8). In order to resolve this conflict, Sabah decides to explore the Indian aspects of her heritage; she travels to India and falls in with her old school mate Rani and her circle of international friends in Delhi. Sabah, indeed, embraces certain aspects of Indian culture as

---

[22] Sunaina Maira, "Making Room for a Hybrid Space: Reconsidering Second-Generation Ethnic Identity," *Sanskriti* 6.1 (1995), http://www.foil.org/resources/sanskriti/dec95/sunaina .html (acc. March 15, 2008).

[23] Maira, "Making Room for a Hybrid Space," 2.

she is introduced to them by her new-found friends, who are in themselves a very mixed and international crowd moving in slightly more elevated social circles; yet she feels herself to be very much the outsider, who attempts to acquaint herself with all things Indian but cannot quite get a grip: "They've finally stopped discussing how strange it is that she looks so Indian but speaks Hindi like a firungi. Now she's just an oddity to be pointed out" (152).

Rani, half-American and half-Indian, inadvertently draws Sabah into her own vortex of unsuccessful transcultural negotiations, thus serving as a projection foil for Sabah to confront her own conflicts, while simultaneously showing her the potential of a returned diasporic's transcultural life-style in a metropolitan setting. Although Rani does not pander to traditional Indian expectations of what an Indian woman should be, she nevertheless tries to integrate into Indian society by agreeing to an arranged marriage into a wealthy Delhi family. She does, however, what she feels she has to do in order to define her own life and her position in Indian society: she is a professional model, for example, something which is normally frowned on by conservative Indian social standards, since a 'proper' Indian woman should never 'put her body on display'.[24] Rani is punished severely for her attempts to return to her Indian roots and to effect a transcultural life-style in what can be perceived as an essentially traditional Indian society as represented by Rani's husband and her in-laws. It should, of course, be noted that this 'tradition' is itself effectively 'transcultural', which raises the question of who defines what 'tradition' is, and to what ends and purposes.

Sabah is drawn to Rani on a personal and emotional level and is forced to confront her own preconceptions of India and their possible influence on her diasporic life-style. Indeed, her fascination with Rani concerns her discovery of her own potential homosexual orientations – another issue Meer chooses to treat in great detail in the person of Sabah's cousin Adam. A significant aspect of Sabah's friendship with Rani is that Sabah herself feels sexually attracted to her childhood friend and is occasionally disturbed to realize that she has homosexual tendencies, despite her more than obvious sexual appetite for heterosexual males. Sabah, who had been raped by one of her uncles in the USA at the age of sixteen, appears distant with regard to her sexual en-

---

[24] This is reminiscent of Sabah's own experiences of being harassed by men when dressed in figure-emphasizing outfits as well as being regarded with distaste by older Indian immigrant women she meets on the streets of San Francisco and who condemn her as a loose woman who shows her body off. See Meer, *Bombay Talkie*, 5–8.

counters with white American men. Yet she seems to enjoy sex for its own
sake without really committing herself to her partner – a rather dubious characteristic for a 'good Indian girl'. Sabah's preoccupation with her own sexuality and the fact that Rani is not at all apologetic about her feminine sexual
attractions are elements pertinent to Sabah's identificatory negotiations. The
question of the Indian diasporic woman's sexual propriety is a significant
matter of debate in the context of identificatory processes of second-generation South Asian-American women; gender and sexuality are often the main
issues, fraught with complex choices regarding cultural resources and their
uses.

In a final Bollywood-type melodramatic explosion, Rani meets with a
tragic end, in a rather cruelly twisted version of bride-burning.[25] In the wake
of Rani's tragedy, however, Sabah decides to go back to the USA, feeling
that she has failed in her quest for a sense of belonging in India. This, too, is
an instance of failed transculturality, since India's cultural value systems as
defined by those around Sabah and Rani appear to have interfered with Rani's
and Sabah's attempts at leading self-defined transcultural lives in India.
Sabah does take charge of the decision-making in her life, however, instead
of allowing her parents to dictate what she is to do and complying in order to
become as Indian as possible (218–19).

Conclusion

In the film and the novel, we see that "modernity is disavowed even as it is
endorsed; tradition is avowed even as it is rejected".[26] Lucia and Sabah attempt to exploit the cultural resources available in India to serve their strategies for facilitating certain transcultural life-styles acceptable to themselves,
but these attempts are not always tolerated. This tension between perceptions

---

[25] Meer, *Bombay Talkie*, 205–10. In *Dislocating Cultures: Identities, Traditions and
Third World Feminism* (London & New York: Routledge, 1997), Uma Narayan has pointed
out that domestic violence and wife murders are not just confined to the cultural context of
India, where dowry-murders are sadly often to be heard of. Dowry murders are also a frequent occurrence in diasporic communities and have acquired a certain 'Indianness', which
allows Western perceptions to grade these crimes as 'Third World gender issues'. The
crime of wife murder, whether by fire or by firearms, can be considered a transcultural
problem, in the sense that this malady crosses cultural boundaries and is not confined to just
'Indian culture' alone (101–102).

[26] Mishra, *Bollywood Cinema*, 4.

of modernity and of tradition is constantly visible both in the *Bombay Talkie* film and the *Bombay Talkie* novel.

Even though the film and novel seem completely different at first, they both end in instances of failed transculturality, since both protagonists have to abandon their attempts to shape new identities through their strategies of return to and possible instrumentalization of India for their own ends. It is their attempt to control the selection process of cultural resources that fails in the end, since transculturality involves interaction and not just individual choice. Thus, one protagonist turns out to be a rootless female 'orientalist' while the other is an American-Born Confused Desi; both these conditions could even be valid modes of transcultural living in themselves, however.

Returning to my initial premise that roots and transculturality are not mutually exclusive and that roots can in themselves be transcultural, *Bombay Talkie*, in both of its manifestations, shows us that trying to find one's routes to the roots, while a seemingly plausible method of effecting transcultural negotiation, is not necessarily the best way of 'authenticating' one's identificatory processes. Indeed, perhaps a 'return' as such may not be necessary at all – one might not have to look very far to discover resources that enable one to live transculturally. In this vein, I would like to end with a pertinent quote from Vijay Mishra: "I had come to India in search of the pot of gold only to find that the pot had been buried deep in my unconscious."[27] Thus a return to the roots may work for some but not necessarily for others, depending very much on one's own transcultural trajectory and the interactive negotiatory strategies employed.

WORKS CITED

Black, Don, Raza Jaffrey, Preeya Kalidas & A.R. Rahman. "Bombay Dreams," from the musical *Bombay Dreams*; lyrics on http://www.allthelyrics.com/lyrics/bombay_dreams_soundtrack/bombay_dreams-lyrics-75250.html (accessed 15 March 2008).
——. "The Journey Home," from the musical *Bombay Dreams*; lyrics on http://www.allthelyrics.com/lyrics/bombay_dreams_soundtrack/the_journey_home-lyrics-75246.html (accessed 15 March 2008).
Bombay Talkie, dir. James Ivory, writ. Ruth Prawer Jhabvala & James Ivory (Merchant Ivory, USA, 1970; 112 min.).
Crist, Judith. "*Bombay Talkie*" (review), *New York* (23 November 1970): 77.

---

[27] Mishra, *Bollywood Cinema*, x.

"Festivals of India: The Rakshabandhan Festival," http://www.kamat.com/kalranga/festive
    /rakhi.htm (accessed 15 March 2008).
"Hinduism: Rakhi: The Thread of Love," *The Economist*, http://hinduism.about.com/library
    /weekly/aa080800a.htm (accessed 15 March 2008).
"Indian Spirituality: The Swamis" (18 December 2003): 5.
Krishnan, Vish, "The History of Hindi Filmi Music," http://www.cs.colostate.edu/~malaiya
    /music_hist.html (accessed 15 March 2008).
Maira, Sunaina. "Making Room for a Hybrid Space: Reconsidering Second-Generation
    Ethnic Identity," *Sanskriti* 6.1 (1995): online http://www.foil.org/resources/sanskriti/dec95
    /sunaina.html (accessed 15 March 2008).
Meer, Ameena. *Bombay Talkie* (London: Serpent's Tail, 1993).
Mishra, Vijay. *Bollywood Cinema: Temples of Desire* (London: Routledge, 2002).
Narayan, Uma. *Dislocating Cultures: Identities, Traditions and Third-World Feminism*
    (London & New York: Routledge, 1997).
Roy, Arundhati. *The God of Small Things* (London: Flamingo, 1997).
Rushdie, Salman. *Midnight's Children* (1981; London: Vintage, 1995).
Russell, Elizabeth. "Cross-Cultural Subjectivities: Indian Women Theorizing in the Dia-
    spora," in *Caught between Cultures: Women, Writing and Subjectivities*, ed. Elizabeth
    Russell (Cross/Cultures 52; Amsterdam & New York: Rodopi, 2002): 77–98.
Shah, Deepa. "Hooray for Bollywood," *The Observer* (24 March 2002): online http://www
    .observer.co.uk/Print/0,3858,4380329,00.html (accessed 15 March 2008).
Syal, Meera. "Prepare for Planet Bollywood" (30 May 2002): online http://www.thisislondon
    .co.uk/theatre/article-575209-details/Prepare+for+planet+Bollywood/article.do (accessed 15
    March 2008).
Takhar, Jennifer, "Bollywood Cinema in Rushdie's Fiction," http://www.postcolonialweb
    .org/pakistan/literature/rushdie/takhar16.html (accessed 15 March 2008).
Welsch, Wolfgang. "Transculturality: The Puzzling Form of Cultures Today," in *Spaces of
    Culture: City, Nation, World*, ed. Mike Featherstone & Scott Lash (London: Sage, 1999):
    194–213.

◄❖►

Beyond the Contact Zone?
— Mapping Transcultural Spaces in Tomson Highway's *Kiss of the Fur Queen* and Eden Robinson's *Monkey Beach*

KATJA SARKOWSKY

MARY LOUISE PRATT'S CONCEPT of the 'contact zone' as "social spaces where disparate cultures meet, clash, and grapple with each other, often in highly asymmetrical relations of domination and subordination" has had a profound impact on the reading of contemporary Native writing in Canada and the USA and has provided a tool for the analysis particularly of processes of transculturation in Native literatures.[1] Pratt's and other critics' conceptualizations of hybridization and transcultural processes are distinctly spatial both in geographical and in metaphoric terms, most notably, of course, Homi Bhabha's notion of the Third Space.[2] Taking up the spatial aspects of these concepts and paying attention to the implications of their spatiality can highlight the role of space constructions as a means of transcultural negotiations in Native texts. Space, as numerous critics have argued, does not merely provide a background for cultural arrange-

---

[1] Mary Louise Pratt, *Imperial Eyes: Travel Writing and Transculturation* (London & New York: Routledge, 1992): 4.

[2] Homi Bhabha writes: "It is that Third Space, though unrepresentable in itself, which constitutes the discursive conditions of enunciation that ensure that the meanings and symbols of culture have no primordial unity or fixity; that even the same signs can be appropriated, translated, rehistoricized and read anew"; *The Location of Culture* (New York & London: Routledge, 1994): 37.

ments; rather, it is an integral part of cultural and political processes. This, as I hope to show, extends beyond 'space' as the bone of contention of territorial struggles, beyond questions of cultural location, and beyond spatial meta-phors of resistance. A close look at spatiality understood as a dynamic pro-cess of simultaneity and its functions in literary texts, I argue, may reveal how the complex cultural agendas of contemporary Native literature are negotiated not 'in' but 'through' the construction of different narrative spaces. These spaces are not static cultural containers, but present ambivalences and contra-dictions and are constitutive of transcultural processes.

Narration, Space, and Spatial Practices in the Literary Text

Mary Pat Brady's insistence on the centrality of space in Chicana literature – and on the specific ways of *textual* and aesthetic space construction – is equally valid for Native American/First Nations writing:

> [Native] writing offers an important theoretics of space, one that, like many critical space studies, implicates the production of space in the everyday, in the social, but that unlike many space theories suggests the relevance of aesthetics, of 'the literary mode of knowing' for understanding the intermeshing of the spatial and the social. And [Native] literature argues for and examines the relevance of race, gender, and sexuality – as well as class – to the making of space.[3]

Like these diverse categories – 'gender', 'ethnicity', 'sexuality', and 'class' – 'space' is a construct, is produced socially, economically, politically, cultural-ly, and also aesthetically in literature and art. And like these categories, space as a construct is not stable but in process. Therefore, I understand 'space' with the cultural theorist and historian Michel de Certeau and the sociologist Martina Löw as a dynamic, actively produced, and constantly shifting relative arrangement between people, places, and cultural and social goods; in the context of literary texts, textual elements in the widest sense present elements of space construction that are being put narratively into relation to one another. As James Clifford points out with respect to de Certeau, "'space' is never ontologically given. It is discursively mapped and corporeally prac-

---

[3] Mary Pat Brady, *Extinct Lands, Temporal Geographies: Chicana Literature and the Urgency of Space* (Durham NC & London: Duke UP, 2002): 6.

ticed."[4] This inseparable connection between space and practice is central. Space is constituted through movement, produced through use, simultaneously a means and a result of action or practice.

This practice depends on the *interdependence* of, hence analytical distinction between, 'space' and 'place'. The difference and relation between space and place has been addressed by a number of cultural and postcolonial critics; for Bill Ashcroft, for instance, 'space' is the (modern) invention of colonialism that literally displaced the colonized, 'place' in contrast is the precolonial sense of belonging in time, community, and landscape, a sense that postcolonial transformation seeks to recover, if in the 'delocalized': i.e. 'spatialized' form of global consciousness.[5] A similar distinction can also be found in Native literary studies: 'place' is often seen as the concrete manifestation of Native myth, history, culture, and community in the land; 'space', implicitly, and in a similar dynamic to what Ashcroft describes, is the colonial construction of the land as open, raw, inanimate, to be conquered by the colonizer – the construction of 'the West', the 'frontier', or 'the North'. 'Place', at least implicitly, frequently functions as the grounded opposition to colonial 'space'.

However, this kind of perception of literary space as empty, abstract, and colonial reinforces interpretations exclusively along the lines of ethnic conflict, of colonizer and colonized. The variety of cultural dynamics active in the construction of space and its role in transcultural processes are ignored, deadlocked in the perpetuation of essential cultural difference and opposition. Thus, without wanting to deny neither the modern institutionalization of 'empty' or 'abstract' space nor its instrumentalization in the colonial enterprise, I suggest with de Certeau and Löw a different analytical separation of space and place. "*Space is a practiced place,*" de Certeau emphasizes.[6] In turn, place is spatialized by practice. For the sociologist Löw, space is "a relational arrangement of living beings and social goods in place."[7] Place is both element and result of spatial practices. A place can harbour a number of spaces; spaces incorporate places as elements and, simultaneously, are groun-

---

[4] James Clifford, *Routes: Travel and Translation in the Late Twentieth Century* (Cambridge MA: Harvard UP, 1997): 54.

[5] See Bill Ashcroft, *Post-Colonial Transformation* (London & New York: Routledge, 2000): 15.

[6] Michel de Certeau, *The Practice of Everyday Life*, tr. Steven Rendall (*Arts de faire*, 1980; Berkeley: U of California P, 1988): 117 (emphasis in the original).

[7] Martina Löw, *Raumsoziologie* (Frankfurt am Main: Suhrkamp, 2000): 271. (My tr.)

ded in place. Löw and de Certeau thus formulate a *relational*: i.e. *processual* understanding of space that includes places as constitutive parts, as results, and as material grounding.

Löw's and de Certeau's concepts do differ in certain respects – while both see a close connection between space and place, place for de Certeau is the 'dead' opposite of 'living' space. For Löw, by contrast, it is an integral part of space construction. Nevertheless, they both share a notion of space as actively constructed and attribute utmost importance to space constituting practices – practices as disparate as walking, building, seeing, touching, producing topographical maps, etc. In the literary text, spatial practices work on different narrative levels; central to all is 'storytelling' in the widest sense. As de Certeau argues, story "does not express a practice. It does not limit itself to tell about a movement. It *makes* it."[8] The Laguna author Leslie Marmon Silko has emphasized that the telling, retelling, and refiguring of stories is a central way in which human beings participate as agents in the construction of space, and she means this explicitly with respect to the physical and spiritual environment;[9] for Silko, the world is story, and story, the production of meanings through the use of language, is a powerfully creative – and potentially destructive – spatial practice. Stories – no matter whether they are told by an authorial narrative voice or by any of the characters, as narrative practice and 'objects' – arrange elements into spatial ensembles and are themselves elements of these (or other) ensembles.[10]

Both Eden Robinson's *Monkey Beach* and Tomson Highway's *Kiss of the Fur Queen* present a large number of different spaces – reserves, urban spaces, domestic spaces, institutional spaces, etc. – and deploy various narrative strategies of space construction. Besides storytelling and closely linked to it, 'mapping' is one such device that can be productively analysed in terms of what Graham Huggan has called 'literary cartography', which, he writes, "not only examines the function of maps in literary texts, but also explores the operations of a series of territorial [spatial] strategies that are implicitly or

---

[8] De Certeau, *The Practice of Everyday Life*, 81 (emphasis in the original).

[9] See Leslie Marmon Silko, "Interior and Exterior Landscapes: The Pueblo Migration Stories," in Silko, *Yellow Woman and a Beauty of the Spirit: Essays on Native American Life Today* (New York: Simon & Schuster, 1996): 25–47.

[10] This process is multilayered: not only are stories and storytelling being used in the literary text – the text itself presents a story/a set of stories as well, presenting an aspect that is not further considered in the context of the present essay.

explicitly associated with maps."[11] Mapping, as Huggan has shown, is not necessarily a strategy only of territorial appropriation; rather, mapping can fulfil a number of different functions simultaneously and thus makes obvious the close connection between the production of narrative spaces and places and the transcultural negotiations carried out in the texts.

Maps, Itineraries, Places: Eden Robinson's *Monkey Beach*

The story of Eden Robinson's *Monkey Beach* is told by Lisa Hill, a young Haisla woman travelling down Douglas Channel in British Columbia in a small motor boat in order to join her parents in the search for her younger brother Jimmy, who has gone missing at sea. The story alternates between the present – Lisa's trip and the days preceding it – and flashbacks from the past, stories of Lisa's and Jimmy's childhood and youth, of the deaths of Lisa's beloved uncle Mick and her grandmother, as well as of Lisa's sensitivity towards and perception of spirits and ghosts as part of everyday life.

Different forms of mapping abound in the novel, both metaphorical and more literal. The most immediate is early on, when the narrator–protagonist locates the novel's plot and her home town Kitamaat by referring to a topographical map:

> Find a map of British Columbia. Point to the middle of the coast. Beneath Alaska, find the Queen Charlotte Islands. Drag your finger across the map, across the Hecate Strait to the coast and you should be able to see a large island hugging the coast. This is Princess Royal Island [...]. Princess Royal Island is the western edge of traditional Haisla territory. Ka-tee-doux Gitk'a'ata, the Tsimshians of Hartley Bay, live at the mouth of the Douglas Channel and surrounding areas just north of the island. During land claim talks, some of this territory is claimed by both the Haisla and the Tsimshian nations – this is called an overlap and is a sticky topic of discussion. But once you pass the head of the Douglas Channel, you are firmly in Haisla territory.[12]

---

[11] Graham Huggan, *Territorial Disputes: Maps and Mapping Strategies in Contemporary Canadian and Australian Fiction* (Toronto: U of Toronto P, 1994): 31.

[12] Eden Robinson, *Monkey Beach* (London: Abacus, 2000): 4. Further page references are in the main text.

The narrator here conflates two spatial strategies that de Certeau has called 'maps' and 'itinerary' – the 'map' as an arrangement of places in relation to each other and the 'itinerary' as a description of how to get from one place to another.[13] The itinerary is doubled: it is performed by both the narrative voice and by the reader, either mentally or actually with a finger on a map. Map and itinerary are not at the opposite poles of experience, as de Certeau has it, but the itinerary retakes the territory the map has supposedly frozen in time and space: through reference to land disputes between indigenous nations, the 'map-itinerary' not only serves the reader as orientation, but the narrative map addresses its own indeterminacies, the struggle for borders and territory. It thereby catapults the reader directly into the close relationship between maps and colonial history, between space and time, into the historicity of spatial arrangements.[14]

This extends to the issue of place-names; naming is a powerful strategy of inscription and also of appropriation. Thus, names are a vital part of the places' connection to history and to the confusion and struggle of different (kinds of) borders. The narrator explains:

> Early in the 19th century, Hudson's Bay traders used Tsimshian guides to show them around, which is when the names began to get confusing. 'Kitamaat' is a Tsimshian word that means people of the falling snow, and that was their name for the main Haisla village. [...] The name got stuck on the official records and the village has been called Kitamaat ever since, even though it should be really called Haisla. (5)

The language confusion is indicative: not only is it part of the struggle over land, resources, and political and cultural agency, the issue of language is

---

[13] For de Certeau, the map 'colonizes' the itinerary: "The map thus collates on the same plane heterogeneous places, some received from a tradition and others produced by observation. But the important thing here is the erasure of the itineraries which, presupposing the first category of places and conditioning the second, makes it possible to move from one to the other. The map, a totalizing stage on which elements of diverse origin are brought together to form the tableau of a 'stage' of geographical knowledge, pushes away in its prehistory or into its posterity, as if into the wings, the operations of which it is the result or the necessary condition" (*The Practice of Everyday Life*, 121, emphasis in the original).

[14] "Spatial history," Bill Ashcroft paraphrases Paul Carter's project as laid out in *The Road to Botany Bay*, "examines place as a palimpsest on which the traces of successive inscriptions form the complex experience of place, which is itself historical" (*Post-Colonial Transformation*, 155).

also, for Lisa herself, a constant theme of contemplation, closely linked to her attempts to make sense of her being able to acknowledge simultaneous realities. As in the case with the geographical territory of her home community, Lisa approaches language with a double strategy: through reference to and citation of 'scientific explanation' and through her experience of and her struggle with it – Lisa's Haisla is rudimentary, but it is nevertheless strongly connected to things and events of her everyday life (particularly those having to do with food!) and even more so with her grandmother. Thus, like the geographical area itself, its history, the history of disputes over borders, and the struggle over language emerge as part of a highly personal space. In her map-itinerary, Lisa narrows down the intended focus of her reader's attention: from B.C. she 'zooms into' Haisla territory and further down to her home town, Kitamaat – which the reader knows first as the result of name-confusion and only then through its relation to other places, as part of territory and map.

> If your finger is on Prince Rupert or Terrace, you are too far north. If you are pointing to Bella Coola or Ocean Falls, you are too far south. If you are pointing in the right place, you should have your finger on the western shore of Princess Royal Island. To get to Kitamaat, run your finger northeast, right up to the Douglas Channel, a 140-kilometre-long deep-sea channel, to its mouth. (5)

Lisa continues to describe the islands the reader should pass on this finger-on-paper journey, ending the map reference with a pointer to her immediate surroundings: "At the end of the village is our house. Our kitchen looks out onto the water. Somewhere in the seas between here and Namu – a six-hour boat ride south of Kitamaat – my brother is lost" (5). This shocking and, in the context of the verbal map, unexpected ending of the passage redefines its purpose: by placing the unknown spot of Lisa's younger brother's disappearance in the immensity of British Columbia's landscape, it shifts from seeming 'background information' to giving the reader an idea of the territory's role in a family tragedy, of Jimmy's agony and of the difficulty of Lisa's search for him. This contextualization turns the coast from topography into a space created by relationships: between people, language, history, the coast, and the sea, as well as between family members. Family issues and 'place' formed by history and story are closely linked; the history of the area and the set-up of the map are central to the narrative formation of place in the novel, first and foremost the home of Lisa's family, and later of Monkey Beach, the place where the different strands of the narrative culminate. A seemingly detached and scientific strategy of space construction is used here to create an intimate space that implicitly questions what is being defined as personal by conflating it partially with 'history'.

The mapping strategy deployed here is a verbal one but in ways that, through its direct address, demand from the reader immediate visualization. As Huggan argues, "the process of matching map to text, or text to map, involves the reader in a comparative that may bring to the surface flaws or discrepancies in the process of mimetic representation."[15] This forced comparison works: no matter whether or not the reader consults a topographical map, it results in the reader's confrontation with a mere illusion of thorough spatial knowledge, for it is the story of Lisa's trip, the stories linked to this trip and to the places she passes on her way, that offer a more complex form of bodily and spiritually experienced knowledge of space.

This does not mean that these different kinds of spatial conceptualization are diametrically opposed; rather, the ways in which the experience of space and of simultaneously existing (material and spiritual) spaces is conveyed rely heavily on apparently impersonal forms of verbal mapping. For instance, the framing narrative of Lisa's trip down the Channel itself serves as a map:

> Going south is faster, even though the channel twists and turns, because I'm aiming for the inside passage, a stretch of water sheltered by islands from the extreme surf and chancy weather of the open Pacific Ocean. To get there, I'll be traveling down the Verney Passage. I'm going by Ursula Channel so I pass Monkey Beach first, then the ghost town of Butedale, then Bella Bella and finally Namu. (180)

Lisa's mapping of her trip in the speedboat connects the places she passes not only through the narrative of the trip itself but also through the flashbacks that inscribe them through story and connect them to a web of spatial references covering the entire novel.

Of central importance here is yet another form of mapping: that of the body and bodily experience, which begins, like Lisa's journey, in the second chapter of the novel (entitled, significantly, "The Song of Your Breath") and is closely linked to the passages narrating her trip towards Namu. Like geographical territory, like language, the body presents an intersection and overlap of different struggles; it is part and agent of the various spatial constructions in the novel, and often enough it presents a border territory and contested space between different realities (spatial, material, spiritual) and be-

---

[15] Huggan, *Territorial Disputes*, 22.

tween different (scientific and mythological) explanations of these realities. Like the reference to the map of British Columbia, Lisa's mapping of the body and/or its vital organs is directed at the reader:

> Make your hand into a fist. This is roughly the size of your heart. If you could open up your own chest, you would find your heart behind your breastbone, nestled between your lungs. Each lung has a notch, the cardiac impression, that the heart fits into. Your heart sits on a slant, leaning into your left lung so that it is slightly smaller than your right lung. Reach into your chest cavity and pull your lungs away from your hart to fully appreciate the complexity of this organ. (163)

Lisa's verbal dissections of the heart – or rather, her directions to the reader: "Pull your heart out of your chest. Cut away the tubes that sprout from the top. Place your heart on a table. Take a knife and divide it in half, lengthwise" (191) – tell parallel stories of an attempt to explain her grandmother's heart failure on the basis of anatomical science and of mapping the body as the intersection between different realities: Lisa sees ghosts, spirits, the dead; she sees the world in "double exposure," she sleepwalks and leaves her body even when awake. Her narrative trip through the body culminates in 'heartbreak', making it obvious that the "complexity of the organ" does not only refer to the mechanical workings of the heart (or its failures) but also to the metaphoric layers attached to it:

> Heartbreak happens when less than 40 percent of the heart is damaged. [...] If too much of the heart is damaged, there is usually not enough pumping power left to maintain the circulation. Shock sets in: the patient becomes pale, cold and sometimes blue, and is mentally confused. Death often follows within the next few hours. (275)

'Heartbreak' is also one of the central themes in Lisa's life – dealing with loss, with the drowning of her beloved uncle Mick, and with her grandmother's death. 'Heartbreak', the fear of further loss, leads Lisa to Monkey Beach to look for her brother, whom she has seen at the Beach in her dreams. In the fragmented structure of the novel's flashbacks and narrative insertions of body maps, Lisa arrives at Monkey Beach directly after the passage quoted above. It is here, at probably the most intensely inscribed place of the novel, that different kinds of insertions – the dissection of the heart and the protagonist's instructions to the reader of how to contact the dead – merge and the body becomes a territory between life and death:

Remove yourself from the next sound you hear, the breathing that isn't your own. It glides beneath the bushes like someone's shadow, a creature with no bones, no arms or legs, a rolling, shifting worm-shaped thing that hugs the darkness. It wraps its pale body around yours and feeds. Push yourself away when your vision dims. Ignore the confused, painful contractions in your chest as your heart trip-hammers to life, struggles to pump blood. Ignore the tingling sensations and weakness in your arms and legs, which make you want to lie down and never get up. (366)

At Monkey Beach, a place of family outings and of looking for the Sasquatch, "the wild man of the woods," as children, a place of stories and of healing, Lisa enters the "Land of the Dead," as the final chapter is entitled. Her earlier narrative mappings make it possible to conceive of this entering as neither 'metaphorical' nor 'real' but as a simultaneity of different realities that intersect in the place of Monkey Beach. The body is both anatomical construct and part of the spirit world; it is itself liminal. This liminality is also part of simultaneously existing and constantly shifting spatial structures, structures and arrangements that are narratively produced by various means, by different mapping strategies that are not mutually exclusive; it is impossible to, for instance, simply oppose the 'colonial' topographical map and 'Native' story places. Rather, these different kinds of spatial productions – often contradictorily – coexist, comment on one another, draw on one another, and thus form a web of cultural references and codes.

Of Monsters and Malls: Story Mapping in Tomson Highway's *Kiss of the Fur Queen*

This web of cultural references is also characteristic of the narrative spatial constructions in Tomson Highway's *Kiss of the Fur Queen*. Set in Manitoba and Ontario, the semi-autobiographical novel tells the story of the Cree brothers Jeremiah and Gabriel Okimasis. The narrative begins in northern Manitoba shortly before the older Jeremiah's conception in 1951, with his father winning the "Millington Cup World Championship Dog Derby" (and receiving a kiss from the Fur Queen, the winner of the festival's beauty pageant) and it ends with the younger Gabriel dying of an AIDS-related illness in a Toronto hospital in 1987. The text follows the protagonists from their youth in northern Manitoba through years of residential school down south to Winnipeg and Toronto; Jeremiah becomes a concert pianist before turning to social work and later to writing, and Gabriel works as a dancer and choreographer.

Like Robinson's novel, *Kiss* also deploys a number of different mapping strategies, including references to topographical maps: the most obvious example is to be found at the end of the second part. Here, the text moves from the residential school (chapter) to the city (chapter); the narration simultaneously maps time and space, the way from the reserve to school and then further to Winnipeg over the course of six years:

> Jeremiah's sixteenth [sic] notes played on. For six years, they played without pause. Sprouting wings, they lifted off Kamamagoos Island that autumn, honked farewell to Eemanapiteepitat twenty miles to the north, they soared in semi-perfect V-formation over the billowing waves of Mistik lake, past the village of Wuchusk Oochisk, over the craggy rocks where the Mistik River joins the Churchill River, past Patima Bay, Chigeema Narrows, Flin Flon, and – following the route Abraham Okimasis had raced back in February 1951 – through Cranberry Portage to Oopaskooyak, where they touched down to slake their thirst on the memory of the Fur Queen's kiss.[16]

Mapping Jeremiah's trip to Winnipeg, the notes he plays on the piano at school turn into a flock of migratory birds travelling south, the image suggesting frequent returns. While there is no direct address to the reader and no mention of a map of Manitoba, this passage – similar to what Robinson's narrative does – presupposes the reader's (at least rudimentary) knowledge of Manitoba's topography. It merges 'map' and 'itinerary', plane overview and description of movement: The depiction of the protagonist's travel 'on a map' becomes visual, in a verbal imitation of a movie strategy that shrinks time in favour of space. This space is created by drawing lines between places, locations on the map, but also through references and allusions. This map mixes places that carry personal meaning for the protagonist with locations that are named here only once and have no further significance in the novel beyond their function as spatial signposts.[17]

---

[16] Tomson Highway, *Kiss of the Fur Queen* (Toronto: Doubleday, 1998): 96. Further page references are in the main text.

[17] The reference to Abraham's race and thus to family history has a number of dimensions: a temporal one (drawing a connection to Jeremiah's conception); a spatial one (partly tracing the very same way Abraham had taken); and a narrative one, connecting family history, the trickster (the fur queen), and the foreshadowing of both brothers' own victories later on, which are phrased as direct citations of Abraham's victory (see Highway, *Kiss of the Fur Queen*, 6, 214, 237).

Two different but significant spaces overlap at Oopaskooyak; despite the time that lies between the events named, the map verbally pins them down. The place refers simultaneously to Abraham's race and victory and to Jeremiah's time at residential school and to the different spatial constructions in which these events are embedded:

> After a detour of some years at the Birch Lake Indian Residential School twenty miles west of Oopaskooyak, the music curved south until it levelled onto the great Canadian plain and landed, just so, in the city of Winnipeg, Manitoba, eight hundred miles south of Eemanapiteepitat, in the pink salon of another woman in white fur. (96)

The 'map' bridges the years that lie between the protagonists' time at the residential school and Jeremiah's arrival in Winnipeg. 'Winnipeg' is thus first characterized in spatial relationship to the reserve – Jeremiah's and Gabriel's home – and the school and through the way that is charted between these places. 'Music', the notes Jeremiah repeats over and over, *is* Jeremiah and his charting of space in the text. Like Robinson's strategy, Highway's also demands or at least evokes visualization. However, the function of the map reference is a different one: in Robinson's novel, the map-itinerary serves to contextualize and place (geographically as well as historically) Lisa's hometown of Kitamaat and provides a background for the following mappings, such as Lisa's trip; in *Kiss*, the map reference collapses time (the years between school and the arrival in Winnipeg) and distance (between Eemanapiteepitat, Birch Lake/Oopaskooyak, and Winnipeg) and thus connects significant phases in Jeremiah's life.

But there is also a more metaphorical kind of mapping, a kind of mapping that relies more directly on the verbal and on the corporeal. How storytelling and bodily spatial movement can comment on each other or even be partly conflated is illustrated by Jeremiah and Gabriel's trip through Polo Park Shopping Mall right after Gabriel's arrival in Winnipeg. Jeremiah introduces Gabriel to the urban experience via the mall. Through clothes shopping, Gabriel is physically transformed from someone looking like he "just crawled out of the bush" (116) into a "rock star with a tan" (119):

> At Wrangler's, Gabriel wedged his lithe frame into a pair of blue jeans so tight that Jeremiah expressed concern. At Popeye's, the black patent-leather belt with a large silver buckle cost less than ten dollars. At Sanderson's, the red cotton shirt with pearl-white buttons became number one in Gabriel's heart. At Jack and Jill's, it

was the red, white, and blue silk baseball jacket with striped knit wrists and collar, to Jeremiah's puzzlement. (119)

The names of the stores serve as landmarks, as points of orientation forming a spatial arrangement – shops and brand names replace place-names and loca-tions; they connect the mall to the transnational world of global capitalism where the mall as a shopping experience ideally could be anywhere.

While trying to find their way through the mall – and, if the mall is seen as *pars pro toto* of their new environment, metaphorically through the city – the brothers tell each other a story of the Cree trickster Weesageechak who, dis-guised as a weasel, kills the cannibal monster Weetigo by eating it up from the inside. The brothers' movement through the mall in combination with the story 'maps' the mall and thus constructs different overlapping spaces. The story sketches a way through the beast of the mall by paralleling the way of the trickster Weasel through the entrails of the beast Weetigo.

Jeremiah and Gabriel tell the story together, complementing each others' knowledge; in the attempt to deal with the onslaught of the mall's bad air and "unkind lighting" (118) they begin to recount their Aunt Susan's story of Weesageechak and the Weetigo. As a reaction to the mall as an overwhelm-ing and pre-arranged space of consumption, the telling of this story can be productively analysed as a spatial practice. The parallels between the trickster story and the brothers' situation in the mall are obvious: like the trickster, the brothers work their way through the monster. At first, the story only parallels the way of the brothers. Eventually, though, after Gabriel's transformation is completed the mall is explicitly identified with the monster, and, by parallel-ization, Gabriel and Jeremiah with the trickster: "Which is when they came across the belly of the beast – one hundred restaurants in a monstrous, seeth-ing clump" (119). 'Eating' or, rather, 'devouring' and 'greed' are central terms in both the context of the cannibal monster stories and the context of critiques of capitalist society, of which the mall serves as an embodiment:

> Never before had Gabriel seen so much food. Or so many people shovelling food in and chewing and swallowing and burping and shovelling and chewing and swallowing and burping, as at some apocalyptic communion. The world was one great, gaping mouth. [...] The roar of mastication drowned out all other sound, so potent that, before the clock struck two, the brothers were gnawing away with the mob. (119–20)

Jeremiah and Gabriel become part of the monster by eating – like the trick-ster, to a certain extent. The trickster in the story kills the monster by chewing

"the Weetigo's entrails to smithereens from the inside out" (120), and the
trickster, as the brothers' recall, kills the Weetigo for eating people, for its in-
satiable hunger and greed.[18]

But the parallelization goes even further. In the story, the trickster comes
out of the beast "covered with shit" (121) and is cleaned by God, held by the
tail so the tip stays dirty. Having been 'processed' and 'digested', the brothers
also leave the monster/mall 'covered with shit': "Grey and soulless, the mall
loomed behind them, the rear end of a beast, that, having gorged itself, expels
its detritus" (121). But Gabriel and Jeremiah are not only "covered with the
shit of a white capitalistic culture" as Mark Shackleton has suggested;[19]
having gorged themselves inside the beast, they take on another trickster
characteristic – excess: "They ate so much their bellies came near bursting.
They drank so much their bladders grew pendulous" (120). Thus, the mall is
not simply a metaphor of capitalism and its legacy of colonial displacement
and alienation; Gabriel and Jeremiah are not merely the innocent victims of
the monster. The narrative arrangement of the dialogically told story links
walking to telling, traces their steps, serves as a comment on what they do
and where they do it. Their physical movement through the mall turns it from
place into an ensemble of spaces; their story changes the space of the mall,
appropriates it, turns it, to a certain extent, from a prearranged space of capitalist consumption, of certain social rules and stratification, into a space with
different rules. The story serves as a map. It produces (cultural) sense; it replaces a certain kind of insider knowledge and practical competence with
another. And while the brothers' story space is certainly in a subaltern position, the narrative nevertheless questions and transforms this embodiment of a
'white' city by offering a powerful alternative to the story of shopping. Since

---

[18] Terry Goldie analyzes the theme of 'eating' in terms of Gabriel's homosexuality. He
points out that against the background of Gabriel's masochism, "the Weetigo as figure in
the novel is not so simply negative. While for the most part he is as evil as usually shown in
Cree mythology, he also has an attraction, particularly for Gabriel. His swallowing oblite-
rates but also enraptures." Gabriel's homosexual desire is indeed addressed at the very end
of the chapter: in the men's room (of the 'monster mall'), he for the first time acknowledges
his desire outside of residential school. See Terry Goldie, *Pink Snow: Homotextual Possibilities in Canadian Fiction* (Peterborough, Ontario: Broadview, 2003): 213.

[19] Mark Shackleton, "The Trickster Figure in Native North American Writing: From
Traditional Storytelling to the Written Word," in *Connections: Non-Native Perspectives on
Canadian Native Writers*, ed. Coomi Vevaina & Hartmut Lutz (New Delhi: Creative
Books, 2003): 122.

the brothers participate in both, however, these mall spaces are not separate but embody the ambivalence of urban space as claimed by indigenous people: a man-eating monster and opportunity for personal transformation.

What happens in both novels – in my view – is not so much a struggle between two disparate cultures, Euro-Canadian and Native (Cree, Haisla), but a struggle for meaning in the context of cultural constellations that draw on different cultural resources and codes. This does not mean ignoring the fact that both *Monkey Beach* and *Kiss of the Fur Queen* do explore what it means to be Haisla or Cree in contemporary Canada, and that some of the realities in the texts are constructed as 'Native'; neither does it mean leaving aside the long-term consequences and damages of colonization and racism: both novels are very clear in the ways in which they name these damages, particularly the devastating impact of residential schools. However, the attention to spatial arrangements and space constructions as part of transcultural processes helps to analyse these negotiations as grounded in place, as simultaneous, as potentially contradictory in ways that do not require cultural conflicts and political tensions to be resolved but that present them as productively dynamic and as going beyond the mere contact zone.

WORKS CITED

Ashcroft, Bill. *Post-Colonial Transformation* (London & New York: Routledge, 2001).

Bhabha, Homi K. *The Location of Culture* (London & New York: Routledge, 1994).

Brady, Mary Pat. *Extinct Lands, Temporal Geographies: Chicana Literature and the Urgency of Space* (Durham NC & London: Duke UP, 2002).

Carter, Paul. *The Road to Botany Bay: An Essay in Spatial History* (London: Faber & Faber, 1987).

Certeau, Michel de. *The Practice of Everyday Life*, tr. Steven Rendall (*Arts de faire*, 1980; Berkeley: U of California P, 1988).

Clifford, James. *Routes: Travel and Translation in the Late Twentieth Century* (Cambridge MA: Harvard UP, 1997).

Goldie, Terry. *Pink Snow: Homotextual Possibilities in Canadian Fiction* (Peterborough, Ontario: Broadview, 2003).

Highway, Tomson. *The Kiss of the Fur Queen* (Toronto: Doubleday, 1998).

Huggan, Graham. *Territorial Disputes: Maps and Mapping Strategies in Contemporary Canadian and Australian Fiction* (Toronto: U of Toronto P, 1994).

Löw, Martina. *Raumsoziologie* (Frankfurt am Main: Suhrkamp, 2000).

Pratt, Mary Louise. *Imperial Eyes: Travel Writing and Transculturation* (New York & London: Routledge, 1992).

Robinson, Eden. *Monkey Beach* (London: Abacus, 2000).

Shackleton, Mark. "The Trickster Figure in Native North American Writing: From Traditional Storytelling to the Written Word," in *Connections: Non-Native Perspectives on Canadian Native Writers*. Ed. Coomi Vevaina & Hartmut Lutz (New Delhi: Creative Books, 2003): 109–28.

Silko, Leslie Marmon. "Interior and Exterior Landscapes: The Pueblo Migration Stories," in Silko, *Yellow Woman and a Beauty of the Spirit: Essays on Native American Life Today* (New York: Simon & Schuster, 1996): 25–47.

❖

The Long Shadow of Tacitus

— Classical and Modern Colonial Discourses in the Eighteenth- and Early-Nineteenth-Century Scottish Highlands

SILKE STROH

T HIS ESSAY AIMS at contributing to the establishment of Britain's so-called 'Celtic' fringe as part of the field of (post)colonial and transcultural studies – not as a mere marginal note to a discipline whose 'proper' and 'main' concern is clashes and contacts between European and overseas cultures, but as a highly central part of the colonial project and of the discursive universe concerned with inter- and transculturality, civilizational hierarchies, ideological colonization, and decolonization. One important reason for this centrality is the fact that so-called 'Celts' had played a vital role in European discourses on civilization and colonization ever since these discourses began in Classical Antiquity; when the first British overseas colonies were established many centuries later, discourses on 'Celticity' served as a fundamental precedent and model for the textualization of encounters with indigenous populations overseas. At the same time, old and new discourses on barbarity were applied to the 'internal colonization' of Britain's 'domestic' fringes such as Ireland or Scotland, and particularly their Gaelic populations. It was here that colonial discourses from Classical Antiquity first came to be adapted to the ideological needs of a modern nation-state aiming at internal homogenization as well as overseas colonial expansion.

These intra-British margins thus form a transcultural meeting-point where several kinds of colonialism, and several kinds of colonial discourse, intersect: ancient and modern, intra-European and overseas. Just as anglophone discourses from the 'centre' (especially in the eighteenth and nineteenth centuries) often likened ancient and modern 'Celts' to indigenous populations of overseas colonies, anti- and postcolonial discourses have engaged in transperipheral comparisons and alignments – e.g., when Highland historians declare solidarity with Native Americans and Third-World peoples as 'fellow victims' of Anglo-British imperialism,[1] or when 'native' Scots ironically refer to English people who have moved to (or own holiday homes in) Scotland as 'white settlers'. However, such Scottish attempts at transperipheral alignments seem to be mainly a product of the twentieth century, and even then have, of course, never been uncontested. One of the main objections commonly cited is the deep involvement of Scottish, Irish, and Welsh people as colonizers in the overseas Empire, and this point is obviously hard to deny – as parts of this essay will again illustrate. Britain's internal fringes have indeed occupied a very *ambivalent* position in a multilayered global hierarchy of power, as a site where the roles of colonized and colonizer overlapped. But perhaps it is this very interstitiality that makes these internal 'fringe' regions such interesting material for postcolonial approaches, especially as the discipline of postcolonial studies has in recent years increasingly distanced itself from older simplistic cultural and political dichotomies, moving towards an ever-greater preoccupation with hybridity and transculturalism – a framework into which Britain's 'Celtic' fringes, with their long history of anglicization, hybridization, and transperipheral contacts and clashes, appear to fit remarkably well.

In what follows I would like to give some examples of how these various transcultural complexities have been negotiated in discourses about 'Celticity' and the Scottish Highlanders. First, there will be a brief sketch of the Classical framework and of the way in which such Classical models were recycled in eighteenth- and early-nineteenth-century anglophone British identity constructions and colonial discourses, with regard to both 'ignoble' and 'noble' savagery. This will be followed by an exploration of the question of how these discourses are reflected in Gaelic poetry of the time, especially

---

[1] For instance, see James Shaw Grant, "Highland History – A British Asset," *Transactions of the Gaelic Society of Inverness* 52 (1980–1982): 460–79, James Hunter, "Preface to the New Edition," in *The Making of the Crofting Community* (1976; Edinburgh: John Donald, 2000), 9–10, and Hunter, *Glencoe and the Indians* (Edinburgh & London: Mainstream, 1996), e.g., dedication (unpaginated), 34, 189.

regarding the internalization of 'mainstream' constructs of 'noble savagery' and its implications for overseas colonialism.

Classical Greek and Roman discourses on cultural identity, social evolution, civilization, and foreign Others display several features which are also found in modern mainstream European discourses on these subjects. One feature that they have in common is the self-confidence of relatively urbanized societies which were internationally preeminent trading powers and possessed a highly literate and technologically advanced culture that made them feel superior to their 'neighbours', whose societies often appeared to be technologically, militarily, and partly also economically less 'advanced' and whose culture was largely an oral one. This sense of discrepancy led the self-styled Greek and Roman 'navels of civilization' to evolve concepts of social development which subsumed all cultures under the same unilinear teleology of historical progress and the same hierarchical ladder of civilizational achievement, with the urban cultures of the 'centre' invariably at the top. An additional factor which was particularly pertinent to the Roman context is the establishment of colonies and the development into a military super-power whose empire lasted for centuries and which entailed the enforcement of so-called 'civilizing missions' on conquered 'barbarian' populations.

The category 'Celtic'[2] was a blanket label used in Classical discourses to designate barbarians living to the northwest of the 'civilized centre', and the peoples thus labelled often functioned as archetypal *arch*-barbarians providing a model for the evaluation and textualization of other kinds of savages elsewhere. 'Celticity' is thus from its very inception essentially a category of othering, and a concept inextricably associated with the representation of foreign cultures as civilizationally inferior and as in many ways the exact opposite of what was perceived to define the 'civilized centre'. The ignoble traits which Greek and Roman texts frequently ascribe to 'Celtic' and other barbarians include many features which also recur in modern colonial discourses, such as disorder, irrationality, ignorance, rudeness, historical stasis, excessive warlikeness, violence, cruelty, fickleness, strong passions, moral corruption, untrustworthiness, treacherousness, cowardice, and cannibalism. However, the theme of 'noble savagery' likewise occurs: several Classical writers criticize refined and luxurious metropolitan culture for its potentially

---

[2] The Greek equivalents of the term were Greek Κελτοί (keltoi) and Γαλάται (galatai); the Latin ones were Celtae and Galli.

degenerating effect on the morality of its population and the valour of its armies, while idealizing the 'primitive' Other for its allegedly uncorrupted moral purity, its virtue-inducing frugal life-style (often linked to rougher climatic and soil conditions), and its military prowess.[3]

The two Classical authors with the greatest direct influence in modern Scotland are probably Julius Caesar and Publius Cornelius Tacitus. Caesar had never been to Scotland, but his famous account of his conquests in *The Gallic War* (*Bellum Gallicum*, c. 51 BC) made influential statements about Gaulish and southern English 'Celts', whom modern readers often considered as ancestors or at least close cousins of the Gaels. Tacitus seems to have visited Britain himself, perhaps even as far as Scotland, during Agricola's military campaigns in the first century AD, and wrote about the island in the biography *Agricola* (c. 98 AD). His comments on the Roman attempt to conquer Caledonia became one of the most important reference-points for Scottish historiography and ethnographic perspectives on the Gaels. While both these authors reiterated several of the conventionally assumed 'ignoble' traits of Celtic barbarism mentioned above, they also expressed anxiety about the slackening effect which Roman civilized over-refinement might have on the hardihood of its soldiers, while praising the 'primitive' life-style of certain 'barbarians' as conducive to morality, physical fitness, and military valour.[4]

---

[3] See Klaus E. Müller, *Geschichte der antiken Ethnographie und ethnologischen Theoriebildung: Von den Anfängen bis auf die byzantinischen Historiographen*, 2 vols. (Wiesbaden: Franz Steiner, 1972, 1980), abbreviated repr. in 1 vol. as *Geschichte der antiken Ethnologie* (Reinbek: Rowohlt, 1997): 91–130, 170–95 and 387–477; Malcolm Chapman, *The Celts: The Construction of a Myth* (Basingstoke & London: Macmillan; & New York: St Martin's, 1992); and Bernhard Kremer, *Das Bild der Kelten bis in augusteische Zeit: Studien zur Instrumentalisierung eines antiken Feindbildes bei griechischen und römischen Autoren* (Stuttgart: Franz Steiner, 1994).

[4] My reading of these two authors is based mainly on the following English editions: Caesar, *The Gallic War*, tr. Carolyn Hammond (Oxford & New York: Oxford UP, 1996); Tacitus, *Agricola*, tr. Anthony R. Birley, in *Agricola and Germany* (Oxford: Oxford UP, 1999): 3–34. References to these works will not be identified by page numbers but by chapter, as these chapters are often shorter than a page and thus offer the easiest possible way of identifying passages, even in different editions. For instances of ignoble savagery in Gaul and Britain, see Caesar, *Bellum Gallicum*, book I, ch. 2–15, 30; book II, ch. 4; book IV, ch. 5, 13; book V, ch. 14; book VI, ch.16, 19, 34; book VII, ch. 4–5, 20, 30, 38, 42, 77–78; and Tacitus, *Agricola*, ch. 30, 34. For Caesar, the most 'uncorrupted' barbarians are mainly Belgae and Germans, who are praised for their resistance to the corrupting temptations of civilization, e.g., by refusing to import Roman wine. Moreover, he also seems to

Both texts were to become important influences on modern concepts of noble savagery. In Tacitus's *Agricola*, the most unromanized, anti-Roman, and freedom-loving specimen of barbarism are located among the Northern Britons, whose fierce, independent spirit is considered much greater than that of the slackened and romanized populace inhabiting the south of the island.[5] His concept of noble savagery becomes even clearer in his ethnography of Germany (*Germania*), which is likewise pertinent to the Scottish case because he considers the Caledonians to be of German stock.[6] Rather than reflecting a sincere wish to *completely* renounce 'civilization', Tacitus's praise of unromanized barbarian virtues clearly implies the hope that the Romans will eventually be able to unite the best of both worlds, by selectively (re-)adopting only a limited number of 'barbarian' qualities: i.e. stricter moral standards and greater military hardihood. Thus he idealizes unconquered, unhybridized foreigners in terms of the military interests of the Roman Empire, and not in terms of cultural relativism.

These Classical discourses on 'Celtic' and other, both 'noble' and 'ignoble', barbarians were to cast a long shadow on Europe's subsequent history of ideas. In the seventeenth and eighteenth centuries, when the modern British nation-state embarked on projects of internal homogenization, prided itself on its own dynamic social progress, and was developing into a global colonial super-power, it appropriated Classical texts on civilization as a lens through which to see itself as well as its own 'barbarian' Others. As enlightened metropoles like London and Edinburgh proudly identified themselves as the intellectual centres of neoclassical progressive civilization, ancient Greek and Roman texts on barbarism, ethnology, and civilizational development had a considerable influence on Enlightenment theories of social evolution. Moreover, as Britain's colonial possessions grew, its anglophone mainstream increasingly liked to see itself as following in the footsteps of the Roman Empire, which provided a prestigious historical precedent and popular reference-

---

admire Germanic society's strong emphasis on freedom (I.1, II.15, IV.1–2, VI.21–24, 28, 35). See also Kremer, *Das Bild der Kelten bis in augusteische Zeit*, 134–48 and 199–201.

[5] Tacitus, *Agricola*, ch. 11, 16, 21.

[6] "Rutilae Caledoniam habitantium comae, magni artus Germanicam originem adseverant" ("their red-gold hair and massive limbs proclaim German origin," *Agricola*, ch. 11). Latin text quoted from Alfons Städele's bilingual Latin/German omnibus edition of *Agricola* and *Germania* (Düsseldorf & Zürich: Artemis & Winkler, 2nd rev. ed. 2001). For noble savagery among the Germans, see *Germania*, ch. 6, 18–20, 22.

point for modern colonizers. In the course of these developments, the Classical concept of 'Celticity' was rediscovered as an ethnic blanket label for
northwestern barbarians and applied to the 'primitive' populations of modern
Britain's own northern and western fringes, who likewise spoke Celtic languages and were thus seen to be essentially still the same as their Continental
European 'ancestors' who had fought the Greeks and Romans over one and a
half millennia before. Having thus equated Classical Antiquity's 'Celtic'
colonized with modern Britain's internal cultural 'fringes' (which were also
considered to be in need of quasi-colonial subjugation and assimilation), the
next logical step along this associative chain was to compare 'Celtic' barbarians (whether ancient or modern) to the likewise 'barbarian' or 'savage' indigenous populations of the new overseas colonies. Celticist[7] discourses thus
provided a vital 'missing link' between ancient and modern imperialism, and
as such formed a crucial component of modern British imperial identity constructs presenting the UK as the modern heir of the glory of Classical Rome.

    One example of the conflation of Classical and modern barbarians is Mar-
tin Martin's *Description of the Western Isles of Scotland* (1703), which traces
relatively recent Gaelic customs (such as inauguration ceremonies for clan
chiefs) all the way back to Caesar's Gaul.[8] Moreover, Martin also refers to
Tacitus's report on the Germans, suggesting that the latter were very similar
to the Gauls in religion and language.[9] Another explicit link to Classical
barbarism can be found in Walter Scott's novel *Waverley* (publ. 1814, set in

---

[7] The term 'Celticism' is often used in deliberate analogy to 'orientalism' as analysed in
Edward W. Said's *Orientalism* (London: Routledge & Kegan Paul, 1978). Although the
word 'Celticism' in fact pre-dates Said's book, since the latter's appearance critics have
employed the term 'Celticism' more frequently and often with explicit reference to Said, to
reflect the similarities between (mainly outsiders') discourses about the so-called Celts and
those about Europe's oriental and overseas colonial Others. The first critic to use the concept of 'Celticism' in this way seems to have been W.J. Mc Cormack in *Ascendancy and
Tradition in Anglo-Irish Literary History from 1789 to 1939* (Oxford: Clarendon, 1985):
219–38. Further examples can be found in three essays published in *Celticism*, ed. Terence
Brown (Amsterdam & Atlanta GA: Rodopi, 1996): Joep Leerssen, "Celticism," 3, 6–7; Patrick Sims–Williams, "The Invention of Celtic Nature Poetry," 98; and George Watson,
"Celticism and the Annulment of History," 207.

[8] Martin Martin, *A Description of the Western Isles of Scotland* (1703), in *A Description
of the Western Islands of Scotland by Martin Martin, Including A Voyage to St. Kilda by the
same author and A Description of the Western Isles of Scotland by Sir Donald Monro*, ed.
Donald J. MacLeod (1934; Edinburgh: Birlinn, 1994): 166–69.

[9] Martin, *Description of the Western Isles of Scotland*, 168.

1745–46), where the abode of a Highland cattle-raider is referred to as a "Scythian camp"[10] – though Scythians were no Celts, they were another 'barbarian' ethnic grouping frequently mentioned in Ancient Greek and Roman discourses. Scott's comparisons move on to the modern colonial era and overseas when a makeshift shelter erected by Highlanders is referred to as a "wigwam,"[11] which aligns Highlanders with Native North Americans. Similarly, a Gaelic soldier on a secret scouting mission is described as "crawling on all fours with the dexterity of an Indian."[12] The Society in Scotland for the Propagation of Christian Knowledge likewise more than once referred to Highlanders and Native Americans in the same breath – for example, in a report on the limited theological knowledge of Gaels, which claimed: "They know no more than by heresay, that there is a God [...] were they to be asked anything further they would be found to be as ignorant as the wild Americans."[13] Religious missionaries were not the only 'metropolitans' who drew such parallels: economic and agricultural modernizers did so as well. For instance, an agricultural report written in the 1790s by William Marshall likened Scotland's Central Highland region to the wildernesses of America and stressed the need to "retriev[e] it from a state so disgraceful to a civilized nation."[14] Another economic modernizer was Patrick Sellar, who referred to the Gaels as "savage"[15] and "barbarous hordes"[16] whose "relation to the enlightened nations of Europe"[17] was

---

[10] Walter Scott, *Waverley; or, 'Tis Sixty Years Since* (1814; Harmondsworth: Penguin, 1985): 146.

[11] Scott, *Waverley*, 189.

[12] *Waverley*, 281.

[13] SSPCK minutes of the Directors of the Society, March 20, 1755, Scottish Record Office GD.95/2/7; quoted from Robert [D.] Clyde, *From Rebel to Hero: The Image of the Highlander, 1745–1830* (East Linton: Tuckwell, 1995): 58. Another example is the title of the Society's pamphlet *State of the Society in Scotland for Propagating Christian Knowledge, giving a brief Account of the Condition of the Highlands and Islands of Scotland, [...] Together with Some Account of this Society's Missionaries for converting the Native Indians of America* (Edinburgh 1741); quoted from Fiona J. Stafford, *The Sublime Savage: James Macpherson and the Poems of Ossian* (Edinburgh: Edinburgh UP, 1988): 21.

[14] William Marshall, *General View of the Agriculture of the Central Highlands of Scotland* (London: T. Wright, 1794): 52; quoted from Peter Womack, *Improvement and Romance: Constructing the Myth of the Highlands* (Basingstoke & London: Macmillan, 1989): 73.

[15] Patrick Sellar, note concerning Sutherland, May 1816; published in *Papers on Sutherland Estate Management, 1802–1816*, ed. R.J. Adam, 2 vols. (Edinburgh: T. & A. Constable for the Scottish History Society, 1972), vol. I: 185, 187.

not very different from that betwixt the American Colonists and the Aborigines of
that Country. The one are the Aborigines of Britain shut out from the general
stream of knowledge and cultivation, flowing in upon the Commonwealth of
Europe from the remotest fountain of antiquity. The other are the Aborigines of
America equally shut out from this stream; Both [sic] live in turf cabins in common
with the brutes; Both are singular for patience, courage, cunning and address. Both
are most virtuous where least in contact with men in a civilized State, and both are
fast sinking under the baneful effects of ardent spirits [alcohol].[18]

Comparisons to the indigenous populations of Oceania likewise occurred –
for example, in the following comments made by a 1799 visitor to St. Kilda:

Nothing in Captain Cook's voyages comes half so low. The natives are savage
[…].
    A total want of curiosity, a stupid gaze of wonder, an excessive eagerness for
spirits and tobacco, a laziness only to be conquered by the hope of the above-
mentioned cordials, and a beastly degree of filth, the natural consequence of this
render the St Kildian character truly savage.[19]

Many of these transperipheral comparisons between 'Celts' and overseas
colonized peoples emphasized mainly the 'negative' qualities of 'primitive-
ness', urging colonization and civilizing missions. This highly critical perspective on 'savagery' dominated mainstream discourses about the Scottish
Highlands for much of the eighteenth century and never entirely disappeared,
persisting with varying popularity and vehemence far into the nineteenth century and even beyond. However, during the second half of the eighteenth
century an alternative perspective emerged: the Gaelic Other underwent a
transformation from ignoble to noble savagery. This alternative perspective
was likewise to endure into the following centuries, but perhaps reached its
greatest preeminence in Celticism during the Romantic Age, in the late-eigh-
teenth and early-nineteenth century. One of the factors that facilitated the
emergence of the 'noble savage' pattern in discourses about the Scottish

---

[16] Sellar, letter to Lord Advocate Colquhoun, 24 May 1815; published in *Papers on
Sutherland Estate Management, 1802–1816*, ed. Adam, vol. I: 156.

[17] Sellar, note concerning Sutherland, 175.

[18] Sellar, note concerning Sutherland, 175–76.

[19] Lord Brougham; quoted from Derek Cooper, *Road to the Isles: Travellers in the
Hebrides, 1770–1914* (London: Routledge & Kegan Paul, 1979), 31.

Highlands was the considerable success which 'civilizing', pacifying, and assimilating missions in Scotland and its Gaidhealtachd seemed to show during the second half of the eighteenth century: the homogenization and stabilization of the British nation-state was so advanced that remaining vestiges of internal otherness no longer seemed dangerous. Thus, Scottishness and Gaelicness could now not only be tolerated and romanticized as harmless complementary *alternatives* to anglocentric British mainstream culture, but could even be seen to benefit the British 'centre' itself. The latter move is related to shifts in Britain's self-perception as a colonizing world-power. Parallels between the British and the Roman empires were often a source of pride, but this Classicist model also had a flipside: the Roman Empire had eventually declined. In a sense, its very success had been its downfall, as its immense wealth and its material conveniences seemed to have corrupted military watchfulness and civic virtues, while its size made both the centralist administration and the defence of the vast realm impracticable. The Roman Empire had fallen and had been overrun by the very barbarians to whom it had deemed itself so vastly superior.

This historical fact loomed ever larger in the British consciousness as Rome's modern British imitator accumulated successes, wealth, and territories of its own. Optimism at least partly gave way to anxiety, and the corrupting influences which civilization and wealth could have on morality, taste, and power became a commonplace in late-eighteenth-century thought. What could the British Empire do to remain an Empire without repeating the mistakes that had been made by Rome? Britain seemed fortunate – it remembered that it had been built on 'barbarian' foundations: in Roman times it had been a barbarian periphery, and parts of Britain (such as Scotland and the 'Celtic' fringes) had retained vestiges of 'barbarism' far into modern times, even right into the eighteenth-century present. If these barbarian traditions could be instrumentalized for the benefit of the British and imperial mainstream, a successful *amalgam* of noble savagery and civilized polish might help the UK to avoid the sad fate of Rome.

Tacitus's admiration for the military valour of barbarian peoples and their readiness to defend their freedom by force of arms played a crucial role in this context, as this became reinterpreted in favour of the UK and its Empire. The Highlanders' noble savagery now marked them for appropriation by the 'centre' as elite soldiers for the imperial army and as pioneer colonizers overseas, predestined by the hardihood-inducing roughness of their homeland and the extraordinary cohesiveness and loyalty allegedly engendered by the clan system. Relatedly, Highland dress and the bagpipes, previously despised and banished, now became symbols of national and imperial pride.[20] Thus, Scotland's Gaels evolved from a despicable Other into either a praiseworthy Other or a national Same. This development is reflected in a military song by the officer Sir Harry Erskine entitled "The Highland Character" (pre-1766), which was allegedly translated from a Gaelic composition authored by one of his comrades, and whose Classical allusions recall both Caesar's Gaul and Tacitus's Caledonians:

> In the garb of old Gaul, wi' the fire of old Rome,
> From the heath-cover'd mountains of Scotia we come,
> Where the Romans endeavour'd our country to gain,
> But our ancestors fought, and they fought not in vain.
> Such our love of liberty, our country, and our laws,
> That, like our ancestors of old, we stand by Freedom's cause;
> We'll bravely fight, like heroes bold, for honour and applause,
> And defy the French, with all their art, to alter our laws.
> No effeminate customs our sinews embrace,
> No luxurious tables enervate our race;
> Our loud-sounding pipe bears the true martial strain,
> So do we the old Scottish valour retain.
> [...]
> We sons of the mountains, tremendous as rock,
> Dash the force of our foes with our thundering strokes.
> Quebec and Cape Breton, the pride of old France,
> In their troops fondly boasted till we did advance;
> But when our claymore they saw us produce,
> Their courage did fail and they sued for a truce.[21]

---

[20] As Christopher Harvie has pointed out, this "militarism and imperialism [...] distinguished Scottish Celticism [...] from its pacifistic Welsh and rebellious Irish contemporaries" (Harvie, "Anglo-Saxons into Celts: The Scottish Intellectuals 1760–1930," in *Celticism*, ed. Brown: 246). See also Hunter, *The Making of the Crofting Community*, 46–48, and Hunter, *Last of the Free: A Millennial History of the Highlands and Islands of Scotland* (1999; Edinburgh & London: Mainstream, 2000): 244–46; Stafford, *The Sublime Savage*, 33–35, 154; Womack, *Improvement and Romance*, 27–31, 39, 46; Charles W.J. Withers, "The Historical Creation of the Scottish Highlands," in *The Manufacture of Scottish History*, ed. Ian Donnachie & Christopher Whatley (Edinburgh: Polygon, 1992): 148–50; and Clyde, *From Rebel to Hero*, e.g., 177.

[21] Quoted from Thomas Crawford, "Political and Protest Songs in Eighteenth-Century Scotland," *Scottish Studies* 14 (1970): 30.

Intriguingly, Antiquity's colonizers and colonized are here collapsed into one, and both are used to describe the achievements of modern Gaels. Another interesting aspect is the fact that in this song the alien invader who threatens the freedom of the Gaels is not the British centralist state (the most likely candidate for the role of modern 'colonizer' in the Highlands) but Britain's foreign competitors for global power, the French. Thus, external enemies appear to weld Lowlanders, Highlanders, and Englishmen together into one nation. In this song, the defence of 'freedom' means not to fight *against* a 'colonizing power' (the Romans or the British centralist state), but *for* one: defending the UK and its empire against foreign rivals.

These discursive shifts in anglophone Celticism were also reflected in Gaelic poetry. On the one hand, mainstream contempt and the various coercive and 'civilizing' measures inflicted on the Highlands had given rise to a considerable tradition of 'anticolonial' Gaelic literature which criticized Britain's 'internal' colonialism in the Gaidhealtachd.[22] On the other hand, even these critical Gaelic voices at that time did not yet form transperipheral alignments with overseas colonized peoples – although, as has been shown, *anglophone* discourses often drew parallels between 'internal' and 'overseas' fringes. Instead, once mainstream Celticism had begun to privilege 'noble' over 'ignoble' savagery, some Gaelic poets internalized these mainstream concepts of noble savagery into their own self-perception and took pride in their new integration into the national and imperial project. This is most lucidly illustrated by the work of Donnchadh Bàn Mac an t-Saoir, which clearly echoes both classical and modern notions of noble savagery – for example, in "Oran do'n t-seann Fhreiceadan Ghàidhealach" ("Song to the Old Highland Watch"):

> Bha onoir nan Gàidheal
> An earbsa r' an tàbhachd,
> Bha sin mar a b' àbhaist,
> Gun fhàilinn [...]

---

[22] Examples can be found in Iain Lom (c. 1620–1710), *Orain Iain Luim: Songs of John MacDonald, Bard of Keppoch*, ed. Annie M. Mackenzie (Edinburgh: Scottish Gaelic Texts Society, 1964); *Highland Songs of the Forty-Five / Òrain Ghàidhealach mu Bhliadhna Theàrlaich*, ed. & tr. John Lorne Campbell (1933; rev. repr. Edinburgh: Scottish Academic P & Scottish Gaelic Texts Society, 1984); and Iain Mac Codrum (c. 1700–79), *The Songs of John MacCodrum*, ed. & tr. William Matheson (Edinburgh: Oliver & Boyd / Scottish Gaelic Texts Society, 1938).

Tha urram an dràsd
[...]
Le feabhas an àbhaist,
An nàduir 's am beus:
Bhith dìleas d' an càirdean,
Cur sìos air an nàimhdean

(the honour of the Gaels was dependent on their prowess, and that had, as usual, no
flaw [...]. Now there is honour [...], through the goodness of their habits, their
nature and code: to be loyal to their friends and to humble their foes.)[23]

The poet portrays the Gaels as having remained essentially unchanged from
time immemorial, and shows the same stress on picturesqueness as that often
found in anglophone texts:

Sliochd fineachan uasal
A ghin o na tuathaich,
[...]
[...]
Gach seòl mar a chleachd iad,
Le 'n còmhdacha dreachmhor,
Le 'n osana breaca,
'S le 'm breacana 'n fhéil'

(Descendants of noble clans, begotten of north men [...] in every way, they appear
as they used to, with their colourful garments, their hose of diced patterns and their
belted plaids.)[24]

Another poem by Donnchadh Bàn, "Oran do'n Rìgh" ("Song to the King"),
celebrates the successes of the British army abroad, both in Europe and in the
overseas colonies, such as India. The Highland regiments are singled out in a
passage which delineates the great transformation from ignoble to noble
savage that the Gael had recently undergone in the mainstream's imagination:

Anns a h-uile [...] cunnart
'S mór an t-urram a fhuair na Gàidheil;
'S bhathas greis 'gan cur an duileachd

---

[23] Donnchadh Bàn Mac an t-Saoir, "Oran do'n t-seann Fhreiceadan Ghàidhealach"
("Song to the Old Highland Watch"), in *The Songs of Duncan Ban Macintyre*, ed. & tr.
Angus MacLeod (Edinburgh: Oliver & Boyd/Scottish Gaelic Texts Society, 1952): 254–63.
[24] Donnchadh Bàn Mac an t-Saoir, "Oran do'n t-seann Fhreiceadan Ghàidhealach"
("Song to the Old Highland Watch").

Mar nach buineadh iad do 'n phàirtidh;
Ach 'n uair fhuair iad mios is creideas
[...]
'S iad bu sheasmhaich' air an onoir

(In every [...] danger great is the respect the Gaels have won; yet for a time they were held suspect, as if they were alien to the nation; but once they won esteem and trust [...] they were the truest in their honour.)[25]

The mission of the British 'centre' is envisaged as a global one with beneficial effects both on its domestic and its foreign peripheries:

An ceithir àirdean an t-saoghail
Tha fearann is daoin' aig Deòrsa;
'S tha chinn-eaglais anns gach àite
Chum an sàbhaladh o dhòbheart;
Tha lagh is pàrlamaid aca
Chumail ceartais riutha is còrach,
'S tha mhèirl' an déidh a casgadh
Sguir na creachan is an tòrachd.

(In the four quarters of the globe, [King] George has territory and subjects; and his prelates are in every place to save them from misdemeanour; they have law and parliament to ensure them justice and equity; thievery has been arrested, forays and feuds have ceased.)[26]

As "creachan" is also the common Gaelic term for the cattle-raids for which traditional clan society had been so notorious before the mid-eighteenth century, the line "Sguir na creachan is an tòrachd" ("forays and feuds have ceased") seems to refer to internal Scottish unrest entailed by the decentralized forces of Highland feudalism and its political and military agendas in the years before the British government had asserted its monopoly of power. The colonizing drive of the modern nation-state is thus shown to aim in two directions: both inward (towards internal peripheries and minority cultures) and outward (foreign and overseas conquest). Donnchadh Bàn's "four quarters of the globe" present a Gaelic equivalent to the proud anglophone formu-

---

[25] Donnchadh Bàn Mac an t-Saoir, "Oran do'n Rìgh" ("Song to the King"), in *The Songs of Duncan Ban Macintyre*, 26–33.
[26] Donnchadh Bàn Mac an t-Saoir, "Oran do'n Rìgh" ("Song to the King").

lation which presented Britain's colonial possessions as 'the Empire where the sun never sets'.

In conclusion, it is to be hoped that these examples help to illustrate the centrality of Scotland and the so-called 'Celtic fringes' as a transcultural link between ancient and modern forms of colonialism, as well as between 'domestic' and overseas imperialism. Discourses on Scottishness and 'Celticity' form an integral component of British imperial identity which helped the modern nation to put its own colonial ambitions into historical perspective. However, it should also be borne in mind that – in spite of all the parallels which could be and have been drawn between the predicaments of internal and external fringes – Scots or 'Celts' could shift more easily from Other to 'Same'. Thus, they often could more easily be made acceptable to the 'mainstream' than many overseas (post)colonial subjects and their cultures, especially where issues of more obvious 'racial' difference seemed to preclude seamless assimilation and easy identity-switching. This is illustrated with particular clarity by late-eighteenth-century Gaelic poetry: the latter's adoption of the noble savage trope and embrace of empire run contrary to several more recent Gaelic and Scottish identity discourses from the last few decades of the twentieth century, whose claims to (post)colonial status sometimes tend to minimize the fact that Scotland's involvement in the British Empire was a highly ambiguous experience as both internally colonized and overseas colonizer. The Gaelic poems here examined serve as a useful reminder that claims of transperipheral or transcolonial solidarity made in the twentieth or twenty-first century do not necessarily reach back to the beginnings of the colonial era.

The necessity of complementing an awareness of transperipheral commonalities with a recognition of interperipheral differences is aptly expressed in a passage by the author with whom this essay began: Tacitus. His Agricola reports a remark which was allegedly made by the Caledonian commander Calgacus about the Roman Empire and the relations between its various subject peoples:

> ac sicut in familia recentissimus quisque servorum etiam conservis lubibrio est, sic in hoc orbis terrarum vetere famulatu novi nos et viles in excidium petimur.
>
> (In a private household the latest newcomer among the slaves is the object of derision even to his fellow slaves. So too, in this slave-household, to which the

whole world has long belonged, we are the new ones, the cheap ones, who are picked out to be destroyed.)[27]

In the eighteenth- and nineteenth-century British Empire, however, the 'Caledonian' Scots were no longer the 'latest newcomer' in the household of colonized subject peoples. Instead, they were among the oldest ones, who would now take their turn to look down upon the new subject populations overseas. Only in the twentieth century, when even the most recent overseas 'slaves' had been part of the imperial household for some time and when the entire household was starting to fall apart, did the solidarity between 'Celtic' and overseas subjects against their ailing master seem to gain the upper hand.

WORKS CITED

Adam, R.J., ed. *Papers on Sutherland Estate Management, 1802–1816*, 2 vols. (Edinburgh: T. & A. Constable for the Scottish History Society, 1972).

Brown, Terence, ed. *Celticism* (Amsterdam & Atlanta GA: Rodopi, 1996).

Caesar, Iulius. *Bellum Gallicum* (51 BC), tr. by Carolyn Hammond as *The Gallic War* (Oxford & New York: Oxford UP, 1996–98).

Campbell, John Lorne, ed. & tr. *Highland Songs of the Forty-Five / Òrain Ghàidhealach mu Bhliadhna Theàrlaich* (1933; rev. repr. Edinburgh: Scottish Academic Press & Scottish Gaelic Texts Society, 1984).

Chapman, Malcolm. *The Celts: The Construction of a Myth* (Basingstoke & London: Macmillan; & New York: St Martin's, 1992).

Clyde, Robert [D.]. *From Rebel to Hero: The Image of the Highlander, 1745–1830* (East Linton: Tuckwell, 1995).

Cooper, Derek. *Road to the Isles: Travellers in the Hebrides, 1770–1914* (London: Routledge & Kegan Paul, 1979).

Crawford, Thomas. "Political and Protest Songs in Eighteenth-Century Scotland," *Scottish Studies* 14 (1970): 1–33, 105–31.

Donaldson, William. "Bonny Highland Laddie: The Making of a Myth," *Scottish Literary Journal* 3 (1976): 30–50.

Donnachie, Ian, & Christopher Whatley, ed. *The Manufacture of Scottish History* (Edinburgh: Polygon, 1992).

Grant, James Shaw. "Highland History: A British Asset," *Transactions of the Gaelic Society of Inverness* 52 (1980–1982): 460–79.

Harvie, Christopher. "Anglo-Saxons into Celts: The Scottish Intellectuals, 1760–1930," in *Celticism* (1996), ed. Brown, 231–56.

Hunter, James. *The Making of the Crofting Community* (1976; Edinburgh: John Donald, 2000).

---

[27] Tacitus, *Agricola*, ch. 31.

——. *Glencoe and the Indians* (Edinburgh & London: Mainstream, 1996).

——. *Last of the Free: A Millennial History of the Highlands and Islands of Scotland* (1999; Edinburgh & London: Mainstream, 2000).

Iain Lom. *Orain Iain Luim: Songs of John MacDonald, Bard of Keppoch*, ed. Annie M. Mackenzie (Edinburgh: Scottish Gaelic Texts Society, 1964).

Kremer, Bernhard. *Das Bild der Kelten bis in augusteische Zeit: Studien zur Instrumentalisierung eines antiken Feindbildes bei griechischen und römischen Autoren* (Stuttgart: Franz Steiner, 1994).

Leerssen, Joep. "Celticism," in *Celticism* (1996), ed. Brown, 1–20.

Mac an t-Saoir, Donnchadh Bàn. *The Songs of Duncan Ban Macintyre*, ed. & tr. Angus MacLeod (Edinburgh: Oliver & Boyd / Scottish Gaelic Texts Society, 1952).

Mac Codrum, Iain. *The Songs of John MacCodrum*, ed. & tr. William Matheson (Edinburgh: Oliver & Boyd / Scottish Gaelic Texts Society, 1938).

Mc Cormack, W.J. *Ascendancy and Tradition in Anglo-Irish Literary History from 1789 to 1939* (Oxford: Clarendon, 1985).

Martin, Martin. *A Description of the Western Isles of Scotland* (1703), in *A Description of the Western Islands of Scotland By Martin Martin, Including A Voyage to St. Kilda By the same author and A Description Of The Western Isles of Scotland By Sir Donald Monro*, ed. Donald J. MacLeod (1934; Edinburgh: Birlinn, 1994): 59–391.

Müller, Klaus E. *Geschichte der antiken Ethnographie und ethnologischen Theoriebildung: Von den Anfängen bis auf die byzantinischen Historiographen*, 2 vols. (Wiesbaden: Franz Steiner, 1972, 1980), abbreviated repr. in 1 vol. as *Geschichte der antiken Ethnologie* (Reinbek: Rowohlt, 1997).

Said, Edward W. *Orientalism* (London: Routledge & Kegan Paul, 1978).

Scott, Walter. *Waverley; or, 'Tis Sixty Years Since* (1814; Harmondsworth: Penguin, 1985).

Sellar, Patrick. Letter to Lord Advocate Colquhoun, 24th May 1815; published in *Papers on Sutherland Estate Management, 1802–1816* (1972), ed. Adam, vol. 1: 155–61.

——. Note concerning Sutherland, May 1816; published in *Papers on Sutherland Estate Management, 1802–1816* (1972), ed. Adam, vol. 1: 175–87.

Sims–Williams, Patrick. "The Invention of Celtic Nature Poetry," in *Celticism* (1996), ed. Brown, 97–124.

Stafford, Fiona J. *The Sublime Savage: James Macpherson and the Poems of Ossian* (Edinburgh: Edinburgh UP, 1988).

Tacitus. *Agricola* (98 AD), in *Agricola and Germany*, tr. Anthony R. Birley (Oxford: Oxford UP, 1999): 3–34.

——. *Agricola*, in the bilingual Latin/German omnibus ed. of *Agricola* and *Germania*, ed. & tr. Alfons Städele (Düsseldorf & Zürich: Artemis & Winkler, 2nd rev. ed. 2001): 6–77.

——. *Germania* (c. 98 AD), in *Agricola and Germany*, tr. Anthony R. Birley (Oxford: Oxford UP, 1999): 35–62.

Watson, George. "Celticism and the Annulment of History," in *Celticism* (1996), ed. Brown, 207–20.

Withers, Charles W.J. "The Historical Creation of the Scottish Highlands," in *The Manufacture of Scottish History*, ed. Ian Donnachie & Christopher Whatley (Edinburgh: Polygon, 1992): 143–56.

Womack, Peter. *Improvement and Romance: Constructing the Myth of the Highlands* (Basingstoke & London: Macmillan, 1989).

❖

TEACHING TRANSCULTURALITY

Inter- and/or Transcultural Learning in the Foreign Language Classroom?
— Theoretical Foundations and Practical Implications

SABINE DOFF

T HIS ESSAY AIMS at contextualizing and evaluating the concept of transculturality with regard to its application to the teaching of English as a foreign language (EFL). On taking a closer look at recent methodological approaches of teaching culture in the EFL classroom (1), it shows that they are flexible enough to easily include transcultural aspects (2). This thesis is illustrated by a practical example in the final section of the essay (3) which gives teaching suggestions for E. Pauline Johnson's short story "A Red Girl's Reasoning."

Culture in the EFL Classroom
Since the 1980s: The State of the Art

In this section, a brief summary will be presented of major developments and research results concerning the role of intercultural learning in the EFL classroom in Germany over the past two decades. It provides a starting point for a discussion of different ways of integrating transcultural aspects into the EFL classroom that will be outlined in the following section.

Since the mid-1980s, the umbrella term 'Interkulturelle Didaktik' (intercultural teaching methodology) has been widely used in Germany to refer to distinct approaches to teaching foreign languages which focus on facilitating and supporting encounters with foreign cultures in the classroom:

> Responding to new communicative needs following the extensive internationalisa-
> tion of business and everyday life, their [different approaches to intercultural teach-

ing methodology] common general objective was to expand the existing goals of the communicative language teaching approaches [...]. While the latter intended to build up a communicative competence aiming at the competence of a native speaker, *Interkulturelle Didaktik* aims at a specific 'communicative competence for intercultural situations' [...]. These two approaches partially overlap. The main difference is that *Interkulturelle Didaktik* emphasises systematic links between cultural backgrounds and linguistic behaviour and its situational effects, caused by the interpretations made by speakers with different cultural backgrounds.[1]

The shift from communicative language teaching to intercultural teaching methodology has had significant practical consequences for teaching and learning in the EFL classroom;[2] however, the limited scope of this essay permits only some of the most important to be outlined in this section. The main aim of foreign language teaching since the 'communicative turn' of the 1970s has been to extend communicative competence[3] to include the intercultural dimension. Key competencies have been refined and directed towards intercultural (communicative) competence;[4] this concept has taken into account the fact that communicative acts in the target language will most likely not take place between two native speakers but, rather, in interactions across frontiers between speakers from different countries.[5]

---

[1] Bernd Müller–Jacquier, "Interkulturelle Didaktik," in *Routledge Encyclopedia of Language Teaching and Learning*, ed. Michael Byram (London: Routledge, 2000): 303.

[2] Edmondson's and House's dismissal of the concept of intercultural learning as superfluous or even harmful can therefore be considered outdated. See Willis Edmondson & Juliane House, "Interkulturelles Lernen: Ein überflüssiger Begriff," *Zeitschrift für Fremdsprachenforschung* 9.2 (1998): 161–88. Cf. Rachel Baron, *Interculturally Speaking* (Munich: Langenscheidt–Longman, 2002): 98–105, Lothar Bredella & Werner Delanoy, "Was ist interkultureller Fremdsprachenunterricht?" in *Interkultureller Fremdsprachenunterricht*, ed. Lothar Bredella & Werner Delanoy (Tübingen: Gunter Narr, 1999): 11–12, and Adelheid Hu, "Interkulturelles Lernen: Eine Auseinandersetzung mit der Kritik an einem umstrittenen Konzept," *Zeitschrift für Fremdsprachenforschung* 10.2 (1999): 277–303.

[3] Communicative competence is defined in terms of linguistic, sociolinguistic, and discourse competences. See: Jan van Ek, *Objectives for Foreign Language Learning*, 1: *Scope* (Strasbourg: Council of Europe, 1986).

[4] See: Michael Byram, *Teaching and Assessing Intercultural Communicative Competence* (Clevedon: Multilingual Matters, 1997): 48.

[5] As a consequence, in the field of teaching English as a foreign language, a controversial discussion about the role of the native speaker was initiated. See: Werner Hüllen, "Interkulturelle Kommunikation: Was ist das eigentlich?" *Der fremdsprachliche Unterricht* 26 (1992): 9–10; Claire Kramsch, "The privilege of the intercultural speaker," in *Language*

Accordingly, the overall aim of intercultural learning and teaching is to provide students with the necessary insights and skills to become successful intercultural speakers and help them acquire intercultural competence:

> Intercultural competence is the ability to interact effectively with people from cultures that we recognise as being different [...]. Interacting effectively across cultures means accomplishing a negotiation between people based on both culture-specific and culture-general features that is on the whole respectful of and favourable to each.[6]

Working towards achieving this general goal, the role of intercultural learning in foreign language teaching has been growing continually over the past two decades in three interdependent and overlapping domains: language, factual knowledge of culture(s), and awareness of culture(s).[7] In the EFL classroom, the cultural dimension of language learning is present in many areas – for example in word semantics, associations with words in the foreign language, and through the training of lexical and grammatical as well as contextual foreign language competence and proficiency. Furthermore, the foreign language in the EFL classroom serves to transmit information about another culture, "to gather and display facts and figures [...] about the history, the society, the culture of the country, topics and ideas, characters and plots in literary texts."[8] Facts about target culture(s) in the EFL classroom should not only refer to a country's history, architecture, geography and society (Culture with a capital 'C'), but also to everyday life (culture with a lower-case 'c'). They constitute pupils' '*Orientierungswissen*', knowledge that makes their orientation in the target culture(s) possible and thus facilitates processes of comparison and identification within and across culture(s). Lastly, the EFL classroom offers unique opportunities to stimulate pupils' awareness of cul-

---

Learning in Intercultural Perspective: Approaches through Drama and Ethnography, ed. Michael Byram & Michael Fleming (Cambridge: Cambridge UP, 1998): 16–31.

[6] Manuela Guilherme, "Intercultural competence," in *Routledge Encyclopedia of Language Teaching and Learning*, ed. Michael Byram (2000; London: Routledge, 2004): 297.

[7] See Lothar Bredella, "Zielsetzungen interkulturellen Fremdsprachenunterrichts," in *Interkultureller Fremdsprachenunterricht*, ed. Lothar Bredella & Werner Delanoy (Tübingen: Gunter Narr, 1999): 85–120, and Friederike Klippel, "Zielbereiche und Verwirklichung interkulturellen Lernens im Englischunterricht," *Der fremdsprachliche Unterricht* 25 (1991): 15–21.

[8] Claire Kramsch, *Context and Culture in Language Teaching* (Oxford: UP, 1993): 242.

tural variety and to foster their tolerance towards different ways of living and interpreting the world.[9]

Media, realia, teachers themselves or new media like email and the Internet play a pivotal role in this field: new media in particular have made encounters with target cultures comparatively easy and have provided an abundance of authentic material which can have significant motivating effects on EFL learners.[10] However, this does not mean that literary texts have become obsolete in the EFL classroom:

> More than any other texts, it is said, the piece of literary prose or poetry appeals to the students' emotions [...] and makes them partake in the memory of another speech community. In my view, the main argument for using literary texts in the language classroom is literature's ability to represent the particular voice of a writer among the many voices of his or her community and thus to appeal to the particular in the reader. After years of functional approaches to language learning that helped learners approximate the voice of the target speech community, there is a renewed interest for the individual voice and the creative utterance.[11]

By studying a suitable literary text in the EFL classroom, all three domains of intercultural learning summarized above – language, factual knowledge, and awareness – can be encompassed.[12] Before highlighting this with the example of the short story by E. Pauline Johnson, the possible role of transculturality in the framework of intercultural learning according to a standard EFL model will be examined in the following section.

Intercultural Competence in Terms of Objectives Extended: The Transcultural Dimension

First, the concept of transculturality needs to be defined before its role in the EFL classroom can be investigated. The philosopher Wolfgang Welsch intro-

---

[9] See Barry Tomalin & Susan Stempleski, *Cultural Awareness* (Oxford: Oxford UP, 1993).

[10] See Matthew Peacock, "The Effect of Authentic Materials on the Motivation of Second Language Learners," *English Language Teaching Journal* 51 (1997): 144–56.

[11] Kramsch, *Context and Culture*, 130–31. See also: Liesel Hermes, "Fremderfahrung durch Literatur: Ein Beitrag zum interkulturellen Lernen," *Fremdsprachenunterricht* 51 (1998): 129–34.

[12] For a related discussion of this issue in a different context, see Sabine Doff, "'The first nation of hockey' and 'The best part of North America': Introducing Canada to the EFL classroom," in *Cultural Studies in the EFL Classroom*, ed. Werner Delanoy & Laurenz Volkmann (Heidelberg: Winter, 2006): 119–30.

duced the term 'transculturality' to designate today's altered cultural constitution.[13] He argues that the concept of interculturality, which is based on Herder's traditional concept of single cultures, defines cultures as homogeneous
and separated spheres or islands and is thus inappropriate for describing today's coexisting and cooperating cultures:

> Cultures de facto no longer have the insinuated form of homogeneity and separate-
> ness. They have instead assumed a new form, which is to be called transcultural
> insofar that it passes through classical cultural boundaries. Cultural conditions
> today are largely characterized by mixes and permeations. [...] Henceforward there
> is no longer anything absolutely foreign. Everything is within reach. Accordingly,
> there is no longer anything exclusively "own" either. [...] Today in a culture's ex-
> ternal relations – among its different ways of life – there exists as much foreignness
> as in its external relations with other cultures.[14]

Welsch's concept of interculturality is quite narrow and does not match the
notion of all the models of intercultural learning that will be shown later in
this section. Nevertheless, his controversial definition offers a good starting-
point from which to investigate the roles of interculturality and transculturality and their adoption in the EFL classroom.

The concept of intercultural learning, as described in the first section of
this essay, is based on the hermeneutic principle that understanding other cultures is more than understanding utterances in a foreign language. According
to Gadamer, the act of understanding is based on the polarity between
foreignness and familiarity: foreignness makes understanding necessary,
whereas familiarity makes it possible.[15]

One of the key questions which has been discussed on the basis of these
insights into the field of teaching and learning foreign languages is whether

---

[13] See Wolfgang Welsch, "Transculturality: The Puzzling Form of Cultures Today," in
Spaces of Culture: City, Nation, World, ed. Mike Featherstone & Scott Lash (London: Sage
1999): 194–213. However, Welsch himself points out that the idea of transculturality is in no
way completely new, but already has a long tradition in history.

[14] Welsch, "Transculturality," 196.

[15] See Peter J. Brenner, "Interkulturelle Hermeneutik: Probleme einer Theorie kulturellen
Fremdverstehens," in *"Interkulturelle Germanistik": Dialog der Kulturen auf Deutsch?* ed.
Peter Zimmermann (Frankfurt am Main & New York: Peter Lang): 35; Hans–Georg
Gadamer, *Wahrheit und Methode: Grundzüge einer philosophischen Hermeneutik* (1960;
Tübingen: Mohr, 1972): 279.

"understanding the other"[16] (other cultures) is possible at all. As the following paragraphs will show, the answer to this question is directly linked to the possibility of embracing aspects of transculturality, as defined by Welsch, in the EFL classroom.

There are two schools of thought on this question. The first rejects the possibility of understanding a foreign culture altogether. Members of this group claim that we cannot step beyond our own culture, since our understanding is based on our personal knowledge and experience. The aim of intercultural learning thus cannot be an understanding of the Other, which must remain foreign, but a critical reflection of the framework in which encounters between cultures take place[17] and an acknowledgement of our inability to understand the Other.[18] It is noteworthy that the goals of intercultural learning, as defined by these scholars, completely exclude the transcultural dimension as defined by Welsch; in fact, they simply negate its existence.

There is, however, a second school of thought that acknowledges the variety of problems involved in understanding other cultures, but nevertheless argues that an understanding among cultures is possible "because we all inhabit a common world."[19] In interacting with foreign cultures, these scholars claim that students do not have to forget their prior experiences and knowledge but, rather, have the chance to become aware of their values, clarifying and relativizing them.[20] In this line of thought, cultural symbols: i.e. areas of experience that are universal to humankind – for example, concepts of space, love, and friendship, death or illness – play an important role, since they can facilitate understanding between cultures when learners are aware of them.[21]

---

[16] Friederike Klippel, "Cultural Aspects in Foreign Language Teaching," *Journal for the Study of British Cultures* 1 (1994): 50.

[17] See Brenner, "Interkulturelle Hermeneutik," 52.

[18] See: Hans Hunfeld, "Zur Normalität des Fremden," *Der fremdsprachliche Unterricht* 25 (1991): 50-52; Hans Hunfeld, "Noch einmal: Zur Normalität des Fremden," *Der fremdsprachliche Unterricht* 26 (1992): 42–44.

[19] Klippel, "Cultural Aspects," 54.

[20] See Lothar Bredella, "Towards a Pedagogy of Intercultural Understanding," *Amerikastudien* 37 (1992): 559–94.

[21] See Byram, *Intercultural Communicative Competence*, 22; Christine Schwerdtfeger, "Kulturelle Symbole und Emotionen im Fremdsprachunterricht: Umriß eines Neuansatzes für den Unterricht von Landeskunde," *Informationen Deutsch als Fremdsprache* 18.3 (1991): 237–51.

This notion of how cultures in the EFL classroom can be encountered thus embraces aspects of transculturality as defined by Welsch, even if it is labelled *inter*cultural. The definition of intercultural learning according to this school is therefore notably wider than Welsch's notion of interculturality described above. In the next part, this thesis will be illustrated by investigating the objectives of this approach to intercultural learning in more detail. According to Michael Byram, one of the most influential scholars of the school of thought that favours intercultural understanding, intercultural competence is the main aim of intercultural learning. His comprehensive concept of intercultural competence defined in terms of objectives,[22] which can be considered standard in the context of EFL methodology today, therefore embraces aspects of transculturality. Before this is illustrated using an example in part three of the essay, Byram's original model will be briefly explained in an adapted and visualized form in the following figure. According to Byram, intercultural competence can be defined in terms of the following areas of objectives within an educational context:

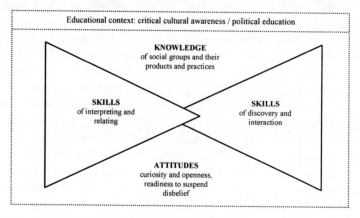

INTERCULTURAL COMPETENCE DEFINED IN TERMS OF OBJECTIVES

The term 'objective' is used here

---

[22] See Byram, *Intercultural Communicative Competence*, 49–55. The four areas of objectives are explained in more detail and by practical examples in section three.

to designate a range of skills, knowledge and attitudes which may not necessarily
be the outcome of learning directly related to language learning, since they may
include phenomena already present in the learner before language learning begins.
Furthermore, the objectives need not necessarily be formulated as observable and
measurable behaviours or changes in behaviour.[23]

These objectives can, in principle, be acquired by individuals through direct
experience and reflection outside the classroom – for example, by going
abroad. However, if they are acquired within an educational context, the
teacher can embed the learning process within a broader educational philosophy that includes, for example, political education and the learners' critical
cultural awareness as one of its most important outcomes.[24]

Within Byram's model, the transcultural dimension, as defined by Welsch,
could be emphasized by an approach to EFL teaching that stresses the cul-
ture-general rather than culture-specific features and that at the same time
critically investigates the roles of stereotypes in interactions between members of different cultures. By offering factual knowledge not exclusively
about Great Britain and the USA but also about examples of the large variety
of many other cultures in which English is the first or second language, transcultural elements could also be included. The same would be possible on a
language level by opening up the EFL classroom further to different standards and varieties in written and predominantly in spoken English. The
transcultural dimension, which in this context is seen as a change of perspective rather than as a profound conceptual change, can thus be strengthened by
the choice of topics, texts, and materials in the EFL classroom.

Native America is, for example, a topic offering mulifaceted possibilities
of intercultural learning and of including the transcultural aspects discussed
above; an example is given in part three of this essay. Visual material, websites, texts, and other resources provide excellent opportunities to investigate
Native and non-Native cultures living side by side in North America. This en-
compasses the differences, social practices, values and their meaning across
these cultures as well as people who mediate more or less successfully be-

---

[23] See Byram, *Intercultural Communicative Competence*, 49.

[24] For a detailed account of intercultural learning and teaching within an educational
framework and an analysis of the main features of critical language pedagogy, see Bredella
& Delanoy, "Was ist interkultureller Fremdsprachenunterricht," 13–14; Byram, *Intercultural
Communicative Competence*, 43–47; Kramsch, *Context and Culture*, 239–47.

tween them. This is illustrated in the next section of this essay using a literary text set in the second half of the nineteenth century entitled "A Red Girl's Reasoning," a story of colonization and a system of antagonisms which is created by a mix of members of different ethnic groups and religions.

A Transcultural Approach to Teaching Native America to Advanced EFL Students: The Story "A Red Girl's Reasoning" (1893) by the Canadian Author E. Pauline Johnson

The following teaching suggestions can serve as a first orientation and a guideline for the EFL teacher. However, due to the limited scope of this essay, suggestions can only be made with reference to the content of the story "A Red Girl's Reasoning" and to the teaching objectives in the frame of a transcultural approach. Nevertheless, the following outline will attempt to show that "A Red Girl's Reasoning" offers broad methodological potential for advanced EFL learners which the individual teacher can expand upon.

THE AUTHOR: EMILY PAULINE JOHNSON (1861–1913)[25]

---

[25] The information and the photographs are taken from www.nancympeterson.com /work1.htm (accessed 20 March 2008) and from www.humanities.mcmaster.ca/~pjohnson (accessed 20 March 2008), where there is also a lot more background information on E. Pauline Johnson, her life and her works.

Both pictures show the Canadian writer and actress Emily Pauline Johnson (1861–1913), the first one in her favourite dressing-gown, the second in a Native dress wearing a necklace made of bear claws. She was born as the daughter of a Mohawk Native Canadian father and an English mother in Brantford, Ontario, and became one of Canada's most popular and successful entertainers at the turn of the century.

Pauline Johnson used the Mohawk name Tekahionwake ("double life"). It is a fitting name, because, in a way, she led a double life. Although she was officially an Indian according to the Canadian government, as her father was a Mohawk, the environment of Chiefswood where she grew up was largely non-Native. Pauline considered herself to be purely Native. She even called white people "palefaces." Pauline could and did fit into the white world, but found that she had to assert her Native identity when she was in white society.

At the age of thirty-one when her society expected her to marry and have children, she began to tour the country. She gave popular recitals of her poetry, and performed comedy routines and plays from Halifax to Vancouver. She was the first Native poet to have her work published in Canada. She was also one of the few female writers at the time who could make a living out of what she wrote and performed.

"A RED GIRL'S REASONING": BACKGROUND, CONTENT SUMMARY AND TEACHING SUGGESTIONS

Background Information: The Mohawks in Canada – Then and Now[26]

The Five Nations and the Great Law of Peace
The term 'Iroquois' refers to the Five Nations who originally inhabited key lands south of Lake Ontario. From east to west, the Five Nations were Mohawk, Oneida, Onondaga, Cayuga, and Seneca. Together, these Five Nations

---

[26] Adapted from Will Ferguson, *Canadian History for Dummies: A fun and Informative Ride through Canada's Past* (Toronto: CDG Books, 2000): 15–17, 410–11. Some recent history books offer critical information on Native American History and provide excellent starting points for a transcultural teaching approach in the EFL classroom, see James W. Loewen, *Lies My Teacher Told Me: Everything Your American History Textbook Got Wrong* (New York: Touchstone, 1995), and Liz Sonneborn, *Amazing Native American History: A Book of Answers for Kids* (New York: John Wiley & Sons, 1999).

formed a powerful and important confederacy, one that played a crucial role in the early development of Canada.

The founding of the Iroquois Confederacy (also known as the League of Five Nations) can be traced back rather accurately to 1451 by a reference to a solar eclipse that occurred in the region. By the time the first Europeans arrived, the Confederacy was well established, giving the Iroquois both a united front and considerable political power. They were united by the Great Law of Peace that would bring the various nations "under one roof." The Mohawk had been the first to accept the law, and thus were known as "the elder brothers" of the Confederacy. The Great Law of Peace was, in effect, the working constitution of the Iroquois Confederacy.

The Oka Crisis and the Formation of the Royal Commission on Aboriginal Peoples (RCAP)

In March 1990, Mohawk protestors in the Oka region outside of Montreal occupied forests which were about to be cut down to make room for an expanded golf course. The forest, and the graveyard nearby, were considered sacred by the Mohawk, who had already seen their land reduced to one percent of what they had originally been granted more than 260 years earlier. When the Mohawk barricaded the roads, the Mayor of Oka sent in the police and a fierce gun-battle started. When an officer with the Quebec provincial police force was killed, the situation spiralled out of control. The army was called in and the conflict lasted well into September. The remaining Mohawk protestors eventually laid down their arms and tried to walk away, at which point panic broke out.

The Oka Crisis led directly to the formation of the Canadian Royal Commission on Aboriginal Peoples (RCAP) in 1991. The commission was to examine the relationship between Canada's First Nations and the government, as well as Canadian society as a whole; it reported back in 1996 after an exhaustive five-year study, and the recommendations it made were complex and far-reaching.

Content Summary: "A Red Girl's Reasoning"

Charlie McDonald, a civil servant at the local Department of Agriculture who has a strong interest in Native cultures, marries the beautiful Christine, daughter of an English trader at Hudson Bay and his Native wife. It is a love marriage on both sides, celebrated in a Christian wedding ceremony which also includes some Indian-American elements.

Joe, the bridegroom's brother, moves in with the young couple at their home in the provincial capital. One evening at a local dance, Christine reveals that her parents at Hudson Bay were married according to Indian rites at the Trading Post twenty years before. Members of the local 'high society' are horrified, as they do not consider this to be a legal marriage. In a heated discussion between the young couple at home the same night, Charlie admits that he agrees with this point of view. He accuses Christine of having "disgraced" him with her scandalous revelation and of having brought shame on them both and her parents. When he indicates that, had he known about this piece of information earlier, it might have affected his relationship with her and his future plans, she takes off her wedding ring and declares their marriage "as empty to me as the Indian rites to you." Joe prevents the situation from escalating by sending his brother away to gather his senses and by calming down Christine. The next morning, Charlie, feeling very sorry for his rude behaviour and ready to apologize to his wife and his brother, finds a farewell note Christine has left for Joe on his door handle.

After several months searching, Charlie finally finds Christine in a small town in Ontario where she is making her own living through embroidery and sewing. He apologizes to her and declares his love for her in a dramatic scene, but she dismisses everything he says, claiming she has not loved him since he expressed his uncertainty about their relationship. The story ends with Charlie lying on the floor of his hotel room sobbing in despair.

Main Characters and Relationships

The main characters in the story are Christine, her husband Charlie, and his brother Joe, who live together in one house. The changing relations between them are depicted in a triangle which could provide a model for analysing the story. The *cultural dimension*, which is of obvious importance, could, for example, be investigated by comparing the marriage of Jimmy Robinson to "Mrs. Jimmy" with the relationship of their daughter Christine to Charlie McDonald. A further discussion-point could be to look more closely at the relationship between men and women as well as between whites and Native Americans in this story. As well as the cultural dimension, the *use of the erotic* also plays a key role in the story; there is a homoerotic relationship between the two brothers, for example, and an obvious attraction between the younger brother and Christine.

Teaching Suggestions[27]

An investigation of both dimensions, the cultural and the erotic, might start with the following *questions* in an EFL classroom:

- Why does Charlie get so upset with Christine?
- Why does Christine leave Charlie?
- Why does she leave a note for his brother, not for him?
- Why does she not return to him, even when he begs her to?
- What is the "lie in her soul"?

Some of the *main motives of the story* which can be closely linked to Byram's objectives and which can be targeted at stressing the aspect of transculturality with advanced EFL learners are the following:

- the changing relationship between Christie, Joe and Charlie (can be depicted using a triangle)
- the concept of marriage as the core of society and the criticism of this concept in the story
- the role of law and legality in different cultures
- the interplay of the subconscious human mind and of conscious actions
- the connection between Christianity and colonization
- the problem of religious dominance in the Americas
- the key question of respect for the human individual (which for Christine is a *trans*cultural value, ie, to be appreciated beyond cultures, religions, and races)

❮❖❯

---

[27] For more detailed teaching suggestions (including background information, worksheets, and keys) on "A Red Girl's Reasoning" and a variety of other topics related to Canada, see *O Canada! History, Country and Cultures from Sea to Sea*, ed. Sabine Doff (Munich: Langenscheidt ELT, 2006).

OVERVIEW: OBJECTIVES OF INTER-/TRANSCULTURAL LEARNING IN "A RED GIRL'S REASONING"[28]

Knowledge of social groups and their products and practices, and of the general processes of societal and individual interaction in different cultures – for example, knowledge of the processes and institutions of socialization and their traditions: Knowledge of Native and non-Native cultures (and their history) living side by side in Canadian society during the nineteenth century which could be compared to other 'multicultural' Western societies and to the situation in Germany, past and present.

Skills in interpreting and relating documents or events of another culture / other cultures – for example, identifying areas of misunderstanding and dysfunction in an interaction and explaining them in terms of each of the cultural systems present: Skills in interpreting the meaning of marriage rites, law, and legality in different cultural groups in Canada around the turn of the nineteenth century and relating this interpretation to the plot of the story.

Skills in discovery and interaction used to acquire new knowledge of a culture and cultural practices; the ability to use knowledge, attitudes, and skills under the constraints of real-time communication and interaction – for example, in investigating the concepts and values of events and developing an explanatory system susceptible of application to other phenomena: Skills in discovering how Christine must feel living in the two (Native and non-Native) cultures and discovering what her final decision could be based on; this could be compared to the situation of other people living in more than one culture (for example, German immigrants).[29]

Attitudes: Curiosity and openness, readiness to suspend disbelief about other cultures and belief about one's own – for example, willingness to question the values and presuppositions in cultural practices and products in one's

---

[28] The objectives of intercultural learning have been adapted to this story from Byram's matrix discussed in the previous part of this essay and have been extended to the transcultural dimension. See Byram, *Intercultural Communicative Competence*, 49–54.

[29] This could, for example, be achieved through a creative-writing task in which pupils have to write entries for Christine's diary at different stages of the story, with reference to 'intercultural' (for example, marriage) and 'transcultural' (for example, respect) practices and values and their influence on her actions. Skills in real-time interaction can perhaps be trained in the classroom (for example, in role play); it is, however, easier to immerse pupils in authentic real-time interactions outside the classroom – for example, in what Byram calls fieldwork or independent learning. See Byram, *Intercultural Communicative Competence*, 68–70.

own environment: Openness to the story's critical stance towards marriage as the core of society and readiness to critically examine the role of marriage in modern German society or other Western cultures.

Summary

A critical investigation of recent methodological approaches has demonstrated that conceptualizing culture(s) has significantly influenced the theoretical foundations of foreign language teaching and its practical implications over the past two decades. In this context, the changing role of English as a world language is a decisive factor in facilitating worldwide contact between people from many different linguistic and cultural groups. Consequently, *inter*cultural (communicative) competence has been highlighted as one of the main aims of foreign language education. This essay has, I trust, shown that the EFL standard model in which Michael Byram defined *inter*cultural competence in terms of concrete objectives for foreign language learning and teaching is flexible enough to include the concept of *trans*culturality and transcultural learning as a process. The theoretical discussion as well as the practical example in this essay suggest that the implementation of transcultural aspects in the EFL classroom should not be interpreted as a profound conceptual shift but, rather, as a change of perspective which can be easily accomplished and which provides a good opportunity to enrich teaching and learning (about) cultures in the EFL classroom.

WORKS CITED

Baron, Rachel. *Interculturally Speaking* (Munich: Langenscheidt–Longman, 2002).

Bredella, Lothar. "Towards a Pedagogy of Intercultural Understanding," *Amerikastudien* 37 (1992): 559–94.

Bredella, Lothar. "Zielsetzungen interkulturellen Fremdsprachenunterrichts," in *Interkultureller Fremdsprachenunterricht*, ed. Lothar Bredella & Werner Delanoy (Tübingen: Gunter Narr, 1999): 85–120.

——, & Werner Delanoy. "Was ist interkultureller Fremdsprachenunterricht?" in *Interkultureller Fremdsprachenunterricht* (1999), ed. Bredella & Delanoy, 11–31.

Brenner, Peter J. "Interkulturelle Hermeneutik. Probleme einer Theorie kulturellen Fremdverstehens," in *"Interkulturelle Germanistik": Dialog der Kulturen auf Deutsch?* ed. Peter Zimmermann (Frankfurt am Main: Peter Lang, 1989): 35–55.

Byram, Michael. *Teaching and Assessing Intercultural Communicative Competence* (Clevedon: Multilingual Matters, 1997).

Doff, Sabine. "'The first nation of hockey' and 'the best part of North America': Introducing Canada to the EFL classroom," in *Cultural Studies in the EFL classroom*, ed. Werner Delanoy & Laurenz Volkmann (Heidelberg: Winter, 2006): 119–30.

——, ed. *O Canada! History, Country and Cultures from Sea to Sea* (Viewfinder Topics Students Book and Resource Book; Munich: Langenscheidt ELT, 2006).

Edmondson, Willis, & Juliane House. "Interkulturelles Lernen: Ein überflüssiger Begriff,"
    Zeitschrift für Fremdsprachenforschung 9.2 (1998): 161–88.
Ek, Jan van. *Objectives for Foreign Language Learning 1: Scope* (Strasbourg: Council of
    Europe, 1986).
Ferguson, Will. *Canadian History for Dummies: A fun and informative ride through
    Canada's past* (Toronto: CDG Books, 2000).
Gadamer, Hans–Georg. *Wahrheit und Methode: Grundzüge einer philosophischen Herme-
    neutik* (1960; Tübingen: Mohr, 1972). Tr. by Joel Weinsheimer & Donald G. Marshall as
    Truth and Method (New York: Crossroad, 2nd rev. ed. 1990).
Guilherme, Manuela. "Intercultural competence," in *Routledge Encyclopedia of Language
    Teaching and Learning*, ed. Michael Byram (2000; London: Routledge, 2004): 297–300.
Hermes, Liesel. "Fremderfahrung durch Literatur: Ein Beitrag zum interkulturellen
    Lernen," *Fremdsprachenunterricht* 51 (1998): 129–34.
Hu, Adelheid. "Interkulturelles Lernen: Eine Auseinandersetzung mit der Kritik an einem
    umstrittenen Konzept," *Zeitschrift für Fremdsprachenforschung* 10.2 (1999): 277–303.
Hüllen, Werner. "Interkulturelle Kommunikation: Was ist das eigentlich?" *Der fremd-
    sprachliche Unterricht* 26 (1992): 8–11.
Hunfeld, Hans. "Zur Normalität des Fremden," *Der fremdsprachliche Unterricht* 25 (1991):
    50–52.
——. "Noch einmal: Zur Normalität des Fremden," *Der fremdsprachliche Unterricht* 26
    (1992): 42–44.
Johnson, Pauline E. "A Red Girl's Reasoning," in Johnson, *The Moccasin Maker* (1893;
    Toronto: William Briggs, 1913); available at www.humanities.mcmaster.ca/~pjohnson
    /5reason.html (accessed 20 March 2008).
Klippel, Friederike. "Zielbereiche und Verwirklichung interkulturellen Lernens im Eng-
    lischunterricht," *Der fremdsprachliche Unterricht* 25 (1991): 15–21.
——. "Cultural Aspects in Foreign Language Teaching," *Journal for the Study of British
    Cultures* 1 (1994): 49–61.
Kramsch, Claire. *Context and Culture in Language Teaching* (Oxford: Oxford UP, 1993).
——. "The Privilege of the Intercultural Speaker," in *Language Learning in Intercultural
    Perspective: Approaches Through Drama and Ethnography*, ed. Michael Byram &
    Michael Fleming (Cambridge: Cambridge UP, 1998): 16–31.
Loewen, James W. *Lies My Teacher Told Me: Everything Your American History Textbook
    Got Wrong* (New York: Touchstone, 1995).
Müller–Jacquier, Bernd. "Interkulturelle Didaktik," in *Routledge Encyclopedia of Lan-
    guage Teaching and Learning*, ed. Michael Byram (2000; London: Routledge, 2004):
    303–307.
Peacock, Matthew. "The Effect of Authentic Materials on the Motivation of Second Lan-
    guage Learners," *English Language Teaching Journal* 51 (1997): 144–56.
Schwerdtfeger, Christine. "Kulturelle Symbole und Emotionen im Fremdsprachunterricht:
    Umriß eines Neuansatzes für den Unterricht von Landeskunde," *Informationen Deutsch
    als Fremdsprache* 18.3 (1991): 237–51.
Sonneborn, Liz. *Amazing Native American History: A Book of Answers for Kids* (New
    York: John Wiley & Sons, 1999).
Tomalin, Barry, & Susan Stempleski. *Cultural Awareness* (Oxford: Oxford UP, 1993).
Welsch, Wolfgang. "Transculturality: The Puzzling Form of Cultures Today," in *Spaces of
    Culture: City, Nation, World*, ed. Mike Featherstone & Scott Lash (London: Sage 1999):
    194–213.

❮❖❯

Towards a Cosmopolitan Readership
— New Literatures in English in the Classroom

MICHAEL C. PRUSSE

I T IS AN UNDENIABLE FACT that Western European classrooms are no longer occupied by homogenous groups of white teenagers born and bred in the country in which they now attend school. The reality faced by most teachers nowadays is one of heterogeneous classes that include a colourful mix of diverse ethnic backgrounds, biographies, and experiences of migration. Many English teachers encountering these changed conditions fall back on traditional values and resort to literature lessons that draw on established texts from the canon.[1] While it can be reasoned that literature as such serves intercultural purposes because it demands identification with characters and understanding different perspectives, and because it explores ambiguities and invites divergent interpretations, there are two reasons why the reaction of these teachers is inadequate.[2] First, these teachers ignore a poten-

---

[1] Ansgar Nünning speaks of an unofficial canon and names William Golding's *Lord of the Flies*, J.D. Salinger's *The Catcher in the Rye*, Aldous Huxley's *Brave New World*, and George Orwell's *Nineteen Eighty-Four* as belonging to it; see "Literatur ist, wenn das Lesen wieder Spass macht!" *Der fremdsprachliche Unterricht* 31.3 (1997): 4–12. An informal poll among grammar-school teachers in Switzerland reveals an equally uniform canon of 'suitable' texts for the classroom: apart from the first two from Nünning's list, John Steinbeck's *Of Mice and Men* and F. Scott Fitzgerald's *The Great Gatsby* were mentioned, complemented by plays such as *The Glass Menagerie*, *Cat on a Hot Tin Roof*, and *A Streetcar Named Desire* by Tennessee Williams, *Death of a Salesman* by Arthur Miller, and *An Inspector Calls* by J.B. Priestley.

[2] See also Ralf Weskamp, *Fachdidaktik: Grundlagen und Konzepte – Anglistik Amerikanistik* (Berlin: Cornelsen, 2001): 188.

tial that is almost innate in a class whose individual members may have experienced quite a few of the matters that postcolonial or transcultural authors write about. And secondly, most curricula describing the goals of English language instruction demand that pupils be familiarized with the cultural background and customs of English-speaking people in general.[3] These directives clearly do not limit the scope to the UK or the USA or to both of these: on the contrary, they invite teachers to adopt a global vision of English and, as a consequence, they ought to incorporate what is presently called the "New Literatures in English" into their teaching repertoire.

The questions that need to be addressed here briefly are, first, how teachers can be made aware of cultural diversity – the answer is clearly that this has to become part of their training and/or of further training – and, secondly, how they can introduce this topic into their classrooms by means of literary texts. Ideally, the stories and novels provided for this purpose would serve as a framework of girders to which other content might be attached. The selection of stories to be discussed in the course of this essay is well-equipped in that respect. The need to educate teachers and pupils for this purpose is self-evident but, as a study by Arun P. Mukherjee demonstrates, far from being met. Mukherjee was appalled by the fact that her students at Canadian universities simply ignored political and social realities when interpreting a specific short story but focused on universally acute problems instead:

> I realized that these generalizations were ideological. They enabled my students to efface the differences between British bureaucrats and British traders, between colonizing whites and colonized blacks, and between rich blacks and poor blacks. They enabled them to believe that all human beings faced dilemmas similar to the ones faced by the two main characters in the story.[4]

Such attitudes can be found not only among students: unfortunately, there is still a certain resistance to postcolonial and transcultural topics and theory even among institutions of tertiary education. In her introduction to *Colonialism/Postcolonialism*, Ania Loomba suspects that apprehensions about "aca-

---

[3] See, for example, the Curriculum for Primary Schools in the Canton of Zurich: Lehrplan für die Volksschule des Kantons Zürich (Überarbeitete Fassung gemäß BRB vom 3. Oktober 2000): 117 & 169.

[4] Arun P. Mukherjee, "Ideology in the Classroom: A Case Study in the Teaching of English Literature in Canadian Universities" (1986), extract in *The Post-Colonial Studies Reader*, ed. Bill Ashcroft, Gareth Griffiths & Helen Tiffin (London: Routledge, 1995): 449.

demic discussions can often be traced to a reluctance to expand or change one's political and conceptual vocabulary."[5] Broadening one's horizons, however, is helpful not just to students or pupils, but also to teachers and lecturers. All the actors in the classroom situation, both teachers and pupils, should, according to Susan Bassnet, ideally undergo a development that involves the following two stages: "The process of working on texts involves an understanding of otherness which implicitly challenges their taken-for-granted perceptions of themselves and their world."[6] Once the pupils have understood that their vision of life is merely one possibility among many, they will have to take the second step. which "requires a reassessment of their perceptions of a specific society, and introduces the issues of cultural relativity."[7] The supreme aim of such a course ought to be that pupils in European classrooms reach the stage of what is here tentatively described as cosmopolitan readership.

The path leading to that destination can be smoothed by introducing into the classroom narratives by authors who have themselves experienced migration and resettlement. Reading these texts will offer some of the pupils a source of identification, while others will discover a wealth of insights into distinct cultures and perceptions of the world. Furthermore, the study of such narratives may help to overcome ethnocentrism and to make pupils aware of paternalistic attitudes and stereotypical views. Pupils might even realize that the Canadian notion of every person as a mosaic may also be usefully applied to themselves and that transculturalism, based on the meeting and intermingling of different peoples and cultures, will enrich rather than threaten them. Before proceeding to the actual discussion of fiction suitable for this purpose, the question of cosmopolitan readership must be considered in more detail.

The projected "cosmopolitan readership" in the title of this article is not meant as an allusion to Homi K. Bhabha's essay "Unsatisfied: Notes on Vernacular Cosmopolitanism," in which he establishes his vision of cosmopolitanism in the contemporary world and in the context of globalization.[8] Rather

---

[5] Ania Loomba, *Colonialism/Postcolonialism* (London: Routledge, 1998): xiii.

[6] *Studying British Cultures*, ed. Susan Bassnett (London: Routledge, 1997): 58.

[7] *Studying British Cultures*, ed. Bassnett, 58.

[8] Homi Bhabha, "Unsatisfied: Notes on Vernacular Cosmopolitanism," in *Text and Nation: Cross-Disciplinary Essays on Cultural and National Identities*, ed. Laura Garcia Moreno & Peter C. Pfeiffer (Columbia SC: Camden House, 1996); repr in *Postcolonial Discourses: An Anthology*, ed. Gregory Castle (Oxford: Blackwell, 2001): 38–52.

than to Bhabha, the title of these reflections is indebted to a paper by Donald
Cuccioletta in which he analyses the current discussion of multicultural issues
in Canada and in which he argues that transculturalism "places the concept of
culture at the center of a redefinition of the nation-state or even the disappearance of the nation-state."[9] It is manifest that migrants who have become
cosmopolitan by moving from one country to another are difficult to pigeon-
hole in national categories. Consider, for instance, the case of literature: if
authors are classified according to nationality, the legitimate question may be
raised whether Rohinton Mistry is Indian or Canadian; similarly, does Michael
Ondaatje belong to Sri Lankan or Canadian literature and does Amitav
Ghosh, by marrying an American and opting to live in New York, still remain
an Indian writer or does he become an American one? The problem is not
new but involves far more countries than in the days when it was mainly a
choice between British and American citizenship with novelists and poets
such as Henry James and T.S. Eliot. Furthermore, the question of nationality
is not nearly so interesting as the fact that these authors, by moving across
boundaries and in distinct societies, shed light on a number of phenomena
that might otherwise have remained undetected. Thus, the prediction of a
future in which the concept of the nation-state begins to lose its significance
and might ultimately cease to exist is not altogether utopian.[10] Contemporary
literary studies would then no longer be divisible into neat categories according to national borders and, as a result, the subject of enquiry might well
transform into 'Literatures in English', and the present categories 'English
Literature', 'American Literature' or 'New Literatures in English' could then
be abandoned.

Today, cosmopolitanism tends to be read as class-related, because the acquisition of a particular attitude that transcends national borders and allows
certain people to become citizens of the world, where they feel at home in
more than one place, is closely connected to privileged access to such resources as power, capital, and education. Cosmopolitanism is usually ascribed
to individuals who qualify for this status according to specific criteria such as
being residents of more than one country. The vision of a cosmopolitan

---

[9] Donald Cuccioletta, "Multiculturalism or Transculturalism: Towards a Cosmopolitan
Citizenship," *London Journal of Canadian Studies* 17 (2001–2002): 9.

[10] In a. essay entitled "Transnationale Kultur als Herausforderung für die Literaturwissenschaft," Frank Schulze–Engler has also anticipated such a change as conceivable; see
Zeitschrift für Anglistik und Amerikanistik 50.1 (2002): 65–79.

readership that is outlined here ought to adopt a more democratic focus; however, it cannot be denied that the present situation is not entirely promising: most teachers in secondary education and probably all the teachers in higher education normally just encounter the privileged – those whose background and intelligence permit them to attend classes in which topics such as literature are taught. Despite this valid reservation, there are arguments in favour of striving towards a cosmopolitan readership as a useful goal in those privileged Western European classrooms, even if merely to further the notion of literature as a possible agent of change that succeeds in crossing physical borders and in breaking down mental barriers. The postcolonial critic Ania Loomba perceives the function of literature in a similar way:

> Literature is an important 'contact zone' [...] where 'transculturation' takes place in all its complexity. Literature written on both sides of the colonial divide often absorbs, appropriates and inscribes aspects of the 'other' culture, creating new genres, ideas and identities in the process. Finally, literature is also an important means of appropriating, inverting or challenging dominant means of representation and colonial ideologies.[11]

While Loomba stresses the significance of the subversive effect of literature – namely, that it succeeds in defying overbearing discourses – Stuart Hall emphasizes the irreversibility of the historical and cultural processes that were initiated by the colonizing experience and points out that the "differences, of course, between colonizing and colonized cultures remain profound. But they have never operated in a purely binary way and they certainly do so no longer."[12] The binary aspect is, nevertheless, deeply ingrained in postcolonial discussions, and one of the challenges in the classroom is to make pupils aware of this fact. One possible solution is to read the following lines from "Stanzas from the Grande Chartreuse" by Matthew Arnold. The excerpt implies that is hard to move from one environment to another, although the poet most probably did not have the migrant experience in mind:

> Wandering between two worlds, one dead
> The other powerless to be born,

---

[11] Ania Loomba, *Colonialism/Postcolonialism* (London: Routledge, 1998): 70–71.

[12] Stuart Hall, "When was 'the Post-Colonial'? Thinking at the Limit," in *The Post-Colonial Question: Common Skies, Divided Horizons*, ed. Iain Chambers & Lidia Curti (London: Routledge, 1996): 246–47.

With nowhere yet to rest my head,
Like these, on earth I wait forlorn.[13]

In Arnold's lines, it is clear that apart from the two worlds, the dead one and the 'unborn' one, there is also a transitory state in the no-man's land in-between. And this particular space that recurs ever so frequently in postcolonial literature is often the most rewarding aspect to explore. Moreover, in a globalized world it is very often the case that people do not just wander between two cultures but maybe among three or even more.

The impact of literature dealing with the experiences of transcultural migrants is certainly so deep because these texts actually mirror situations that are already prevalent in many Western European classrooms (and not only there, of course). These situations arise as a consequence of migration that transports both individuals and groups of people into new environments where – apart from inevitable conflicts – one result is that exciting cultural syntheses are sparked off by these encounters. Writers and other artists are to be found at the forefront of this development and, as was pointed out above, their biographies often reflect precisely what they are writing about. The Pulitzer Prize-winning American author Jhumpa Lahiri, for instance, was born in London, grew up in Massachusetts, and regularly visits her extended family in Calcutta. Thus she is at home in more than one culture and her writing unquestionably benefits from the contact as well as the fusion of the cultures she is familiar with. Comparing the situation of her parents with her own, she writes:

> For immigrants, the challenges of exile, the loneliness, the constant sense of aliena-
> tion, the knowledge of and longing for a lost world, are more explicit and distress-
> ing than for their children. On the other hand, the problem for the children of
> immigrants, those with strong ties to their country of origin, is that they feel neither
> one thing nor the other. The feeling that there was no single place to which I fully
> belonged bothered me growing up. It bothers me less now.[14]

---

[13] Matthew Arnold, "Stanzas from the Grande Chartreuse" (1855), in Arnold, *The Complete Poems*, ed. Kenneth Allott (London: Longman, 1979): 305–306.

[14] Anon., "An Interview with Jhumpa Lahiri," http://www.readinggroupguides.com /guides_I/interpreter_of_maladies2.asp#interview (accessed 12 April 2008).

Similar feelings are expressed in Frank Sargeson's short story with the telling title "The Making of a New Zealander." The narrator informs his readers about the thoughts of an immigrant apple farmer he talks to: "Nick was saying he was a New Zealander, but he knew he wasn't a New Zealander. And he knew he wasn't a Dalmatian any more. He knew he wasn't anything any more."[15] This negative perception of the migrant's situation is probably as significant as the more positive vision of transcultural enrichment. One of the famous aphorisms by the French philosopher and mathematician, Blaise Pascal, might be useful in this context: "On ne montre pas sa grandeur pour être à une extrémité, mais bien en touchant les deux à la fois."[16] Similarly, the meeting of cultures will automatically produce both clashes and exciting new syntheses and quite a range of consequences between these poles. It is essential to understand that these outcomes are to be anticipated and that all of them contribute to the discovery of new insights into human lives.

The lack of roots and the feeling of homelessness mentioned above by Lahiri can certainly be interpreted as a negative element; however, as Pascal seems to imply, the opposite must also be true, and there are critics who perceive it in this fashion. Basing his arguments on Bhabha's writings, John McLeod holds that migrants are in an enviable situation:

> Standing at the border, the migrant is empowered to intervene *actively* in the transmission of cultural inheritance or 'tradition' (of both the home and the host land) rather than *passively* accept its venerable customs and pedagogical wisdom. He or she can question, refashion or mobilise received ideas. The migrant is empowered to act as an agent of change, deploying received knowledge in the present and transforming it as a consequence.[17]

While quite a number of academics and thus inherently privileged citizens of the world would probably subscribe to what McLeod and Bhabha propagate: namely, that transcultural experiences and texts should be seen as enriching and mind-opening assets, critical voices should not be suppressed. Aijaz Ah-

---

[15] Frank Sargeson, "The Making of a New Zealander" (1939), in Sargeson, *Collected Stories* (London: MacGibbon & Kee, 1965): 102.

[16] "We do not display greatness by going to one extreme, but in touching both at once, and filling all the intermediate space"; Blaise Pascal, *Pensées sur la Religion et sur quelques autres sujets*, ed. Louis Lafuma (Paris: Delmas, 1952), No. 229.

[17] John McLeod, *Beginning Postcolonialism* (Manchester: Manchester UP, 2000): 218–19 (emphasis in the original).

mad, looking at the situation from an ideologically altogether different per-spective, regards the notion of transcultural cosmopolitan citizens as the pro-duct of deluded minds:

> That one is free to invent oneself and one's community, over and over again, as
> one goes along, is usually an illusion induced by the availability of surpluses – of
> money-capital or cultural capital or both. That frenzied and constant refashioning
> of the Self, through which one merely consumes oneself under the illusion of con-suming the world, is a specific mode of postmodern alienation which Bhabha mis-takenly calls 'hybridity,' 'contingency,' 'postcoloniality.'[18]

Although the significance of roots cannot be doubted and despite the fact that capitalism and its – in Fredric Jameson's words – "cultural logic" raise rather than solve certain problems, Ahmad's rejection may be necessary as a counter-stance, but is nevertheless too emphatic. Transculturalism is viable and, at least for some, this moving between different cultures is a rewarding experi-ence.

In order to put the process of "an understanding of otherness" into practice, teachers have to develop a certain sensibility for the topic in their pupils. This can be achieved by various means; in an ideal world, teachers would invite guest speakers and travel with their pupils to other countries and let them experience 'the Other' themselves. In realistic classroom situations, simula-tion games by intercultural trainers such as Sivasailam Thiagarajan can be exploited for this purpose, or teachers can resort to literary texts.[19] Experience has shown that the ubiquitous prejudices that can be found in Louis de Ber-nières's short story "Stupid Gringo" are an ideal starting-point for this pur-pose. De Bernières, best known for his novel *Captain Corelli's Mandolin*, may be a surprising name in the context of postcolonial literatures, but "Stupid Gringo," based on the author's experiences in Colombia, provides much food for thought for young minds in Western European classrooms, in which a lot of travel-weary junior tourists are often wary of the teacher's input. The story describes how Jean–Louis Langevin, a French businessman,

---

[18] Aijaz Ahmad, "The Politics of Literary Postcoloniality," *Race & Class* 36.3 (1995): 1–20; repr. in *Contemporary Postcolonial Theory: A Reader*, ed. Padmini Mongia (London: Arnold, 1996): 291.

[19] See Sivasailam Thiagarajan, *Simulation Games by Thiagi* (Bloomington IN: Work-shops by Thiagi, 5th ed. 1996).

is sent to Colombia to set up a branch office for his company in Bogotá. De Bernières's choice of a French protagonist is deliberate, since this allows him to include the following stereotypes about the British:

> The boss laughed; 'The English only ever say "I love you" to their dogs. To each other they only say "Shall we have tea?"' The boss clasped an imaginary English-woman in his arms and gave her a cartoon kiss. 'O chérie,' he exclaimed, 'Let's go to bed and have tea.' The boss turned to Jean–Louis and said 'How the English have children, only the Good Lord knows.'
> 'It's virgin birth,' replied Jean–Louis. 'Perhaps it's more common as a miracle than one might suppose.'
> 'Anyway,' said the boss, 'they say that an Englishwoman can be tremendous as long as she's drunk. I was told this by a Greek. Englishmen are all homosexuals, of course.'[20]

The author's intention is evident: his readers, bombarded with absurd and biased statements, should realize that the ensuing comments on Colombia, although familiar because they are recurrent in the media, are equally biased and untrustworthy. The protagonist arrives in Colombia brimming with pre-conceptions that are bound to be disappointed:

> The cuisine had surprised him; he had been told that he would be eating llamas and guinea pigs marinaded in spices that burned holes in the oesophagus, but actually the cuisine was wholesome and even a bit bland.[21]

The narrative is cleverly constructed and lets the reader experience, along with the main character, how feelings and impressions can change swiftly but also how, ultimately, prejudice is so deep-rooted that in extreme situations it bursts to the surface again. The inhabitants of Bogotá are equally prone to preconceived notions and, interestingly enough, Jean–Louis is offended when he himself becomes the victim of such stereotyping: "Wasn't 'gringo' an insulting sobriquet for a yank? 'If he just wants to insult me, then I won't stop,' thought Jean–Louis, who certainly bridled at the thought of being mistaken for an American."[22] The end of the story reveals how the protagonist has yet

---

[20] Louis de Bernières, "Stupid Gringo," in *Enigmas & Arrivals: An Anthology of Commonwealth Writing*, ed. Alastair Niven & Michael Schmidt (Manchester: Carcanet, 1997): 7.

[21] De Bernières, "Stupid Gringo," 9.

[22] "Stupid Gringo," 11.

again been deceived and is taught a lesson that he will not forget: the man trying to stop him, whom Jean–Louis takes to be a 'thieving native', actually wants to hand his lost wallet back to him. The pupils are given questions to think about in groups:

1.) There are different versions of Bogotá in the story. Describe these versions.
2.) Make a list of the various stereotypes that surface in the narrative.
3.) Characterize Jean–Louis Langevin. What kind of person is he?
4.) What effect does the author create with this story? How does he succeed in achieving it?

By helping pupils with the analysis and having them detect the strategies behind the construction of the story, teachers can bring their pupils to the point where they begin to question their own set of values, beliefs, and pre-judices. This is not a simple process, but one which, according to Abdul JanMohamed, can only succeed up to a certain point:

> Faced with an incomprehensible and multifaceted alterity, the European theore-tically has the option of responding to the Other in terms of identity or difference. If he assumes that he and the Other are essentially identical, then he would tend to ignore the significant divergences and to judge the Other according to his own cultural values. If, on the other hand, he assumes that the other is irredemiably dif-ferent, then he would have little incentive to adopt the viewpoint of that alterity: he would again tend to turn to the security of his own cultural perspective. Genuine and thorough comprehension of Otherness is possible only if the self can somehow negate or at least severely bracket the values, assumptions, and ideology of his culture.[23]

The main purpose of reading "Stupid Gringo" would consist in urging the pupils to take this step at least partly and in making them aware of the prob-lematical nature of the matter. Having established this basic alertness, more complex texts can be introduced to widen and deepen the discussion. The number of suitable texts is immense; for the purposes of this essay I have

---

[23] Abdul R. JanMohamed, "The Economy of Manichean Allegory: The Function of Racial Difference in Colonialist Literature" (1985), excerpts in *The Post-Colonial Studies Reader*, ed. Bill Ashcroft et al. (London: Routledge, 1995): 18.

selected "Borders" by Thomas King, "Japanese Girl" by Gopal Baratham, and "Interpreter of Maladies" by Jhumpa Lahiri.

In *The Location of Culture*, Homi Bhabha emphasizes the significance of borders and their function as locations of opposites and ambiguities. Border-lines separate and link at the same time and in-between there is the no-man's-land that travellers have to cross in order to pass from one country into another. According to Bhabha, this process of crossing is a stage of transition:

> the 'beyond' is neither a new horizon, nor a leaving behind of the past [...] we find ourselves in the moment of transit where space and time cross to produce complex figures of difference and identity, past and present, inside and outside, inclusion and exclusion.[24]

It is precisely this experience that Thomas King captures in his short story "Borders," in which he offers a precise analysis of certain consequences of colonialism that are too often ignored. At the same time, he shows how many borders exist in daily life and how hard it can be to cross some of them. King's physical description of the two border towns already displays the de-ceptiveness of outward appearances when the narrator muses that one would expect a name like Sweetgrass to belong to Canada because there you also find such poetic names as "Medicine Hat and Moose Jaw and Kicking Horse Pass." By contrast, "Coutts, which sounds abrupt and rude, would be on the American side. But this was not the case."[25] This is just the first instance in the narrative where outward appearances prove deceptive. The conflict in the story can be seen in outline in the following exchange between the mother of the narrator and the American border guards:

> "Good Morning."
> "Where you heading?"
> "Salt Lake City."
> "Purpose of your visit?"
> "Visit my daughter."
> "Citizenship?"
> "Blackfoot," my mother told him.

---

[24] Homi K. Bhabha, *The Location of Culture* (London: Routledge, 1994): 1. See also John McLeod, *Beginning Postcolonialism* (Manchester: Manchester UP, 2000): 217.

[25] Thomas King, "Borders," in King, *One Good Story, That One* (New York: Random House, 1993): 135–36.

"Ma'am?"

"Blackfoot," my mother repeated.

"Canadian?"

"Blackfoot."

It would have been easier if my mother had just said "Canadian" and been done with it, but I could see she wasn't going to do that.[26]

When the mother continues to refuse to reveal her nationality, the Americans send her back to the Canadian border, where the situation repeats itself. The media eventually bring this spectacle in the no-man's-land between the borders to an end when they sniff a story and the situation of mother and son is broadcast into homes all over North America. Ironically, it is the TV reporters who ask the most revealing question when they want to know from the narrator what it feels like "to be an Indian without a country."[27] They – as much as the border guards and the majority of the TV watchers – would be hard put to understand that the mother is proud of her tribal identity and that the First Nations were there before a border was established between Canada and the USA. The line was drawn according to the needs of the two nations, but did not take into consideration the needs of the native population, whose homelands were divided and who were forced to accept a 'nationality'. In the globalized present with its numerous migrants moving from one corner of the planet to another, King's narrative raises the question of belonging and of being torn between cultures and loyalties. Hybridity, one of the central concerns of postcolonial criticism, can thus be explained to pupils who might not have come across the concept before.

While "Borders" is about negotiating space and identity, "Japanese Girl" by the Singaporean author Gopal Baratham deals with culture and powerful emotions. The narrative opens ominously enough with the following sentence: "I was not present at my father's execution. That is not to say that I was spared its details. Mum made sure of that. *She* was."[28] The details that the narrator's mother provides are shocking enough and bring to light how the father, a Eurasian doctor in Singapore, was brutally tortured and in due course

---

[26] King, "Borders," 137.

[27] King, "Borders," 145.

[28] Gopal Baratham, "Japanese Girl," in *The City of Forgetting: The Collected Stories of Gopal Baratham*, ed. Ban Kah Choon (Singapore: Times Books International, 2001): 360 (emphasis in the original).

shot by the Japanese secret police because he helped to protect rich local Chinese businessmen in the Second World War. In consequence, the narrator grows up hating the Japanese and extends his abhorrence to every Japanese product:

> Their commercial success made matters worse. Seiko was the turning of thumb-screws, NEC the electrical generators they used to torture dad, Mitsubishi made the zeros that flung bombs at us from the sky and also the bullet that smashed through dad's brain.[29]

Then his wife introduces him to Kaori, the Japanese girl of the title, and he falls in love with her. The ensuing affair has him discover passion – not just for the girl but also for the culture she comes from. There is no happy ending, however, since Kaori eventually returns to Japan to get married. The narrator finds comfort in his own way: "I have become a local expert on Japanese language and art. Not without purpose. I look in them for the smell and taste of Kaori but I know I will not find them there."[30] This story beautifully illustrates how personal experience may modify what people know just because they have heard it. The narrator's hatred for the Japanese is based on his mother's story and even though it is in all probability factual he discovers a further dimension to reality when he not only gets to know a representative of the Japanese but also falls in love with her. With a little help by their teacher, in particular by means of questions such as the ones given below, pupils will be able to interpret the story themselves.

1.) What cultures are mentioned in the story?
2.) In what way are these cultures portrayed?
3.) Please comment on the names that are used in the story.
4.) How does the narrator change in the course of the story? In what way can his experience be a lesson?

The names that are referred to in question 3 are significant, since the narrator's name is Christian and his father's was Jasper Cuthbert; everybody

---

[29] Baratham, "Japanese Girl," 363.
[30] "Japanese Girl," 367.

called him JC, however, which is obviously a reference to Jesus Christ. This
lends the story a further dimension that is worth paying attention to.

Jhumpa Lahiri's "Interpreter of Maladies" is beyond doubt the most transcultural of the stories selected. It relates the fantasies and experiences of an
Indian driver and tour-guide, Mr Kapasi, who has a second job that involves
interpreting for a doctor in order to enable him to understand his patients' ail-
ments. Mr Kapasi drives an American–Indian couple, Mr and Mrs Das, and
their children to a famous temple and imagines that the wife is paying him
more than the usual attention. His imagination running wild, he foresees a
future with her, whereas she is only seeking advice from him, interpreting his
job as a qualification in this respect; she reveals a secret to him. Both are disappointed in their expectations: Mrs Das because Mr Kapasi is at first speech-
less and then, instead of providing comfort, appears to pass judgement on her
behaviour; Mr Kapasi because she no longer corresponds to the romantic
picture he had created in his mind. The ensuing unpleasant encounter that one
of her children has with a group of monkeys upsets her even more and Mr
Kapasi, although saving the boy, cannot get back into her good books.

The transcultural element comes into the story in various guises: "The
family looked Indian but dressed as foreigners did" is a first hint; Mr Kapasi
next notices various modes of behaviour that do not suit an Indian family,
such as Mr Das's using the first name of his wife when talking to his daughter.[31] The Das family is a mixture of India and the USA, and the tour guide
takes careful note of how much their behaviour differs from that of Indians
like himself. Mr Kapasi's picture of the USA is, as he says himself, based on
his watching of the TV series *Dallas*, which "went off the air," as Mr Das
explains to his children who have never heard of it.[32] It is hardly astonishing
that the intercultural encounter does not turn out to be a success.

Jhumpa Lahiri's text is an excellent opportunity for teachers who feel trapped in strict curricula. If they are fortunate enough to have to deal with E.M.
Forster's *A Passage to India*, then Lahiri's short story offers itself as an ideal
companion, since the young American writer appears to have written "An
Interpreter of Maladies" in homage to Forster's novel. The parallels are
striking: Dr Aziz and his failed quest for the friendship of Miss Quested,
which basically arises from intercultural misunderstandings, is rewritten into

---

[31] Jhumpa Lahiri, "Interpreter of Maladies," in *Interpreter of Maladies* (London: Flamingo, 2000): 43, 45.

[32] Lahiri, "Interpreter of Maladies," 48–49.

Mr Kapasi's equally unsuccessful bid for the affections of Mrs Das. The fateful moment in the Malabar caves is replaced by a conversation in a "bulky white Ambassador" car. Only, this time the cultural gap opens between a traditional Indian and a westernized American Indian or, as Lahiri describes this type of person in an essay, an ABCD (this acronym "stands for American born confused 'desi' – 'desi' meaning Indian").[33] The sexual overtones, highlighted by the erotic figures that Mrs Das and Mr Kapasi contemplate at the temple at Konarak, are a link to David Lean's film version of *A Passage to India* where he has Adela Quested discover similar stone friezes in a dilapidated temple in the jungle.

The four stories discussed so far all touch on different aspects of encountering the 'Other' and provide plenty of opportunities for pupils to experience the complexity of the problem. Should teachers intend to continue in this vein, they might want to look into V.S. Naipaul's "The Nightwatchman's Occurrence Book," which focuses on the power of the English language and how it can be used as a means of oppression.[34] It is also a wickedly funny story that reveals how Britons and Americans exploit and abuse the Caribbean islands. The focus on language prevalent in the narrative could be usefully combined with a reading of Ngũgĩ wa Thiong'o's essay "The Language of African Literature."[35] Tim Winton's "Neighbours"[36] has nothing to do with the famous Australian television soap opera but portrays multicultural life in the inner suburbs of Australian cities where an Anglo-Australian couple encounter immigrants from various countries and learn to appreciate their neighbours' diversity.[37] This story, like "Japanese Girl," shows how prejudice can be assuaged by close encounters with alterity. Another eminently 'teachable' text is Alice Munro's "A Wilderness Station," a narrative in letters that

---

[33] Cited in Pashupati Jha & T. Ravichandran, "Bicultural Ethos and Conflicting Claims in *Interpreter of Maladies*," in *Jhumpa Lahiri: The Master Storyteller – A Critical Response to "Interpreter of Maladies"*, ed. Suman Bala (New Delhi: Khosla, 2002): 83.

[34] See V.S. Naipaul, "The Night Watchman's Occurrence Book," in Naipaul, *A Flag on the Island* (1967; Harmondsworth: Penguin, 1982): 52–61.

[35] Ngũgĩ wa Thiong'o, "The Language of African Literature," in Ngũgĩ wa Thiong'o, *Decolonizing the Mind: The Politics of Language in African Literature* (London: James Currey, 1986): 4-33.

[36] Tim Winton, "Neighbours" (1985), in Winton, *Scission* (London: Picador, 2003): 84–88.

[37] See Rudolf Bader, "Australian Literature," in *Companion to the New Literatures in English*, ed. Christa Jansohn (Berlin: Erich Schmidt, 2002): 164.

demonstrates how women were written out of pioneering history but how, in truth, it was their contribution that made the conquest of the wilderness at all possible.[38] This particular story can be employed as a vehicle that proves how the discourses of oppression and subversion function in a similar fashion with regard to women and colonized subjects. A theoretical framework, depending on the pupils' abilities, could be established by referring to Gayatri Chakravorty Spivak's essay "Can the Subaltern Speak?" and by discussing her argument that "both as object of colonialist historiography and as subject of insurgency, the ideological construction of gender keeps the male dominant."[39]

Teachers fortunate enough to find that curricula *do* allow them space for a detailed look into the new literatures in English might want to consider Amitav Ghosh's *The Glass Palace* (2000). However, 552 pages are probably too much for most classrooms and so the use of excerpts is recommended. The outlay of the novel as well as its themes and discussions seem to reflect much of the theory discussed in postcolonial criticism: in an interview, Ghosh admitted that he was familiar with the texts of Homi Bhabha but also said that his own writing was not influenced by this knowledge.[40] *The Glass Palace* addresses issues of complicity – how Indian soldiers "collaborated" in the conquest of Burma – and hybridity:[41] Rajkumar, one of the protagonists, is torn between Burma and India and also has business interests in Malaya. In the course of the narrative he becomes a typical transnational, whose identity is formed in the "interstices of race, class and nation."[42] Uma Dey, a significant minor character in the novel, also becomes transnational but only after being swayed from the grasp of imperial cultural hegemony by a number of eye-opening experiences, one of which is quoted below:

---

[38] Alice Munro, "A Wilderness Station" (1992) in Munro, *Open Secrets* (1994; London: Vintage, 1995): 190–225.

[39] Gayatri Chakravorty Spivak, "Can the Subaltern Speak?" (1988), excerpt in *The Post-Colonial Studies Reader*, ed. Bill Ashcroft, Gareth Griffiths & Helen Tiffin (London: Routledge, 1995): 28.

[40] Neluka Neluka & Alex Tickell, "An Interview with Amitav Ghosh," in *Amitav Ghosh: Critical Perspectives*, ed. Brinda Bose (Dehli: Pencraft International, 2003): 215.

[41] See Melita Glasgow & Don Fletcher, "Palimpsest and Seduction: *The Glass Palace* and *White Teeth*," *Kunapipi* 27.1 (2005): 75–87.

[42] Rakhee Moral, "'In Time of the Breaking of Nations': *The Glass Palace* as Postcolonial Narrative," in *Amitav Ghosh: Critical Perspectives*, ed. Brinda Bose (Dehli: Pencraft International, 2003): 144.

One night, plucking up her courage, Uma remarked: 'One hears some awful things about Queen Supayalat.'

'What?'

'That she had a lot of people killed … in Mandalay.'

Dolly made no answer but Uma persisted. 'Doesn't it frighten you,' she said, 'to be living in the same house as someone like that?'

Dolly was quiet for a moment and Uma began to worry that she'd offended her. Then Dolly spoke up. 'You know, Uma,' she said in her softest voice. 'Every time I come to your house, I notice that picture you have, hanging by your front door…'

'Of Queen Victoria, you mean?'

'Yes.'

Uma was puzzled. 'What about it?'

'Don't you sometimes wonder how many people have been killed in Queen Victoria's name? It must be millions, wouldn't you say? I think I'd be frightened to live with one of those pictures.'[43]

Exchanges such as this one also have the potential to serve as eye-openers with regard to pupils who are only familiar with their own culture while, at the same time, lending support to those who have moved from one culture to another and are already accustomed to this 'double vision'. Lothar Bredella emphasizes the fact that "aesthetic reading directs our attention to the interaction between text and reader and encourages us to explore how the text affects us."[44] Postcolonial and transcultural narratives have a great affective potential that will challenge pupils to contribute their experiences, recollections and associations which in turn are transformed by the reading process: i.e. to quote Bredella again, "the aesthetic experience also modifies what is brought to the text."[45] If, at the end of the course, more pupils have acquired one or several new perspectives, teachers have planted a seed that might bear fruit much later. This is particularly relevant if the pupils belong to the privileged classes that tend eventually to become leaders in politics, the economy, and science; hence, the education of these future decision-makers into cosmo-

---

[43] Amitav Ghosh, *The Glass Palace* (London: HarperCollins, 2000): 113–14.

[44] Lothar Bredella, "The Anthropological and Pedagogical Significance of Aesthetic Reading in the Foreign Language Classroom," in *Challenges of Literary Texts in the Foreign Language Classroom*, ed. Lothar Bredella & Werner Delanoy (Tübingen: Gunter Narr, 1996): 18.

[45] Bredella, "The Anthropological and Pedagogical Significance of Aesthetic Reading in the Foreign Language Classroom," 18.

politan readers is extremely important. The laying of foundations in creating a greater empathy for distinct ways of life and cultures makes it possible, to fall back on a well-worn metaphor, to establish bridges across cultures. The New Literatures in English offer prospects for essential conversations – a necessity that is also strongly felt among authors from formerly colonized societies: "The need for the postcolonial to converse with that world, as it were, prevails over the other more blind need to resist the old world."[46]

WORKS CITED

Ahmad, Aijaz. "The Politics of Literary Postcoloniality," *Race & Class* 36.3 (1995): 1–20; repr. in *Contemporary Postcolonial Theory: A Reader,* ed. Padmini Mongia (London: Arnold, 1996): 276–93.

Anon. "An Interview with Jhumpa Lahiri," http://www.readinggroupguides.com/guides_I /interpreter_of_maladies2.asp#interview (accessed 12 April 2008).

Arnold, Matthew. "Stanzas from the Grande Chartreuse" (1855), in Arnold, *The Complete Poems,* ed. Kenneth Allott (London: Longman, 1979): 301–11.

Bader, Rudolf. "Australian Literature," in *Companion to the New Literatures in English,* ed. Christa Jansohn (Berlin: Erich Schmidt, 2002): 137–74.

Bala, Suman, ed. *Jhumpa Lahiri: The Master Storyteller – A Critical Response to "Interpreter of Maladies"* (New Delhi: Khosla, 2002).

Bassnett, Susan, ed. *Studying British Cultures* (London: Routledge, 1997).

Bhabha, Homi K. "Unsatisfied: Notes on Vernacular Cosmopolitanism," in *Text and Nation: Cross-Disciplinary Essays on Cultural and National Identities,* ed. Laura Garcia Moreno & Peter C. Pfeiffer (Columbia SC: Camden House, 1996); repr. in *Postcolonial Discourses: An Anthology,* ed. Gregory Castle (Oxford: Blackwell, 2001): 38–52.

——. *The Location of Culture* (London & New York: Routledge, 1994).

Bredella, Lothar. "The Anthropological and Pedagogical Significance of Aesthetic Reading in the Foreign Language Classroom," in *Challenges of Literary Texts in the Foreign Language Classroom,* ed. Lothar Bredella & Werner Delanoy (Tübingen: Gunter Narr, 1996): 1–29.

Childs, Peter, & R.J. Patrick Williams. *An Introduction to Post-Colonial Theory* (Hemel Hempstead: Prentice Hall, 1997).

Cuccioletta, Donald. "Multiculturalism or Transculturalism: Towards a Cosmopolitan Citizenship," *London Journal of Canadian Studies* 17 (2001–2002): 1–11.

de Bernières, Louis. "Stupid Gringo," in *Enigmas & Arrivals: An Anthology of Commonwealth Writing,* ed. Alastair Niven & Michael Schmidt (Manchester: Carcanet, 1997): 6–14.

Glasgow, Melita, & Don Fletcher. "Palimpsest and Seduction: *The Glass Palace* and *White Teeth,*" *Kunapipi* 27.1 (2005): 75–87.

Ghosh, Amitav. *The Glass Palace* (London: HarperCollins, 2000).

---

[46] Moral, "'In Time of the Breaking of Nations'," 153.

Jha, Pashupati, & T. Ravichandran. "Bicultural Ethos and Conflicting Claims in *Interpreter of Maladies*," in *Jhumpa Lahiri: The Master Storyteller*, ed. Bala, 68–85.

Hall, Stuart. "When was 'the Post-Colonial'? Thinking at the Limit," in *The Post-Colonial Question: Common Skies, Divided Horizons*, ed. Iain Chambers & Lidia Curti (London: Routledge, 1996): 242–60.

JanMohamed, Abdul R. "The Economy of Manichean Allegory: The Function of Racial Difference in Colonialist Literature" (1985), excerpt in *The Post-Colonial Studies Reader*, ed. Bill Ashcroft, Gareth Griffiths & Helen Tiffin (London: Routledge, 1995): 18–23.

King, Thomas. "Borders," in King, *One Good Story, That One* (New York: Random House, 1993): 132–47.

Lahiri, Jhumpa. "Interpreter of Maladies," in Lahiri, *Interpreter of Maladies* (London: Flamingo, 2000): 43–69.

Lehrplan für die Volksschule des Kantons Zürich [Curriculum for Primary Schools in the Canton of Zurich] (überarbeitete Fassung gemäss BRB vom 3. Oktober 2000).

Loomba, Ania. *Colonialism / Postcolonialism* (London: Routledge, 1998).

McLeod, John. *Beginning Postcolonialism* (Manchester: Manchester UP, 2000).

Moral, Rakhee. "'In Time of the Breaking of Nations': *The Glass Palace* as Postcolonial Narrative," in *Amitav Ghosh: Critical Perspectives*, ed. Brinda Bose (Dehli: Pencraft International, 2003): 139–53.

Mukherjee, Arun P. "Ideology in the Classroom: A Case Study in the Teaching of English Literature in Canadian Universities" (1986), extract in *The Post-Colonial Studies Reader*, ed. Bill Ashcroft, Gareth Griffiths & Helen Tiffin (London: Routledge, 1995): 447–51.

Munro, Alice. "A Wilderness Station" (1992), in Munro, *Open Secrets* (1994; London: Vintage, 1995): 190–225.

Naipaul, V.S. "The Night Watchman's Occurrence Book," in Naipaul, *A Flag on the Island* (1967; Harmondsworth: Penguin, 1982): 52–61.

Ngũgĩ wa Thiong'o. "The Language of African Literature," in Ngũgĩ wa Thiong'o, *Decolonizing the Mind: The Politics of Language in African Literature* (London: James Currey, 1986): 4-33.

Nünning, Ansgar. "Literatur ist, wenn das Lesen wieder Spass macht!" *Der fremdsprachliche Unterricht* 31.3 (1997): 4–12.

Pascal, Blaise. *Pensées sur la Religion et sur quelques autres sujets*, ed. Louis Lafuma (posth. 1670; Paris: Delmas, 1952).

Sargeson, Frank. "The Making of a New Zealander" (1939), in Sargeson, *Collected Stories* (London: MacGibbon & Kee, 1965): 97–103.

Schulze–Engler, Frank. "Transnationale Kultur als Herausforderung für die Literaturwissenschaft," *Zeitschrift für Anglistik und Amerikanistik* 50.1 (2002): 65–79.

Spivak, Gayatri Chakravorty. "Can the Subaltern Speak? Speculations on Widow Sacrifice" (1988), excerpt in *The Post-Colonial Studies Reader*, ed. Bill Ashcroft, Gareth Griffiths & Helen Tiffin (London: Routledge, 1995): 24–28.

Thiagarajan, Sivasailam. *Simulation Games by Thiagi* (Bloomington IN: Workshops by Thiagi, 5th ed. 1996).

Silva, Neluka, & Alex Tickell. "An Interview with Amitav Ghosh," in *Amitav Ghosh: Critical Perspectives*, ed. Brinda Bose (Dehli: Pencraft International, 2003): 214–21.

Weskamp, Ralf. *Fachdidaktik: Grundlagen und Konzepte – Anglistik Amerikanistik* (Berlin: Cornelsen, 2001).

Winton, Tim. "Neighbours" (1985), in Winton, *Scission* (London: Picador, 2003): 84–88.

◄❖►

Teaching Hanif Kureishi

LAURENZ VOLKMANN

1. Why Hanif Kureishi?

I T WAS ONLY A FEW YEARS AGO that one of the most prominent
German *Anglisten* lamented the "ossification" of the canon of novels or
short stories used in the EFL classroom at German schools.[1] Others
have dubbed the sclerotic list of traditional novels "The Catcher of the Flies".
Scoffing at the petrification of reading habits at German schools of higher
education has become an easy, arguably all too facile exercise. So is bashing
the old generation of teachers who for the umpteenth time put their dog-eared
Stundenblätter (ready-made 'teacher's notes') to use in a classroom in which
students are bored stiff with dinosaur novels written at a time when their
teachers had experienced or were about to experience the growing-pains of
puberty. Notwithstanding the fact that, as I would maintain, some of the classics of EFL teaching have stood the exacting test of time thanks to their
intrinsic merits, new textual galaxies are there to be explored – and one does
not even need to be bold to launch into this enterprise. It goes without saying
that each generation must discover its own Orwell, Golding or Salinger. New
contenders for official, unofficial or 'secret' lists of set texts at grammar
schools have been suggested and their relative merits and chances in the
struggle for canonical survival in the classroom have been weighed. There
are, of course, the usual suspects – Ian McEwan, Julian Barnes, Peter Ack-

---

[1] Ansgar Nünning, "Literatur ist, wenn das Lesen wieder Spaß macht!" *Der fremdsprachliche Unterricht Englisch* 27.3 (1997): 4–13.

royd, and Graham Swift, to mention just four in the category of British heavy-weight novelists.[2]

In recent years, a new great British-Indian hope has stolen the limelight – by leaps and bounds. This contender has everything teachers of English novels, short stories, and plays could hope for. This is confirmed by his personal story, one of 'mixed background', early success, and increasing establishment status. Born of an Asian father and an English mother in Bromley in 1954, Hanif Kureishi escaped the suburbs to write plays for the Royal Court during the 1970s and film screenplays for Stephen Frears in the 1980s (including *My Beautiful Laundrette* and *Sammy and Rosie Get Laid*). In the early 1990s, he set himself on the more solitary course of writing fiction. The first novel, *The Buddha of Suburbia* (1990), was made into a television series by the BBC; a second followed, less hailed by critics and less popular with readers – *The Black Album*. Recent years have seen a steady outpouring of slimmer novels and short stories – with Kureishi's critics discerning a sort of achievement-and-decline pattern with regard to his latest offerings. His fame rests, and will increase, with some 'classics' of the 1990s, usually set in the two preceding decades. They will be the focus of this article.

2.   Which Kureishi for the Advanced EFL Classroom?

Of course, in the classroom teachers are eager to present the representative of an ethnic minority group, the "Englishman born and bred, almost,"[3] as Karim Amir, the protagonist of *The Buddha of Suburbia*, calls himself in the famous opening lines of the novel. Or are they? It seems obvious that a focus on Kureishi's generally positive concepts of 'hybrid' identity questions exactly those categories one initially sets out to find in narratives by members of an ethnic minority group – the insignia of 'authenticity' or 'ethnicity'. Rather, Kureishi favours all shades of the 'in-between' status, portrays most of his characters and all his protagonists as 'fluid identities', unfinished, unfixed – searching for meaning, identity, and a sense of belonging, yet never achieving it. Right here one of the main challenges of teaching Hanif Kureishi unfolds.[4]

---

[2] Hanif Kureishi, *The Buddha of Suburbia* (London: Faber & Faber, 1990). 3.

[3] Ansgar Nünning, "Literatur ist, wenn das Lesen wieder Spaß macht!" *Der fremdsprachliche Unterricht Englisch* 27.3 (1997): 4–13.

[4] On the challenges and advantages of teaching literary texts to gain cross-cultural understanding, see Klaus Stierstorfer, "Literatur und interkulturelle Kompetenz," in *Interkul-*

Because Kureishi's chief narrative focus is constantly on taking both sides into account, black and white, straight and gay, cultural assimilation and rejection, his work amounts to an unmitigated case of what conservatives would call relativism, scepticism, even nihilism – at best, hedonism.

These principles seem to fly in the face of time-honoured didactic principles – that students expect (moral) guidelines from books, not conflicting and confusing ethical stances. However, such arguments could apply to almost any canonized work of literature for the classroom; even classics such as *Lord of the Flies* or *The Catcher in the Rye* have been called defeatist, nihilistic etc. The question might thus be asked: Are students reading Kureishi during puberty or adolescence – i.e. at a difficult phase in their lives – cast into utter confusion or are they taught the wrong values of consumer society, drug abuse, and sexual promiscuity? In other words, are teachers placing a Trojan horse in front of their students? According to this view, guided by the best of intentions, teachers use literature to teach insights into and empathy with members of ethnic minority groups. Against their intentions, however, they might be sowing the seeds of doubt. Frustration, indifference, and even a sense of powerlessness might be the result, given Kureishi's preference for a globalized pop culture as the backdrop to his characters' fumbling for meaning in life and his refusal to take sides or to offer any sign of moral touchstones.

However, it is precisely this hybridity as a state of mind and the philosophical framework of Kureishis's texts that could become the focus of teaching and could initiate thought-processes in the students' minds leading to what could be called greater cultural sensitivity, a heightened awareness of both cultural differences and cultural commonalities – and this applies not just to race, but also to gender, class, etc. Additionally, tolerance in the sense of Keats's 'negative capability' could be fostered: learning to be less rigid – not only in the construction of the self, but also in the process of encountering the Other.[5]

---

turelle Kompetenz: Theorie und Praxis des fremdsprachlichen Unterrichts, ed. Laurenz Volkmann, Klaus Stierstorfer & Wolfgang Gehring (Tübingen: Gunter Narr, 2002): 119–41.

[5] For discussions of these issues, see Laurenz Volkmann, "Universal Truths or Ethnic Peculiarities? On Tensions Inherent in the Reception of Post-Colonial and Minority Literature," in *Intercultural Encounters: Studies in English Literatures – Essays Presented to Rüdiger Ahrens on the Occasion of His Sixtieth Birthday*, ed. Heinz Antor & Kevin Cope (Heidelberg: Winter, 1999): 131–52; Laurenz Volkmann, "Interkulturelle Kompetenz als neues Paradigma der Literaturdidaktik? Überlegungen mit Beispielen der postkolonialen

3.   Introducing Hanif Kureishi – Pre-Reading Activities

It goes without saying that teachers should not throw their students in at the deep end, so to speak. Reading, interpreting, and discussing texts must be preceded by so-called *pre-reading activities* which provide motivation and background information to facilitate reading and enable students to put Kureishi into a wider, non-literary as well as literary context. On principle, I would suggest that students approach Kureishi by means of group work. Each group, according to the intellectual level and interests of its members, takes on the task of collecting, selecting, and evaluating information on a specific topic related to Kureishi. Teachers provide material and act as mediators or facilitators, asking their student groups to report to the rest of the course after group work. Thus, as with a puzzle, each group adds its piece of information in order to gain a more comprehensive view of the author, his themes, and the texts. Thus the ground for an encounter with the text is prepared.

I suggest that students split up into five groups. Each group deals with one of the following thematic angles on Kureishi:

a) *The "Sex & Drugs & Rock'n'Roll" approach*. Students are provided with (or find information on the Internet on) material on changes in rock music during the 1980s and 1990s. A focus is on the shift from glam rock (David Bowie) to punk rock (Sex Pistols) – this is most prominently reflected in *The Buddha of Suburbia*, with Charlie Hero serving as a David Bowie-like character. Additionally, depending on the class, changes in sexual mores, fashion, leisure activities etc. during those decades can also be taken into account. Life-style magazines would be the best source, also rock'n'roll encyclopaedias etc.[6] Since students tend to get side-tracked into presenting either a potpourri of 1980s and 1990s pop phenomena or exhibiting encyclopaedic knowledge of this era, tutors should make sure that the focus stays on music as a reflection of its age, especially of shifting social phenomena such as attitudes towards authority, material success, social issues, sexuality or gender constructions.

Literatur und Minoritätenliteratur," in *Wie ist Fremdverstehen lehr- und lernbar? Vorträge aus dem Graduiertenkolleg "Didaktik des Fremdverstehens"*, ed. Lothar Bredella et al (Tübingen: Gunter Narr, 2002): 164–90.

[6] An obvious source for students is *The Faber Book of Pop*, ed. Hanif Kureishi & Jon Savage (London: Faber & Faber, 1995).

b) *The "Pop Star Kureishi" approach.* Students learn about Kureishi as a 'cultural icon', a much-feted celebrity, and about his views on literature, race, sex, or family. The best source here is, of course, his website (http://www.hanifkureishi.com). This fosters a true 'human interest' angle, for Kureishi's star quality is not to be underestimated in today's 'promotional culture', which, of course, extends to the classroom. So why not make the most of it in this approach (though embellishing classroom walls with Kureishi posters might be one step too far)?

c) *The "Kureishi's Books as 'Landeskunde' Material" approach.* Here students research the most important facts and figures about contemporary Britain's ethnic minority groups. This provides the factual background to Kureishi's fictions. Students should be encouraged to go beyond enumerating statistics to research how ethnic minority groups actually experience life in Great Britain. David Mason's rather factual study book from 2000 could be a source providing statistics and sociological interpretations.[7] The best source in this respect is, of course, the Internet, where students will find that some project groups from German schools on minorities in Great Britain have already posted their findings on the net. In addition, there are a number of official websites on the topic.

d) *The "If a Man is Tired of London ..." approach.* Since most of Kureishi's novels and short stories are set in London, students are given the task of doing research about London – with special emphasis on matters of class, ethnic minority groups, and 'in-places'. In developing their own 'mental maps', students learn about one of the main categories of recent cultural-studies interests: the construction of 'space', specifically urban space (versus rural space) as a means of fashioning identity.[8] Differences between German and other ideas of (urban) space can be discussed, such as the British (and American) concept of suburbia vs. the city, which has no real equivalent in the German *Vorstadt* und *Stadt*. Semantic connotations of "suburbia" and the much-

---

[7] David Mason, *Race and Ethnicity in Modern Britain* (Oxford: Oxford UP, 2nd ed. 2000).

[8] For deeper insights into mental or cultural mapping, see Doris Teske's chapters "Raum in den Cultural Studies" and "Das Aufbrechen britischer Identitäten," which provide useful information on historical as well as contemporary aspects of London's topography; Teske, *Cultural Studies: GB: Anglistik – Amerikanistik* (Berlin: Cornelsen, 2002): 103–86. This introduction can also be used by students.

dreaded humdrum existence of suburbanites as expressed in *The Buddha of Suburbia*, for instance, can be explained by actively listening to and discussing songs by the British group The Pet Shop Boys – for example, "Suburbia" or "West End Girls." Here the connection with approaches 1 and 2 is obvious.

e) *The "Who was Rudyard Kipling" approach*. It seems impossible to understand *The Buddha of Suburbia*, let alone concepts of postcolonialism and othering, without reference to the man who has become the representative of Victorianism, colonialism, imperialism and othering – Rudyard Kipling. It is recommended to ask students to find out more about Kipling, the man, his works (especially *The Jungle Book*), and the myth. Internet research could also entail gleaning information on Joseph Conrad and E.M. Forster. Additionally, interested students might be asked to report on Conrad's *Heart of Darkness* and Foster's *A Passage to India* – thus presenting two key texts of (anti)colonialism in class. Further, films or excerpts from films based on Conrad's stories (*Apocalypse Now*) or Forster's novels (*A Passage to India*) are still much appreciated by students, as personal experience has taught me. As a basic introduction to Kipling and imperialism, students would be asked to present to the others a seminal stanza from one of Kipling's poems and comment on two much-quoted lines. Here is the first stanza of "The White Man's Burden" from 1899, originally directed at the USA with regard to the Philippines:

> Take up the White Man's burden –
> Send forth the best ye breed –
> Go bind your sons to exile
> To serve your captives' need;
> To wait in heavy harness
> On fluttered folk and wild –
> Your new-caught, sullen peoples,
> Half devil and half child.[9]

The two infamous lines are, of course, line 1 ("Take up the White Man's burden") and line 8 ("Half devil and half child"). While the former encapsulates the sense of quasi-religious mission pertinent to Victorian imperial-

---

[9] Rudyard Kipling, "The White Man's Burden" (1899), in Kipling, *Selected Poetry*, ed. Craig Raine (Harmondsworth: Penguin, 1992): 127.

ism, the latter provides the conventional Victorian image of natives or indigenous people and their de-individualized character as oscillating between vicious, devious rogue and naive, undeveloped child of nature.

After these preparatory activities, students will be able to connect their readings of Kureishi's texts with various strands of 'cultural knowledge', thus creating a more lasting and increasingly tightly woven 'web of knowledge'. Their involvement with Kureishi will not take place in a mental vacuum; rather, they will be able constantly to link literature, film, art or information about contemporary Britain with previously acquired knowledge.

In the remainder of this essay, two ways of working with Kureishi's texts will be introduced. Using the example of "My Son the Fanatic" as the short story most likely to be used in the classroom from about form 10 upwards, they propose two completely different ways of dealing with literature. The first task is designed to introduce students to some of the mechanisms of othering, as analysed by theories of postcolonialism, alterity or discourse analysis. However, instead of being overwhelmed by recent ramifications of cutting-edge theory, students become involved in the simple mechanics of creating meaning by means of binary oppositions – which they later apply to Kureishi's story to achieve new skills in unravelling meanings in texts. While this task aims at more cognitive objectives, the ensuing part suggests two methods of working with literary texts by taking them off the page, responding to them by turning them into performance and role play. Here not only oral skills – reading skills, skills in extemporizing and improvising – are promoted, but also awareness of the role of non-verbal features such as gestures and body language in communication. Holistic in its scope, drama work is influenced by theories of group and gestalt therapy and aims at fostering a stronger sense of involvement, thus helpings to motivate students and encourage them to learn through active participation.

4.   How Binary Oppositions Work (or Don't): Pre-Reading and Reading Activities for "My Son the Fanatic"

One of the accepted tenets of theories of postmodernism, structuralism, post-structuralism, gender studies, and postcolonial studies is the fact that the standard ordering strategy of Western culture is the organization of our thoughts in binary pairs. Our prioritizing of one pole of this opposition determines the

way we think – specifically, how we inadvertently construct our sense of the
Self versus the Other. Following Jacques Derrida's linguistic theories, postcolonial critics have drawn attention to the presence, and inadequacy, of such
an ordering system in the context of colonial or postcolonial encounters, or in
our general interaction with the Other – either assimilating or 'othering' it.
Theories of hybridity aim at breaking open traditional, inadequate dependencies on binary pairs which are used to generate these rigid ordering-systems.
By contrast, authors such as Kureishi aim at constructing a more fluid, flexible ordering system which reflects the individual's personality and is conducive to more openness, mutability, and tolerance. In his texts, Kureishi does
not give us an answer to whether this postmodern world of fluidity and
constant change is morally better or whether it shapes the individual for better
or for worse. He does not even provide answers to the question of the extent
to which individuals have a choice in actively shaping their lives. Kureishi
remains the chronicler of this age of dissolving binary oppositions, of slipping
certainties, and of both exuberant and confusing arrays of life-choices.

Working like a gigantic deconstruction apparatus, Kureishi's texts constantly question the hierarchical binaries on which we base our assumptions
about race, class, and gender; and they constantly undercut our desire as
readers to achieve coherent meanings, values, and beliefs – both traditional
hierarchies and newly evolving ones remain in flux, unfinished, and exposed
to constant change. How these binary oppositions work both in texts and in
our daily lives can be discussed with students by involving them in a series of
pre-reading activities, leading up to an interpretation of "My Son the Fanatic." This interpretation centres on how binary oppositions are both established here and reversed – so that the reader is left in the end with the puzzling question as phrased by son Ali, "So, who's the fanatic now?"[10] Thus
reading becomes an exercise in deconstruction. As several obvious binary
oppositions are reversed, the text must be interpreted on several levels and
students learn that no reading can ever be complete or finished. This openness
and the ongoing nature of interpretation can also be demonstrated with reference to other texts by Kureishi. The example of "My Son the Fanatic" has
been chosen here for reasons of brevity and easy illustration.

---

[10] Hanif Kureishi, "My Son the Fanatic" (1994), in *Many Voices – Many Cultures: Multicultural British Short Stories*, ed. Barbara Korte & Claudia Sternberg (Stuttgart: Reclam,
1997): 165. Abbreviated in the following page references in the text as SF.

One method of raising awareness of the ubiquitous nature of hierarchical binary structures could be to ask students to think about some obvious oppositions which seem to be mutually exclusive. For instance, on the blackboard the following binaries could be put in opposition:[11]

LAND : SEA

CHILD : ADULT

US : THEM

Reflecting on how these binaries function to structure our perceptions of the natural and social world into order and meaning, students are asked to mention and discuss examples of how this generation of meaning by opposition is the underlying assumptions of stories in newspapers and in television news. Questions could ensue, such as: How do these oppositions separate parties involved in a conflict or dispute and generate ideological meanings? After this first step in raising awareness of how signifying systems work and how one category is privileged over another, students are asked whether there are any ambiguities or overlaps between the stark oppositions discussed so far. It becomes clear that between land and sea there is an in-between, ambivalent category, the beach – sometimes land, sometimes sea:

> It is *both* one and the other (sea at high tide; land at low tide), and neither one nor the other. Similarly, between child and adult there is another ambiguous category: youth. And between us and them there are deviants, dissidents and so on.[12]

It has been suggested that the area of overlap shown in the figure below is impossible according to the system of binary oppositions. It is not only a deviant category; it is a breaking of taboo, subject to both repression and ritual – it is a "scandalous category."[13] This becomes all the clearer in the case of US : THEM, where an ambiguous inter-category evolves which cannot be identified with 'them' or 'foreigners':

---

[11] The following observations on binary oppositions are indebted to John Hartley, *Communication, Cultural and Media Studies: The Key Concepts* (London & New York: Routledge, 2002), 19–21.

[12] Hartley, *Communication, Cultural and Media Studies,* 19–20.

[13] *Communication, Cultural and Media Studies,* 20.

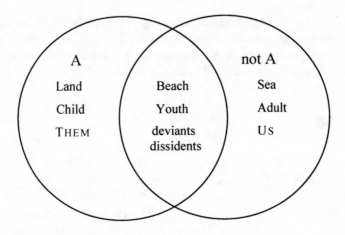

Figure: 'Overlapping' binaries and the spaces in-between

As a third step, having established the nature of binary systems and the 'scandalous' status of ambiguity, students may be asked to look at one of the basic human binaries, MASCULINITY : FEMININITY. They are asked to order qualities or characteristics which they find invested with female or male connotations in a table with two columns. Some 'typical' terms indicated by students are listed below:

FEMININITY : MASCULINITY

MAN : WOMAN

BOY : GIRL

MODEL TRAINS : DOLLS

MARS : VENUS

FASHION : SOCCER

As becomes quite obvious when the list turns to more concrete items, traditional binaries have become extremely dubious as categories for providing order and meaning for individuals. In fact, students will find the topic of gender construction one of the most apparent cultural areas in which conservative patterns are in the process of dissolution.

However, binary oppositions are still highly productive as generators of ideology, in the media as well as in everyday life. Having discussed binaries in two essential cultural fields (US : THEM for race, MALE : FEMALE for gender), students can turn to "My Son the Fanatic." As the story lends itself to such an approach, they can use the grid of binaries to equip themselves with a powerful interpretative tool to analyse other texts and cultural phenomena. Thus this interpretation of Kureishi's short story provides students with the basics of structuralist modes of interpretation. What is more, they learn about basic deconstructionist reading strategies. In this case, the deconstruction of meaning – of binaries – is presented by the text itself, by means of the closing words of the story, which dismantle all formerly clear-cut oppositions: "So, who is the fanatic now?" Reading and discussing the text, students could adhere to the following steps of deconstructive reading, which I have adapted from Charles E. Bressler's useful introduction *Literary Criticism*:[14]

> Discover the binary operations that govern "My Son the Fanatic" [if your students need help, ask them to start with West vs. East or father vs. son].
>
> Describe the values, concepts, and ideas beyond these operations.
>
> How does the text reverse the present binary operations?
>
> Does the text dismantle previously held worldviews?
>
> Does the text favour one of the two perspectives or levels of meaning?
>
> Is the message of the text, as true deconstructionists would have it, the following: "Allow the meaning of the text to be undecidable"?

A more abstract pattern of the binary logic at work in "My Son the Fanatic" might resemble the following oppositions:

FATHER : SON

MODERN : TRADITIONAL

ASSIMILATION : SEPARATION

WESTERN VALUES : TRADITIONAL VALUES

"ANYTHING GOES" : FUNDAMENTALISM

INDIVIDUALISM : COLLECTIVISM

This apparently neat pattern is, of course, suddenly disrupted by the following opposition:

---

[14] Charles E. Bressler, *Literary Criticism: An Introduction to Theory and Practice* (1994; Upper Saddle River NJ: Prentice Hall, 2003): 131.

To take this activity one step further and to highlight the 'marginalized' voices in this text, it could be useful to ask students to elaborate on another inherent, yet less obvious binary in the story: MEN : WOMEN. The pattern would look like this:

$$
\begin{array}{cc}
\text{PARVEZ} & \text{MOTHER / WIFE} \\
: \quad \text{MEN} : \text{WOMEN} & : \\
\text{ALI} & \text{BETTINA}
\end{array}
$$

With regard to this pattern of juxtapositions, 'Western' and 'Eastern' attitudes towards masculinity and femininity can be discussed. Finally, the role of women as the (in the case of Parvez's wife 'suppressed') voice of the Other can be discerned as one of the strategies of the text to create meaning – there seems to be noa way out of the double bind of binary oppositions, even if a text deconstructs one pair of them.

5.   Taking Kureishi "Off the Page": Sculpting, Tableaux and Working with Cue Cards

Interpreting short stories, novels, and films is often the only way of dealing with them in the classroom. There is, however, an alternative, additional way of working with texts – taking them *off the page*. Asking students to write scripts from a non-dramatic text, act out or perform, is often an excellent way of creating emotional responses. In addition, cohesion and cooperation in a group are fostered. Students do not necessarily have to engage with a complete literary text, but could be encouraged to choose a pivotal scene to work with. "Act it out or just do it!" – this is Albert Rau's recommendation for getting students involved in drama-related activities.[15] Of the many choices of what to do with literary texts *in action*, two will be suggested here: sculpting or creating frozen tableaux, and acting with the aid of cue cards.[16] A scene

---

[15] Albert Rau, "Short Texts in Action – More than Action in the Classroom," *Der fremdsprachliche Unterricht Englisch* 42.6 (1999): 7.

[16] A useful introduction to drama techniques is offered by *Drama Techniques in Language Learning: A Resource Book of Communication Activities for Language Teachers*, ed. Alan Maley & Alan Duff (Cambridge Handbooks for Language Teachers; Cambridge: Cambridge UP, 1983).

from "My Son the Fanatic" which lends itself to such forms of dramatization is the "restaurant episode" (SF 155–59), which in the story is narrated by Parvez in retrospect. In this scene, father and son face each other, with their differences and conflicts coming to a head. Controversial issues such as alcohol, pork, gambling, drugs, prostitutes, working to achieve a better life for one's child, obedience to parents, patriotism (or love of England), praying, the *jihad* etc. are tackled, with both sides defending their positions. As some of the arguments are only reported in indirect speech and some issues of the debate are just hinted at in the passage, students are asked to fill in the arguments in this 'standoff' between fundamentalist son and westernized father revolving around Ali's accusation of his father: "You are too implicated in Western civilisation" (SF 157). The staging of the following activities encourages students to get involved in the controversial debate about opposing value systems.

Activity 1: Turning the restaurant scene from
"My Son the Fanatic" into a tableau

Frozen tableaux or sculpting scenes enhance students' understanding of literary texts. As Albert Rau has pointed out, students can visualize the scene depicted by taking on the roles of the characters and can create character constellations by interpreting the relationships between the protagonists involved; in order to create a composite picture expressing all the features and relations of the characters, students need detailed knowledge, which suggests that this task should be tackled after the text has already been dealt with in some detail in class.[17] Working with "My Son the Fanatic," a number of 'frozen tableau' activities can be put into practice. All exercises should avoid contortions, as students must be able to hold their pose for a minute or so.

a) *First activity involving one 'sculptor'*: The teacher asks his students: "We need someone to shape us into a picture." A volunteer comes forward. "Right, you may bring the characters into your sculpture in any order." The volunteer decides who will represent Ali and Parvez, Bettina, and Parvez's nameless wife (Ali's mother). No one may speak and the characters must be physically loose and pliable. The sculptor moulds them into the image by placing them in the group, curling a little finger here, tilting a head there, turning the corner of one character's mouth, etc. Then students discuss what this sculpture re-

---

[17] Rau, "Short Texts in Action," 7.

veals about the individual character's personality and the relationship between the characters.

b) *Second activity involving more 'sculptors'*: No sculptor is chosen, but the
students enter the tableau, one at a time. They themselves decide which character from the text they represent. They may 'sculpt' any alterations they may
wish to those already assembled. Again, there must be no spoken instructions
or requests; everything must be sculpted.

c) *Third activity, using tableaux based on quotations*: Students are sent off in
pairs (Ali, Parvez) or in groups of four (including Bettina and mother/wife)
with their texts to choose a significant quotation from the restaurant scene
(for instance, when Ali rejects alcohol, "But it is forbidden", SF 156). After
careful discussion of the line, students must find a physical way of presenting
it to the rest of the group, who will try to guess the actual quotation.

d) *Fourth activity, speaking tableau*: After activities one and/or two, the
students describe how they feel about being the characters they represent.
They also describe how they feel towards the other characters of the tableau.

Activity 2: Re-enacting the restaurant scene from
"My Son the Fanatic"with the help of cue cards

Using cue cards could be a useful method of furthering students' skills in
improvisation and impromptu speech in a foreign language. It is a sort of
'guided task' during which students respond to stimuli and create, as in this
case, an exchange of opinions and ideas. The restaurant scene from "My Son
the Fanatic" would seem to be an ideal scenario for such an exercise, as father
and son confront each other with conflicting opinions, ranging from concrete
things (drink, pork etc.) to abstract ideas (attitudes towards women, religion
etc.). Students may be asked to make a list of the 'bones of contention' which
are bound to come up during such a confrontation – apart from the matters
mentioned in the text. Then they act out the confrontation. Two students sit
down at the table; other students may remain standing behind them, providing
them with cues and prompts or acting as Bettina and mother/wife. Then the
'waiter' hands the actors cue cards – each time 'Ali' or 'Parvez' voices his or
her opinion on the subject-matter presented to them. To help students slip into
their roles, it is advisable to start with tangible, actual things first and then go
on to more abstract matters. The goal is to make students 'slip into a role' and
present opinions on a range of issues in a consistent manner. Here we have a
debating society of sorts, but with a difference. Cue cards could first prompt
responses on alcohol, pork, cigarettes, Western movies, whores, or amenities
of Western life-styles. Then they could elicit responses to the father's plans

for his son: school, stereo-equipment, VCR, computers, girlfriend, sports, or college. Increasingly, the conversation could turn to general issues such as assimilation vs. separation, or fitting in vs. fundamentalism. Students should also be encouraged to find an ending to this performance, culminating in reconciliation or separation. After the performance, students should discuss not only the pros and cons of the arguments presented, but also how *they* felt about this performance. Did it create more tolerance? Did it reconfirm existing prejudices? They might also go on to speculate about Ali's reasons for becoming a fundamentalist – which are only hinted at in the text.

In sum, Hanif Kureish's oeuvre is a treasure trove of up-to-date material on multicultural Britain. His narratives, deeply ingrained in popular culture and taking into account the reading and viewing habits of our visual age, provide excellent opportunities and stimuli not only for more traditional ways of textual analysis but also for activities which are geared towards furthering oral, communicative, performative, and emotional skills.

WORKS CITED

Bressler, Charles E. *Literary Criticism: An Introduction to Theory and Practice* (1994; Upper Saddle River NJ: Prentice Hall, 2003).

Hartley, John. *Communication, Cultural and Media Studies: The Key Concepts* (London & New York: Routledge, 2002).

Kipling, Rudyard. *Selected Poetry*, ed. Craig Raine (Harmondsworth: Penguin, 1992).

——. *The Jungle Book* (1894; Oxford: Oxford UP, 2007).

Kureishi, Hanif. *The Black Album* (1995; London: Faber & Faber, 2000).

——. *The Body and Seven Stories* (London: Faber & Faber, 2002).

——. *The Buddha of Suburbia* (London: Faber & Faber, 2000).

——. *Gabriel's Gift* (London & Boston MA: Faber & Faber, 2001).

——. *Intimacy and Other Stories* (London & Boston MA: Faber & Faber, 2001).

——. *Love in a Blue Time* (1997; London & Boston MA: Faber & Faber, 1998).

——. *Midnight All Day* (1999; London & Boston MA: Faber & Faber, 2000).

——. *My Beautiful Laundrette: A Screenplay*, ed. Merle Tönnies & Claus–Ulrich Viol (1986; Stuttgart: Reclam, 1999).

——. "My Son the Fanatic" (1994), in *Many Voices – Many Cultures: Multicultural British Short Stories*, ed. Barbara Korte & Claudia Sternberg (1994; Stuttgart: Reclam, 1997): 147–65.

Maley, Alan, & Alan Duff, ed. *Drama Techniques in Language Learning: A Resource Book of Communication Activities for Language Teachers* (Cambridge Handbooks for Language Teachers; Cambridge: Cambridge UP, 1983).

Mason, David. *Race and Ethnicity in Modern Britain* (1995; Oxford: Oxford UP, 2000).

Nünning, Ansgar. "Literatur ist, wenn das Lesen wieder Spaß macht!" *Der fremdsprachliche Unterricht Englisch* 27.3 (1997): 4–13.

Rau, Albert. "Short Texts in Action: More than Action in the Classroom," *Der fremdsprachliche Unterricht Englisch* 42.6 (1999): 4–11.

Stierstorfer, Klaus. "Literatur und interkulturelle Kompetenz," in *Interkulturelle Kompetenz: Theorie und Praxis des fremdsprachlichen Unterrichts*, ed. Laurenz Volkmann,
Klaus Stierstorfer & Wolfgang Gehring (Tübingen: Gunter Narr, 2002): 119–41.

Teske, Doris. *Cultural Studies: GB: Anglistik – Amerikanistik* (Berlin: Cornelsen, 2002).

Volkmann, Laurenz. "Universal Truths or Ethnic Peculiarities? On Tensions Inherent in the
Reception of Post-Colonial and Minority Literature," in *Intercultural Encounters: Studies
in English Literatures – Essays Presented to Rüdiger Ahrens on the Occasion of His
Sixtieth Birthday*, ed. Heinz Antor & Kevin Cope (Heidelberg: Winter, 1999): 131–52.

——. "Interkulturelle Kompetenz als neues Paradigma der Literaturdidaktik? Über-
legungen mit Beispielen der postkolonialen Literatur und Minoritätenliteratur," in *Wie ist
Fremdverstehen lehr- und lernbar? Vorträge aus dem Graduiertenkolleg "Didaktik des
Fremdverstehens"*, ed. Lothar Bredella et al. (Tübingen: Gunter Narr, 2000): 164–90.

❮❖❯

A New Dialogue at the Periphery?
— Teaching Postcolonial African, Black American, and Indian Writings in India

KANAKA BASHYAM SANKARAN

I

HAVING TAUGHT ENGLISH as a second language and English literature for more than twenty-five years now as an English teacher at university level, I have followed the historical development of these literatures from a defensive and hesitant beginning to their current state, where they have gained acceptance and respectability and have come to occupy an important place in the curriculum for English studies in our universities.

Before the late 1960s, English literary studies as a subject of specialization at universities meant learning only classical English literature, the social and literary history of England providing a backdrop. Initial academic debates regarding the status of New English Literatures in the realm of English literature had to do with, for example, the legitimacy of using English in a non-English context and questions of readership and nomenclature. University bodies responsible for formulating syllabi were generally disinclined to include these literatures as part of the university curriculum. After a lot of deliberation and sustained efforts on the part of some scholars in this area, a hesitant beginning was made in the late 1960s when what was then called 'Commonwealth Literature' was made part of the university curriculum. With regard to Indian writing, initially the three doyens, R.K. Narayan, Raja Rao, and Mulk Raj Anand, were placed on pedestals and looked upon as the only writers worthy of study. Other genres such as poetry or drama were not taught, nor were later generations of writers included in the syllabus. In a sense, the development regarding the status and acceptance of these writings has gone through phases not unlike those observed in postcolonial literatures worldwide.

A lot of water has flowed down the Ganges since, and now we are so 'emancipated' as to offer special papers on Indian writing in English to students majoring in English literature. Most of us teach such courses, although we still do not have B.A. or M.A. programmes devoted exclusively to these literatures. Students are quite wary about majoring in these programmes because of the fear of being dubbed a scholar of 'only' these programmes – a symptom of the underlying prejudices and condescension. Still, we have come a long way. In fact, in the meantime, there are a few centres in the country which are entirely devoted to teaching and research in New English Literatures. In the late-1950s, the teacher and those being taught were chiefly occupied with the 'Indianness' or 'Africanness' of a prescribed text. I shall endeavour to show in the next section of my essay that this no longer holds true in our classes. This is because we currently deal with writings of a different character, which are perceived differently and evoke new responses from our students. Naturally, the pedagogic methodology has to adapt and conform to these new concerns and responses. Hence, new methodological approaches are indispensable for a proper understanding and appreciation of these works.

II

My own teaching experience has essentially been undergraduates in the age group of 17–20 years. This comprises two sub-groups: (1) the first learns so-called "General English," an obligatory second-language course at Indian universities in which English is taught with the help of literary texts; the programme is more a skills-oriented one. (2) The second group majors in English literature and is taught the entire range of concerns, including literary history and criticism. The first group, learning general English, is large and heterogeneous with regard to their language skills, aptitude, and social background. The second group, consisting of only female students in my college, is compact and exhibits a fairly high level of language proficiency. Nevertheless, one should bear in mind that the social backgrounds of the students would reflect a very broad spectrum characteristic of a multi-ethnic society in which significant class distinctions and educational standards exist. This social and cultural heterogeneity has a high degree of relevance in the context of pedagogy and critical methodology of teaching the New Literatures in English.

Traditional Hindu society was an extremely complex entity with respect to its polyethnicity and the myriad castes and sub-castes embedded in its fabric. Social organization was based on a one-to-one correspondence between castes and classes. With the introduction of English education and the variety of occupations that arose from it, this class structure came to be redefined, at least in urban India, as elsewhere in the world, in terms of education, occupation, and income. This not only made the entire caste–class correlation more complex, but in its wake ushered in a new urban middle class in Indian metropolitan regions. New laws were passed in post-Independence India, with a view to uplifting the so-called lower castes socially and economically. This loosened the caste–class correlation, enabling members of the lower castes to climb the social ladder by virtue of their education and occupation. Thus, the new urban middle class in India is more heterogeneous than before, since it now incorporates multiple strata of caste and class affiliations. If we accept the basic premise that modernization and globalization have shaken up societies worldwide, leading to new value systems, such changes have affected developing economics and traditional societies like India even more violently. Since the pace of modernization has been uneven in India and since traditional values, at least some of them, are still sacrosanct to most Indians, it is extremely difficult to define cultural identity even within a given social or ethnic group. In other words, a peculiar kind of multiculturalism prevails in the Indian context.

Our students are largely drawn from urban India with its innumerable shadings of caste–class affiliations. We have, for example, some students who have spent a few years abroad with their parents and some whose parents live abroad temporarily or permanently. We also have a small percentage of students who migrate from rural areas for the sake of higher education. It is interesting to observe that India also attracts students from Sri Lanka, Malaysia, and sometimes even Iran. These students (I will call them literature students from now on) possess both passive and active language skills, but are drawn from different social classes and religions and ethnic groups. Since caste affiliation still plays a dominant role in the upbringing and cultural background of these students, we see how multiculturalism of a peculiarly Indian kind or what I call cultural heterogeneity characterizes these groups.

III

I should now like to discuss teaching New Literatures and the responses they evoke from students in the context of the aforementioned heterogeneity. Our syllabi prescribe texts that cover a broad range of topics from different parts of the world. In the course of my long teaching career, I have come to realize that the cultural specificity of topics and their treatment are slowly breaking down. By this I mean that these literatures, viewed from a literary perspective, transcend national and sometimes even ethnic boundaries and address readers far beyond the indigenous society in which they are placed. This changing perception can be understood in terms of, or ascribed to, two significant developments in the postcolonial world, particularly in the last fifteen to twenty years. First, the current New English Literatures tend to be increasingly preoccupied with a realistic and socio-critical depiction of themes, of human destinies and predicaments (thus moving away from concerns that characterized these writings thirty years ago). Secondly, modernization and globalization have brought about enormous social and economic changes in postcolonial societies, producing a new Third-World generation of cosmopolitan readers and learners. Thus, the transcultural validity and appeal of the New English Literatures defies earlier classifications or categorizations such as African subject-matter or an Indian or black-American setting.

To put it more explicitly, if topics like decolonization, democratization, and conflicts between tradition and modernization had a relevance to the entire postcolonial world, one could argue that nepotism, social unrest among the poor and the underprivileged, women striving for emancipation, and the misery of slum-dwellers can no longer be dubbed as mere black-American reality. The reality of an employed mother demanding social recognition or resigning herself to its denial cannot be prescribed as specific or peculiar to a coloured woman. Similarly, the struggle of a working woman to combine career and family, as dealt with in Shashi Deshpande's novels and short stories, is not just an Indian problem. Likewise, Achebe's concern with racism in his novels and critical writings, or issues such as the persecution of minorities, tradition versus modernity, nostalgia about the demise of an old order, changing ethnicities and modes of femininity, and the validity of traditional norms and moral codes cannot be stamped as having currency only in an Indian or black-American setting. Nor can the representation of rural communities undergoing social and economic changes – as in Lamming's fiction – be confined to the Caribbean society of the 1960s. Indeed, all these issues are of relevance to all societies in a globalized world.

Thus, these texts address the students more directly than ever before owing to this sense of transcultural immediacy and validity. The term 'immediacy' implies that the literary experience lies at least partly, if not wholly, close to what the students can perceive themselves. If topics like the burden of colonialism, oppression through political and economic power, or conflicts arising between crumbling old and emerging new orders are perceived as generally relevant, the students are able to identify themselves even better with themes such as corruption, racism, and the predicament of women in societies undergoing rapid transformation where traditional values still hold. This is, however, not to deny or simplify the diversity of these writings as reflected in the modes of narration or the use of language. The students definitely need pedagogic help to perceive how subtle and delicate these elements are and to become aware of their significance for a comprehensive understanding and appreciation of the texts. Let me turn to the critical responses from our students on which our teaching methodology is based.

Since most of the texts prescribed are realistic fiction or drama, the initial reaction of the students is, predictably, to respond to the 'familiar' depicted in the text. Due to the cultural heterogeneity among the students, the proximity of the experience portrayed is bound to differ from student to student or from group to group. After the initial phase of subjective and spontaneous response, the students are helped by us to take cognizance of the subtle nuances underlying the broad multicultural context and transcultural validity of the texts. By examining the language or voice given to the protagonists and the endings of the plots, students try to discern how realistic the work is and what the artistic compulsions are, and to what extent, if any, the two elements are mingled. This sort of scrutiny provides a method for understanding or justifying endings or solutions of plots in stories. As a teacher, I have come across a number of interesting responses, which will be discussed briefly below in the context of critical methodology. While reading the texts, a certain 'tension' arises between the transcultural nature of the texts and their multicultural audience. This tension, peculiar to the New Literatures in English, stimulates an interaction that enables the readers to perceive both their proximity to the texts and the diversity of the latter. This transcultural dialogue, I submit, is a new parameter in critical assessment, which occurs at two levels: among students and between students and the texts they read. This leads to the next step, of evaluating the degree of authenticity of the experience or episode depicted, which, in fact, constitutes the key to the understanding of the artistic message. These responses are partly tutored and party spontaneous.

In order to elicit a 'proper' response from the students they are taken through the following steps:

First, the subjective sense of familiarity is assessed by taking into account the social background of the writer and his/her work. In order to bridge the

gap between the student and a literary work that may contain elements that
are strange or alien, we give lectures on the socio-historical background of the
author and his/her work. We lay special emphasis in our lectures on aspects
of traditions and conventions as well as on the vocabulary and idiom used in
the text that are culture-specific and peculiar to the ethnic or dialectal register.
We notice time and again how the sensitivity to the experience depicted can
suffer if students are not well-informed about the socio-cultural background. I
have already alluded to the vast socio-cultural diversity among our students
that renders it a challenging task to make them receptive to the nuances of, for
example, African cultures. Although the secondary sources of reference in the
area of transcultural studies are meagre, we still strive to give our students
adequate guidance on how and where such materials may be found. As we
have a fairly good library in our college, we give a list of both primary and
secondary sources of materials the students ought to read before we start our
classroom discussions.

The actual discussion of the text starts with an exchange of initial impressions. Then we turn to an examination of the nature of realism – whether the
novel, short story or play reflects absolute adherence to social reality or
whether there is a mix of real and fictional elements. Here, the depiction of
the main plot and its resolution (which I term an ending) is discussed as well.
We try to see if the author is socio-critical while depicting reality or if he tries
to go beyond social reality by resorting to a radical or an ideal ending. As a
final step, the language or voice given to the central character is examined to
determine whether the author allows them to speak their mind and act accordingly or if they merely have the freedom to think but not to act according to
their expressed convictions. Time permitting, we also discuss whether there is
a social constraint on the part of the author not to venture beyond what is
socially permissible for his characters. Taking Achebe's two novels *Things
Fall Apart* and *A Man of the People*,[1] the students' initial reaction was that
the human predicament and the socio-cultural situation in postcolonial
Nigeria of the 1950s and 1960s were by no means peculiar to the African
continent. The nostalgia in the first of these novels about 'the good old times'
and the fear of 'a new global order' are authentic and can be extended to other
postcolonial societies as well, opined the students. However, they could not

---

[1] Chinua Achebe, *Things Fall Apart* (London: Heinemann, 1958); *A Man of the People*
(London: Heinemann, 1966).

understand the protagonist Okonkwo's consistent opposition to change and reform and his suicide. We had to repeatedly grapple with the special problems of a closed society like that of the Ibo people. Most of the students finally agreed with the view that Okonkwo's destiny was authentic, since Achebe's primary concern in the late-1950s after decolonization was a realistic documentation of Ibo society.

Identification with the protagonist Odili in *A Man of the People* and coming to terms with the political situation in Nigeria was easier for the students. They could see how the author once again resorts to a realistic portrayal of his society in the 1960s. It was apparent to the students that the problems encountered were not peculiar to Ibo society. The emergence of new power structures, abuse of power, corruption in politics, and declining moral standards are all characteristic of a society struggling to modernize itself. The destiny of Odili, his futile fight against all these evils, and the general tone of pathos and despair in the use of language were found 'real' and 'familiar'. In the light of this analysis, we discussed the following questions in the context of both Africa and India: the role of the educated in politics; the application of moral values in a slowly changing society; whether the views expressed in the novels have a localized 'black' significance or whether they could be extrapolated to India.

The theme of race and religious relations as projected in the short story "Debbie Go Home" (1961) by Alan Paton or in *The Interpreters* (1965) by Wole Soyinka visibly created 'the tension' referred to above and provoked a lot of discussion, since parallels were drawn to Indian society and its class affiliations and caste prejudices. In our reading of *Goa* (1970) by Asif Currimbhoy, the students compared the tragic end of Krishna, a Hindu, falling in love with Rose, a Christian, to the fate of the Muslim protagonist marrying a Christian girl in *The Interpreters*. But teaching Lorraine Hansberry's *A Raisin in the Sun* (1959) seemed particularly challenging because the cultural background in the play seemed inaccessible to our students. After several discussions, the students were helped to perceive the subtle differences between the nervous American coloured man and the self-confidence of the African coloured man. The students tried to see if the crucial black experience can be related to Indian history during the freedom movement. Some interesting questions that came up for consideration were:

1.   What kind of reader competence is required to comprehend texts that have a special multidimensional context like *Raisin in the Sun*?

2. Is there verbal deprivation in language that could betray the social class of a character?

3. Can theatre or drama bridge cultural barriers because it actively integrates language and literature in a way other genres cannot?

While reading Buchi Emecheta's *The Joys of Motherhood* (1979) and Asare Konadu's *A Woman in Her Prime* (1967), the students responded critically to the glorification of motherhood. They found the theme and its treatment very socio-critical and drew parallels with Indian fiction and society. Here radical or ideal solutions to the stories were worked out both in the language given to the female figure(s) and the ending. The way Nnu walks away from a childless marriage and commits to one that endows her with motherhood, the students said, was provokingly depicted. The subtle use of irony showed that the author was not only documenting a social reality but was also critical about it. The protagonist in *A Woman in Her Prime* suffers a childless marriage and obediently succumbs to several rituals as well as purification ceremonies to get rid of her barrenness, but is allowed to gain strength and courage in the course of the novel, until in the the end she is able to reject the stigma of childlessness and find fulfilment and happiness in her childless marriage. We had lively discussions regarding the use of language in the two novels and their endings. Whereas the ending in *The Joys of Motherhood* was perceived as purely realistic, that in *A Woman in Her Prime*, the students felt, bordered on utopia. In our subsequent discussions, we raised the argument that the use of language helped to establish the character of the protagonist in Konadu's novel without idealizing her, thus making the end realistic and plausible. The novel's message was that any change should come both from within and from without. As a student put it, any social change for women can only happen if women wanted it. We also discussed whether the author was questioning marriage and the status of women in African society and whether there are factors peculiar to their situation as African women.

When we began reading Shashi Deshpande's fiction it was striking to see how familiar and immediate the destiny of her protagonist was to our students even before the author's social background was known. Students found both Sarita of *The Dark Holds No Terrors* (1980) and Jaya of *That Long Silence* (1988) contemporary and socially authentic. The projection of an educated and employed woman feeling trapped in marriage and torn between her culturally conditioned need to be a wife and mother and her personal aspiration for autonomy and selfhood reflected the social and cultural reality of most of our students. Responding to the very aggressive and emancipatory language given to both Sarita and Jaya to voice their hopes, misgivings, and fears, most of the students said that they could identify with this female predicament as easily as they could with the endings in both the novels, in which these two women return to their families. However, some students felt that the final reversal to their roles as wives and mothers stood in contradiction to the way they were made to see their situation in the novel. An interesting question posed was if this ending had something to do with the fact that the author also belongs to the social class from which her figures are drawn.

I have tried to show how our pedagogy is based on a shift of emphasis in critical analysis from the conventional mode of exclusively assessing a work of art for its literary merits to assessing the same in its entire socio-ethnic and cultural contexts. The text is both a work of literary art and a socio-cultural document. Transcultural texts like those discussed above become interpretable only when one is able to unravel the text within its linguistic, ethnic, and anthropological frameworks. The decoded text carries with it the historical, political, and economic factors of its age. It is then redundant in my view to ask if literatures can be taught as if they were anthropological documents; instead, I would argue that these literatures can be used to teach both literature and anthropology.

WORKS CITED

Achebe, Chinua. *Things Fall Apart* (London: Heinemann, 1958).
———. *A Man of the People* (London: Heinemann, 1966).
Currimbhoy, Asif. *Goa* (Calcutta: Writer's Workshop, 1970).
Deshpande, Shashi. *The Dark Holds No Terrors* (1980; Penguin India, 1993).
———. *That Long Silence* (London: Virago, 1988).
Emecheta, Buchi. *The Joys of Motherhood* (London: Allison & Busby, 1979).
Hansberry, Lorraine. *A Raisin in the Sun* (1959; New York: Samuel French, 1988).
Konadu, Asare. *A Woman in Her Prime* (London: Heinemann, 1967).
Paton, Alan. *Debbie Go Home: Stories* (1961; Harmondsworth: Penguin, 1965): 7-22.
Soyinka, Wole. *The Interpreters* (London: André Deutsch, 1965).

◄❖►

Look, See, and Say

— Photographs of Africa in a Cultural Perspective

DETLEV GOHRBANDT AND GISELA FEURLE

> But you must surely concede that at a certain level we speak, and therefore write, like everyone else. Otherwise we would all be speaking and writing private languages. It is not absurd – is it? – to concern oneself with what people have in common rather than with what sets them apart.[1]

---

[1] J.M. Coetzee, *Elizabeth Costello* (London: Secker & Warburg, 2003): 8.

I: Transcultural Communication, Poetics and Viewer Response in Photography

DETLEV GOHRBANDT

1.   Africa in Newspaper Photographs

THE STUDY OF PHOTOGRAPHY, like that of any other symbolic medium, raises problems in hermeneutics, aesthetics, and ethics. The theme of Africa compounds these problems by adding historical, political, and economic issues. My perspective, that of a non-African student of postcolonial culture in Africa, who is at the same time a language teacher (of future language teachers), may seem to complicate matters still further, but will perhaps allow me to focus on selected aspects of the overall topic.

I shall be addressing, first, three general questions about photography, then three specific ones about photographs of Africa: What is a photograph and how does it represent? What activities are involved in looking at or reading a photograph? What is the relation between visual image and verbal text? How do (some) photographs represent Africa? In what way is photography transcultural and/or culture-specific? How do photographs tell what needs to be told about Africa, and how can I tell if it is necessary? This final question will always be in the background as I investigate the others, even as I remind myself that the quest for the grounds of truth or authenticity may be misunderstood and could lead me into all kinds of traps, like naturalism or essentialism, or the arrogation of authority. I do want to say that this quest seems to me necessary in face of the many untruthful, misleading, and inauthentic pictures of Africa that have played such an important part in the development of colonialist ideology and have deeply tainted the Western mind with false images.[2] If we can identify (as we so often do) such a thing as the inauthentic, should there not also be something we can class as authentic?

With this in mind, let us look at a recent photograph from my local newspaper, which, though not blatantly stereotyped, is fairly representative of the way Africa is presented to us every morning in the newspapers and every evening on TV.[3]

Photograph no. 1 "Argungu Fishing Festival." AFP.

The AFP photograph shows a scene from the Argungu fishing festival held annually in mid-March in the town of Argungu in Kebbi State, Northern Nigeria. One will recognize a few things, like the fishermen and their hand nets, and be uncertain about others, such as the big round gourds, open at the top, which presumably serve as pails. The context is invisible: namely, that the festival dates from 1934, when it was organized "in an attempt to broker peace" between the Sultan of Sokoto and the Emir of Argungu, whose people,

---

[2] The desire to correct this false image of Africa is the driving impulse behind Chinua Achebe & Robert Lyons, *Another Africa* (New York: Doubleday Anchor, 1998).

[3] "Petri Heil in Afrika," *Saarbrücker Zeitung* (22 March 2004): A6.

the Kabawa, the sultan had been trying to subjugate. In 2004, the festival is being promoted as part of a drive to attract tourists to the area, and it coincides with the bicentenary of Dan Usman Fodio's *jihad* of 1804. I derive this information from a Nigerian paper, the *Weekly Trust* of Kaduna, as available on the internet,[4] and much the same information is given by the *Saarbrücker Zeitung*. This, however, adds three characteristic touches: first, the photograph is presented on a "News of the World" page without any further African context. Second, the editors have added an untranslatable German title, "Petri Heil in Afrika" (i.e. 'Hail Peter in Africa'), based on a traditional German formula wishing successful fishing that refers to the Apostle Peter, who was originally a fisherman. And third, the descriptive caption closes with the following remark: "A tradition which offers a welcome change in this abjectly poor African country." So three familiar strategies are involved: first, the photograph is largely decontextualized, as is so often the case with the snippets of news we are given about Africa; second, the "Petri Heil" title assimilates the decidedly foreign image to a cosy German cultural context, imposes a Christian frame of reference on an image of Muslim culture, while implying a dubious transcultural community of ideas which Clifford Geertz called "a lowest common-denominator view of humanity."[5] Finally, the caption, using the rather trivial idea that all human beings need a bit of relaxation, perpetuates the cliché of African misery. I shall expand on the issue of transcultural understanding later and only want to suggest here, as a word of warning, that in its naive form it has a potential for falsification, for misrepresenting its ostensible subject. It seems to me that this photograph, presented in this way, actually deludes the unwary newspaper reader into a pleasantly vague sense of understanding and empathy, while actually (and even more pleasantly) confirming his prejudices about 'poor naked Africans' using primitive tools.

---

[4] "Argungu, Revival of a Grand Fishing Festival," *Weekly Trust*, http://allafrica.com /stories/printable/200403150523.html (accessed 5 May 2008). The photograph is accessible on the *Sydney Morning Herald Online* under www.smh.com.au/ftimages/2004/03/21 /1079823237709.html (accessed 5 May, 2008), where the caption is simply "Gone fishing … participants at the Argungu fishing festival in Kebbi State, northern Nigeria."

[5] Clifford Geertz, *The Interpretation of Cultures: Selected Essays* (1973; London: Fontana, 1993): 43.

2. The Cultural and Transcultural in Photography and Writing: Two Pictures of Africa at School

According to David MacDougall, the Australian ethnographic filmmaker and theorist in visual anthropology, there is a basic difference in the way cinema and photography on the one hand and writing on the other relate to and affect the reality of what they aim to record: "Pictures and writing produce two quite different accounts of human existence."[6] Writing, being tied to language, tends to representations of general and abstract ideas, and is further limited, by being tied to a single language, to what that language can express. Writing tends to concentrate selectively on certain particulars that contribute to an argument (i.e. ethnographic writing's aim to identify difference), but often omits or reduces "many sensory details that might shock or repel us if we were to confront them directly" (246). In writing, "the ordinary features and substructure" of a scene are mostly not spelled out, but given by way of implication, as something that the reader can fill in on the basis of his or her own experience. Pictures are quite a different matter, though a rather paradoxical one: they are, MacDougall says, "staggeringly particular and indiscriminate in detail, but they constantly reiterate the general forms in which the particular is contained" (246). In other words, pictures show specific details, but always (or almost always) place these within general visual and verbal schemes. This coexistence of details, in part selected and in part accidental, and general thematic schemes can be observed in almost any photograph of a topic we are familiar with – for example, Peter Magubane's "Pupils at Lofentse Girls' High School, Orlando East" (overleaf).

This shows all kinds of intentional and accidental particularities – girls from Soweto, with different faces and hair-does, dressed in their blue school uniforms, standing in a quadrangle of their school, and led in morning prayer by one of their teachers. Compared with the details of any British or American school assembly, some of these particulars look familiar and some express difference, a difference modified by the commonalities in which the particulars are embedded: the concepts of school, school assembly, prayer, uniform, etc. A closer look reveals that teacher and girls are clapping their hands to some unheard but imaginable rhythm and melody, and if we recognize this clapping to be a difference, we will refer to practices of clapping in

---

[6] David MacDougall, "Transcultural Cinema," in *Transcultural Cinema*, ed. & intro. Lucien Taylor (Princeton N J : Princeton U P, 1998): 246.

our own cultures and be able to attribute some sense to what we see, if only in an approximative manner. Thus, as MacDougall says, "photographs and films, by reiterating the familiar and recognizable, constantly transcend and reframe their own specificity" (245). Photographs and films, he says, show "the visible continuities of human life" (245)and it is these that we understand across boundaries.

Photograph No. 2: Peter Magubane, "Pupils at Lofentse Girls' High School, Orlando East." Photo reproduced from Peter Magubane, *Soweto*, texts by Charlene Smith (London: Struik, 2001): 64.

The concept of boundaries can serve to remind us that we come to most photographs, especially of foreign parts, from the distance of our own particular time and place, so that looking at a photograph does not just mean travelling from our place and time to that place and time but being in two places and times at once. These visible continuities linking different places and times, as MacDougall says, run counter to anthropology's traditional focus on cultural difference and distinctiveness. Thus, when a photographic image simultaneously marks difference and elides it in favour of similarity, we find two senses of the transcultural: first, of crossing cultural boundaries of place and time in order to focus on the commonalities and continuities of human living; and, second, of "defying such boundaries" (245)by foregrounding their tenuous and permeable nature, and pleading that comparative judgements on the value of what we find beyond the boundary should be deferred in favour of an attitude of empathy.

The distinctions MacDougall makes are important for workers in the field of the new anglophone cultures because they suggest that as a result of our dominantly philological training and Western culture's privileging of the written we may in the past have been relying altogether too much on the slanted evidence of written records. It is no doubt a fertile approach to link the imperialist project with textuality, with the colonizers' strategy of writing and reading stories and, still more, stories of exploration and appropriation, as well as inscribing Western claims and institutions in other worlds, but that does not justify the widespread neglect of the various visual modes of symbolization – drawing, engraving, photography – that were regularly employed to support the texts, add documentary evidence, and attract viewers as well as readers.[7] Perhaps it was the very popularity of certain illustrated accounts of Empire, such as J.W. Buel's *Heroes of the Dark Continent* of 1890, "Illustrated with 500 of the Grandest, Most Beautiful and Wonderful Engravings," that helped to cause this disparagement.[8] Boehmer's emphasis on textuality, of course, derives from Edward Said, whose "constructionist frame"[9] is evident when he discusses at length the narrative structures and strategies of Edwards William Lane's *Manners and Customs of the Modern Egyptians* (1836) without even a passing glance at the role of photography in Lane's work.[10] In the case of sub-Saharan Africa, with no indigenous writing sys-

---

[7] See Elleke Boehmer's chapter on "Imperialism and Textuality" in her *Colonial and Postcolonial Literature: Migrant Metaphors* (Oxford & New York: Oxford UP, 1995): 12–59, in which every single reference to visuality is metaphoric.

[8] An illustration from this popular book (Richmond VA: B.F. Johnson, 1890) is used by Indira Ghose to open her discussion of "Conrad's *Heart of Darkness* and the Anxiety of Empire" in *Being/s in Transit: Travelling, Migration, Dislocation*, ed. Liselotte Glage (Cross/Cultures 41, ASNEL Papers 5; Amsterdam & Atlanta GA: Rodopi, 2000): 93–110. As usual, no attention is paid to the illustration as a visual artefact.

[9] Edward Said, "In Conversation with Neeladri Bhattacharya, Suvir Kaul, and Ania Loomba," in *Relocating Postcolonialism*, ed. David Theo Goldberg & Ato Quayson (Oxford: Blackwell, 2002): 11.

[10] See Edward W. Said, *Orientalism* (1978; Harmondsworth: Penguin, 1991): esp. 158–66. On Lane's cooperation with photographers, see Anne Krauter, "Imagination und Dokument: Die eigene Kultur im photographischen Abbild der fremden Kultur," in *Exotische Welten, Europäische Phantasien*, ed. Herrmann Pollig (Stuttgart: Institut für Auslandsbeziehungen/Württembergischer Kunstverein/Cantz, 1987): 202.

tems but many forms of visual culture, this neglect of the visual is particularly strange.

I would like to follow up these ideas on verbal and visual representation and underline the political significance of photography in imperialist discourse via another school picture, which stands in a peculiar relation to its accompanying text. In order to appreciate the difference between looking and reading I will consider these activities separately, artificial though this may be.

Photograph No. 3: Ilse Steinhoff, *Afrika wartet*,
ed. Joachim Fernau, Kurt Kayser & Johannes Paul
(Potsdam: Rütten & Loening, 1942): 98.

An African girl in a pretty cotton frock is shown in a half-figure close-up, so that her expression of intense concentration dominates the picture. Another girl is just visible on her left, and in the row behind them two boys can be seen. They are all practising writing on slates, the kind of slates my generation learned to write on, but which in Germany gave way to plastic boards in the 1960s and have long since been replaced by exercise books. In Britain, slates fell into disuse much earlier, around the end of the nineteenth century. Unfortunately, I cannot quite make out what the girl has written on her slate, but I can tell that she is tracing the letters very carefully, perhaps copying

them from the blackboard. What we are being shown, it seems, in this ele-
mentary-school classroom, through synecdoche and metonymy, is how well
the virtues of industry and application augur for Africa's future. The accompanying text reads:

> Should blacks be educated? English colonial policy answers this question by train-
> ing black doctors and lawyers and so creating the direst problems. An organic
> development of native culture makes sense, but it is a long way from reading and
> writing to black academics.[11]

The photograph was taken by Ilse Steinhoff in German South-West Africa
around 1940 and published in 1942 in a volume called *Afrika wartet* ('Africa
is waiting'), a title implying that Africa was waiting for the Germans to return
and lead it into the right kind of future. In this instance, it is striking how the
commentary overturns the picture, invades it, to borrow a phrase from Victor
Burgin.[12] Looking at it sixty years after, can we on the evidence of our eyes
come to the conclusion that this is as far as education needs to go for African
children? Through images and texts we have learned that exactly the opposite
applies, and so the texts that any one of us might append to the photograph,
however they might differ from each other, would be more or less unanimous
politically. This points to a very difficult relation between picture and text,
one quite different from caricature, for example, where the artist is usually responsible for the caption and will make sure that drawing and wording support each other. Many photographers seem to be extremely wary of the word
and offer only very reduced captions, sometimes none at all. Others, like
Peter Magubane in his *Soweto*, have a professional writer (Charlene Smith)
supply the texts, or, like David Goldblatt and Nadine Gordimer, pool their
respective resources without themselves making direct connections between
picture and text. In an interview with Okwui Enwezor, Goldblatt responds to

---

[11] The German original reads: "Soll der Schwarze gebildet werden? Die englische
Kolonialpolitik beantwortet diese Frage, indem sie schwarze Ärzte und Rechtsanwälte
heranbildet und damit die schwierigsten Probleme schafft. Eine organische Fortentwicklung
der Eingeborenenkultur ist vernünftig, aber vom Schreiben und Lesen bis zum schwarzen
Akademiker ist noch ein weiter Weg." See *Afrika wartet: Ein kolonialpolitisches Bildbuch*,
ed. Joachim Fernau, Kurt Kayser & Johannes Paul (Potsdam: Rütten & Loening, 1942): 98.
[12] Victor Burgin, "Seeing Sense," in *The End of Art Theory* (1986), quoted by W.J.T.
Mitchell, *Picture Theory: Essays on Verbal and Visual Representation* (Chicago & London:
U of Chicago P, 1994): 282.

a description of his captions as "very precise and elaborate" with a careful distinction:

> DG: I'm sorry you regard them as elaborate. Precise, yes; all photographs come out of a context, and because of the nature of most of my subjects, I think it's important to explain something of that. My photographs are not self-contained. I favour brevity but try to impart what I regard as critical information.[13]

Fully self-contained photographs would be transcultural, but photographs of locally specific subjects cannot produce meaning fully and entirely out of themselves, except perhaps for contemporary and local viewers, and so they require verbal supplementation. This "critical information" remedies a want, but simply by being supplementary also produces a surplus and an instability, in that a single picture can produce a large number of texts which may be different and contradictory.[14] The supplementation answering to a want is a case of what Bernhard Waldenfels has called "reciprocal excess" (*wechselseitiger Überschuß*):[15] i.e. the text goes beyond the picture and reveals the insufficiency of the visual, and, vice versa, "the objects [that] images record, and certainly many aspects of social experience, are not finally translatable."[16] For Mieke Bal, it is this "impurity" of the visual, specified as the act of looking, in which seeing and saying are "mutually permeable," that properly constitutes the discipline of visuality, or visual cultural studies.[17] It is a consequence of photography's fertile impurity that picture and text should not be subordinated to each other;[18] in particular, the visual should not be abused as

---

[13] Okwui Enwezor, "Matter and Consciousness: An Insistent Gaze From a Not Disinterested Photographer," interview with David Goldblatt, in Goldblatt, *David Goldblatt Fifty-One Years* (exh. cat.; Barcelona: Museu d'Art Contemporani de Barcelona/Actar, 2001): 39.

[14] The instability caused by the captions changing in different books of Goldblatt's is an interesting issue; see Michael Godby description of Goldblatt's practice of editing his work depending on whether it was to be shown in exhibitions, magazines or monographs ("David Goldblatt: The Personal and the Political," in Goldblatt, *David Goldblatt Fifty-One Years*: 414.

[15] Bernhard Waldenfels, *Der Spielraum des Verhaltens* (Frankfurt: Suhrkamp, 1980): 90.

[16] MacDougall, "Transcultural Cinema," 266.

[17] Mieke Bal, "Visual Essentialism and the Object of Visual Culture," *Journal of Visual Culture* 2.1 (2003): 9.

[18] See Bal, "Visual Essentialism...," 10, for a critique of false hierarchies and the corrective idea that "far from the photographs illustrating the text or the words 'explicating' the

a mere occasion for language, as all too often happens, whether in the class-room or in the worlds of reviewing and criticism. Ethically speaking, a verbal commentary or narrative should not be produced without a sense of responsi-bility for its origin in looking (reflecting the photograph's same origin) and without an awareness that, whatever is said about it, the picture continues to exist and engender new meanings beyond any yet put into words.[19] Finally, let us note that in none of these photographs do the people portrayed ever speak for themselves. They are voiceless, have been kept voiceless by a poli-tical system, which the photographer may resist, but whose strategy of un-voicing he unwittingly colludes with, as do the viewers who take it upon themselves to speak unbidden for the mute image. But since the silenced voices are unlikely ever to be recovered, the photographer's and the viewer's captions and commentaries will have to stand in for them as best they can, always ready to revoke themselves, or, as in the case of the text accompany-ing Steinhoff's school photograph, to be revoked by later viewers.

3. Photography as a Medium: Two Photographs of Beds

How does a photograph work as a medium with its own characteristic ways of meaning? We must not regard a photograph as just another form of text, which can be 'read' in the same way as a newspaper report or a short story. Taking Roland Barthes as our guide, the first thing to bear in mind is that "a specific photograph [...] is never distinguished from its referent (from what it represents), or at least it is not immediately or generally distinguished from its referent."[20] Barthes refers to the characteristic fact that every photograph re-mains tied to what it shows, quite unlike a description in words, and initially just means what it shows because this adheres to it. Usually when we look at a photograph, we do not really look at the photograph itself, at the medium,

---

images, the simultaneity between the photographs and images and their appeal to the viewer's entire body [i.e. all his senses] operates by means of the enigmatic discrepancies between these two main registers."

[19] See J. Hillis Miller, *The Ethics of Reading* (Wellek Library Lectures; New York: Columbia UP, 1987): 4–5, 8, 9–10, and esp. 43. When Miller defines the "ethical moment" as "not a matter of response to a thematic content asserting this or that idea about morality" but rather as "a much more fundamental 'I must' responding to the language of literature in itself" (9–10), he is very close to Barthes' distinction between *studium* and *punctum*.

[20] Roland Barthes, *Camera Lucida: Reflections on Photography*, tr. Richard Howard (*Chambre Claire*, 1980; tr. London: Vintage, 1993): 5.

but look through it – as if it were transparent – at the referent, and as we do so
we tend to assume that we are experiencing this referent in an unmediated
form in all its reality. This is not wholly an illusion, since the peculiar effect
of a photograph vitally depends on this seeming presence of the real, but it is
illusory nonetheless if it seduces the viewer into forgetting that the photograph never shows reality entire. As John Berger insists, a photograph shows
a particular detail at a particular moment, "cuts across time and discloses a
cross-section of the event or events which were developing at that instant."[21]
This relation to time causes what Berger calls "the shock of discontinuity":[22]
i.e. the separation or isolation of the photograph's moment from the flow of
time before and after. Both the adherence of the referent and the temporal discontinuity of the single photograph remind us that photography uses processes of selection, omission, focusing, emphasis etc. which are even more
radical than those that writing employs. Thus we must be alert to what is, out
of necessity, absent from the photograph. We have to be prepared to search
for it via the traces it has left and to ask what its absence means.

We have seen that there is more to a photograph than the visual. A second
point that Barthes makes with respect to this supplementarity of the photograph (as I will call it, using a term from Derrida's *Grammatology*)[23] is that a
photograph "is verbalized at the very moment it is perceived; or better still: it
is perceived only when verbalized," because its referent so firmly adheres to
it.[24] Furthermore, since a verbalization adopts an attitude of judgement or "all
language accommodates itself to things," the verbalized picture "exists socially only when immersed in at least a primary connotation."[25] In other words,
the moment we look at a photograph we speak *of* it and *to* it and *about* it and
thus supplement it with at least three levels of speech, assigning meanings
that are not there in the picture. Looking is literally response, and response is

---

[21] John Berger & Jean Mohr, *Another Way of Telling* (1982; New York: Vintage,
1995): 120.

[22] Berger and Mohr, *Another Way of Telling*, 86.

[23] Defining 'supplement', Peggy Kamuf says that it "floats between its two senses of that
which is added on and that which substitutes for and supplants"; Jacques Derrida, *A Derrida Reader: Between the Blinds*, ed. & intro. Peggy Kamuf (New York: Harvester Wheatsheaf, 1991): 33.

[24] Roland Barthes, "The Photographic Message," in *The Responsibility of Forms: Critical Essays on Music, Art, and Representation*, tr. Richard Howard (1985; Berkeley & Los
Angeles: U of California P, 1991): 17.

[25] Barthes, "The Photographic Message," 17.

supplementary. Because our responses are supplements and because first responses are so rapid and culturally predetermined, they always contain a
margin of error. These are some of the main points Barthes' poetics of photography makes about medium, reference, and verbalization.

I would now like to apply Barthes' ideas to a fourth photograph of Africa,
this time by the South African photographer David Goldblatt.

Photograph no. 4: David Goldblatt, "Miners' Bunks,"
from David Goldblatt & Nadine Gordimer, *Lifetimes: Under Apartheid*
(New York: Alfred A. Knopf, 1986).

As one looks at this picture, one cannot help asking: what does it represent?
The close-up photograph, taken in the relentless bright light of the Witwaters-
rand, at first sight shows nothing but an almost abstract repetitive geometrical
pattern of light and dark, from which one can with difficulty infer depth in a
three-dimensional structure. No living thing, neither animal nor vegetable, is
visible; there is nothing to serve as a measure of size. Here discontinuity is
such that reference does *not* seem to adhere. Many photographs, through their
subject-matter and by the use of camera techniques, allow us to infer sounds,
smells, and the feel of material surfaces, but here there is a bleak and silent
formality. Describing the picture in this way, we are taking the problem of absence into account, the absence of life, of use, of significance. Looking at the

photograph insistently, not giving in to the temptation to look away and turn to something more easily rewarding (which is what tends to happen in an exhibition or when leafing through an anthology), this tentative, groping description of the photograph is undertaken in the hope of producing meaning. As Goldblatt himself says, "for as long as a building or structure is, it may 'tell' something of the needs, imperatives and values of those who put it there, of those who used it, and of the ideologies upon which their beliefs and lives may have been contingent."[26] The photographed structures are therefore metonymic of meanings we have yet to discover, meanings which lie in what Barthes calls "the blind field" of an image:[27] i.e. in the not visually represented conjectural space outside the picture. In a first approach, we only sense that there are such meanings, which may be constructed on the quality of emptiness we see here, on the absence of the human scale.

On this basis, we can now turn to the caption, which tells us: "Miners' bunks in the Chinese compound, Simmer and Jack Gold Mine, Germiston, July 1965."[28] So what we see here is beds, concrete beds, with little ledges in the second and third storeys to prevent the miners from falling out – or is it just their mattresses or blankets? I find it difficult to imagine people resting from a hard day's labour in what forcibly reminds me (a Barthesian connotation, this) of a Mediterranean graveyard, and my wife of images of a concentration camp – both of us are reminded of death rather than rest. How can they possibly sleep here? Why aren't they given proper beds, proper rooms? For the practically-minded, wondering how to get into the top berths, the handles visible on the vertical wall in the middle of the picture may give a hint. But speaking from my cultural position I can only guess at such things: I am unable, in a gesture of transcultural empathy, to transfer my European experience of beds to the claim that these are beds, too. Since there is no further information from the photographer (or his co-writer), I may be very mistaken in my ideas about this picture. Still, the photograph, one of a series of fifty-six photographs which, together with Gordimer's seven-page essay, form a

---

[26] Goldblatt, *David Goldblatt Fifty-One Years*, 291.

[27] Barthes, *Camera Lucida*, 23, 57.

[28] Goldblatt, *David Goldblatt Fifty-One Years*, 100, with a text (101) by David Goldblatt from his and Nadine Gordimer's first collaborative work *On the Mines* (Cape Town: Struik, 1973). In *Lifetimes: Under Apartheid* (New York: Alfred A. Knopf, 1986), the second collaboration between Goldblatt and Gordimer, the caption was changed to "Bunks in a compound for black miners, Simmer and Jack Gold Mine, Germiston, 1965."

narrative account of mining in the 1960s, opens up paths of enquiry, speculation, and debate about the history of gold mining in South Africa, about the
role of immigrant labour, about conditions of work and pay, holidays and
social security, but mainly about what is fit for human living, and finally
about a concept of humanity.

   Clifford Geertz has argued that any enquiry into human universals must
"descend into detail" as the only way to get "past the misleading tags, past the
metaphysical types, past the empty similarities" which have dogged the enterprise of comparative anthropology.[29] The "Miners' Bunks" picture shows one
such detail, but only one, so I would like to compare it with another photograph with a related motif and possibly theme, Goldblatt's picture of "Margaret Mcingana at home on a Sunday afternoon, Zola, Soweto, 1970."[30]

Photograph no. 5: David Goldblatt, "Margaret Mcingana,"
Lifetimes: Under Apartheid, 43.

---

[29] Geertz, *The Interpretation of Cultures*, 53.
[30] The caption in Goldblatt, *David Goldblatt Fifty-One Years*, reads: "Margaret Mcingana who later became famous as the singer Margaret Singana, Zola, Soweto, October
1970." Details about her career are to be found at the The South African Rock Encyclopedia
under www.rock.co.za/files/ms_index.html. This reveals that Margaret Singana enjoyed
some success during the 1970s, suffered a stroke in 1978, and after a brief comeback in 1986
died in poverty on 22 April 2000, aged 63.

First and foremost, this picture is visibly and, to my masculine gaze, attractively populated, and for another it shows what I recognize as ingredients of civilized comfort, a real bed (or folding couch), a patterned blanket, a vase on the embroidered and hemstitched tablecloth, a carpet on the linoleum, a neatly arranged pair of shoes. But then there is the expanse of empty wall which, like the sky in a classical landscape, takes up two-thirds of the picture. It is a rough brick wall only very incompletely plastered or white-washed, a wall which should be on the exterior, not the interior of a home, so that one wonders what the building containing this room looks like from the outside: would I recognize it as a home at all? The photograph reminds me of a passage I read in a recent novel of intercultural experience, Monica Ali's *Brick Lane* (2003); Hasina writes from Dhaka to her sister Nazneen in London about the room she is currently living in: "We have concrete floor very smooth and walls will be plaster inside soon. My room have one wall is already half plaster."[31] For Margaret as well as for Hasina, the wall, like any other empty or unfinished surface, conceals an untold story, which demands to be filled, either inscribed or camouflaged with graffiti or a wall-hanging or a poster. But its occupant, about whom I know so little, has done no such thing, making her statement through the furnishings of the small inhabited zone, as well as through her posture, relaxed, pensive, and dignified. It is left to the viewer to fill the empty wall with questions, conjectures or researched facts, all of which must be informed by the stark contrast of rough, hard wall and soft, living body – the visual values of the photograph.

4. The Use of *studium* and *punctum*: Pictures of Africa At Work

Roland Barthes was often concerned to define the nature of semiotic systems and to discover by what processes they were decoded and understood. His distinction between 'readerly' and 'writerly' texts, made in the very first section of *S/Z*, is germane to our inquiry. It is enough to quote a single thesis here: "To interpret a text is not to give it a (more or less justified, more or less free) meaning, but on the contrary to appreciate what *plural* constitutes it."[32]

---

[31] Monica Ali, *Brick Lane* (London: Doubleday, 2003): 121.
[32] Roland Barthes, *S/Z*, tr. Richard Miller (*S/Z*, 1973; tr. Oxford: Blackwell, 1990): 5 (emphasis in the original).

Some texts and pictures are "incorrigibly plural," as Louis MacNeice once put it,[33] others possess a very limited plurality and seem to be exhausted by attributing a single meaning to them. In *Camera Lucida,* Barthes approaches photographs of the second kind with an attitude that he labels with the Latin term *studium.* "The *studium* is that very wide field of unconcerned desire, of various interest, of inconsequential taste" – something that he terms "liking" rather than "loving" (27). To adopt the attitude of *studium* towards a photograph means "to encounter the photographer's intentions, to enter into harmony with them, to approve or disapprove of them, but always to understand them" (27–28). Barthes calls this "cultural participation" (26): i.e. in the mode of *studium* I relate to a photograph as an immediately recognizable product of my own culture. When this 'studied' response occurs with regard to photographs from a different culture, then that would be a case of transcultural participation: i.e. an understanding across boundaries in which the sense of difference is muted, relegated to a minor factor, held to be unproblematic.

Sometimes something happens to upset the *studium,* however, to break or fragment it, and leads to a completely different attitude or kind of attention, a different way of looking and reading. Barthes calls this contrary and complementary attitude the *punctum,* a word that signifies an "element which rises from the scene, shoots out of it like an arrow, and pierces me" (26). In other words, there are photographs that are distinguished by some special quality, a quality that holds my attention, makes me linger, wonder, and speculate, because I feel it as a "sting, speck, cut" (27). Using Shylock's words, I could say: it pricks me, and makes me bleed. Less metaphorically, the *punctum* is caused when all of a sudden I am jolted in my neutral, docile attitude of *studium* and am hit by some "detail which attracts or distresses me" (40), which makes me intensify my way of looking and also changes the quality of the picture, giving it a "higher value" (42). When a viewer is struck, unsettled, pierced by such a detail or "partial object" (43), which the photographer may only have included in his picture because he had to, because it was there (and which a painter and most certainly a writer might have left out), he becomes active in search of plural meanings (49). Looking at the picture in the attitude of *punctum,* he assumes a "'thinking eye' which makes [him] add

---

[33] Louis MacNeice, "Snow" (1935), in MacNeice, *Collected Poems,* ed. E.R. Dodds (London: Faber & Faber, 1966): 30.

something to the photograph" (45), a supplement to make good the absence or incompletion marked by the *punctum*, and to make the picture *scriptible*, writerly. Punctuated pictures can be ascribed more than one meaning, they are inexhaustible. On the other hand, there is Barthes' insight that "What I can name cannot really prick me" (51), meaning that the unsettling quality of *punctum* can disappear if one verbalizes it in too facile a manner and wrongly assumes that such verbalization could be permanent. Any naming of the *punctum* must be temporary, a mere approximation to what still needs to be said. In the photographic representation of Africa, this quality of response to the *punctum* is of particular importance, because it would seem to be our best guarantor for authenticity.

It seems clear that any photographer of Africa who is consciously seeking for truth will try to create pictures that possess this quality of *punctum*, at least for an alert and sensitive viewer, pictures which resist a simplistic and merely habitual reading that in the last resort is authoritarian by too confidently ascribing a definite, limited meaning. I would like to discuss this with reference to two further photographs, both on the topic of work.

Photograph no. 6: David Goldblatt, "Frederick Jillie, Ironing"
Lifetimes: Under Apartheid, 78.

It was the concentrated and ambiguous expression on the man's face that first caught my attention in this photograph, though it is not a portrait. Then, distracting me from the picture itself, the caption took over and forced me to consider its reference and implication:

> Frederick Jillie, migrant worker, irons his dustcoat in the Jabulani Men's Hostel, Soweto. He sees his wife and children at his home in Queenstown, nearly 800 kilometres (500 miles) away, for two and a half weeks during his vacation each year. When the photograph was taken, in 1972, he had been living like this for thirteen years.[34]

There would be a lot to say about this, and about the details of the photograph, such as the cardboard boxes labelled "Cape Apples," the contents of which are of uncertain origin, the ancient iron and the protective handkerchief, the tin mug, and the barely recognizable cigarette stub on the bench next to the table. There is also the issue of gendered work, a man compelled to do the ironing, recalling Buchi Emecheta's description of "Nnaife the washerman" in *The Joys of Motherhood*.[35] But what really got me thinking was something I did not see till my eyes had repeatedly returned Frederick Jillie's speaking gaze and then followed the horizontal line of the brickwork from his head to the right of this rather lop-sided picture. And there I discovered what is technically known as a 'ghost': i.e. "a blurred, faint, residual impression" of an object that has moved during exposure.[36] It is hard to tell what has caused this image, a freshly ironed shirt perhaps, or why it is blurred, but it is there, and the photographer has not edited it out by trimming the negative. This blurred object is my *punctum*, for it reminds me over and over again that, however sharp the focus of the rest of the picture may be, however penetrating my gaze (let alone Frederick Jillie's), and however well I am able to recognize even a tiny detail like the cigarette end, there are things in and beyond the photograph that I cannot see properly. The blurred object tells me how limited my understanding of this man and his plight is, how much I still need to get into focus.

---

[34] Goldblatt & Gordimer, *Lifetimes*, 78.

[35] Buchi Emecheta, *The Joys of Motherhood* (1979; London: Flamingo, 1988): 60.

[36] Gordon Baldwin, *Looking at Photographs: A Guide to Technical Terms* (Los Angeles & London: J.Paul Getty Museum / British Museum P, 1991): s.v. 'ghost.'

The second photograph of a man working is taken from Peter Magubane's *Soweto*. The older photographs in the book, going as far back as 1954, are in black-and-white, the contemporary ones are in colour, contrasting "Soweto's Evolution" with "Soweto Today."

Photograph no. 7: Peter Magubane, "Vegetable Hawker," from *Soweto*, 105.

This photograph is one of three on a double page, the other two showing a 'chicken seller' and a 'second hand clothes retailer'. Photographs often have such a photographic context, and derive some of their meaning from it. The narrative text, written by the Johannesburg journalist Charlene Smith, tells us that all three show an open-air market at Freedom Square, so named because it was there on 26 June 1955 that thousands gathered to adopt the ANC's Freedom Charter, "the programme of the South African liberation struggle."[37] Smith explains that these traders "are exercising their rights in terms of section three of the Charter: 'The people shall share in the country's wealth'" and that the Charter further proclaims that "all people shall have equal rights

---

[37] Heidi Holland, *Born in Soweto: Inside the Heart of South Africa* (Harmondsworth: Penguin, 1994): 1.

to trade where they choose, to manufacture and to enter all trades, crafts and professions."[38] So the civil rights background is clear enough, and it gives the photograph a depth of meaning it would not otherwise have. But as I look at the picture and bring to it my images and memories of the many comparable markets in Europe I have visited for shopping and amusement over the years (is the camera-armed tourist walking towards us from the background my alter ego?), I notice all the differences that prevent this from being a wholly transcultural experience. To me, the most striking anomaly is the pink plastic plates on which the pyramids of mass-produced tomatoes have been so carefully erected. The trader no doubt knows his customers, and is appealing to their taste and habits, but he does not know me, who would rather buy home-grown tomatoes displayed in wicker baskets, harvested earlier the same morning. And why is he selling nothing but tomatoes? Why does Charlene Smith call him a "hawker," a term which in British usage designates an itinerant trader of the lowest category? It is these differences that signify, and override the simple commonalities. I only *seem* to know what I see when I contemplate this photograph, but in truth I am ignorant of what it really means in its South African context.

5.   Conclusion: Not Accepting the World As It Looks

It would seem, then, that photographs, because they are so immediately referential, and because they record what is there less selectively than writing, tend to foreground the features of everyday life, bodies at work and play, people eating, sleeping, shopping, and doing all the things all of us do and which are therefore recognizably similar all over the world. There are exceptions, which work consciously against this tendency, as documented here by Goldblatt's semi-abstract photograph of miners' bunks. The examples have also shown that behind the familiar there is often, especially when we look long and attentively enough, something puzzling, strange, and foreign, something that unsettles our initial response of recognition. The transcultural aspect may hide a wealth of cultural difference. Both Susan Sontag in *On Photography*[39] and John Berger and Jean Mohr in *Another Way of Telling*

---

[38] Magubane, *Soweto*; text by Charlene Smith (Cape Town: Struik, 2001): 104.
[39] Susan Sontag, *On Photography* (1977; Harmondsworth: Penguin, 1979).

(1982)[40] describe how photographic images give a highly discontinuous account of the world, owing to the fact that they have sharply defined borders which cut off the adjacent reality in an arbitrary fashion. "Through photographs, the world becomes a series of unrelated, freestanding particles," Sontag says in *On Photography* (22–23). This causes two effects. The first effect is that "the camera makes reality atomic, manageable, and opaque" and "confers on each [photographed] moment the character of a mystery" (23), a view which takes up Barthes' notion of the transparency of the photographic surface. The second effect is that this discontinuous opacity points to something beyond the image:

> The ultimate wisdom of the photographic image is to say: "There is the surface. Now think – or rather feel, intuit – what is beyond it, what the reality must be like if it looks this way." (23)

Sontag relates this twofold effect to man's fate of "linger[ing] unregenerately in Plato's cave" (3), where all he can perceive is shadows of true forms but never the forms themselves. After all, a photograph is just a shadowy record of objects exposed to the sun, it shows "mere images of the truth" (3). Photographic shadows can thus never give direct evidence of the world, and the observer who is in search of reality must be prepared to go beyond the photograph. Sontag calls this attitude "the ability to say no":

> Photography implies that we know about the world if we accept it as the camera records it. But this is the opposite of understanding, which starts from *not* accepting the world as it looks. All possibility of understanding is rooted in the ability to say no. Strictly speaking, one never understands anything from a photograph. (23)

The observer who says no to a photograph has already begun speaking about it, and will have to continue speaking in justification of this beginning. Let us apply this insight to a final example, again a photograph by David Goldblatt. It is a quiet, sunny day, and a woman and her child are resting on a bed. Behind them we see a table, full of kitchen utensils, an armchair and a chair and many other household items. All these are placed, it seems, in the middle of the bush. This cannot be, I say, and find myself "not accepting the world as it looks" here.

---

[40] John Berger & Jean Mohr, *Another Way of Telling* (1982; New York: Vintage, 1995).

Photograph no. 8: David Goldblatt, "Mother and Child," 1984,
from *South Africa: The Structure of Things Then*
(New York: Monacelli, 1998): 43.

The caption briefly explains the circumstances:

> Mother and child in their home after the destruction of its shelter by officials of the
> Western Cape Development Board, in pursuance of apartheid regulations prohibi-
> ting Africans from the Western Cape, Crossroads, Cape, 11 October 1984.[41]

One can just about imagine what must have happened, but the photograph
does not tell the story, does not show what things looked like before the demolition squad arrived, nor what will happen after. For information about the
before we must turn to a witness like the American journalist Adam Hochschild, who visited Crossroads in the 1980s:

---

[41] Goldblatt, *South Africa: The Structure of Things Then* (New York: Monacelli, 1998):
43. In a section with "extended captions," Goldblatt tells us that some time after the de-
struction of her home the woman "got up and began to cut and strip branches of Port Jack-
son bush to make a new framework for her house. The child slept" (185).

> The African huts I walk past are made of corrugated zinc, tarpaulins, plastic sheet-
> ing, or pieces of the walls of demolished buildings, with painted advertisements
> still on them. […] But what strikes me most is the walls. They are wallpapered with
> the shiny paper from Sunday newspaper ad supplements.[42]

A single photograph cannot show this, nor the demolition, but it does provide
indexical signs of what happened. It can and does set me on the road to finding out what happened there (as opposed to the place where I am), who was
responsible, who suffered, and what followed. By a subtle interplay of looking at and looking through, seeing and naming what I see and finding words
for what I do not see, recognizing the familiar and being startled by difference
and absence, the photograph leads me to a certain knowledge of Africa that I
could not have discovered in any other way. It offers evidence of transcultural
commonalities and at the same time opens up perceptions of cultural difference, including the conditions and limits this imposes on my striving to
understand. In this way, the cultural study of photographs helps to show that
cultural studies can be relocated in-between and above these opposites, confirming Mieke Bal's diagnosis that "confronted with visuality's many ten-
tacles" the notions of culture as local, universal, global, or judgemental
should give way to a concept of the cultural as "situated, polemically, between global and local, retaining the specificity of each" in order to explore
the processes of cultural understanding and misunderstanding.[43]

WORKS CITED

Achebe, Chinua, & Robert Lyons. *Another Africa* (Garden City NY: Doubleday/Anchor,
    1998).
Ali, Monica. *Brick Lane* (London: Doubleday, 2003).
"Argungu, Revival of a Grand Fishing Festival." *Weekly Trust*, http://allafrica.com/stories
    /printable/200403150523.html (accessed 5 May 2008).
Bal, Mieke. "Visual Essentialism and the Object of Visual Culture," *Journal of Visual Cul-
    ture* 2.1 (2003): 5–32.
Baldwin, Gordon. *Looking at Photographs: A Guide to Technical Terms* (Los Angeles &
    London: J. Paul Getty Museum & British Museum P, 1991).
Barthes, Roland. *Camera Lucida: Reflections on Photography*, tr. Richard Howard
    (*Chambre claire*, 1980; tr. London: Vintage, 1993).

---

[42] Adam Hochschild, *The Mirror at Midnight: A South African Journey* (New York:
Viking Penguin, 1990): 24.

[43] Bal, "Visual Essentialism…," 17.

——. "The Photographic Message," in *The Responsibility of Forms: Critical Essays on Music, Art, and Representation*, tr. Richard Howard (1985; Berkeley & Los Angeles: U of California P, 1991): 3–20.

——. *S/Z*, tr. Richard Miller (*S/Z*, 1973; tr. Oxford: Blackwell, 1990).

Berger, John, & Jean Mohr. *Another Way of Telling* (1982; New York: Vintage, 1995).

Boehmer, Elleke. *Colonial and Postcolonial Literature: Migrant Metaphors* (Oxford & New York: Oxford UP, 1995).

Buel, J.W. *Heroes of the Dark Continent* (Richmond VA: B.F. Johnson, 1890).

Coetzee, J.M. *Elizabeth Costello* (London: Secker & Warburg, 2003).

Derrida, Jacques. *A Derrida Reader: Between the Blinds*, ed. & intro. Peggy Kamuf (New York: Harvester Wheatsheaf, 1991).

Emecheta, Buchi. *The Joys of Motherhood* (1979; London: Flamingo, 1988).

Enwezor, Okwui. "Matter and Consciousness: An Insistent Gaze from a Not Disinterested Photographer," interview with David Goldblatt, in Goldblatt, *David Goldblatt Fifty-One Years* (2001), 13–45.

Fernau, Joachim, Kurt Kayser & Johannes Paul, ed. *Afrika wartet: Ein kolonialpolitisches Bildbuch* (Potsdam: Rütten & Loening, 1942).

Geertz, Clifford. *The Interpretation of Cultures: Selected Essays* (1973; London: Fontana, 1993).

Ghose, Indira. "Conrad's *Heart of Darkness* and the Anxiety of Empire," in *Being/s in Transit, Travelling, Migration, Dislocation*, ed. Liselotte Glage (Cross/Cultures 41, ASNEL Papers 5; Amsterdam & Atlanta GA: Rodopi, 2000): 93–110.

Godby, Michael. "David Goldblatt: The Personal and the Political," in Goldblatt, *David Goldblatt Fifty-One Years* (2001), 407–25.

Goldblatt, David. *South Africa: The Structure of Things Then* (New York: Monacelli, 1998).

——. *David Goldblatt Fifty-One Years* (exh. cat.; Barcelona: Museu d'Art Contemporani de Barcelona / Actar, 2001).

——. *David Goldblatt 55*, ed. Lesley Lawson (London: Phaidon, 2001).

Goldblatt, David, & Nadine Gordimer. *On the Mines* (Cape Town: Struik, 1973).

——. *Lifetimes: Under Apartheid* (New York: Alfred A. Knopf, 1986).

"Gone fishing," *Sydney Morning Herald Online*, www.smh.com.au/ftimages/2004/03/21/1079823237709.html

Hochschild, Adam. *The Mirror at Midnight: A South African Journey* (New York: Viking Penguin, 1990).

Holland, Heidi. *Born in Soweto: Inside the Heart of South Africa* (Harmondsworth: Penguin, 1994).

Krauter, Anne. "Imagination und Dokument: Die eigene Kultur im photographischen Abbild der fremden Kultur," in *Exotische Welten, Europäische Phantasien*, ed. Herrmann Pollig (Stuttgart: Institut für Auslandsbeziehungen / Württembergischer Kunstverein / Cantz, 1987): 202–09.

MacDougall, David. "Transcultural Cinema," in *Transcultural Cinema*, ed. & intro. Lucien Taylor (Princeton NJ: Princeton UP, 1998): 245–78.

MacNeice, Louis. "Snow" (1935), in MacNeice, *Collected Poems*, ed. E.R. Dodds (London: Faber & Faber, 1966): 30.

Magubane, Peter. *Soweto*; text by Charlene Smith (Cape Town: Struik, 2001).

"Margaret Singana," *The South African Rock Encyclopedia*, http://www.rock.co.za/files/ms_index.html.

Miller, J. Hillis. *The Ethics of Reading* (Wellek Library Lectures; New York: Columbia UP, 1987).

Mitchell, W.J.T. *Picture Theory: Essays on Verbal and Visual Representation* (Chicago & London: U of Chicago P, 1994).

"Petri Heil in Afrika." *Saarbrücker Zeitung* (22 March 2004): A6.

Said, Edward W. "In Conversation with Neeladri Bhattacharya, Suvir Kaul, and Ania Loomba," in *Relocating Postcolonialism*, ed. David Theo Goldberg & Ato Quayson (Oxford: Blackwell, 2002): 1–14.

——. *Orientalism* (1978; Harmondsworth: Penguin, 1991).

Sontag, Susan. *On Photography* (1977; Harmondsworth: Penguin, 1979).

Waldenfels, Bernhard. *Der Spielraum des Verhaltens* (Frankfurt am Main: Suhrkamp, 1980).

◄❖►

II: Teaching and Learning with Photographs of Africa

GISELA FEURLE

1.   Photographs and Africa in the English Classroom

FOR ENGLISH TEACHERS, the use of pictures and photographs in
their lessons is daily bread. There are various purposes for this: to
introduce a new topic or a pre-reading phase, to motivate students, to
stimulate oral expression, and so forth. When starting a new topic, I sometimes display a number of photographs or postcards referring to the theme
and ask the students to choose one and write or speak about it. This approach
has proved very productive, but I have also been aware that it does not deal
with this visual medium in its own right, that it remains at its surface, that it
neglects the potential of photographs for teaching and learning English in a
cultural perspective. I have made a start to change this – last but not least
under the influence of the project on African photography developed by Detlev Gohrbandt and myself.

As English teachers, we all know that in recent years dealing with audiovisual media and developing media competence and visual skills has gained
great importance: in the curriculum guidelines, in textbooks, and in our teaching. The aim is to develop media literacy and critical media competence.
Besides the new technologies, this mostly only refers to audiovisual media:
feature films, video-clips, documentaries, TV news.

I think that, as a visual medium, photography can and should play an important role, too, for developing visual skills and critical media competence in
a world where we are flooded with pictures and images of all kinds every day
– young people even more than the older generations. Susan Sontag's reflections support this didactic choice:

> Nonstop imagery (television, streaming video, movies) is our surround, but when it comes to remembering, the photograph has the deeper bite. [...] The photograph is like a quotation, or a maxim or proverb.[1]

However, we do not only come across photographs in the public media – in the newspaper on the breakfast table, in magazines, museums or holiday brochures; photos can also play a very personal role in one's life, conserving and creating memory and experience – for example, in one's family album or as tourists taking photos.

In class photographs can easily stimulate and concentrate verbal responses – often more easily than texts and films because of their immediate intensity. Thus they are a productive medium for developing and practising speaking and writing skills, interpretative and creative abilities.

This essay is concerned not only with photography in the English language classroom in general but also with photographs of Africa in an intercultural and transcultural approach in particular. One of our aims in teaching English is to develop cultural, political, and historical knowledge and to stimulate intercultural learning not only about Britain and the USA, but also about other parts of the world. It is Africa in particular that is widely presented and represented with stereotypes and one-sided images in the West, and to a large extent these are transmitted by pictures. Reflecting on stereotypical images, on the colonial gaze, and on eurocentric perspectives, getting to know African perspectives and learning 'how photographs work' are therefore important objectives. I would like to show how a literary or historical approach can not only be fruitfully complemented by dealing with photographs of Africa, but how this medium opens up particular ways of learning and intercultural self-reflection. In a nutshell, my aims in teaching and learning with photographs in the English classroom are developing visual skills and critical media competence, language skills, and the ability of verbal response as well as intercultural competence – here: with regard to images of Africa.

2. Theoretical Concepts and Didactic Approach

In the following, I'll take up some of the theoretical concepts and questions that Detlev Gohrbandt developed in his essay. They guided my didactic ap-

---

[1] Susan Sontag, *Regarding the Pain of Others* (London: Hamish Hamilton, 2003): 19.

proach and my methods and the reflection of my teaching experiences. My own essay is a result of this process of collaboration and of the interplay of theory and practice: applying the theoretical concepts to the analysis of concrete photographs in a didactic context and communicating with students about the "act of looking" and the "experienced image."[2] It is work in progress.

I will first explore some of the theoretical concepts underlying my teaching and show how I 'translated' them into questions to guide the process of interpretation and discussion in the classroom. This will be followed by a presentation of my teaching experience with some selected photographs.

The extent to which the specific character of photography as a medium that both represents and interprets reality can be addressed theoretically and explicitly in the classroom depends on the teaching context. Theoretical statements may be discussed – by Roland Barthes, for example, who describes this double character of the photograph, the "photographic paradox," as the "coexistence of two messages, the one without a code (the analogue), the other with a code (the 'art', or the treatment, or the 'writing', or the rhetoric, of the photograph),"[3] and any opportunity during practical analysis should be grasped to make students aware of these ideas. For example, when a student concluded, in my lesson, that a certain arranged photo was not natural, whereas a snapshot would have shown the reality, I took this as the starting-point for a discussion about the character of the medium. We looked at the photo as 'cultural construction', but also at the question of a culturally determined reception, and we read and discussed what the photographer Lyons says about his work: "I continuously choose *that moment, that light, that gesture*, and *that framing* to construct the image."[4] Such questions – and many more

---

[2] When Mieke Bal asks "what happens when people look, and what emerges from that act?" she distinguishes between "the visual event" and "the experienced image"; Bal, "Visual Essentialism and the Object of Visual Culture," *Journal of Visual Culture* 2.1 (2003): 9.

[3] Roland Barthes, *Image, Music, Text*, tr. Stephen Heath (tr. 1977; New York: Hill & Wang, 1977): 19. I may also take a quotation from John Berger: "Are the appearances which a camera transports a construction, a man-made cultural artifact or are they like a footprint in the sand, a trace naturally left by something that has passed? The answer is, both." John Berger & Jean Mohr, *Another Way of Telling* (1982; New York: Vintage, 1995): 92.

[4] Robert Lyons & Chinua Achebe, *Another Africa* (Garden City NY: Doubleday, 1998): 118.

referring to the context and the function of a photograph – are important in the context of developing a critical media competence.[5]

Another basic aspect of teaching with photographs is the relation of pictures to language: the idea that the picture is not a 'pure medium', that in fact all media are mixed. W.J.T. Mitchell underlines the "interaction of pictures and texts" in visual and verbal representations.[6] But not just the relation of the photo to its accompanying caption or text has to be considered; one's own language has also to be taken into account. Barthes' idea that "the photograph is verbalized in the very moment it is perceived; better, it is only perceived verbalized"[7] can help to illuminate the very common task of describing a picture. When students are asked to describe what they see, it becomes obvious that describing: i.e. verbalizing, and seeing are interrelated: the first spontaneous verbal response, in particular, shows the culturally determined connotations. One's first impressions may be corrected, developed, pluralized etc. by verbalizing what is seen.

My own interpretation of photographs in the classroom is also guided by (overlapping) questions which I derived from theoretical concepts or reflections.

a) Asking about *the particular detail*. This is based on Barthes' distinction between the attitudes of *studium* and *punctum* in dealing with photography. It is the *punctum* of a photograph that "pierces me," strikes me or attracts me as a viewer. It is the disturbing detail that makes me acquire a "thinking eye" and makes me aware of the plurality of meanings in the photograph.[8]

b) Asking about *the visible and the invisible*. This refers to Susan Sontag's insight that photographs show us the world as a series of discontinuous particles, that the photographic image tells us: "There is the surface. Now think – or rather feel, intuit – what is beyond it, what the reality must be like if it

---

[5] There are many dimensions that are important for critical media competence which I have not dealt with here: for example, the meaning, function, and context of photographs taken by 'embedded' and 'unembedded journalists' – a debate that is crucial with regard to the American army in Iraq. For a similar question, the manipulation of pictures, see also the exhibition and catalogue *X für U: Bilder, die lügen* (X for U: Pictures that lie), ed. Haus der Geschichte der Bundesrepublik Deutschland (Bonn: Bouvier, 1998).

[6] W.J.T. Mitchell, *Picture Theory: Essays on Verbal and Visual Representation* (Chicago & London: U of Chicago P, 1994): 5.

[7] Roland Barthes, *Image, Music, Text*, 28.

[8] Roland Barthes, *Camera Lucida: Reflections on Photography*, tr. Richard Howard (*Chambre claire*, 1980; tr. London: Vintage, 1993): 26–27.

looks this way."[9] David Goldblatt expressed this in the following way: "as a photographer I wasn't at all that interested in events. I was and am far more engaged by the states of being that lead to events."[10] When asked by Okwui Enwezor how conflict in South Africa is represented in his photographs, he answered: "Probably by an awareness I have tried to convey in my work, of the immanence and imminence of conflict in much of what passes for the everyday in South Africa."[11]

c) Asking about *ambiguity*. Ambiguity to convey the complexity of reality plays a great role in David Goldblatt's photographs: "I would like to imbue these pale, two-dimensional rubbings of reality [...] with something of the subtlety and ambiguity of our shifting and frequently contradictory perceptions of reality."[12] For John Berger, the ambiguity of the photograph arises out of the discontinuity, the photo arresting the flow of time: "All photographs are ambiguous. All photographs have been taken out of a continuity."[13] He says: "Meaning is discovered in what connects, and cannot exist without development. [...] When we find a photo meaningful, we are lending it a past and future."[14]

d) Asking about the *theme*, the *meaning* or the *plurality of meanings*. Goldblatt says about Walker Evans: "In one photograph, he would reveal a whole world in most subtle and complex ways, and yet achieve it with elegant simplicity."[15] For John Berger, "a photograph that achieves expressiveness [...] works dialectically: it preserves the particularity of the event recorded and [...] articulates a general idea."[16] Goldblatt stresses that for him meaning is always embedded in a context: "I took these photographs because I was engaged in a dialogue – between the subject and me."[17] He often works with indirect meaning and irony: "my work became more oblique. I sought out

---

[9] Susan Sontag, *On Photography* (Harmondsworth: Penguin, 1979): 23.

[10] Okwui Enwezor, "Matter and Consciousness: An Insistent Gaze From a Not Disinterested Photographer," interview with David Goldblatt, in Goldblatt, *David Goldblatt Fifty-One Years* (exh. cat.; Barcelona: Museu d'Art Contemporani de Barcelona/Actar, 2001): 19.

[11] Enwezor, "Matter and Consciousness," 27.

[12] "Matter and Consciousness," 35.

[13] Berger & Mohr, *Another Way of Telling*, 91.

[14] *Another Way of Telling*, 89.

[15] Enwezor, "Matter and Consciousness," 26.

[16] Berger & Mohr, *Another Way of Telling*, 122.

[17] Enwezor, "Matter and Consciousness," 17.

irony and tried to impregnate pictures with a sense of it, for it often reveals the nuances and complexities of our life in South Africa."[18]

e) Asking about the relation of *image and caption or text*. Goldblatt explains about his personal work: "I recognise that the caption is a continuation of the process that began when I selected the moment to take the picture; it may be vital to the weight and balance of the image for the viewer. So I tell what seems necessary."[19] To quote Berger: "Yet often this ambiguity [of the photograph] is not obvious, for as soon as photographs are used with words, they produce together an effect of certainty, even of dogmatic assertion."[20]

f) Asking about *transcultural and intercultural aspects* – about similarity and difference, familiarity and unfamiliarity, stereotypes. David MacDougall states: "Visual representation [...] has intercultural as well as transcultural implications"[21] – transcultural in the sense that the photograph not only crosses but also defies cultural boundaries. "The photo is overwhelmingly physical and psychological before it is cultural. It therefore transcends 'culture' in a way most written ethnographic descriptions do not."[22] For MacDougall, the conclusion that visual anthropology "is counter-cultural (in the anthropological sense) by drawing attention to the significance of the non-'cultural'" plays a significant role in the context of recent criticism – also in anthropology – of the 'culture concept':

> the tendencies that it [the culture concept] encourages in its users to treat abstractions as realities, to view humanity as made up of discrete and bounded entities, to imply a uniformity and coherence that societies do not have, to deny social groups a place in time and history, and (a criticism made by Said and Appadurai in particular) to perpetuate colonial distinctions between Western intellectuals and all non-Western 'others'.[23]

These problematic implications and tendencies can also be found in the everyday use and idea of the term 'culture' and often contribute to the creation or persistence of stereotypes. To counteract this in the context of teaching

---

[18] Enwezor, "Matter and Consciousness," 22.

[19] "Matter and Consciousness," 40.

[20] Berger & Mohr, *Another Way of Telling*, 91.

[21] David MacDougall, *Transcultural Cinema* (Princeton NJ: Princeton UP, 1998): 261.

[22] MacDougall, *Transcultural Cinema*, 252.

[23] *Transcultural Cinema*, 260.

I try to convey the idea of culture as being dynamic, ambiguous, and continuously changing, as being closely linked to the historical, political, socioeconomic, and global context and to relations of power. Photographs can be a very productive medium in this respect, but this greatly depends on the kind of photograph and on the reflection of one's reception. MacDougall emphasizes that visually based media have "undermined stereotypical perceptions of national identity,"[24] but he notes that they may also reinforce cultural boundaries and perpetuate stereotypes. Thus intercultural reflection is essential and implies reflecting on our connotations and on our (historical, cultural etc.) background and the knowledge determining our reception. Roland Barthes says: "Thanks to the code of connotation the reading of the photograph is [...] always historical; it depends on the reader's 'knowledge' just as though it were a matter of a real language (langue), intelligible only if one has learned the signs."[25]

Concepts 'translated' into questions for the classroom
Interpreting the photograph
1. Is there any detail that strikes or disturbs me, arouses questions or makes me think?
2. Does the photo reveal anything of the reality beyond the picture, 'behind the surface'? What is visible and invisible (for me) in the picture? Is there anything conveyed that is invisible?
3. Is there anything ambiguous in the photo? In which respect?
4. What is the theme of the photograph? What does the portrait or the scene express? Is there one or are there many meanings?
5. Is there a title, a caption or an accompanying text? Would the meaning or effect of the photo be different without the caption/ text? How?

Inter- and transcultural reflection
6. Is there anything familiar in the photograph for me? Are there similar situations, aspects or characters in my experience?

---

[24] MacDougall, *Transcultural Cinema*, 261.
[25] Barthes, *Image, Music, Text*, 28.

7. What is unfamiliar or strange for me (perhaps because of my different socio-cultural or historical context)?
8. Is the photo different from stereotypical images and representations of 'Africa'? In which respect?

I had these questions – or some of them – guide the students' individual reflection and interpretation, their analysis and discussion in groups and in the
plenary.[26] As a complement to analysis, a creative or production-oriented
approach also implies interpretation and takes into account the specific character of the medium. For example, writing a story – what happened 'before
and after' the picture? Creating a fictitious dialogue – for example, between
the subject and photographer, between the persons in the picture, or between
oneself and the subject.

3.   Presentation of and Reflection of the Teaching Experience

3.1. Didactic Context of 'Photo-Units'

I taught a short photo unit of about three double lessons in two different
courses. In one English course (grade 12), I began with the question of stereotypical representations and images of Africa in order to have a familiar and
also contrasting starting-point and to create a reference base for intercultural
reflection.[27] My method in brief: I used the collection of photographs on
Africa by Misereor[28] and displayed pictures of all kinds (of rural and urban
Africa) on the desks. The students were asked to select one that they thought
was typical of the 'common image of Africa' in the media, in the public
realm. When we compiled the various choices and characterizations, they
boiled down to three basic one-sided or stereotypical images: beautiful and
exotic Africa (of nature, animals and rituals); terrible Africa (of war, cata-

---

[26] I also had questions drawing attention to basic aspects of the 'construction' of the
photograph: to the background and foreground, the framing, contrasts, colours, the light, the
angle and distance of the photographer, to the kind of lens, the focus, the order of perception, etc.

[27] In the other course, an interdisciplinary course in English on the topic "The City of
Gold – Johannesburg in literature and history," the photo unit was one dimension to develop the theme and interpretative abilities.

[28] *Bildkartei: 'Bilder über Afrika und uns'*, ed. Bischöfliches Hilfswerk Misereor
(Aachen: Misereor Vertriebsgesellschaft, 1987).

strophes and famine); and needy Africa (asking for help). Against the distorting reduction of Africa to such images and themes and the implied eurocentric perspectives, I introduced the topic of 'everyday life' and 'other'
photographs of Africa by the photographers David Goldblatt, Peter Magubane, and Robert Lyons.

3.2. People's Bodies: Images and Ambiguities

When the students described the photograph "Margaret Mcingana at home on
a Sunday afternoon, Zola Soweto, 1970"[29] by David Goldblatt in detail
(photograph no. 5),[30] they came across the contrasts: the nice shiny vase, the
embroidered tablecloth, the carpet on the one side and the bare, ugly wall on
the other. The 'detail' that struck most and prompted a lot of questions and
meanings – and thus meant the *punctum* – was the bare and ugly wall, which
was often perceived first or second after the woman's face. They discussed
and argued: "Why is it not painted?" – "She is too poor to buy paint, it's a
sign of poverty" – "But she is smoking, so she can't be so poor" – "Smoking
doesn't mean you are rich, homeless people in Germany also smoke" –
"Maybe she has other worries than buying paint?" "There is so little in her
room," one student said, "as compared to my room, my walls."

As for the woman, Margaret Mcingana: in one group some students' first
impression was that she was a prostitute because of her way of lying on the
bed, her smoking, her dress: "Maybe she is thinking about her customer."
There was a discussion of whether the caption "at home on a Sunday afternoon" – which not all had noticed! – did not contradict this. In the other
course, the idea 'prostitute' was not mentioned. When I brought up the idea,
two students explained that they also had thought so at first, but hadn't said it,
because they felt it was a typical stereotype of a black woman, a white and
Western gaze. They wanted to be careful with judgements. The students won-
dered what the photographer had said to the woman: "He must have known
her [...] Perhaps he said: 'Find yourself a comfortable position'" – "It is a
very private and intimate situation (at home, lying on the bed) – is the viewer
not intruding?"

---

[29] Nadine Gordimer & David Goldblatt, *Lifetimes Under Apartheid* (New York: Alfred
A. Knopf, 1986): 43.

[30] See Detlev Gohrbandt's section of this article. The numbers refer to the photographs
reproduced in these two sections of *Look, See and Say*.

The discussion showed that the wall and the contrasts pointed at the reality beyond the picture: the poverty in Soweto and how people deal or live with it.[31] It contradicted the idea that there is only one face of poverty (e.g., in slums or refugee camps) and raised the question "what does poverty mean?" The photo left questions, riddles, ambiguities. It was important to share the different impressions, to speak about them in order to further the process of understanding. As for transculturalism: the unfamiliar setting was in the foreground for the students, but at the same time references to one's own experience ("my room") showed that "the strangeness of the most exotic subject was counterbalanced by a sense of familiarity."[32]

I think the discussion "how does poverty show" is important, because stereotypical images of Africa can often be found here. For the Western eye, poverty in Africa is often only known or seen in its extreme: when children are naked and people are in rags, half-starved, in slums, expressing despair and hopelessness. These are the pictures we get when the media turn their attention to Africa, the continent of catastrophes. I also came across this question of poverty in two students' written responses to Peter Magubane's photo of the drinking boy (photograph no. 9 overleaf):

The students described the poverty expressed by the shacks in the background, by the outside communal tap, but they thought "the boy has rich parents" or "is living in relatively good conditions" because of the "good clothes" he is wearing. I think pictures of everyday life in Africa can also teach about different shades and meanings of poverty and about ways of dealing with it (e.g., to dress as well as possible, to iron one's shirt although, or because, one lives in a shack). For another student, the transcultural commonality was in the foreground: "Peter Magubane may want to show us that children of South Africa are the same as in Europe. They drink, when they are thirsty, and eat when they are hungry."

---

[31] In *David Goldblatt*, ed. Lesley Lawson (London: Phaidon, 2001), where this photo is also reproduced (47), Lawson's text following the caption reads: "For Goldblatt this photograph is symbolic of many aspects of Soweto life and is one of the few that hang in his own home. It encapsulates what he sees as the astonishing ability of Sowetans to achieve a sense of ease and normality in the harshest of environments. Mcigana, who later became known as the singer Margaret Singana, relaxes in obvious enjoyment of her own sensuality, while above her looms a wall that seems to bear the scars of violent assault" (46).

[32] MacDougall, *Transcultural Cinema*, 245.

Photograph no. 9: Peter Magubane, *Soweto* [33]

When dealing with David Goldblatt's photo "Miss Lovely Legs Competition" (photograph no. 10 overleaf), I realized once more how difficult it
often is for students to see and accept ambiguity, and that photographs in
particular require the exchange of different views so that students do not get
stuck with first impressions or remain on the surface, but experience the
'*punctum* effect' of other or deeper meanings of one representation.

For one students' group, the photo immediately expressed "the oppression
of blacks," as "they are not allowed on the stage, only whites are there." The
plenary discussion and further study of the photo created doubts about such a
one-dimensional message and reception. They now realized that it was a
mixed crowd of black and white people and noticed the critical expression of
the black spectators. They then studied the different expressions of the girls
and found them uncertain, shy or proud. "It is upside down from what usually
happens," a student stated, "not whites look at black women and judge their
bodies, but it's the other way round."

---

[33] Peter Magubane, *Soweto*, 69.

Photograph no. 10: David Goldblatt, "Miss Lovely Legs Competition
at the Pick 'n' Pay Hypermarket, Boksburg 1980"[34]

Another idea of oppression was realized: the female body as object in beauty
shows. Some students referred to similar events in our society and culture –in
fact, globally: "Miss Germany, Miss World, Choose a Superstar." However,
it was the particular setting and meaning that were in the foreground and required information on the social and historical context in South Africa.

3.3. Buildings: Image and Text –
The Visible and the Invisible – the Reality Beyond

Without caption, the photo "Bunks in a compound for black miners"[35] by
David Goldblatt (photograph no. 4 in Detlev Gohrbandt's essay above) presented a riddle for the students, though it already had some strong effects: for
some students, the picture evoked coffins, Spanish graveyards. Adding the
text created a lot of inner images; the invisible became visible: the living

---

[34] Gordimer & Goldblatt, *Lifetimes under Apartheid*, 107.
[35] Full caption: "Bunks in a compound for black miners, Simmer and Jack Gold Mine,
Germiston, 1965," in Gordimer & Goldblatt, *Lifetimes under Apartheid*, 11.

conditions of the miners, the atmosphere. The students described it with words such as "cold, hard, claustrophobic, no privacy, so many men" and imagined two possible effects: aggression, or unity and solidarity. It raised questions about the context of apartheid, the situation of migrant workers, and the reality beyond the photo. Showing it first without caption made the students aware of the effect of the text and of the interplay of image and text.

Another example that made students experience how texts can change their way of looking is Robert Lyons' photo of the beach with palm tree and house (the caption for which can only be found at the back of the book).

Photograph no. 11: Robert Lyons[36]

The students' first impression and culturally determined connotation was: holidays, beach, relaxing. There was a discussion about whether one could see the sea or not. But then there was the ugly wall in the corner. In a nice holiday picture, the photographer would have avoided that sight. What does it mean to include it? It is the irritating detail in the photo that makes you think,

---

[36] Lyons & Achebe, *Another Africa*, 41 (caption: "Embarkation point of slaves to the new world, Ouidah, Benin, 1994": 120).

that creates the *punctum* Roland Barthes speaks of. On reading the caption, "Embarkation point of slaves to the new world, Ouidah, Benin, 1994," one student suddenly noticed the footprints in the sand or realized their relevance. The footprints assumed another significance – one of history, of brutality; they became symbolic and raised the question of the traces of the past.

3.4. People's Work: Before and After –
Transcultural and Intercultural Aspects

The photo "Frederick Jillie, Ironing" by David Goldblatt[37] (photograph no. 6 in Detlev Gohrbandt's essay, above) with its detailed caption quite obviously presents us with an excerpt from a 'story'; the moment 'conserved' by the photographer has a 'before' and an 'after'. This raised questions about the past and future of Jillie's life. What did Frederick Jillie do before and after ironing his dustcoat? Students wrote: "I think he is working for 12–13 hours a day or more for his money and he thinks his terrible life will never end"; or: "Why can't F.J. have another job to be with his family?" There is also the immediate past and future of the situation the photo was taken in, so that students asked themselves what the photographer might have asked Frederick Jillie and how Jillie feels. It was Frederick Jillie's facial expression that mainly triggered these questions and different responses. Some students found it sad and desperate, others just serious, or querying; yet others interpreted it as angry, or: "he looks as if he hates this world." When exchanging their views, the students experienced the ambiguity of body language – on the one hand, there is the transcultural aspect of understanding it; on the other, there is the need to know details about the concrete situation and the cultural context.

The body language of the black worker in Goldblatt's photo "Meeting of the worker–management liaison committee of the Colgate Palmolive Company, Boksburg 1980" (photograph no. 12, next page) also made an ambiguous impression: Some students interpreted his attitude as being uncertain (the way he is folding his arms), others as resisting or provocative (e.g., the outstretched legs). Immediately there was a discussion in class about the pos-

---

[37] The full caption reads: "Frederick Jillie, migrant worker, irons his dustcoat in the Jabulani Men's Hostel, Soweto. He sees his wife and children at his home in Queenstown, nearly 800 kilometres (500 miles) away, for two and a half weeks during his vacation each year. When the photograph was taken, in 1972, he had been living like this for thirteen years." Gordimer & Goldblatt, *Lifetimes Under Apartheid*, 78.

sible meaning of folding one's arms. As compared to the manager who is talking actively (and who has papers in front of him), the worker is listening, is passive or receptive at the moment of the photo. The students observed that the two are also divided by the gap of the door.

Photograph no. 12: David Goldblatt, "Meeting of the worker–management liaison committee of the Colgate Palmolive Company, Boksburg 1980"[38]

I had the students imitate and act out the different positions and body languages to get a feel for the attitudes and their meaning. There were still different views, but all agreed that the worker's attitude was not subservient. The acting-out of the body language in some way takes up Mieke Bal's analysis of the "the act of looking" as "profoundly 'impure'."[39] She describes looking as sense-directed like other activities: listening, reading, tasting, smelling. The body is involved. This photo was another good example to show that ambiguity is also caused by the fact that the photo presents an in-

---

[38] Gordimer & Goldblatt, *Lifetimes under Apartheid*, 61.
[39] Bal, "Visual Essentialism and the Object of Visual Culture," 9.

stant of an event, that it "cuts across the appearances,"[40] as Berger says, which makes the viewer think about the past and future of the instant. A creative assignment can be to write a narrative or a dialogue that includes and thus interprets the instant seen.

When asked if they could think of situations in Germany that looked like this, one student made an association with a pedagogical conference at a school, teachers talking with a student about his performance. This transfer picked up the transcultural aspect: the hierarchical situation and the ambivalent attitude of the worker/student, but the uncertainty about the meaning or the meanings of the photograph in its social and historical context remained.

4.   Two Brief Conclusions

There are special opportunities for intercultural learning with the medium of photography of and from Africa (or other societies). The stimulation of a 'thinking eye', the quality of ambiguity, the plurality of meanings, remaining riddles, and the immediacy of responses to photos have proved productive for intercultural reflection and self-reflection, and for the development of visual skills and of a differentiated image of Africa. With their transcultural properties, photographs can undermine essentialist and static concepts of culture, which are a basis for stereotypes.

My second brief conclusion refers to teaching methods: interpreting and communicating about one and the same photograph in various constellations (individually, in groups, in the plenary) makes sense. It not only allows the students to share their visual experiences and reflections, but it also opens up further perspectives, making them aware of ambiguities or a variety of meanings and individual responses, and can thereby reveal the complexity of a photographic representation and interpretation of reality and of the reality behind.

---

[40] Berger & Mohr, *Another Way of Telling*, 120.

WORKS CITED

Bal, Mieke. "Visual Essentialism and the Object of Visual Culture," *Journal of Visual Culture* 2.1 (2003): 5–32.

Barthes, Roland. *Image, Music, Text*, tr. Stephen Heath (1977; New York: Hill & Wang, 1977).

——. *Camera Lucida: Reflections on Photography*, tr. Richard Howard (*Chambre Claire*, 1980; tr. London: Vintage, 1993).

Berger, John, & Jean Mohr. *Another Way of Telling* (1982; New York: Vintage, 1995).

Enwezor, Okwui. "Matter and Consciousness: An Insistent Gaze from a Not Disinterested Photographer," interview with David Goldblatt, in Goldblatt, *David Goldblatt Fifty-One Years* (2001), 13–45.

Goldblatt, David. *David Goldblatt Fifty-One Years* (exh. cat.; Barcelona: Museu d'Art Contemporani de Barcelona / Actar, 2001).

Gordimer, Nadine, & David Goldblatt. *Lifetimes Under Apartheid* (New York: Alfred A. Knopf, 1986).

Haus der Geschichte der Bundesrepublik Deutschland, ed. *X für U: Bilder, die lügen* (Bonn: Bouvier, 1998).

Lawson, Lesley, ed. *David Goldblatt 55*, tr. Suzan Depping, Ute Peters & Gerd H.Söffker (2001; Berlin: Phaidon, 2001).

Lyons, Robert, & Chinua Achebe. *Another Africa* (Garden City NY: Doubleday, 1998).

MacDougall, David. *Transcultural Cinema* (Princeton NJ: Princeton UP, 1998).

Magubane, Peter. *Soweto*; text by Charlene Smith (London: Struik, 2001).

Misereor, Bischöfliches Hilfswerk, ed. *Bildkartei – 'Bilder über Afrika und uns'* (Aachen: Misereor Vertriebsgesellschaft, 1987).

Mitchell, W.J.T. *Picture Theory: Essays on Verbal and Visual Representation* (Chicago & London: U of Chicago P, 1994).

Sontag, Susan. *Regarding the Pain of Others* (London: Hamish Hamilton, 2003).

——. *On Photography* (Harmondsworth: Penguin, 1979).

◄❖►

Notes on Contributors

SABRINA BRANCATO studied Modern Languages and Literatures at the Istituto Universitario Orientale di Napoli (1995) and earned a doctorate in English from the Universidad de Barcelona (2001), specializing in literature and cultural pluralism. She has taught courses and published on women's literary history, postcolonial and migration literatures, contemporary poetry, Caribbean and black British fiction and poetry. She conducted a comparative study of Afro-European narratives as a Marie Curie Intra-European Fellow in the Department of New Anglophone Literatures and Cultures at Johann Wolfgang Goethe University, Frankfurt.

NADIA BUTT has an M.A. in British and American literature from the University of the Punjab, and has recently completed her doctoral dissertation on "Overlapping Territories, Intertwined Histories: Transcultural Memory and the Indo-English Novel" in the Department of New Anglophone Literatures and Cultures at Johann Wolfgang Goethe University, Frankfurt.

SABINE DOFF is Professor of Didactics at Goethe University Frankfurt. She studied English and German literatures as well as philosophy at the universities of Glasgow and Munich, where she obtained her doctorate in 2002. She was a Visiting Fellow at the University of British Columbia and the University of Illinois at Chicago. Her publications include *Englischlernen zwischen Tradition und Innovation* (2002) and *Englischdidaktik in der BRD 1949– 1989: Konzeptuelle Genese einer wissenschaftlichen Disziplin* (2008) as well as a number of co-written books and co-edited volumes such as *Fremdsprachendidaktik im 20. Jahrhundert: Entwicklung einer akademischen Disziplin im Spannungsfeld von Theorie und Praxis* (2006), and *Fremdsprachendidaktik heute: Interdisziplinäre Impulse, Methoden und Perspektiven* (2007).

GISELA FEURLE teaches English and African literatures within an interdisciplinary context (literature/history) at the Oberstufen-Kolleg of the University of Bielefeld. She also taught English in Zimbabwe and has published a study on processes of intercultural learning on the occasion of students'

trips to Southern Africa (*Annäherungen an das Fremde*). Together with Detlev Gohrbandt, she has translated Bessie Head's novels *Maru* and *When
Rainclouds Gather* into German. Her research interests relate to teaching the
literatures (as well as cartoons and photography) of Southern Africa, and
intercultural learning.

PASCAL FISCHER is assistant professor of English and American Literature at Würzburg University. He studied German and English studies as well
as history and was a visiting scholar at Columbia University, New York City
in 2002. His publications include *Yidishkeyt und Jewishness: Identität in
jüdisch-amerikanischer Literatur unter besonderer Berücksichtigung der
Sprache* (2003).

DETLEV GOHRBANDT teaches Cultural Studies and Didactics at the University of Koblenz–Landau at Landau, Germany. Publications include articles
on the history of the English fable, George Eliot, and anglophone literature in
and about Africa. He was involved in the Saarbrücken Modern Self-Refer-
ential Poetry Project, documented in *Self-Referentiality in 20th Century British and American Poetry* (1996, ed. with Bruno von Lutz) and *Seeing and
Saying: Self-Referentiality in British and American Literature* (1998, also ed.
with Bruno von Lutz). More recently, he has worked on theories of genre and
reading, as in *Textanlässe, Lesetätigkeiten: Poetik und Rhetorik der Unab-
geschlossenheit* (1998). Translations include stories and poetry by Dylan
Thomas and Bessie Head's *Maru* (1998, with Gisela Feurle) and *When Rain
Clouds Gather* (2000, again with Gisela Feurle). He is currently focusing on
topics in visual culture and preparing a critical edition of English *Struwwel-
peter* satires from 1899 to 1999.

SISSY HELFF works as an assistant professor of English Literature and
Postcolonial Studies in the Department of New Anglophone Literatures and
Cultures at Johann Wolfgang Goethe University, Frankfurt. She was a Visit-
ing Fellow at the Institute for Colonial and Postcolonial Studies at Leeds University, where she started working on a postdoctoral project focusing on the
representation of refugees in the media and literature. Her publications include *Unreliable Truths: Indian Homeworlds in Transcultural Women's
Literature* (Rodopi, forthcoming), the co-edited volume (with Elisabeth
Bekers and Daniela Merolla) *Transcultural Modernities: Narrating Africa in
Europe* (in the *Matatu* series; forthcoming, Spring 2009), as well as a number
of essays on Australian, Indian, African, and black British literature.

KERSTIN KNOPF works as an assistant professor of North American Studies at the University of Greifswald. She received her doctorate from Greifswald University with the dissertation "Decolonizing the Lens of Power: A

Study of Indigenous Films in North America" (Rodopi, forthcoming, Spring 2009). Her main research interests are Indigenous literature and filmmaking and North American media culture.

RUTH MAYER is professor of American Studies at the University of Hannover. Her publications include her monographs *Selbsterkenntnis, Körperfühlen: Medizin, Philosophie und die amerikanische Renaissance* (1997), *Artificial Africas: Images of Colonialism in the Times of Globalization* (2002), *Diaspora: Eine kritische Begriffsbestimmung* (2005), and the co-edited volume (with Vanessa Künnemann) *Pacific Interactions: The United States and China, 1880–1950* (forthcoming, 2009).

MICHAELA MOURA–KOÇOĞLU has a master's degree in English Studies from Johann Wolfgang Goethe University, Frankfurt, and has recently completed her doctoral dissertation on "Narrating Indigenous Modernities: Transcultural Dimensions in Contemporary Māori Literature" in the Department of New Anglophone Literatures and Cultures at the same university. She currently lives in the USA.

MIKE PHILLIPS was born in Georgetown, Guyana. He came to Britain as a child and grew up in London. He worked for the BBC as a journalist before becoming a lecturer in media studies at the University of Westminster. He is best known for his crime fiction, including four novels featuring the black journalist Sam Dean, and his most recent novel, *A Shadow of Myself* (2000). He also co-wrote *Windrush: The Irresistible Rise of Multi-Racial Britain* (1998) to accompany a BBC television series telling the story of the Caribbean migrant workers who settled in postwar Britain. His book *London Crossings: A Biography of Black Britain* (2001) is a series of interlinked essays and stories, a portrait of the city seen from locations as diverse as New York and Nairobi, London and Łodz, Washington and Warsaw. His latest book is *Kind of Union* (2005).

EVA ULRIKE PIRKER read Latin, English and American Studies, and Philosophy and is currently enrolled as a doctoral student at Tübingen University. Since 2003 she has been working as a research and teaching assistant in the English department of Freiburg University. She is part of the research group History in Popular Culture of Knowledge. Her interests are black British culture and history, cultural studies, film studies, and narratology.

MICHAEL C. PRUSSE is professor of Didactics and Literatures in English at the Zürich University of Teacher Education. His research interests range from contemporary British and postcolonial fictions to the genre of the short story and children's literature. He has published on J.G. Farrell, E.M. Forster,

Amitav Ghosh, William Golding, Ernest Hemingway, Jhumpa Lahiri, John McGahern, Paul Scott, Graham Swift, and Nigel Williams.

VIRGINIA RICHTER is professor of modern English literature at the University of Bern, Switzerland. She studied English literature, comparative literature, and German literature at the University of Munich, where she also held various teaching and administrative posts in English and Comparative Literature. She was a Visiting Fellow at the University of Kent at Canterbury and the University of Leeds, and taught English literature at the University of Göttingen. Her publications include *Gewaltsame Lektüren: Gender-Konstitution und Geschlechterkonflikt in "Clarissa", "Les Liaisons dangereuses" und "Les Infortunes de la vertu"* (2000) and an annotated translation of Margaret Cavendish's *The Blazing World* (2001). She is co-editor of *Zwischen Revolution und Emanzipation: Geschlechterordnungen in Europa um 1800* (2004) and *Theater im Aufbruch: Anfänge des europäischen Dramas in der Frühen Neuzeit* (2008).

KANAKA BASHYAM SANKARAN is a reader in the department of English at Seethalakshmi Ramaswami College Tiruchy, India.

KATJA SARKOWSKY is junior professor of New English Literatures at the University of Augsburg. She completed her doctorate in American Studies at Johann Wolfgang Goethe University, Frankfurt in 2003 and worked as an assistant professor at the Centre for North American Studies at the same university from 2003 to 2007. She has published widely on indigenous North American literatures and Canadian and American literature and culture. Her publications include *AlterNative Spaces: Constructions of Space in Native American and First Nations Literatures* (2007) and the co-edited volume *Öffentlichkeiten und Geschlechterverhältnisse: Erfahrungen, Politiken, Subjekte* (2005).

BARBARA SCHAFF is professor of English Literature and Culture at Göttingen University. She studied English and Slavic literature at the universities of Munich, Edinburgh, and Passau and has held teaching posts at the universities of Tübingen, and Munich, and Vienna. Her postdoctoral project focused on World War I, gender, and memory. Her book publications include *Autorschaft: Genus und Genie um 1800* (1994) and a co-edited volume on *Bi-Textualität: Inszenierungen des Paares* (2000).

EDITH SHILLUE, born in the early 1960s and having no direct experience of the Vietnam War, arrived in Ho Chi Minh City (Saigon) in September 1993 from her native Massachusetts to begin work as a university lecturer in English and American history. Her books include *Peace Comes Dropping*

Slow: Conversations in Northern Ireland (2003) and *Earth and Water: Encounter in Viet Nam* (1998).

FRANK SCHULZE–ENGLER is professor of New Anglophone Literatures and Cultures at the Institute for English and American Studies at Johann Wolfgang Goethe University, Frankfurt. His publications include his doctoral thesis *Intellektuelle wider Willen: Schriftsteller, Literatur und Gesellschaft in Ostafrika 1960–1980* (1992) and the co-edited volumes *African Literatures in the Eighties* (1993, with Dieter Riemenschneider), *Postcolonial Theory and the Emergence of a Global Society* (1998, with Gordon Collier and Dieter Riemenschneider), and *Crab Tracks: Progress and Process in Teaching the New Literatures in English* (2002, with Gordon Collier), as well as numerous essays on African literature, comparative perspectives on the New Literatures in English, postcolonial theory, transnational culture, and the cultural dimensions of globalization.

AXEL STÄHLER is lecturer in Comparative Literary Studies in the School of European Culture and Languages at the University of Kent, Canterbury, UK. He has published widely on Jewish authors from the anglophone and German-speaking diasporas and from Israel as well as on early modern festival culture. He has edited *Anglophone Jewish Literatures* (2007) and has just completed a book-length study on anglophone Jewish writing and Jewish postcoloniality.

MARK STEIN is professor of English Literature and postcolonial studies at Münster University. He read English Studies, American Studies, and Political Sciences at the Universities of Frankfurt, Oxford Brookes, and Warwick and holds an M.A. from the University of Warwick (1994) and a doctorate from Johann Wolfgang Goethe University, Frankfurt (2000). He has taught anglophone literatures and cultures at Frankfurt, Bremen, and Saarbrücken Universities, was a visiting training fellow at the University of Kent at Canterbury, and a research fellow at the Postcolonial Studies graduate school (Graduiertenkolleg) of Ludwig Maximilians University, Munich. From 2002 to 2006 he was junior professor for Theories of Non-European Literatures and Cultures at the University of Potsdam. His book publications include *Black British Literature: Novels of Transformation* (2004) and the co-edited volumes *Can 'The Subaltern' Be Read? The Role of the Critic in Postcolonial Studies* (1996), *Postcolonial Passages: Migration and Its Metaphors* (2001), and *Cheeky Fictions: Laughter and the Postcolonial* (2005).

SILKE STROH is an assistant professor of English literature and postcolonial studies at the University of Münster. She studied anglophone literatures, German literature, political science and Celtic studies at the universities of

Aberdeen and Frankfurt, where she obtained an M.A. in 2000 and completed her doctoral dissertation "(Post)Colonial Scotland? Literature, Gaelicness and the Nation" in 2005. She also taught British and postcolonial studies as well as Gaelic language classes at the University of Frankfurt and Giessen. Her research interests include postcolonial theory, black and Asian British as well as African literature and culture, Scottish studies, images of Celticity, English literature, film, and TV as well as strategies for teaching transcultural competence in English as a foreign language courses.

PETER O. STUMMER recently retired as senior lecturer in the English Department of the University of Munich, where he was active in the postgraduate programme on English-speaking countries. He has taught at the Universities of Aberdeen, Cologne, Trento, and Passau, and has published widely on contemporary English literature, political discourse, and African, Australian, and Indian literature in English. His publications include the edited volume *The Story Must Be Told: Short Narrative Prose in the New Literatures in English* (1986) and the co-edited volume *Fusion of Cultures?* (1996; with Christopher Balme).

CHRISTINE VOGT–WILLIAM taught at the Department of New Anglophone Literatures and Cultures at Johann Wolfgang Goethe University, Frankfurt and took a doctorate on Indian Diasporic Literature at the University of York, where she was a Marie Curie Fellow. Her research interests include Indian diasporic literature, Bollywood films, and food cultures. She currently lives in the USA.

LAURENZ VOLKMANN is professor of Didactics at Friedrich Schiller University, Jena. He studied at Erlangen University, Germany, where he also received his doctorate in English literature. His publications include *Wildnis und Zivilisation: Britische Romanschriftsteller des späten 19. und 20. Jahrhunderts und das Internationale Thema* (1991), *Homo oeconomicus: Studien zur Modellierung eines neuen Menschenbilds in der englischen Literatur vom Mittelalter bis zum 18. Jahrhundert* (2003), and *The Global Village: Progress or Disaster?* (2005). He has also edited and co-edited numerous volumes on teaching English literature and culture and has published numerous articles on a wide range of topics, from Shakespeare in the EFL classroom and Madonna as an icon of postmodernism to German techno music.

GISELA WELZ is professor of cultural anthropology and European ethnology at the Institute of Cultural Anthropology and European Ethnology at Johann Wolfgang Goethe University, Frankfurt. She was assistant professor at Tübingen University and visiting fellow at New York University (1992–93), and the University of California at Los Angeles (1996). Her research interests include anthropological perspectives on city life, globalization, transnationalization, and modernization (particularly on European peripheries), the staging of cultural traditions in Europe, and the production and dissemination of knowledge in expert and lay cultures. She has published widely in all of these fields; among her most recent publications are co-edited volumes on *Divided Cyprus: Modernity, History, and an Island in Conflict* (2006) and *Gesunde Ansichten: Wissensaneignung medizinischer Laien* (2005), and a co-edited *Encyclopedia of Cultural Anthropology* (2005).

WOLFGANG WELSCH is Professor of Philosophy at Jena University. He has taught at the universities of Bamberg and Magdeburg and has held numerous visiting professorships and fellowships at German and European universities, at Stanford University and Emory University in the USA, and in Japan. His major research interests include epistemology, anthropology, philosophical aesthetics and the theory of art, cultural philosophy, contemporary philosophy, Aristotle, and Hegel. His wide-ragimg publications include *Vernunft: Die zeitgenössische Vernunftkritik und das Konzept der transversalen Vernunft* (1995), *Undoing Aesthetics* (1997), and *Unsere postmoderne Moderne* (2002), as well as numerous edited and co-edited volumes on aesthetics, philosophy, modernity, and postmodernity.

DIRK WIEMANN is Professor of English Literature at the University of Potsdam. He has held posts at the Central Institute of English and Foreign Languages (Hyderabad, India) and the University of Delhi, and has taught English and New English Literatures and Cultural Studies at the Universities of Magdeburg and Tübingen. He has published widely on English literature, culture, and politics in the seventeenth century, the New Literatures in English, Empire and national culture, modernity and transmodernity, critical theories of narrative, history and ideology, media and film studies, and subcultures. His publications include *Exilliteratur in Großbritannien 1933–1945, Genres of Modernity: Contemporary Indian Novels in English* (2008), and the co-edited volumes *Global Fragments: (Dis-)Orientation in the New World Order* (2007), *Only Connect: Texts – Places – Politics: A Festschrift for Bernd–Peter Lange* (2008), and *Transcultural Britain* (2008).

◄❖►

CPSIA information can be obtained at www.ICGtesting.com
Printed in the USA
LVOW081940210812

295325LV00010B/5/P